Crossroads of the Revolution

Trenton, 1774 - 1783

Other Books by William L. Kidder

The Pleasant Valley School Story: A Story of Education and Community in Rural New Jersey (2012)
(Winner of the 2013 Scholarship and Artistry Award presented by the Country School Association of America)

A People Harassed and Exhausted: The Story of a New Jersey Militia Regiment in the American Revolution (2013)

Farming Pleasant Valley: 250 Years of Life in Rural Hopewell Township, New Jersey (2014)

Edited by William L. Kidder

Meet Your Revolutionary Neighbors (2015)

by

William L. Kidder

KNOX PRESS

Cover image is the N.C. Wyeth mural *Reception To Washington on April 21, 1789, at Trenton on his way to New York to Assume the Duties of the Presidency of the United States* and is used with permission of Wells Fargo Bank, N. A.

CROSSROADS OF THE REVOLUTION: Trenton 1774 to 1783
by William L. Kidder
This edition published in 2017

Published by Knox Press
A Division of New England Publishing Associates, Inc
PO Box 66066
Lawrence Township, NJ 08648

ISBN 978-1-94849-608-7
LCN 2017936857

Bibliographical references and index
1. American Revolution. 2. Biography. 3. Military

For more information on Knox Press, visit us at:
https://www.Knoxpress.com

Published in conjunction with Winged Hussar Publishing, LLC

Cover design by CarolSullivanDesign.com

Dedicated to

the many students
over my long teaching career whose interest and questions have continually expanded my interest in and understanding of history,

and especially to my daughters, Susan and Debi, who continue to enjoy history and teach me, as well as their students.

Acknowledgements

Researching and writing this book has been a very enjoyable experience both because of the fascinating story it uncovered and because of the help from so many interested and interesting people.

Talks with Richard Hunter convinced me to take on the project and helped keep me going. Richard's work on the history of Trenton through his many archaeological projects was a real inspiration for this book. The Hunter Research project reports contain a huge amount of vital information about Trenton in this time period and were tremendously helpful. His support throughout the project is greatly appreciated.

Richard Patterson, Executive Director of the Old Barracks Museum, was also an inspiration and strong supporter of this work. Rich's notations on chapter drafts and conversations about them were extremely helpful and insightful. Staff members at the Old Barracks, especially Rebecca Heiliczer, Ashur Lurie and David Niescior, were all very supportive and helpful.

Inspiration for the project also came from attending and participating over several years in the events of Patriots Week organized by the Trenton Downtown Association.

The David Library of the American Revolution provided a tremendous amount of information as well as encouragement. Librarian Kathie Ludwig was always ready to help, guide, and encourage, as was her husband David with whom I always enjoy talking. Chief Operating Officer Meg McSweeney and staff and volunteers including Brian Graziano, Rich Wood, and Paul Davis were all supportive and encouraging.

The New Jersey State Archives provided a vast array of important documents and the staff always made visits there productive and pleasant.

The staffs at the Department of Rare Books and Special Collections at Princeton University Library and at the Special Collections and University Archives, Rutgers University Libraries were also very helpful and welcoming.

The Trentoniana Room at the Trenton Free Public Library has a wonderful collection on Trenton history and archivist Laura Poll was enthusiastically supportive and helpful.

The Swan Historical Foundation collection at the visitor center at Washington Crossing State Park provided several important documents and artifacts and I greatly appreciate the help and conversations with Clay Craighead, Mark Sirak, and Kels Swan that both guided and encouraged me. My many friends in the Washington Crossing Park Association of New Jersey have been valuable supporters of this project.

During my research I met a number of historical researchers who shared ideas and resources with me. I would mention especially Don Billig on the evacuation of items and people from Philadelphia to Trenton in September and October 1777, David Bosted on the Battle of Trenton, Dave Hart who helped me greatly with the story of Samuel Tucker, and Pat Millen who helped me understand the tannery operations of Stacy Potts and others in Trenton.

This book is in some ways an outgrowth of my volunteer work for the Crossroads of the American Revolution National Heritage Area and its Meet Your Revolutionary Neighbors project. Executive Director Noreen Bodman and Program Manager Kate Knowles-Brindle have both been extremely encouraging of this work that focuses on the experiences of individual people in the story of Trenton.

I am greatly indebted to my publisher, Roger S. Williams, for his enthusiasm and support for this project. It has been a joy to work with him and his comments and suggestions on the draft manuscript really made me think and make improvements. Copy editor David Price helped me keep consistent and clear in my writing.

As always, I have to thank my wife, Jane, for putting up with my concentration on this project that must have seemed an all-consuming obsession at times. And, I cannot omit acknowledging the contribution of my cat, Izzy, who so enjoys being with me when I work that she literally told me to get to work each day. She is purring on my shoulder as I write this.

While all these people, and no doubt others I failed to mention, have helped to improve this work, any errors are my responsibility and I welcome having them pointed out to me.

Note on Illustrations

The map of Trenton Town 1774-1783 is based on a map produced by Hunter Research, Inc. as part of its *Trenton in 1775 Mapping Project* (2007). This map and information about individual properties is available online at http://www.trentonhistory.org/Document.html. The map of Functional Trenton is based on the map produced by Hunter Research, Inc. for a project on Trenton in 1784. The examples of stoneware made by James Rhodes were recovered from archaeological excavations at the William Richards kiln site on the Lamberton waterfront and the Rhodes kiln on the current Eagle Tavern site. More about Rhodes can be found in: Rebecca White, Nadine Sergejeff, William Liebknecht and Richard Hunter. *A Historical Account and Archaeological Analysis of the Eagle Tavern, City of Trenton, Mercer County, New Jersey*. Trenton: Hunter Research, 2005. The archaeological reports written by Hunter Research, Inc. on their website at www.hunterresearch.com contain a vast amount of information from both documentary and archaeological sources about Trenton during the Revolution and at other time periods. These reports were tremendously helpful during the research and writing of this work.

The musket from the John Fitch shop is from the collection of the Swan Historical Foundation on exhibit at the Visitor Center at Washington Crossing

State Park in New Jersey and is used with permission of the Foundation. The collection includes a number documents and artifacts relating to Trenton during the Revolution, as well as the Revolution in general.

The drawings and paintings chosen to illustrate this book represent the work of 19th and early 20th century Trenton artists picturing places and events in the history of their town during the Revolution. Three artists lived at the time of William S. Stryker whose primary researches into the Revolutionary history of Trenton were monumental and these men sought to portray buildings and events with historical accuracy, based on the evidence available to them at the time. If not completely accurate, they do represent how Trenton artists have helped us to understand the history of their city. Archivist Laura Poll at the Trentoniana room of the Trenton Free Public Library was very helpful with locating images of Trenton and information about the artists.

Oliver L. Kemp was born in Trenton in 1876 and died in 1934 in Lansing, Michigan. He studied art under Howard Pyle and did many covers for magazines such as the *Saturday Evening Post*. His illustrations included here were apparently done for William Stryker's 1898 book *The Battles of Trenton and Princeton*.

George Bradshaw was born in Trenton in 1881 and died in 1968. He was on the faculty of the School of Industrial Arts in Trenton from 1921 until 1945. He did the etchings included here for the 1929 Trenton Historical Society history of Trenton.

William E. Pedrick was born in 1868 and died in 1927. He was associated with the School of Industrial Arts in Trenton for more than 20 years and served in the New Jersey National Guard for more than 30 years, rising to the rank of colonel. He was a well-known artist and in 1923 wrote a critique of the accuracy with which various artists had portrayed the Battles of Trenton and Washington's Crossing of the Delaware. Images of the paintings are used with permission of the Old Barracks Association which owns them.

Illia Barger is a contemporary artist well-known in the Trenton area who has done several historical mural projects on buildings in the city to heighten the awareness of Trenton's historic roles in the American Revolution. Her dramatic mural included in this book represents an event that took place directly across the street from the building on which the mural was painted during Patriots Week in 2006. Her enthusiastic support for this book is greatly appreciated.

Contents

Maps

Illustrations

Introduction

Most Americans today have heard the story of Washington's surprise attack on Trenton in December 1776, after his famous crossing of the Delaware River, and the capture of the Hessian soldiers occupying it. But, does the fuller story of Trenton in the years 1774 to 1783 have anything to contribute to a deeper understanding of why the war for independence succeeded? The stories of people living in or passing through the town during ten years of protest and war reveal that Trenton continuously played several little known but very important roles in New Jersey politics and as a military post (featuring a major supply depot and Continental hospital) that contributed to Washington's main strategy of keeping his army together and in the field until the expense of trying to stifle the fight for independence became unbearable for the British government. Trenton's contributions were the product of that strategy combined with the British army occupation of New York City from July 1776, about the same time that independence was declared, until the withdrawal of the British army at the end of the war in 1783. That occupying army continually threatened New Jersey and required Washington to keep Continentals in and near New Jersey throughout the war to counteract any British movement from New York, while Washington looked for a way to retake the city, his constant, unfulfilled, dream. Trenton, a river port at the head of navigation on the Delaware River on the main road between New York and Philadelphia, became a major thoroughfare for troops, supplies, diplomats, and other traffic – a crossroads of the Revolution.

In our story, we meet Trenton's craftsmen, merchants, mill owners, innkeepers, ministers, lawyers, farmers, and laborers, as well as politicians and soldiers. Equally important, we meet their wives, children, apprentices, servants, and slaves. Trentonians contributed to a long string of military events that intertwined with a myriad of political, economic, social, and cultural changes evolving during the late 18th century. Trenton's position also allowed it to function frequently as an unofficial state capital, the role it would officially play beginning in 1790. The stories of people who traveled through, or spent some time in Trenton, speak to the significance of the town and deepen our understanding of both the inhabitant's experiences and the wider revolution. Each story adds to the rich tapestry of individual experiences encountered during the Revolution.

As a town in the middle colonies, Trenton exhibited the diversity of that region. Today, we identify Americans as a culturally diverse people and the middle colonies already displayed this trait during the Colonial and Revolutionary eras. Although diverse, people living in the middle colonies tended to see themselves as patriotic citizens whose liberties, economic opportunities, and general prosperity were supported by the British Constitution, an enlightened monarchy, and the strong British navy and army. This partly explains why the people of Trenton, along with others in New Jersey, lagged behind the northern and southern colonies, especially Massachusetts and Virginia, in developing Revolutionary leadership and commitment. However, the cultural diversity also created the conditions for a bitter civil war fought as part of the War for Independence.[1]

People living in Trenton between 1774 and 1783 lived in their present, not ours. They had no conception of the Constitution we live under today, nor could they envision that we would become a continent-spanning country of 50 states united as one country with worldwide importance rather than a loose confederation of 13 states, or foresee other aspects of the United States that have evolved politically, economically, and socially over some 240 years and are part of our history. The events of 1774 through 1783 were experienced as rapidly changing current events, with unknown consequences, and their historical background was British, Northern European, and British colonial. Our current concepts and understandings of freedom have evolved over the past 240 years, while the political freedoms discussed so hotly in late 18th century Trenton were part of a long struggle between King and Parliament that included the Magna Carta, an unwritten constitution, a long period of "salutary neglect," unsuccessful rebellions in Scotland and Ireland, European imperial rivalries, the English civil war, European wars, the Reformation, the Enlightenment, etc. Their story is even more compelling when viewed from their perspective.

Trentonians in the 18th century lived in a culture based on human, animal, wind, and water power; giving the town an atmosphere very different from ours today. Critical to the development of several Trenton industries were the water and waterpower provided by Petty's Run[2], a stream defining the western edge of town, and the Assunpink Creek. The variety of businesses at Trenton ranged from large fisheries, grist mills, fulling mills[3], tanneries, and iron and steel works to small shops of tradesmen, such as silversmiths, coopers, blacksmiths, potters, cabinet-makers, tailors, shoemakers, and hatters. Trenton-made products were sold locally in small shops and numerous general stores, while also distributed to other towns and cities such as Philadelphia, and exported to other areas of the British North American colonies and the West Indies.

Horses were ubiquitous on the streets, as well as in stables on house lots and tavern yards. Residents and visitors were immersed in the clomping, snorting, rumbling, squeaking sounds, and the sweaty, harness leather oil, wagon grease, and animal sweat and excrement smells associated with horses and the wooden vehicles with iron rimmed wheels that they pulled. To these sensory stimulants were added the farm sounds and smells produced by oxen[4], dairy cows, chickens, and the occasional sheep or hog, kept in town or brought to town for sale. The farm sounds and smells mixed with industrial ones produced by blacksmith forges, a plating mill, a steel furnace, several tanneries, grist mill stones, and water wheels. The constant burning of wood for cooking and heat created a smoky haze, but also produced the appetizing smells of cooking and baking, offset somewhat by odors from the many privies. Conditions of the dirt roads in town constantly changed, as the weather and traffic created surfaces that varied from smooth dry dusty to muddy or frozen ruts. Compared to today, life in 18th century Trenton was very earthy and close to nature.

Colonial New Jersey developed from several isolated settlements that were initiated by the Dutch in the northeast on the Hudson River, opposite New Amsterdam, and by Swedes in the southwest, on the Delaware River. Great Britain took possession of these colonies in 1664, created the two proprietary colonies of East and West Jersey, and combined them into a single Royal Colony in 1702. Much of the proprietary culture persisted, including maintaining two alternating capitals throughout the British colonial and Revolutionary years: Perth Amboy in the east, and Burlington in the west. Both capitals were commercial ports that functioned as satellites of the major seaports at New York City and Philadelphia but never rivaled them in importance.

Mahlon Stacy, a tanner from Handsworth, Yorkshire, accompanied by fellow Quakers Thomas Potts and Thomas Lambert, came up the Delaware River from Burlington in the spring of 1679 with a group of English Quakers, mostly from Nottinghamshire, Derbyshire, and South Yorkshire, and settled land on both sides of the Assunpink Creek, a tributary of the Delaware. This settlement was at the "falls" of the Delaware River, a stretch of shallow, rocky rapids marking the head of navigation. This location, also the southernmost fording point on the river, had drawn humans to it since Native Americans found it attractive for settlement, probably more than ten thousand years before any Europeans arrived. Attractions for Europeans included the potential industrial water power provided by the Assunpink Creek entering the Delaware near the falls, abundant fish, building stone, freshwater springs, trading opportunities with Native Americans, and good agricultural land spreading back from the river bank.[5]

Additional settlers followed Stacy's group, and he wisely built a grist mill on the south bank of the Assunpink to grind their grain into flour for shipment downriver to Philadelphia and then to the West Indies.[6] As the population served by the mill grew, Nottingham Township was established in 1688, between the Assunpink and Crosswicks Creeks, and when Burlington County was formed in 1694 it included the settlements at the falls on both sides of the Assunpink. The population continued to increase and Hopewell Township was organized in 1700 on the north side of the Assunpink, thus dividing the settlers around Stacy's mill between Hopewell and Nottingham townships.[7] In 1714, William Trent, a Philadelphia merchant originally from Scotland, purchased 800 acres, including the mill, and played a major role in the economic and political development of the town that soon bore his name. Hunterdon County was carved out of Burlington County, north of the Assunpink, in 1714, and Trenton Township out of Hopewell Township in 1719, at which time the developing town of Trenton was made the county seat of Hunterdon. These actions divided the growing and prosperous community of Trenton between two townships and counties.

By 1774, Trenton was a prosperous market town of between 500 and a thousand inhabitants, diverse in terms of ethnic heritage, religion, comparative wealth, and the variety of crafts and businesses pursued. On the north side of the Assunpink was Hunterdon County and Trenton Township, with the market town of Trenton anchoring the southern border. On the south side of the Assunpink was Burlington County and Nottingham Township, containing Kingsbury manor, Trenton Ferry, and Trenton Landing (or Lamberton), which combined with the market town to make up "functional" Trenton. The vast majority of Trentonians lived and worked on the north side of the Assunpink in the compact market town. Some residents owned land on both sides of the Assunpink and dealt with two local governments. Ironically, William Trent's home was located in Nottingham Township. For our story, we will consider Trenton to be the broader "functional" community on both sides of the Assunpink Creek.[8]

We begin our story in 1774 because New Jersey citizens began to participate more fully with other colonies in the political protest movement that had been developing since at least 1763. In 1774, Trenton's residents were reasonably content British citizens, living relatively prosperous lives in the technological and social culture of the 18th century, and loyal to a government they believed to be the best in the world. The desire for political and economic independence gradually increased during 1775 and 1776, and many, but certainly not all, people developed a loyalty to the newly declared independent state of New Jersey acting under the authority of the Continental Congress. By 1783, Trenton's people were fully committed to independence from Great Britain, provided a welcoming safe haven for the Congress of the Confederation, and saw their town as a potential capital for the new nation. Trenton's story helps us understand that the War for Independence involved much more than just the stories of the armies, leaders, and major battles, even the justly famous Battle of Trenton. An equally important part of the story is how Trenton's residents and visitors constantly adapted to or resisted, contributed to or hindered, and suffered or benefited from the various events of the political Revolution and War for Independence that changed their lives and world view.

Trenton was a busy community with people coming and going all the time; stage coaches and mail express riders followed regular schedules, river vessels carried goods and people between Trenton and Philadelphia, and a variety of craftsmen, merchants, and farmers conducted business in town, along with the judges, lawyers, and other officials living in, or coming to, town because it was the county seat. Visitors of all sorts found lodging at the inns, or took meals at them before travelling on, and shopped in the many stores. All this activity brought news that stimulated Trenton's inhabitants to discuss social, economic, and political affairs, including the controversial acts of Parliament after 1763 and the growing protest movement against them. Those protests developed into a war for independence in 1776 that turned Trenton into a necessary military post and brought participants in the war through town on a regular basis, making it the crossroads of our Revolution.

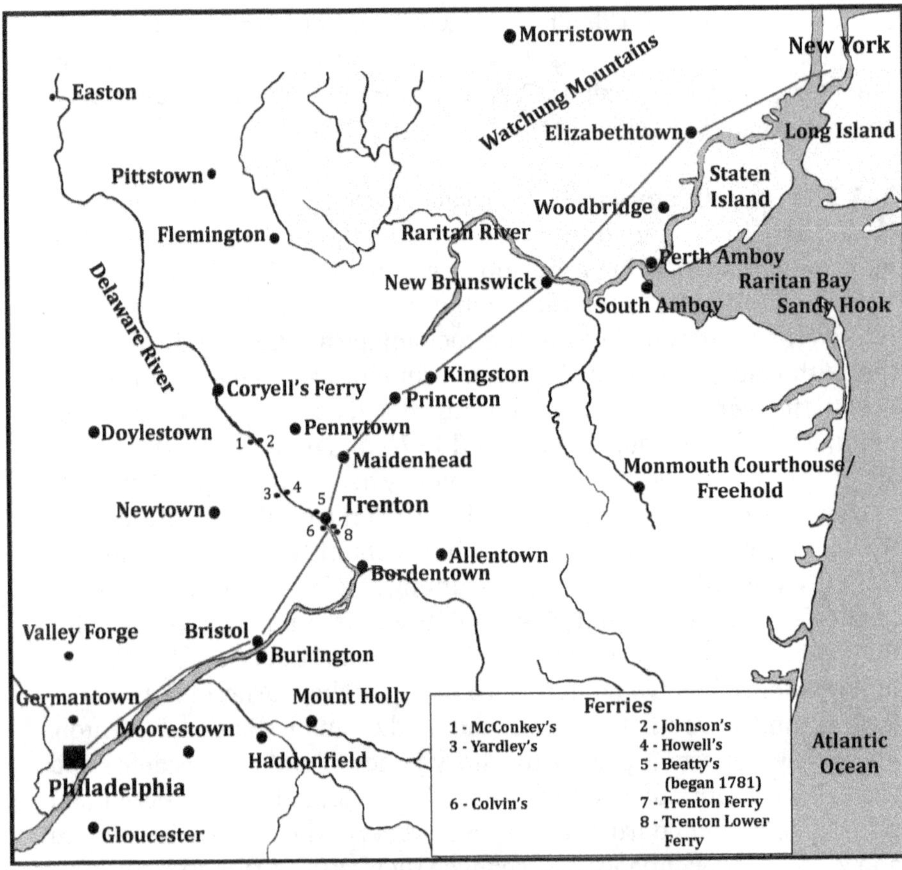

Central New Jersey: 1774-1783

This map shows how Trenton was positioned on the main road between New York City and Philadelphia. The line of the road is simplified and does not represent the exact path it took.

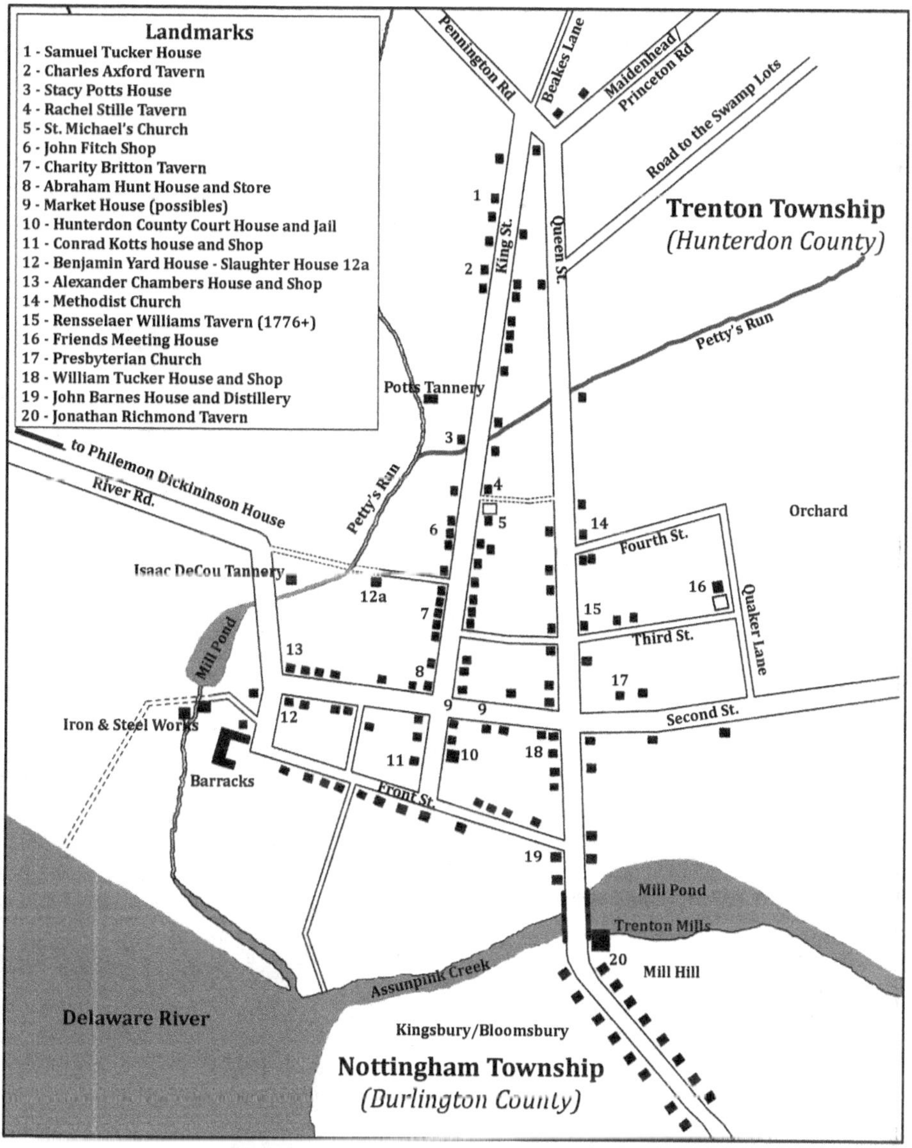

Trenton Town: 1774-1783

The compact market town of Trenton was the county seat of Hunterdon County and provided traveler services as well as stores, craft shops, tanneries, and mills. While the Assunpink Creek formed the boundary between Hunterdon and Burlington Counties, the people living in the social and economic communities on both sides of the creek identified with Trenton.

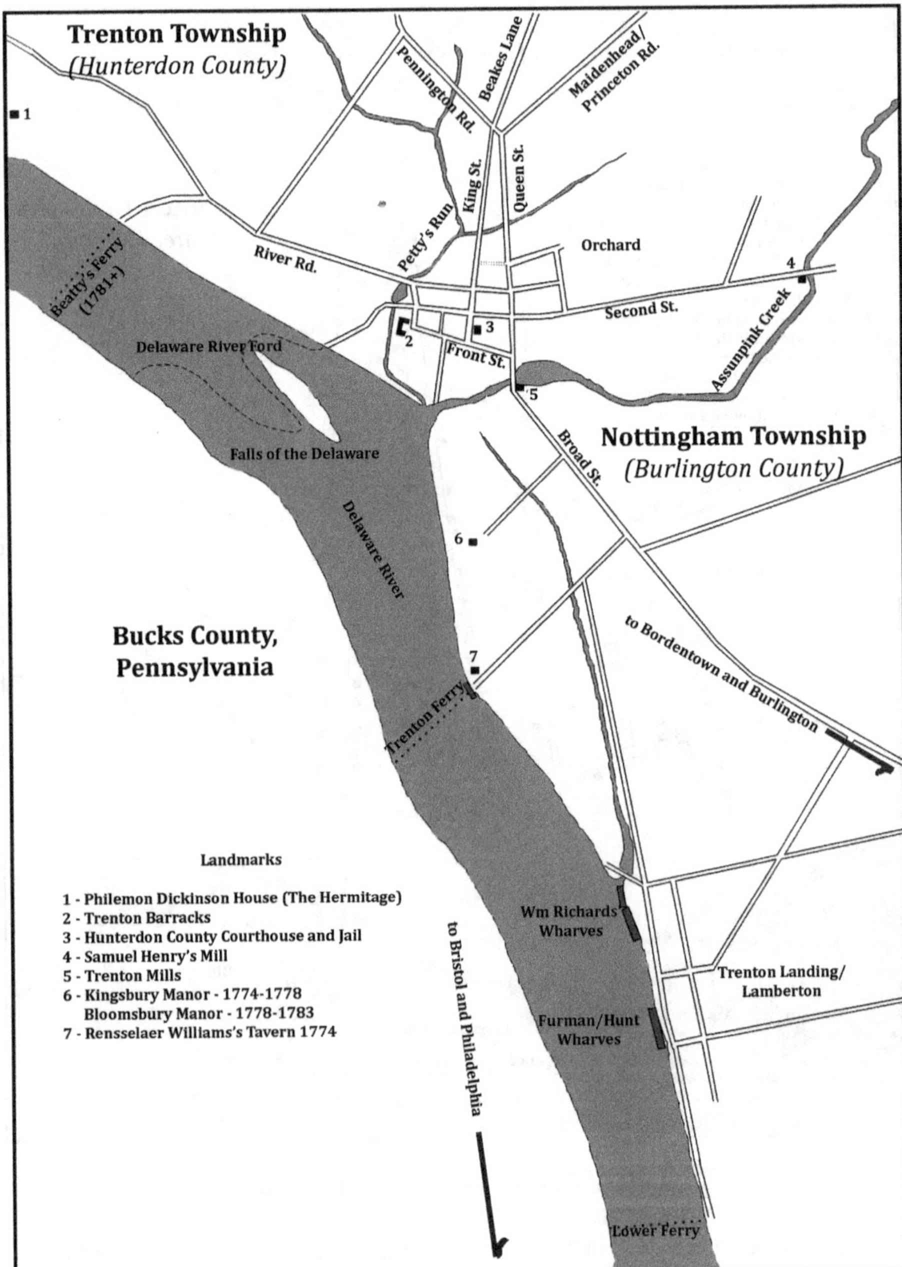

Functional Trenton: 1774-1783

This map shows the geographical extent of social and economic Trenton that was split politically by the Assunpink Creek.

Chapter 1

1774

In the heat of late August 1774, thirty-nine year old John Adams, his older cousin Samuel Adams, Thomas Cushing, Robert Treat Paine, and their four servants rode in a swaying, jolting four-horse coach on a rough, dusty dirt highway heading to Philadelphia as delegates to a Continental Congress, called to develop coordinated responses to recent acts of Parliament that many North American colonists found obnoxious. They spent Saturday and Sunday, August 27 and 28, in Princeton visiting with Rev. John Witherspoon and other local leaders at the college in Nassau Hall. The next morning, they rode twelve miles south, through the village of Maidenhead, crossed the bridge on the Shabakunk Creek, went up into a woods and after crossing a large clearing and a little hollow rode up onto high ground and into another woods. Coming out of the woods, they could see the town of Trenton below them. They descended again, as the road gradually turned to the right, and reached the first houses of Trenton.[1] After passing through town and crossing the stone bridge on the Assunpink Creek, they paused for breakfast at Rensselaer Williams's Royal Oak Inn at Trenton Ferry.[2] During their leisurely stop, John Adams was struck by "four very large black walnut trees standing in a row behind the house." They caught his interest because, as he wrote in his diary that night, "all the black walnut timber which is used by our cabinet makers in Boston is brought from the Southern Provinces," and to him, anything south of New England was a southern province. Adams found Trenton to be "a pretty village" and the largest of the towns he passed through on the road in New Jersey.[3]

Connecticut delegates Silas Deane and Roger Sherman travelled together on the same road and were passed at Princeton by East New Jersey delegates William Livingston and Stephen Crane. Deane wrote to his wife, Elizabeth, that the weather was "extremely hot, without the least breath of air stirring," so they stopped at one of Trenton's taverns to spend the night. The New Jersey delegates also spent that night in Trenton and paid a social call on their fellow delegates, bringing along Trenton's Presbyterian minister, Rev. Elihu Spencer, the brother of well-known Connecticut Colonel Joseph Spencer. The gathering was convivial, but Deane wrote Elizabeth that "for my part, I never underwent more to keep up my part of the conversation." He was anxious to get to bed, "sick, worn out with the heat and dust, headache, and anxiety of mind; but so it was, I could not retire until past eleven, when, as fond as I am of sleep, the night and bed were worse to me than to have proceeded on my journey. I turn'd, and turn'd, and groan'd, while Judge Sherman who lodged in the same chamber snored in concert." When morning finally came, Deane told Elizabeth, "I got up, wash'd my feet in hot water, and without eating a mouthful set out on my journey." His misery did not keep him from observing Trenton to be "the prettiest town I have seen in the Jerseys." [4]

The New England delegates came through Trenton because it was on the main inter-colony road, a King's Highway, connecting New York and Philadelphia, and by extension New England and the Southern colonies. The people of Trenton knew the road by several functional names, such as the Upper Road or the York Road, i.e., the road to New York. Like other colonial roads, it evolved haphazardly from a "bridle way" just wide enough for a man on horseback, or leading a packhorse, and travelers regularly noted its poor condition. The colonial legislature periodically discussed plans to make roads wider, straighter, faster, and safer to travel, but seldom enacted legislation to carry out a plan. One plan was derailed in 1765 when the Stamp Act controversy diverted attention from it.[5] Consequently, roads in 1774 still meandered across the countryside, uneven, strewn with rocks and stumps, marked by ruts and holes that filled with water in wet weather, and lacking direction posts or milestones except where some inhabitant took it upon himself to provide them. Travelers encountering rivers, creeks, or streams, faced bridges of uncertain condition, ferries, or simply fords through shallow water. Royal Governor William Franklin signed the latest law to improve the roads on March 11. It contained a clause requiring each male resident to annually contribute one to three days of road labor.[6]

The bridge crossed by the delegates over the Assunpink Creek at the Trenton Mills connected two townships and counties.[7] The colonial government ordered Nottingham to construct a bridge over the creek in 1688.[8] When Hunterdon County was formed, responsibility for the bridge was shared and by 1763 the southern half of the bridge was constructed of stone and the northern half of wood. Trenton's William Morris warned the Assembly that the bridge had become dangerous. The Assembly ordered Hunterdon County in 1765 to reconstruct the entire bridge with stone, taking responsibility for two-thirds of the cost, while Nottingham assumed one-third. Merchants Abraham Hunt and Thomas Barnes of Trenton worked with managers from Nottingham to build the stone bridge.[9] The March 11 road act continued the two-thirds, one-third ratio for maintaining the bridge.[10]

Although there was a ford through the shallows at the Trenton falls, it could be treacherous, so Trenton Ferry was established in Nottingham Township below the falls.[11] A "large, commodious, and well finished" inn accommodated travelers on a 242 acre tract of fertile soil with meadow for hay, woodland for timber, a fruit orchard, a barn, stables, a coach-house, store-houses, and two other houses. Daniel Coxe purchased the tract in 1770 and leased the ferry with its inn to Rensselaer Williams in September. In 1772, Patrick Colvin purchased the ferry opposite it in Pennsylvania and the two ferries were jointly known as Trenton Ferry.[12]

In 1774, Elijah Bond operated a competing ferry south of Trenton Ferry. Daniel Coxe petitioned the governor and his council in 1773 to charge Bond with usurping the authority of the Crown to grant ferry licenses, by operating without one. Attorney General Cortland Skinner drew up charges,[13] but Bond's ferry did not go away. In a March newspaper advertisement, Williams and Colvin included thinly veiled references to Bond's unlicensed ferry stealing their customers with lower rates. They pledged to "ferry all persons, horses, carriages, &c. upon the same terms, and at as low a rate and price as any ferry within the distance of four miles on the river." They touted "the superior conveniences" of their ferry and their shorter crossing distance. They hoped these advantages, combined with their sacrificially lowered fares, would lead people to "favour ... an old established ferry."[14] Both ferries competed for business throughout the next decade.

New Jersey had not provided leadership in the protests against the acts of Parliament after 1763,[15] but interested Trenton residents knew all about the acts and protests from conversations with the many travelers passing through their town and the readily available Philadelphia and New York City newspaper articles. The residents developed their opinions and some participated in the protests. In response to the Grenville Acts of 1764, which increased import duties on British textiles, members of the Union Fire Company[16] unanimously agreed on May 6, 1765 to "expend no lamb in their families this season." Keeping sheep alive for their wool promoted home and local production of cloth, reducing the need for imported British cloth. The fire companies, a library company, several schools, and other organizations provided opportunities for political discussion and action.[18] Reaction to the Stamp Act in 1765 shut down a number of critical services. By February 1766, Hunterdon County had a Sons of Liberty group planning to resume legal services on April 1, without using the stamps, whether or not the act had been repealed by then.[19] Between 1763 and 1774, the people of Trenton, like those throughout New Jersey, were generally united in challenging unpopular acts of Parliament.[20]

The argument over "no taxation without representation" symbolized the conflict over how much local self-government was appropriate for the colonies. The people of New Jersey believed they were subjects of the King but should be governed by their local colony, county, and township governments in which they participated directly. Like other colonies, New Jersey's political structure allowed for a degree of self-government, but Parliament always retained ultimate authority. The colonial governor, appointed by the King, exercised many powers as chief executive and commander-in-chief, including deciding when to hold elections to the Assembly, calling or dissolving Assembly meetings, and appointing officials such as judges, justices of the peace, sheriffs, and coroners. The legislature consisted of two houses. The Provincial Council, appointed by the King with input from the governor, represented the interests of the proprietary upper class, the royal governor, and the British government. The General Assembly contained men owning at least 1,000 acres of land, elected by men owning at least 100 acres. The Assembly could initiate laws and then negotiate with the council and governor to enact them, exerting pressure when needed through its power to withhold funding for the government, including the governor's salary. The two houses ultimately had to work together to fund the government.[21]

The General Assembly met in Burlington in February and March with Trenton merchant Samuel Tucker serving as a delegate, and the Provincial Council met with Trenton lawyer Daniel Coxe as a member.[22] On February 8, the Assembly discussed letters from other colonies "respecting the common rights of the colonies" and resolved unanimously and heartily to maintain communication with "our Sister Colonies." Ten colonies had previously established Committees of Correspondence, beginning in 1772, so New Jersey was one of the last to finally join the network.[23] The Assembly elected Samuel Tucker to its nine-man Standing Committee of Correspondence and Inquiry, unanimously appointed by the Assembly "to obtain the most early and authentick intelligence of all Acts and Resolutions of the Parliament of Great Britain, or the proceedings of administration that may have any relation to or may affect the liberties and privileges of His Majesty's subjects in the British colonies in America." The Assembly charged the Committee to maintain communication with the other colonies on these issues and report back periodically.[24] No one knew where this step would lead, but if anyone expected that committee activities would be limited to acquiring and disseminating factual information, the reality was soon different. In the words of historian John Ferling, these committees of correspondence "also acted as propaganda machines, tirelessly broadcasting the warning that the imperial government plotted to curtail liberty in America," and helped mold ideas about the rights of Englishmen into something like a political party platform. Although some people believed at least some members of Parliament sincerely sought to resolve the colonists issues fairly, others believed Parliament was powerfully moving towards tyranny.[25] Creating this Committee of Correspondence took the Assembly beyond its authority to deal with internal matters and become engaged in arguably extralegal cooperation with other colonies on common issues relating to their relationship with the Mother Country.

As the everyday work of the Assembly and Council continued, Tucker reported in the Assembly on a bill, entitled "An Act to regulate the Packing of Beef and Pork, and to ascertain the Size of Casks." Tucker also served on the Committee for Public Accounts, helped individual citizens resolve problems, and took bills passed by the Assembly to the Governor's Council for its concurrence.[26] He was fully serving in the colonial government, while simultaneously working with other leaders, inside and outside the government, to redress colonial grievances.

Fifty-three-year-old Samuel Tucker was a prominent Trenton merchant with ties to Philadelphia merchants such as Thomas Riche and John Reynell. Tucker procured flour, apples, flax seed, hair, and lumber among other items and shipped them to Riche in Philadelphia, while Riche sent Tucker sugar, wine, salt, lemons, saltpeter, coffee, and molasses. Tucker helped Riche avoid a £10 Pennsylvania duty by landing slaves imported directly from Africa in New Jersey and selling them at Trenton in the 1760s.[27] Tucker's correspondence with prominent Quaker merchant John Reynell speaks of family matters as well as business. As early as 1755, he was trading in nails, textiles, horses, and other items. Tucker's wide-ranging interests included shipping goods to New England and the West Indies, while also buying and selling land.[28] When Tucker was about 30 years old, Attorney General Joseph Warrell described him as "a man of good understanding, a man of probity and veracity," noted for his "good substance reputation and honesty." In the 1760s, Tucker served as a justice of the peace and for some time as sheriff of Hunterdon County. He was elected to the Assembly in 1768, where his attempts to reform the practice of law incurred the wrath of lawyers, who disingenuously retaliated by successfully prosecuting him for charging excessive fees while serving as sheriff. Tucker lost no credibility in this somewhat frivolous action.[29]

Thirty-four-year-old Daniel Coxe, serving on the Council, was descended from Dr. Daniel Coxe, a London physician and one of the original 1674 West Jersey proprietors. Dr. Coxe remained in England, but his son, Colonel Daniel Coxe, came to New Jersey with its first royal governor in 1702. Colonel Coxe lived in Burlington and then Trenton, where he married and started his family. Active in colony politics, he became hated due to disputes concerning titles to land his father had sold to farmers in Trenton and adjacent townships. Although threatened by angry farmers, he died of natural causes in 1739. Colonel Coxe's son, also Daniel, was less involved in politics and resided on his large estate along the Delaware River in Hopewell Township until his death in Trenton in 1757. This Daniel's son, again Daniel, lived in Trenton where he owned several properties.[30]

While Tucker and Coxe served as representatives in colony-level government, the eligible inhabitants of Trenton north of the Assunpink participated directly in the government of their township and met for their annual town meeting on March 8. People living south of the Assunpink met separately with the other inhabitants of Nottingham Township for their annual meeting and voted on similar issues and officers. Trenton's voters agreed to raise £100 to cover town expenses for the coming year and elected township officials.[31] They elected tannery owner Stacy Potts to be Town Clerk; innkeeper Charles Axford, Jr., Assessor; Ralph Jones, Collector; and David Clark and Stacy Potts county Freeholders. Ralph Jones and merchant Benjamin Smith were elected Overseers of the Poor whose duties included examining the clothing of the poor and maintaining a consistent quality of clothing for each person during the year. Daniel Clark, Charles Axford, Jr., and Stacy Potts agreed to provide the poor with all other necessities, except "phisick and doctoring," and would pay for the funerals of any poor who died during the year. But, they made it clear they would not be liable for any legal expenses incurred by the poor.[32]

Township road maintenance had always been a local responsibility; John Howell and Joseph Tindall were elected surveyors of the roads and a local resident was elected overseer of road repair for each public road of the township. Merchant David Pinkerton became overseer for the Trenton town roads. These surveyors and overseers called out residents to contribute their annual one to three days of labor to keep the roads in good condition and dig ditches and drains as necessary.[33]

Fifty-four-year-old town clerk Stacy Potts was a devout Quaker descended from the families of two early Trenton settlers, Mahlon Stacy and Thomas Potts. He had four children from his first marriage and in September 1774, second wife Marguretta gave birth to their first child.[34] His tannery required large amounts of water from Petty's Run flowing through his lot and involved placing animal hides in large lime vats dug into the ground, and pits of water containing ground-up, tannin-releasing bark. Potts used mostly oak bark, stored in a large bark house and pulverized at his bark mill. He purchased quantities of oak from Nathan Beakes, Thomas Tindall, Hugh Runyon, and others. The tannery provided a number of full and part-time jobs for skilled and unskilled workers to soak, scrape, place hides in pits, monitor the hides, remove the hides, and make them flexible and finished by pounding, drying, stretching, oiling, and rubbing. In addition to hiring skilled labor, Potts often hired local laborers for a day or so and sometimes paid masters for the work of their slaves. His workers sometimes lacked the qualities of "sobriety and diligence." He recorded in his day book on November 22, 1766 that George Stuart "lost 3 days drunk the forepart of this week." In 1773, Potts advertised for "a few good breeches and glove makers, either men or women, also, a good journeyman tanner." Potts also paid local craftsmen for making leather items, such as when Lott Dunbar made six bridles.[35]

Potts supplied "both shopkeepers and others, with skins, breeches, gloves, and shoe leather of all kinds, on the most reasonable terms,

George Bradshaw's c1929 etching of the Stacy Potts house on King Street next to the lot containing his tannery. (THS, Trenton)

either wholesale or retail."[36] Trenton shoemaker William Tucker, Samuel Tucker's brother, was a frequent customer, purchasing tanned hides suitable for shoe soles and others suitable for uppers. Potts even sold leather to a blacksmith for his bellows. Local customers, such as Dr. Isaac Smith, purchased completed pairs of leather hunting breeches and other clothing.

In an economy that was partly barter, customers received credit for untanned hides. Local merchants, such as tailor Conrad Kotts, brought in hides that they had accepted as payment for services. Thomas Yardley once brought in one dry hide, some good calf skins, "2 dry calf skins spoiled with worms," one sheep and one lamb skin, two green hides, and a dog skin. Potts also accepted agricultural produce as payment, including corn, turnips, potatoes, dried apples, and cider, in addition to animal products such as wool, hogs, and beef tongues.[37]

In mid-May, Massachusetts protest leader Paul Revere rode through Trenton carrying a troubling message from the Boston Committee of Correspondence to Philadelphia. Parliament had passed the Boston Port Act to punish the town for the tea destroyed in its harbor the previous December. Revere carried copies of a broadside, printed on black-bordered paper decorated with a skull and crossbones and a liberty cap, stating the Committee's defiant call for a ban on all British imports in response to Parliament forbidding ships to load or unload in Boston harbor until recompense had been made for the tea. Revere distributed copies of the broadside at taverns and villages along his route.[38] Because the Port Act punished every citizen of Boston, rather than just those who destroyed the tea, it was viewed as an affront to all Bostonians, who possessed the rights of Englishmen. If this could happen to Bostonians, it could happen to any Englishman in the colonies.[39] The Boston Port Act was just the first of several laws frequently called Coercive Acts by the British (and only in the 19th century became labeled the Intolerable Acts).[40] These actions convinced many colonists that advocates for a tough stance to end their protest actions were firmly in control of Parliament.[41]

About this time, Trenton silversmith John Fitch became a confirmed supporter of the protest movement. He wrote in his autobiography, "As soon as the Parlement of Great Britain declared that they had a right to bind us in all cases whatever I became a violent opponent to that declaration." Fitch had not previously developed a strong opinion about the dispute; however, he "became so zealous" he declared that he would have sacrificed everything to save his "Country and done it cheerfully."[42]

Looking for a new start in life, and perhaps to escape a nagging wife, twenty-six-year-old Fitch arrived in Trenton in 1769 and boarded first with tinsmith Matthew Clunn. Silversmith James Wilson lived next door and, at Clunn's suggestion, hired Fitch even though he was not a trained silversmith. Wilson himself was not well trained in his craft and was living off money inherited from his father. Fitch described him as "a man not possessed with a lively sensation of honor" who was unable to control "his passions[;] in particular in drinking and was seldom if ever sober." Fitch was a quick learner and knew surveying, working with brass, and watch and clock repair. Soon he was a successful travelling clock repairman and took up lodging with William Smith where he made brass and silver buttons in addition to performing his repair work. When Wilson fell into extreme debt, Fitch purchased his silversmith tools and then compassionately employed him as a journeyman. Fitch soon established himself as a first-rate silversmith and hired several additional journeymen, including John Cochran and James Graves.[43] At his shop on King Street in 1774, Fitch made buckles, tea tongs, milk pots, spoons, pincushions, tankards, buttons, soup ladles, lockets, and seals, and also did watch repairs. Fitch made items for Rensselaer Williams, some undoubtedly for his

Pitcher made by Trenton silversmith John Fitch.
(Courtesy of a private collector in New Jersey)

inn, and made purchases from merchant Abraham Hunt, as well as selling him a dozen tea spoons.[44]

The feeling was growing that an injury to one colony, was an injury to all. Six members of the Committee of Correspondence met at New Brunswick on June 1 to study letters from Boston describing conditions created there by the British army occupation. The Committee answered the letters, declaring that because New Jersey might "eventually [be] in the same predicament with Boston," they would do "everything which may be generally agreed on." Hunterdon County leaders sent letters to every county in New Jersey urging each to appoint a Committee of Correspondence.[45]

Parliament passed a new Quartering Act on June 2, which applied to all of the colonies and allowed for troops to be quartered in occupied dwellings, in addition to taverns and deserted buildings as previously authorized in 1765-1766. This must have grabbed the attention of Trenton residents, who had lived for years with a large, stone military barracks on the edge of town that, with or without their approval, could be used to house British soldiers. The new Quartering Act undoubtedly raised fears that British troops might soon arrive, causing Trenton to suffer like Boston. Nobody wanted soldiers of any army quartered in their town, except possibly for defense in times of imminent danger.

The barracks had been built in 1758-59, during the French and Indian War, after the colonial legislature heard petitions, including one from Trenton citizens, objecting to providing shelter for soldiers. Many residents had quartered soldiers of the 48th Regiment of Foot, veterans of Braddock's defeat in Pennsylvania in 1755, over a number of months in 1757 and 1758. These included: Samuel Tucker, who quartered two soldiers for 26 weeks and four days, two for 16 weeks and four days, four for four days, and three for two weeks; Hezekiah Howell, one soldier for 16 weeks; Conrad Kotts, two soldiers for more than 20 weeks; Nathan Beakes, two soldiers for 22 weeks and one soldier for 11 weeks; Benjamin Yard, a variety of soldiers totaling 67 weeks; and Mary Dury, soldier John Baker for 21 weeks and two days. Innkeeper Charity Britton took in six soldiers for 21 weeks and five days, two soldiers for 13 weeks, and three soldiers for a week and five days. Altogether, 124 vouchers were issued to Trenton area inhabitants for quartering soldiers over various lengths of time.[46]

The Trenton petition noted that because Trenton was on "so great a thoroughfare," numbers of soldiers were "continually passing and repassing upon their severall commands and quartered upon us night and day." Because the soldiers were dispersed in town, officers had difficulty keeping "their stragling soldiers under due command and subjection." Fifty-seven citizens, including Moore Furman, Andrew Reed, Charles Axford, Alexander Chambers, Samuel Bellerjeau, and Samuel Tucker, signed the petition asking the Assembly "to enable them to build a barracks." Most of the signers still lived in Trenton in 1774 and perhaps had second thoughts.[47]

On the positive side, the local economy was boosted when troops were billeted at the barracks and food and supplies for them were purchased from Trenton merchants and nearby farmers. The barracks also provided a small income for several Trenton residents who served as barrack masters, or commissioners, and could hire local men to maintain the building and grounds. Merchants Alexander Chambers, William Clayton, and Abraham Hunt had regularly served in this capacity.

Chambers, living at Chambers' Corner, was a turner, spinning wheel, and chairmaker who maintained a store in an old house his father built, adjoined by the brick house he had built on the corner of Second Street and River Road near the barracks.[48] William Clayton was a well-known hatter, with his shop on the northeast corner of Second and King Streets.[49] Abraham Hunt was the junior partner in the merchant firm of Furman and Hunt. Moore Furman had been shipping goods since the 1750s to and from Lamberton, where he maintained wharves and warehouses, establishing himself as a distinguished merchant with strong ties to prominent Philadelphia merchants. His wharves at Lamberton accommodated numerous shallops and other small vessels transporting goods between Trenton and Philadelphia.[50] In 1762, Furman became a partner in two new firms – Furman and Hunt, and Coxe and Furman. As senior partner in the first, Furman took on Abraham Hunt. In the second, Furman was junior partner to William Coxe of Philadelphia, the son of Daniel Coxe. Coxe and Furman was an international import/export business, with Coxe primarily supplying the capital and Furman overseeing the company's diverse operations, buying, selling, importing, and exporting a huge variety of goods, as well as buying, selling and operating various types of merchant sailing vessels. Furman resided in Philadelphia and relied on Hunt to operate the Trenton stores, thus making Furman and Hunt the Trenton affiliate of Coxe and Furman.[51] Hunt became one of the most important merchants in town, and his store offered a large variety of products for sale, sold lottery tickets and paid lottery prizes, took subscriptions for magazines and items for publication in them, and took subscriptions for books being published.[52]

Beginning in 1765, the barracks commissioners were ordered to keep the board fence around the barracks lot in good repair and submit an account, with cost estimates, of any needed repairs. They were paid £10 per year but were liable for any expenses incurred from damage to lands adjoining the barracks if the fence was not kept in good repair.[53] Over the years, they supplied the barracks with blankets, beds, firewood, small beer or vinegar, and other items necessary for the comfort of troops living there. To help fund their work, after 1763 they were authorized to sell some excess items at public auction and rent out the building when no soldiers were using it.[54]

Assembly actions appointing commissioners and funding maintenance, repair, and supply of the barracks were often disallowed by Parliament when they conflicted with its policies. The Assembly obviously bristled over footing the bill for an imperial structure used by troops doing more than just defending New Jersey.

William Pedrick's 1912 painting of the Trenton Barracks with a Parade of Redcoats. The painting shows the building after its first restoration and is thought to depict the Inniskilling Regiment marching out in April 1759. Although Pedrick always strove for historic accuracy, there are some discrepancies in this depiction. (Collection of the Old Barracks Association)

During June and July, politics heated up along with the temperature and several New Jersey counties held public meetings to organize committees of correspondence. In Hunterdon, people gathered on July 8 at John Ringo's tavern in Amwell, about 20 miles from Trenton. Some members of the Assembly attended, although it was not a government-sanctioned meeting. Assemblyman Samuel Tucker was elected chairman and the group unanimously passed a series of resolutions, the first of which declared their deep loyalty to King George as the symbol of their English political culture and declared that it was their duty to defend him "to the utmost of our power, against all attempts upon his person, crown, and dignity." They listed their grievances arising from those legislative actions of Parliament they believed were violations of their rights as Englishmen.

Referring to taxes, they declared that "it is the undoubted hereditary right of an English subject to give and grant what is absolutely his own, either by himself or his representatives" and "the only lawful representatives of the freemen of this Colony are the persons they elect to serve as members of the General Assembly thereof." Parliament could not tax them because they did not have representatives elected by them in that body.

In response to the actions taken against Boston under the Administration of Justice Act, they stated that a person accused of any crime committed within "this Colony" must be tried by a "jury of this vicinage," because it was unconstitutional and "subversive of the rights and liberties of the free subjects of this Colony" to have cases tried in another colony, or Great Britain, by "Commissioners or any Court constituted by Act of Parliament or otherwise." Combined with the Massachusetts Government Act, these laws were seen as evidence that Parliament was determined to take away all aspects of self-rule, just as the most radical protestors had been warning for the past decade. Believing they were acting within their rights, and not as rebels, the men stated clearly that protesting was the "indispensable duty" they owed "to our King, our country, ourselves and our posterity" by using "all lawful ways and means in our power, to maintain, defend and preserve our loyalty, rights and liberties, and to transmit them inviolate to the latest generations." They were not trying to exact new freedoms, but were protecting for themselves, and their descendants, the long-established, and hard-won, liberties central to British citizenship that, in their opinion, made Britain the best nation in the world.

The freeholders and inhabitants then stated unanimously that they would join any effort to restore "the liberties of America," including if the several colonies jointly agreed "not to purchase or use any articles of British manufacture, nor any commodities imported from the East Indies, under such restrictions as may be agreed on by a general congress of delegates from all the colonies." Hunterdon County stood ready to elect delegates to such a general congress, "whose resolutions and determinations we will most strictly adhere to, and abide by." This was to be the first such general, Continental Congress. Among the nine chosen to meet with men from other county committees of correspondence to elect New Jersey's delegates, were Samuel Tucker, Dr. Isaac Smith, and Abraham Hunt of Trenton.[55]

The county Committees of Correspondence met in New Brunswick on July 21 as the Convention and chose four delegates to the Continental Congress, two from Elizabethtown in east New Jersey and two from Burlington County in west New Jersey. New Jersey was one of eight colonies that established such conventions or provincial congresses in 1774 as the first institutions of local government subordinate to the Continental Congress, rather than Parliament.[56] Like the men who met at Ringo's Tavern had done, the Convention swore loyalty to the Crown but protested unfair taxation. In addition to electing representatives to the upcoming general Congress, the Convention also authorized several men, including Abraham Hunt, Samuel Tucker, and Dr. Isaac Smith, to collect contributions from throughout the colony to send to the people of Boston who were suffering severe shortages as a consequence of the Boston Port Act. Because important men from Trenton were directly involved in the Convention's debates and actions, all of Trenton was undoubtedly abuzz with discussions about them.

As political developments intensified, Britain found that its theory of empire and the reality of how it actually worked were two different things. While Britain proclaimed the supremacy of Parliament and centralized authority, this was in stark contrast to the way the colonies had developed from their beginnings with a certain amount of local authority that had become ingrained during the long period of "salutary neglect." In the words of historian Jack Rakove, "the reality was that British authority did not penetrate deeply into the American countryside. It was merely a thin template resting on distant societies where governance had always been highly decentralized. Had the empire and Parliament really exercised the authority they claimed, Americans would need no reminders of where sovereignty resided." Places like Trenton really had not experienced any immediate difficulties, but protest leaders became concerned about what Parliament might do in the future. While some leaders on both sides believed they had more to gain by resolving their disputes than from pushing things to even more violent confrontation, Britain's forceful and negative responses increasingly pushed the colonists towards unification and coordinated actions in defiance of Parliament, such as calling a Continental Congress that began meeting in Philadelphia on September 5.[57]

The Suffolk Resolves, passed in Massachusetts on September 9, called for colonists to refuse to obey the provisions of the Coercive Acts and the officials responsible for enforcing them, stop paying taxes and trading with Britain. Also, each colony should form a militia and each town elect a committee to enforce the restrictions on importation, consumption, and exportation of British goods. Paul Revere again saddled up and left Milton, Massachusetts on September 11, arriving in Philadelphia with the Resolves on September 16, after passing through Trenton on his ride of almost 350 miles on the rough and winding colonial roads. Congress adopted the Resolves the next day after only brief debate, and Revere began his return journey on September 18. Revere made another round-trip between Boston and Philadelphia from September 29 to October 19, apparently riding part of the way in a sulky, perhaps to relieve his overused horse-riding muscles, and again passed through Trenton both ways.[58] In late September, some of the more conservative delegates attempted to convince the Congress to accept Joseph Galloway's "Plan of a Proposed Union between Great Britain and the Colonies." Under this proposal, the colonies would govern their internal affairs, while still operating under the authority and approval of Parliament. Galloway's plan was narrowly defeated and then expunged from the record shortly before Congress adjourned.

On October 14, the Congressional delegates declared the rights of Americans and denounced the Coercive Acts and the recent Quebec Act as unjust, cruel, and unconstitutional. The earlier acts passed by Parliament after 1763 related to raising revenue and other issues were also criticized. Then on October 18, they agreed that the colonies would not trade with England until the objectionable laws were repealed. This agreement created the Continental Association, by which all thirteen colonies would: stop the importation of British goods and the slave trade beginning December 1, 1774; begin non-consumption of British goods and some foreign luxuries on March 1, 1775; and, stop exportation from the colonies to Britain, Ireland, and the West Indies on September 1, 1775. This graduated implementation was geared to help prevent serious problems for local economies. Just three days after passing the Association, a broadside was printed in Philadelphia informing citizens "that the Congress request the merchants and others, in the several colonies, not to send to Great Britain any orders for goods, and to direct the execution of all orders already sent, to be delayed or suspended, until the sense of the Congress, on the means to be taken for the preservation of the liberties of America, is made public." Copies of this broadside undoubtedly reached and were posted in Trenton within a few days.[59]

By telling each community to establish an enforcement committee, the Congress was encouraging the development of extralegal government agencies that would not have been tolerated if the royal colonial government was functioning properly. Congress, in effect, was hastening the transfer of power from the colonial governments to the hands of local people. The people of Trenton were expected to support and enforce the Association, and thereby acknowledge the authority of the Continental Congress. Protest leaders believed that uniting in action under the Association would convince Parliament to change course, but the delegates agreed to meet again on May 10, 1775 if their grievances had not been resolved by then. Before adjourning on October 26, Congress debated whether the colonies should make military preparations, an idea that abhorred conservative members still hoping for a peaceful resolution. Congress compromised and simply requested that each colony put its militia in readiness.[60] The extralegal Continental Congress essentially told the legal New Jersey Assembly, along with the other 12 colonies, to make sure the local militia laws were being enforced so that the men were well armed and trained. In New Jersey, the colonial militia laws had been widely neglected for years.

While Trentonians jealously guarded their rights and freedoms, they continued to deny human rights to the slaves in their community. From its beginning, Trenton had been home to men, women, and children of African descent, forcibly brought to the colony and owned as slaves by inhabitants of the town and vicinity.[61] Most slave owners had from one to three such individuals, but a few owned several more. Some individuals, especially Quakers, denounced slavery, and on October 6, 1774, Trenton Quaker Mary Dury freed two slaves; forty-three-year-old James and twenty-three-year-old Bedford. Freeing slaves was discouraged by a 1769 law that required former masters to put up £200 in security and forbade freedmen from owning property. Very simply, communities did not want to become responsible for supporting former slaves. Because New Jersey slaves usually worked in close proximity to their owners, personal relationships between slaves and their master's family could become very close, but this did not eliminate instances of harshness and cruelty.[62]

Even in small towns like Trenton, slaves needed agricultural skills because most house lots were mini-farms. Advertisements describing male slaves for sale reveal skills valued in Trenton, including: farmer, gardener, horseman, farrier, carriage driver, bricklayer, waiter, blacksmith, general laborer, and house servant. One house servant had the extra skills of speaking French and the ability to dress hair. Horse care was the most frequently mentioned skill, indicating the degree to which horses were a part of everyone's life. Skills needed for work at one of Trenton's various industries are not often mentioned, but one man was touted as able to work in either a saw or grist mill.[63] Female slaves usually performed household tasks such as general housework, cooking, washing, ironing, spinning, sewing, and care of children. Some women also had farm skills their masters needed, especially in dairying.[64]

In this relatively small community, many sales may have been arranged without surviving documentation. The New Jersey Gazette, published in Trenton beginning in 1778, contained advertisements for sales. It was not unusual for a slave to be listed among other items being sold, clearly showing that slaves were considered commodities. Male slaves for sale ranged in age from boys of seven years to men of about forty. The majority were teenagers or in their twenties, but several were in their thirties and one about forty. Females were also young, most in their teenage years or twenties. Sometimes slaves were sold as families. Randle Mitchell of Nottingham Township advertised a man and woman "with two children, one a girl two years old the other a boy on the breast." They would be sold to a person willing to take the whole family. The only reason Mitchell was selling them was to "lessen his family," in other words, to save money.[65]

Individual slaves might be sold simply because the owner needed money or he didn't have enough work to justify keeping them. If lack of work was the issue, the owner might not sell the slave outright but rather hire him out for a time, even for a full year. In some cases, the owner was leaving the area and had no further need for the slave.[66] To ensure that a potential buyer did not think the slave was being sold because of misconduct, advertisements frequently stated that the slave was being sold for "no fault" on the slave's part. Owners usually sold their slaves directly or through an agent, such as printer Isaac Collins at his print office. The number of advertisements giving Collins as the contact agent make it appear that he was a very active slave trader, in conflict with his Quaker religion. Slave sales, though, were just one of many transactions for which he served as the contact. Everyone knew where to find the printer. Other merchants, including Abraham Hunt, also served sometimes as agents for slave sales.[67] Trenton and Nottingham residents who sold one or more of their slaves included Jonathan Richmond, Bernard Hanlon, Benjamin Smith, Mary Pinkerton, Daniel Coxe, Rensselaer Williams, Hezekiah Howell, Robert Singer, and Randle Mitchell.

Newspaper advertisements reveal only a handful of runaways, and most occurred during the last three years of the war. Reasons for the runaway are not often given, but several advertisements speculate it was to reach British controlled areas or to return to an area where they had previously lived. At least some may have simply taken advantage of the chaos of war to take their fate into their own hands and seek a new life. Descriptions of the men focus mostly on the clothing they were wearing, plus any additional clothing they were known to have taken with them. In one case, the runaway took with him "an English fuzee and silver mounted ivory handled sword," but taking weapons seems to have been unusual.[68] The list of owners who had slaves run off is a who's who of Trenton society and includes: Jonathan Richmond, A. Lambert, Rev. Elihu Spencer, William Chambers, Patrick Colvin, Samuel Henry, and Hezekiah Howell.

The Trenton jail often housed runaways from outside Trenton waiting to be claimed by their masters, and a number escaped from the jail.[69] When a suspected runaway slave of an unknown owner was brought to the Trenton jail, he was advertised and a date given for when he would be sold, if not claimed earlier. The confined, supposed runaways often tried to convince the jailer that they were really free men, always a possibility as there were free blacks in the population.[70]

While essentially ignoring the contradiction inherent in seeking the return of their perceived rights while denying them to their slaves, the people of New Jersey slowly joined the protest actions that characterized the decade between 1763 and 1774. The New Jersey colonists opposed Parliament's actions that they regarded as unconstitutional, but no one publicly advocated independence as a goal, and all continued to hold the King in high regard.[71] In 1774, most people still favored a moderate approach to resolving the problems, but the growing disillusionment with the British government was accompanied by resentment at being considered second-class citizens and unsophisticated colonials. This contributed to a growing sense among colonists that they had a separate identity from Britain.[72]

Over the following decade, the geographical importance of Trenton gave it a front-row seat and a variety of important roles in the more radical and violent Revolution that was gaining momentum. As colonial protests transformed into armed conflict the people of Trenton often suffered but sometimes benefitted from the Revolutionary events that brought various groups and individuals through town.

Chapter 2

1775

On January 13, 1775, Daniel Coxe and Samuel Tucker attended a Joint Meeting of the Assembly and Council at Perth Amboy to hear an address from Royal Governor William Franklin. Coxe and Tucker held strongly conflicting opinions in the debates over how best to deal with the acts of Parliament. Daniel Coxe opposed the protest movement and believed the problems could, and should, be resolved through legal channels, while Samuel Tucker was one of several men serving in the colonial government while also on one or more extralegal committees. Franklin told the legislators, "It would argue not only a great want of duty to His Majesty, but of regard to the good people of this Province, were I ... to pass over in silence the late alarming transactions in this and the neighbouring colonies, or not endeavor to prevail on you to exert yourselves in preventing those mischiefs to this Country, which, without your timely interposition, will, in all probability, be the consequence." He did not risk giving any legitimacy to the Continental Congress or the Convention by detailing their specific actions. Everyone knew what they were anyway. Franklin, the illegitimate son of Benjamin Franklin, was a colonial whose career was firmly tied to the British political establishment. He encouraged the legislators to address the people's grievances, rather than encourage formation of extralegal, in reality illegal, organizations such as the committees, Convention, or Continental Congress and reminded them that they were entrusted by their constituents with "a peculiar guardianship of their rights and privileges."

Both Coxe and Tucker fully understood this mandate but disagreed whether it was best served at present by the legal or extralegal structures. Franklin warned the legislators that, "You have now pointed out to you, Gentlemen, two roads – one evidently leading to peace, happiness, and a restoration of the publick tranquility – the other inevitably conducting you to anarchy, misery, and all the horrors of a civil war." Franklin did not gloss over the rising tide of anger and demands for action. However, after commenting that the legislators might receive short-term popularity by taking the misguided, extralegal road, he sermonized that, "It is a most infallible symptom of the dangerous state of liberty, when the chief men of a free country shew a greater regard to popularity than to their own judgment." Again, both Coxe and Tucker could assure Franklin that their opinions and actions, although in complete opposition, were based on judgment and principle rather than seeking popularity. The Council confirmed its support of the Governor's message on January 26. The Assembly's response would take more time and be another matter. [1]

Kevin Phillips writes compellingly that the events surrounding the vote for independence in 1776 can only be fully understood as the culmination of changes taking place in the 1760s and early 70s, reaching a crescendo in 1775. As violent protest escalated into more formal warfare in New England, and as extralegal committees and congresses began to displace colonial governments throughout the colonies, all Americans struggled with which forms of protest and what ultimate goal they could support. The issues were extremely complex, with elements of philosophy, tradition, and self-interest intertwined with complexities of family and social relationships, all blending into a unique combination for each individual and leading to a wide variety of very personal responses that could switch quickly in response to changing situations.[2]

Dr. Benjamin Rush of Philadelphia wrote that the winter of 1774-75 "was a period of uncommon anxiety among the citizens of America" who were awaiting the King's response to a petition that would "determine whether reconciliation, or a civil war, with all its terrible and distressing consequence, were to take place." The intense stress caused by this uncertainty could even lead to death. Rush observed that all colonials believed a limited monarchy was essential to a free and safe government and that people were more passionate about the liberties they had been born with than any new ones they might seek. The deep ties to England through common kinship, laws, religion, commerce, language, interest, and a mutual sense of national glory resulted in an equally deep resentment over lost liberties. Rush felt that "an indifferent, or neutral spectator of the controversy, was scarcely to be found" in any colony. In short, "The controversy was conceived to be the most important of any that had ever engaged the attention of mankind."[3]

While struggling with questions of rights, Trenton's residents dealt with the issues of daily life. In January, Daniel Coxe was looking for someone to lease Trenton Ferry beginning March first. The same month, John Pemberton advertised Trenton steel products for sale "either in blister or faggot; mill saws, tanners shaving knives, cart and wagon boxes, cogs for wheat fans, &c." In addition, he offered one half of the steel furnace for sale, a substantial stone building with a frame building on an adjoining lot.[4] The iron and steel complex had been created in the 1730s by Benjamin Yard on Petty's Run and included a plating mill, steel furnace, one or two smith's shops, a coal house, and the waterpower system.[5] Parliament had passed laws beginning in 1750 aimed at preventing the growth of a colonial iron industry, so this was one of the few such complexes in the colonies. By the 1770s, advertisements stated "American steel, manufactured by John Zane, at Trentown, [was] esteem'd quite equal, if not better in quality than what is imported from England."[6]

Silversmith John Fitch made an agreement in January with John Cochran to work as a journeyman for forty shillings per week plus meals and in March haggled over the pay of another worker, James Graves. Fitch's shop was busy making many articles, including buckles for tavern owner Rensselaer Williams.[7] William Smith had to deal with his runaway indentured servant, Irish born butcher Daniel Murrin, who took off "with a sum of money that he was intrusted with."[8] The community lost young attorney Joseph Warrell, who died at the age of thirty-six and was buried in the Presbyterian churchyard cemetery. He was known for his "affability, good humor, and generosity, [that] endeared him to all those who had the pleasure of his acquaintance."[9] Peggy Spencer, daughter of Presbyterian Reverend Elihu Spencer, married Jonathan Dickinson Sergeant, an up-and-coming young lawyer of Princeton on March 14.[10] Furman and Hunt had for sale the newly published *Letters of Abelard and Eloisa*.[11]

Samuel Tucker took time away from the Assembly to attend a January 18 meeting of the various Hunterdon County Committees of Correspondence at Ringo's Tavern in Amwell Township. This meeting endorsed the Continental Association created by the Continental Congress, agreed to abide by it, and then chose Samuel Tucker and others as the county Committee of Correspondence to attend a meeting in Trenton on March 29 to select delegates to a second Continental Congress.[12]

Six days later, Tucker attended the General Assembly when it learned about, and then unanimously approved, the actions of the extralegal Continental Congress and then, without the concurrence of the Council or governor, reappointed the same four delegates from the first Continental Congress to attend the second one; negating the need for the March 29 extralegal meeting to select them. These delegates were charged "to propose and agree to every reasonable and constitutional measure for the accommodation of the unhappy differences at present subsisting between our Mother Country and the Colonies."[13] The Assembly was working with the extralegal committees seemingly in an attempt to maintain its legislative authority while striving for leadership in the protest movement.

The Assembly finally responded on February 3 to Governor Franklin's message. Members expressed disappointment that Franklin felt as he did and pretended uncertainty regarding which specific actions he felt were wrong. They again expressed their loyalty to the King and the British form of government, and their hope for a happy resolution to the difficulties. They did, however, say they "are warmly attached to that liberty, which, as subjects of our august Monarch, we apprehend ourselves to be justly entitled to" and pledged to do whatever was needed to preserve it. Governor Franklin was frustrated with their response but tried to keep discourse on a civil level, even though some people were attributing less than honorable intentions to him. He reassured them that "the advice I gave you was totally uninfluenced by any sinister motive whatever, it came from an heart sincerely devoted to my native Country, whose welfare and happiness depend, as I conceive, upon a plan of conduct very different from what has been hitherto adopted." He agreed that changes needed to be made, but that extralegal methods would not achieve the best results.[14]

Like Franklin, many people were growing very concerned about the extralegal events taking place. On February 8, the Assembly considered a petition from a number of inhabitants of Nottingham Township, including Jesse Waln, Isaac Quigley, and Elijah Bond. The petitioners expressed great alarm at the conflict between Great Britain and the colonies "which is now brought to the most alarming crisis, and in all probability will involve this once happy country in all the horrors of a civil war" unless prevented by the "legislatures of the colonies." Resolution of the issues was in everyone's interest, and they wished that measures would be adopted to end the "unnatural" dispute "and reestablish tranquility and union, on a solid and constitutional foundation." They agreed that in addition to paying taxes to cover the expenses of "our internal government," they also had a responsibility to pay for the "expences necessary for the defence of the Empire, in proportion to our circumstances and situation." However, decisions should be made by their representatives, not Parliament. They expressed qualified support for the protest actions of the Convention and Continental Congresses saying, "such regulations as have already been taken, for the security of our liberties, we will for the sake of internal quiet faithfully, observe, but we disavow all violent proceedings." At all times, they would work to prove themselves "loyal subjects of our Gracious Sovereign, friends to the liberties of our country, and promoters of peace and good order."[15] That would prove to be an impossible combination.

The Nottingham petition was considered by the committee preparing one from the entire colony to the King. A lengthy draft petition was presented on February 13 stating again that their complaints did not arise from any disloyalty to the King or "a disposition to withdraw ourselves from a constitutional dependance on the British Crown," but rather "from well grounded apprehensions that our rights and liberties are intimately affected by the late measures" of Parliament. The petition then enumerated over a dozen grievances, ranging from keeping an army in the colonies ever since the French and Indian War without the consent of the Assemblies, to the laws concerning Admiralty and Vice-Admiralty courts, customs inspections, dissolution of Assemblies, the imposition of duties for the purpose of raising revenue, and the wrongs inflicted by the Coercive Acts. While few of the protested actions immediately affected New Jersey, the assemblymen feared future actions would directly impact their colony, and all of these actions by Parliament "necessarily tend to reduce us to a state of servitude, from which our affection for the English Constitution, and duty to ourselves and our posterity, loudly call upon us to avert by all means in our power." They outlined the concrete ways New Jersey had acted to support the British Empire and pay the costs of government. In conclusion, they beseeched the King to intervene on their behalf to redress their grievances. On the question of whether the Assembly Speaker, Cortland Skinner, should sign the petition, Samuel Tucker joined the overwhelming number of "Yea" votes. However, Skinner dissented from approving it and moved that his dissent be entered on the record. Tucker voted "Nay" on Skinner's motion. The votes were evenly split and Skinner used his tie-breaking vote to pass his motion. Demonstrating an increasing sense of local autonomy, the Assembly ordered that the extralegal Committee of Correspondence should transmit the petition to the colony's agent, ignoring the normal concurrence and communication route of Council and Governor to British government.[16]

After two months dealing with both internal concerns and the wider concerns of the protest movement, neither house of the colonial legislature met during March.

In April, Stacy Potts was looking for a "good journeyman blacksmith" and "also a person who understands the glove making business, either a man or woman."[17] Daniel Coxe attended a one-day meeting of the Council at Perth Amboy on April 8 dealing with several routine matters.[18] Then on April 19, seven days after publication of Stacy Potts' want ad for craftsmen and two days after John Fitch agreed to pay John Cochran by the piece and five shillings per week to take care of the shop, British soldiers and American minutemen exchanged shots at Lexington and Concord in Massachusetts. News of the encounters arrived by express rider in Trenton at about nine o'clock on the morning of April 24. Samuel Tucker and Isaac Smith of the Trenton Committee of Correspondence forwarded the letter by express rider to the Philadelphia Committee.[19] Later that day a notice about Lexington and Concord appeared in a supplement to *The Pennsylvania Packet* and boldly stated, accurately or not, that the British had fired "without any provocation."[20] This addressed the colonists' need to be the victim, but to this day it cannot be stated conclusively who fired first.[21] Two days later, at about six-thirty in the morning, an express rider brought additional news that the British troops at Boston had been reinforced and were surrounded by about twenty thousand militiamen digging entrenchments, with ambushes and casualties reported on both sides. Tucker, Smith, and Abraham Hunt forwarded the letter to Philadelphia.[22]

The exchange of shots at Lexington and Concord set off a sharp rise in anti-government feelings and a desire among some New Jersey inhabitants to take up arms – a rage militaire.[23] This rage was encouraged by the naïve belief that virtue and bravery exhibited by a large proportion of men, acting as militiamen willing to die for their beliefs like those in Massachusetts, could bring about a redress of grievances. While reactions to Lexington and Concord blew oxygen on the smoldering idea of American independence, the Declaration of Independence was still more than a year away and the concept remained only an ember for a longer period of time in New Jersey and the other middle colonies, where the population contained a larger percentage of people with doubts about the course the rebellion was taking.[24]

While many people still hoped for a peaceful resolution, the rage militaire led some men to join ad hoc militia companies, separate from the required militia established by the colonial government, as a tool of protest, similar to companies that had formed during land title conflicts in the 1730s and 40s.[25] The Provincial Committee of Correspondence met at New Brunswick on May 2, with Samuel Tucker and Abraham Hunt attending, and called for a Provincial Congress to meet at Trenton on May 23 to consider what steps to take in response to recent British actions.[26] Parliament passed a Restraining Act in April that directly affected New Jersey by banning its vessels from the North Atlantic fisheries and restricting its trade to Great Britain and the British West Indies.[27]

Another group of New England delegates rode into Trenton, dined, and crossed at the ferry on their way to the second Continental Congress scheduled to meet on May 10.[28] About the same time, Trenton fish merchant Jonathan Richmond was advertising his "choice pickled sturgeon, at ten shillings the two gallon keg, and twelve shillings the three gallon keg, cured after the Baltic manner," and touting his thirteen years of experience.[29] Fishing had been important from the earliest days of human habitation at the falls and in addition to Richmond, Benjamin Yard, Elijah Bond, and William Richards had established local fisheries. Sturgeon, shad (a type of herring), and other species ascended the Delaware River in large numbers each spring to spawn. Beginning in the late seventeenth century, European colonists established fishing and processing facilities to take advantage of markets in other British colonies such as Barbados. High-level skills were required to pickle the fish, pack them in crates or barrels, and ship them to market or preserve them for up to two years by curing in salt brine and smoking. The fish could also be rendered by boiling and cleansing to produce oil, glue, or isinglass (a very pure gelatin used as a clarifying agent made from fish air bladders).[30] In his ads, Richmond included instructions for using his barrels of preserved fish properly, telling customers to "draw off the liquor at the bung into a clean pan, then take out the head that is branded, harden on the hoops, and pour to it again its own pickle, and if at any time there is a supply wanting to cover the fish, add some good neat vinegar."[31]

The *Hartford Current* announced on May 8 that William Goddard was organizing an alternative postal service to the Royal one. Goddard had engaged a post rider to proceed from New York with mail for Philadelphia and the colonies to the south. One of the new post offices Goddard created was at Trenton and administered by the Trenton Committee of Correspondence.[32]

The Second Continental Congress began meeting on May 10 and voted to issue three million dollars in paper money and raise a Continental army of twenty thousand men. Almost immediately, some delegates raised questions about the goal of the fighting. Was it to restore rights or achieve "independency?"[33] New Jersey did not immediately contribute troops for the new army and remained opposed to independence.

Governor Franklin delivered another long address to the colonial legislature on May 16, favorably describing a recent House of Commons resolution and reiterating the many ways the British government had supported the colonists and their justifiable responsibility to help fund those benefits. It called for calmer heads to prevail and work out solutions rather than call for trade embargoes and independence. The governor "lamented that there is so much truth in the observation, that mankind generally act not according to right, but according to present interest, and most according to present passion." Peaceful resolution was only possible "if men come together sincerely disposed to serve their country, unbiased by any sinister views or improper resentments." He urged the legislators not to reject Parliament's resolution outright, because that would reinforce "what has been lately so often mentioned in publick, 'That it is not a dispute about Modes of Taxation—but that the Americans ... mean to throw off all dependence upon Great Britain.'" Franklin warned that independent colonies would have to pay a great deal more for protection than they were being asked to contribute by Parliament and, showing his misunderstanding of the complex conflict, optimistically summed up his message saying, "taxation being the principal source of the present disorders, when that important point is once settled, every other subject of complaint which has grown out of it will, no doubt, of course, be removed." In spite of Whig propaganda to the contrary,

Franklin had found "the whole tenor" of letters he received from the King's ministers to be "that his Majesty and they have nothing more at heart than to have these unhappy differences accommodated on some just and honourable plan," one "which shall at the same time secure the liberties of the people without lessening the necessary power and dignity of Parliament."[34]

After the joint session, Samuel Tucker put before the Assembly a pamphlet printed in England containing a purported letter from Governor Franklin to the Earl of Dartmouth the previous February concerning his unsuccessful efforts to prevent the General Assembly from approving the actions taken by the Continental Congress. This revelation was clearly timed to embarrass the Governor and discredit his public comments.

Tucker and another Assemblymen waited upon the governor on May 19 to set up a time for the Assembly to deliver its response to his May 16 message. Part of the Assembly's response was a statement of their reluctance to respond to Parliament's resolution before communicating with the Continental Congress. They had no intention "to desert the common cause, in which all America appears to be both deeply interested and firmly united," recognizing the strength of united action. They found nothing new in Parliament's resolution and did not appreciate the governor's insinuation that their actions represented self-interest, or present passion, and hoped the governor would choose to be a positive force "in settling of the present unhappy differences." This response greatly frustrated Franklin who felt he had done all that he could, would always work toward reconciliation, and had been honest with them. Franklin strongly pointed out that their desire to avoid acting counter to the policies of the Continental Congress violated their declaration not to let any of their constitutional rights be usurped by "any person or persons whatsoever."

The pamphlet Samuel Tucker had introduced was the last item considered before the Assembly adjourned. When the Assembly inquired of Franklin about the legitimacy of the letter, he gave them a scathing response denying he wrote it, pointing out several reasons to question its authenticity, and castigated them for not sharing it with him before entering it into their minutes. Franklin was particularly angry with Tucker, who apparently had acted for a member of the Assembly who wanted to remain anonymous. The Assembly denied any attempt to embarrass the Governor, but rather to provide him the

Oliver L. Kemp's c1898 sketch of the Trenton Friends Meeting House. (Stryker, Trenton and Princeton)

"opportunity of exculpating himself from the charge of writing the said letter." The Assembly then named Tucker to a committee formed to consider the Governor's response and report at the next meeting in June at Burlington, and adjourned.[35]

Three days later, the new Provincial Congress convened at Trenton, instead of one of the two colonial capitals, making Trenton effectively the capital of Revolutionary New Jersey and at least some of its meetings were held at the Friends Meeting House. The Provincial Congress replaced the Convention, which had coordinated protest actions, with a protest government acting in parallel to the colonial Assembly. Leaders were chosen, including Assembly member Samuel Tucker as Vice-President. Because its work would profoundly affect the people of New Jersey, the Congress requested the town's ministers, Rev. Elihu Spencer of the Presbyterian Church

George Bradshaw's c1929 etching of the Trenton Presbyterian Church during the time of the Revolution. (THS, Trenton)

and Rev. George Panton of St. Michael's Anglican Church, to attend alternately each morning at eight o'clock to open the meetings with prayer.[36] Spencer, a strong supporter of the protest movement, was a graduate of Yale, had served as a missionary to the Oneida Indians in New York, developed congregations in North Carolina, and served several congregations in New Jersey before coming to Trenton in 1770. He had been a trustee of the College of New Jersey in Princeton since 1752.[37] Panton was born in Scotland and became pastor in Trenton in 1774. He did not support the protest movement and later wrote that from the beginning of "the commotions which terminated in the late unnatural revolt" he had "cooperated with the Principal Loyal Characters in New York, Jersey, Pennsylvania and Maryland, in counteracting the popular system and endeavouring to maintain the civil government, traversing these several provinces at his own expense for that purpose."[38] However, hoping for a peaceful solution, both ministers provided opening prayers for the work of the Provincial Congress.

While the Provincial Congress was only called to determine "measures to be pursued in defending those inestimable rights and privileges to which, by our happy constitution, the inhabitants of the Province are justly entitled," whether the members saw it then or not, they were initiating the process by which the Provincial Congress would eventually replace the colonial legislature. The Provincial Congress complimented the General Assembly for adopting the Continental Association and other measures of the Continental Congress. It also approved the delegates to the Second Continental Congress chosen by the Assembly, but stated it would choose future delegates. The Congress developed a Continental Association document on May 31 that was both a loyalty oath to the Provincial and Continental Congresses and a pledge to support their actions, while not renouncing British citizenship. It was to be signed by the inhabitants of each township.[39]

Even though the Provincial Congress was still a parallel, extralegal legislature, it passed a tax in June to raise £10,000 to pursue the protests and prepare for war if necessary. This tax was similar to the existing property tax except that money would be collected by the extralegal county committees instead of the colonial government. This tax was in addition to any tax imposed by the colonial government and was not well received. Many people refused to pay, including Quakers, who opposed paying taxes that supported war, and those who considered themselves "the friends of government." In October, orders went to the county collectors to seize and sell enough property of tax delinquents to pay their bills. This did not completely solve the problem, and efforts to collect unpaid taxes were still being pursued in 1777. By fall, dissension was rampant. People did not want to pay taxes to two governments. Because of the ill feeling, the Provincial Congress decided in October to simply delay paying for any war expenses. Rebuffed by the Continental Congress when it tried to borrow money, the Provincial Congress issued £30,000 in paper money with 1784 designated as the year when tax revenue would begin to support it.[40] This inaugurated a series of actions resulting in rampant inflation that damaged the economy and made it extremely difficult to financially support the war effort.

Neither the Provincial Council nor the General Assembly met in June, essentially leaving government in the hands of the Provincial Congress, which received requests to enact guidelines on forming local militia companies. A local community defense militia established by the colonial government had existed for a century, but this would be a new militia organized by the people to help bring about a restoration of rights. A brief militia law passed on June 3 was more suggestive of a system, based on the colonial model, rather than laying things out in detail. One or more companies of eighty suitably armed men aged 16 to 50, capable of bearing arms, were to be formed immediately in each township with a captain, two lieutenants, and an ensign elected by the members. The company officers must appoint sergeants, corporals, and drummers and help elect a colonel, lieutenant colonel, major, and adjutant for their regiment. Captains were to keep muster rolls and assemble their companies at least once a month for training. Since both the legal and extralegal militias consisted of the same men, the Provincial Congress effectively took control of the militia from the colonial government. During 1775 the Provincial Congress gradually usurped the governing powers of the colonial government and this new militia would enforce its actions, as well as the policies of the Continental Congress. Also on June 3, the Provincial Congress named Samuel Tucker to a new Committee of Correspondence, superseding the one established previously by the Assembly, authorized to convene the Provincial Congress.[41]

As early as June 26, militiamen under Captain Robert Hoops of Trenton "escorted to Elizabethtown four wagons with ninety-eight quarter casks of a necessary article, placed in eight hogsheads, to be forwarded to Cambridge," Massachusetts. The "necessary article" was gunpowder.[42] Some men from Trenton who had land and interests in several locations joined military units in other colonies or counties. These included Moore Furman who was commissioned a captain in the Third Battalion of the Philadelphia Associators.[43] Events were moving rapidly, and Samuel Tucker wrote on June 18 to his friend, merchant John Reynell, in Philadelphia that "Publick affairs realy weare [wear] a melancholy aspect." Express riders arrived daily with news "and unless the Allwise Governor of the Universe interposes and commands order and peace[,] no human creature can possibly tell where these terrible calamities will end."[44]

In June, John Fitch balanced his accounts with his journeyman, Joseph Toy.[45] Toy was very active in the Methodist Church, leading Trenton's first Methodist Class by 1772 and apparently attracted Fitch to the group.[46] Money had been raised in 1772 to build a "preaching house" by people attracted to Methodism, and subscribers included members of other churches, including Benjamin Yard, Sr., John Yard, Abraham Hunt, Isaac DeCou, Isaac Smith, Samuel Bellerjeau, and Jonathan Richmond.[47] The Methodist Church, just the third built in America, was completed in 1774 on the northeast corner of Queen and Fourth streets. Tailor Conrad Kotts, formerly a Quaker, became the first Methodist Steward.[48]

Word of the June 17 Battle of Bunker Hill had just reached Trenton when General Washington crossed the Assunpink bridge on June 23 or 24 and passed through town on his way to take command of the newly constituted Continental army. Life was not nearly as stressful in Trenton as around Boston but still had its usual difficulties. On June 19, twenty-year-old Irish indentured servant James Lio ran away from Trenton mill owner Samuel Henry and headed up the Delaware River.[49]

While neither of the parallel legislatures met in July, the militia continued to form. John Fitch made regimental buttons while also cleaning a sword and putting a mounting on a scabbard for Lieutenant Elias Hunt of Maidenhead. Fitch also purchased a pair of shoes from Trenton shoemaker William Tucker, an officer in the Trenton militia company.[50]

People opposed to the protests felt threatened. Council member Daniel Coxe fully supported the British government, whose policies had benefitted his family for four generations, and after the war touted "his invariable opposition to the late seditious usurpations in America & particularly in his own Province," which made him "frequently subject to much personal insult & danger." When protests heated up after Lexington and Concord, he "opposed the measures of the insurgents in his conversation at all public meetings," resulting in threats of "tarring & feathering." When presented with "an Association paper," he refused to sign it. Exactly one year before the Declaration of Independence, Coxe wrote, "What then have men of property not to fear and apprehend, and particularly those who happen and are known to differ in sentiment from the generality? They become a mark for popular fury, and those who are esteemed friends to Government devoted for destruction. They are not even allowed to preserve a neutrality, and passiveness becomes a crime."[51]

After the war, deposed royal governor William Franklin commented that Coxe was actually rather passive during the protests and although always "loyally disposed," was "one of two or three of the council who were so disposed but not active to embark in matters of risqué; they declined to do some things proposed by the Governor as too hazardous, alleging they were unsupported." Franklin summed up Coxe's passivity saying, "he did nothing to encourage the disaffection but was not active in preventing it." Still, Coxe was branded an arch Loyalist by the Whigs and suffered just like those who opposed the Revolution more actively.[52]

Supplies coming from the south, ordered by the Continental Congress for its newly created army in Massachusetts, began passing through Trenton. Six and a half tons of gunpowder ordered by Congress on July 25 were sent from Philadelphia under convoy to General Washington. Two officers and thirty riflemen, raised in Pennsylvania for the Continental army, met the powder wagons at Trenton and escorted them to Cambridge.[53]

The Provincial Congress met at Trenton on August 5 and ordered all township committees to submit the names of people who refused to sign the Continental Association or who "have refused to pay their respective apportionments." In this way, leaders put pressure on people to demonstrate support for the cause or risk being publicly identified as an enemy of it.[54]

Congress tried to resolve problems generated by the hastily passed militia law with a second act on August 16. Now, any qualified man between the ages of 16 and 50 who refused to enroll and bear arms would be fined. Service in its militia was now a requirement imposed by the extralegal government, almost a year before independence was declared and while the colonial government was still in place. This law put Quakers in a difficult situation. In July and August, William Plaskett and Joseph Milnor were dismissed from their Meeting because they obeyed the militia act and did not repent.[55] The new law also instituted a body of volunteer minutemen recruited from the militia. The Provincial Congress appointed Philemon Dickinson of Trenton as brigadier general of militia and John Fitch created a mounting for his sword, in addition to attaching mountings on a musket for militiaman William Read and a sword scabbard for an unknown militiaman. Fitch also made a hanger and belt for Robert Quigley of Nottingham Township and another for Captain George Green of Maidenhead, as well as swords, hangers, etc. for others. He repaired and polished a hanger for militia Major Ephraim Anderson of Trenton.[56]

Ad hoc companies of light infantry competed for men with the newly legislated militia, and Congress co-opted them by requiring such companies to obtain the consent of their local militia regiment field officers and their county or township committee. Thirty-five-year-old Irishman Charles Harrison of Trenton formed one of these light infantry companies and his election as captain was certified on August 30, along with John Yard as first lieutenant, James Matthews second lieutenant, and innkeeper Henry Drake third lieutenant. Doctor Isaac Smith, apparently already serving as colonel of the First Hunterdon militia regiment, signed the certification as required.[57] Thirty-five-year-old Doctor Smith was an early member of the New Jersey Medical Society,[58] and a member of the prestigious American Philosophical Society since 1768.[59] Elected colonel on the basis of his character and social standing, rather than military experience, Smith's election reflected the hope that violence could still be avoided. Before Congress adjourned, it created a Committee of Safety, including Samuel Tucker, to operate during its recess.[60]

While traveling on the road to Trenton in August, Benjamin Franklin overtook a wagon loaded with gunpowder and thought it was part of a shipment forwarded to Boston by the Philadelphia Committee of Safety. However, at New Brunswick, Franklin learned that four wagon loads had passed through the previous Friday. Now believing the Friday wagons carried the promised powder he wrote a quick note to the wagoner he had passed, instructing him to return to Philadelphia. He sent the note by a man "just setting out for Trenton" and asked him to intercept the wagon. As a result, that wagon of powder, with its possibly very confused driver, went through Trenton in both directions.[61]

Trentonians may have been impressed by the 80 "remarkably stout and hardy men" of Captain James Ross's Pennsylvania Rifle Company raised in Lancaster County. Many were over six feet tall and all wore "white frocks or rifle shirts and round hats" when they passed through Trenton in August.[62] The company officers purchased food and services from several Trenton businesses, including tavern keepers Charles Axford, Charity Britton, Joseph Clunn, and Rachel Stille, telling them to submit bills to the Continental Congress. Congress later ordered the bills paid, but in the case of Mrs. Stille's bill, the Congress charged the expense to Captain Ross "until he makes it appear to be just and reasonable that the same be charged to the Continent." Congress must have felt Ross had lived a little too well in Trenton.[63]

About September 30, six wagons carrying gunpowder, escorted by 24 light infantry and some riflemen of the First Pennsylvania regiment, came through Trenton, where the escort was changed.[64]

Trenton's taverns not only provided meals and lodging for the many people and horses stopping in town but also space for meetings, making them centers of social life and communication for local people. The first tavern encountered in Trenton when entering on the Maidenhead Road was the Fox Chase Tavern, at the northern entrance to the village. After turning onto King Street, Charles Axford, Jr.'s King of Prussia Tavern was on the right. A short distance down the hill was Charity Britton's Indian King Tavern; this was a large, two-story frame house with four rooms on each floor and an entry through the first floor. A large kitchen adjoined it. The property also had a wood house and shed, a two story stable accommodating upwards of forty horses, and a young orchard with more than 50 trees bearing grafted fruit. Petty's Run, a never-failing stream of water, ran through the property. Charity Britton's tavern license applications cover 1763 through 1779, and her 1772 application stated that she had been in business for many years "for the entertainment of straingers, travelers and others, and keeps good entertainment for men and horse, and keeps good orders in her house."[65] Charity was Samuel Tucker's sister and had married Henry Bellerjeau, with whom she had nine children. After Henry's death, she married shoemaker Joseph Britton, with whom she had three children. Joseph pursued his shoemaking business while she operated the tavern. After Joseph died in 1755, Charity continued her tavern.[66]

Joseph Clunn applied for a tavern license on May 2, 1774, stating that he had taken "that house in Trenton now known by the Sign of the Ship & Castle in which a tavern has been keep [sic] many years past."[67] This was a small, one-and-a-half story, stone building located

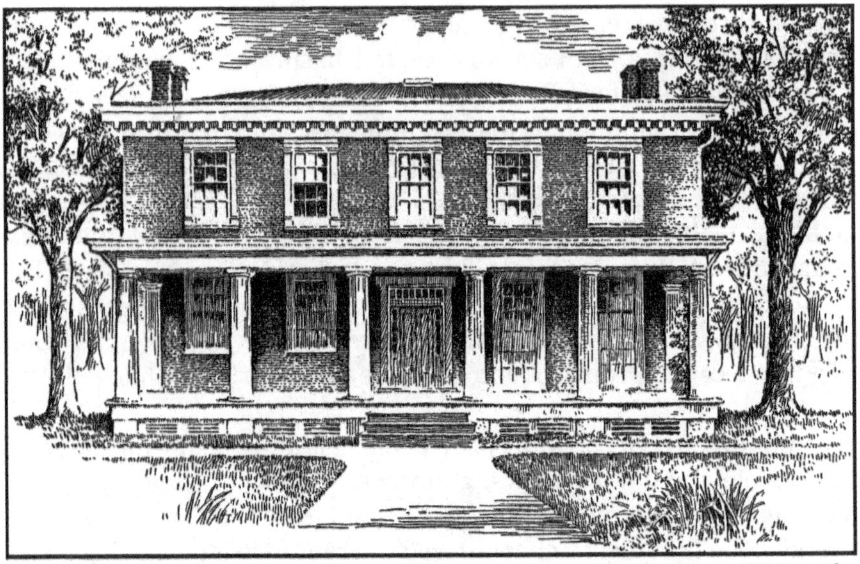

George Bradshaw's c1929 etching of Kingsbury Manor, built about 1719 as the home of William Trent. During the Revolution it was first the home of the Loyalist Dr. William Bryant and then Colonel John Cox who served as an assistant quartermaster general to Nathanael Greene. (THS, Trenton)

on the north side of Front Street, just east of the intersection with King Street.[68]

Rachel Stille's tavern, located on the northwest corner of the intersection of Queen and Second Street about a block east of King Street, where Captain Ross ran up his questionable bill, had existed for many years under several names.[69] The brick house was thirty-five-feet square with four rooms on the lower floor and a spacious entry through it. The second floor had three rooms, including a well-appointed assembly room with a door opening on a balcony fronting Queen Street. The third story contained lodging rooms. Close by was a large two-story brick kitchen containing a wash house. The lot had a large yard, a garden with an excellent well, and large stables fronting on Second Street, also known as Market Street, in addition to cow houses, hen houses, and pigeon houses.[70]

Trentonians eager to honor the Battle of Bunker Hill became subscribers to a proposed printing of "an exact view of the late Battle at Charlestown, (June 17th, 1775) to be printed on a good crown

Oliver L. Kemp's c1898 sketch of the tavern at the corner of King and Second Streets in the heart of the Trenton commercial district. (Stryker, Trenton and Princeton)

imperial paper, either plain or colored, and delivered to subscribers in about ten days." Subscriptions were available from Trenton merchant James Emerson in September.[71]

When the Provincial Congress assembled again at Trenton on October 4, Samuel Tucker was elected its president. Rev. Spencer opened the meeting with prayer "so that peace, unanimity and harmony may be happily re-established between both countries upon a permanent foundation." The Congress heard a petition that day from some inhabitants of Nottingham Township, requesting permission to join Captain Charles Harrison's light infantry company in Trenton. The militia law, organizing regiments based on counties and companies on townships, had not anticipated divided communities like Trenton's. Permission was granted, but only to residents of the settlement called Kingsborough, or Kingsbury, just south of the Assunpink. Dr. William Bryant had purchased William Trent's 1719 home, called Kingsbury, in 1769. It was a two-story brick building with a separate two-story brick kitchen containing four apartments for servants and an avenue of English cherry trees leading down to the ferry.[72] Bryant was a highly respected doctor who had been elected to membership in the American

Philosophical Society on January 21, 1774 and presented a paper entitled an "Account of an Electrical Eel or Torpedo from Surinam."[73] He had been selling lots to develop the village of Kingsbury "between Trenton and the Ferry, on the east and west sides of Broad, and on the north side of Delaware streets," a "good neighborhood" where he had laid out streets for a town.[74]

Another petition from members of Captain Harrison's company came before the Provincial Congress on October 24 from men who were not from Kingsbury but wanted to continue in the company. Their Nottingham company had been combined with another in the township, so they now lived closer to the mustering site of the Trenton company. Their request was granted on October 25. Congress also granted John Matthews, apparently one of the Nottingham men, a lieutenant's commission in Harrison's company. Jonathan Richmond, Hugh Runyan, and Rensselaer Williams were several of the men involved.[75]

Units of the Continental army had been sent north under General Richard Montgomery and Benedict Arnold to take Canada from the British, but New Jersey had not yet raised any Continental regiments. The Continental Congress asked the Provincial Congress on October 9 to help enlarge the Continental army by immediately raising two regiments of eight companies, each containing 79 officers and men enlisted for one year. Recruits would have to supply their own arms like the militia and, instead of a cash bounty, receive a felt hat, a pair of yarn stockings, and a pair of shoes. No uniform was specified so recruits would wear their civilian clothing.[76] Although not yet authorizing enlistments, the Provincial Congress voted on October 13 to give each man a hunting shirt and blanket in order to encourage enlistments and provide some sort of uniform. These were not to be part of the enlistment agreement because their procurement was questionable.[77]

Word that New Jersey Continental regiments had been requested spread quickly and men reacted to it in the spirit of the rage militaire. The only known minuteman company raised in the Trenton area was Captain Joseph Brearley's of nearby Maidenhead and several Trenton and Nottingham men had joined it, including George Beatty, Martin Scott, Henry Garrison, Jacob Keen, Joseph Skirm, and John Wilmot.[78] Captain Brearley offered his services and those of his entire company for Continental service on October 13, while his lieutenants, Jonathan Phillips and Philip Moore, also petitioned the Provincial Congress, stating that the company was fully manned and "the greatest part of 'em desirous of going at this juncture upon the service of their Country." Three high-ranking militia officers from Trenton, Brigadier General Philemon Dickinson, Colonel Isaac Smith, and Major Ephraim Anderson, along with Major Joseph Phillips of Maidenhead, signed a recommendation on October 25 supporting Captain Brearley's request that he and his minuteman company be taken into a Continental regiment. They supported Brearley "as a very suitable person for a captain of a company" based on their knowledge of "his character, patriotism & zeal in the American Cause."[79]

Samuel Tucker told the Continental Congress on October 21 that many men had applied for commissions in the new regiments, but the Provincial Congress would not grant commissions or recruit men until questions were answered about whether the Provincial or Continental Congress was responsible for financing these regiments and appointing their field officers. Samuel Tucker, as President of the Congress, signed an October 14 letter to the Continental Congress asking about the source for money to purchase arms, ammunition, and other essential articles. Requests for commissions continued to come in from petitioners who called on anyone with influence to help them.[80]

In the middle of this activity, John Fitch submitted a bill to Samuel Tucker for mending a pair of gold buttons and making a pincushion hoop and chain, and a scissors chain for his wife. Fitch also repaired a hanger for an unknown militiaman and considered applying for a Continental commission himself, so he could "render as much service to my country as possible." However, after submitting his petition, Fitch asked that it be rejected because he objected to the requirement for recruits to "furnish themselves with armes and cloathing." He knew "the soldiers were the poorest class of people and could not equip themselves and put themselves on an equal footing with the British troops." Fitch believed it was partly due to his protestations that the law was soon changed to provide the men with arms and clothing. He stayed in the militia and became very active at his shop making muskets for the Continentals and militia.[81]

The Provincial Congress finally advertised on October 26 for enlistments in the two Continental regiments and authorized warrants for recruiters to begin enlisting men.[82] Trenton's Thomas Yard almost immediately requested a commission as either lieutenant or ensign.

His petition was endorsed by prominent Trenton militia officers - General Philemon Dickinson, Colonel Isaac Smith, Lieutenant Colonel Abraham Hunt, Major Isaac DeCou, Captain William Tucker, and Captain Charles Harrison, plus important Trenton merchants Hezekiah Howell, David Pinkerton, Charles Axford, Jr., and Benjamin Smith.[83] Joseph Brearley was awarded a captain's commission in the Second New Jersey Regiment and undoubtedly knew Yard, who was commissioned October 28 as his first lieutenant.[84]

Second New Jersey Regiment enlistments began in earnest in November, and some local men entered companies organizing in Trenton at the barracks. Barney Johnson enlisted in Captain Brearley's Company on November 4, Joseph Skirm of Nottingham on November 3, Martin Scott on November 4, and James Monjoy on November 11.[85] Dennis Cain enlisted on November 5 and Henry Garrison on November 3 in Captain James Lawrie's company. Benjamin Moore enlisted November 27 in Captain John B. Scott's Company, and Ephraim Anderson was commissioned lieutenant for Captain Joseph Stout's Company on October 28. The four captains began receiving various sums of money from Provincial Congress President Samuel Tucker on November 23 to purchase arms for their men. Payments continued in December.[86]

Still solidifying the militia structure, the Provincial Congress unanimously commissioned Philemon Dickinson on October 19 as First Brigadier General of the militia. Two brigadiers were needed because militia duty was part-time and only one brigadier was expected to be on duty at a time. Dickinson would be the senior of the two. The various county militia regiments made up the brigade the general would command. Before adjourning on October 28, the Provincial Congress passed yet another militia act seeking to clarify and strengthen the previous laws. It appointed Trenton merchants Samuel Tucker, Abraham Hunt, and Alexander Chambers as commissioners for the western division of New Jersey, to purchase supplies for the militia and pay the men. The Provincial Congress named the field officers for the two New Jersey Continental regiments and approved the resignation of Major Ephraim Anderson from the militia after he accepted a commission as a lieutenant in the Second New Jersey Continental Regiment. Samuel Tucker was named to the powerful Committee of Safety for New Jersey created that day, and also continued as president of the Provincial Congress. Several housekeeping items were addressed. The Congress gave thanks to Trenton Reverends Spencer and Panton for their services and to their churches "who have been pleased to accommodate this Congress with the use of their respective places of worship." Samuel Tucker was authorized payment for the expenses he personally incurred for "firewood, candles, pens, ink and paper, for the use of this Congress, during the present sitting." That day, the Continental Congress authorized payment to Rachel Stille for expenses incurred by a guard staying at her inn while protecting some gunpowder at Trenton, and on November 16 approved payment to John Hider for expenses incurred securing a boat and five men for two days carrying gunpowder to Trenton on its way to the army.[87]

Although the Provincial Congress did not meet in November, President Samuel Tucker was still busy with its business, even while continuing to serve in the General Assembly where he was conveniently able to meet with other protest leaders also serving in it. The colonial government was still in place, although having lost its grip on things.[88] The combined Council and Assembly heard yet another message from Governor Franklin on November 16 at Burlington, repeating his concerns, frustrations, and commitment to cooperate with any endeavor toward "peace, order, and good government." After this meeting, the Council did very little until adjourning on November 24. The Assembly continued to meet on routine business during the month, and Tucker worked on a committee charged with developing a bill for the financial support of the government and also for preparing a petition to the King, "humbly beseeching him to use his interposition to prevent the effusion of blood; and to express the great desire this House hath to a restoration of peace and harmony with the parent State on constitutional principles."[89]

The first British soldiers encountered by the citizens of Trenton during the Revolution arrived in town on or about November 17. Major Joseph Stopford, Captain Brice, Lieutenants Hamar, Harrison, and Shuttleworth, one surgeon, and 83 non-commissioned officers and men of the 7th Royal Fusiliers, along with some of their wives and children, arrived as prisoners of war captured by Continental forces in Canada at the fall of Fort Chambly on October 19. These prisoners were soldiers of the British government being held by the extralegal Continental Congress and presenting a most unusual situation with a number of questions about how to treat them. Their captor, General

Montgomery, had threatened to retaliate for the cruel treatment inflicted by British General Richard Prescott on the captured American officer Ethan Allen, but thought better of it.[90] The British prisoners were to be well treated. Major Stopford was granted requests for his band of music and sutler to accompany him. General Schuyler at Ticonderoga ordered Captain John Hulbert to treat the prisoners well and take them to Trenton, where he was to provide them with good lodgings and see them properly settled before proceeding to Philadelphia to report to Congress about what he had accomplished and take any orders they might have for him.[91] While the commissioned British officers were put up at inns, the non-commissioned officers and privates were quartered at the Trenton barracks with their families. Shortly after arriving in Trenton, one of the British officers wrote about the good treatment they received. He attributed this to everyone seeming "happy they have it in their power to convince us, by their behavior, of the benevolent principles on which they wish this unnatural contest may be conducted." This led him to believe that "it is the sincere sentiment generally of the Americans, that a happy and honourable accommodation between Great Britain and her Colonies may speedily take place." The Continental Congress ordered the Trenton Committee of Safety to have the prisoners sign paroles pledging they would "not to go to or near any seaport town, nor farther than six miles from my place of residence, without leave from the Continental Congress" and also not to carry on any "political correspondence whatever, on the subject of dispute between Great Britain and these Colonies, so long as I remain a prisoner."[92]

While the British prisoners were getting settled, the New Jersey Continental Regiments were forming and needed space in the barracks. The colonial General Assembly passed a bill to assign barracks masters in early December, but, in Samuel Tucker's words on December 10, it "was condemned or d_d in the Council, so that we must now do as well as we can with them." The troops were being raised by authority of the Continental Congress while the colonial government was still in place and not inclined to assist.[93]

The Trenton barracks had been designed to accommodate 300 men and contained 20 fifteen-square-foot rooms quartering 12-15 men each. Each room had a single door, two windows, and a brick fireplace for heat and cooking. The two-level wooden bunk beds held two men on each level, and the room also had wood benches, a trestle table, bedding, a candlestick, a chamber pot, and cooking utensils. The walls and ceiling were white washed plaster and the woodwork painted Spanish brown. The officers' residence was much more sophisticated, with seven rooms and a cellar kitchen.[94]

Amid the rapidly evolving events and preparations for war, a number of citizens were alarmed at how things were progressing. The Assembly received a petition dated November 23 from a number of Burlington County freeholders expressing this alarm and lamenting that the radical leaders on both sides seemed to "dwell so much on their own dignity or importance" that reasonable propositions could not be developed. They were especially "alarmed at the sentiments of independency which are openly avowed by too many people at this time." The petitioners believed that "an effectual opposition may be made against the measures now pursuing by the Ministry and Parliament of Great Britain without changing the Constitutional form of government in the British Empire established." Independence, on the other hand, would lead to the "destruction of the interests of the whole British Empire and a perpetual barr to every door of peace & reconciliation between the parent state and the colonies." The Assembly was encouraged to use peaceful ways to resolve the issues and "discourage an independency should such a measure be attempted, and also make such provision for the support of the civil government of this colony as heretofore." They were solemnly protesting against changing the "form of government as by law established & declaring that it is not, nor never was their intention to vest any congress or body of men whatsoever with that power."[95] The petitioners may have supported the extralegal bodies as protest vehicles, but that did not mean they favored changing the government. A number of factors helped put New Jersey at the center of moderation rather than radicalism, including the population diversity that raised fears of disruption and struggles for power among the various groups should a new political order be created.[96]

Governor Franklin communicated to the Assembly again on November 30, stating that "I return you my thanks for your resolution of support of His Majesty's Government, and cannot but approve your determination to promote peace and good order." Recently, royal governors in other colonies had been removed from office and forced to flee, but the Assemblymen said they were surprised to hear that Franklin had been advised to seek asylum also. Franklin found this disingenuous and told them, "your surprise that any persons could advise me to seek an asylum, when so many Governours and Crown officers had been before compelled to do the like, is as extraordinary as your supposition that those persons must therefore be no friends to the Colony." Franklin told the Assembly he would not relate to the King "any remarks on your sentiments respecting the present unhappy situation of public affairs," but he would convey their "opinion of the Resolution of the House of Commons." Franklin obviously disagreed with their opposition to the Resolution and told them they were "greatly mistaken" if they believed negotiations based on it would have failed to produce "some plan of accommodation, on terms that Americans have heretofore solemnly and repeatedly declared would give them full content."

Franklin then challenged the Assembly to act responsibly regarding the soldiers confined at Trenton "by some supposed unlawful authority," and allow them to apply to the colonial Supreme Court for "an habeas corpus." He felt they had committed no offense against the legitimate government. After hearing Franklin's message, a motion was made to ask the governor to dissolve the Assembly at the end of the present session and give the people an opportunity to elect new representatives, presumably including more members of the Provincial Congress. The vote on the motion was equally divided. Samuel Tucker voted "Yea," and Speaker Cortland Skinner again broke the tie with a "Nay" vote.[97]

The Continental Congress was informed in early December that "Major Stopford notwithstanding his parole is endeavouring to debauch the minds of the people," that is, encouraging people to remain loyal to the British government and disown the policies of the rebel government.[98] Samuel Tucker, Colonel Isaac Smith, Lieutenant Colonel Abraham Hunt, and Captain Robert Hoops from the Trenton Committee of Safety were directed to look into this and reported on December 9 that they had examined the situation and found the prisoners were abiding by their paroles. The only problem had been that Doctor Huddleston had been "unguarded & imprudent in his discourse." This had caused the other prisoners "great uneasiness" and they hoped that if Congress could not overlook Huddleston's "indiscretion," at least "their innocence may not suffer by it, as they have never failed to reprove him, and often times severely, for it." They feared that they would all be removed from Trenton. The Committee of Safety reported there was "not the least danger" to the cause because the prisoners were behaving well. Also, they would not find much sympathy if they did encourage disaffection, because "the people in and about Trenton, as early fixed their principles upon proper knowledge & rational conviction & have as steadily maintained them, as any people on the Continent."[99] The people of Trenton were hardly as unified in their support of the cause as the Committee portrayed, but it strengthened morale to say so.

The day after the Committee of Safety wrote its report, John Adams left Philadelphia to go home on leave from Congress and on December 10 rode to Trenton where he crossed at the ferry and breakfasted at Rensselaer Williams's tavern before riding on to Princeton, dealing as always with "very miry and dirty" roads, but the weather was pleasant and not very cold for that time of year.[100]

Recruiting for the two New Jersey Continental regiments was well underway in December. Enlistments slowly increased in Colonel William Maxwell's Second New Jersey Regiment, with four companies forming at the Trenton barracks and four at Burlington. They were badly needed in Canada and getting them ready to send off was a priority. On December 2, Lord Stirling, commanding the First New Jersey Regiment that was organizing in eastern New Jersey, wrote to Colonel Maxwell that the Continental Congress was "extremely pressing and anxious" to get at least some troops in motion, even if only three companies from each of the two regiments. Stirling was sending off one of his companies the next Wednesday, with another to follow soon, and he begged Maxwell to send off three companies from his regiment. However, it would be some time before any troops left Trenton.[101]

Making soldiers of the recruits was hampered by the fact that they were not entering into a well-structured organization with established expectations, routines, and a cadre of veterans. For most, their only military experience was with the part-time militia, which had been routinely neglected under the colonial regime. In addition, the officers also were learning their jobs, and the lack of uniforms and complete sets of standardized equipment slowed their transition from civilian to military life. On December 8, all soldiers in Trenton were ordered to turn out for roll call in the barracks yard upon the beating of the drum each morning and at sunset. Violators would be confined and punished. Every man was to be in his quarters at nine o'clock each evening unless he had received leave from the commanding officer. These orders were expanded the next day and required every soldier to mount guard in his turn. Each night at roll call, every man was to be as clean as possible, with shoes blacked and hair combed. How they should appear between their shoes and hair was not stated. The regiment was still establishing routines on December 11, when Trenton's Lieutenant Ephraim Anderson was officer of the day, and the orderly sergeants from each company were ordered to make out regular rolls of the men in their companies and have them delivered to the Quarter Master when requested. Soldiers were ordered on December 14 to keep their side arms in their quarters and not wear them, except when on duty. Although it was cold, the soldiers were ordered on December 15 not to wear their blankets over their shoulders during daytime, because the blankets were to be used as bedding. These directives and all others that followed were ordered to be read every evening at roll call.[102]

Colonel Maxwell wrote a letter of frustration to Lord Stirling on December 14, telling him he had written to the Continental Congress seeking to have a surgeon appointed for his regiment, and to see if Congress could do something about giving orders to repair the barracks – even though that should be a Colonial legislature concern. Maxwell was concerned that the Burlington and Trenton barracks did not have the capacity to hold a complete regiment, especially because the British prisoners from Canada occupied part of the Trenton barracks. Maxwell was outraged that the non-commissioned officer prisoners "have possession of the officers' rooms, and most of the bedding and utensils." He needed those spaces and materials for his officers and men. Maxwell also believed the prisoners were "unfit companions for our soldiers" because "they may infuse bad sentiments into their minds that will not be easily removed." Maxwell also had heard the local people speak "loudly of it, that Trenton is a very improper place for the prisoners, it being so much of a thoroughfare."[103]

Supporting Maxwell, Stirling wrote to Congress on December 17, confirming that Maxwell's regiment could not be fully provided with the barracks at Trenton because there were "about seventy or eighty non-commissioned officers and private soldiers, prisoners from Canada, with their women, &c.," who had "taken possession of the best rooms in the barracks, with all the furniture, and behave in a most insolent and improper manner, exciting mutiny and dissension among the men of Colonel Maxwell's regiment, posted there." Based on the comments of the Trenton Committee of Safety, Stirling greatly exaggerated any problems of inciting "dissension" in order to strengthen his case to get them out of the barracks. He then joined in with those who believed "that it is very improper those prisoners should remain at Trenton, or in the Province" where Loyalists "have of late assumed fresh courage, and talk very daringly."[104] Maxwell also had other problems: he needed powder and flints; the companies were still not complete in numbers; those enlisted did not have sufficient arms or clothing; and "a great many of our best arms want repairs." His troops were not in any condition to head north to Canada.[105]

Maxwell commented on December 26 that a member of Congress who passed through Trenton on his way home had told him that the delegates in Philadelphia had discussed the prisoners at Trenton outside of their formal meetings, and all agreed Trenton was not "a proper place for them." On a positive note, he reported the people of Trenton and Burlington had been requested to repair and provide their barracks with necessities, and they had complied. He believed that "when I get them in repair, they will be large enough to hold my regiment; and it will be very handy to exercise them." Hunting shirts had been authorized to serve as a uniform back in October but had not yet been procured for Maxwell's men, so he asked Lord Stirling to send him by stage coach "one of your best frocks for a pattern" and he would return it.[106]

Reverend Spencer applied in December to his Presbytery for permission to accept the invitation of North Carolina to journey there with Rev. Alexander MacWhorter to preach and talk with the "exceedingly ignorant" settlers in the back country about the reasons for the Revolution and the need to stand together to support it. He would be revisiting areas where he had been a missionary in the 1760s. The Presbytery approved, and on December 20 the Continental Congress resolved to pay their expenses, and to have them also visit the remote parts of Virginia, Georgia, and South Carolina.[107]

As 1775 neared its end, everyone was talking about finding peaceful solutions while also engaging in what had become full-scale organized warfare. Trenton was now home to British prisoners of war, who were treated very civilly while a Continental regiment was being raised and competing with them for housing at the military barracks. By the end of 1775, colonial governments throughout the colonies were crumbling, although in New Jersey Governor William Franklin still retained some small semblance of authority. While no military action had yet taken place in New Jersey, there was concern among many people that its geographic position would make it a battleground if the war expanded. There were still many people, even some in positions of Whig leadership, who continued to hope for some kind of reconciliation short of independence.[108] But there were other people who favored independence because of an unforeseen result of the colonial experience. John Ferling describes these colonists as having "unthinkingly grown to be Americans, not merely English living in America. They were Americans who had come to understand that colonial dependency meant an intolerable second-class status, and they yearned to strike out on their own and seek their American destiny."[109]

Chapter 3

1776
Winter and Spring

Colonel William Maxwell was extremely frustrated by the obstacles delaying the complete outfitting of his Second New Jersey Regiment at the barracks in Trenton and Burlington during January. Forming since late October, after three months it was still not ready to take the field. He told Congress that "altho I cannot make arms & other necessaries for the men, I am endeavouring to make them soldiers as quick as I can." Maxwell received orders in mid-January to begin his march to Canada "immediately" and wanted to obey because he was a good soldier and loyal to the cause, but his troops lacked proper clothing and equipment. They did have hats, shoes and stockings, for the most part, but needed "much warmer cloathing to go into Canada." He had unsuitable, lightweight frocks for about half the regiment and on January 23 still needed about 200 muskets and 400 bayonets. Many of the muskets he did have were in need of repair and had been distributed to many gunsmiths. He did not have enough cartridge boxes and cross belts to supply each soldier, and among other necessary items that he had not seen yet were axes, tomahawks, camp kettles, canteens, moccasins, and caps.

He had done everything he could to inform Congress of his needs but still had not received necessary items. Commissary Stephen Lowrey at Trenton had contracted to have needed articles made at various locations, but there was an apparent lack of materials.[1] Samuel Tucker and the Trenton Committee of Safety had been supportive, and Maxwell knew that Tucker's letters to Congress detailing his need for arms and blankets had been very clear. Maxwell believed the problem was the inefficient Continental supply system. To help himself, Maxwell had recently sent a lieutenant into the country to buy blankets. He had purchased about 50 from farmers, enough to complete Captain Stout's company, and reported there were plenty of blankets available.

Upon his return to Trenton from a trip to Burlington to assess the needs of the men there, Tucker found that Captain Scott, having taken two prisoners to Congress, had returned with $4,000 for purchasing muskets. Although Maxwell already had his marching orders, he would *first go to Philadelphia to see if arms could be purchased there. Tucker optimistically promised to find money to purchase any arms Maxwell found.*[2] *However, if his troops were to march immediately, it was too late for his officers to go out "to the different parts of the province" looking for muskets and "gather them up and have them repaired." If he did set off, he wondered if the canteens and camp kettles, along with other camp equipment they completely lacked, would follow them in time.*

Maxwell was making herculean efforts to send off the first company in the first week of February. He warned that "they will make but a poor figure[,] but I cannot help it." He assured Congress that "they are as likely a battallion of men as any in the Continental service" and should perform well, but he implored Congress "for God's sake do not let them be disgraced for want of their necessaries." Because he was sending his companies piecemeal, he asked for orders regarding which company he should escort. He deeply wanted to be with the first company that marched, because he was "distressed beyond measure to have so fine a parcel of men under my command & yet so unfit for doing their country service when it is so much wanted."[3]

As 1776 began, the war was still distant in Massachusetts and Canada, but life in Trenton was complicated by the presence of four companies of Continental troops organizing at the barracks and the continuing presence of British prisoners of war living in town. The colonial government continued to exist but was progressively superseded by the Provincial Congress. The continuing protest movement against the acts of Parliament was increasingly challenged to become a movement for independence and Trenton people became involved in supporting the growing war effort in various ways.

Men had not exactly been rushing to the colors. By the end of October 1775, Joseph Brearley had only himself, one lieutenant, his ensign, two sergeants, two corporals, and eight privates enrolled in his company. He gained another lieutenant, two more sergeants and corporals, his fifer, and 61 privates during November. However, few men appear to have enlisted from his minuteman company even though all had been promised. In December, he gained six privates and in early January three more, for a total of 75. The companies of Captains Joseph Stout, John B. Scott, and James Lawrie showed similar patterns, with each eventually containing between 73 and 78 privates.[4] The numbers were fluid though, because not everyone who enlisted stayed in the army. Some men deserted or were discharged for various reasons. In one case, an eighteen-year-old bored and adventure seeking Trenton apprentice named Philip Bevan enlisted in December with a "view of going to Quebec." His master found and reclaimed him, and he was discharged after serving about six weeks.[5]

The Provincial and Continental Congresses struggled to work together in the effort to create an effective system for supplying arms and equipment for the New Jersey regiments. The Continental Congress ordered they be provided with the same types and quantities of firewood, camp equipment, and barrack utensils as allowed to battalions raised in Pennsylvania and ordered Commissary Lowrey to supply them with the many stockings they were lacking. However, to do that he would need to somehow obtain money, locate a supply, collect the items, and transport them. Even supplying something simple required a complex system. Congress also noted the "defenceless condition of the colony of New Jersey" and asked the Pennsylvania Committee of Safety to supply New Jersey "four hundred weight of powder."[6]

On January 11, twenty-three-year-old John Yard (one of several John Yards in Trenton) enlisted in the First New Jersey Regiment along with three other men between the ages of 38 and 48 who gave Trenton as their residence.[7] Why they went clear across the colony to enlist instead of joining the Second New Jersey Regiment at Trenton is not known. By January 19, nearly half the men in the two Continental regiments were still without arms, and the colony had no money to purchase any. Samuel Tucker acknowledged that $6,000 advanced by Congress had been spent and $4,000 more was needed to completely outfit the regiment.[8] At the end of January, Maxwell's troops still needed: "near one-half their arms; leggings; a number of warm waistcoats; some coats and breeches; stockings to make two pair per man; some shirts; Canada caps for the whole regiment; [and] moccasins, [which] may be had at Albany." He acknowledged that Commissary Lowrey had provided "about one pair of stockings per man," but he had no orders from Congress to provide the other missing items and even "if he had, they could not be purchased in Jersey."[9]

Meanwhile, an inadequate number of troops desperate for reinforcements continued the siege of Quebec. In Trenton, the recruited soldiers needed to get moving for their own morale. Maxwell received complaints that his soldiers were throwing snow balls and breaking windows, and had to order that any soldier seen throwing a snow ball was to be confined in the guard house for 24 hours on bread and water. He also forbade his bored soldiers to play cards in their rooms "as such gaming practices is a means of breeding frequent disorders in their quarters." Clothing supplies were relieved just a bit when Lieutenant John Yard delivered locally made hats to Brearley's company on January 11.[10]

Several Second New Jersey officers tried to improve their position in the army by applying for higher-ranking commissions when a third New Jersey Continental regiment was authorized in February. On January 12, Second Lieutenant Ephraim Anderson wrote to Samuel Tucker of the Provincial Committee of Safety requesting a field officer's commission in the new regiment. He made sure to note that he had formerly been a field officer in the Hunterdon County militia and was now regimental adjutant, an administrative position for which he received extra pay for the additional duties. Anderson also touted that his request was motivated by his desire to be "as usefull as in his Power (to the common cause)." He would even take a pay cut if necessary "for the good of the Service." However, he was not promoted and remained a second lieutenant and adjutant in the Second Regiment.[11] Ensign Thomas Ryerson sought a captain's commission and was endorsed by the captains of the four companies at Trenton and the ever self-promoting Lieutenant Ephraim Anderson. However, Ryerson had no more luck than Anderson and also stayed in the Second Regiment.[12] Officers jockeying for better positions must have hindered the effort to get the first two New Jersey regiments into combat readiness.

Maxwell's troops were badly needed in Canada. To supply his regiment with blankets and get them moving, the Continental Congress ordered Abraham Hunt and Alexander Chambers on February 2 to determine the value of the blankets belonging to the Trenton barracks so they could be appropriated for the Continentals.[13] Maxwell was still desperate for muskets so the Provincial Congress ordered any county that owned some muskets for their militia to deliver them to officers appointed by Maxwell.[14] Maxwell dispatched officers who "rode night and day to expedite the business." Philadelphia merchant Clement Biddle tried to obtain some canteens and kettles belonging to a Pennsylvania militia company for Maxwell. In spite of the many issues, Maxwell praised Commissary Stephen Lowrey, Rev. Spencer's son-in-law who lived with him, as one who "has ever been indefatigable in his department to compleat the troops under my command." After ranting to Congress in January about his many unfulfilled requests, Maxwell now said it was at least partly his fault that Lowrey had not been completely informed of his needs.[15]

Still short of muskets and having canteens and camp kettles for only two companies, Maxwell ordered Captain Brearley's company to march north on February 5 and Captain Lowrie's on February 6, with the others to follow as soon as possible.[16] At this critical time, Lieutenant Ephraim Anderson was losing his 240-acre farm, a big part of his wealth, at sheriff's sale because of his debts.[17] Captain Stout's company was no doubt preparing to march on February 10 when Anderson made out his will, authorizing his wife, Rezine, to dispose of what remained of his property as she saw fit "if I never return from service to my country."[18] Several weeks later, Captain Howell's company came up to Trenton from the Burlington barracks and was furnished with whatever clothing and equipment was available before leaving for Canada on February 28.[19]

The Continental Congress continued to ask the Trenton Committee of Safety to relocate the British prisoners. Just who was responsible for paying the expenses of the prisoners, especially the officers, continued to be an issue. On January 4, the Continental Congress authorized payment to Furman and Hunt for provisions and hiring horses, and asked the Committee of Safety to inquire into the "manner the prisoners of war at Trenton live, who supplies them, and upon what terms." With no defined system in place, Congress was concerned that expenses were unequal and in any case should not be a burden on its budget. Congress felt the officers' "manner of living, [was] exceedingly extravagant, they being boarded at taverns, and the inn keepers supplying them in a luxurious manner, on the credit of the Continent." Innkeeper Rachel Stille's bill of £158.17.7, for subsistence of the officers up to January 4, was ordered paid; but in the future, Congress would only "allow two dollars per week for the board and lodgings of officers," believing that amount would enable them to have "decent lodgings." However, the officers were required to repay all previous and future bills before their release and innkeepers were to no longer accept any charges on the credit of the Continent. The Committee of Safety was ordered to remove the officers to some place of their choosing, "at a proper distance from the public post road."[20] However, no immediate action was taken.

Samuel Tucker, Isaac Smith, and Abraham Hunt of the Trenton Committee of Safety collected bills from the officers staying at Rachel Stille's tavern so Congress could repay her. Taking an action that could be interpreted as accepting the legitimacy of the Continental Congress, the British officers petitioned to be relieved of bearing the cost of their maintenance, arguing that Captain Hulbert placed them at the tavern when he brought them to Trenton. After reporting to Congress, Hulbert returned and told the tavern keeper and the Trenton Committee that the officers were to live at the expense of the Continental Congress until informed otherwise. Congress had been too busy to formalize arrangements at the time but now was making the officers responsible for their expenses.[21]

Midshipman Richard Symonds of the British Navy, taken prisoner on board a small tender at Barnegat, joined the British prisoners in January and was put on parole under the same terms.[22] In mid-January, the officer prisoners, including their musicians and servants, chose Bordentown for their place of residence, but still nobody moved.[23] Continuing the saga, the Continental Congress resolved the officers should "be boarded in farmer's houses (not exceeding six miles) west of Trenton, and that the soldiers there with their wives and children remain at Trenton." Samuel Tucker tried to find quarters for the prisoners in Bordentown, but he "could neither hire a house or get them boarded on any terms in that town."[24] Meanwhile, the enlisted prisoners were suffering from the loss of clothing items, and Major Stopford ordered his sergeants to make up a return of lost-clothing items. Socks and shoes led the list, followed by shirts, breeches, and waistcoats, with fewer numbers of hats, winter caps, and gaiters. He requested restitution for these losses, in addition to a whole year of clothing for each man, but with unknown results.[25]

Dr. Richard Huddleston, the man who had caused so much concern in December with his questionable behavior, raised the issue on January 23 that "amongst all civilized nations at war," it was common to release captured medical officers immediately because they were "esteamed a friend to both sides" by offering relief to any wounded soldier. Why he waited two months to make this request is not known. He asked to return to Quebec, where there was a shortage of surgeons, and assured Congress that he would not transmit any intelligence to the British. He wanted to create cooperation between Britain and America and felt that his release would result in a similar release for any captured American military surgeons.[26] The Trenton Committee sent a letter to the Continental Congress recommending that Huddleston be released immediately and Congress agreed.[27]

Two officers captured by General Montgomery in Canada, Brigadier General Richard Prescott and Captain Chase of the captured schooner *Gaspée*, were brought to Trenton on their way to Philadelphia. Prescott was despised for his ill treatment of Ethan Allen when he was captured in Canada. Now that Prescott was a prisoner, Washington and Congress warned the British that Allen's future treatment would determine Prescott's. The Trenton Committee of Safety told Congress that Prescott had been brought to town, permitted to stay overnight at his request, but then refused to give his parole and was confined to his room under guard provided by Colonel Maxwell.[28] The two officers were sent on to Philadelphia "in a light covered wagon" guarded by a detachment of Maxwell's Continentals under the command of Captain Scott,[29] and Congress thanked the Trenton Committee for the excellent way its "orders relating to Gen. Prescot & Capt. Chace had been executed."[30] Captain Chace was sent back to Trenton to join the other officer prisoners there, but Prescott remained imprisoned at Philadelphia.[31] Captain Scott returned to Trenton on January 25 with the $4,000 requested by the Committee of Safety on January 19 to buy muskets for the New Jersey Continentals.

Colonel Isaac Smith, Lieutenant Colonel Abraham Hunt, and Captain Robert Hoops on behalf of the Trenton Committee of Safety reported to Congress on February 22 that the prisoners had not yet been removed from Trenton. They attached a complete list of prisoners and complained that they were not getting clear instructions from Congress, first being told the prisoners could "chuse the place of their residence" but then receiving orders to remove them to Bound Brook. The list of prisoners and dependents was sent to help Congress determine whether Bound Brook could accommodate them. They apologized for troubling Congress with small matters but wanted to carry out is directions in an "immediate and punctual" manner.[32]

One of the British prisoners removed himself from Trenton by enlisting in Maxwell's regiment on February 19 and returned to Canada with it, no doubt causing consternation among the other prisoners who now viewed this man as a deserter, even though he may have been planning to desert the Americans once he was back in Canada. His departure left 26 soldiers, 10 women, and 20 children at Trenton.[33]

Isaac Smith and Abraham Hunt alerted Congress to trouble caused by seventeen-year-old prisoner Lieutenant William Barrington of the 7th Regiment, the nephew of the British Secretary of War. Barrington was under the guardianship of, and serving as aide-de-camp to, General Prescott, who had been so difficult when he came through Trenton as a prisoner. Apparently a young man of great "vanity and indiscretion," General Schuyler wanted Barrington sent to where Prescott was being held. The Trenton Committee sent Barrington on to Philadelphia but stated "his insignificance, we apprehend, renders a guard or any other ceremony unnecessary; and we presume will apologize for the mode of his transmission." The Trenton men seem to have had little regard for the spoiled young man and were glad to be rid of him.[34]

The Continental Congress believed that by various means "divers honest and well-meaning, but uninformed people" had been "deceived and drawn into erroneous opinions respecting the American cause, and the probable issue of the present contest." Not wanting to lose the support of anyone who was simply "uninformed" rather than lacking in "virtue or public spirit," Congress ordered in early January that the various committees and "other friends to American liberty" were to treat the uninformed "with kindness and attention." They should educate these people about the "origin, nature and extent of the present controversy," using everything available in print from England and the colonies that supported their cause, so they could see how proper the protests had been and how the colonists' petitions had been ignored. Congress was sure this approach would convince right-minded people how "just and necessary [is] our present opposition to ministerial tyranny."[35]

However, a different approach should be taken with "unworthy Americans" who, without regard for "their duty to their Creator, their country and their posterity," have cooperated with the government oppressors, hoping for personal gain, and misrepresented "the conduct and principles of the friends of American liberty" while "opposing every measure formed for its preservation and security." Local committees aligned with the Provincial Congress were instructed to disarm these "enemies" and keep those considered to be a particular danger either in custody or "bound with sufficient sureties to their good behavior." And, in contrast to the barbarity of British actions, the committees must ensure "that cruelty should find no admission among a free people."[36]

In response, the New Jersey Committee of Safety ordered each township to disarm enemies of the rebellion and keep the most dangerous ones in safe custody or paroled with sufficient surety.[37] Forty-six-year-old Dr. William Bryant was known as a "friend of government" and retired British army surgeon on half-pay whose request for permission to join the British at Boston was denied. It may actually have been an effort to save his half-pay, rather than a real effort to go to Boston. He was not considered a serious threat and Samuel Tucker, Chairman of the Trenton Committee of Safety, took Bryant's parole on January 22 in which he promised not to "go farther than 12 miles from my present place of residence except to Philadelphia without leave of the Congress." His parole gave him somewhat greater freedom of movement than others were granted because he had patients in Princeton and business at Philadelphia.[38]

As ordered by the Provincial Congress, on February 26 the Trenton Committee of Safety submitted a list of people in the township who had signed the Continental Association and a separate list of those who refused to sign.[39] Knowing who supported the protest movement, generally called Whigs, and who opposed it was not always easy. Trenton Whigs could find themselves suspected of being Loyalists when travelling in areas where they were not known. Twenty-eight-year-old Absalom Hart was well regarded in Trenton as a Whig who served diligently in the militia. Sometime in late 1775, he travelled alone into Monmouth County at the invitation of his friend, tavern keeper Henry Drake, who had gone to Monmouth County with his wife to visit a young lady named Susan. Henry, playing matchmaker, sent for Absalom to come meet her, but on his way Absalom was picked up by the Whig militia in Monmouth as a stranger without a pass signed by a Whig committee. Absalom's excuse for being in Monmouth, that he had come "a courting," did not impress them and Drake, known there because of his wife, had to intercede and convince them that Absalom was "a good Whig."[40]

Still trying to acquire enough muskets for the New Jersey Continentals, the New Jersey Committee of Safety resolved on March 22 that local committees should disarm persons who were "notoriously disaffected to the cause of America, or who have not associated, and refuse to associate, to defend by arms the United Colonies, ..." The arms seized were to be given to the Continental troops raised in New Jersey as a first priority, then to any provincial troops, and anything left to the militia. Items taken were to be appraised by "indifferent persons," and those arms given to the Continentals would be paid for by the Continental Congress and those given to New Jersey troops by the Provincial Congress or Committee of Safety.[41]

At the March town meeting, obeying a directive from the Provincial Congress to choose a town Committee of Observation & Correspondence, the town chose Dr. Isaac Smith, Samuel Tucker, Abraham Hunt, John Mott, Benjamin Yard, Benjamin Clark, Daniel Howell, Philemon Dickinson, Daniel Scudder, Alexander Chambers, and David Pinkerton for its committee.[42] Like several of the others, Abraham Hunt was wearing many hats, including lieutenant colonel of the militia and postmaster at Trenton.[43]

Taking care of numerous pieces of business at the end of February, the Provincial Congress, continuing to take over functions from the colonial government, ordered the treasurers of the colony, Samuel Tucker and John Dennis, to each put up a security bond; named Alexander Chambers as one of the commissioners for purchasing arms and military stores and paying the militia; appointed Alexander Chambers and Captain William Tucker to be barracks masters at Trenton; and approved incorporating the no-longer-needed minute man companies into the regular militia.[44] Captain Tucker received £125 on March 23 from his brother, Provincial Treasurer Samuel Tucker, and began work on cleaning the barracks, hiring George Ely to work on repairs, no doubt necessary after quartering the British prisoners and Continental recruits. Before the month was over, he purchased forage from Elijah Jones, boards from William Clayton and Joseph Milnor, and sundries from Harrison & DeCou, and David Pinkerton. He hired John Cade to do some masonry work and William Reeder to do some carting. Then on May 25, he paid for washing the beds and blankets of the barracks.[45]

Robert Treat Paine, member of a Continental Congress committee to improve the militias, submitted a report on muskets in December 1775, stating the great difficulty in obtaining them from outside the colonies and highlighting the "indispensably necessary" task of manufacturing enough muskets in the colonies, not only to arm "such troops & forces as are raised & put into pay," but also to arm "every freeman." Ideally, surplus muskets would be manufactured in order to replace losses and supply new immigrants with arms. The committee felt there were enough "artificers" with the skills to manufacture muskets and they only needed encouragement "to carry on & enlarge" their businesses. Each colony was directed to identify specific craftsmen skilled at making musket locks (the firing mechanism) and induce them to manufacture double-bridled locks[46] as their sole business, employing the best journeymen and teaching apprentices. Colonies should also identify craftsmen "skilld in making musket barrels & to induce them also to sett up & carry on the manufacture of musket barrels 45 inches long, carrying an ounce ball & bearing proof in firing, & also bayonets[,] long steel ramrods & worms." Appropriate craftsmen should be contracted to employ journeymen and apprentices and "engage skillful persons" to assemble the muskets with a wooden stock mounted with "proper pipe strings & bell Swivels."[47] The Continental Congress allotted $10,000 on March 8 for the manufacture of muskets and bayonets.[48]

Paine learned that Benjamin Yard was capable of making gun barrels and asked him on March 9 if he would agree to make some, as well as bayonets and other needed metal parts except locks. Paine wrote the same day to Abraham Hunt, Yard's brother-in-law, requesting his assistance in contracting with Ebenezer Cowell for the manufacture of gunlocks. Cowell agreed to manufacture double-bridled gun locks at three dollars each and deliver them each week to Hunt, who was recommended to Paine as the best man to coordinate securing musket components.[49]

Cowell advertised his immediate need for "a number of good workmen, who are well acquainted with forging and filing of gun-locks. All those who apply well recommended for sobriety, industry and diligence, may expect to meet with great encouragement and good pay." Cowell also noted his hearty desire "to promote the present most glorious defence of his country." To increase production, he took on apprentices and devoted his business solely to manufacturing gun locks.[50]

Craftsmen such as John Fitch assembled the muskets from the parts collected by Abraham Hunt. In March, Fitch recorded cleaning and repairing a musket for militia Captain Philip Phillips and making a bayonet for Robert Forman, both of Maidenhead. Fitch had no training as a gun smith, but took up the craft because, "fealing myself deeply interested in behalf of my Country and being frequently solicited by several members of the Committee of Safety to enter into

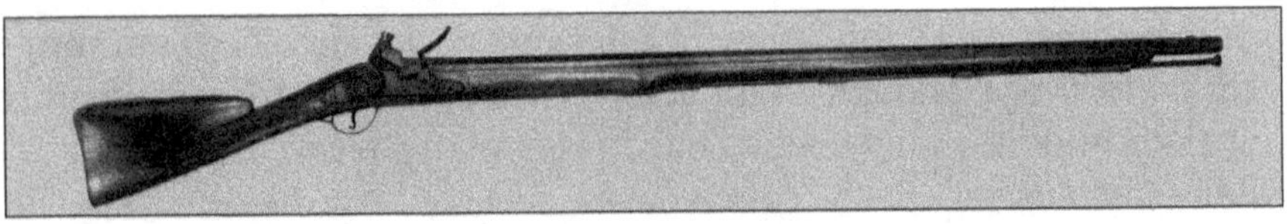

Military musket made in the shop of John Fitch in 1776 and exhibited currently at the visitor center at the Washington Crossing State Park at Washington Crossing, New Jersey. (Courtesy of the Swan Historical Foundation)

the gunsmiths business I at length consented tho' it was against my judgment." He stipulated that to do this he needed a loan of £50 and the men he hired must be exempt from militia service so he would have a steady workforce. Fitch, however, continued to serve in the militia as a lieutenant and boasted he was "anxious to meet my enemy in the field." However, he did not have "the malignant disposition against what they called Tories as some had." Fitch had proven himself to be a resourceful, skilled craftsman and businessman who could be entrusted with this important work.[51]

The people of New Jersey, including Trenton, were still sympathetic to the suffering endured by the people of Boston, even though the occupying British troops left on March 17. On April 4, the monthly women's meeting of the Chesterfield Friends heard a report on the money collected by the local Quakers to help the people of Boston.[52]

Efforts to fully equip the troops were never ending. Alexander Chambers received £201 on May 9 from Provincial Treasurer Samuel Tucker to "purchase armes for the men of New Jersey,"[53] and on May 11, Tucker paid a bill submitted by Dunbar & Smith for 300 cartridge boxes.[54] The committee appointed by Congress to contract for muskets was directed on May 23 to order the manager of the continental firearm factory at Lancaster and the manager of the gun lock factory at Trenton to deliver to Colonel John Shee of the Third Pennsylvania Continental Regiment all the muskets and gun locks they had ready.[55] On June 17, merchant David Pinkerton was named a Commissioner for the Western Division to purchase tents and camp equipage such as knapsacks, haversacks, canteens, and camp kettles.[56] And, on June 27, Alexander Chambers paid DeCou & Mount's bills for sundry entrenching tools.[57]

On May 21, Trenton merchant William Richards was appointed "Ships' Husband" of the Pennsylvania State Navy to oversee the upkeep and provisioning of the 57 river craft in the fleet, utilizing his mariner's background and merchant connections. Richards was born in Barbados and had long experience as a ship owner, ship captain, and merchant at Perth Amboy and Philadelphia. As part of his duties, Richards requested Betsy Ross of Philadelphia to make flags for the Pennsylvania Navy during the winter of 1776-77.[58] About June 20, the commodore commanding the Pennsylvania State Navy was instructed to "immediately take an exact survey of its present condition," and report "whatever may be wanting in its equipment" to Captain William Richards.[59]

In addition to a Philadelphia store, Richards owned a store, warehouse, smokehouse, mustard and chocolate mill, cooper shop, bakery, pottery, fishery, and possibly a gristmill at Lamberton. His pottery was operated by James Rhodes between 1774 and 1778, after which Rhodes opened his own business nearby in Nottingham Township where he produced excellent grey salt-glazed stoneware.[60] Richards's fishery was predominant at Trenton during the Revolution.[61] Fish were "in abundance to be taken in their several seasons, either with the sein or hook."[62] His businesses at Lamberton made it a place "from whence shallops constantly ply to and fro from Philadelphia." One of his ships was the appropriately-named sloop Herring, which sailed frequently to Barbados. In the mid-1770s, his stores in Philadelphia and Lamberton sold many items imported from London and were especially noted for their stock of medications.[63] In 1774, he put a new schooner into service, the *Lamberton Packet*, which he used throughout the War of Independence.[64] A list of freight rates between Trenton and Philadelphia charged by Richards and his associate Thomas Ashmore reveals that at various times he carried: soldiers, iron items, boards, barrel staves, stoneware, earthen ware, crates, bran and shorts, Dutch fans, bales of cotton, bundles of deer skins, bullocks horns, window glass, scythes, textile bolts, sugar, rum, molasses, tobacco, beef, pork, cider, flax seed, rice, wine, grain trunks, bales, cases, boxes, bags, chests, bricks, reams of paper, and other items.[65]

On a stage-coach trip from Elizabethtown to Trenton in early April there was a heated discussion among the passengers resulting in charges against one of them for promoting the enemy cause and disparaging the American forces. A passenger recounted how the British prisoners at Trenton had run up £150 in expenses in just one

Pottery made by James Rhodes in Trenton during the Revolutionary War period. Rhodes worked for William Richards before operating his own shop and created a range of grey salt-glazed stoneware items including the bowl, chamber pot, tankard, and coffee pot shown here. Examples of the distinctive applied molded faces and floral decorative motifs that Rhodes used are also shown. (Images courtesy of Hunter Research, Inc.)

week and spoke disrespectfully of them for being so extravagant. In return, a Mr. Peter Dubois attacked the complainer "with all names and abusive language" and went on to so severely criticize aspects of the American cause that his conversation became "intolerable." The stage stopped at Rachel Stille's tavern, and at dinner "Mr. Dubois came into the room, and declared he had been to see some gentlemen who were prisoners there – had been in their room, and been invited to dine with them, but chose to dine with the company who came in the stage with him." Dubois generally made himself unpopular but later claimed that he was only making comparative comments, not disloyal ones. It was difficult to carry on a conversation between people holding differing opinions without someone ending up charged with being a traitor.[66]

On May 13, the Continental Congress authorized reimbursement to Rachel Stille for boarding prisoners, including a bill from Captain Chace, and another for providing waggonage. Congress reimbursed Hunterdon County High Sheriff John Barnes of Trenton on May 22 for boarding some of the British officer prisoners. The Congress also charged some of the British officer prisoners for unspecified purchases. Congress was still authorizing payments for services to the prisoners on June 6 when it authorized payment to Benjamin Smith for prisoner board and the cost of accommodations incurred before the limitations set by Congress.[67]

Samuel Tucker wrote to John Hancock on June 30 about two of the British prisoners at Trenton whose families had difficult situations back in Quebec. They did not ask for release, only to be among the first to be exchanged whenever an exchange was finally authorized. The letter was delivered to Hancock by Trenton militia Captain William Tucker.[68]

The Yard family received a letter from First Lieutenant Thomas Yard, dated March 30, 1776 at Camp Quebec. He reported that the army had about 1,700 men of which 700 had the small pox while others were sick with different diseases, so that there were only about 700 fit for duty. Describing the siege, he wrote, "The cannon play by day and shell by night, but do us no hurt. We have two batteries that will be opened the second of April which will make some sport. If they do not surrender before the fourteenth of April we shall begin the storm; then thee will hear how the matter goes." As for his own condition, he wrote, "Dear Brothers and Friends, I am in good spirits, but how it will be in the storm I cannot tell, but with the blessing of God I will fight a good fight and gain all the honors possible for brothers, friends and the flower of the world – dear Trenton – the place of my nativity." He closed saying, "Give my love to my only uncle – Benjamin, --my loving sister, my brother and friend, Samuel Bellerjeau [who married his only sister, Achsai], my brother William, and my dear fatherless and motherless brother Daniel."[69] Undoubtedly, other Trenton families received similar letters from their men serving in Canada.

The British troops in Boston had been forced to evacuate when Washington placed cannon, brought from Fort Ticonderoga, on the heights overlooking Boston and its harbor. They left in March for Nova Scotia, and in June were reported to be on their way to attack New York. On June 10, Washington questioned the advisability of keeping two Pennsylvania battalions at Philadelphia when the British army was on the verge of landing at New York. As a result, Colonel John Shee's Third Pennsylvania was transported to Trenton and then marched on to New York City where it arrived about June 18. Shee's thirty-four-year-old Lieutenant Colonel Lambert Cadwalader had been born in Trenton in 1742 and the previous March had purchased parts of the original Cadwalader family holdings in Trenton, renewing the link between this important Philadelphia family and Trenton.[70] James Fergus in an 84-man volunteer Cumberland County, Pennsylvania rifle company came from Philadelphia by sloop to Trenton, and his company marched through town in their dark purple hunting shirts and pantaloons, each man equipped with "a good rifle & powder horn & shot pouch, a tomahawk & belt" he had supplied himself. From Trenton, they marched to Maidenhead and on to Perth Amboy.[71]

The Provincial Congress began a session at Burlington on June 10, with both Samuel Tucker, again elected president, and militia general Philemon Dickinson representing Hunterdon County. The Congress discussed requests from the Continental Congress to raise militia and Continental units for the defense of New York City and for a "flying-camp" as a flexible backup force. Dickinson was appointed to a committee to develop plans responding to these requests. To reinforce the army at New York, on June 14 the Provincial Congress authorized raising 3,300 volunteer militiamen for five-month tours of service as full-time soldiers.[72] Innkeeper Henry Drake signed on as Second Lieutenant under Maidenhead's Captain Benjamin Van Cleve, although he was a volunteer tag-along for just two months rather than a commissioned officer. Several Trenton men from both sides of the Assunpink enlisted. William Morris, a tailor of Nottingham, volunteered as a drummer, John McCollum as a sergeant, and John James as a private.[73] Asa Adams enlisted under Captain John Anderson, and his friend Robert Carson watched his company march off to New York from Mill Hill.[74]

Several units of the five-month militia levies came through Trenton on their way to New York in June. Colonel Silas Newcomb's regiment rendezvoused at Haddonfield, Gloucester County on June 18, boarded boats at Cooper's Ferry on June 27, proceeded up the river to Trenton, and from there marched through Princeton to New Brunswick, where Samuel Tucker and William Paterson, president and secretary of the Provincial Congress, signed the officers' commissions.[75]

Other local men became involved with the Continental army in various ways. Samuel Wooley lived on Mill Hill. He had been born in England and came to New Jersey to live with his uncle, Jonathan Richmond, who had asked for him to come. Wooley and his friend, Matthew Mount, enlisted as teamsters in the summer of 1776 under Continental wagon master Benjamin Hendrickson. Wooley received regular pay and rations, but his pay went to his uncle who was his guardian and had sent him out for this service. They drove wagons belonging to the government and considered themselves to be the same as Continental soldiers in terms of their commitment and obligation to service.[76]

The campaign in Canada turned even uglier with the American defeat at Quebec in May and while American troops, including the Second New Jersey, were retreating and militiamen were being recruited for the five-month levies to defend New York, the collapse of New Jersey's royal government was completed with the arrest of Governor Franklin by militiamen commanded by Colonel Nathaniel Heard. In mid-June, the Provincial Congress passed a motion to refuse to obey Governor Franklin's call for a meeting of the General Assembly on June 20. Trenton's Philemon Dickinson was one of the handful of delegates who voted against the motion. Dickinson also voted with the minority against a motion authorizing the immediate arrest of Franklin for violating resolves of the Continental Congress regarding the suppression of British government powers in the colonies. He did, however, vote to stop pay for the governor and require the treasurers of the colonial government to make an accounting to the Provincial Congress for the money in their hands. Colonel Heard was appointed to take the governor into custody, but "with all the delicacy and tenderness which the nature of the business can possibly admit."[77]

On June 17, Samuel Tucker received word from Colonel Heard that Franklin refused to leave his house and the next day wrote to Congress suggesting it would be best to get Franklin out of New Jersey and kept in custody in Pennsylvania or Connecticut, where he could do less "mischief." The Provincial Congress unanimously agreed that Franklin should be confined in a place designated by the Continental Congress, and he was removed to Connecticut.[78] Power was now firmly in the hands of the Provincial Congress. On June 22, the Congress elected new delegates to the Continental Congress and authorized them to vote for independence.[79]

Even before the departure of Governor Franklin, the New Jersey Committee of Safety, including Colonel Isaac Smith and Lieutenant Colonel Abraham Hunt, was deciding whether to allow prominent "friends" of the British government to remain in their homes under parole, as was done with Dr. Bryant in Trenton, or force them to leave the area, as with Governor Franklin.[80] A number of Loyalists were brought to town and imprisoned while Congress determined how to deal with them. On June 26, Colonel Abraham Ten Eick was ordered to apprehend 26 suspected Loyalists in Hunterdon County and bring them before the Congress or Committee of Safety, then in recess. The men were to be brought to the Trenton jail and kept "in close and safe confinement" until the jailor received further orders from the Congress or Committee of Safety.[81]

The expected arrival of the British fleet and army at New York shattered the relative calm of the past few months and increased the importance of the defenses along the New Jersey coast opposite Staten Island. The people of New Jersey, including Trenton, could no longer look at the war as something taking place far away in New England or Canada and posing no immediate threat to them. General Dickinson reported that he was sending on to New York what he had of the still incomplete five-month levies and that many of the regular militia would simply not turn out when called, because it was near the height of the wheat harvest season and the five-month levies had reduced the workforce. Captain Tucker's First Hunterdon Company, with John Fitch as first lieutenant, Isaiah Yard as second lieutenant, and Joseph Clunn as ensign, along with several other companies from the First Hunterdon were ordered east with whatever men had turned out.[82] David Van Norden was "drafted" at Trenton, and John R. Hart went out with Captain Charles Harrison's Light Infantry Company.[83]

Business carried on as usual in Trenton even with the imminent arrival of the British at New York. On June 14, Coxe, Furman, and Coxe in Philadelphia, an expansion of the Coxe and Furman company, sent a shallop carrying 44 barrels of common flour upriver to Abraham Hunt, their storekeeper at Trenton. Hunt frequently forwarded such items to company customers in New York and New England. From Trenton, he sent the flour in wagons to Brunswick and where it was put on "stage boats" for New York to be delivered to merchant James Parsons.[84] Trenton transactions with New York merchants would soon be disrupted for the duration of the war.

Chapter 4

1776
Summer and Fall

Dr. James Clitherall wrote in his diary on July 2, "This glorious day that threw off the tyranny of George III, and greeted the Colonies as free united and independent states, I left Philadelphia, having yesterday heard that an attack on New York was expected hourly." Clitherall and several companions rode all day and passed through Trenton on their way to New Brunswick undoubtedly telling everyone they met as they rode through town about the successful vote on independence.[1]

The Provincial Congress moved its meetings from Burlington back to Trenton on July 5 and Trenton received a copy of the Declaration of Independence by post rider on the morning of July 8. According to tradition, Provincial Congress President Samuel Tucker read the Declaration and the new state constitution, passed on July 2, from the steps of the Hunterdon County Courthouse on King Street,[2] *and both "were received with loud acclamations."* Dunlap's Pennsylvania Packet *reported, "The members of the Provincial Congress, the gentlemen of the Committee [of Safety], the officers and privates of the Militia under arms and a large concourse of the inhabitants attended on this great and solemn occasion," and local business people, including innkeeper Rachel Stille, contributed to the celebration. The paper exclaimed that "the people are now convinced, of what we ought long since to have known, that our enemies have left us no middle way between perfect freedom and abject slavery."*[3] *Now, every resident of Trenton had to weigh the benefits they enjoyed as citizens of the British Empire against venturing into the unknown to create a new political structure that would inevitably and unpredictably change over time.*

Isaac DeCou resigned his major's commission in the militia on July 5. Why he resigned is not documented, but he might have been opposed to fighting for independence. He continued on the militia rolls as a private but apparently paid fines rather than turning out when called. Another reason could be that DeCou, like many militia officers, had been chosen on the basis of community status, rather than military knowledge. Now,

Illia Barger's Winds of Change *mural depicting Samuel Tucker reading the Declaration of Independence from the porch of the Hunterdon County Courthouse on July 8, 1776. This was possibly the first public reading of the Declaration to citizens of the new states. (Illia Barger, Winds of Change, acrylic on stucco, 2006, image courtesy of the artist)*

with a serious war looming, he may have been making way for someone with more military experience. Whatever his reason, he remained a well-regarded citizen of Trenton throughout the war for independence.[4]

Captain Charles Harrison was devastated by the Declaration of Independence. The thirty-six-year old Irishman was very active in the protest movement until July 8, when he resigned his militia captain's commission and immediately joined the Loyalist military forces. He was one of many people who wholeheartedly supported efforts to restore

American liberties by protesting the acts of Parliament, but who could not support a complete break from the British Empire.[5]

The Declaration created a serious dilemma for Rev. Panton and the vestry of St. Michael's Church. Like all Anglican clergymen, Panton took a sacred oath of loyalty to the King as part of his ordination. When independence was declared, he was faced with either making changes in the liturgy, such as omitting a prayer for the King, or closing up his church. The St. Michael's vestry met on Sunday, July 7, the day before the Declaration was read publicly, and passed a resolution to suspend services, partly out of fear for the safety of Rev. Panton and members of the church who were split between supporters and opponents of the war for independence. Services would not resume until October 1783, over seven years later.[6]

The Declaration of Independence and the military activity taking place in and around New York City impacted all events in Trenton during the summer and fall of 1776. Trenton residents learned on the morning of July 4 that 10,000 British troops were landing on Staten Island adding to the 7,000 to 10,000 troops under General Howe that had landed and taken possession of every pass on the island on July 2, the same day Congress voted to declare independence. British troops were stationed at each ferry crossing between New Jersey and Staten Island, in addition to two regiments and several pieces of artillery opposite Perth Amboy.[7] Through the late summer and early fall, the British army took control of New York City, establishing it as headquarters for British military activities. This created a threat to eastern New Jersey, and Trenton militiamen were called out frequently to help protect the area from British foraging parties and other incursions. Men from Trenton in the five-month levies served alongside Continental army regiments from July through November during the unsuccessful campaign to prevent the British occupation of New York City that included the battles of Long Island, Haarlem Heights, and White Plains.

Anticipating the vote for independence, the Provincial Congress wrote and adopted a constitution for New Jersey. However, it contained an escape clause, perhaps initiated by Samuel Tucker, stating it was null and void if a still hoped for reconciliation with Britain occurred. A general election in August would select government officials for the now independent State of New Jersey, and every voter would be required to renounce, under oath, all allegiance to the King of England and pledge to uphold the laws adopted by the State Legislature and Continental Congress.[8] The Provincial Congress was officially renamed the Convention of the State of New Jersey on July 18, to be the interim legislature until the elections. It met at the Friends Meeting House or one of Trenton's taverns, with local resident Daniel Bellerjeau serving as doorkeeper.[9] When elected in late August, the new governor would be commander in chief of the militia, but until then General Washington communicated primarily through General William Livingston who kept him informed of the status of the militia.[10] In early July, with the British army digging in at New York, General Livingston needed to know the condition of each county militia regiment and ordered colonels to send him a list of their field officers and where each lived, the other commissioned officers, and the number of privates and muskets in each company. Not every man owned the musket required by the militia law, and there was still a great need for additional muskets to be manufactured or purchased.[11]

So many New Jersey militiamen were in the five-month levies at New York that too few remained to guard the coast opposite Staten Island. Samuel Tucker asked the Continental Congress just how New Jersey was to be defended when the "eastern part of our Colony is now unhappily exposed to the ravages of the enemy, a large army being in possession of Staten-Island, which is divided from us by a narrow river only."[12] To help New Jersey, on July 5 the Pennsylvania Committee of Safety ordered several companies of volunteer militia, known as Associators, to march immediately to Trenton or New Brunswick. They were to remain in service until relieved by the Flying Camp, a corps of ten thousand troops from Pennsylvania, Maryland, and Delaware being raised to defend New Jersey and provide potential reinforcements for Washington in New York. The committees of inspection for Pennsylvania counties were ordered to march their troops raised for the Flying Camp to Trenton. The Continental Congress elected a muster master general for the Flying Camp and ordered the militiamen to rendezvous at Trenton.[13]

Maryland militia units for the Flying Camp now marched through Trenton almost daily on their way to Amboy.[14] Sixteen shallops, carrying perhaps eleven hundred Maryland men, arrived at Trenton Landing about July 14, as did six or seven companies of Pennsylvania militia, all reported to be in high spirits. Two Pennsylvania artillery companies with their field pieces and baggage wagons came through Trenton, and another twelve shallops with Maryland troops landed about July 21.[15]

On July 13, Pennsylvania militiamen were in motion, but not completely sure of their ultimate destination or how long they would be out. They did know they would encamp first at Trenton, probably for a few days, before crossing the state.[16] Colonel William Montgomery's Chester County militia regiment came through on July 18 and 19.[17] John Cochran enlisted in a Chester County militia company that was reviewed at Trenton by General Thomas Mifflin before proceeding to Princeton and on to Perth Amboy for their two month tour of duty.[18] Peter Yokum was drafted into a Pennsylvania militia company that marched to Philadelphia, loaded into shallops, sailed to Trenton, and marched on to Bergen Point. After two months, they walked home and presumably passed again through Trenton.[19]

One group of soldiers passing through town asked to use the Friends Meeting House for temporary quarters, but the Friends only permitted it after the soldiers threatened to break down the doors. They did not honor the Friends' explanation that such a use of the meeting house was "inconsistent with our religious principles against wars and fightings." Afterwards, the Friends resolved to resist any similar future use of their meeting house by troops, even if it brought on suffering.[20]

The Flying Camp did not work out as envisioned, and Samuel Tucker complained to the Continental Congress on July 9 that New Jersey had to call out large numbers of militia to defend itself from the British on Staten Island even though the state had contributed large numbers of militiamen for the five-month levies to defend New York. Tucker forcefully argued that the New Jersey militia was doing Continental business in New York and, therefore, the other states should step up and provide for New Jersey's defense with money and troops.[21]

Militia duty was taking on a completely different character than it had in colonial times. No longer just a community defense force, militiamen were called on to travel long distances from home too often to maintain their full-time occupations and support their families. The numerous disruptions affected not only individual militiamen but their entire families and communities.[22] The next day, Tucker notified

Congress that there had been a very uneven militia turn out in New Jersey. This was partly a protest at the number of men being called out for what many considered was a Continental responsibility, but was also due to the time of year. Tucker reinforced the critical need for the Pennsylvanians, encamped uselessly at Trenton awaiting orders, to be sent east quickly to relieve New Jersey's militiamen, so they could return home to harvest the wheat crop, "the support of the Colony" and in great danger of being lost.[23] Washington backed Tucker and wrote to Congress on July 14 that he had "sent orders to the commanding officer of the Pennsylvania Militia to march to Amboy, because remaining at Trenton can be of no service."[24] Because the Flying Camp did not raise enough men, on July 18, the New Jersey Convention (formerly the Provincial Congress) reluctantly passed an ordinance calling out two thousand militiamen for the Flying Camp, hoping it was just a stop-gap for one month.[25]

The problem continued, and a follow-up ordinance on August 11 required half of each militia regiment to turn out in alternate months for duty with the Flying Camp until further notice. Under this system, half of the First Hunterdon Regiment combined with half of the Third Hunterdon each month to form a composite regiment. The colonel of the First Hunterdon would command one month and the colonel of the Third Hunterdon the next. Muskets were in such short supply that men staying home one month were encouraged to loan muskets to men going out and then get them back for their month of duty. The value of loaned muskets was determined ahead of time so that owners could be reimbursed for losses. John Fitch, because he knew "the guns in the township" and because no one else would do it, went around collecting muskets for men in the first group sent out who did not have one. He was able to convince everyone he asked to loan a musket, except for Alexander Chambers who refused. Fitch stated "having then about 20 hands at work I collected these arms and had them put in order with bayonets and all compleat in about three days and armed upward of fifty men as compleat as ever marched out of Trenton." Out of his concern for the poorer men, Fitch noted that several of the men were too poor to even supply themselves with blankets. He applied to Alexander Chambers, the barracks master, for about "10 or 12 English blankets in the barracks," but only got them when he went over Chambers's head. Chambers was also reluctant to provide knapsacks needed by the militia unless Fitch signed a note that he would personally be accountable for them and return them after use. Fitch finally talked him into giving him the knapsacks on his pledge to do his best to return them. Fitch believed that his confrontations with Chambers turned a friend into an enemy, and Chambers "being a man of great influence I soon felt the weight of his resentment." Whatever the accuracy of Fitch's feelings of persecution by Chambers and others, he was unflagging in his support of the poorer men in the militia.[26]

Under the revised militia system reinforcing the Flying Camp captains did not command their usual men and many men served under officers they did not know well and had not elected. This only added to the discontent over being called out at harvest time. William Tucker's composite company of men from Trenton and nearby areas paraded at Trenton and marched to Princeton where it quartered that night, and the next day they marched through New Brunswick and Woodbridge to their guard station at the New Blazing Star Ferry opposite Staten Island, arriving on August 25th. It looks like Tucker's company had some sickness or possibly discontent. He started out with 54 men, but the number fluctuated for several days before settling in at 45.[27]

Samuel Tucker sent General Livingston a letter on July 12 by Lieutenant Ephraim Anderson. Anderson must have been visiting family and friends back in the Trenton area while recovering from severe burns he had suffered during the fighting in Canada. Tucker's postscript referred to him as "Col Anderson" now appointed "Deputy Adjutant General." The titles of colonel and deputy adjutant general sounded very impressive. However, Anderson was still a second lieutenant who, until recently, had served as adjutant for his regiment. Adjutant was not a rank, but rather an administrative position held by officers of various ranks, usually junior ones. The self-promoting Anderson continued to use the title after he left the regiment to recover because it sounded to the uninformed much loftier than second lieutenant.[28]

The troops at New York and in the Flying Camp in New Jersey needed supplies of all types, and Trenton began a long period of service as a supply depot for the American army. The Continental Congress directed Colonel Clement Biddle on July 14 to use every method he could to forward flour collected at Trenton to the places where it was needed. He was also ordered to employ armorers for the army in New

Jersey, make application to the New Jersey Provincial Congress for all the lead they could supply and to the Pennsylvania Committee of Safety for as many musket cartridges as they could spare for the Flying Camp and militia in Jersey.[29] On July 16, the State ordered township committees to collect lead to be cast into musket balls, including lead weights from house windows and clocks, one pound and greater lead weights from shops, stores and mills, and any other available lead and forward it to commissioners Alexander Chambers, Lieutenant Colonel Abraham Hunt, David Pinkerton, or Captain William Tucker, who would pay for it at the rate of six pence proclamation money[30] per pound plus any reasonable expenses.[31]

Alexander Chambers purchased military equipment for the army throughout the year. He paid various local people for such items as muskets, cartridges, lead, flints, shovels, pick handles, cartridge boxes, and knapsacks. He purchased one or two muskets each from G. Wilson, Furman & Hunt, Plaskett & Clayton, Samuel Appleton, John Ruston, and Steven Burrowes. John Machett sold him 100 cartridge boxes, and Hopewell saddler Steven Burrowes was paid for cartridge boxes and for making up cartridges. Chambers and Jonathan Richmond also supplied cartridges. Merchant James Emerson was paid for supplying lead and flints. Ironically, Captain Charles Harrison was paid on July 4 for supplying lead and flints, just four days before he resigned and went over to the Loyalist cause, and for one musket on August 12. Benjamin Smith, Lott Dunbar, and William Yard respectively made 200, 82, and 80 knapsacks. Lyndon Brown provided 112 canteens, J. Somers six camp kettles, and Neil Livingston 15 shovel and pick handles. Local men also helped move supplies. Trenton merchants Brown and Reeder carted gunpowder to New Brunswick, and militiaman Daniel Yard guarded it. William Coxe provided a baggage wagon, and Neil Livingston arranged for carting militia baggage to Elizabethtown.[32] On July 4, Benjamin Yard received £51 for 12 muskets and on July 15 £1 and 14 shillings for 17 scabbards delivered to Hunterdon County commissioner Abraham Hunt.[33]

On July 2, Colonel Isaac Smith took charge of 14 Loyalists apprehended in Hunterdon County, brought them to the jail in Trenton, and used his militiamen, no doubt some from Trenton, to keep them under guard until further orders.[34] Fifty-nine-year-old Trenton grist mill owner Samuel Henry, born in Ireland about 1717 and living in Trenton since 1738, came under suspicion of disloyalty and on July 11 was ordered "committed to the common gaol of Hunterdon" and kept in close confinement. Colonel Smith employed one of his militia officers, probably William Tucker or one of his company officers, to arrest Henry and deliver him to the jail. Henry's large, stone grist mill was located further up the Assunpink Creek from Trenton Mills on 335 acres that included good crop land, a good wood lot, a farm house, a cedar-covered barn, and two large, framed corn cribs. This mill had "two pair of the best Esopus stones" that produced quality flour.[35]

Henry appeared before the New Jersey Convention on July 16; the charges against him were read, several witnesses examined, and further action deferred until the next day.[36] Henry proclaimed that he wanted to make amends for "any rash expressions that Convention may conceive he has been guilty of, and for every part of his conduct that has been, in their opinion, exceptionable." He was determined to conduct himself in the future in a positive way and was ready to "give any security the Convention may think necessary to require" so he could be released from confinement. The Convention took him at his word and discharged him from confinement on July 20, requiring him to provide £2,000 as a bond "for the faithful performance of his parole" and to stay within two miles of his mill, unless given leave by the Convention or future legislature.[37]

A number of suspected Loyalists came to Trenton to explain themselves to the Convention and hopefully obtain parole rather than jail or banishment.[38] Trenton militia Lieutenant Ellet Howell was ordered on July 12 to take two privates and proceed immediately to Burlington and bring a Loyalist under guard to Trenton and place him in jail.[39] It could be difficult for a man who was himself "a friend of government" to arrest suspected Loyalists and the High Sheriff of Hunterdon County, John Barnes of Trenton, who had been appointed by Royal Governor Franklin, resigned his office on July 18 because he opposed the efforts of the new government to control suspected Loyalists. Barnes was a distiller who lived for many years on Queen Street and during the colonial wars had been a lieutenant in Captain John Dagworthy's company of New Jersey troops. Although Barnes was well respected, Ebenezer Cowell, Jr. accused him of refusing to receive and execute arrest writs for suspected Loyalists. Two days after this resignation, busy Captain William Tucker was named to replace Barnes until a new sheriff was chosen in the upcoming election.[40]

During the first week of July, Samuel Tucker received word that the Continental Congress wanted the British officer prisoners sent to York, Pennsylvania. This relieved Tucker, who had been in the middle of the seemingly endless stream of conflicting orders, "from any more anxious thoughts on acct of those gentry."[41] However, Captain Ibbetson Hamar, one of the original British 7th Regiment prisoners, did not want to leave the area due to a budding romance and wrote to John Hancock from "Kingsberry near Trenton" about his fear that this move would supersede the permission he had been granted to live near Princeton. Samuel Tucker recommended that he apply to Congress "for leave to remain in the same quarters for some time longer with permission to come as far as Trenton." Hamar was surprisingly and curiously housed with a known British supporter, Dr. William Bryant.[42] The Continental Congress continued for some time to settle accounts with Trenton residents and firms, such as Furman and Hunt, for necessaries they furnished to the British prisoners from Canada.[43]

The Pennsylvania militia companies coming to Trenton as a staging area needed supplies. Commissary Carpenter Wharton at Trenton noted two thousand Pennsylvania militia had arrived in mid-July and that Colonel John Dickinson's[44] battalion had just marched off to Woodbridge and would be followed by the whole body of Pennsylvania militia. Wharton supplied them with one day of provisions, and they would receive additional provisions at Princeton to last them to Woodbridge. Wharton had just received 150 head of oxen, 500 head of sheep, and 1,500 barrels of flour, but these would only supply the many troops passing through Trenton for a short time. Wharton needed an additional $15,000 if he was to provide supplies for the Maryland and Pennsylvania troops.[45] At least some of the Pennsylvania militia came through town without a full supply of arms and camp equipage.[46]

Captain Rudolph's Company of Colonel Paschall's battalion arrived by shallop on the evening of August 16 and, probably like many others, lodged for the night in the barracks before marching on to Princeton.[47] Some 70 Associators of Captain John Young's company of the Third Battalion of Philadelphia County militia passed through on August 19 heading to northeastern New Jersey. They came from Philadelphia on a shallop normally used to carry bran, which caused a foul odor to permeate the vessel. For a variety of reasons, mostly contrary winds, they spent several unpleasant days on the water.

Some men disembarked and chose to walk the last few miles to Trenton rather than ride the stinking craft with their baggage. First Lieutenant Algernon Roberts wrote in his journal that the shallop arrived at Trenton Landing about seven o'clock in the morning, "to our unspeakable joy being heartily tired of our voyage." Roberts wrote that "after unloading our baggage we got a wagon to carry it to Amboy [and] drew rations which we took to a [Presbyterian] church yard at the upper end of Trenton whare we coock't them[,] it being the first time that we had an opportunity of regularly trying our hands at that business." Even though their initial effort at cooking was "not performed in the best order," they still found it "an agreeable repast" due to "a good stomack supplying the place of sauce." After their meal, "all [men] that kept journals got journallising on a tomb stone erected to the memory of Joseph Worrel [Warrell]," the young attorney who had died March 6, 1775 at age 36. After contemplating a variety of tombstones, Roberts and his company marched on to Princeton.[48]

While Pennsylvania militiamen were passing through Trenton on their way east, others were travelling west, having left their posts to return home before their tours were completed. Flying Camp commander General Hugh Mercer ordered General Dickinson on August 10 to post one militia company at Trenton, one at Princeton, and one at New Brunswick to stop these deserters.[49]

August was election month, and the newly elected Legislative Council and General Assembly held their first meetings at Princeton on August 27. John Hart of Hopewell, a signer of the Declaration of Independence, was chosen Speaker of the Assembly. Samuel Tucker had been elected Second Justice of the Supreme Court instead of to the Assembly[50] and the Grand Jury of Burlington County expressed its confidence in Tucker's "integrity and assiduity" and congratulated him on his election, only wishing that "your country had called you to so important an office in times less perilous and dangerous." Pleased with their "good opinion" of him, Tucker expressed his hope that his "future conduct will be such as will meet with the approbation of every freeman in the State of New Jersey." He would soon be severely tested.[51]

A Joint Meeting of the new State Legislative Council and General Assembly on September 1 elected William Livingston as New Jersey's first governor. Several days later, on September 7, a subsequent legislative Joint Meeting elected civil officers for Hunterdon County, including William Clayton and Dr./Colonel Isaac Smith as a judge and justice; Moore Furman and Alexander Chambers as justices of the peace; and, Ebenezer Cowell, Jr. as Clerk of the Peace and Pleas.[52]

While the new government was forming, Sergeant John Dougherty of Captain Tucker's Company was serving a one-month tour with the Flying Camp. While posted near the New Blazing Star Ferry on September 2, he accidentally discharged his musket and put the ball through his right hand. Because he was a tailor by trade, this wound rendered him incapable of earning a living. When the company got back to Trenton, Captain Tucker wrote a note for Dougherty that he could take to the General Assembly in the hope that they would take him under "Further Care."[53] There was no system yet for addressing this kind of need.

Another Trenton resident who came home from military service in September was innkeeper Henry Drake, who had been serving in the five-month levies as a volunteer lieutenant. After the August 27 battle on Long Island, desertion increased and Drake found himself accused of leaving the army without permission and being absent for twenty days. At his court martial on September 26 at Harlem Heights on Manhattan, Drake made the very unusual defense that he could not be guilty because he was not commissioned and was a civilian volunteer who had publicly stated when he joined that he would serve for just two months, rather than five. He had left the army when his two-month agreement expired, coincidentally just after the disastrous Battle of Long Island where the Trenton men in the five-month levies saw heavy action. Since he had not requested nor accepted any pay or rations from the army, he considered "himself at liberty to return home." Fellow innkeeper Ensign Joseph Clunn served as adjutant for the regiment and testified in support of Drake's explanation. Drake was acquitted, but his case shows just how confused things were at that time. Apparently even his regimental commander, Joseph Phillips of Maidenhead who undoubtedly knew him, was not aware of his actual status with the army.[54]

General Philemon Dickinson informed Governor Livingston on September 23 that the heavy calls upon his militiamen, combined with the dismissal of the Pennsylvania militia after their six weeks of service, made it difficult to get the next rotation of New Jersey militia for the Flying Camp to turn out. The numbers were so small that it no longer made sense to have two brigadier generals on duty. He asked for Livingston's and the Legislature's approval for some time off, noting the custom for militia officers to alternate duty and that he had been out on continuous duty for a long time. Matthias Williamson had recently been commissioned a brigadier general and could replace him for a while. One reason Dickinson wanted leave was that his wife had been confined to their house and bed in extreme pain for the past two months and Dickinson admitted that when he had gone out on duty, he never expected to see her alive again. Not wanting his personal life to affect his performance of duty, he had gone out with his troops in spite of his concerns for her.[55]

John Fitch was among the men from Trenton who dutifully turned out for the second division, but he became embroiled in a dispute over officer elections in the composite company. When he lost the election for first lieutenant to John Yard, a person he held in contempt as an officer, he left the company and marched back to Trenton alone. This dispute also involved Alexander Chambers, Jr. for whom Fitch had no use. In his anger, Fitch briefly considered abandoning the cause of independence but said, "finally [I] concluded not to resent my wrongs on my Country for the rashness of a few inconsiderate boys. Therefore [I] made the best of it I could." Fitch then focused his efforts on making and repairing muskets, remarking, "My return to Trenton was absolutely necessary as the troops came daily in from all quarters who wanted armes repaired. And I believe I expedited the business much faster than any foreman would. ... I gave the closest attention to business that summer as perhaps ever man did and from the first dawn of the day to 10 – 11 – 12 and one oclock at night was always persueing it with unremitted industry." He even worked on Sundays, which "gave great disgust to the Methodists of whose society I then was a member." Fitch had 12 to 15 men working for him in June and July as silversmiths or gunsmiths.[56]

In early August, the Assistant Deputy Quartermaster General at Trenton, John Shaw, received a large shipment of military items for the Flying Camp from Colonel Biddle in Philadelphia by way of John Clunn and his vessels based at Trenton Landing. The shipment included two kegs of barley, two kegs oatmeal, one bag of hops, 63 tents, 369 sets of tent poles, 155 camp kettles, 12 pieces of iron cannon – four and six pounders, eight kegs of buckshot, six casks containing sundry military stores, 30 dozen cartridges, 10 worms and ladles for six pounders, 10 ladles and five worms for six pounders, a quantity of round shot for six and four pounders, and 13 ladles.[57] Another shipment, again via John Clunn, included one hogshead containing artillery supplies such as match, linstocks, port fire stocks, tompions, calipers, compasses, copper powder measures, gunners slings with powder horns, priming irons, and other items along with 100 knapsacks and 86 haversacks and a barrel containing 40 blank books, 750 blank returns, and 500 blank passes in addition to 26 pair of men's shoes, a pair of shoes for Major Ross, a saddle cloth, and four yards of gingham for General Mercer. A barrel of flints and some blankets arrived at Trenton on August 22.[58] In September, Hugh Runyon of Nottingham Township was preparing to take over from John Shaw as Assistant Deputy Quartermaster at Trenton.[59]

To increase the number of desperately needed muskets as rapidly as possible, on August 18 the Convention resolved that "all the workmen of this State actually employed in the manufacture of fire-arms be excused from going out with the militia when called upon."[60] Benjamin Yard had been hard at work on muskets and on August 19 was approved payment for 14 muskets and on August 21 for 19 muskets delivered to Abraham Hunt.[61]

One of William Richards's tasks outfitting the Pennsylvania Navy was to provide flags for harbor defenses, pilot boats, and the armed galleys of the fleet. He was frustrated in August that he could not provide them because he had not been given designs for the galley flags which would help distinguish them from enemies in battle.[62]

Troops and supplies coming through town greatly increased business at the two Trenton ferries. The Convention resolved on August 11 that troops in the service of the United States or any state, along with their baggage, ammunition, wagons, and other supplies would pay no more than one-third of the usual ferry fees. Although the ferry operators would no doubt have appreciated receiving full fares, the troops and supply wagons represented a bonus to their normal business. Civilians supplying the army with provisions and other stores still paid full price because they were not part of the military and profited from the ferried supplies.[63]

John Adams passed through Trenton again on Sunday, October 13, on his way to Boston from Philadelphia. Setting out in the morning from Philadelphia, he dined at Bristol and crossed at Trenton Ferry "long before sun set, drank coffee at the Ferry House on the east side of Delaware." Adams says he put up for the night at the familiar inn "partly to avoid riding in the evening air, and partly because 30 miles is enough for the first day, as my tendons are delicate, not having been once on horse back since the eighth day of last February."[64]

When militia "division one" was called out for the second time, Lieutenant John Fitch was apparently appointed by Colonel Isaac Smith to lead one of the three composite companies. Since only two captains turned out, Smith was putting a lieutenant in command of the third company. When several key men opposed the appointment and recommended Ralph Jones, a younger man, to lead the company, Colonel Smith decided to leave it to a vote of the officers. The officers chose Jones, and Fitch told Colonel Smith that he would not serve under him. Fitch did not mean this as an affront to Smith's authority, but he intended to take his case to the Committee of Safety on appeal. Fitch then returned home and instead of appealing, he offered his services to Colonel Smith as his adjutant. However, Smith rather brusquely declined the offer. Fitch did not attend the next militia muster day in Trenton, causing Colonel Smith to order Captain Tucker not to recognize him as an officer and elect another lieutenant. Fitch asked for a court martial to defend himself, but more important military matters came first. However, General Dickinson and Colonel Smith must have been mighty tired of him by this point.[65]

Colonel Thomas Lowry, Assistant Commissary at Trenton, greatly needed salt in late October to furnish much needed provisions to the army at Kingsbridge on the northern end of Manhattan. The main army was then moving out of Manhattan, except for a force left at Fort Washington. Lowry had purchased a large number of beef cattle, but lacking forage, he needed to butcher them and salt down the meat.[66] Salt was in short supply, and while William Richards was trying hard to get the design for the Pennsylvania Navy flags, he noted that the people "in and about Trenton, are in great distress for the want of salt." Richards was willing to get the salt to Trenton, but if the Committee of Safety did not want to give him salt then he asked them to "order it to the Committee of Trenton." Richards brought 500 bushels of salt in his shallop to Trenton and delivered them to David Pinkerton, Clerk of the Trenton Committee of Safety, on November 16. The Committee sold it according to instructions in the amount of a half bushel per person who applied for it. Pinkerton was grateful because the need for salt in New Jersey was "extremely urgent."[67] However, Lowry was still without salt in the middle of November when he petitioned Congress directly. It was early December before two thousand barrels of salt beef were ready for the army.[68]

As the New York campaign worsened in October, General Nathanael Greene decided to establish supply magazines in New Jersey at Aquakanonk (Passaic), Springfield, Bound Brook, Princeton, and Trenton, with the principal ones at Aquakanonk and Trenton. Noting that all these posts were inland and secure, he made up an estimate of the amount of provisions needed at each post to support troops passing through the state. If his estimates seemed high, he explained "very little or no loss can arise, as the articles will be laid in at a season when the prices of things are at the lowest rates; and the situations will admit of an easy transportation to market by water." For the magazine to be set up at Trenton Landing, Greene recommended collecting 3,000 barrels of flour, 3,000 barrels of beef and pork, 300 tons of hay and 10,000 bushels of grain. He felt this would subsist 20,000 men for three months.[69] All this took place about the time of the Battle of White Plains on October 28 when it was looking like the army would need to retreat to New Jersey.

New Jersey's new government passed an act in October to control disaffected persons by outlawing any verbal or written statement, or any action to "maintain and defend the authority, jurisdiction or power of the King or Parliament of Great-Britain, heretofore claimed or used within this State." Violation could result in a fine of up to £300. Repeat offenders would be "set in the pillory, and imprisoned for any term not exceeding one year." Also prohibited were actions contemptuous of the State government or Continental Congress, or "which will encourage disaffection, or manifestly tend to raise tumults and disorders in the State," or "maliciously and advisedly spread such false rumours" concerning military affairs, or attempt to "alienate the affections of the people from the government." Anyone judged potentially dangerous by any two justices of the peace could be summoned by the justices and required to take an oath of abjuration renouncing British authority and an oath of allegiance to the new State, as set forth in a law of September 19. Anyone refusing to take these oaths would be taken to court.[70]

In spite of the fact that the primary military action was taking place north of New York City, General Charles Lee informed Congress on October 12 that a large contingent of Hessians had been removed from Staten Island and this could be preliminary to an attack on Trenton or Burlington. He said, "They will infallibly proceed either immediately up the River Delaware with their whole troops or what is more probable, land somewhere about S. Amboy or Shrewsbury and march strait to ... Trenton or Burlington." Washington's army was not in position to deal with this threat, so "for Heaven's sake let ten thousand men be immediately assembled and station'd somewhere about Trenton." Lee said he was on his way to headquarters to communicate his concerns and urge Washington to send troops, if he had any to spare, to help prevent this. Of course, Washington did not have any spare troops, and the British were not threatening Trenton yet. The people of Trenton, though, were no doubt wondering if or when they might be attacked.[71] The Continental Congress resolved on October 14 that some Virginia troops currently on the march to New York should halt at Trenton until further orders.[72]

Fear about how the war was proceeding must have been great in Trenton. On November 4, "A Friend to American Freedom" at Trenton wrote a letter to the editor of *The Pennsylvania Evening Post* noting efforts by New York Loyalists to reestablish the old colonial constitution of New York and make peace with England, something he considered a "breach or attempt of the utmost importance to the peace and well-being of every State."[73]

In November, the British army pursued the American army across the Hudson River, captured Fort Washington on Manhattan and Fort Lee across the river from it in New Jersey, and followed the American retreat across the State towards Trenton. The people of Trenton were in the direct path of the British army if it was headed for Philadelphia as everyone suspected. General Charles Lee at Phillipsburg, New York wrote to Dr. Benjamin Rush criticizing the army, commenting that the British may attempt to go to Philadelphia, and again called for a "Corps of Observation" at Trenton, recognizing its strategic importance in the line of communication.[74]

The Board of War had ordered General Adam Stephen and his Virginia brigade to Trenton in late October.[75] By November 7 they were at Trenton but needed quickly opposite Staten Island.[76] General Stephen set off to join the main army on November 8 but left behind 324 sick and convalescent men in the military hospital at Trenton.[77] The Trenton hospital was one of half a dozen established in New Jersey that summer and fall, and patients began to arrive in August.[78] Just what building, or buildings, contained the hospital at this point is not known, but it may have been the barracks and several additional buildings.

When Fort Washington surrendered to the British, several men with ties to Trenton, including John Beatty, Thomas Janney, Hamilton Martin, and Timothy Ryan of the Fifth Pennsylvania Regiment were among the captured soldiers.[79] Lambert Cadwalader was captured but released without parole and sent home in return for a kindness his father had shown to British General Prescott when he was a prisoner in Philadelphia. Cadwalader considered himself honor bound to secure the release of a British officer of equal rank before he would take up arms again. A collection of circumstances prevented this and he remained inactive until January 1779, when he resigned his commission so as not to stand in the way of promotion for other officers.[80]

On November 18, Governor Livingston directed Colonel Isaac Smith at Trenton to detach some men to go to Shrewsbury to prevent local Tories from communicating with the British fleet. Smith thought Livingston had asked him to send 100 men and replied that the half of his regiment currently serving in the Flying Camp had not returned yet from their monthly tour. He also noted that they had been out six of the last nine months. The other half of his regiment was on its way to relieve them and, because weapons were shared between the two divisions when necessary, he said "there are not arms enough now at home to arm" the needed troops. The most men that Smith thought he could get armed and together was one company, far fewer than 100 men. Smith apologized that he had to represent the facts so bluntly, but he did not have the resources to carry out the orders as he understood them. Livingston clarified on November 21 that what he really needed was a detachment of one company of 50 men for the duty at Shrewsbury and that Smith should comply as soon as possible. However, the developing retreat across the State made Livingston's request obsolete.[81]

When news of the November 16 capture of Fort Washington, opposite New Jersey's Fort Lee on the Hudson River, first reached Trenton, Samuel Tucker commented to Governor Livingston that it was not believed.[82] But things got even worse on the night of November 19, when about six thousand British troops crossed the Hudson, landed unopposed about five miles above Fort Lee, and climbed the New Jersey Palisades in the dark through a rainy mist and captured Fort Lee the next day, along with most of the supplies stored there. The American troops began to retreat across the State with the British in pursuit. John Anderson had turned out under Captain Tucker and began his tour at Bound Brook near the Raritan River, but when the British crossed into New Jersey, Tucker's men joined the retreat towards Trenton along with the other militia and Continental troops in eastern New Jersey.[83]

While the army was retreating across New Jersey, a Joint Meeting of the Legislative Council and General Assembly on November 29 named officers for the three new Continental regiments being raised to replace those whose enlistments were almost up. Thomas Yard and Ephraim Anderson were named captains in the Second Regiment. There were no fully active New Jersey regiments in the State at this time, and men in the original three New Jersey regiments were discharged as their enlistments expired. The next day, the Joint Meeting elected delegates to the Continental Congress and one was Jonathan Dickinson Sergeant, son-in-law of Trenton's Rev. Spencer.[84]

As the American troops retreated across New Jersey with the British in pursuit, Trenton lawyer Joseph Taylor abandoned his home and property and joined the British Army at New Brunswick from fear he would be imprisoned by the American troops nearing town. He was a known "friend of government," had refused to sign the Association, and had been fined for not turning out with the militia. In an effort to save at least some of his possessions, he "removed his furniture books &c to the house of a friend in Burlington County" before he left Trenton.[85] Former sheriff John Barnes also left Trenton in November, leaving behind his wife and his large, two-story house, its stables, and other outbuildings on one and a half acres next to the Assunpink Creek at the foot of Queen Street. He joined with the British army and was commissioned major in the Loyalist First Battalion of the New Jersey Volunteers.[86]

November 30 was a desperate and busy day. Washington had little hope of help from the New Jersey militia and the five-month levy enlistments would expire on December 1 along with the tours of some of the militia serving under General Mercer in the Flying Camp. In addition, a number of Continentals were deserting before their enlistments expired on January 1. To discourage and apprehend deserters, Washington asked Livingston to immediately "give orders to the officers of militia on the roads and ferries over Delaware to take up and secure every soldier that has not a regular discharge or pass." These guards included Trenton militiamen at the town ferries.[87] The same day, brothers General William and Admiral Richard Howe announced an amnesty for anyone taking an oath of allegiance to England. As many as 2,700 people, including some from Trenton, took advantage of this offer to gain protection from British depredations.[88]

Chapter 5

1776
December 1-8

Trenton lawyer Daniel Coxe, fourth generation scion of one of the wealthiest and most politically influential, and often hated, proprietary families from the first days of British ownership of New Jersey, was in the habit of taking his family to Philadelphia for the winter. With the American army approaching town in late November and wanting to "escape arrest and imprisonment" for his support of the Royal Government, Coxe decided it would be a good time to get out of town. Trenton's Mary Poynton decided to stay in town although equally concerned for her safety, acknowledging that the rebels "at this period were particularly active in seizing upon all the friends of government in the Province." Coxe left quickly, not taking time to secure his property beyond leaving it in the care of his servants and tenants, and took his Trenton Ferry across the river on December 1. His widowed mother, who had lived in Trenton for over 40 years "in comfort and affluence," went with him and later sought asylum in New York before removing to England in 1778. After the war, Coxe defended his abandonment of New Jersey, writing that he left "firmly intending himself to return and join the Royal Army the first favourable opportunity," but was prevented "by the American seizure of all the boats and communication on the river." He was "rendered totally unable, at that time, from either returning, or saving any part of his property not before sent off to another estate near Trenton." Former Royal Governor William Franklin believed Coxe's removal to Pennsylvania at this time was his way to "live quiet" and avoid taking real action. It appears Coxe kept a low profile in Pennsylvania until the arrival of the British army in 1777. He never returned to New Jersey.[1]

As one of the State Treasurers, when Samuel Tucker heard on November 30 that the British army was nearing town and that Washington planned to cross to Pennsylvania and leave Trenton exposed to the British, he decided to remove many of his papers and valuable possessions from town. He collected all his bonds, deeds, books of accounts, papers dealing with several estates for which he was executor, all his plate, his and his wife's clothes, and other valuable items. He also gathered up a quantity of New Jersey paper money and some Maryland and New Jersey Loan Office money. The New Jersey paper money had two signatures but required Tucker's as a third signature before it was legal tender. By not signing the notes before hiding them, they would have no value if discovered by the British or anyone else. He quickly packed everything in several chests and boxes, loaded them on his phaeton[2] , and drove about five miles to the most secure place he could think of, the house of twenty-nine-year-old John Abbott in Nottingham. He put what he believed to be about £6-7,000 of unsigned money in a small box with his deeds and hid it in Abbott's bed chamber on the upper floor, returned to Trenton, and hoped for the best.[3]

George Ewing limped into town on or about December 1. He had sprained his ankle about three days earlier at Pennington while walking home to southern New Jersey from Fort Ticonderoga after the expiration of his one-year enlistment in the Second New Jersey regiment. He had enlisted at Burlington on November 2, 1775 and then marched off on February 28, 1776 from the Trenton barracks, where his company had been furnished with clothing and equipment for the Canadian campaign. Ewing only got as far as Albany, where he took sick and was left behind to recuperate. He had rejoined his regiment during its retreat from Canada in May. Before heading home, Ewing stayed in town for a day or two and no doubt shared stories with people about the sad events and condition of the men in the northern army.[4]

Ewing must have blended right in with the Trenton militiamen returning home from their active duty with either the five-month levies or the Flying Camp. Tavern owner Joseph Clunn was back in town after serving his five months as ensign in Captain Joab Houghton's company and adjutant for Colonel Joseph Phillips's regiment. With him was his company's twenty-two-year-old drummer William Morris, a young tailor in Nottingham. Together with the other exhausted and ragged men who had experienced a series of defeats at the hands of the professional British and Hessian troops, they spread the word in and around Trenton of the desperate situation of the American army and the imminent approach of the British regulars and Hessians.[5] Among the disheveled men passing through Trenton were others like Ewing whose enlistments in Continental regiments had expired, or who were fed up and deserting, heading for the ferries that would take them to Pennsylvania.

There were said to be about 4,334 ragged and dispirited men from Hugh Mercer's, Adam Stephens's, James Ewing's and Edward Hand's brigades of the American army at and near Trenton as December began, but this was perhaps an overly optimistic count.[6] Their presence did little to reassure the people of Trenton, who were anticipating some kind of destructive encounter with the British troops. Almost everyone believed the British objective was actually Philadelphia, but no one knew whether that attack would take place in the current campaign or be delayed until the spring. The inhabitants pondered whether Washington would invest the town with his desperate army and try to hold it against a determined British assault, or whether he would pass through, cross over to Pennsylvania, and leave the British in control of the town and subject its people to British and Hessian occupation and plundering. Either scenario was potentially catastrophic for individuals and their property. The war was becoming very personal, and everyone faced questions of survival that interwove with whatever viewpoint they held on the importance and validity of the conflict. Each person weighed carefully the offer of amnesty and protection provided by General Howe and imagined how accepting or rejecting it might affect their survival in the short and long term. The cultural and economic benefits of Trenton's location on the main road between New York and Philadelphia did not seem so enviable in the present situation.

Washington firmly decided at New Brunswick on December 1 to cross the Delaware with what was left of his army, rather than make a stand there, at Princeton, or at Trenton with his back against the river. To avoid repeating the recent disaster at Fort Lee in which the post was abandoned without removing all the important military supplies, his first objective was to get his army and all its supplies out of Trenton and across the river. He knew it would require many boats making many trips to carry everything across the river successfully, and it was also absolutely crucial to make it impossible for the British to cross after him when they arrived, unless the river froze solidly enough for an army to get across it. Washington wisely became almost obsessed with securing and controlling anything on the river usable for ferrying the men and supplies of his army across it. He asked Governor Livingston to send militiamen to the Trenton ferry landings to assist with crossing his army and to dispatch other parties to gather up every kind of watercraft and secure them under guard on the Pennsylvania side of the Delaware. It is very likely he called on Trenton militiamen who were very familiar with where boats were kept along the river and its tributaries at Trenton, as well as north and south of the town for some distance.[7]

Washington also ordered Colonel Richard Humpton of the 11th Pennsylvania Continental Regiment to go to the two ferries near Trenton and ensure that suitable boats were "put in the best order, with a sufficiency of oars and poles" to transport the troops and their baggage over the river "in the most expeditious manner." Washington instructed Humpton to be especially attentive to the Durham boats, "which are very proper for this purpose," and promised him every assistance from the quartermaster general and his staff. In addition, he ordered Humpton to collect "every other craft" up and down the river from the ferries and secure them on the Pennsylvania side, stressing the "infinite importance" of preventing the British from having the means to cross to Pennsylvania and march on Philadelphia. No time was to be lost. The baggage was to be taken over before the men crossed and placed somewhat back from the river. Washington's messages to Livingston and Humpton were essentially redundant, a reflection of the urgency of the mission, and put plenty of manpower, both Continentals and local militia, into motion to carry out this essential task quickly and completely.[8] Washington issued additional orders throughout the week to ensure that the British would find no boats on or near the Delaware within 40 miles north or south of Trenton.[9] Joshua Mersereau recalled, "I was ordered with my father to examine the river and bring off all the boats from the Jersey shore to prevent the British from pursuing & was engaged in that capacity for some days." One family tradition says they found several sunken boats that the British could have raised had they not been found by members of the family.[10]

The men sent ahead to locate boats found a variety of vessels. Washington was only partially correct that the Durham boats were especially suited for the purpose at hand. These boats were designed to carry bulk cargo the length of the river, not across it. They could carry baggage and men very well, but horses, wagons, and artillery could not be loaded onto them. Washington wisely crossed the river at well-established ferries where the proper types of long, low, flat-bottomed ferry barges were available to transport army horses and vehicles, just as they routinely did with similar civilian horse-drawn traffic. To move so much in so short a time, it is likely a variety of craft were used in some way. Any craft not used was taken across the river and secured.

Washington expected to be reinforced by General Lee[11] and some Pennsylvania militia. The Pennsylvania Council of Safety ordered militia units to join Washington at Trenton, and William Richards was ordered to provide "every necessary for accommodating the militia on their passage from here [Philadelphia] to Trenton, to have Oars fixed to each Shallop, and proportion the number of men each can carry."[12] Washington also hoped the New Jersey militia would turn out and gather at Trenton "that they may be ready to join us and act as occasion may require."[13]

Trenton lawyer Isaac Allen and his family abandoned their home about the same time the American army entered town and travelled the short distance to an area controlled by the oncoming British. Allen accepted General Howe's protection papers and on December 3 was commissioned as a lieutenant colonel in the New Jersey Volunteers, a Loyalist brigade of regiments organized by Cortland Skinner, the former colonial attorney general and speaker of the General Assembly.[14]

Washington left a rearguard of two brigades at Princeton under Lord Stirling, positioned to give him timely warning of a British approach, and arrived at Trenton on December 2, where he found that Colonel Humpton and others had the necessary boats ready, while everything else that could float was rapidly being cleared from the river. Washington reported from Trenton on December 3 that "immediately on my arrival here, I ordered the removal of all the military and other stores and baggage over the Delaware," and because boats had been ready at both Trenton Ferry and Elijah Bond's ferry, "a great quantity are already got over." He expected the arrival of armed Pennsylvania State Navy row galleys that William Richards had helped outfit, and as soon as they arrived he would order them loaded so that everything could be taken over that night, and on the next day if the British did not suddenly advance. Good weather assisted this huge operation with temperatures on December 2 and 3 in the low to mid-40s, and aside from some wind on the afternoon of the third, there were just a few clouds on otherwise sunny days.[15] Feeling the pressures of his desperate situation, Washington noted rather somberly that "after being disencumbered of my baggage and stores, my future situation will depend entirely upon circumstances."[16]

Militiaman William R. Green of Trenton Township had been in almost continuous service since March 1, but when Livingston called out the entire militia in late November, he had gone to New Brunswick with his friend John Burroughs and arrived just in time to retreat with the army. Because he had experience as a ferryman, he was one of those ordered ahead to assist at the Trenton ferries.[17] Israel Hunt was not out on duty in December, but he turned out with seven other men who joined a makeshift company formed under Maidenhead Captain Phil Phillips at Trenton. Israel recalled that they "were marched to Lamberton ... a little below Trenton and were employed in getting the baggage of Genl. Washington's army across the Delaware River..." before crossing themselves. For the next five days, Trenton militiamen assisted with the crossing. In addition to the supplies traveling with the army, the supplies gathered for the Continental magazine at Trenton also needed to be removed. Commissary Stephen Lowrey made an estimate on December 2 of the provisions at and near Trenton. These included: 2,000 barrels of flour; 40 hogsheads and 100 barrels of beef (62,000 lbs), and 250 bushels of salt at Trenton Landing; 33 hogsheads of beef (33,000 lbs) and 100,000 pounds of bulk beef at Samuel Tucker's store; 35 hogsheads of rum in various stores; 150 boxes of soap and candles in his office cellar; 1,020 cattle in various places on the east side of the Delaware; 300 barrels of pork at Pennington; 500 barrels of pork at Flemington; and 100 barrels of pork at Jacob Service's on the Delaware.[18] Trenton residents may have recognized at least seven of the wagons, drivers, and horses bringing army supplies to the ferries, because they belonged to Hopewell men impressed into service on December 2 to cart for the army.[19]

The small fleet of Pennsylvania State Navy row galleys under Commodore Thomas Seymour arrived at Trenton to assist with the crossing. These river craft were forty to fifty feet long, flat bottomed, pointed at both ends, painted black and yellow, and powered by two lateen sails on short masts, in addition to a double bank of twenty-two-foot oars. Each galley carried either an 18, 24, or 32-pounder cannon, as well as swivel guns along its bulwarks. The people of Trenton saw galleys with names like *Congress, Franklin, Washington,*

Burke, Camden, Chatham, and *Ranger,* but what flag the vessels flew is unclear because William Richards still had no design information. The galleys may have flown a variety of colors, including a white flag with a green pine tree in the center and the motto "Appeal to Heaven" as they helped cross the baggage and men. Another redundant order, this time from Congress and the Pennsylvania Council of Safety, had Captain Thomas Houston with the row galley *Warren* proceed up the Delaware from Philadelphia and remove all "river Craft, Vessels & Boats" to the Pennsylvania side of the river as far up as Trenton.[20]

Crossing the baggage continued on December 3, while the soldiers of the American army, a combination of veterans and reinforcements described by contemporaries "more as a tatterdemalion mob," awaited in and about Trenton for their orders to cross.[21] The town of Trenton must have been in turmoil from the influx of men more than doubling the population and seeking services, lodgings or campgrounds, forage for horses, and wood for fires while churning up the dirt roads and causing property damage. Unlike most Americans, the people of Trenton saw firsthand, and up close, the terrible condition of their army resulting from the disastrous New York and Canadian campaigns and the lack of supplies.

The First Hunterdon Regiment under Colonel Isaac Smith was disheveled, and the men were torn between protecting their families and forming up in their companies. Many of the officers and men had served in the five-month militia levies, and after their recent discharge needed to reenter the regiment. Others had been serving rotating months of duty in the Flying Camp composite companies rather than their normal ones. The regiment needed to be reconstituted, but the confused and threatening conditions made this impossible leaving men to find ways to assist the army in small bands or as individuals on their own initiative.[22] John Coleman came to Trenton in December as a guide with a party of militia and then joined a scouting party organized by local militiamen under Joseph Brearley, recently returned from his one-year stint as a captain in the Second New Jersey Regiment in Canada. They operated between Trenton and Princeton throughout December.[23] Having been a First Hunterdon captain before his Continental commission, Brearley was betwixt and between but was doing what he could to organize local militiamen to assist Washington while the British occupied his community.

Ferrying the army's supplies continued in good weather on December 4, while Washington continued to hope for reinforcements. A heavy overnight rain and temperatures rising into the 50s made for muddy roads, but there was sun and mixed clouds during the day.[24]

General Nathanael Greene wrote to Rhode Island's governor reviewing recent events and highly criticizing the New Jersey militia system. He sent the letter by way of Captain Skinner of the Connecticut Light Horse, because the mail posts were uncertain and sometimes intercepted. Basic structures supporting normal life in New Jersey were breaking down and Trenton was becoming isolated.[25]

The sick and wounded in the military hospital at Trenton were evacuated across the river about December 4 to more permanent hospitals at Easton, Allentown, Bethlehem, and Philadelphia, to get them out of the way of danger and also to free up space needed by the troops in Trenton.[26]

General Greene wrote to his wife, Catharine, known as Caty, trying to give her accurate information without sounding too gloomy about the future. He began by saying, "The situation this army was in when I wrote you last must naturally alarm your fears. The enemy have since pressed us very hard from place to place. The time for which our troops were engaged expired and they went off by whole brigades notwithstanding the enemy lay within two or three hours march of us and our [remaining] force not near half equal to theirs. The virtue of the Americans is put to a trial." More optimistically, he noted the militia of Pennsylvania, particularly Philadelphia, were reinforcing the army greatly. Then, in seeming contradiction to everything going on around him, he said, "In a day or two I hope to advance upon the enemy and drive them back as fast as they drove us on. We are making every disposition to advance upon the enemy and by tomorrow I hope the General will issue his orders to move forward." Greene welcomed the expected advance as an opportunity "to stop the ravages of the enemy; [as] their footsteps are marked with destruction wherever they go. There is no difference made between the Whigs and Tories – all fare alike. They take the cloaths off of the peoples back. The distress they spread wherever they go exceeds all description." Caty had hoped to join him, but he discouraged this saying, "I hope to God you have not set forward for this place from what I wrote you last. Continue at home my dear if you wish to enjoy the least share of happiness." Lastly, with all the troubling things going on around him, he asked for news from her and how the spirits of the people of Rhode Island were and whether she had any successes to report, especially of privateers intercepting British ships.[27]

Ferrying the baggage and supplies continued on December 5 with temperatures back down in the 40s and the weather fair. Contemplating a possible stand at Princeton, which explains why Greene thought a movement against the enemy was imminent, Washington decided that with almost all the baggage safely removed from Trenton, he would "face about with such troops as we have fit for service and march back to Princeton" where he would "govern" himself "by circumstances." Washington was glad that a recently recruited regiment of Pennsylvania and Maryland Germans had arrived as reinforcements that day and believed he now had about 1,200 men, that when combined with Stirling's men at Princeton would total about 2,400. He planned to go to Princeton himself, still hoping for additional reinforcements and very angry about the lack of response from the New Jersey militia "and the principal men of the country."[28]

The abandonment of Trenton ahead of the approaching British soldiers caused a near panic as well-known Whigs attempted to get out of town. John Fitch fled Trenton with as many of his tools as he could fit in one small wagon and took refuge in Bucks County. He thought about rejoining his old militia company and asking to be reinstated as a lieutenant, but wisely decided against it. Even though his services as a gunsmith were highly valued and could exempt him from military duty, some of his enemies had unfairly declared him to be a militia deserter. Avoiding the inevitable disputes, he enrolled instead in the Bucks County militia as a new resident of Pennsylvania and did not reside in New Jersey during the remainder of the war.[29]

Sergeant William Young of Captain Thomas Fitzsimmons's company of the Third Battalion of Pennsylvania militia marched into Trenton that night after travelling by schooner from Philadelphia to Bristol and marching overland to Trenton. Young had difficulty finding lodging for himself, but "Providence directed me to Mr. Brown's who kindly let us lodge in his stove room." The next day, Friday, December 6, his company paraded together and marched to Major Samuel Meredith's, "where we were kindly treated, had a good lodging-room, warm and comfortable."[30]

The British had not yet left New Brunswick on December 6, so Washington planned to depart Trenton for Princeton "unless something should occur to prevent me, which I do not expect." However, he did not leave until the next day.[31] The weather was not the problem, as temperatures were in the 40s and it was fair.[32] Still not knowing when the British would advance towards him, Washington wrote to Trenton born Pennsylvania militia Colonel John Cadwalader on December 7, telling him that his troops could be accommodated better at Trenton than Princeton. Washington told him to remain in Trenton "till the whole of your Brigade comes up. In the meanwhile, keep me regularly advised of their arrival, that I may endeavor to time other matters thereby." He expected Cadwalader to lose no time getting them properly arranged, supplied with ammunition and three days of cooked rations so they would be ready "to march at a moments warning." Cadwalader should also take the sailors and marines coming from Philadelphia under his care and let Washington know if they "came out resolved to act upon land or mean to confine their services to water only."[33]

After sending off this letter, Washington finally set out for Princeton on the morning of December 7 in fair weather and temperatures that rose again into the 40s. Ahead of him in Princeton, Nathanael Greene learned the British were on the march from Brunswick to Princeton. He dashed off a note to Washington and sent it by express rider to Trenton, and Stirling's troops marched off for Trenton. Sergeant James McMichael of Colonel Miles' Pennsylvania Rifle Regiment was part of Stirling's rearguard, and his regiment was paraded at 2:00 pm and marched off toward Trenton. Galloping ahead of them, General Greene's express rider intercepted Washington on the road. Upon learning of the enemy advance, Washington quickly turned his force around and headed back to Trenton, where the men began crossing the river to Bucks County. Sergeant McMichael's company finally arrived in Trenton at 10:00 pm, took up quarters, and did not cross until the next morning.[34] Enoch Anderson had been promoted from lieutenant to captain by Colonel Haslet of the Delaware Continentals just three days earlier and his regiment also left Princeton, reaching Trenton at dusk. To slow the British pursuit, Anderson and others from Haslet's regiment tore up bridges and cut down trees. After spending the night in Trenton, he reported, "In the afternoon of the next day, we crossed the Delaware into Pennsylvania."[35]

Shortly after arriving in Trenton, Sergeant Young's Third Battalion of Associators, under Cadwalader, was ordered "to move our quarters and retreat over Delaware" because "Howe's advance party was near at hand." They went over after dark on the 7th and "lay on the shore very cold – and with much difficulty got some wood to make a fire." All this renewed a cold that Young came down with while coming up the river to Trenton.[36]

While the troops were crossing on December 7, Washington sent Major Robert Hoops, the former Trenton militia company captain and now brigade major for General Dickinson, as express rider with an urgent message for General Lee to hurry up with his troops and join the main army. Lee disregarded this message and was captured several days later by a British patrol. Fortunately, his men did eventually join with Washington after the crossing to Pennsylvania.[37]

Civilians continued to leave Trenton in fear of the British advance. Rev. Spencer was warned in the night that he needed to make his escape. After his work in the southern colonies for the Continental Congress, the British had put a price of 100 guineas on his head.[38] But, Spencer had more than just himself to worry about. His daughter, Margaret, had married Continental Congress delegate Jonathan Dickinson Sergeant in March 1775.[39] The Sergeants lived in Princeton in their recently built home, but Jonathan was attending Congress in Philadelphia, leaving Margaret and their young daughter at home. Fortunately, Margaret was warned by her neighbor, Dr. Absalom Bainbridge, of the near British advance at two in the morning and he made sure she set off immediately in the family carriage heading to a Delaware River ferry. Dr. John Witherspoon knew of her departure and, during his own escape to Trenton that night riding his sorrel horse, met Rev. Spencer coming up the road to find Margaret. Witherspoon told him to return to Trenton and remove the rest of his family to safety. Spencer locked up his house without removing any contents, left his cattle without being able to provide care for them, loaded his entire household into a large carriage, and drove north to Howell's Ferry.

Leaving his family at Howell's, Spencer continued north to Johnson's Ferry, across from McConkey's Ferry, where he found his daughter and her party. He returned to Howell's to bring up his family, and they all crossed at Johnson's. Spencer's daughter, Lydia, was left with indelible images of that night and to her "youthful imagination they called up the day of judgment: so many frightened people were assembled, with sick and wounded soldiers, all flying for their lives, and with hardly any means of crossing the river." Most of the local boats had been diverted to Trenton, and Margret recorded, "We were unspeakably delighted when we got over safely, and into a little hut, where we spent the night with a company of American soldiers, on their way to join General Washington."[40]

Charles Willson Peale, leading a company of Philadelphia Associators, spent the night of December 6 at Bordentown and marched to Trenton the morning of December 7, arriving there about one o'clock in the afternoon. They had only rested a short time and eaten when their heavy baggage was ordered sent across the river, each man was given "his complement of cartridges," and they were ordered to prepare to march. Peale wrote, "I expected we were to advance toward the enemy, but it was to retreat across the river, which we accomplished in the evening. We put up a few tents for the night on the [Pennsylvania] shore."[41]

After crossing, Peale looked back at the troops continuing to cross and through his artist's eyes found it "the most hellish scene I ever beheld. All the shores were lighted up with large fires, boats continually passing and repassing, full of men, horses, artillery and camp equipage ... The sick and half naked veterans of the long retreat streamed past," providing additional images of despair. The noises were also terrifying and "the hollowing of hundreds of men in their difficulties of getting horses and artillery out of the boats, made it rather the appearance of Hell than any earthly scene." At one point, a passing soldier approached him who was so dirty and bedraggled, his face disfigured by long beard and sores, that he only recognized his brother James when he spoke. The people who remained in Trenton experienced these "Hellish" images and sounds as well.[42]

The British troops occupied Princeton while boats filled with Washington's men made repeated trips across the Delaware through the afternoon and night of Saturday, December 7, finishing late on the morning of the 8th. General Greene had estimated that it would require about forty boats, properly manned, under the care of solid officers, making multiple crossings each, to get the troops over expeditiously.[43]

Commodore Seymour had apparently withdrawn all or part of his squadron of row galleys from Trenton before the troops crossed, and on December 8 the Pennsylvania Executive Council directed him to take his squadron up to Trenton immediately and place himself under the orders of General Washington. However, by the time he got to Trenton, the crossing had been completed.[44]

Pennsylvania Rifle Sergeant James McMichael paraded with his company at 4:00 am on December 8 "and at dawn crossed the Ferry into Pennsylvania."[45] The crossing continued during the morning, and the last of the soldiers and supplies got across to Bucks County very shortly before the British arrived in Trenton. In addition to his army, Washington had been able to remove all his stores, except for a few boards.[46] The Americans left nothing at the Trenton ferries that could be used by the British to cross after them. The owner of Trenton Ferry, Daniel Coxe, later complained that his two large scows (ferry boats) and two batteaus (small boats), along with their oars, poles, and hooks were all taken away. The Americans also took his horse and carriage to prevent the British from having the use of them.[47]

Just after crossing at Trenton Ferry, Henry Knox wrote to his wife Lucy, opening with, "You may be surprised my dating from this place but it is [due] to a combination of unlucky circumstances [which] have oblig'd us to retreat from before the enemy, however we shall soon I hope be able to face them[.] we are now making a stand on the side of the Delaware towards Philadelphia."[48] Like, Greene, Knox was itching to retake the offensive against the British.

Samuel Tucker left Trenton on December 8, taking with him an additional £1,504:4:0 of unsigned public money and about £1,000 that he held in trust as an executor for several estates. He paid the public money to the other State Treasurer. However, he did not cross the river like so many other well-known Whig leaders, but went into hiding outside of Trenton and placed the money and papers in places he felt were as secure as possible.[49] Some of those papers related to a number of fines levied on "friends of government" and their paroles.[50] His family stayed at their home in Trenton. It is unclear why Tucker did not cross to Pennsylvania or at least make sure the public money got across. Like everyone else, he was faced with the questions of what to do about one's family, property, and person, and each person did what seemed appropriate at the time amid all the fears, rumors, and confusion. As with many decisions in life where there was no perfect solution, many people looked back later and wondered if they had done the right thing. At this point, Tucker could only hope he had acted most appropriately.

Even in the confusion of the river crossing, some things continued as usual in Trenton, including taking care of military business. Alexander Chambers continued to make out pay vouchers to various Trenton citizens who had sold him arms and military stores for the army. Several of these vouchers went to Benjamin Yard for 36 guns, John Royell and Jeremiah Woolsey for lead, Lott Dunbar for strapping canteens, and Josiah Appleton for coopering powder casks. Chambers also made a pay slip out to himself for his purchase of various sundries, along with one gun, 13 gun locks, and 11 axes and handles. These locally made items probably crossed to Bucks County with the army or militia if they were not damaged, used up, or lost in the recent campaign.[51]

The temperatures on December 8 were again in the upper 40s and the weather fair, so the final crossing of troops was not impeded.[52] Shortly after the last boats crossed to Pennsylvania, about two or three o'clock in the afternoon, the sounds of martial music preceded the colorful sight of British infantry, light infantry, and Hessian grenadiers entering town. The advance guard was led by Hessians commanded by Major Friederich von Dechow and the 1st battalion of Light Infantry. Dechow says, "the last ¾ of a mile the jägers[53] took at a trot, in order to fall upon the enemy's rearguard, which had not all got over the Delaware yet. We, however, found nothing further on this side, except a few rebels who had been left behind, and who were here and there hidden in the houses, - which we took prisoners."[54]

Hessian Captain Freiderich Meunschausen, an aide to General Howe, recorded in his diary that upon reaching the outskirts of Trenton, some of the residents ran out and encouraged them to hurry so they could capture some of the enemy at the river. General Howe was suspicious, though, suspecting that the rebels had established artillery on the far side of the river and would bombard his troops when they got to the open plain below Trenton. Therefore, he ordered his troops to halt, except for some light infantry and Hessian jägers. Meunschausen recorded that, "with these troops, General Howe, Lord Cornwallis, and three of us aides, went through Trenton and down to the plain. Just as we arrived, the rebels opened a terrific fire upon us with all their batteries, containing 37 cannon. The light infantry and jägers were forced to retreat in the greatest hurry to the valley at the left. On their way, in the blink of an eye, they lost 13 men."[55] Other eyewitnesses estimated from eight to eighteen cannon fired on them and three soldiers were wounded. Sergeant McMichael was able to look back across at Trenton and said the British at the shoreline "were soon dispersed by several messengers sent from an 18-pounder of ours."[56]

General Howe rode in plain view of the Americans across the river and Meunschausen wrote he "stayed there with the greatest of coolness and calm for at least an hour, while the rebels kept their strongest fire going. Wherever we turned, the cannon balls hit the ground, and I can hardly understand, even now, why all five of us were not crushed by the many balls.... Just as General Howe was about to move into the town, a ball landed so close to him in soft ground that dirt splattered his body and face."

Meunschausen did not escape unscratched and recorded, "I had the honor to receive a small contusion on my knee. We were just standing still when a ball took away the hind leg of my horse, and hit some stones on the ground, one of which hit me in the knee and caused my leg to swell up. I was lucky, for my horse fell to the ground with me with great force, and feeling the blow on my knee just then, I believed that I was really seriously wounded. Afterwards General Howe gave me a superb English horse to replace mine." Finding no boats had been left behind, General Howe refused to begin building boats or pontoons. However, that evening he detached Lord Cornwallis with four regiments to occupy Pennington and as Meunchausen recorded, "It was hoped that he would find boats or perhaps a good ferry so that he could cross over" the Delaware the next day.[57] By evening, Hessian Colonel Carl von Donop and his brigade had established quarters in Trenton with a battalion of British light infantry bivouacked at Trenton Ferry. Other units were at posts nearby.[58] Trenton became an armed camp with the arrival of the Hessian and British soldiers, who quartered themselves at taverns and the homes of residents who had fled. Trenton lawyer Joseph Taylor, who had left town and joined with the British Army, came back to the area with them.[59] The Hessian brigade commanders, von Donop and Johann Rall, requested to pursue the Americans to Philadelphia, but were told to just keep their brigades in readiness, presumably to cross when the Delaware froze.[60]

The British 17th Regiment of Foot arrived in Trenton after setting out from Princeton at 8:00 am and took up quarters in the Trenton barracks. General orders established their daily routines for the immediate future: two sentries were posted "to prevent the men going out after 7 in the evening;" the field behind the barracks was designated the alarm post; all arms and accoutrements were to be arranged so that "the men can get to them without inconveniency;" the army was to be ready to march on short notice; and assembly "must be done without confusion by companys from the right. Capt Scotts first and so on." The barracks was "to be kept as cool as possible, the windows put up & no fire in the barrack room." This may seem harsh in December, but it was standard military practice when troops moved from tents to buildings in cold weather so that the transition to heated quarters was moderated to prevent the onset of "inflammatory maladies."[61] Cooking was to be done in the church yard, presumably the Presbyterian, or near it. Rooms were to be swept every morning by 9:00 am and the men were to use their watch coats and blankets as bedding, since "no straw can be got." Cooking kettles were to be boiled every day at 12:00 pm. Guards were to mount at 9:00 am and the regiment parade at 10:00 am. To prevent trouble with civilians, officers who wanted to buy anything from civilians were ordered to do it themselves, perhaps accompanied by a soldier servant, but not to send servants alone.[62]

Important merchant Abraham Hunt, Lieutenant Colonel of the First Hunterdon militia, stayed in Trenton rather than crossing with the American army and received protection papers. This act was just one of many that seemed to confirm the opinion of Samuel Adams that the people of New Jersey were determined to give up the cause, and Hunt's actions undoubtedly led some local people to assume that he had switched sides just as other prominent men had. He was certainly in a delicate situation, to say the least. Even with his long Whig pedigree, he was somehow able to convince General Howe very quickly that he was once again devoted to King and Parliament. There are essentially two explanations for his action. One possibility is that he ingratiated himself with the side he now expected to win the war; that he was the clever, opportunistic, self-serving individual pictured by some historians, who always looked out for himself and went with the flow. Another intriguing possibility is that he was going undercover to be in position to help the Whig cause at some point during the British occupation. Whichever of these scenarios was in play, the only way he could achieve his aim was to obtain a protection paper. It was a bit unusual that he did not first sign a loyalty oath to secure the protection, but he may have played on his value to the British as a local merchant and the offer of his home to house Hessian officers. At any rate, the second in command of the First Hunterdon militia regiment lived comfortably in his own Trenton home, cooperating with and entertaining the enemy, while other officers and men of his regiment suffered in their camps across the river at Yardley while their homes, families, farms, and businesses were subject to British depredations.[63]

Any residents remaining in Trenton like Hunt knew they would now have to deal with the enemy army, but they did not know for how long. Would the British be able to overcome Washington's efforts to prevent them from crossing after him? Or, would they stay for the winter before advancing on Philadelphia? Would they win the war and dash all hopes of independence? The future did not look positive.

Chapter 6

1776
December 9 – 25

An unidentified Hessian soldier arriving in Trenton in December to take up winter quarters wrote in his journal that there were many empty houses, because "the inhabitants, like those at Princeton, are almost all fled, so that we occupy bare walls." He estimated that Trenton "consists of about one hundred houses, of which many are mean and little, and it is easy to conceive how ill it must accommodate three regiments." As for his own quarters, he wrote, "my friend Sheffer and myself lodge in a fine house belonging to a merchant, and we have empty rooms enough." Some of the fleeing residents left their slaves behind and he commented that, "last evening I gave one a box on the ear for his sausiness [sic]; I bid him bring me a candle, and he replied, if I wanted candles, I should have brought them with me. I was furnished with a candle, but nothing else." A lack of good wine troubled him because, "Here is no wine, except Madeira at three shillings and sixpence sterling a bottle."

Although the occupying soldiers were separated from the American army by the "extremely rapid" Delaware River, the Hessian wrote they were "obliged to be constantly on our guard, and do very severe duty, though our people begin to grow ragged, and our baggage is left at New-York." Even though the strong British army had "marched across this extremely fine province of New-Jersey, which may justly be called the garden of America, yet it is by no means freed from the enemy, and we are insecure both in flank and rear." The British troops were subject to hit-and-run ambushes that made life stressful and the Hessian believed that his brigade, Colonel Rall's, had "incontestably suffered the most of any," and now was stationed at the most advanced point. He hoped that "as soon as the Delaware freezes we may march over and attack Philadelphia, which is about thirty miles distant." Even though the Hessians were tired and worn down from the heavy campaign against Washington's army fought since their arrival in America the previous summer, they were not going to have any down time during December. Just the opposite.[1]

The first full day of the British occupation of Trenton - Monday, December 9 – was spent in fair weather with temperatures in the mid to upper - 40s.[2] Many inhabitants had fled their homes and British troops began seizing houses for use as quarters, regardless of the owners' political stance. Trenton residents and British soldiers alike expected, and hoped, the army would somehow get across the river soon and march to Philadelphia. Howe sent out troops to search for boats and before the end of the day received word that a detachment sent out under Lord Cornwallis to Coryell's Ferry, 15 miles above Trenton at today's Lambertville, New Jersey and New Hope, Pennsylvania, failed to find any. John Williams, one of the many Loyalists who joined with the British army at Trenton, guided those troops to Coryell's Ferry.[3] A detachment sent out to reconnoiter closer to Trenton received cannon and musket fire from across the river.[4] Continuing on to Philadelphia was looking problematic for the British.

Still hoping to cross the river, the men of the British 17th Regiment of Foot, temporarily quartered in the barracks, were ordered to be ready to march "upon the shortest notice," no one was to wander from his quarters for any reason, the roll was to be called every hour, and the troops were immediately issued four days provisions. In the usual round of garrison duties, the 17th Regiment supplied a corporal and 17 privates for the picket detail that evening and a corporal and five men paraded at 4:00 pm as the cattle guard to secure the fresh meat travelling with the army. The 17th also provided General James Grant's guard and orderly.[5]

On December 8, some 500 men of the British 37th Regiment of Foot commanded by Lieutenant Colonel Robert Abercrombie had set up camp for a week at Randle Mitchell's house in Nottingham. Abercrombie learned about the items that Samuel Tucker had taken to the Abbott house and ordered Lieutenant Thomas Hackshaw to march there around noon on the 9th with about 20 soldiers of the 5th Regiment. Trenton Loyalist Mary Poynton, wife of British army officer Brereton Poynton, was at the Abbott house with a wagon, "to bring off some goods she had" there. John Jolly guided the soldiers to the Abbott house after simply being asked if he knew the way, because the British knew exactly where to go and Tucker believed that Mrs. Poynton had informed the British officers where his goods were hidden. Daniel Coxe later wrote that Mrs. Poynton "rather spoke her mind too plain." The soldiers seized Tucker's property, pressed Abbott's wagon into their service and, except for one small chest belonging to Tucker's slave, loaded everything onto it, including the unsigned money. Hackshaw also took possession of Tucker's phaeton and a horse that he had left with Abbott. John Abbott, Jr. received his protection papers that day at Trenton.[6]

Hackshaw brought the items back to Randle Mitchell's and some officers showed Mitchell letters addressed to Tucker. Mitchel asked where they had got them and was told they had information about Mr. Tucker's goods that he had concealed. That evening, Abercrombie summoned Mitchell and inquired about Tucker, specifically whether he had been a "violent rebel." Mitchell described Tucker as "a man of character and considerable fortune ... that he was a member of the Provincial Congress, and had been president thereof; that he had formerly been sheriff of Hunterdon County, and a member of Assembly, but believed he had never been a violent Rebel." He believed, in fact, that Tucker had been "the chief cause of the last clause [the escape clause] being inserted in the Constitution of New Jersey." In other words, Tucker was a highly respected man who actively supported the Whig cause but had not taken up arms and had been among those hoping for a peaceful settlement. Abercrombie then showed him a square black trunk containing a number of papers and parchment deeds, saying that Tucker must be a man of "considerable consequence." The officers then showed Mitchell "a large parcel of printed paper on the floor" commenting on the "fine parcel of money they had got." They asked Mitchell to look at it, and he noted the signatures of two, rather than the required three, officials. After Mitchell refused to give them anything for the worthless money, they told him they were going to repack the trunk and send it to General Howe. Afterwards, Mitchell saw some of the officers again reading letters addressed to Tucker. Hackshaw went to New Brunswick to report to General Howe, and soon after part of Tucker's clothes and linen were sent back to his house and his wife's watch was delivered to her by Abercrombie.[7] While all this was taking place, Tucker was in hiding, fearing what might happen to him and his family.

Rev. George Panton of Trenton's St. Michael's Church had sought refuge with the British garrison at New York after suffering "a variety of dangers and hardships" supporting the British government at "great expense and personal hazard." From there, he had facilitated "the progress of the Royale Army by personal communications & otherwise" and assisted with the "protection of his Majesty's subjects, by accompanying the ... Army in its progress thro the provinces of New York and New Jersey."[8] He was now back in Trenton and found his church building had been taken over to quarter British troops.

The weather continued fair on December 10, but temperatures dropped into the mid-30s.[9] People still expected the British to construct vessels to cross the river, if necessary using lumber from the wooden houses and nails and iron from John Rickey's hardware store and blacksmith shops such as those of Joseph and Samuel Lanning, Joshua Newbold, and Hezekiah Howell. British army engineer Captain John Montressor asked Joseph Galloway, who was sharing quarters with British Deputy Quartermaster Thomas Gamble at the house vacated by John Barnes on Queen Street near the Assunpink Creek, to inquire about materials at or near Trenton suitable for building pontoons, boats, or rafts. Galloway found "48,000 feet of boards, a quantity of iron, and there was timber enough about Trenton for that purpose." He also heard about, but never actually saw, two boats, large enough to carry 50 or 60 men, sitting in a mill pond near Trenton. Given the extensive American efforts to remove all boats, this may have been misinformation. Although the Americans had feared that the British would bring boats from New Brunswick, none were brought and no boats were constructed using the materials Galloway found. Both the British soldiers and the residents of Trenton wondered just what moves, if any, Howe was considering before ending the campaign.[10]

Six Philadelphians friendly to the British forces slipped through the American lines on December 10 with information for Howe.[11] American raiding parties were already making life unsafe for the British and capturing baggage wagons and animals collected to feed the occupying soldiers.[12] British soldiers killed a sheep near Trenton Ferry but they could not retrieve it because whenever they came near the river's edge, American riflemen shot at them from the protection of houses on the Pennsylvania side.[13] Orders for the 17th Regiment on December 10 tightened up procedures to resolve problems that developed among the troops who were not particularly happy about living in cold barracks in Trenton, rather than heading for the comforts of Philadelphia. General Howe was endeavoring to win the hearts and minds of the local people with his amnesty and protection papers, but the protections were not preventing harassment by his soldiers. His orders on the 10th strongly stated that he would severely punish anyone molesting inhabitants who had protections. The 17th, 40th, and 55th regiments continued to supply officers and privates for various pickets and guards. The evening picket and the cattle guard were strengthened.[14]

After a bit of snow overnight, the weather continued fair with temperatures in the mid-30s, on December 11.[15] Hessian Colonel von Donop left Trenton two hours before daylight leading 500 or 600 jàgers and grenadiers to reconnoiter a cantonment site at Bordentown and look for boats.[16] A spy sent by Joseph Reed, the Continental army's Adjutant General, came into Trenton to gather intelligence, especially to learn if the British had plans to cross the river and where they would cross.[17] Reed had been born in Trenton in 1741, attended the College of New Jersey in Princeton, and then spent most of his life in Philadelphia. The three British regiments again provided picket and guard details, several of which now had drummers assigned.[18]

The usual picket and guard posts were manned and a guard on the Assunpink Creek bridge was added on December 12. Because so many men needed shoes, officers were ordered to report the number wanted to the Quartermaster General.[19] A man leaving Trenton ran into some American light horse sent across the river by Joseph Reed to gather intelligence. He told them that "General Howe was with the main body of his army ... that they are certainly waiting for boats from Brunswick; that he believed they would attempt a landing in more places than one. ... They are collecting horses from all parts of the country. Some movement was intended yesterday morning but was laid aside."[20]

This information reflected what people in Trenton believed, but given the onset of winter and the actions Washington had so carefully taken to prevent the British from following him across the river, Howe had decided not to move on Philadelphia until the next campaign season and to establish a chain of cantonments in New Jersey extending west to Trenton and Bordentown. This would give him control of central New Jersey and a large portion of the important road leading from New York to Philadelphia. Howe believed his troops would be well-received in Trenton and the many residents taking advantage of his amnesty would feel protected. Howe poisoned this scenario when he assigned Hessian troops to occupy Trenton. Trenton was on the left end of the British line of cantonments, the normal Hessian position in the line of battle, so to place other troops there, Howe believed, would create "jealousies between the Hessian and British troops." Howe also had great confidence in the Hessian professionalism demonstrated during the New York campaign. However, the German soldiers he assigned to Trenton lived among people whose culture and language they did not understand while they were in daily hostile contact with the American army across the river.[21]

That night, long after dark, Colonel von Donop and his reconnoitering party returned to Trenton from Bordentown. He had delayed leaving for Trenton until five in the afternoon, partly to rest his men and partly so they would not receive enemy cannon fire from across the Delaware River.[22]

The British army was made up of volunteers and, unlike the navy, could not be expanded by drafting or impressing men into it. To augment their forces, the government had often hired foreign regiments. The three regiments that Howe ordered into winter quarters at Trenton were hired from Hesse-Cassel and had arrived in America in mid-August, shortly before the Battle of Long Island. Military service was expected and honored in their homeland, and all able-bodied men were required to undergo military training before either making the military a career or serving in the part-time militia. Men expendable from the civilian economy were recruited for the army between the ages of 16 and 30, while men in certain designated occupations and situations could not be recruited, even if they wanted to serve. The agreement of January 31, 1776 between Great Britain and Landgraf Friedrich Wilhelm II, of Hesse-Cassel was a mutual defense treaty, since Hesse-Cassel was essentially left defenseless. But, the income from the agreement could help this small state deal more effectively with its rural overpopulation and poverty. For the soldiers involved, receiving the same pay as soldiers in the British army meant a substantial increase. The Hessian soldiers expected the war to be short and successful, consisting mostly of skirmishes, followed by two or three years of garrison duty. There should be few casualties, because the enemy was merely untrained rabble.[23]

The Hessian officers had received training that was very practical and discouraged innovation. They were generally enthusiastic about the war, being eager for active service with its opportunities for recognition and promotion. Many of the junior officers were older, long-time veterans, such as Lieutenant Andreas Wiederholdt, who was 43 years old with 24 years of service. He had come up through the ranks, promoted from sergeant major in 1760. Quartermaster Muller was 52 years old and had served 31 years. The non-commissioned officers were generally over 40 years old and very experienced, but susceptible to illness and the fatigues of the hard life of a soldier on campaign.[24]

Like their American counterparts, the Hessians had been through hard service the past four months, and these men, their uniforms, and equipment had taken a beating. The Hessian battalions were under strength due to heavy combat losses and many officers were either sick or convalescing from wounds.[25] While the officers had quality uniforms, the soldiers' uniforms were cheap, coarse cloth. The lapels and cuffs were narrow strips of coarse cloth sewn to the coat. Soldiers in all three regiments wore heavy, long, black cloth gaiters with metal buttons. From a distance their uniforms looked impressive, but a close look revealed patches, tears, and areas worn thin. At their best, the uniforms were uncomfortable, too hot in summer and not warm enough in cold winter weather. Overcoats, or watch coats, were only supplied in numbers to provide a bit of warmth for men on duty as sentries.[26]

Each soldier carried a knapsack, a tin canteen on a white leather strap slung over the right shoulder, a black cartridge box with a metal plate attached to a white belt over the left shoulder, and a sword on a white buff waist belt. In their knapsacks, the men carried things needed to keep their uniform and equipment in proper condition. For off duty times they might carry a few Hessian and English coins, a clay or wood pipe and a twist of tobacco, and perhaps a Reformed Church prayer book, among other personal items. Their cartridge boxes carried cartridges, extra flints, a wire for cleaning the musket lock priming hole, and a rag for wiping the musket. Each soldier took his turn carrying a haversack with rations for four men, a tin camp kettle, or a canvas bag holding tent pegs or other camp equipment, and a shovel.[27]

Each Hessian regiment had five companies and each company was assigned to five or six houses in Trenton. Some larger houses held up to 50 men. Over 1,000 soldiers were quartered in and around

Trenton; if they had not used public buildings it would have taken almost every private home in town to accommodate them.[28] Loyalist Mary Poynton, Daniel Coxe's friend, later recalled that as soon as the British army entered Trenton, "Mr. Coxe's dwelling house and offices, and his other houses in the town were taken and occupied as quarters and barracks for the Hessian Troops, who ... drove out his servants." Mary Barnes, spouse of Loyalist John Barnes, later wrote that Coxe's house was made a barracks, just "as every other house in Trenton was." Coxe owned two other houses rented to tenants, and these were taken also.[29] Rall tried to avoid quartering men in places close to the river where they would draw fire from the American artillery on the Pennsylvania side.[30] This included the barracks, so it was available and possibly used by the Hessian dependents and civilian Loyalists who came to Trenton during the occupation.

Colonel Rall's regiment contained many young farm boys and a large percentage of recent recruits, unlike a typical grenadier battalion made up of select men in elite flank companies. The Landgraf had taken the best and taller men for his guards. The men wore dark blue uniforms and tall brass grenadier helmets. Seventeen-year-old, five-foot-one-inch-tall grenadier Johannes Reuber arrived with the Rall Regiment after spending the previous unpleasant night sleeping out in the open at Kingston. Reuber was one of the younger Hessians, who averaged about 28 to 29 years old.[31] He was, however, considered an ideal soldier – loyal, brave, enduring, and never questioning the actions of his superiors.[32] Reuber said of Trenton, "It was quiet here and we did the usual duties, as watches, etc." He was encouraged by the freezing weather, believing it meant that the river would freeze and they would march across and take Philadelphia.[33] Rall's grenadiers were billeted at the courthouse and jail, the post office, Henry Drake's Bull's Head Tavern on Second Street, William Pidgeon's and Abraham G. Claypoole's houses on King Street, and other dwellings in the same area.[34]

The Knyphausen Regiment, commanded by Major von Dechow, wore blue coats, lined red, with black lapels and cuffs, sporting rows of plain bright brass buttons over a straw-colored vest and breeches. Their impressive fusilier's caps had a brass front plate shaped like a gothic arch and decorated with cannon, spears and symbols unique to Hesse, most prominently a lion carrying a sword in his right hand, a crown over his head, and under him the initials "FL" referring to "Frederick Landgraf." The men did not wear mustaches, but on formal occasions they tallowed their hair and wore it down their back in a queue. Their uniform was calculated to give the illusion that they were taller than they actually were. For example, the long black leggings gave the illusion of long legs, while the fusilier cap added height. To keep their heads erect, they wore a high black neck stock. On parade the soldiers marched with the "goose step" to further their formidable appearance, keep them standing straight, and move together with grace. The regiment took up station in the vicinity of the corner of Queen and Second streets with the men occupying the Presbyterian Church and school next to it. They occupied the houses of militia Captain William Tucker, Ellet Tucker, and Joseph Milnor on the corners of Queen and Second streets, and those of Thomas Tindall, John Bellerjeau, Thomas Ryall and Joshua Newbold.[35]

The Lossberg fusilier regiment in their blue coats with orange lapels and cuffs, commanded by Lieutenant Colonel Francis Scheffer, was last to arrive and not impressed with the crowded town. Scheffer was 54 years old, married, and a 35-year veteran of service in the Hessian army. His regiment took up quarters in northern Trenton on King Street, north of the Rall Regiment. The regimental headquarters remained there, but many men were scattered in quarters around the town. Two companies were billeted in St. Michael's Church and the house of Hunterdon militia Major Micajah How on the east side of the street and at the houses of Colonel Isaac Smith, Thomas Barnes, and Miss Rebecca Coxe on the west side. How and Smith were presumably with the Hunterdon County militia at Yardley's Ferry under General Dickinson. Captain von Altenbockum's company took up quarters at the house of Alexander Calhoun and also at his store just northwest of town on the Pennington Road. Major von Hanstein's company quartered at Jonathan Richmond's inn just over the Assunpink bridge near Trenton Mills.[36]

Fifty Hessian jägers were quartered north of town near the river at the Hermitage, the home General Philemon Dickinson had purchased on July 30. The jägers were light infantry recruited from foresters and huntsmen known for their individual field craft and marksmanship, carrying short rifles rather than muskets, wearing black cocked hats edged with black lace, and sporting a green silk cockade; green coats with crimson collar, cuffs, and lapels; and green waistcoats and breeches.

Three small artillery detachments, comprised of new men recruited specifically for the American expedition, in their blue coats

Oliver L. Kemp's c1898 sketch of Jonathan Richmond's tavern near the Trenton mill at the Assunpink Creek bridge. Used as quarters by the Hessians and one of the several buildings that Washington used for headquarters between December 30 and January 2. (Stryker, Trenton and Princeton)

with white-bordered crimson lapels, were housed in the Methodist Church on Queen Street and in St. Michael's Church, known locally as the English Church, on King Street; for the first four days, their six brass cannon were kept in the St. Michael's graveyard.

The Hessians established their hospital in the parsonage of the Presbyterian Church, recently abandoned in haste by Rev. Spencer.[37]

Twenty troopers and an officer of the British 16th Light Dragoons made their quarters at the Friends' Meeting House, against the Friends' wishes. After its use by the Hessians and British dragoons, "footprints, cuts, and places where they stuck their bayonets" were visible for many years after.[38] The dragoon troopers were impressive in their red coats with blue lapels and cuffs. Their breeches and waistcoats were white, and they wore knee-high black leather boots, and red horse hair crested brass helmets painted black, with a black front piece displaying their badge and motto. Each trooper was armed with a short musket hooked on a white belt slung over the left shoulder and a sheathed sword on a white waist belt. Two pistols filled holsters at the front of the saddle, and the saddle cloth was white with a variety of colorful trimmings and badges.[39]

Arriving in town with the troops were their baggage wagons and several wives and children accompanying their husbands and fathers. One of the wives was seven and another was eight months pregnant. During the march across New Jersey, the Hessian women had earned a reputation for cruel plundering, perhaps even greater than the brutal reputation of the Hessian soldiers.[40] It is possible the women and children were quartered in the barracks.[41]

Trenton residents were now living shoulder to shoulder with the Hessian soldiers, British light dragoons, and Hessian women and children, and constantly fearing harm from them. Some local people sought protection by accepting General Howe's offer to take an oath of loyalty. Trenton Ferry operator David Howell took his oath before General James Grant on December 12.[42] The same day, Loyalist Brigadier General Cortland Skinner was in Trenton and insisted Abraham Hunt, whom he had known for years as a Whig leader, take the loyalty oath in his presence, making a notation to that effect on the reverse of Hunt's protection papers. Skinner may not have trusted Hunt's apparent return to Crown loyalty as much as Rall did.[43] Other people did believe Hunt had turned traitor to the cause of independence and he was later charged by Trenton Township residents Nathaniel Furman and James Burrows, through Trenton's Ebenezer Cowell acting for the State, with encouraging people on December 13 to take British protection. He was also reputed to have said that the presence of General Lee's army in New Jersey was keeping some people from doing so and that if Lee left the State, people would begin to seek protection within three days. He was vividly, perhaps viciously, described in the Grand Inquest document as "being a pernicious & disaffected man and a person of a turbulent mind and seditious disposition and conversation, and contriving, practicing and falsely, maliciously, advisedly and seditiously intending to terrify and disunite the good subjects of this State, and dispose them to favour the pretentions of the enemy, and to alienate the affections of the people from the present Government." The case did not go to trial so Hunt was never acquitted or found guilty.[44]

Hessian Major Baurmeister generally distrusted all protection seekers noting that, "A great many [people] came to headquarters in Trenton, were accepted, and dismissed with a protection. Unfortunately, it was not discovered until too late that many, on the other hand, had come only to look around and spy."[45] Howe's loyalty oaths proved to have little value when taken by people who felt threatened by an enemy army of occupation. Some men who signed oaths suffered later, because they were considered either weak or outright traitors to the cause, while others, who signed in order to survive to fight at another time, or to put themselves in a position of being able to spy on the enemy, did not suffer socially or politically. In general, Abraham Hunt's reputation and community trust did not suffer and he may well have been putting himself in position to spy or help the cause in some other way at Washington's request or with his approval.

Raids on the Hessian outposts began immediately after their arrival and about 15 Pennsylvania row galleys came up the Delaware on December 12 and fired on their outposts. The Hessians did not have the heavy artillery needed to counter them.[46] Away from the river, raids and ambushes conducted by ununiformed local farmer militiamen harassed British and Hessians patrols in the surrounding townships and took a toll on Hessian health and morale. This irritated General Howe into invoking longstanding rules of warfare that forbade civilians from attacking uniformed soldiers of an enemy army. Howe was well aware that militiamen, operating under the Whig militia act, did not wear uniforms. The militia had always been a last resort, community-defense force of trained civilians, not a group of campaigning soldiers, but the realities of the Revolution were causing them to take on new roles as auxiliaries of the Continental army. Even while trying to win the hearts and minds of the local residents, Howe ordered on December 12 that "small straggling parties not dressed like soldiers & without officers not being admissible in war who presume to molest or fire upon soldiers or peaceable inhabitants of the country will be immediately hanged without trial as assassins."[47] The raids and ambushes continued as before.

Those residents who had stayed in town anticipated a winter of British occupation with dread. Martha Reed, recalling her childhood, said, "we had heard a great deal about the Hessians, who were objects of dread on account of their lawless brutality." Picturing them as "scarcely one remove from brutes," the townspeople had heard many stories of "their savagery" and believed "no house, nor home, no woman, nor child was safe from their wanton cruelty; they pillaged and destroyed as they chose, only stopping short of absolute murder." Martha remembered, "We lived in momentary dread of their appearance, and our worst fears were soon fulfilled." On a cold night when the Hessians were settling into their quarters, "mother, and we two children were gathered in the family room; a great fire blazed in the chimney place, and mother sat with her feet on the low fender talking to us about father, who was away with the army." The family heard the sound of many feet outside, then the door opened, "and in stalked several strange men, and a couple of women, who looked like giants, and giantesses to us they were so tall." She recalled "they jabbered away in harsh, guttural tones, and coming to the fire, spread out their hands to the blaze." The frightened Reed children "jumped up screaming, and clung to our mother" who stood up, pointed to the door, and told the intruders to leave. They refused. Then, Martha recalled, "as they crouched about the fire, one of the women caught sight of the large silver buckles which mother wore in her shoes, as was the fashion of the time, and made signs for her to take off the shoe. Seeing her hesitate, the woman snatched at the buckle, and pulling off the shoe, rapped my mother in the face with the heel." The buckle snatcher was rebuked by one of the men, who appeared to be the captain, and he told Martha's mother "that they had been sent to secure quarters" for an officer and his suite and "our house seemed suitable."

In order to obtain better treatment, Martha's mother convinced the Hessians that her husband was an officer in the British army. After that, Martha said, "they treated us with rough kindness, and permitted us to go to our beds in safety. But there was little sleep for us, as we heard them rummaging in the closets, and finding what they could to eat." The next morning, the soldiers demanded that the store room be opened "and they helped themselves liberally to its contents." Martha recalled, "nothing was sacred to these marauders, they killed a hog, and cut it up on the mahogany dining table," while "pickles and preserves, and our winter stores, vanished away; as they devoured our substance like a pest of locusts." Although still in fear, the family was thankful to have their lives and be permitted to stay in their house.

One of the Hessian women picked up a sugar bowl that was made "of heavy dark blue glass, shaped like a tulip" and the "handle on the cover was a little lamb." This bowl had been a gift to Martha and she called it "the pride of my heart." Martha became very angry when she saw the bowl in the "coarse grip" of the woman and tried to grab it back from her. However, when Martha "wrenched away the bowl," the cover broke and she ran away and hid the bowl, "but cried long for the loss of the little lamb which was its greatest charm."[48]

A number of residents experienced Hessian plundering, as well as quartering. Jacob Keen had served in Joseph Brearley's minuteman company, then the First Hunterdon militia. He was probably with the Hunterdon militia camped across the river when a party of Hessians entered his home on King Street, where his wife Hannah, "a woman of great courage and resolution, had locked her valuable silver in a bureau." When the Hessians entered, she sent one of her children to find an officer and stood before her bureau, holding the keys in her hand. The Hessians demanded that she open the drawers. She pretended not to understand them, and they angrily began to break the drawers with their musket butts until her child returned with an officer and the men left.[49]

Even the property of Loyalists was not safe. Daniel Coxe later wrote that "notwithstanding his well-known public and loyal character and every remonstrance of his friends and servants to the contrary, his rooms, closets, stores and cellars were all broken up, ransacked and pillaged and every species of furniture, china, glass, liquors, etc. plundered, destroyed or taken away, his servants compelled to fly for safety elsewhere, and most wanton desolation committed on his property and estate."[50]

The weather continued partly cloudy with temperatures in the upper-30s, on what must have seemed to the people of Trenton an exceptionally unlucky Friday the 13th. Word spread that General Charles Lee, widely believed to be one of the best American generals, if not the best, had been captured. The British and Loyalists no doubt celebrated this news, but Whigs might well have felt that this was yet another severe blow and the rebellion might effectively be over. The Hessians continued to organize their occupation and General Howe placed Colonel von Donop in command of both his own brigade, to be stationed at Bordentown, and Rall's brigade at Trenton.[51] Von Donop saw Trenton as merely an outpost to be manned by about 150 men, rotated frequently, rather than the three-regiment command Rall insisted on as a reward for his gallant service in the New York campaign.[52] Rall was a fairly junior colonel but became commander of his brigade when two of the four officers senior to him became ill, one died of dysentery, and one was wounded.[53]

The 17th, 40th, and 55th British regiments of foot at Trenton received orders to march the next morning at 8:00 am to Princeton for their winter quarters. They manned the Trenton guard posts for the last time and company officers made returns to the quartermaster of their men's needs, attempting to see that each man was "immediately provided with at least one pare of good shoes." The daily orders made it official that the troops were going into winter quarters and Howe ineffectively ordered his commanders to particularly attend "to the protection of the inhabitants & their property in their several districts." On the morning of the 14th, the British regiments marched to Princeton.[54] General Howe breakfasted with Colonel Rall at 10:00 am before setting off for Princeton.[55]

Before von Donop left for Bordentown, he showed Rall the general locations for two redoubts he wanted constructed for Trenton's defense. At the same time, he gave Rall "a copy of the orders of the General-in-Chief and also gave him further detailed information of the surrounding country and explained other precautions which were necessary to be observed for the better secrecy of the place."[56] Von Donop's instructions did not impress Rall who believed he was fully capable of making his own decisions about how to defend Trenton.

While the Hessians were settling in during falling temperatures and some snow on the 14th, Samuel Tucker was in hiding at William Newbold's house where he received a message by Robert Pearson from his wife begging him to return home as soon as possible because family members were suffering from illness. He set out for home and about a mile from the Crosswicks Bridge was overtaken by about 20 men, known in Crosswicks as the Tory Light Horse, led by John Leonard and Anthony Woodward. Leonard approached Tucker, put a pistol to his breast, told him in "very ill language" that he had General Howe's order to take him prisoner, and if he made a move he "would put a brace of balls" into him. Leonard then took him to Robert Pearson, who gave his word to keep Tucker at his farm until given further orders.[57]

The British pursuit of the American army across the state encouraged many Loyalists to take similar actions. A group in Monmouth sought to disarm local "rebels" and requested help from the British to attack the Monmouth County militia at Freehold. They threatened Whigs that they would be turned over to the British at Trenton if they did not surrender their weapons and abusively encouraged them to sign loyalty oaths and receive protection papers. One of the Loyalists, Jesse Woodward, was reputed to have told the British in Trenton about December 12 that he "had disarmed sixteen or seventeen of the rebels." Another man, Richard Robins, working with Woodward, came to Trenton where he "did publicly damn" William Imlay, whom they had disarmed and forced to go to Trenton, for being "an old Presbyterian" and "the cause of all this bloodshed." Robins also reputedly stated publicly that the rebels "would have to answer for the lives of all the regular troops that should be killed." Loyalists generally believed that the supporters of the Continental Congress had "commenced the war in order to make estates and aggrandize themselves." They had issued money "which they were changing at a great undervalue for gold and silver" in order to make a profit for themselves.[58] Moses Ivins was reportedly seen at Trenton celebrating the Loyalist exploits with British soldiers, displaying "a mug of cyder in one hand and a gun in the other."[59]

Woodward and Robins had come to Trenton with a group of "near 100" Loyalists "in a body & armed" from Upper Freehold in Monmouth County to provide "every aid & assistance in their power for the suppression of the Rebellion." General Howe's aide-de-camp, John Montressor, gave Woodward and Leonard a certificate on December 14 authorizing them to procure wagons, horses, and provisions needed by the British. They went into the countryside to find these items and impress them from rebels if necessary.[60] Richard Robins' father butchered some 40 hogs for the British, but before they could be brought to Trenton, they were plundered by American forces who had learned of them.[61] Leonard had appeared before the Provincial Congress in June because he had "rendered himself obnoxious" to the supporters of the Congress "for influencing the people against the measures of Congress." He had been found guilty but was allowed to go home after giving a £500 bond with two securities "to remain quiet."[62] These may be the Loyalists that tradition says were temporarily housed for a period of time in the Trenton barracks during December.[63]

These Loyalists expressed a number of the beliefs that influenced men to remain loyal to the Crown. They complained of political disenfranchisement inflicted on those who did not sign the Association and other documents as ordered by the rebel government. They frequently acknowledged the support they received from the British and their belief that the British government would reward men who aided the war against the rebels with grants of land taken from the Whigs. They did not go to the extreme of killing their opponents and basically used the same tactics and methods the "Associators," those enforcing compliance with the Continental Association, had employed against Loyalists early in the war.[64] The Monmouth Loyalists who joined the British at Trenton were of relatively high social status and reputation and not the evil and desperate men portrayed in Whig propaganda.[65] All this activity demonstrated that the war was a civil war with all its dark aspects.

General Howe ordered Rall to establish a formal headquarters in Trenton to mark his honor and authority. Rall chose Stacy Potts' King Street house that stood on a half-acre lot adjoining his two-and-a-third-acre tan yard. The house had four rooms on each of its two floors and the lot was fenced with cedar posts and boards to protect its garden.[66] The six Hessian cannon were positioned one behind the other in the middle of narrow King Street in front of the designated guardhouse just north of St. Michael's Church and across from Colonel Rall's headquarters.[67] Lieutenant Andreas Wiederholdt criticized this placement, writing that "the guns which ought to have been stationed on avenues or on places where they might have been put to instant use, were all drawn up in front of [Rall's] quarters and every morning two of them had to be dragged to the upper town; only to cause a constant noise and turmoil."[68] Rall was a thirty-six-year military veteran who had performed with distinction as a combat leader. One of his fellow officers believed that Rall was born to be a soldier but not a general. He possessed courage and skill on the battlefield, but lacked the ability to make a sound decision and keep a cool mind. He was recognized as a generous and sociable man who enjoyed a good party, often enjoying his evenings well into the early morning hours and then sleeping until 9:00 am. Troops routinely formed up at his quarters between 10:00 and 11:00 am and then stood in formation for a half hour, waiting to change the guard until Rall finished his morning bath.[69]

Rall did not always appreciate information from his officers about problems they encountered. Shortly after billeting their men, Lieutenant Colonel Sheffer and Major von Dechow informed Colonel Rall that the men in their regiments did not have enough shoes and clothing for the approaching winter and asked him to send to New York for more. Rall made light of their request, still erroneously believing that they would soon be crossing the river and on their way to Philadelphia. The officers were greatly depressed by their commander's indifference and believed their soldiers were in an unsafe condition, making it impossible to carry out their mission effectively.[70] Sufficient clothing was just one of the issues that Rall's subordinate officers were worried about. They recognized theirs was the most vulnerable of the British cantonments, necessitating heavy security duties, and Trenton was really not big enough to comfortably house the whole force.

During the first days of occupation, the duty men turned out every day at 4:00 pm in front of their commander's quarters and stacked their arms under guard of a sentinel. They then returned to their quarters and remained fully dressed, including all belts, throughout the night. They were only allowed to remove their leggings. Some companies remained under arms for three consecutive nights, before being allowed a night off. For over a week, no man experienced two consecutive nights without being called out for something. Under these exhausting conditions, the hospital at the Presbyterian Parsonage was well populated. After a week or so, the system was modified so that each regiment was only on duty for 24 hours every third day. The artillery horses, though, were kept harnessed day and night in readiness for immediate hitching to the guns.[71]

Lieutenant Wiederholdt found little of importance in the theatrical sentry and picket changes that he believed produced nothing more than "just a lot of restless commotion around ... headquarters all day long." The crowning moment of useless and tiring requirements occurred when, "around two in the afternoon the guards were relieved and at four o'clock the pickets. All the commissioned and non-commissioned officers had to participate and to be around his [Rall's] quarters so that it might look grand and like a real headquarters." Wiederholdt believed "our poor, worn-out soldiers, denuded of small clothes and uniforms" had a harder time recovering their strength in these winter quarters than if they had been active in the field. But, in spite of the excessive ceremonial duties, Wiederholdt was dismayed that "not the least precautionary measure was taken; no rendezvous or alarm was prescribed in the case of a surprise. Still less was the possibility taken into consideration, that an attack might be made," because Rall never discussed with his officers the practical problems involving "security and welfare of the garrison," as other commanders did.

As long as watches were relieved with proper ceremony and all was well with his regimental band of music, Rall was happy, but he was apparently unconcerned with sloppy off-duty dress; having adequate clothing; keeping muskets cleaned, polished and in good repair; and, keeping ammunition ready. His musicians got very little rest because the main guardhouse was only half a dozen houses down the street from his quarters and he could not get enough of their music. Wiederholdt describes a daily ritual held at the English Church in which Rall "had the officer and picket march first around a church which was enclosed by a fence rail and just faced his lodgings - this looked just like a Roman Catholic procession, and to be complete it only lacked the cross, -- banners and a number of little girls and boys marching in front and singing. He would always follow the parade as far as the guard-house, only to hear the music during the relief."[72]

The main picket post for Trenton was manned at the Fox Chase Tavern on the Maidenhead Road. The duty picket consisted of one commissioned officer, three noncommissioned officers, and about 70 men who provided the sentinels and watch parties in the town. A Pennington Road picket with one corporal and 15 men was posted at the house and cooper shop of Richard and Arthur Howell, relieved periodically by men from the Maidenhead Road post. Jäger Lieutenant von Grothausen commanded the River Road post at General Dickinson's Hermitage and maintained a picket of one officer and 15 men behind the barn near the house and posts at the greenhouse, in the garden towards the Delaware, and on the road along the Delaware towards Pennington. Small groups of men were also regularly supplied to several posts south of the Assunpink Creek near the house of Dr. Bryant and the ferry. Grothausen sent patrols up the river periodically, and each morning several British dragoons came to the post and reconnoitered up the river as far as Yardley's Ferry.[73] The post at the Assunpink Creek bridge consisted of a sergeant and 18 men responsible for sending a patrol to Dr. Bryant's grand house every half hour during the night. Sentinels were posted on the north side of the bridge, at George Bright's bakery on the south end of the bridge, and at Major von Dechow's quarters near the bridge on Queen Street. One commissioned officer, five noncommissioned officers and 22 men made up the picket at the old tavern at Trenton Ferry and provided the sentinels posted at Dr. Bryant's house and the Trenton Ferry landing. Any guards posted close to the river were ordered to stay under cover and not draw fire from American troops on the opposite bank.[74] One night, Pennsylvania militia officer Solomon Bush led a harassing attack on the ferry tavern picket post. After crossing back to Pennsylvania, he looked back and "distinctly observed the Hessians on their return to the post set fire to the Ferry House, the property of Daniel Coxe, which was totally consumed."[75] The most distant post was at the drawbridge over Crosswicks Creek four miles from Trenton. Although the post was closer to Bordentown, von Donop assigned it to Rall's brigade. Rall sent 100 men and two officers of the Knyphausen Regiment, along with their baggage, to the drawbridge where they were to take up quarters in the nearby houses.[76]

These picket posts were important, but when von Donop marched for Bordentown, he left behind his engineer, artillery Captain George Pauli, and another officer to plot out the two defensive redoubts he wanted built as positions to retreat to and defend if the Americans crossed from Pennsylvania and attacked in force.[77] The temperature dropped into the 20s overnight and there was a hard frost. On Sunday afternoon, December 15, the temperature only rose to about 32° and a brisk wind made it feel even colder.[78] Colonel Rall, Lieutenant Colonel Scheffer, and the two engineer officers marked out the location for a redoubt, with flanking angles for cannon, on the high ground where King and Queen Streets joined with the Pennington and Maidenhead roads.[79] They then rode down to Trenton Ferry and identified an elevated spot for a small fortification near the bridge over a stream flowing beside Dr. Bryant's house. Rall ordered some fascines[80] made but never ordered construction of the redoubts and when reminded by von Donop, he brushed it off, considering the rebels too weak to be a serious problem. He had consistently defeated them in battle and knew they were in bad shape. Several of Rall's officers offered to build the redoubt at the ferry, and the frustrated von Donop stressed that it would cost nothing to build the redoubts, so it would do no harm if it turned out they were not needed. But Rall, stubborn in his ways, was not persuaded to act, even though Trenton was on open ground with a number of roads leading into it. Without fortifications, its only defense from a surprise attack was constant vigilance and active patrolling.

Even without orders from von Donop, standing Hessian infantry orders read, "When a regiment or battalion is posted in a village, which is not far from the enemy, the chief or commander must immediately cause a redoubt to be erected on a chosen spot or height, or where it is in some other way advantageous, which is large enough that the regiment or battalion has space for itself within." This was the standard expectation of Frederick the Great, highly admired by the Hessian officers, who also emphasized the need for troops to guard against surprise attacks when in winter quarters, "because that is what they have to fear most." Rall did order active patrolling and kept one company under arms and one regiment fully dressed and ready to turn out each night.[81]

Rall also neglected to gather intelligence concerning rebel movements and simply lacked respect for the number and skill of his opponents; considering them nothing but a bunch of farmers. He refused to listen to his officers when they argued otherwise and was supported by his superior, Major General James Grant at New Brunswick. It was left to Rall's subordinates to endure the stress of worry over what kinds of actions the rebels might take. While Rall neglected to gather intelligence, Major Justus Matthaus criticized him for issuing protection papers to people like Abraham Hunt, whom Rall saw as wealthy and influential residents, but whom Matthaus, like Major Baurmeister, suspected were gathering information for the rebels to use in an attack on the town.[82]

One such attack occurred early on the cloudy Monday morning of December 16, with temperatures just at or about freezing, when three boats loaded with about 30 Americans crossed at Trenton Ferry under covering fire from 18-pounder artillery. The troops landed near a house where the Hessians had a sergeant and six soldiers posted and forced them to withdraw. Rall sent an officer and 30 men to reinforce the post, but by the time they got there the American party had left taking only a "prize" pig that had just been killed by the Hessians. The same day, a British officer with 20 dragoons arrived in town and Rall sent out a patrol of six dragoons to Pennington.[83]

Hessian Lieutenant Broom was sent to Robert Pearson's house and ordered Samuel Tucker to return to his home in Trenton. Upon arriving, Tucker inquired about his papers and found that part of them were at Colonel Abercrombie's lodgings in Princeton. He sent a letter by his niece, Elizabeth G. White[84], requesting the return of his property and papers, especially those belonging to the estates he was settling. Abercrombie replied that they could not be returned until Tucker's loyalties were known. Still loyal to the Whig cause, Tucker was in a tough situation; he needed his papers back, worried about his sick wife, feared for the safety of his family, and was aware that many other Whig supporters had sought protections and that the Whig cause was in desperate straits. Needing to act quickly, Tucker applied for protection and it was granted by Colonel Rall on December 17. Like others though, he still lost four cows and a number of other items to the occupation troops.[85] His decision hurt his reputation for the rest of his life and seems to exemplify what Dr. Benjamin Rush meant when he wrote, "The friends and enemies of the American Revolution must have been more or less than men, if they could have sustained the magnitude and rapidity of the events that characterized it, without discovering some marks of human weakness, both in body and mind."[86]

The morning of December 17 was a fair day with temperatures in the upper-20s and a Hessian sergeant and six men from the cattle guard took 40 oxen to Bordentown. Rall's regimental quartermasters prepared to set off for New York to bring back badly needed supplies, but had to wait for the quartermasters from von Donop's brigade at Burlington. The six dragoons sent by Rall to Pennington the previous day had not returned, but there was word that one of them had been seen mortally wounded ten miles from Trenton, so Rall sent a surgeon to attend to him.[87]

Scheffer and Dechow wrote to General von Heister on December 17 about the condition of the Lossberg and Knyphausen regiments. They noted, "We have not had enough quiet leisure to have so much as a pair of leggings made. We had counted on having time and opportunity here to put our ragged men once more in order, and to have enjoyed a little peace and repose, instead of which each single company has been given four uninhabited houses and some of them are very small." The bad quarters were not the worst part, though. They also had to supply 100 men from each regiment for daily duty, and every night each company spent the whole time in one house fully clothed. While this may be necessary, "it is a step backwards," because the soldiers "will not be in any state to hold out against an enemy, if this continues." Turning out on constant alarms from enemy harassment attacks increased the sick list and only about 100 men per regiment were fit for duty, threatening disaster. "It is impossible for the tailors and the shoemakers to do any work on the clothing which is so sorely needed to protect our men from the cold, and for want of this proper clothing illness is daily increasing." The two commanders found themselves in an active outpost, rather than in winter quarters providing rest for their men. They asked for relief "before the ruin which we see before our eyes overwhelms us. We should be greatly to blame if we did not report this deplorable state of affairs to your Excellency."[88] Reporting their concerns did not change anything.

December 18 was another cloudy day with temperatures barely reaching above freezing and the wind making it seem much colder.[89] The missing dragoons returned, having left the mortally wounded man behind, and told Rall that they had come across "a party of rebels about one hundred strong, who opened on them a terrific fire." Rall sent out another patrol to Pennington with a wagon to "bring in the wounded man if possible."[90] The anonymous Hessian recorded in his diary the same day that "seventy rebels came over the water, and we were obliged to turn out. But they only carried off a family who went willingly, with three cows and some furniture." Once again, the rebels landed 50 men at daybreak at the jäger post near Trenton Ferry and drove the jägers back "by a fire of 18 [pounder] shots from their cannon" before they disembarked, but they returned back across the river almost immediately.[91] These morning raids were becoming so frequent that heavy patrols were sent down to the ferry early each day. General Alexander Leslie sent reinforcements from Princeton on several occasions because of these raids, and on December 18 he sent some light infantry to Trenton and over 300 other troops to Maidenhead, to be used if needed.[92] Grenadier Reuber wrote in his diary, at "nights, negroes and others wanted to beat us up, but it was not too bad, had a guard on the Delaware, but the Americans came across and put houses on fire and then returned to their side. But we had to watch out."[93] A group of Americans crossed at Howell's Ferry about four miles above Trenton and a patrol of 12 jägers and 2 dragoons were sent out in that direction to get more information.[94]

Monmouth Loyalist Anthony Woodward returned to Trenton on the 18th with four wagons loaded with 50 barrels of pork and 11 barrels of flour, 10 wagons with two horse teams, and 16 wagons drawn by single horses. He turned them over to James Stockton, clerk for James Christie of the British Quartermaster General's Department at Trenton.[95]

Just before daylight on December 19, a fair day during which the temperature never got out of the 20's, a heavy patrol moved out from the Fox Chase Tavern on Maidenhead Road and marched down Queen Street to Church Alley where it combined with an artillery detachment of two cannon. The patrol marched over the Assunpink Creek bridge to the house of Dr. Bryant and Trenton Ferry, just in case the Americans attacked there again.[96] Later, three men of the Lossberg Regiment left town to look for forage and two miles up the road to Maidenhead were captured by the Americans. Incidents like these prompted Rall to request General Leslie to post additional troops at Maidenhead to keep the lines of communication open.[97]

Thomas Paine's *The American Crisis* was published as a pamphlet in Philadelphia on December 19 and was read to the American troops across the river from Trenton, but whether it was read in Trenton is not known.[98] In any event, the people of Trenton supporting the cause of independence were directly experiencing the crisis Paine discussed while Rall's officers saw their own crisis developing.

The weather continued well below freezing on December 20 with the overnight snow continuing in the morning and changing to freezing rain in the afternoon.[99] Rall was increasingly concerned that his right flank was too exposed. He was tied down by the enemy activity and apologized that "the constant alarms and troubles I have here prevents me going to Bordentown today as I had hoped." That morning, a grenadier of the von Linsingen battalion called on Rall to report that he alone was in charge of some battalion baggage that had been at Trenton for four days waiting for a wagon from his battalion at Bordentown to pick it up. From his post at Philemon Dickinson's estate Lieutenant von Grothausen led a patrol of 20 jägers from his company and four dragoons. He advanced four miles up the Delaware and encountered a force of 150 Americans that retreated after a short skirmish resulting in the death of a dragoon horse and one American taken prison. They brought the prisoner back and placed him in the Trenton guard house.[100] The prisoner may have been Arthur Howell, son of Richard Howell, whose Pennington Road house was a Hessian picket post. Howell frequently told the story to his family and friends that he had been captured by Hessians shortly before the Battle of Trenton, had been ill-treated and threatened with hanging on December 26. He was able to escape, however, and rejoin the militia forces. If it was Howell who was captured, the 150-man American force included members of the First Hunterdon militia regiment and perhaps other men from Trenton as well.[101]

Grenadier Reuber wrote in his diary that "the ice was rather thick on the Delaware, but not strong enough to cross. We had to have patience. The inhabitants of the city circulated a rumor that the rebels wanted to surprise us. We did not have any idea of such a thing and thought that the rebels were unable to do so."[102]

About this time, Isaac Pearson of Nottingham fell victim to British and Hessian plundering. His widow later testified that she "saw a quantity of hay, oats, & sheep taken from the house & farm" by Hessian troops and "a team with two horses & two oxen was impressed by the Hessians and kept in their service a considerable time." The Hessians did not pay for these items, and she submitted claims to the British government after the war, citing Assistant Commissary Thomas Watson as the man responsible for taking 11 quarters of beef on December 20 and five quarters on December 24. She also enumerated 21 days that her four-horse team and driver were used to carry 60 bushels of oats, six tons of hay, and 14 "fatt sheep" to the Hessians at Trenton.[103]

The weather warmed just a bit on December 21, but there had been wind, rain, and snow during the night and temperatures in the mid-30s during the day were accompanied by wind.[104] With so many Loyalists, who might recognize local Whigs, working with the Hessians, General Dickinson was frustrated in his efforts "to prevail with some intelligent person to go down into Trenton" to get accurate, up-to-date information.[105]

Reuber noted on December 21 that "early in the morning Commander Rall selected a strong force from his brigade, also a cannon, and we must march in 2 divisions, along the Delaware, to see about the Americans making an effort to cross the Delaware for an aggression. There was no sign of it and we marched to near Frankfurt, which was situated on the other side of the Delaware.

There we could see Americans. Rall stopped us and we joined with the other Divisions and returned to Trenton. All was quiet again."[106] Some of Rall's officers, including Lieutenant Colonel Scheffer, thought that the frequent skirmishes at Trenton Ferry were designed to divert attention from guarding against forays at Howell's and Johnson's Ferries, which he was neglecting. In Scheffer's opinion, Rall put too much emphasis on garrison routines at Trenton and devoted too few resources to watching and securing the ferry crossings up and down the river from the town.[107] Reuber also recorded that "an order came that every evening every company must stop in front of a certain house and place the guns 3 and 3 together in front of the door, and watch, and the soldier must be fully dressed like he was on watch. The officers and sergeants must enforce this order and so it was quiet."[108]

By December 21, Colonel Rall felt surrounded and in danger, writing to Colonel von Donop that "I have the enemy before me, behind me and at my right flank. The road from here to Princeton is very unsafe so that I have to send your letters by an escort of fifty men."[109] Rall had sent a routine letter to General Leslie by two dragoons who were shot at in the woods about three miles from Trenton. One dragoon was killed, and the survivor returned to Trenton within an hour of leaving and reported the incident.[110] Rall immediately ordered a force of one captain, three other officers, 100 men, an artillery piece and its artillerymen to carry the letter to Princeton. Lieutenant Wiederholdt went with this force and noted "It was exceedingly bad weather, too. We delivered our letter, slept that night on the bare ground, and returned the next morning without having seen or heard anything." Wiederholdt felt Rall had greatly overreacted, exemplifying his inability to make sound decisions. While Rall had underreacted to the American threat by refusing to build redoubts, he overreacted to this messenger problem. Wiederholdt was embarrassed when the British soldiers at Princeton laughed at them, but he accepted the fact that "truly it was laughable; a simple non-commissioned officer with 15 men would have been sufficient to do this errand, as the entire distance between the two garrisons was only 16 miles."[111] The number of rebels making the road unsafe was estimated to be 40 by some and 150 by others. Von Donop advised that sending messengers at unpredictable times would be an easier solution than sending larger escorts.[112]

The frequent American harassing attacks from across the river and from militiamen in the countryside exhausted the Hessian soldiers. One American officer leading these raids was Trenton's Ephraim Anderson, recovered from his wounds suffered at Quebec and making the transition to captain in the new version of the Second New Jersey Regiment. He led mostly militiamen from the First Hunterdon Regiment on his forays back into New Jersey, and "gained great honour" from these actions against the Hessians.[113]

General Grant expressed his regrets on December 21 that Rall's brigade was so fatigued. He reassured him that the rebel army in Pennsylvania was no larger than 8,000 men and they had neither shoes nor stockings, lacked proper clothing, and were dying of the cold without blankets and adequate provisions. There were no more than 300 men on the New Jersey side of the river, and they were divided into small groups led by officers below the rank of captain, like Ephraim Anderson, and their chief activity seemed to be ambushing the dragoons. General Howe did not approve of stationing any troops at Maidenhead.[114] In general, both Howe and Grant contributed to Rall's contempt for the American forces and did not take seriously the warnings of the other Hessian officers nor act on intelligence that was often accurate, but may have seemed redundant by indicating almost daily attacks.[115]

The quartermasters of both the Rall and Donop brigades were finally all together at Trenton on December 21, ready to leave for New York City to obtain pay and supplies for their regiments. They left Trenton with an escort of 80 men, mostly from the Lossberg Regiment. At New Brunswick, they met some supply wagons under a small escort heading to Trenton. When informed of the poor security on the road to Trenton they returned back to New York.[116]

On December 21, Rall refused to act on von Donop's request to send one of his regiments to reinforce the Hessian troops at Bordentown, because "he was in momentary expectation of being attacked by the enemy and must hold himself in readiness for the same, for he had them on his right flank as well as on his rear." There were also other American troops that might attempt to attack him, "but in the future he hoped to be able to circumvent them by means of ambuscades." If he gave up one regiment, he would be so understrength that he could not defend Trenton and would be forced to evacuate the town "and go into bivouac with the other two battalions and remain so."[117]

Weather was fair with temperatures in the mid-30s on December 22.[118] David Lanning of Trenton Township was a cooper at Captain John Mott's grist mills just upriver from Trenton. Lanning and Mott were members of the First Hunterdon militia then with General Dickinson at Yardley's Ferry. Several days before Christmas, probably while on a reconnaissance mission, Lanning was confronted and taken into custody by a British scouting party near the Delaware River, marched to Trenton, and confined in one of the houses at Tucker's Corner. The resourceful Lanning took advantage of a commotion distracting his guards, slipped out the back door of the house and after negotiating a high board fence in the back yard, made his way to the house of Quaker merchant Stacy Potts, Colonel Rall's headquarters. Potts had risked condemnation by both sides in the conflict by not swearing allegiance to one or the other, but on this occasion he concealed Lanning from the British. The next morning, Lanning covered himself with an old ragged coat and floppy hat, put an axe under his arm, and headed out assuming a limp and bowed head. Appearing to be an elderly wood cutter, he passed safely through the Hessian sentries and was not spotted by any local Loyalists. At the Pennington and Scotch road intersection he felt safe, threw down the axe, entered Dickinson's swamp and escaped across the river to rejoin his militia company and report his findings to General Dickinson.[119]

A patrol of the British 1st Light Infantry battalion marched into Trenton from Princeton at 10:00 am on December 22 to assist Rall. However, Colonel Rall decided he didn't need them, so, as grenadier Reuber noted, "they were ordered to turn around again and march back to Princeton." Reuber added that at night "100 men were placed all around town. In the middle of a dark night suddenly we heard alarm shots from our watch posts. The American patrol or avant-garde came too close to our watch." This caused all three Hessian regiments to "get busy right away." Colonel Rall with two companies and a piece of artillery "marched forward through woodland and looked around but could not detect a thing."[120] While Rall firmly believed that the American forces were too weak to attack him in force, he must have expected that his troops were in for a long winter of harassment attacks and turning out on false alarms.

The weather continued fair on December 23 with temperatures hovering around freezing.[121] About eleven o'clock in the morning

Dr. Bryant came into town from his Kingsbury estate seeking Colonel Rall. He met thirty-year-old Lieutenant Ernst Schwabe, a sixteen-year veteran of the Lossberg Regiment, on King Street, but together they were unable to find Rall. Dr. Bryant told the lieutenant that he would return later in the day. When Bryant returned, they located Rall, and Bryant passed on intelligence from one of his slaves, who had returned from a trip across the river, that the American army had been issued rations for several days in anticipation of an attack on Trenton. Colonel Rall dismissed the report as "old woman's talk."[122]

To improve the morale of Rall's troops, von Donop reported that the commissaries "would soon make the necessary arrangements for having beer brewed at Trenton as well as at Bordenton." Intelligence on December 23 indicated many rebels were sick and many near the end of their enlistments who were determined not to extend their time. The only sizeable force in New Jersey was led by Colonel Chambers of the Third Hunterdon militia regiment near Howell's Ferry with 80 men.[123]

The weather continued fair on December 24, but the temperature dropped into the mid-20's.[124] A man described as a "proper person" by General Dickinson was in and about Trenton gathering intelligence about the Hessian guard posts on the various roads leading into Trenton, the number of guards on the Assunpink Creek bridge, the location and number of the cannon, and the number of troops actually in Trenton or expected there. Dickinson believed the enemy troops in Trenton amounted to about 2000, mostly Hessians.[125]

Loyalists Leonard and Woodward had not been able to collect enough supplies even though they worked diligently. Acting Deputy Quartermaster General Gamble put out a circular to the people of Hunterdon and Burlington counties, stating that the residents had not brought in enough forage and stores for the British troops at Trenton and Bordentown, as well as the forces at New Brunswick, and listed prices the British would pay for hay, oats, Indian corn, wheat, flour, bran, pork, and beef. Higher prices were listed for products delivered by a farmer or mill, and lower ones if the army had to come get them. Inhabitants living near Trenton could deliver produce to Mr. Palmer, the commissary there. The circular also carried the blatant threat that if not enough supplies were brought in, there was the "disagreeable alternative of having them seized by foraging parties."[126]

Colonel Rall was growing very concerned about his brigade's worsening fatigue from the continuous hit-and-run harassment by the enemy in the cold weather. Fatigue led to illness, and he had only two officers in his regiment that he considered fit for duty. While all three regiments had similar complaints, the Lossberg Regiment was in especially bad shape, having suffered more than any other regiment in the recent campaign.[127] General Grant rather understatedly communicated to Rall on December 24 that "Washington has been informed that our troops have marched into winter quarters, and has been told that we are weak at Trenton and Princeton, and Lord Sterling expressed a wish to make an attack upon these two places. I don't believe he will attempt it but be assured that my information is undoubtedly true, so I need not advise you, to be on your guard against an unexpected attack at Trenton."[128]

The Christmas day weather was fair with sunshine and clouds, but the temperatures were again only in the 20's.[129] Major von Dechow reported to Colonel Rall that the baggage and supplies of the brigade were vulnerable if the town should be suddenly attacked and urged him to have them removed to safer places. Rall was very irritated by the frequent concerns expressed by his subordinates and simply told von Dechow that if the rebels came and were successful, which he sincerely doubted, they could "have all the stores and the baggage to my very last wagon." In his opinion, the best the rebels could hope for if they attacked Trenton was to retreat successfully.

On Christmas morning, Colonel Rall received a message from General Grant that an American detachment under General Stirling was near Trenton and might make some kind of attack that day. Rall dismissed this and it was in fact erroneous information, but he did ride around the outskirts of town with some troops, visiting guard posts and pickets. He returned to his quarters late in the afternoon after finding everything quiet. Rall struck up a game of checkers at his quarters with his host, Stacy Potts. During the game, at about 7:30 pm, shots were heard from the northwest part of town - a single volley followed by a few scattered shots. It was enough to alarm the town and came from an American party of about 30 Virginia Continentals from General Adam Stephen's brigade attacking the picket post on the Pennington Road. Not knowing the size of the American force and whether the attack would continue, the Hessians prepared for action.[130]

The Lossberg Regiment gathered under arms at their company quarters. The Rall Regiment formed up in front of the English Church and marched to the head of King and Queen Streets. The Knyphausen Regiment on southern Queen Street and a company of the Lossberg Regiment south of the bridge gathered by their quarters. Picket posts were reinforced. The Altenbockum Company stayed all night in the houses of John Chambers and Warrell Cottnam near their captain's quarters. The regimental officers assembled to report their situations and Rall decided that this attack had been made by the force General Grant had warned him about or by some local farmers who had gotten together just to annoy him. Six Hessian soldiers had been wounded and several muskets and some ammunition captured by the Americans. Meeting at the head of King Street, Major von Dechow urged Rall to send out a heavy patrol to all the ferries and up the roads, but Rall thought it could wait until morning. Von Dechow, extremely angered by Rall's lack of concern, took care to put sentinels at each of the houses occupied by soldiers of his regiment and ordered his men to remain in their quarters and be prepared for an alarm.[131]

Lieutenant Wiederholdt with nine men and one noncommissioned officer was sent to reinforce the picket post at the Howell cooper shop. He later criticized Rall for not sending out patrols as far as the ferries while defending his own actions that night, saying, "as soon as I came to my post, I detailed seven pickets as well as I could manage it during the night; I had patrols after patrols walk about, thus to protect myself from any surprises."[132]

Rall apparently found the checkers game with Potts to be a less enjoyable way to spend what was left of Christmas day than a more lively party at the home of Abraham Hunt down the street. There, Rall relaxed with the thought that all was well. The very stormy weather that developed also put his mind at ease about any further attack, and he enjoyed his games of cards while eating and drinking in Mr. Hunt's comfortable home. According to tradition, a Loyalist from Bucks County came to the house seeking Colonel Rall to give him information on more extensive American movements that night, but either Rall could not be bothered or he looked at the note and thought it referred to the small force encountered earlier in the evening. He put the note in his pocket and continued his relaxing evening well into the early morning before returning to his quarters at Stacy Potts's house and expecting to sleep late the next morning, as was his usual habit.[133]

Chapter 7

1776
December 26 – 31

Cannon and musket fire killed men and horses during the battle in Trenton on December 26 as Washington's forces pressed the Hessians from all sides with deadly shots, many coming from inside houses and cellars, or behind trees and fences. Some Hessians believed that even civilians shot at them from houses, and one reported seeing a woman mortally wound a Hessian officer.[1] *This mystified the Hessians, used to more formal battlefield warfare, and one captured Hessian commented to the son of Rev. Henry Muhlenberg that when they had "entered Trenton and occupied the region, the inhabitants swore their allegiance to the king of Great Britain" in response to General Howe's offer of amnesty and protection. However, the Hessian told him that when the American troops entered town, residents shot at the Hessians from their houses. Muhlenberg felt that if this was true, "it corroborates the proverb which says that oaths obtained by force are an outrage to God. The submissiveness, obedience, and loyalty which are obtained by force do not have the permanence of the virtues which have their basis in love, righteousness, and justice."*[2]

Overnight and during the day on December 26, there was wind-driven hail, snow and freezing rain with temperatures in the low-30s, making the ground semi-frozen mud.[3] At four in the morning, Hessian artillery Lieutenant Friedrich Fischer began his normal routine and ordered horses hitched to the two brass cannon in front of the guard post on King Street. He then sent men to report to Colonel Rall that all was ready for the morning patrol to the "Doctor House," the Kingsbury home of Dr. Bryant near Trenton Ferry. These men returned with word that the patrol was cancelled for that day, so the horses were unhitched and returned to their stables. At five o'clock, three Hessian jägers made an early morning patrol from the guard post at Philemon Dickinson's house up the river as far as the home of grist miller and militia Captain John Mott. They reported no sign of the enemy. Normally, there would have been more men and they would have patrolled out further from Trenton.[4]

On the road to Pennington near the edge of town, a resident was out chopping wood in the early morning storm when he was surprised by two riders who came out of the storm and asked him where the Hessian picket was stationed. Any hesitation he felt ended upon being told that it was General Washington who needed to know, and he pointed towards the house and cooper shop of Richard Howell.[5] For Lieutenant Wiederholdt, commanding that picket post, the night had passed quietly. A patrol returned about an hour after sunrise and reported everything was quiet and that the jägers had withdrawn men from night posts between his post and the river. Wiederholdt later wrote that, "if I had not just stepped out of my little guard-house and seen the enemy, they might have been upon me before I had time to reach for my rifle, as my sentinels did not keep a very sharp lookout any more as it was broad daylight, and the advance-guard did not expect the enemy from that direction [since they normally came across the river below town].... I was thus quickly under arms and awaited the approach of the enemy with fortitude, thinking that it was merely a skirmishing party." Wiederholdt was joined immediately by some of his men, tired from the night and morning patrols, who ran out of the cooper shop while trying to get on their coats and slip their equipment belts over their shoulders. Wiederholdt said the enemy "charged with three rounds of rifle fire [at] me and my 17 men, who stood still under their arms. After the third discharge I gave the order to fire and fought with them until I was almost surrounded by several battalions."[6]

After the stormy Christmas night of wind-driven snow, sleet, hail, and rain, Martha Reed recalled, "Then, in the grey dawn, came the beating of drums, and the sound of firing. The soldiers quartered in our house, hastily decamped, all was uproar, and confusion."[7] Lieutenant Jacob Piel of the Lossberg Regiment had been up since five o'clock at his quarters in the house of Miss Rebecca Coxe, next door to Colonel Rall's quarters on King Street. As Rall's adjutant, he had tried unsuccessfully to wake his commander at six and then again at seven. That was pretty normal, but when he heard the unexpected firing at the edge of town that had awoken Martha, he ran across the street to the main guard post where men were turning out to support the upper picket post which was apparently under attack. Then Piel knocked loudly on Colonel Rall's door, and a sleepy Rall in his night-clothes opened an upper window and shouted down, demanding to know what the problem was. When told of the firing, which he could now hear himself, he said he would be out in a minute, and in a very short time he appeared.[8]

The residents of Trenton were just as surprised as the Hessians by the appearance of the American troops out of the storm and reacted instinctively. Martha Reed says, "My mother, and we children hid in the cellar to escape the shots that fell about the house, and remained until quiet was restored." She recalled that "our next door neighbor was killed on his doorstep, a bullet struck the blacksmith as he was in the act of closing himself in his cellar, and many other townspeople were injured by chance shots."[9] One of Stacy Potts's daughters was slightly injured while running home from a neighbor's house, when a musket ball hit and sent flying the comb in her hair.[10]

Neither civilians nor Hessians knew the size of the force that was attacking the edge of town. It was General Nathanael Greene's division that made the first contact at the upper picket post, and within minutes General Sullivan's division engaged the jàger picket at Dickinson's Hermitage. Both divisions had crossed to New Jersey at McConkey's Ferry and marched to Trenton during the night guided by militiamen from the First Hunterdon Regiment, including David Lanning.[11] The night march was so harrowing that Massachusetts Colonel Paul Dudley Sargent later commented that only the difficulties of obtaining a veteran's pension in 1826 gave him "more pain, anxiety, and fatigue, than my March to Trenton Decr 26 1776, thro' one of the most boisterous nights ever experienced by Man."[12] Captain John Flahaven's 40 recruits for the First New Jersey Regiment led the attack on the jàger's and drove in the pickets. The jàgers were also the targets of ten ineffective cannon shots from across the river fired by American troops who had not been able to cross due to the ice on that part of the river.[13]

The jàger's retreated hastily toward town, leaving their knapsacks at the Hermitage. Near the barracks, they formed with some reinforcements and delivered just one volley before the Americans were upon them. Not having bayonets on their short rifles, they retreated hurriedly along Front Street heading for the bridge over the Assunpink Creek at the old gristmill. In fear of being cut off by the

William Pedrick's 1893 painting The Opening of the Battle of Trenton, Pennington Road, King and Queen Streets *as viewed from the site of the present Trenton Battle Monument. Historian William S. Stryker provided historical information about the action and the houses shown in the distance that stood there in 1776. (Collection of the Old Barracks Association)*

large force attacking them, some tried to ford the creek while most continued on toward the bridge still held by their picket. One jäger was captured in the race to the bridge, but the others escaped over it and headed to Bordentown, apparently joined by the 19-man picket detail at the bridge.[14] Once over the bridge and in Kingsbury on the Bordentown Road, at the corner of Ferry Street they may have briefly rested at the house of Robert Waln, owner of the Trenton Mills at the bridge.[15] The sentry in front of Major von Dechow's quarters just up from the bridge on Queen Street was killed. The 20 British dragoons also quickly left town by way of the Assunpink Creek bridge. John Cadwalader, observing things from the Pennsylvania shore, said, "the Light Horse & Hessians were seen flying in great confusion towards Bordentown but without cannon or wagons, so that the enemy must have lost the whole – a party of our men intercepted about a dozen Hessians in sight of our people on this side & brought them to the [Trenton] Ferry & huzza'd."[16]

At the northwest corner of town General Greene's forces continued pushing the Hessians from the picket post at the Howell's shop on

Pennington Road. Retreating Hessians sought sheltered firing positions wherever they could, including house lot gardens, but they could not relieve the pressure from the advancing Americans.[17] Lieutenant Wiederholdt retreated under fire until reaching Altenbockum's company, which he said "had rallied during my engagement and had taken up a position straight across the street in front of the Captain's quarters. I posted myself at their right wing and together we charged the enemy, but we were again forced to retreat in the same manner as before, so as not to be cut off from the garrison." Loyalist Major John Barnes was back in Trenton, apparently staying at the house where Altenbockum's squad was posted, and watched this attack, later testifying that Altenbockum "behaved well, and made a retreat which redounds to his honour."[18] The two detachments gained time for the main garrison to form up.[19]

Wiederholdt became angry that "nobody came to see what was going on, no one came to our assistance with reinforcements," not even Rall's regiment that was the duty regiment that night. Still, he "took up [his] position in front of one of the first houses of the town and fired at the enemy who was just forming in battle order on the upper side of the town." Wiederholdt, not a great fan of Rall's, said afterwards that it was only at this point that Rall, "made his appearance and he seemed to be quite dazed. I considered it my duty to report what had happened outside of the town, as he was ignorant of everything." Wiederholdt reported that the enemy was strong and was attacking from both sides as well as the head of the town. Rall asked Wiederholdt how strong the enemy was, and he answered, "I could not possibly tell that with accuracy as I had had to look after my men, however I had seen about 4 or 5 battalions advancing from the woods and from three of these I had withstood the firing before I had abandoned my post." Wiederholdt then stated that Rall shouted to his regiment, "'Forward, March, Advance! Advance!' and he tottered back and forth without knowing what he was doing."[20]

When Greene's division reached the point where King and Queen Streets met at the northern end of town, an intersection known as "the gateway,"[21] artillery pieces were placed in position to rake King and Queen Streets. Washington placed himself where he could oversee the town and observe enemy movements on high ground on the road leading out of town to Nathan Beakes' plantation.[22] Washington and his aide could see the frenzied commotion of "men running here and there, officers swinging their swords, artillerymen harnessing their horses."[23] The falling sleet did not help his view, and the smoke of battle further obscured it. Nathanael Greene later wrote to Caty that, "It rained, haild and snowd and was a violent storm. The storm of nature and the storm of the town exhibited a scene that fild the mind during the action with passions easier conceived than describd."[24] The wet, freezing conditions made it very difficult for soldiers on both sides to fight effectively. Washington's troops had tried, with only partial success, to protect their firing mechanisms and powder during the long overnight march, but during the fighting in town both sides experienced many misfires. Lieutenant Colonel Scheffer later reported that, "It rained cannon balls and grapeshot here, and snow, rain, and sleet came constantly into our faces. In short, none of our muskets would fire any longer."[25]

Henry Knox wrote that early in the battle, "we ... entered the town with them pell-mell, and here succeeded a scene of war of which I had often conceived but never saw before. The hurry, fright, and confusion of the enemy was [not] unlike that which will be when the last trump shall sound. They endeavoured to form in the streets, the heads of which we had previously the possession of with cannon and howitzers. These, in the twinkling of an eye, cleared the streets. The backs of the houses were resorted to for shelter. These proved ineffectual: the musketry soon dislodged them." Knox was glad that although "the storm continued with great violence" it was at the backs of his artillerymen and "consequently in the faces of our enemy."[26] Private Cornelius Sullivan remembered that many of the Hessians turned out and "entered the action with nothing but their shirts on," while Thomas Forrest, who referred to the Hessians as "the Brass Caps and Crous Cuops" noted the lack of shoes and watch coats among the Hessians.[27] They were not unlike most of the Americans, who like John Boudy of the Second Maryland Regiment in Greene's division "was but thinly clad, and entirely barefoot all the while."[28]

After alerting Colonel Rall, Lieutenant Piel got his friend, Second Lieutenant Zoll, who was quartered with him at the Coxe house, to cross the street to the English Church and get the artillerymen and Lieutenant Colonel Scheffer's company out into the street. He also retrieved the regimental flags being kept in the church. Scheffer had been very sick for five days but left his sick bed to go on duty. Rall ordered the Lossberg Regiment to form up on Church Alley behind a row of poplar trees, essentially in the cemetery, and then rode down King Street to where his regiment was forming up under Lieutenant Colonel Batthas Brethauer, facing east with their center in front of Pinkerton's Alley. As the Hessians began to advance up King Street, they met cannon shot flying down the street and breaking their ranks. At the same time, they were exposed to strong musket fire on their left from General Mercer's soldiers who entered the rear of Stacy Potts's tannery and moved among its bark house, mill house, bark mill, beam house, stone currying shop, leather house, stable with hay loft, and chaise-house, which provided them with protective cover.[29] The Hessians also received fire from American troops on the Queen Street lots of William Tindall and William Smith. Lieutenant Colonel Brethauer was weak from severe illness and left the field when his horse was shot from under him. By this time, the American artillery fire was scattering any troops trying to resist.[30]

The two Hessian brass cannon stationed on King Street in front of the main guardhouse were hitched to their horses and ordered forward. They got north of the small bridge over Petty's Run, perhaps to Charles Axford's tavern, under destructive artillery fire from the head of the street and bullets from the marksmen posted behind the fences around Potts's tan yard. The Hessian artillery got off six rounds in spite of suffering heavy casualties. With too few men left to move the guns and five horses killed, they fired one last round of canister[31] at the Americans across Stacy Potts' tan yard. The few Hessian artillerymen still uninjured dropped their equipment and fled toward Church Alley and Queen Street. By the time they had gone 40 steps from stay maker Richard Norris' house, what they called the "broken-down house," the Americans had captured their two brass cannon.

Artillery Sergeant Joseph White recalled, "The 3d shot we fired broke the axle-tree of the piece, -- we stood there some time idle, they firing upon us. Col. Knox rode up and said, my brave lads, go up and take those two held pieces sword in hand." White joined the attackers led by Captain William Washington and Lieutenant James Monroe and recalled, "the party inclined to the right. I hallowed as loud as I could scream, to the men to run for their lives right up to the pieces. I was the first that reach them." The Hessians had abandoned the cannon, "except one man tending vent – run you dog, cried I, holding my sword over his head, he looked up and saw it, then run[.] We put in a canister of shot, (they had put in the [powder] cartridge before they left it,) and fired. The battle ceased." General Adam Stephen of Virginia remembered a little differently that, "We had a Christmas frolick at Trenton, ... You never saw so many good shot made in your life time – We drove the enemy from their cannon in our shooting." He saw how one "brave" German remained at his artillery piece and "was loading her by him self after the rest had left him – A Virginian as brave as he, would not let him but run up knockd him down wt the butt of his gun & took him prisoner." Both Captain Washington and Lieutenant Monroe were wounded in this action, Washington with a bullet wound to his wrist and Monroe with a bullet "through his breast and shoulder." Washington and Monroe were carried to the same house and were ministered to by Dr. John Riker, who had joined the army during its march to Trenton the night before. Dr. Riker saved future president Monroe's life by stopping the bleeding from a severed artery in his shoulder.[32]

Grenadier Reuber of Rall's regiment later recalled that, "After the first salvo we had to get busy and arranged our battle position. Suddenly the rebels advanced unbelievably severe against us. Next to Major Rall's quarters was a wooden wall, and in front of same stood our 2 cannons in a street in front of 7 American cannons and one of the American cannons damaged and blew in pieces one of ours. They advanced to the wooden wall and captured our cannons in front of the regiment."[33]

Lieutenant Patrick Duffey of Thomas Proctor's Pennsylvania artillery regiment was in the thick of the fighting on the main street "in front of the savages" and "sustained the fire of several guns from the houses on each side, without the least loss, must attribute my protection to the hand of Providence."[34] In the heat of battle, at least one American soldier, a sergeant, was heard singing one of his favorite songs that contained words something like: "Exert yourselves with power and might, See how American boys can fight, Drums are beating, colours flying, Cannon roaring, men lie dying, These are the known effects of war." At the time he was totally unaware that he was singing and only learned of it later when told by those who heard him.[35]

Having no battle plan or defensive positions such as redoubts to man, the Hessians had to improvise in reaction to developing and changing situations. Hessian troops sent forward continued to be forced back down Queen Street under heavy fire from artillery and advancing American troops, as well as from muskets fired through openings in the board fences that sheltered other Americans. Hessian artillery and infantrymen retreated rapidly down Queen Street heading for the creek while receiving fire from some of Colonel Glover's men stationed behind a red board fence standing between the Assunpink Creek and the house owned by Loyalist John Barnes on the west side of Queen Street. Some Hessians were able to escape, though, by crossing the Assunpink bridge and heading to Bordentown.[36]

Rising casualties among the Hessian officers, whose number was already depleted by illness, made it difficult to maintain military order and discipline. Sullivan's division was rapidly taking possession of the southern part of town. Colonel John Stark's New Hampshire regiment, accompanied by an artillery detachment, turned at Alexander Chambers' at the corner of Second Street and River Road and marched toward the Knyphausen Regiment marching toward them from the Bull Head Tavern. In the advance, a captain, sergeant, and 16 men of Stark's regiment captured 60 Hessians. The rest of the division headed to Front Street to take possession of the barracks and then cut off access to the bridge over the Assunpink. Colonel Glover's brigade crossed the bridge and established a position on Mill Hill.[37]

The Rall and Lossberg regiments retreated through an area of the town known as "the swamp." They were ordered to turn and attack the town once again. The brigade band began to play in an attempt to raise the morale of these men, who were taking heavy casualties from the musket fire coming from houses. The officers urged their men on and they got back to Queen Street below Church Alley. The Knyphausen Regiment engaged St. Clair's Continentals on Second Street. The Hessian troops were receiving fire from all sides and becoming demoralized, although some men made heroic efforts to counter the American onslaught. Captain von Lowenstein's company of the Lossberg Regiment marched along Second Street toward the intersection of King Street, and encountered heavy American fire in front of Mr. Davies' house. Everyone was now moving by various paths towards the bridge over the Assunpink and the smoke of battle, even with wet powder problems, combined with the storm precipitation to make identifying friend or foe difficult. Hessian Second Lieutenant Ernst Christian Schwabe of the Lossberg Regiment was shot through the thigh, turned over command to his ensign, and was carried to safety behind Isaac Yard's house.[38]

Some Hessian units fragmented and recombined in new formations, forcing officers and privates to adapt while fighting for their lives. Ensign Christian von Hobe of the Lossberg Regiment was disabled by a wound to his leg from a spent bullet and hobbled to the Methodist meeting house on the corner of Queen and Fourth streets for shelter. Lieutenant Piel's friend, Second Lieutenant Zoll of the Lossberg Regiment, took a bullet in the spine and lay bleeding in the street.[39]

Lieutenant Wiederholdt says, "Colonel [Rall] moved with his regiment to the right of the town under the apple-trees, intending only to charge the enemy on the Princeton road. But when he was reminded, I do not know by whom, of the loss of the baggage left behind in the town, he changed his mind and with his own regiment and that of Lossberg he attacked the city which he had just left." Wiederholdt, again criticizing Rall said, "What madness was this! ... A man of a little common sense and of very small experience in the business can here see his weakness."[40] Grenadier Reuber wrote that when they withdrew from the city to the fields, "Major Rall commanded: 'All my Grenadiers, forward.' We were then storming the city, and the enemy retracted. As we were in the city again, the rebels marched around us, and as we wanted to return to our positions, the enemy had again seven cannons on the main street. We had to get through, but was it hard to overcome this predicament."[41]

By the time Colonel Rall was ready to order his troops to retreat to the Assunpink Creek bridge, the Americans controlled it. By that time, two cannon manned by General Sullivan's division had begun firing on Queen Street from the corner of Second Street. Rall ordered a retreat out Third and Fourth Streets toward the apple orchard and then almost immediately fell from his horse, having received two severe wounds in his side. He fell in front of Isaac Yard's house on the west side of Queen Street about 200 feet north of Pinkerton's alley. Two soldiers lifted Rall and helped him painfully walk to the Methodist Church. On the way, they passed the seriously wounded Lieutenant Zoll.[42]

The retreat to the east on the two short streets found the troops in confusion. With Rall out of action, Lieutenant Colonel Scheffer ordered the troops to break through anywhere they could and escape the town. Captain Altenbockum was struck in the head by a bullet but was able to mount Colonel Rall's horse and retreat toward the orchard. He was captured by an American officer and carried to the quarters of Lieutenant Colonel Brethauer, who was still quite ill. Ironically, they found a Hessian medical officer bleeding Brethauer to cure him, while throughout the town many Hessians were bleeding to death from wounds.[43]

While Hessian units retreated toward the orchard, stragglers from all three regiments attempted to get to the Assunpink bridge but were encircled and surrendered on Queen Street between Second and Front streets. Colonel Stark led his troops on Second Street driving the Hessians into a field on the edge of the orchard just north of the Assunpink Creek. As the Hessians attempted to form for an attack on the bridge and make their escape, the two cannon of the Lossberg Regiment, serving with the Knyphausen Regiment that day, became stuck in the marshy ground while under heavy fire and had to be abandoned.[44]

Some Hessians began to surrender, including the wounded Major von Dechow who hobbled along toward Queen Street aided by Corporal Kustner who had tied a white handkerchief to a spontoon and held it up as they walked toward Joshua Newbold's house to give themselves up. Major von Dechow apparently surrendered to General Sullivan when he reached Queen Street. Other groups tried to escape, including one group that attempted to ford the ice-cold water in the creek. Some men found themselves up to their necks in the frigid water, negotiating a muddy bottom. The panic of the troops increased from the frantic noises made by the regiments' servants, women, and musicians who were gathered by the creek with much of the brigade's baggage. The Rall and Lossberg regiments were in the orchard east of the Friends' Meeting House on Third Street with the surrounding American forces, including artillery, clearly visible to them. When told to throw down their arms and surrender, Lieutenant Colonel Scheffer called out that they must surrender, and after a few minutes conversation with an American officer they did. The Hessians lowered their standards and grounded their muskets, while the officers put their hats on the points of their swords to hold up as a sign of submission. Some of the soldiers, seeing the surrender as an indignity, broke the stocks of their muskets by striking them against the ground, cut their cartridge pouch straps, or threw their muskets as far as they

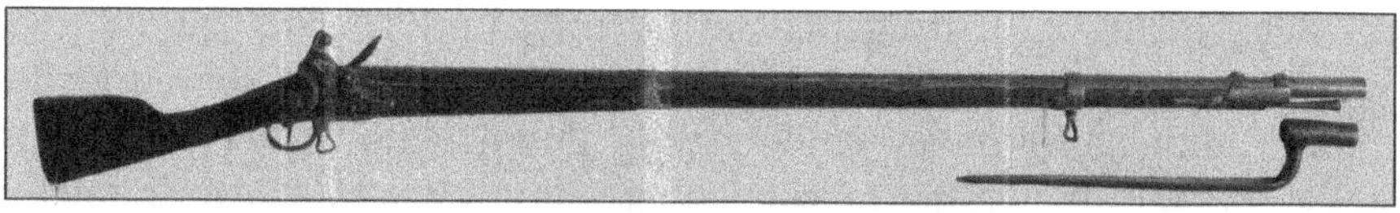

Hessian musket captured at the Battle of Trenton and by tradition retained for use by a Trenton militiaman of the First Hunterdon County Regiment. (Courtesy of a private collector in New Jersey)

could into the woods. By military custom, they should all have simply placed their muskets on the ground in front of them.[45]

A detachment of skirmishers from the Knyphhausen Regiment was sent to high ground towards the back of William Roscoe's house and the Presbyterian Church to see if it was possible to escape across the creek. A number of individual officers and privates attempted to cross with little success, although at least one officer did get across. Several drowned while others found it too deep and turned back. The Americans kept pressing toward the creek to cut off the Hessian retreat. As the Americans closed in, Lieutenant Wiederholdt helped negotiate the surrender for Captain Biesenrodt with General St. Clair. St. Clair agreed to allow the officers to keep their swords and baggage and the noncommissioned officers their swords and knapsacks. However, about an hour after the surrender, their swords and knapsacks were taken from them.[46] After the surrender, some of the American soldiers ran among the prisoners "and after satisfying their curiosity a little, they began to converse familiarly in broken English and German."[47]

Apparently, about the time of the surrender, the officer and 27 Hessian soldiers in the picket at Trenton Landing moved out on the road to Bordentown and reported to the picket at the Crosswicks Creek drawbridge.[48] Private Elisha Bostwick's company of Connecticut Continentals was ordered to pursue any Hessians who had crossed the bridge and headed toward Bordentown. Bostwick said that after about a half-mile march, they were in sight of the Delaware River when they suddenly received fire from American artillery on the Pennsylvania side that mistook them for the enemy. Bostwick's Colonel, Charles Webb, "swang his hat & gave a shout & instantly every hat on both sides of the river was swinging & every voice rais'd with a shout." The regiment mistakenly firing on them, commanded by Colonel Hitchcock, had been unable to cross the river due to the ice.[49]

The heaviest fighting had lasted only between half and three-quarters of an hour. Washington was informed of the surrender by Major James Wilkinson while riding down King Street and some residents within earshot heard him exclaim, "This is a glorious day for our country, Major Wilkinson."[50]

Shortly after the surrender, Colonel Rall was carried on a bench from the Methodist Church through Church Alley to his quarters at the Stacy Potts house. He was visited by Generals Washington and Greene who promised Rall that his men would be treated well. The location of the house had put it in the midst of some of the heaviest fighting and it had been badly damaged by gunshot and cannon ball. One of the panes of glass with a bullet hole through it was kept as a relic of the battle.[51]

When the noise of battle ceased, according to Martha Reed, "the voices of neighbors calling for us, reassured us, to venture out" and with the Hessian occupiers gone, "my mother went all through the house, and found it had been ransacked and pillaged from garret to cellar. Her stores of household linen, mostly of her own spinning and her feather beds were gone - every article of silver had vanished - tables, and chairs were broken, furniture defaced, china and glass utterly ruined, while not a crumb remained of our winter stores." Their sense of loss was tempered by the knowledge that the Hessians had been defeated and most of them made prisoner. Like other families, Martha's now began the slow process of restoring their home "to its usual orderly comfort." They all no doubt hoped that their town would never again be occupied by British and Hessian soldiers.[52]

Loyalists left town as fast as they could to find elements of the British army for protection or to join.[53] Trenton lawyer Joseph Taylor again left the area and sought safety with the British in New York City.[54]

Jane Richardson, who was about 10 years old at the time of the battle, recalled for the rest of her life that after the battle she saw several soldiers "indifferently clad" and "with but parts of shoes to their feet, leaving bloody footprints on the frozen snow and on the floor." Two tired and cold soldiers came to her house, stacked their muskets around the clock in a corner of the sitting room, and warmed themselves at the recently used bake oven.[55]

Artillery Sergeant Joseph White later wrote about what he saw as he walked through town, recalling "my blood chill'd to see such horror and distress, blood mingling together – the dying groans, and 'garments rolled in blood.' The sight was too much to bear; I left it soon, and in returning I saw a field officer laying dead on the ground and his sword by him, I took it up and pulling the sheathe out of the belt, I carried it off. It was an elegant sword, and I wore it all the time I staid in the army."[56]

Coming through town, private John Greenwood's company passed two Hessian brass cannon next to which lay seven dead Hessians and a brass drum. Although Greenwood eyed the drum as a possible souvenir, one of the drummers in his company quickly claimed it and threw away his own drum. However, Greenwood later wrote, "I obtained a sword from one of the bodies, and we then ran on to join the regiment, which was marching down the main street toward the market." Just before reaching the market house, they encountered General Washington who ordered Greenwood's colonel to "March on, my brave fellows, after me!" as he rode forward.[57]

Ensign Beale from Virginia recorded that "as soon as the enemy surrendered there was a guard placed over them and they were marched to the river. The balance of our men fell into the utmost confusion, every man shifting for himself." Beale very nearly engaged in some looting after the battle and wrote, "After I had gotten pretty well refreshed with good old Jamaica and excellent beef and biscuits, I asked Captain Fauntleroy and our adjutant, by name, Kelly, to go to the stable and get us a horse apiece. We did so and all mounted, but it was much colder on horseback than on foot, so seeing Colonel Lawson of the Sixth Regiment in the street, asked him what would become of the property taken here. He told us it was for the general good and not individual advantage, upon which I dismounted and set my horse loose."[58] Private Moses Smith of the 26th Continental Regiment, with one of his friends, captured 20 horses belonging to the British cavalry that they found grazing in a field and delivered them into the American service.[59]

Elisha Bostwick found the prisoners from the Rall Regiment to be "of a moderate stature [with] rather broad shoulders[,] their limbs not of equal proportion[,] light complexion with a b[l]uish tinge[,] hair cued as tight to the head as possible sticking straight back like the handle of an iron skillet. Their uniform blue with black facings[,] brass drums which made a timbling sound[,] their flag or standard of the richest black silk & the devices upon it & the lettering in gold leaf."[60]

Not wanting to risk disaster should a Hessian counterattack come from Bordentown or Princeton, Washington ordered his men and prisoners back across the Delaware that day. The weather remained foul and only began to clear in the evening. One reason given by Joseph Reed for why the army should get back across the river quickly was that "there were great quantities of spirituous liquours at Trenton of which the soldiers drank too freely to admit of discipline or defence in case of attack." One officer reported that "We stove about forty hogsheads of rum we could not carry off."[61] Merchant Jacob Benjamin later submitted a claim for items taken by the Americans, and the list included large quantities of rum, brandy, claret, porter, and gin, as well as large quantities of food for humans and horses, and personal items.[62]

Sergeant White and his gun crew wanted to take their damaged cannon back with them, but Colonel Knox told them "to leave that piece with the broken axle-tree." They regarded the cannon as the best in the regiment and White, determined to salvage it, hired four men, including an experienced mate from a sailing vessel, who were able to rig it to move. They set off, although at reduced speed with their awkward cannon. The rearguard came up with them and the commanding officer told them to abandon the cannon, that he would not take charge of it. White told him that he would rather risk being captured than leave the cannon now that they had come so far. The rearguard left White and his gun crew behind and on their own. Soon after, White's men thought they saw some enemy cavalry approaching but found, "they were nothing but a party of old Quakers; they had handkerchiefs tyed over their hats, for there had been a snow storm all the day." Later, Colonel Henry Knox himself rode up with a party of officers and asked White, "Sergeant what piece is that?" White told him it was the piece Knox had ordered left behind, but that he had wanted the victory to be complete. Knox replied, "You are a good fellow," said he would remember him, and then rode on.[63] Some things did get left behind because of the orders to get out of Trenton quickly. General Lord Stirling, "in order to facilitate the passage of the troops," left behind two of his very fine horses, complete with their saddles and bridles, and they were stolen during the night.[64]

Just how many men and what quantity of weapons and supplies were captured was difficult to determine. It was a good problem to have, but there were all sorts of wild numbers circulating about that were constantly revised. For example, on December 27, Thomas Wharton, President of the Pennsylvania Council of Safety, wrote to John Hancock that "besides the arms mentioned in the enclosed letter to have fallen into our hands we have taken about 200 stand in General Dickinson's house at Trenton." A gallant attempt at very specific numbers of captured soldiers, but admittedly "very rough," was transmitted from Stephen Moylan to Robert Morris on December 27, giving the total number breakdown as one colonel, two lieutenant colonels, three majors, four captains, eight lieutenants, twelve ensigns, two surgeons, 92 sergeants, 20 drums, nine musicians, 25 officers' servants, and 740 rank and file for a total of 918 prisoners. The numbers were further broken down by regiment, including the separate artillery company with 38 officers and men. In terms of captured material, Moylan listed "six pieces of artillery brass double fortified three pounders, twelve drums, four standards, and about 1000 stand of arms." In contrast, Moylan noted, "Our loss very inconsiderable, two or three killed & as many wounded."[65] Other early returns noted the six cannon carriages, three ammunition wagons, four wagons of baggage, 40 horses, and "as many muskets, bayonets, cartouch boxes & swords as there are prisoners."[66] General Ewing at Trenton Ferry reported that one wagon loaded with captured Hessian arms and six captured Hessians were brought down and safely gotten across the river.[67]

After providing for the wounded and refreshing themselves with captured and plundered spirits, the Continentals transported some of the prisoners and their guards over the Delaware at Trenton Ferry, but most of the army and prisoners left Trenton about noon and marched the nine miles back to Johnson's Ferry. The men, both victors and prisoners, were exhausted, wet, cold, and in many cases sick or injured.[68] Among those detailed to guard the Hessian prisoners that crossed at Johnson's Ferry and were taken to Newtown, Pennsylvania were twenty-three-year-old Hosea Husted of Captain Samuel Hugg's Western New Jersey Artillery Company and twenty-six-year-old Cornelius Wells in Captain Maynard's company of Colonel Smallwood's Maryland regiment. Husted was quite sick and remained at Newtown until December 30, when he was discharged because of his health.[69] Re-crossing the river was difficult and Rev. David Avery, chaplain of Colonel John Patterson's 15th Continental Regiment, recalled, "I had the good fortune to cross the river before night, wh[ich] was exceedingly difficult to cross by reason of the abundance of ice. I was extremely chilled, and came near perishing before I could get to a fire."[70]

Colonel Rall and his officers and men too badly wounded to move were left in Trenton and put on parole under the care of Regimental Assistant Medical Officer Freidrich Wilhelm Oliva and Assistant Medical Officer Philip Obenhausen, both of the Lossberg Regiment, who were also put on parole.[71] Lieutenant Zoll, who had been shot in the spine and left lying in the street, survived and stayed in Trenton for several months recuperating. He was 29 years old, unmarried, and had been in the service for 12 years.[72] At least 30-40 seriously wounded men were left at Trenton while those less seriously wounded were among the prisoners taken back across the Delaware. Although the number of casualties varies in different accounts, it can be reasonably stated that at least five Hessian officers and 17 men were killed and six officers and 78 men wounded. Some of the wounded died later of their injuries. By tradition, the dead were buried in a common grave near the Presbyterian Church.[73]

Hessian records indicate that about 48 sick or severely wounded men were captured and paroled at Trenton. Several of them died before the end of the day, including Staff Captain Friedrich Wilhelm von Benning of the Lossberg Regiment and Private Henrich Kothe of the Knyphausen Regiment. Colonel Rall, wounded twice in the lower part of his body, died the evening of the 27th at the Potts house, attended by Medical Officer Oliva, and was reportedly buried in the graveyard of the Presbyterian Church.[74] Private Friedrich Marcus also died on December 27 and then Private Kurt Mensing of the Lossberg Regiment on December 28, followed by Private Friedrich Hartmann of the same company on December 29.[75] Oliva thought there were an "extraordinary number of wounded, especially among our Regiment." On the first day, he "was occupied attending to the wounds of Major von Dechow who was shot in the pelvis from the back, and with Captain [Alten]Bockum who was wounded in the head, and with the transportation of those others who were sent at once to Philadelphia." Only then was he "set free to attend from morning till night to the unhappy wounded who were lying in all corners." He began moving the wounded at once to houses near the hospital at the parsonage, but it took until December 31 before he had them all in the houses assigned for their care. Oliva reported there were "58 wounded privates, and 5 officers", and that "Lieuts. Zoll, Schwabe, and Sternickle had to be daily treated by me."[76]

The wounded Hessians were left with the few civilian residents remaining in the bleak and torn town, already marked by the "stripped and torn to pieces" houses belonging to inhabitants who had fled town, but then further devastated by the morning fighting. Some people had remained in town with their property and many took protections, which were ignored by the Hessians. Tench Tilghman, Washington's aide, learned that some people had sent their property to Philadelphia, believing that if Howe took that city his British troops would better honor the protections. The problem in Trenton had been that he "did not pretend to restrain the foreigners."[77] One casualty for the town was the destruction of the "elegant public Library at Trenton" and perhaps only some of the books out in circulation survived.[78]

Damages to the Presbyterian Church included the loss of "303 feet of board fence three feet high, 45 round posts, and rails, which was round the burying-ground, 11 panel post and 4 rail fence, 140 panes glass, large gates, hooks, and hinges, a silk damask curtain and hangings, a silver can with two handles, and a large plate." Damages done to Rev. Spencer's parsonage, while serving as a Hessian hospital, included "1400 feet of boards stript off the stable, 310 feet board fence, five feet high, 40 posts and rails, round the parsonage garden, 2 large front gates, hooks, and hinges, 1 well-curb, bucket, and chain, 1 table cloth and about ten yards diaper." Another loss inventory included "five hundred and twenty-four panel fence, four rails with post;" as well as "one hundred and sixty-seven panel of red cedar post and rail fence, good as new;" agricultural implements, wheat in the stalk and in the ground, cattle, furniture, maps, clothing, china, glass, three spinning wheels, provisions, and a "stable totally destroyed," possibly for firewood. Of particular grief to Dr. Spencer was the loss of his library, which included school books, a large collection of Hebrew books, a French dictionary and several works in French, Pool's *English Annotations on the Holy Bible*, and many literary and theological works. Spencer's mission on behalf of the Continental Congress to the southern colonies in 1775 had made him, according to his daughter, "very obnoxious to the British, who suffered his library with all the writings of his whole life to be burnt and entirely destroyed."[79]

Anglican Rev. Panton also suffered losses, including more than 200 valuable books taken by the Americans during their attack on the

Hessians, and a huge number of manuscript essays, sermons, belles lettres, criticism, and philosophical investigations either taken or destroyed. Isaac Pearson, who had served in the Provincial Congress, had provided lodging for Rev. Panton and was either "murdered," as his wife Elizabeth attested, or killed somehow within several days after the fighting. After the war, Elizabeth attested that their house was also ransacked by American troops. Only one carpet was saved, and she showed investigators "the remains of the boxes broken open & riffled by the Americans after the murder of her husband."[80] During the British and Hessian occupation, her farm wagon and driver were impressed into service for 15 days and 12 "fat sheep" were confiscated.[81] A number of people claimed they had fence boards torn down and burned, furniture broken up and burned, and clothing, household items, food, livestock, and various items taken away.[82] Just as Stacy Potts' house had suffered window damage, William Plasket had 120 panes of glass in his house broken by cannon fire during the battle. Undoubtedly, other houses experienced broken glass from the concussion of the cannon blasts, if not from musket or cannon ball strikes.[83]

During the last five days of December, the weather was generally fair, although temperatures were below freezing, and there was a bit of snow on the 28th.[84] Ice conditions on the river south of Trenton the night of the 25th had prevented Colonel John Cadwalader's division containing about 1,500 Rhode Island and Massachusetts Continentals and Pennsylvania militia from crossing over the river at Bristol to block the road to Bordentown and help surround the Hessians. On December 27 he crossed the river with his troops south of Trenton and sent Colonel Joseph Reed, with Lieutenant Colonel John Cox and Major Cowperthwaite, to Bordentown and then on to Trenton, where they arrived long before daylight on Saturday, December 28. At Bordentown, Reed found that von Donop had moved his troops to Allentown and saw "all the marks of a savage enemy." The inhabitants were "terrified" and "effectually broken & hardly resembling what they had been a few months before." Reed found Trenton "in a still more wretched condition" than Bordentown and wrote to Washington from Trenton "urging him to cross the river again & pursue the advantages which Providence had presented." Two parties of light troops requested by Reed marched into Trenton about 2:00 pm, and he directed them to pursue von Donop's brigade that had left Allentown that morning for Princeton upon hearing of Cadwalader's crossing to Trenton, harass their rear, and if possible detain them until other American units could join them.[85] Washington was concerned about the lack of food available for his troops at Trenton and ordered Thomas Mifflin to procure all the provisions he could, especially flour, and forward them to Trenton.[86]

About December 28, General Greene crossed at Trenton Ferry and took possession of the town.[87] Rev. David Avery wrote in his diary on December 29 that he crossed back to New Jersey at McConkey's Ferry[88], and Lieutenant James McMichael's company of the Pennsylvania Line crossed at Yardley's Ferry at 10:00 pm and camped out in six inches of snow with no tents or houses to protect them from the very cold weather. They broke camp at 8:00 am and marched into Trenton two hours later. That same morning, Washington crossed back to New Jersey and took post at Trenton while his army, baggage, provisions, and artillery (including the six captured Hessian cannon) crossed at McConkey's, Howell's, and Trenton ferries, although the drifting ice made the passage "extremely difficult and fatiguing, and the rear of the troops did not join him before the next evening." The weather was rather mild, making the roads very muddy. Washington established his headquarters at the house of fugitive Loyalist John Barnes on Queen Street very near the Assunpink bridge.[89]

Expecting the British would seek revenge for the capture of the Hessians, on December 30 Washington ordered all his artillery to be posted on Mill Hill, the rising ground behind Trenton Mills on the south side of the Assunpink Creek in Nottingham Township, with two cannon posted to cover the Assunpink Creek bridge. The troops formed in three lines behind the artillery, with the baggage wagons behind everything. Guard posts with a captain and 40 men were established on each road leading into town and the captains were ordered to keep mounted patrols out to two miles. Horses for these patrols would be supplied by the quartermaster department. Officers were ordered to plan out the areas to quarter their troops, keeping them together as much as possible. Everyone was to hold himself in readiness to move out at a moment's notice.[90]

Joseph Reed led a patrol of the Philadelphia First Troop of Light Horse towards Princeton and brought back a dozen prisoners and word of British preparations for an imminent attack on Trenton.

Lieutenant McMichael was pleased to see the prisoners who were aware of British strength and intentions to attack Trenton. James Wilkinson recognized that their information "left no doubt of the enemy's superiority, and his intention to advance upon us, which would put General Washington in a critical situation."[91]

Nathanael Greene wrote to Caty from Trenton on December 30, noting the importance of the battle a few days previously. He wrote, "This is an important period to America, big with great events. God only knows what will be the issue of this campaign, but everything wears a much better prospect than they have for some weeks past. The enimy are collecting their force at Princeton; whether they mean to attack us or to act upon the defensive." Things were turning around for the army and he told Caty, "I am well in health and hope to continue so. In a few weeks I hope to have a fine army together." He tried to raise her spirits by writing, "should we get possession again of the Jerseys perhaps I may get liberty to come and see you. I pity your situation exceedingly. Your distress and anxiety must be very great; put on a good stock of fortitude."[92]

With his army now assembled in New Jersey, Washington faced the problem on December 31 that many of the Continental troops would be free to leave the next day when their enlistments ended. By offering a bounty to Pennsylvania militiamen, he was able to convince a sizeable number to continue with him for six weeks, and through the force of his personality and the respect he had among the troops, along with a bounty, Washington also convinced many Continentals to stay. He demonstrated his trust in them by not asking these men to sign new enlistment papers. Men from the First Hunterdon militia who were out with the army continued to serve, no matter how long they had been out. They had little choice, because they were defending their very own homes and families.[93] General Knox, promoted to that rank by Congress the day after the battle of Trenton, addressed the troops and urged them to stay with the army a few more days, while General Thomas Mifflin came up from Bordentown to speak with the soldiers also.[94] Chaplain Avery wrote in his diary that "much pains taken to persuade ye continental troops to tarry six weeks after yr inlistment shall be out, wh will be tomorrow. Colo. Paterson's Regt. agreed, generally, to tarry, havg. 10 dollars bounty each soldier."[95]

Corporal David How of Colonel Paul Dudley Sargent's regiment wrote in his diary that they were ordered to parade with other regiments and a general asked them to stay six weeks longer. Although How says a great part of the army agreed to stay, he was one of the men who drew wages and food money on the morning of January 1 and in the afternoon set out for New England. How had been through a lot from April 1775 through the New York campaign, and at the Battle of Trenton took a musket and knapsack from a captured Hessian. Both items remained in his family for many years.[96]

That day at Trenton, Washington also wrote a proclamation addressed to "the Friends of America in the State of New Jersey" that called on the militia to join his reinforced army. To organize the militia, he had sent out several officers ordered "together with some other gentlemen of your State to call together and embody your militia, not doubting but success will attend their endeavours."[97] However, quickly getting out the militia from other parts of the state would be difficult.

That evening, Washington sent a force to Eight Mile Run about six miles south of Princeton to set up a blocking position to delay any British advance towards Trenton.[98] Washington had avoided an all-out confrontation with the British in early December when his back was to the Delaware River but now he appeared to be setting up just such a dangerous confrontation.

Twenty-year-old John Howland, a descendant of Mayflower passenger John Howland, was serving in a Rhode Island regiment camped below Trenton at Crosswicks where he had been convinced to extend his enlistment. The weather turned mild and a thaw began on December 31 when Howland's regiment was paraded in the evening and ordered to march, although "None of us knew where we were bound. We only perceived we were going westward."[99]

Chapter 8

1777
January 1 – 3

On January 2, 1777, twelve-year-old Nancy Shippen sat down at her boarding school in Trenton to write a letter to her mother, Alice Lee Shippen, the sister of Richard Henry Lee who had made the motion in Congress seven months earlier "That these united Colonies are, and of right ought to be free and independent States," and Francis Lightfoot Lee, who had joined Richard in signing the Declaration of Independence. Her father, Dr. William Shippen of Philadelphia, was serving with the Continental army as the chief physician of the Flying Camp. William and Alice Shippen's marriage connected two aristocratic colonial families representing Stratford Hall in Virginia and Shippen House in Philadelphia, and Nancy was being raised to be the belle of the ball in Philadelphia society. Shippen House was a three-and-a-half-story brick house with interspersed black glazed brick and white marble steps and trimmings, a typically opulent house of the colonial American aristocracy. One of the most fashionable schools for training aristocratic young ladies was Mrs. Rogers's School for Young Ladies in Trenton where Nancy was enrolled to prepare her for high-society life. The school had undoubtedly closed during the Hessian occupation but was now open again.

Young Nancy's letter to her mother was short, expressing how much Nancy missed her, hoped that her mother's health was better than when she last saw her, and noted that it had been some time since she had received a letter from her. Alice had been severely weakened the previous August by the difficult delivery of a son, who died shortly after his birth. Nancy wrote, "I am afraid by my not hearing from you that the distance has prevented your receiving my letters, the number being five." She closed by saying that "Mrs. Roger & the young Ladies present their compliments[.] I cant express their kindness to me." Finally, she signed off with "God bless you my dear Mamma & make me a deserving daughter of so good a mother." What Nancy did not comment on in her letter was anything about the sometimes tragic and other times glorious events that had taken place in and around Trenton during the past month, or how her teacher had protected her charges. Neither did Nancy mention that she was in imminent danger from the British army led by General Lord Cornwallis approaching Trenton at that very moment to engage Washington's army in a battle that could either destroy or add to the recent morale-raising capture of the Hessians.[1]

There was a major thaw in the weather on January 1, with low-40s temperatures in the morning rising into the low-50s in the afternoon.[2] While warmer temperatures were welcomed, the frozen roads and fields turned to mud, making travel both unpleasant and extremely difficult. One month earlier, Washington's defeated and crumbling army had retreated into Trenton where Washington opted not to make a stand with his back to the Delaware River. Major James Wilkinson felt Washington had placed himself in a dangerous situation by coming back to Trenton, seemingly in contrast to his usual prudence. He faced an enemy that until recently had forced him to retreat, put the river at his back, and "by this step he threw himself into a 'cul de sac,' with a corps numerically inferior to that of the enemy in his front."[3] Washington knew the British force was larger than his roughly 5,000 men; a mixture of veterans, recently recruited Continentals, and militia. His veteran troops were mere remnants of regiments, debilitated by long marches, hard battles, and great suffering.[4]

Hoping to avoid civilian complaints, Washington posted notices in the areas of New Jersey where American troops were located forbidding both Continentals and militia from "plundering any person whatsoever, whether Tories or others." The notices stated that the property of Loyalists "will be applied to public uses in a regular manner, and it is expected that humanity and tenderness to women and children will distinguish brave Americans, contending for liberty, from infamous mercenary ravagers, whether British or Hessians."[5]

He was much harsher towards those men who had joined the Loyalist military forces. Two Trenton men, Charles Harrison and Peter Campbell, who had left town to take commissions in the Loyalist regiment raised by Trenton's Isaac Allen, were back as prisoners of war and Washington wanted them "closely confined."[6]

Washington was still promising bounties to convince men with expiring enlistments to extend them. Robert Morris of Philadelphia sent Washington $50,000 collected on his own credit from his friends in Philadelphia and from his own resources to supplement money he had sent several days earlier.[7] Lieutenant Elisha Bostwick says, "by the pressing solicitation of his Excellency a part of those whose time was out consented on a ten dollar bounty to stay six weeks longer & altho desirous as others to return home I engaged to stay that time & made every exertion in my power to make as many of the soldiers stay with me as I could & quite a number did engage with me who otherwise would have went home."[8]

Private Moses Smith of the 26th Continental Regiment, who had helped capture 20 British horses after the battle of Trenton, also extended his enlistment for six weeks.[9] Thirteen-year-old fifer Oliver Corey of Colonel Paul Dudley Sargent's Massachusetts regiment, had been detached to serve as fifer for General Sullivan's Life Guard. For the rest of his life, Corey recalled that when Washington, mounted on his horse, made his plea to the men to extend their enlistments, he was near enough to observe tears on the cheeks of Washington and there was "scarcely a dry eye among the soldiers." In contrast "those who left the army for home were hooted at & covered with opprobrium."[10]

Thirty-one-year-old Dr. Benjamin Rush of Philadelphia, a signer of the Declaration of Independence now no longer in Congress, had offered his services to the army after Congress adjourned on December 12. He and Dr. John Cochran joined the army and were with the Philadelphia militia at Crosswicks. Rush described Cochran as possessed of "humanity as well as skill, and is dear to all who know him."[11] Rush has been described as "generous and idealistic to a fault, [but] he was also impulsive, opinionated, and filled with an amount of zeal and self-righteousness that taxed friends and family alike. His public and professional life was punctuated by quarrels, jousts and battles."[12] Just about a year earlier, he had passed through Trenton on his way to marry sixteen-year-old Julia at Morven, the Stockton family home in Princeton. Rush had attended and graduated from the college at Princeton before he was 15 years old and had known Julia since she was four years old.[13]

Rush rode up to Trenton from Crosswicks on January 1 to visit some of the Continental officers and went to General St. Clair's quarters at the Alexander Douglass house in Kingsbury near the Assunpink Creek bridge, where he spent a pleasant day with General Mercer and Colonel Clement Biddle, hearing details of the previous week's battle. He was impressed by their "highly cultivated minds" and Mercer's determination that "he would not be conquered, but that he would cross the mountains and live among the Indians, rather than submit to the power of Great Britain in any of the civilized states."[14]

That evening, Dr. Rush heard the news that British troops collecting at Princeton under Lord Cornwallis planned to attack the American forces at Trenton and Crosswicks. Washington called a council of war to determine how best to deal with the threat. The council could not agree whether or not the troops at Crosswicks should be brought to Trenton or be left there as a diversion to the British. General Knox suggested Dr. Rush be invited to the council because he was connected with Cadwalader's militia. Rush came to the council but did not feel competent to give military tactical advice; although he did tell Washington "that all the Philadelphia militia would be very happy in being under his immediate command." Rush then left the meeting but was called back after a few minutes and given a letter from Washington to deliver to General Cadwalader. Escorted by a Philadelphia light horseman, Rush set off for Crosswicks at 10:00 pm, negotiating the muddy roads on that dark, damp, cold night. Rush got to Cadwalader's quarters about 1:00 am and had him awakened. Cadwalader immediately got up, read the letter, and gave orders to get his brigade moving.[15]

Washington could not expect to defeat the much larger British force coming from Princeton, even with the addition of the troops from Crosswicks. He understood that his only chance was to delay and punish the British for as long as he could and then make them pay a heavy price to attack him on Mill Hill; i.e. make it another Bunker Hill. To delay the British, Washington sent out a force under General de Roche Fermoy which consisted of Fermoy's brigade, Colonel Edward Hand's riflemen, Colonel Charles Scott's Virginia troops, Colonel Nicholas Haussegger's German battalion, and two cannon under Captain Thomas Forest. They established a defensive post at Five Mile Run, a stream crossing the road between Princeton and Trenton, with pickets positioned ahead toward the village of Maidenhead, with orders to harass the enemy soldiers, slow their advance, and not allow them to reach Trenton before evening.[16]

The British relied on various Loyalists for intelligence on Washington's situation. On the afternoon of the Battle of Trenton, Pennsylvania Loyalist John Williams was summoned by General Leslie at Princeton and employed as a spy, going out at night and reporting each day. He went out the night of January 1 to get information on the advanced enemy forces encamped near Maidenhead, but was taken prisoner about midnight and carried to Trenton where he was immediately tried by a court martial, found guilty of spying, and sentenced to be executed at 10:00 am.[17]

After his all-night mission to alert Cadwalader, Dr. Rush got back to Trenton about 7:00 am. He recalled, "I went to Genl. St. Clair's quarters, and begged the favor of his bed for a few hours. Just as I began to sleep, an alarm gun was fired at the General's door. I started up, and the first creature I saw was a black woman crying and wringing her hands in my room. She was followed by Genl. St. Clair with a composed countenance. I asked him what was the matter. He said the enemy were advancing, and 'what do you intend to do?' said I. 'Why, fight them,' said he with a smile. He then took down his sword, and girdled it upon his thigh with a calmness such as I thought seldom took place at the expectation of a battle." Rush followed him out, mounted his horse, and met the Philadelphia militia just below Trenton and rode with them towards town. Riding slowly along with them he asked a militiaman how he felt, to which the man bravely replied, "as if I were going to sit down to a good breakfast."[18]

Charles Willson Peale's Pennsylvania militia company at Crosswicks began marching for Trenton at 1:00 am. He recorded, "The number of troops, badness of the roads, so many runs to cross, and fences to remove, make it a very tedious march. The sun had risen more than an hour before we reached the town, and afterwards, the difficulty of getting quarters kept us a long time under arms. At last we were provided, and had made a fire. I took a short nap on a plank, with my feet to the fire."[19]

Nineteen-year-old Private James Johnston arrived at Trenton from Crosswicks about daylight, and his Chester County, Pennsylvania militia company was ordered to occupy General Dickinson's greenhouse, the former jäger outpost.[20]

Sergeant William Young's company got to Trenton about 9:00 am after marching all night on the muddy roads and Young recalled that upon his arrival, "I was a good deal fatigued on account of the deepness of [the] road, and its being night I could not see my way, the moon gave some light, but it being on my back I could not see so as to get the best road." When he got to Trenton, Young saw the six Hessian cannon captured the week before and he called on Mrs. Brown, "the old Lady at whose house I lodged when I first got to Trentown, December 5." His company was also posted at Dickinson's greenhouse until the alarm gun fired at about 10:00 am and they went to pack up their baggage and get ready for the oncoming British.[21]

Sergeant James McMichael of the Pennsylvania Rifle Regiment wrote in his diary that "at 10 A.M. we received news that the enemy were advancing, when the drums beat to arms and we were all paraded on the south side of the bridge [over Assunpink Creek]."[22] John Howland recalled after marching from Crosswicks, "we found ourselves at Trenton, which we had left two days before. From the badness of the road, the darkness of the night, and accidents to the artillery carriages, or the falling of a horse, &c., we thus consumed the whole night in the march. We quartered in the houses occupied by the Hessians the week before. We had kindled our fires, got on our kettles, and were collecting from our knapsacks or pockets, a stray remnant of bread or tainted pork, when the drums beat to arms. Hungry, tired and sleepy, we swallowed our half cooked food, placed the camp kettles in the wagons, and leaving the comfort of houses which we had not lately enjoyed, formed the line for marching."[23]

Charles Wilson Peale was startled awake from his nap by drums beating the call to arms and paraded with his regiment at their alarm post. Looking about him, Peale was "greatly struck with the appearance of so fine an army. At least a brigade paraded in the same field below the town" across the Assunpink in Kingsbury.[24] James Johnston's militiamen at the Dickinson greenhouse were preparing breakfast when they heard the alarm, hurried back to town, crossed the Assunpink Creek bridge, and formed up with the army on Mill Hill. Johnston recalled Washington ordered about 12 pieces of artillery to be placed behind Trenton Mills.[25]

Young John Cowell had quite a case of hero worship for a family friend, William Morris, a twenty-three-year-old tailor and drummer for the Trenton militia company. One of Cowell's vivid childhood memories was "seeing Morris standing at the head of the main street in this city beating the troops to arms in consequence of the approach of the British army." Cowell recalled telling his mother "what a good drummer Morris was" and then following him across the Assunpink bridge to where the army was forming on Mill Hill and "being pleased with his dexterity as a musician."[26]

Captain Thomas Rodney of the Delaware militia had been called out at 2:00 am at Allentown and ordered to march to Trenton at daylight. He got to Trenton about 11:00 am and "found all the troops from our different posts in Jersey, collected and collecting there under Gen. Washington himself; and the regular troops were already properly disposed to receive the enemy, whose main body was then within a few miles and determined to dispossess us."[27]

Rev. David Avery, chaplain for the 15th Continental Regiment, recorded in his diary that when the alarm was sounded about 11:00 am the army was formed up on the south side of the Assunpink Creek bridge with Sullivan's division guarding several fording places.[28] Due to the alarm, Loyalist spy John Williams's 10:00 am execution was cancelled. Instead, he was marched with several other prisoners to Trenton Ferry, taken across the river, and jailed at Newtown. In all the confusion of the rapidly changing situation, his death sentence apparently did not follow him.[29]

Perhaps about the same time Nancy Shippen was writing to her mother, Henry Knox sat down at Trenton and, because an express rider was about to leave, wrote hurriedly to Lucy. After expressing his affection for her and the hope they would be together soon, he told her that "we are collecting our force at this place & shall give battle to the enemy very soon. Our people have exerted great fortitude & staid beyond the time of their inlistments in high spirits[,] but want arms & clothing." He then announced that, "It will give you satisfaction or pleasure in being inform'd that the Continental Congress have created me a Genl officer - a brigadier with the entire command of the artillery." He told her this promotion was "unsolicited on my part tho' I cannot say unexpected. - People are more lavish in their praises of my poor endeavors than they deserve. All the merit I can claim is industry." After asking to be remembered to his brother, he returned to recent events and lamented that the recent "attack on Trenton was a most horid scene to the poor inhabitants - War my Lucy is not a humane trade & the man who follows at such will s[uffer] with his proper demerits in another world." Less than two hours after writing his letter, Knox learned that the British were near and would soon test the American troops in their defensive positions.[30]

While people in Trenton, like Nancy Shippen and Henry Knox, awaited the inevitable arrival of the British they could hear the combat noises produced by the troops sent up to Five-Mile Run to delay the British for as long as possible. Just as Washington had been aided by the weather the night of December 25/26, the weather helped him again. The heavy overnight rains had turned the roads into quagmires. During the day, temperatures rose to about 40, keeping the roads and fields in deep mud and making life miserable and fatiguing for the men of both armies.[31] Private James Barnett of the Sixth Virginia Regiment had marched from Williamsburg to Trenton in September 1776 and then to Elizabethtown where his unit met Washington's retreating army. At the battle of Trenton, he had been with the advance forces under Captain William Washington. For the past two days, his unit had been posted at Maidenhead as part of the delaying force now slowly falling back to Trenton during the day.[32] The day-long fighting retreat must have been heard with increasing clarity and loudness in Trenton as the fighting grew closer. About half a mile from the first Trenton buildings on the road to Princeton, a last stand was made that included cannon fire and lasted for about twenty minutes. The British column then advanced relentlessly into the heavy American musket and artillery fire.[33]

As the British approached Trenton, both the residents and the American troops there prepared for their arrival. The civilians in Trenton, such as Nancy Shippen and her schoolmates, sought cover, and the American army consolidated its position on Mill Hill on the south side of the Assunpink Creek. When the slowly retreating American troops arrived on the outskirts of Trenton, they entered town with the British in hot pursuit.

General Wilkinson later remarked on the importance of the successful delaying action, saying, "If there ever was a crisis in the affairs of the revolution, this was the moment; thirty minutes would have sufficed to bring the two armies into contact, and thirty more would have decided the combat." The result would have been catastrophic for the Americans.[34]

Henry Knox's letter to Lucy left town about 3:00 pm and about the same time, he later wrote her, "the column of the enemy attacked a party of ours which was stationed about one mile above Trenton. Our party was small & did not make much resistance." Soon after, the British force, led by Hessian grenadiers and jägers, "enter'd the town pell-mell pretty much in the same manner as we had driven the Hessians seven days before."[35] Dr. Rush recalled "a brave and sensible American colonel" who asked his troops as "they came within sight of the enemy who they were. They answered, "Hessians, sir." He asked them *what* they were. They answered, "Men, sir;" and "What are you, my lads?" asked the Colonel. "Why, men, sir." "Then," said the Colonel, 'let not one man be afraid of another."[36]

The Americans continued to harass and delay the British and Hessians as they advanced through town. Henry Knox said "The enemy pushed our small party thro' the town with vigor tho not with much loss."[37] Hessian Colonel von Donop later reported, "in and outside Trenton we had to suffer a heavy cannonade from the enemy, through which however the loss is not great.[38] At some point during the day, Washington changed his headquarters from the John Barnes house to Jonathan Richmond's tavern on the south side of the Assunpink Creek bridge.[39] When British engineer officer Archibald Robertson arrived at Trenton, he observed how the Americans were positioned on Mill Hill and declared that "they were exactly in the position Rall should have taken when he was attack'd from which he might have retreated towards Borden's Town with very little loss."[40] Henry Knox described Mill Hill as completely commanding Trenton "with 30 or 40 pieces of artillery in front." He felt the position was strong, but also hazardous, because "had our right wing been defeated[,] the defeat of the left would almost have been an imediate consequence & the whole thrown into confusion or push'd into the Delaware."[41] General Mercer's brigade was at Phillips Ford, two miles above the Trenton bridge and on the extreme right of the army. Colonel Cadwalader's troops were stationed in a field opposite Samuel Henry's mill, about a mile from the bridge. General St. Clair's brigade and an artillery battery were on the high bank of Mill Hill just east of the Assunpink Creek bridge. The left was on the Delaware River and the troops had dug small earthworks on the ridge and across the road below the Queen Street bridge. A second line was placed behind this.[42]

John Howland's brigade was ordered to cross the bridge back into Trenton and march up the main street to provide cover for the retreating artillery and the other troops coming into the north end of town. When they met the retreating Americans, they opened their ranks to let them pass and then closed back up into a solid, compact column in the narrow street. The British pressed down a parallel street and poured fire into the American right flank from spaces between houses. At this point, according to Howland, "When what was now our front, arrived near the bridge we were to pass, and where the lower, or water street [Front Street] formed a junction with the main street, the British made a quick advance in an oblique direction to cut us off from the bridge." The Americans were closer to the bridge and avoided being cut off, supported by artillery fire from Mill Hill that caused the British to fall back.[43]

Presbyterian minister, Rev. John Rosbrugh, of Allentown, Pennsylvania was serving as chaplain to a Pennsylvania militia regiment that had rushed to join Washington's army. Although beyond militia age, he had served as a private, carrying his own musket, before recently receiving his commission as chaplain. On December 27, he had been at Bristol Ferry, probably waiting on the wharf, when he wrote, in a hurried letter to his wife, "You would think it strange to see your Husband, an old man, riding with a French fusé[11] slung at his back." Anticipating the military action, he noted, "This may be ye last letter ye shall receive from your husband."

On the morning of January 2 he went to Francis Witt's Blazing Star Tavern on the corner of Second and King Street, opposite Abraham Hunt's store, tied his horse in a shed, and entered the tavern for some refreshment. He left hastily when the alarm sounded, but found his horse gone. Hurrying on foot to escape across the Assunpink Creek bridge, he could not get to it and tried to ford the creek, but found it impossible. Turning to hide in a grove of trees, he ran into some Hessians commanded by a British officer. He surrendered as a prisoner of war and offered his gold watch and money to the soldiers, asking them to spare his life for his wife and family. The items were taken, but the soldiers prepared to put him to death. He knelt down under a tree and prayed for his enemies, who proceeded to make him a martyr with bayonet thrusts and sabre slashes. By tradition, the soldier who killed him ran into a tavern and "profanely boasted" to the woman owner that he had killed a rebel minister. When she strongly admonished him, he cursed her and shouted, "If you say another word, I will run you through." He then ran off and reported his actions to some British officers who applauded his deed.[45]

Ensign Robert Beale of the Fifth Virginia Regiment stated that when they had retreated to Trenton, a Major Forsyth ordered them to about face and move off in order. They had only taken a few steps when the word was shouted to "shift for yourselves, boys, get over the bridge as quick as you can." The men took off running under heavy British fire. Several were killed and "a very clever young man, who had but a few days before been made an ensign by Colonel Parker, carried the colors. He was shot down in the street with his thigh broken, but the colors were brought off."[46]

Colonel Christopher Lippitt's Rhode Island regiment was ordered to retreat through town without firing and take a position on Mill Hill. During the retreat, seventeen-year-old private Isaiah Crandall took a British musket ball in the back that knocked him to his hands and knees. The bullet hit his knapsack and put 33 holes through his folded up blanket, but a hard lump of bread stopped the force of the bullet and probably saved his life.[47]

With nowhere to retreat to, the Virginia brigade of three regiments, including Ensign Beale's company, "was ordered to form in column at the bridge and General Washington came and in the presence of us all, told Colonel Charles Scott of the 5th Virginia to defend the bridge to the last extremity." Colonel Scott, renowned for his colorful swearing, answered with an oath, followed by, "Yes, General, as long as there is a man alive."[48]

By one account, Washington, with a small detachment, then moved off a bit on his horse but turned back and looked at Scott and his men, appearing to ponder the importance of what Scott and his men must accomplish. Thinking Washington had departed, Scott told his men, "Well, boys, you know the old boss has put us here to defend this bridge; and by G-d it must be done, let what will come. Now I want to tell you one thing. You're all in the habit of shooting too high. You waste your powder and lead; and I have cursed you about it a hundred times. Now, I tell you what it is, nothing must be wasted; every crack must count. For that reason boys, whenever you see them fellows first begin to put their feet upon this bridge, do you shin 'em." Taking this in, Washington could not help bursting out laughing and when Scott saw him they exchanged "a pleasant glance."[49] Colonel Scott was known both for swearing and for advising his men to aim low so they would not miss the enemy completely by firing too high.[50] By another account, Virginia Captain Richard Parker was told by General Washington, "you well understand Capt. Parker that this bridge must be defended to the last extremity," to which Parker replied, "Sir, we intend to sleep on it."[51]

From their position in a Kingsbury field, Charles Willson Peale's company watched as the British fought their way through town and one of their cannon and a howitzer "played on the town."[52] Pennsylvania militiaman James Johnston recalled that about 3:00 pm, the enemy came down Queen Street, driving the Americans before them and inflicting casualties, while receiving heavy and effective fire from behind houses. When the British reached Tucker's Corner at the intersection of Queen and Second Street, they began to receive artillery fire from the cannon posted on Mill Hill, which caused them to recoil.[53] Colonel Nicholas Hausegger of the German battalion was taken prisoner, but it was always questioned whether he had actually deserted. Another British force marched rapidly down King Street, hoping to close off access to the bridge. They opened fire on the Americans at Front Street but could not prevent their crossing the bridge. The skirmishers who had been fighting all day to slow the British advance got across the bridge and joined the main army on Mill Hill. Crossing the bridge they passed General Washington who had stationed himself on horseback at one end where they were inspired by his display of personal courage and confidence in that place of exposure.[54]

The bridge over the Assunpink was now both the escape valve for the American troops retreating through town and the doorway for the British troops advancing on the American positions in Kingsbury and on Mill Hill. James Wilkinson recalled that the enemy "continued to advance until he forced our corps to retire by the bridge across the Assanpink, I had a fair flank view of this little combat from the opposite side of the Assanpink, and recollect perfectly the sun had set, and the evening was so far advanced, that I could distinguish the flame from the muzzles of our muskets." After this skirmish, Washington, along with Generals Greene and Knox, rode up to the advance party and thanked everyone, especially the artillery, for their services and gave orders to make "as obstinate a stand as could be made on that ground, without hazarding the pieces."[55]

Jacob Bottomer, a private in Colonel Hand's regiment, was wounded in the left side during the delaying action. His lieutenant immediately ordered some soldiers to bring him along and told him not to cry out. When they got almost to the bridge, he fell down and was trampled by an estimated 50 soldiers. After his company crossed the bridge and formed in battle formation along the creek, Bottomer came crawling along although very weak from loss of blood. His wound was thought to be mortal, but he was placed under the care of army surgeons and survived.[56]

The stone bridge was narrow and the Americans crossing it crammed together, giving the pursuing British a tempting target. John Howland was impressed that "the noble horse of Gen. Washington stood with his breast pressed close against the end of the west rail of the bridge, and the firm, composed, and majestic countenance of the general inspired confidence and assurance in a moment so important and critical." Howland crossed the bridge next to the west rail and at the end of the bridge was "pressed against the shoulder of the general's horse, and in contact with the general's boot. The horse stood as firm as the rider, and seemed to understand that he was not to quit his post and station." When Howland was about halfway over the bridge, Washington ordered his commander, Colonel Hitchcock, to form his men as quickly as possible in a field he pointed to on the south side of the creek on the Kingsbury farm. Hitchcock obeyed the order and then advanced his men to the edge of the creek, where they hastily built a temporary breastwork and forced the British to fall back and take cover among the houses in town.[57]

Delaware Captain Thomas Rodney wrote in his diary that "after sunset this afternoon the enemy came down in a very heavy column to force the bridge. The fire was very heavy and the light troops were ordered to fly to the support of that important post, and as we drew near, I stepped out of the front to order my men to close up; at this time Martinas Sipple was about 10 steps behind the man next in front of him; I at once drew my sword and threatened to cut his head off if he did not keep close, he then sprang forward and I returned to the front."[58]

Immediately after the last American troops got over the Assunpink bridge, Sergeant White's battery and all the other American cannon fired together on the advancing British columns. John Howland recalled, "the cannon which had been drawn aside, to leave us a passage, were again placed at the end of the bridge and discharged into the front of the enemy's column, which was advancing towards it; at the same time several pieces placed at the right and left of the bridge, with musketry at the intervals, took them partly in flank." Henry Knox later wrote that after the Americans got over the bridge, "the enemy

George Bradshaw's c1929 etching of the January 2 battle at the Assunpink Creek. (THS, Trenton)

advanced within reach of our cannon who saluted them with great vociferation and some execution." In spite of the concentrated fire, casualties on both sides were small. The enemy was unsuccessful in three attempts to cross the bridge or ford the creek between the bridge and river. The third time, according to White, "We loaded with canister shot, and let them come nearer" before firing together and making the bridge look "red as blood, with their killed and wounded, and their red coats. The enemy beat a retreat, and it began to grow dark." The cannon fire went both ways for about 12 minutes, and one enemy cannon ball killed two men on Mill Hill.[59]

Sergeant Daniel Smith of Stonington, Connecticut, serving in Lippitt's Rhode Island regiment, recalled that as soon as the Americans finished crossing the bridge, "the artillery which was stationed at the end of the bridge opened up on the enemy's van and swept them from the bridge as often as they attempted to cross with grape shot." Each time the enemy was forced back, "Genl Washington rode up and ordered the Army to cheer, which they did several times."[60] When darkness caused the British to call off the assault, Henry Knox wrote that the Americans continued with "a few shells we now & then chucked at them to prevent their enjoying their new quarters ..."[61] The exchange of artillery fire had been so pronounced and characteristic of the battle that participants often later referred to the encounter as a cannonade rather than a battle.[62]

Dr. Rush recalled that "in the afternoon a cannonade began in which several soldiers were wounded. All was now hurry, confusion and noise. General Washington and his aids rode by the Philadelphia militia in all the terrible aspect of war. Genl. Mifflin, in a blanket coat, galloped at the head of a body of Pennsylvania militia. He appeared to be all soul. I recollect the ardor with which he called to them to quicken their steps. His command was not without effect. They ran after him."[63] Rush observed that General Knox "was cool, cheerful, and was present everywhere."[64]

The cannonade continued at intervals after dark, and American artillery fire hit several buildings in Trenton. Charles Axford, Jr.'s home was damaged when at least one ball entered his house and destroyed a walnut tea table. By tradition, the building on William and Ellet Tucker's corner was struck by cannon balls and the courthouse and jail lost part of a wall. Jonathan Richmond's tavern on Mill Hill was hit by a three-pound British cannon ball that embedded in the mortar. Most of the British troops withdrew to the high ground on the Beakes farm just above the town, although a number of soldiers milled about in the town streets.[65]

Dr. Rush was introduced to combat medicine and found that "the scene which accompanied and followed this combat was new me. The first wounded man that came off the field was a New England soldier," probably Moses Smith of the 26th Continental Regiment, who had extended his enlistment for six weeks only two days before. "His right hand hung a little above his wrist by nothing but a piece of skin. It had been broken by a cannon ball." Rush took him under care and got him to a house close to the river that had been taken over as a hospital. Smith had also received a serious leg wound shattering his thigh bone from his knee to his hip. He recalled being taken to a house with other wounded men but that the surgeons, thinking he would not live, removed a large number of limbs from other men before dressing his wound. He did live and was taken to the Philadelphia hospital and remained there until discharged on April 1.[66] David Jackson, a private in the Fourth Battalion Chester County Militia also received a cannon shot necessitating the amputation of his left hand.[67] Private

George Tilson of the First Pennsylvania Regiment was shot through the left leg and the wound was so severe that he was still recovering in an army hospital in September 1778. As late as October 15, 1785, Dr. Bodo Otto attested that his wound would require a long time to heal, if it ever did.[68]

During the evening, Rush and Cochran, with several young men they were teaching, treated about 20 wounded men. Exhausted, they lay down on some straw in the same room as their patients. According to Rush "it was now for the first time [that] war appeared to me in its awful plentitude of horrors. I want words to describe the anguish of my soul, excited by the cries and groans and convulsions of the men who lay by my side. I slept two or three hours."[69] His experience at Trenton led him to study the effects of combat on soldiers. At the beginning of battles, he observed "thirst to be a very common sensation among both officers and soldiers. It occurred where no exercise, or action of the body, could have excited it." Officers, at the beginning of battles, even in very cold weather "felt a glow of heat, so universal as to be perceptible in both their ears." He found that soldiers bore operations immediately after battles "with much more fortitude than they did at any time afterwards." At Trenton, he noticed that Philadelphia militiamen, accustomed to city life, suffered very little illness when sleeping hungry and poorly clothed in tents, barns, or the open cold air and displayed "patience, firmness, and magnanimity." He could only attribute this patriotically "to the vigour infused into the human body by the victory of Trenton having produced insensibility to all the usual remote causes of diseases" and "an insensibility of body produced by an uncommon tone of mind excited by the love of liberty and their country."[70]

Cornwallis called off the attack at dark believing he had his enemy cornered and could easily dispose of him in the morning. He also needed to rest his troops who were greatly fatigued after their long day slogging through deep mud while constantly engaging with enemy forces. Both British and American soldiers made up fires and began cooking supper while sentries were posted by both armies within 150 yards of each other. Engineer Archibald Robertson observed the American positions and was one of several senior British officers worried that Washington was contemplating an attack on the weak garrison Cornwallis had left at Princeton. The British troops lay out at Trenton overnight and two battalions of light infantry provided a picket, without fires, to keep watch over the Americans across the Assunpink Creek.[71] Von Donop set light infantry and jäger pickets in town, while "the remainder of the troops were withdrawn to the hills in the wood, so that there should be no further loss through the fire from the enemy's howitzers."[72] Pennsylvania rifle Lieutenant James McMichael reveled that "our artillery fire was so severe, that the enemy retreated out of town and encamped on an adjacent hill. We continued firing bombs up to seven o'clock P.M., when we were ordered to rest, which we very commodiously did upon a number of rails for a bed. Thus my friend Capt. Marshall and I passed the night until two after twelve o'clock."[73] Captain Thomas Rodney's men retired after the battle to the woods, encamped, and set up fires. Rodney stated, "I then had the roll called to see if any of our men were missing and Martinas [Sipple] was not to be found, but Lieut. Mark McCall informed me, that immediately on my returning to the head of the column, after making him close up, he fled out of the field."[74]

Charles Willson Peale noted that it was quite dark when the firing completely ceased. One or two men of the Third Philadelphia Battalion had been killed by an unlucky cannon shot, and some men of the Cumberland County, Pennsylvania militia were also killed. Peale reported that his company "marched to the skirts of the field, grounded our arms, made fires with the fence rails, and talked over the fatigues of the day; and some, after eating, laid themselves down to sleep." Peale's commander, Captain Bernie, told him that he could not continue in command and had told Colonel Cadwalader that he wanted Peale to take over for him. Bernie had injured his leg some time past, and although he had not been able to march with the company from Crosswicks, he had marched with it during the day of fighting. Peale's first orders to his men were to take some of the baggage from the wagons and send the rest away.[75]

While the British rested and prepared to renew the fight the next morning, Washington held a council of war at the house of Alexander Douglas, where General St. Clair had his headquarters. Washington had abandoned his headquarters at Jonathan Richmond's tavern because it was within range of British artillery.[76] After receiving input from and having discussion with his officers, Washington decided to leave his untenable position and march the army overnight

William Pedrick's 1923 painting of the Council of War *at the Douglass house the evening of January 2 when Washington decided to march his army by a roundabout road overnight to surprise the British troops that had been left at Princeton. (Collection of the Old Barracks Association)*

by a circuitous route towards Princeton in order to make a surprise early morning attack on the British force there. This action avoided any appearance of retreat and it is possible that Washington had this plan in mind when he allowed himself to appear to be trapped in Trenton. The weather cooperated nicely by becoming quite cold overnight with temperatures in the 20s. The muddy roads froze into a hard, though bumpy and slippery, surface on which to march his troops and artillery the 12 or so miles to Princeton.[77] Three First Hunterdon militiamen, who were familiar with the route chosen, were interviewed and selected to be guides for the army that night.[78]

After the firing ceased, Sergeant White's men were "dismissed for an hour or two, to pull down all the fences we could find, to build fires with them - and get some refreshment."[79] Hugh Maxwell recalled that late at night, "An officer, mounted, and wrapped in a military cloak, was now seen silently approaching the commanders of regiments in quick succession. He whispered his orders in a low tone – the colonels started with astonishment, -- they looked – it was their general, and they immediately sent for their captains. Each officer heard the new order with astonishment, but to hear was to obey. The captains whispered it to their orderlies and in twenty minutes after it was communicated to commanders of regiments, the whole army stood upon their feet in battle array. Our tents were struck and our baggage wagons were ready for march." To keep the British unaware of the withdrawal, "The sentinels paced their rounds as though nothing was about to happen. The laugh of the relieved guard was heard above the din of both armies, 'all's well' rang above the night."[80]

Sergeant White recalled that the fires were kept going "to deceive the enemy; to make them suppose that we were there encamped."[81] Trenton militiaman George Yard, son of Benjamin Yard, was detailed to stay back with other men and told "to keep up the fires in order to deceive the British General and induce him to believe the American army was still lying before him."[82] Troops used fence rails to keep campfires burning brightly during the night, while fatigue parties created earthworks by the old mill and strengthened those at the lower ford. The noises from digging these defensive trenches were intended to give the British pickets, only 150 yards distant, the idea that the Americans were digging in for the morning's battle. Guard posts at other fords and the bridge were strengthened and maintained through the night.[83] Twenty-six-year-old Cornelius Wells of Smallwood's Maryland regiment had returned to Trenton that morning from his duties guarding the Hessian prisoners taken on December 26 and joined his company encamped on the Assunpink. After dark, he helped build "double" the usual number of fires.[84] Cary McClelland serving in the Second Pennsylvania Rifle Regiment under Lieutenant McMichael recalled they were ordered to build fires "about two rods apart."[85]

Hugh Maxwell later told how "fresh fuel was now piled upon the campfires – the sentinels were posted in advance – small parties were stationed to guard each ford – the cry, "all's well," the quick challenge, and the prompt answer; the tramping of a returning vidette – and the occasional tapping of a drum in the guard-room, were heard in our camp." From the British camp, "The noise of hammers – the clashing of the armorer's hammer, and the laugh of the artisan and pioneer, came over upon the night-wind and grated harshly upon our sensitive ears."[86]

Shortly after midnight, the heaviest artillery, baggage, and stores were moved out under a strong guard, including Chester County militia, to head to Burlington by way of Bordentown.[87] Charles Willson Peale felt, "by sending away the wagons, and parading at midnight, I really expected a retreat."[88] Sergeant William Young noted that, "as soon as night fell our people lined the wood made large fires, as soon as I could I came to them with the wagon, with the provisions and blankets, and staid with them till 12 o'clock then loaded our wagon set out and joined my two sons whom I left in the wood with some of our men." At one o'clock they were ordered to move out with their baggage to Burlington, which caused "a hurry skurry among all our waggoners."[89]

The officers and crew of the new Pennsylvania State Navy floating battery *Putnam* were with Washington's army and marched to Princeton that night. The men had outfitted themselves but when they marched to Princeton, they became separated from the baggage wagon that contained all their "cloathing and necessary's, save only what was on our backs." They did not see their wagon again until January 23, when they found many things missing, either from loss or theft. They petitioned Thomas Wharton, President of the Supreme Executive Council of Pennsylvania, for reimbursement to replace their lost items. They had individually borne the cost of supplying themselves and then had to replace these losses. The men suffered from lack of clothing during the winter campaign.[90]

Captain Rodney wrote that the orders were given about 2:00 am and when the army was put into motion, no one knew just what Washington had planned. Some thought they were going to attack the enemy in the rear after a short march, while others thought they were headed for Princeton. As Rodney wrote, "the latter proved to be right."[91]

At 1:00 am, according to Charles Willson Peale, his company "began to move, and directed our course through the woods, directly from the road, and after some time northerly. By this, I expected we were going to surround the enemy – but after marching some miles, I learned that we were going a by-road to Trenton [Princeton], marching pretty fast."[92] Pennsylvania rifleman Lieutenant James McMichael also recorded that "at 1 A.M. we all paraded and marched for Princeton."[93]

William Pedrick's painting of Washington Withdrawing from the Assunpink, January 2, 1777 *to march to Princeton. Some soldiers were left behind to keep the camp fires burning and deceive the British into thinking the army was still in place and awaiting the resumption of battle in the morning. (Collection of the Trenton Free Public Library, Trentoniana Room)*

James Johnston's company of Colonel Evan Evans's Pennsylvania militia regiment learned the army was about to move out and Johnston recalled, "Many of the soldiers thinking they were about to be led against the enemy threw away their knapsacks." General Washington came up and "inquired at the rear of the column, who commands here?" Major Bell stated he was in command of the rearguard and he "received orders to remain behind for two hours, carefully observing the enemy." Major Bell sent forward a party that included Johnston "to reconnoiter the enemy." As they moved forward, "they had a full view of the Hessians sitting round their fires smoking their pipes." They were challenged by a British sentry and Johnston "and the others dropped to the ground, and lay quiet until the centinel was heard to resume his walk. They then cautiously retrograded and made report. At the expiration of the two hours Major Bell proceeded to join the main army."[94]

At about 4:00 am, Dr. Cochran stepped out from his quarters but returned quickly when he found the army had left. He and Dr. Rush found wagons, put their patients in them, and headed to Bordentown guessing that the army had retreated in that direction. They heard firing, but were uncertain where it came from. When they heard about the battle at Princeton, they "set off immediately for Princeton and near the town passed over the field of battle still red in many places with human blood."[95]

Not long after Dr. Cochran discovered the American army had left Trenton, several militia officers and privates returned to Mill Hill after spending the night at houses of local people they knew. Expecting to fight in the battle that morning, they were as surprised as Dr. Cochran and headed off towards Bordentown, where they also heard the distant sounds of gunfire from the direction of Princeton.[96]

On the morning of January 3, two British officers came to the house of Samuel Tucker and asked for breakfast. They were "filled with astonishment" that the American army was gone and wondered how Washington could have gotten his army back across the river without being discovered. Just as Tucker poured them coffee, they heard loud cannon fire and immediately departed the house thinking that Washington had renewed the fighting. However, the cannon fire came from near Princeton, and the British troops soon marched off in that direction.[97]

After the British left Trenton, John Hayes, one of Rev. Rosbrugh's parishioners, buried his body somewhere in Trenton. Rosbrugh became an important martyr to the cause, and Rev. George Duffield, who saw the corpse before it was interred, observed, "besides the strokes which had been given him on the head with some edged weapon, he had been stabbed with a bayonet in the back of the neck, and between his ribs on the right side, which last appeared remarkably deep, and from which, even then, there issued a large quantity of blood."[98] Rosbrugh's body was just one of many human and animal casualties that needed proper burial.

In many ways, things needed to be put back together so the routines of life could return. Trenton had been physically damaged repeatedly during December and right up until the British left on January 3. William Richards's buildings at Lamberton had been occupied by part of the American army for use as barracks, hospitals, and slaughter houses. A reputedly accidental fire that day burned down the dwelling-house, destroying "a large quantity of mustard seed, some household goods, and a chocolate mill," along with some other things.[99] During the previous evening's action, a Continental army horse had been taken from in front of the commissary store near Trenton along with its bridle, saddle, and saddle bags. The saddle bags contained "between ten and twelve thousand dollars Continental Money, mostly in sheets of one hundred and thirty dollars." There was also some clothing and an account book belonging to Commissary Stephen Lowrey. A reward was offered for its return.[100]

John Howland reflected on the day's action and wrote that "on one hour, yes, on forty minutes, commencing at the moment when the British troops first saw the bridge and the creek before them depended the all-important, the all-absorbing question, whether we should be independent States, or conquered rebels! Had the army of Cornwallis within that space have crossed the bridge, or forded the creek, unless a miracle intervened, there would have been an end of the American army." Howland felt that anyone who doubted this did not understand "the state of our few half-starved, half-frozen, feeble, worn out men, with old fowling pieces for muskets, and half of them without bayonets, and the States so disheartened, discouraged, or poor, that they sent no reinforcements, no recruits to supply the places of this handful of men, who, but the day before had volunteered to remain with their venerated and beloved commander, for thirty days more."[101]

James Wilkinson summarized the significance of the January 2 and 3 actions noting that even though Washington had put himself into a seemingly indefensible position, "yet under the guidance and protection of that God in whom he placed his trust, he extricated himself from this desperate situation, by converting his fault into a 'ruse de guerre,' which dismayed and disheartened the enemy, and suddenly deprived them of all their acquisitions south of Brunswick." The Revolution had been saved from seemingly inevitable defeat and the people who had remained in Trenton had been part of the experience. While they still were struggling with the philosophical ideas and issues driving the Revolution, their most important questions on January 3 focused on how they would be able to rebuild their town and whether the military actions of the war for independence would continue to invade their daily lives.

Chapter 9

1777

At three in the morning on Friday, September 19, John Adams, attending Congress in Philadelphia, was awakened by fellow Massachusetts delegate James Lovell and told that members of Congress had been leaving town since a little after midnight. A British army that was threatening to occupy Philadelphia could arrive before morning, and there was not a moment to lose if they were to avoid capture. Adams and his roommate, Henry Marchant of Rhode Island, got up, sent for their horses, collected their things, and set off for Trenton in company with Benjamin Harrison, John Witherspoon, and some delegates from New York and New England. At Trenton, Adams drank tea at Rev. Spencer's and then accepted Samuel Tucker's invitation to lodge for the night.

In the morning, Adams breakfasted at Mrs. J.B. Smith's and "the old gentleman, his son Thomas the loan officer, were here, and Mrs. Smith's little son and two daughters." They had an "elegant" breakfast, including "fine Hyson [tea], loaf sugar, and coffee &c." Adams later dined at Rensselaer Williams's "Sign of the Green Tree." Williams had left the tavern at the ferry landing and moved his business to the house on the northeast corner of Queen and Third Streets.[1] Adams drank tea with Mr. Thompson and his lady at Mrs. Jackson's and afterwards walked with James Duane of New York to General Dickinson's house. They found his farm, gardens, and greenhouse still "a scene of desolation" nine months after the Hessians had left. Adams saw, "The floor of the greenhouse is dug up by the Hessians, in search for money. The orange, lemon and lime trees are all dead, with the leaves on. There is a spacious ball room, above stairs a drawing room and a whispering room. In another apartment, a huge crash of glass bottles, which the Hessians had broke I suppose. -- These are thy tryumphs, mighty Britain." Again, Adams spent the evening at Williams's tavern and slept at Samuel Tucker's.

Adams found Elizabeth Tucker quite outspoken, noting in his diary that she had about £1,600 sterling invested in some funds in her native England, and was in great fear of losing it. "She is accordingly, passionately wishing for peace, and that the battle was fought once for all &c." She also complained "private property will be plundered, where there is an army whether of friends or enemies. That if the two opposite armys were to come here alternately ten times, she would stand by her property untill she should be kill'd. If she must be a beggar, it should be where she was known &c." Adams observed "this kind of conversation shews plainly enough, how well she is pleased, with the state of things."

On Sunday, Adams learned that the flight from Philadelphia had resulted from a false alarm and that the British had not yet entered Philadelphia.[2]

After suffering through the Hessian occupation and two battles, there were more disruptions in 1777. The victories at Trenton and Princeton greatly encouraged supporters of the Revolution and as the year began, the Continental army was in transition and rebuilding. Men were discharged as their one-year enlistments expired, such as Joseph Killgore, a veteran of the Canadian campaign and the battles of Trenton and Princeton, who was discharged at Trenton on January 7. While at the same time, the army was enlisting men for three years, or the duration of the war, in continuing, new, or reorganized regiments.[3] Trenton officers commissioned in the 1777 version of the Second New Jersey Regiment included: Captain Thomas Yard, Captain Ephraim Anderson, Second Lieutenant Abraham Appleton of Nottingham, and Ensign Matthew Clunn.[4]

Through the winter and into summer, the main army encamped and reorganized in the vicinity of Morristown and Middlebrook, strategically separated from the British in New York by the Watchung Mountains. Trenton supported Washington's army as a military post with an important supply depot and Continental army hospital. People who had fled town in December began to return, including Rev. Spencer who came home in July after a seven month absence to find his house empty, damaged, and its contents, including his papers, burned by the Hessians.[5] The summer and fall British campaign to take Philadelphia brought American troops through town heading for Pennsylvania, and raised fears of British attacks up the Delaware as well as opposite Staten Island.

William Richards continued to supply the Pennsylvania Navy, and a number of local men, including merchant Abraham Hunt, helped supply the army at Morristown throughout the year.[6] Apprentice John Bell entered service in January as a teamster, driving the teams of his master James Jackson, carrying flour, provisions, forage, and other articles from Trenton to Morristown several times over a period of three weeks. He also collected hay for cavalry and wood for the soldiers from various places around the area. Nottingham's Samuel Wooley began several years of continuous service as a Continental wagoner bringing forage and provisions to the supply depot at Trenton or carting supplies to Morristown.[7] On February 6, the Assembly named Moore Furman as one of three men to receive clothing purchased for the Continental army and deliver it as ordered by the legislature.[8] Furman and Hunt furnished express riders and horses, lead, and cartridge paper.[9]

Trenton militiamen tried to carry on their normal lives, and on a snowy day in February or early March, William Robinson married Sarah Kotts, daughter of tailor Conrad Kotts, to whom Robinson was apprenticed. Kotts was against the marriage, but the ceremony was performed anyway by militia Major Benjamin Van Cleave, who was also a justice of the peace in Maidenhead.[10]

Washington expected the British to probe the area of Princeton and Trenton, so he ordered out parties to keep an eye on them. On January 5, General Israel Putnam ordered Major Aaron Burr to gather intelligence by crossing from Pennsylvania to New Jersey at Trenton and then proceed down to Bordentown. Putnam himself crossed to Bordentown the next afternoon and marched up to Trenton with about a thousand men, including several hundred Continentals and militiamen he found at Bordentown.[11] Several days later, the baggage wagons that had been sent south the night of January 2 rolled back through town on their way to rejoin the army.[12] Virginia General Adam Stephen was back in Trenton on January 8 where he obtained some intelligence from "a man from New York."[13] General Putnam took command of an observation post established at Princeton, and several local militia companies from Nottingham joined him in January. John Coleman marched from Nottingham Township in Captain Robert Quigley's company and served there for several months. James Fergus, serving in a volunteer Cumberland County, Pennsylvania rifle company, had marched through town the previous June and returned home when the company's tour expired. Called out again in December, he passed through Philadelphia, where he saw the recently captured Hessians and soon after arrived in an "evacuated & partly desolate" Trenton after the Battle of Princeton. The next morning, his company marched on to Princeton, where they served under General Putnam until spring.[14]

Trenton became a formal military post on January 16, commanded by Brigadier General Caesar Rodney of the Delaware militia. Rodney still suffered from the disfiguring and painful cancer on his face that had almost kept him from participating in the vote on independence, but he immediately sent out scouting parties to watch for British movements. Rodney ordered artillery Captain Samuel Hugg at Newtown, Pennsylvania to bring his five pieces of brass artillery to Trenton. Captain Isaiah Robinson of the Continental brig *Andrew Doria* at Philadelphia, offered the services of his men for any needed project and was asked by Lord Stirling to help transport additional iron cannon and ammunition from Newtown to Trenton Ferry and to fortify the crossing there by arranging the cannon to cover an American retreat or prevent an enemy crossing from New Jersey, either by boat or on ice.[15]

Rodney was responsible for expeditiously moving forward to the main army the many encamped troops consuming large quantities of food and fire wood. Upon arriving in Trenton on January 19, he ordered an immediate accounting of the number and condition of men in each Continental and militia company. Rodney ordered a troop of Virginia cavalry and four infantry companies to march immediately to Princeton and a full regiment to march the next morning. About 80 or 90 men at Trenton served as the garrison to guard the cannon and military stores. Needing to keep these men disciplined, Rodney established parade and guard procedures, issued provisions, and ordered captains to see that their men had good quarters and kept themselves clean and sober. Finally, observing how the people had suffered terribly from the Hessian occupation, he ordered captains to ensure that their men "do no injury to any of the inhabitants."[16] Describing the results of the British and Hessian actions at Trenton, Rodney declared, "Good God, what havock they have made. He that hath not seen it can have no idea of it."[17]

Shortly after Rodney arrived in town, his younger brother, Captain Thomas Rodney, while returning to Delaware on the road between Princeton and Trenton, met up with Samuel Tucker who informed him that Caesar was at Trenton and was well. When the brothers met in Trenton, Caesar tried to convince Thomas to stay and serve as his brigade major to help keep things under control. However, Thomas wanted to get home and left on January 25, noting that although "horses and wagons crossed the river on the ice yesterday the great rain that fell last night has broken it up and this morning I crossed over in a boat, a little above the island, opposite the town, and at the same time the last troop of Virginia Light Horse were passing over to the camp."[18]

A well-known politician, Rodney wrote to William Killen, Chief Justice of Delaware, on January 27, telling him, "I begin to play the general most surprisingly." But he added, "I would not have you suppose I mean the fighting general. That is a part of duty I have not yet been called upon to discharge. [Rather,] I was directed to take the command at this place – to forward the troops to the army as fast as they should arrive[,] always keeping sufficient for this post – since my arrival I have sent forward near two thousand." Through January and into February, Rodney ordered companies forward to Princeton and Morristown almost daily, including about 1,200 on February 7.[19] He also had to figure out how to deal with the people who had taken British protections although still supporting the cause of independence, men such as Samuel Tucker and William Trent, son of the town's founder, who was deeply involved in western lands as well as local interests.[20]

In early February, Rodney offered to switch commands with Philemon Dickinson, to allow Dickinson to be stationed in Trenton. He was not seeking a "fighting general's" command, but was aware of the severe damage to Dickinson's estate and his concern for his wife and children. However, no swap occurred and Rodney forwarded troops to Dickinson on the Raritan River, where he was very actively preventing the British at New Brunswick from obtaining forage. Rodney ordered the Trenton quartermaster to supply each company he sent with a wagon and four horses to transport its baggage.[21]

By February 12, Rodney expected to be relieved of his duties and wrote to Thomas that he had made friends in Trenton, both men and women, who "do everything in their power to make my time agreeable." He commented that, "I am certainly a man of consequence here, tho of ever so little in my own State, and they have got it in their heads, tho ever so strangely, that I am a gentleman as well as a Whig." Rodney left Trenton on February 19, the day after Washington wrote to thank him for his efforts in forwarding troops, noting Rodney's "cheerfulness to continue in service, though your brigade had returned home," and his acceptance of the call to Trenton at "the most critical period of our affairs."[22]

The wounded Hessians left behind in Trenton had been permitted to maintain their Presbyterian parsonage hospital facilities under their own surgeons, who unfortunately lacked suitable amputating instruments. Hessian medical officer Oliva helped arrange for the less severely wounded and sick prisoners to be transported on January 4 to the Philadelphia hospital. On January 13, Oliva reported 12 of the wounded had died, including Lieutenant Kimm, and there were still 28 wounded men and three officers. Major von Dechow was in critical condition because Oliva had not yet found the bullet that had "pierced both bones of the pelvis."[23]

Hessian quartermaster Muller was back in Trenton on January 10, sent from New York on a mission of mercy with six wagons packed with clothing, including boots, shirts, and stockings for at least 500 of the Hessian prisoners and a bar of gold valued at £900 to provide payment to the men. British officers from New Brunswick went to Morristown to negotiate for these items to be taken to the prisoners, and Washington assigned an officer and two dragoons to accompany Muller. At Trenton, Muller was blindfolded, brought before General Putnam, and reported he was "entertained very well by this general. After enjoying supper, however, we had to continue our march that evening still farther..." While at Trenton, Muller saw the wounded Hessians, which he numbered at 40. After delivering the supplies in Pennsylvania, Muller obtained permission from General Horatio Gates to take three non-commissioned officers, one drummer, four domestics, and three Hessian women with him on his return to New York and they passed through Trenton about February 13 or 14.[24]

Smallpox was rampant in the late 18th century in both the civilian and military populations, and especially in Philadelphia. As early as January 6, General Washington had decided to inoculate the men of his army to prevent its spread and decimation of his men. The threat from the disease was so great that he believed "we should have more to dread from it than from the sword of the enemy." The inoculation process was controversial, based on great fear of spreading the disease if those receiving inoculation could not be isolated during their recovery and receive new clothing. On February 12, the Continental Congress finally authorized Washington to determine the feasibility of such widespread inoculation.[25] Soon after, Dr. Bodo Otto was sent to Trenton, designated as one of a number of inoculation sites, to perform inoculations and take charge of the military hospital. It was unclear if militia were to be inoculated, but any Continentals who had not already gained immunity by surviving the disease were to be inoculated immediately at a place chosen by Caesar Rodney and Dr. Otto. They chose the barracks, very likely because it provided a means to isolate men during their recovery from inoculation. Washington's aggressive approach to inoculation likely saved his army and may have been one his most important military decisions during the war, in addition to being the first major public health initiative undertaken in the newly independent states.[26]

Patients continued to come and go at the hospital's other buildings. Fifty-six-year-old Aeneas MacKay, a veteran of the French and Indian War and colonel of the Eighth Pennsylvania regiment, died in Trenton of putrid fever on February 15 after enduring great fatigue and anxiety marching his battalion nearly 400 miles in January through the snow-covered mountains of Pennsylvania. When his depleted force arrived at camp in northern New Jersey, he and the many ill men were sent to Trenton for care.[27]

By spring 1777, Congress ordered that soldiers sick enough to require different food or lodging from that normally provided must be sent to a Continental army hospital. Trenton treated a number of these patients, including a group from Colonel Daniel Morgan's Eleventh Virginia Regiment from the spring into the fall.[28] On May 29, every sick soldier in Sullivan's division at Princeton who needed special lodging or diet was ordered to the Trenton hospital, "where no cost or pains is spared to make them happy & comfortable."[29] On June 12, the Delaware Regiment officers at Princeton also received orders to remove their sick men to Trenton immediately.[30]

When Samuel Tucker met Thomas Rodney on the road to Princeton, he was searching for his property taken by the British in December. He had been told that some of his papers were seen at Richard Stockton's house where Tucker found many of his bonds and mortgages in a desk drawer and was given a box of his papers that had been swept up by Stockton's "old negro man," after being spat upon and dirtied on the floor. Some of the deeds had their seals cut off and some had been picked up by local people; one woman gave him six very valuable deeds. Tucker was told that Lieutenant Hackshaw had sold his horse to an officer in Princeton and his phaeton had been driven on towards New York, along with his plate, his wife's jewelry, and other items.[31]

The General Assembly and Legislative Council summoned Tucker to Haddonfield in January to discuss a letter he had submitted regarding the loss of the public money in December.[32] Scheduled to appear before the Assembly on February 5, Tucker wrote to Speaker John Hart on the 4th saying that he had ridden out to the Abbott farm the day before to find out for himself the "full slate of facts respecting Lieut. Coln Abercromby seizing the unsigned publick money" and his belongings. He only found his slave's chest. The ride had been so tiring that he needed rest before attending the Assembly. He was, however, able to report a lower figure for the missing unsigned money, £5,818.16.3, and £250 in Loan Office and Maryland money, but he needed to get hold of several sums from various locations before he could make a complete accounting. Tucker sincerely wanted to explain everything and asked that Samuel Abbott and Randle Mitchell also be summoned in order to verify his statements and answer any questions the Assembly may have.[33]

Tucker testified under oath on February 14, answering a series of written questions based on the information in his letter. The Assembly wanted to know the amounts of signed and unsigned money, how it had been secured, why he had not taken it all to the State Treasurer at Burlington or across the river to Pennsylvania, whether he knew if any of the money was circulating, whether he had been asked by the British to sign any of the money, and if so, whether he had? The Assembly deliberated after his testimony and found no evidence that Tucker had been guilty of misconduct in the loss of the money.[34] The next day, Tucker appeared before the Joint Meeting of the Legislature and "proposed to resign his Commission as Second Justice of the Supreme Court of this State." He had been placed on a January 31 list of men who had accepted protection from the enemy and were no longer eligible to serve in public office. Dr. Isaac Smith was elected to replace him on the court. The Assembly resolved on February 17 that the affidavits of Samuel Tucker, Randle Mitchel, and Samuel Abbott concerning the loss of State money would be entered into the

Assembly minutes and the public cautioned against taking any of the missing money if found.[35]

Although life in Trenton was hardly back to normal and not all citizens who fled in December had returned, Trenton's inhabitants held their annual town meeting in March and again elected Stacy Potts as clerk and Charles Axford, Jr. as assessor. Rensselaer Williams was chosen to oversee the town roads. Benjamin Yard was elected a county freeholder and also one of the commissioners for appeals, along with Stacy Potts. Charity Britain's son, Isaac, was chosen one of the constables. Other business was normal, as usual mostly concerning roads and the poor.[36] Potts placed a notice in the *New Jersey Gazette* on May 5 that "some evil disposed persons, at this time of distress and desolation in Trenton, have taken the brass pipes off the two fire engines belonging to the Fire Companies."[37]

The First Hunterdon Regiment went through a major leadership change on March 15. Dr. Isaac Smith resigned as colonel after his election to the Supreme Court and was replaced by Joseph Phillips of Maidenhead, a prominent man with extensive military experience. Lieutenant Colonel Abraham Hunt also resigned. Like Smith, he owed his commission to his prominence and social standing. He was replaced by Joab Houghton of Hopewell who had served as a captain in the five-month levies under Joseph Phillips. New Second Major, Benjamin Van Cleave of Maidenhead had also been captain of a company in the five-month levies under Phillips. Major Isaac DeCou had resigned the previous July and Joseph Brearley of Maidenhead was now elected to replace him as First Major. Once again, DeCou was not a military man, while Brearley brought experience gained in the brutal Canadian campaign during the year he served as a captain in the Second New Jersey Regiment. These changes shifted top leadership from the hands of economically and socially prominent Trenton men to individuals with significantly greater military experience living in the nearby rural townships.[38] Governor Livingston also recommended to the Assembly on March 15 that the two Trenton militia companies be consolidated.[39] The companies must have become small, perhaps due to a combination of some men not returning after leaving town in December 1776, men joining the Continentals or supply services, and wealthier men paying fines rather than turning out.

Trenton became an important supply depot supporting Washington's army and before Caesar Rodney left, he ordered the competent and hard-working militia Captain William Tucker on February 7 to continue acting as Assistant Deputy Quartermaster (ADQM) and that the local wagon master was to follow Tucker's orders. The quartermaster position was only temporary, but Tucker was always contributing to the supply system in some way. Samuel H. Sullivan also served as ADQM at Trenton and Rodney ordered him on February 9 to provide a good wagon to transport the baggage of five companies of militia being sent to Coryell's Ferry.[40]

In addition to supplies for the army, Commissary Thomas Jones at Trenton received an order from Governor Livingston at 9:00 am on March 26 to send off a shipment of bread, beef, and pork to provide rations for 66 Loyalist prisoners for three days. Jones said he would have sent off the wagon immediately "if the Negro had not got drunk" and his horses run away with the wagon. Jones tried to retrieve the wagon from Bordentown, but some of the gear had been lost. He told Livingston he would have to send his own wagon because the driver remained so drunk and apologized, saying, "I thought it safe to send them by him, he deserves to be well punished."[41]

Through the winter, supplies for the army units encamped at Middlebrook, including the Trenton men in the Second New Jersey regiment, came through Trenton from the south. In early June, pork, bacon, corn, peas, and other foodstuffs were in transit to Head of Elk "and so across to Christiana Bridge, thence to Phila & Trenton by water" and then to Middlebrook by wagon.[42] Commissary General Joseph Trumbull estimated that provisions on hand at Trenton on August 8 included: bacon, pork, beef, peas, 1,000 barrels of flour, salted provisions, hard bread, soap, candles, spirits, etc., and part of two thousand barrels of herring.[43] A September 3 list of stores received at the Trenton supply depot included: over 600 barrels of flour, 64.3.6 hundredweight of biscuit, 29.1.25 hundredweight of bacon, 84 hundredweight of soap, 9,407 pounds of soap, at least 2,665 pounds of candles, 90 pounds of pork, 25 tierces of rice, at least 630 pounds of lard, ¾ bushels of peas and beans, 20 gallons of whiskey, 149 barrels of Indian meal, and 1 hogshead of beef. Under notes on quality was recorded "good for nothing."[44]

The supply depot required facilities and personnel to function properly. As the depot evolved, storehouses needed to be rented or built on rented land; pastures for horses needed to be rented; and offices for commissaries, quartermasters, wagon masters, and forage masters needed to be rented or built. Commissaries procured and issued provisions while quartermasters dealt with other supplies and also with transporting them, assisted by wagon and forage masters. A number of local men found employment at the supply depot along with men from other towns who came to Trenton. The patience of the supply depot officials was sorely tested, and there was periodic turnover because of the frustrations they encountered dealing with seemingly impossible problems. Two of the problems most frequently mentioned in letters were the need for money to purchase necessities and the lack of forage to fuel the horses. Several wagons and teams of horses had to always be available to move things around, and there was a continual stream of horse or ox-drawn wagons coming to the depot with purchased supplies or being loaded with supplies to take to the army. The depot developed primarily at Trenton Landing where shallops could land supplies coming up from Philadelphia. While obtaining sufficient quantities of supplies was a primary concern, another equally important and sometimes more difficult problem to solve was procuring wagons, horses, drivers, and forage to move the supplies where needed. It is difficult for us today to understand the huge number of horses required to keep the system going, all needing stabling, feeding, proper harnessing, and shoeing.

Places to slaughter and butcher the many animals needed for meat and hides became something of an issue. Benjamin Yard lodged a complaint concerning the use of his slaughter area. Alexander Chambers investigated and reported to Governor Livingston on September 9 that the available slaughter houses had been sufficient in the past, even "when there was more troops in town." He learned from Abraham Hunt that the butchers had "confessed there was room anuff[,] but they did not like to kill together." If additional space was needed, Chambers had been told that the slaughter yard used by military hospital commissary Conrad Kotts was no longer needed.[45]

Anticipating the opening of the spring campaign, General Benedict Arnold reported on June 1 that troops were being dispatched from Philadelphia with all possible expedition and "boats & men will be ready at or near Trentown, on the shortest notice."[46] Arnold received orders to take command of the post at Trenton, but ever petulantly vigilant that his honor should not be slighted, he protested that there were not enough garrison troops there to justify a brigadier general's command. Arnold explained to Congress in great detail why the assignment was inappropriate for him and hoped his acceptance of it would be favorably noted in the future.[47]

To his credit, Arnold worked diligently at Trenton and informed Congress of an enemy movement from New Brunswick. He set off for Coryell's Ferry on June 15 after receiving reports, which turned out to be erroneous, that the enemy was marching rapidly for that place.[48] While at Coryell's Ferry, he reflected on Washington's order to fortify and guard the fords and ferries on the Delaware and calculated it would take 2,000 militiamen, as a start, to cover everything between Coryell's Ferry and the Bristol Ferry. He drew up plans identifying locations that needed fortification, but also expressed to Congress concerns about calling out the militia during a busy farming season like mid-June.[49] Just a few weeks later, Arnold resigned his commission in a dispute over officer promotions and seniority but was convinced to withdraw the resignation and join the northern army in New York to help counter the British invasion from Canada under General Burgoyne.

Howe sent a force deep into northeastern New Jersey hoping to entice Washington out from behind the Watchung Mountains and into a full battle. The result was the Battle of Short Hills on June 26, followed by the British army's return to New York. Militiaman John Clutch of Nottingham was out on service and although not engaged in the battle, learned that his friend, Captain Ephraim Anderson, had been killed.[50] Rezine Anderson and others in Trenton received the news of his death within a few days. With the British back in New York, speculation resumed about whether the British would send troops north to assist General Burgoyne's movement from Canada towards Albany, or seek to take Philadelphia by landing troops somewhere on Chesapeake or Delaware Bay.

On July 18, Hessian First Lieutenant George Saltzmann of the Rall Regiment was still recuperating in the hospital and gave his "German Improved Song Book" to surgeon John A. Otto with an inscription marking the gift on the flyleaf. There is a family tradition that Saltzmann also gave Dr. Bodo Otto, John's father, a German sword. Reorganization of the army hospitals had encouraged two of

Bodo Otto's sons, Frederick and John, to offer their services as junior surgeon and surgeon's mate. Both were immediately commissioned on July 14 and assigned for duty at their father's hospital at Trenton, where there were "many men sick."[51] Some soldiers were sent from their regiments to assist at the hospital, such as private John Stuart of the Fourth New Jersey Regiment who was sent on command to the Trenton hospital from August 1777 through May 1778.[52]

In late summer, Dr. Benjamin Rush, now physician general, made an inspection tour of the Trenton hospital. He wrote a letter for the signature of Dr. Otto, addressed to William Shippen, Director General of Hospitals. The letter outlined Dr. Otto's urgent need for medicines and other stores for the soldiers under his care. Dr. Otto may have believed he was simply signing a requisition for needed supplies. However, Dr. Rush, who carried on a long feud with Dr. Shippen, kept the letter for almost two years and then produced it at a court-martial for Dr. Shippen, as evidence that the Trenton hospital had not been provided with adequate necessities.[53]

For the court-martial, Conrad Kotts, who served as assistant commissary to the Trenton hospitals from December 1776 until January 1778, testified on behalf of Dr. Shippen that his "constant directions to me were to purchase everything necessary and comfortable for the sick, and he furnished me with money from time to time, for that purpose." Kotts reported, "I was well supplied with sugar, molasses, wine, spirits, rice, and other hospital stores" and also that "Dr. Shippen visited the hospitals several times, inquiring into their condition and giving repeated directions to supply them with every necessity, as well as to see they were kept clean. I seldom missed inspecting once or twice a day, to see they were so." He concluded that, "Dr. Shippen always appeared to me as attentive and humane, to the sick under his care."[54] Shippen was acquitted, but the feud with Dr. Rush continued.

In early summer, Washington wanted to position some of his troops on the Delaware River to counter any British threat to Philadelphia, while still keeping units in place to guard against British movements from New York. On July 16, Washington asked Congress to order General Francis Nash to march his nine regiment North Carolina brigade from Philadelphia to Trenton and wait there for further orders along with Colonel Thomas Proctor's Continental artillery regiment. Washington wanted these troops positioned at Trenton until Howe's intentions were clearly understood.[55] Ten regiments with their requirements for tenting space, food, forage, and wood was a lot to inflict on Trenton at any time, but especially in its still-battered condition.

A British force of 1,600 soldiers boarded ships at New York on July 23 and put to sea. Everyone wondered about their destination, but Philadelphia was a strong possibility. Breaking up winter encampment, Washington arrived at Coryell's Ferry on July 28 and halted there. He had troops also at Howell's Ferry to the south and at Trenton further south. He wanted to keep troops in position either to defend Philadelphia or reinforce General Putnam on the Hudson River watching New York. If the British threatened Philadelphia, the officer commanding at Trenton would advance all his troops towards it.[56] Part of the troops at Trenton on July 30 were the detachments forming Colonel Daniel Morgan's rifle corps[57] and the Continental light horse.[58] Baylor Hill of the First Continental Light Dragoons wrote in his diary that on July 27 that they marched from Middlebrook to Princeton and then after dinner on to Trenton, arriving at dark. They remained in Trenton on July 28 and 29 and on the afternoon of the 29th marched down to Trenton Ferry where they encamped. Hill obtained a short leave on July 30 to go to Philadelphia.[59]

The North Carolina brigade arrived in town on August 9, encamped in the orchard on the edge of town and soon dug "necessaries" ordered "for the purpose of keeping the camp clean." On August 12, the brigade formed under arms at 5:00 am "in order to go through the manoeuvers in Brigade, when it is expected all officers not on duty will attend at their respective stations." Orders issued on August 13 required two men from each company to "clean the camp of everything offensive, and as the camp of the artillery corps hath been observed to be remarkably offensive, by throwing bones, and scraps of meat and other things about their tents, it is hoped they will pay particular attention to this order." The next day, the spread of sickness was noted, perhaps due to bathing in the heat of the day. So the order came out that in the future no soldier or non-commissioned officer was "on any pretence whatever [to] go into the water to bathe between the beating of the troop in the morning & the retreat in the evening." The same day, a new encampment location was laid out and occupied the next morning. The entire brigade received a ration of whiskey the morning of August 19, and the whisky ration was ordered to continue through the current period of "bad weather." Trenton's quartermaster provided a good pasture for the brigade's horses. Daily fatigue parties cut firewood.

Washington told Nash on August 21 to hold his North Carolina brigade ready to march to Princeton on Friday morning but not to leave until he heard from Washington. Nash found the rate of sickness among his men to be "alarming" and ordered the greatest exertions to be made in caring for the sick. On August 22, orders came down for officers "to leave any superfluous baggage they may have at this place." Private baggage had proven to be a problem on previous campaigns. When word was received that Howe's fleet was "high up in the north east part of Chesapeake Bay," and Philadelphia was indeed in danger, Washington changed Nash's orders and told him to take his brigade and Colonel Proctor's artillery south to Chester, by water if possible. Early on the morning of August 24, the brigade struck their tents, folded them up "neatly," and loaded them on wagons. Because of the large number of sick, all wagons not used for baggage were ordered to serve as hospital wagons and the women with the army were prohibited from riding on any of them. There were not enough boats at Trenton to transport the regiment so Nash secured wagons and proceeded by land. Nash had the boats at the upper and lower ferries divided equally and put in order for crossing his wagons, which crossed first, followed by the men in their order of march.[60]

The cavalry units still at Trenton received marching orders on August 22, and Colonel Sheldon's troop was ordered to go to Trenton with Lord Stirling and, after crossing at the ferry, camp three or four miles into Pennsylvania. The Delaware Regiment at Princeton struck its tents at daybreak on August 28 and marched to Trenton, crossing the Delaware that evening. Captain William Beatty's Virginia company came through Trenton and crossed at the ferry on August 30, continuing on to Wilmington.[61]

In addition to the Continental troop movements, the local militiamen continued to be called out so frequently to the east that some had difficulty keeping their economic lives in order. The militia law made it possible for a man to avoid military service by not turning out, if he was willing to risk a fine. Everyone, from company captains to the legislature and the courts, had to evaluate the decisions made by individual men trying to keep the economy going while also required to contribute military service, and fines were often reversed. At the

Hunterdon Court of Common Pleas held at the Courthouse in August, five local men successfully appealed their fines for failing to turn out with the militia on a recent call. David Pinkerton, David Pinkerton, Jr., and Benjamin Smith also appealed their fines and the court ordered that they be given time to prepare their defense.[62]

By early September, with the British army advancing on Philadelphia, all the military stores at the city were ordered removed by water to Trenton. However, it took "a great deal of time" longer than hoped and "the stores got much scattered."[63] Adding to the confusion, 600 Americans were wounded at the Battle of Brandywine on September 11 and those who could walk set off on foot for Philadelphia. Those incapacitated were transported in open wagons to Trenton and Surgeon John Otto accompanied one group of wounded men to his father's hospital. Regimental Surgeon Dr. James Tilton accompanied some wounded to Princeton and later claimed that their temporary quarters at the Trenton barracks hospital had not been cleaned and his patients came down with putrid fever. However, Trenton hospital commissary Kotts, along with John and Frederick Otto, stated the rooms had been cleaned and that there had been no putrid fever at the hospital for three weeks before Tilton's arrival. However, many of Tilton's wounded developed maladies shortly after arriving in Princeton.[64]

One of the Brandywine wounded was Major Joseph Bloomfield of the Third New Jersey regiment, who took a musket ball in the arm. Unable to get immediate medical attention, he rode alone for two miles until he came across a stranger who did his best to dress the wound and wrap his arm in a handkerchief. Bloomfield continued on alone, his arm swelling and painful, until he reached Trenton on September 13 where a surgeon treated him, as he wrote in his journal "53 hours after I was wounded. 20 hours of which it bled." Bloomfield survived, later became the fourth governor of New Jersey, and had a town named after him.[65]

The defeat at Brandywine put Philadelphians in a panic to remove their goods and themselves up the Delaware. Charles Biddle commanded a small armed brig whose owner decided to send it up the Delaware to Trenton. Biddle later wrote, "I took on board every person that applied to go up until we had as many as we could stow. Many of these unfortunate people who were leaving the city knew not how they were to subsist. Some of them had wives and children without a morsel of provision to give them." How many went as far as Trenton and how they survived there is not known.[66] But even Trenton may not have seemed safe enough. The military stores from Philadelphia were collected at Trenton by September 16, but Washington felt that Trenton "in the first instance, was fixed on through necessity, and conveying 'em there was better than to leave them where they were; but I am clear in opinion, that they should not be suffered to remain there a moment longer than can be avoided" and they should be sent on to Allentown, Pennsylvania.[67]

Congress joined the exodus from Philadelphia in the middle of the night on September 19. John Adams left hurriedly along with fellow Congressman Eliphalet Dyer of Connecticut who commented, "we were soon on the wing & made our flight with all speed to Trenton" and James Duane of New York also fled to Trenton where he wrote to his wife about the flight two days later. Congressional President John Hancock wrote from Trenton on September 19 that "I have removed my papers, & am now at this place where I shall tarry 'till I hear further." Prominent Philadelphian Jacob Hiltzheimer was also awakened and went to work dispersing his property, sending his public papers to Abraham Hunt in Trenton. Hiltzheimer didn't depart the city until September 24 when he traveled to Trenton where his family was "kindly received" by Hunt with whom he stayed until October 6. It is likely that many Trenton people opened their homes to Philadelphia refugees.[68]

While refugees were flocking to Trenton, efforts to protect important military items by removing them from Trenton to northeastern Pennsylvania were already underway. On the evening of September 22, the "Congressional Archive" arrived in Bethlehem from Trenton accompanied by 50 cavalry and 50 foot soldiers. Some 700 wagons carrying military stores from camp arrived at Bethlehem, Pennsylvania on September 24, were unloaded, and ordered to Trenton to bring up the stores located there.[69] Three days later, Robert Lettis Hooper, Jr., Deputy Quartermaster General (DQMG) at Easton, received orders to hire or impress 200 teams[70] and send them to Trenton immediately to bring the Continental stores up to Easton. He called on the Hunterdon County militia quartermasters to exert themselves to help him procure as many teams as possible. If teams could not be hired, at least 26 should be impressed and sent directly to the deputy quartermaster at Trenton.[71]

In spite of these efforts, Charles Stewart, Commissary General of Issues, arrived at Trenton Landing on the evening of September 28 and was horrified to discover "an amazing quantity of stores in the different departments unguarded on the wharf[,] in shallops and wagons." There were a number of people about, but no one seemed to be in charge. Stewart ordered all wagons and boats to the Trenton side of the river, but he did not have the power to hire any guards and expected it would be many days before enough wagons were procured to remove the most valuable commodities. He asked Governor Livingston to order a party of 100 or 150 militiamen with good officers to assemble at the Trenton wharves. This action might save the States millions of dollars and prevent the loss of "vast quantitys of powder[,] cloathing[,] spirits & provisions" for the army "who now are much distressed from every necessary."[72] Livingston told Stewart that he had so many demands for militia that he couldn't satisfy them all. But, this request was so important he would do what he could.[73]

After earning praise for his leadership in disrupting British foraging during the winter, Philemon Dickinson had been promoted on June 6 to major general of the New Jersey militia.[74] In September, there were calls to order New Jersey militia to Pennsylvania to help protect Philadelphia and some were sent. However, Dickinson was told that the British planned a movement against Morristown. He met with the officers of Colonel Joseph Phillips' First Hunterdon regiment, the only one he had at Trenton, and they agreed to take men to eastern New Jersey to counter this threat, if necessary. Dickinson had been reliably told that there were 4,000 enemy troops in New Jersey and "the apprehensions of the inhabitants are great." Dickinson wished militia from the western part of the State had not been ordered to Pennsylvania and believed the turnout to his call would be very small. Dickinson informed Livingston that all the Continental cavalry had been sent to Trenton and the enemy would soon know it, endangering the town. Things were so confused that when Colonel Phillips' regiment paraded the evening of September 15, not a single man from the Trenton company showed up and the whole regiment produced only about 200 men. Dickinson reiterated his impassioned plea for a new militia law that would "compel the men to turn out."[75]

About the same time, Dickinson learned that two men had been brought to the Trenton jail who were connected with a group of 70 or 80 "disaffected persons" marching from the upper parts of Hunterdon

County towards Staten Island.[76] This large group of "Tories & refugees" were captured and brought to Trenton. Captain Moses Estey of the Fourth Hunterdon Regiment was on duty at Trenton, unpleasantly quartered at the house of a baker who opposed the revolution and "was unwilling to give quarters or shelter to rebels." Estey received orders to march the prisoners to Burlington and ordered the two leaders to be handcuffed together and the privates tied together with rope around their arms. Estey ordered his men to load their muskets and told the prisoners that they would be shot if there was any attempt to mutiny or escape. After safely conveying their prisoners to Burlington jail, Estey marched his company back to Trenton.[77]

Congress sent three brass and one iron cannon to General Dickinson in September and although lacking any trained artillerymen, he gave certificates to men "who have some knowledge in gunnery" to raise companies from the militia to do 30 days duty in camp as artillerymen. He asked the legislature to commission proper officers to raise at least three artillery companies "to be called out as occasion may require."[78]

In October, Dickinson recommended three men as captains whom he believed would "do honor to the expectations." He personally knew two of the nominees as "men of zeal & proved spirit," but apparently without artillery training or experience, while the other had the required "character." One was Joseph Clunn, the tavern owner and militia veteran, another was Thomas Quigley of Nottingham. To celebrate the joyful news received from New York of Burgoyne's defeat at Saratoga, Dickinson ordered 19 cannon discharges, the militiamen on duty each served a gill of rum, and the town to be illuminated that evening.[79]

Ensign Clunn learned of his appointment as artillery captain while out on duty with Captain Tucker's company at Elizabethtown in October and immediately began recruiting volunteers. The men with Tucker were given permission to join the new artillery company if they wished, and Jabez Ashmore of Nottingham was one who quickly joined. Ashmore was an eager lad of 16 who had gone out in April under Captain Tucker as a substitute for Robert Emley, who paid him $75 in Continental money. Henry Chambers and Israel Yard were chosen First and Second Lieutenant, respectively.[80] Artillery required horses to pull the cannon, and Captain Clunn, along with his cannon and ammunition carts, brought to Trenton in December some "light continental horses which have been in service at Elizabeth Town." There was no immediate use for these horses, and Dickinson asked Livingston whether two of them could be kept at Trenton to pull cannon limbers for the artillery company. If so, Dickinson would appoint a proper person to take charge of them.[81] Taking command of the artillery company was not the only change in Joseph Clunn's life that year. He also removed his tavern from the Ship and Castle to a building on King Street where he operated the Alexander the Great tavern.[82]

Dr. Shippen probably visited his daughter Nancy at her school when he periodically visited the Trenton hospital and his letters reveal a great deal about her education. In addition to sewing, she was also learning French and he noted his pleasure with a letter she wrote in French "which was much better spelt than your English one, in which I was sorry to see four of five words wrong. Take care my dear girl of your spelling and your teeth." Her parents expected Nancy would learn to play the harpsichord, sing, dance, read classics such as Milton, Dryden, Pope, Cowper, Goldsmith, and *The Spectator*, and develop elegant penmanship. Also, her manners and behavior were to be developed to conform to a pattern set by her "tutresses" at school, as well as her parents.

Nancy's mother wrote her on August 31 asking her to "Tell me in your next how you spend your time. Ask Mrs. Roger where she supplys herself with materials for japaning, crowning, painting & if they can be got you shall have them for I would willingly do anything in my power that would assist in your improvement. Much depends on your being improved." Nancy apparently had a "pian[o]forte" at school, but her mother said "Yr matress not ready yet" and "Yr desk shall come when the matress comes."[83]

In spite of all the people fleeing from Philadelphia, Alice Shippen was still there on September 22 and wrote Nancy admonishing her for not writing, even in the midst of the dangerous events currently taking place. She followed with an apology, "I am sorry it is not in my power to get you the things I promised. It was late before I got to Philadelphia the afternoon I left you & the shops were shut the next day. I have looked all over this place but no muslin, satin or dimity can be got." She reminded Nancy to work on the pair of ruffles for General Washington that her father had asked her to make. She then touched on Nancy's education, "Needle work is a most important branch of a female education, & tell me how you have improved in holding your head & sholders, in making a curtsy, in going out or coming into a room, in giving & receiving, holding your knife & fork, walking & seting." She closed with, "There is an alarm here the enemy are said to be coming this way, tis lucky you are not with me," and noted that her uncles in Congress had left for Lancaster and she was leaving for Maryland. Alice was at Reading, Pennsylvania when she next wrote to Nancy on November 8 and indicated she might go to Virginia and bring back one of Nancy's "pretty cousins" to be a pupil with Mrs. Rogers.[84]

By October 1, Washington's concern was growing for the safety of the "vast quantity of stores of different kinds" at Trenton, warning that "if they are left intirely uncovered, it may tempt the Enemy to send up a light party to destroy them." He asked Dickinson to send as large a body of militia as possible to guard the stores until their removal. Washington feared the loss of these stores would be "irreparable" and that recent military activity on the river, including the capture of the frigate Delaware, made Trenton very vulnerable. Knowing it would take some time to remove the stores, he set priorities. The first items moved should be "military stores, articles of clothing and whatever else we are in immediate want of," and that can only be procured with difficulty. Provisions and other readily available items from the country could wait till last, "but not a moment should be lost, nor any industry spared to get the whole off, as speedily as the nature of things will permit." Wagons must be procured by whatever means available, even if not entirely according to regulations, because this was an emergency and "punctilios... must not hinder our doing whatever is essential to the good of the service."[85]

Washington also asked Livingston for assistance in securing wagons and calling out some militia.[86] Livingston replied that, in response to Commissary Charles Stewart's plea of September 28, he had ordered 100 men of the First Hunterdon Regiment to Trenton under Major Benjamin Van Cleve.[87] Things were better by October 6, when DQMG Jonathan Mifflin observed that the British might try to come up to Trenton but they would not get much because "all the valuable stores are gone."[88] Two wagon loads of ammunition had been sent to besieged Fort Mifflin on the Delaware River on October 1. But in the future, ammunition would have to be ordered directly from General Knox because "the ammunition will be removed some distance above Trenton."[89]

In mid-fall, Quartermaster Sullivan, was finding it "impracticable to procure the necessary supplies for the Army without the favourable interposition of the Legislature, or the use of military force." People were not willing to sell items to him at the low prices offered because "extortionate prices" were being paid on the civilian market due to inflation. Everyone was desperately hoping the legislature would do something to regulate prices.[90]

With the British in control of most of the Delaware River, Benjamin Ayres was ordered on October 14 to remove all sails, rigging, and stores from the Pennsylvania Navy vessels at Trenton. Any ammunition was to be sent to Commodore Hazelwood. However, in December, the Pennsylvania Supreme Executive Council had to decide where to lay up the Pennsylvania Navy vessels for the winter. The busy wharves at Trenton Landing, particularly those of Moore Furman and Abraham Hunt, and William Richards who was supplying the fleet, were considered the safest, and also the furthest possible from Philadelphia.[91]

After the Battle of Brandywine and then the October 4 Battle of Germantown, Dr. Shippen was greatly concerned about the wounded men suffering in the Continental hospitals, including the one at Trenton. There was a lack of clothing "and the covering necessary to keep the soldiers clean and warm; articles that at that time were not procurable in the country." He also believed the suffering was partly attributable to "the fact that our army was raw, unused to camp life, exposure, fatigue, discipline and great hardships; [and] from their being obliged to fly before an enemy in a cold and inclement season." In addition, "the sick and wounded were moved great distances in open wagons" from the battlefield to the hospitals. Presbyterian Rev. Elihu Spencer was appointed chaplain for the middle department military hospital on October 20 to help the patients with spiritual if not with physical comfort.[92]

The Assembly and Council held a Joint Meeting at Rachel Stille's tavern at 3:00 pm on November 1 and elected William Livingston to another term as governor and John Hart as Speaker of the Assembly. On November 13, Benjamin Yard and Rensselaer Williams were elected by the Joint Committee to be Justices of the Peace for Hunterdon County.[93]

The Legislature's requirement to swear oaths of abjuration to Britain and loyalty to the new State government put Quakers in a difficult position. Stacy Potts refused to take the oaths on religious grounds and was fined £100. Potts did not oppose the new State government but still had to pay the heavy fine after unsuccessfully petitioning the Assembly for relief in November. The owner of Trenton Mills, Quaker Richard Waln, refused to take the oaths in November. Unlike Potts, he was deemed too dangerous to remain at large. Willing to go with his family into the enemy's lines, he was given five days to do so.[94]

The New Jersey Continentals urgently needed additional clothing for the approaching winter so commissioners were appointed in each county on November 25 to procure and deliver blankets, waistcoats, breeches, stockings, and shoes to the man appointed receiver general, Alexander Chambers at Trenton. Items to be purchased or impressed were specified, and any tailors, weavers, fullers, or shoemakers put under contract to produce clothing for the New Jersey Continentals were exempted from militia duty while so employed.[95]

Soldiers from the First Virginia Regiment who became sick spent time in the Trenton hospital beginning with one man in June and then two in July, two in August, eight in September, two in October, four in November, and one in December. The two privates in July were recent recruits and both died that month.[96] Privates James Reagan and Benjamin Sadler of the same company in the Second Pennsylvania Regiment were in the Trenton hospital in July. Reagan returned to his company only to be killed at Germantown on October 4, while Sadler apparently was discharged in December.[97] Additional space and medical people were needed by November because there were 214 soldiers at the Trenton hospital including 112 sick and 102 convalescent. These included nine men from the Fourth Pennsylvania regiment, three from the Eleventh Virginia,[98] and three privates from John Stuart's company of the Fourth New Jersey Regiment.[99] One soldier was 20-year-old Sergeant Wardwell Greene of the First Rhode Island Regiment who had been wounded on October 12 in an attack on Province Island in the Delaware as part of the operations at Fort Mifflin. He had arrived at Fort Mifflin about October 1, and during the attack "received a musket ball which entered near his throat and passed through his left shoulder." He was carried off the field by his captain, the only officer in the company, and removed to the Trenton hospital where he stayed until December 1. After Fort Mifflin fell in mid-November, Surgeon's Mate John Dickinson came to the hospital to assist. The nineteen-year-old had signed into the Pennsylvania State Navy that spring and was discharged at Trenton after serving about a year.[100]

Colonel Lewis Nicola of the Continental army invalid regiment returned to Trenton on October 2. Invalids were men unfit for duty in the field but fit enough for garrison duty. Nicola had been having trouble controlling his men because his only officer, Ensign Walsh, was sick at Trenton.[101] While commanding the militiamen guarding the military stores in early October, Major Benjamin Van Cleve received a verbal message from the governor by way of Benjamin Yard requesting him to investigate damages done to Yard's smith shop and coalhouse. Van Cleve found the roof of the shop "torn off as high as they could get at it," the doors taken away and destroyed, and the coalhouse completely destroyed. Yard told him the damage had been ordered by Hospital Commissary Hugh James and that his slaughter house was taken from him and forcefully broken open by men of Colonel Nicola's Invalid Regiment.[102] Livingston quickly followed up and requested Hugh James to "acquaint me with the reasons upon which the said order (if any such hath been given) was founded." He wanted to know what extreme situation concerning the hospital facilities had caused him to commit "so injurious a violation of private property," but no reply from James has been found. Because of civilian complaints about property confiscation and destruction, Livingston was very concerned about even the appearance of abuses of military power.[103] Adding to the problem, some of the many American soldiers who passed through town stooped to plunder, such as when some soldiers broke a cellar window at Charles Axford's in 1777 and "carried off two quarters beef and other things."[104]

The "English Church," St. Michael's, also suffered physical damage in November: a large bell carried away; 24 pieces of wainscot pulled down and destroyed together with 24 pair of hinges; 12 common seats removed; 200 panes of glass destroyed when the building was being used as a forage house; and 2,000 feet of boards round the yard and 800 feet of new pine boards taken along with 400 bricks. The pulpit and a reading desk were damaged and one large door and hinges destroyed. While passing near the church, Charles Axford heard hammering and other noise. Curious, he went inside and saw men taking down pews and seats. Doctor William Brown, a deputy under the Director General of the Hospital of the Army, told him the church was being converted into a hospital. Axford was a parishioner with carpenter skills, so Brown told him he could take down pews and seats and carry them to an adjacent brew house for security and safety. However, they were later destroyed and burned by the army.[105]

Nicola had about 40 invalid men at Trenton on November 7 when he was told to supply a guard detail for the military stores at Trenton. Quartermaster Samuel H. Sullivan told him that, "A guard at this post is necessary for every department – for the forage, wood & other stores which are liable to be stolen every night. It [is] likewise necessary for impressing of wagons which upon an emergency can be got in no other way." Assistant Commissary of Issues James Paxton told him the same day that "I should be much obliged to you for a guard at the stores in Trenton as there is salt, soap and other things of value which require a constant guard."[106]

Benjamin Smith petitioned the Assembly on November 14, stating that he was "employed in making harness and other articles for the army, and therefore praying exemption for himself and apprentices from military duty." The request was considered but ultimately rejected. Stacy Potts also requested exemption from militia duty for the men he would employ at the paper mill he was building. His request was also rejected.[107] Frequent requests like these kept the legislature struggling with how to provide military protection and also create items needed for the military and the general economy.

Late in the year, Washington became concerned the Trenton hospital was vulnerable to raids from Philadelphia and ordered Dr. Shippen to transport all the sick from Trenton and other New Jersey hospitals to Lancaster County, to remove them from possible harm's way. Shippen asked for an extension of time because out of concern that some men were so ill that transporting them in winter would prove fatal. However, the sick and wounded were loaded once more into springless, open wagons for transportation to Bethlehem, Allentown, and Easton. Dr. Otto and his son John also transferred to hospitals in Pennsylvania. The move was made with less difficulty than anticipated due to the caring efforts of the hospital officers.[108]

At the close of the year, the British occupied Philadelphia and the Continental army took up winter quarters at Valley Forge. The people of Trenton wondered what the next year would hold in store for them as a military post helping to supply the army and care for its sick and wounded. They greatly feared the British would send troops up from Philadelphia to neutralize their ability to support the army.

Chapter 10

1778

On January 2, 1778, a year to the day after the British retaliatory attack on Trenton, four men, describing themselves as "some of the magistrates of this town and neighborhood," composed and signed a letter they felt compelled to write after they learned about a letter to Governor Livingston from Washington at Valley Forge stating his plan to send Count Casimir Pulaski's brigade of four Continental light horse regiments to Trenton for winter quarters. The magistrates believed Washington must not know that Trenton had not yet recovered from the military activity of the past 13 months. Although Washington told Livingston he was sending the cavalrymen to protect Trenton's inhabitants and the Continental supply depot, he told Pulaski it was to rebuild and get his troopers ready for the next campaign. However, he did encourage Pulaski to regularly send out small patrols, but not at the expense of damaging the health of men or horses, obtaining clothing, or keeping their equipment in good condition and repair. The magistrates feared that if the local people were required to supply shelter and forage for the cavalry mounts, their own animals would suffer, as would the many horses already at Trenton pulling wagons to and from the supply depot. The magistrates expected that life in Trenton would continue to be harsh because its location made it "so necessary a post and so much a thoroughfare" in the war.

To top things off, the Legislature was scheduled to meet in Trenton beginning in February, placing an additional burden on the town to provide quarters and food for the legislators plus shelter and forage for their horses. The magistrates noted that when the Legislature last met in Princeton, the session was cut short, leaving a number of tasks unfinished, because that town could not accommodate the needs of the legislators. This could happen in larger Trenton if it was overcrowded with dragoons competing with legislators for services. William Clayton, Benjamin Yard, and Rensselaer Williams of Trenton, and Benjamin Van Cleve of Maidenhead, signed the letter hoping they had proven their case and that Washington would send the light horse to a different post. They awaited his reply.[1]

The year 1778 brought no reduction in the need for Trenton's war efforts. The Continental army's winter encampment at Valley Forge required the supply depot to stay active. Even though most patients had been removed in December, the military hospital continued to treat sick soldiers, including several from the First Virginia Regiment. At least two men were there in January and February and one stayed until April.[2] There was a constant concern throughout the spring that the British would come up the Delaware River to attack Trenton. The British left Philadelphia in June and marched across New Jersey toward New York, fighting the Americans at the Battle of Monmouth on June 28 - the last major military engagement of the war in the northern theater. This was also the first full year that Isaac Collins' published the *New Jersey Gazette* at Trenton, providing residents with weekly reports on the military and political developments of the war.

About 40 newspapers were published in the colonies when war broke out at Lexington in April 1775, but none were printed in New Jersey where New York City and Philadelphia papers were readily available. Isaac Collins received permission from the General Assembly on November 5, 1777 to publish a State newspaper and printed the first few issues at Burlington.[3] Collins was born into a Quaker family in Delaware, served his apprenticeship, and then worked for a printer in Williamsburg, Virginia before moving to Philadelphia as a journeyman printer. He moved to Burlington in 1770 where he succeeded James Parker as New Jersey's official government printer. Samuel Tucker cast one of the few votes against his appointment by the Assembly. In 1771, he married Rachel Budd of Philadelphia, whose mother was the great-granddaughter of Mahlon Stacy, an early settler of Trenton. Collins moved his business and family to Trenton in February 1778, because the town was larger, economically more advanced, and better located on land and river communication routes. Isaac and Rachel had five young children (one boy and four girls) when they arrived in Trenton. Collins was much more than a printer, publisher, and bookseller. He engaged in a wide variety of enterprises, including a general store, at his printing office on the southeast corner of Second and Queen in the center of town. His office became known locally as the "Quaker Tavern."[4]

Collins petitioned the Legislative Council on March 12, arguing "that paper for the important purposes of schools, for printing the laws and votes, the *New Jersey Gazette*, and other publick business, is become very scarce, dear and difficult to be had." Without some encouragement from the Legislature for its manufacture, paper might become unavailable at any price. He stated that Stacy Potts was nearing completion of a paper mill but needed up to five workers to be exempted from militia service. The Legislature passed an act encouraging paper mills in general on June 20. The inadequate paper supplies forced Collins to announce in April that he could not take any further subscriptions for the *New Jersey Gazette*. He promoted increased paper production by encouraging "every family in this State" to save their rags, whose fibers were used for making the paper, and send them to him, the paper mill at Spotswood, or Anthony Armbruster in Burlington. Rags would be accepted at three pence per pound.[5]

In spite of the magistrates' plea, the light horse came to Trenton and by January 12 the officers were already complaining about a shortage of horses, only having stables for a quarter of the horses they did have, and having no hay available two-thirds of the time they had been in Trenton. Pulaski brusquely ordered the local people "to procure me every convenience necessary for the subsistence of my troops while they occupy this post." This did not sit well with people unable to supply the needs of their families. Ignoring the practical realities, Pulaski expected their patriotism would inspire them to "give satisfaction to those men [his troopers], who from motives of honour, sacrifice themselves to a cause so righteous as that of liberty." Trentonians probably wondered if Pulaski knew of their substantial sacrifices to the same cause. In stark contrast to the tone of Pulaski's demands, the Pennsylvania State Navy advertised in January that its commissary at Trenton was available to purchase beef, pork, flour, wheat, and potatoes from them.[6] Pulaski also expected the inhabitants would give him "the earliest intelligence of any movement of the enemy you may discover towards this quarter." Residents must have wondered why this was necessary if Pulaski's troopers were effectively patrolling.

Washington's instructions to Pulaski emphasized training both men and horses and establishing an indoor facility where training could continue in bad weather. Washington felt it was important "to inspire the men with an affection for their horses, and make them perfect in the management of them." In addition, Pulaski was told to train a troop of lancers and "the lances may be made according to your directions on the spot."[7]

Trenton also accommodated that winter about 75 "Navy" men furloughed from the row galleys of the Pennsylvania State Navy that were submerged for the winter in Watson's Creek near Trenton. Failing to understand that the sailors were not an organized military unit, Pulaski informed Washington on January 20 that "the men of the Navy behave themselves very ill" and their "commanding officer" should be ordered to agree with him on how to handle things. For example, he wanted sailors moved out of a house next to a large stable "in order that the dragoons may be near their horses." Pulaski believed everything should be done to accommodate his troopers, no matter who it inconvenienced - even schoolgirls. Dr. Shippen wrote to his daughter Nancy on February 9, just a couple of weeks before her 14th birthday, telling her he had "spoken to Mr. Barclay about Genl Pulaski & am in hopes no more troops or horses will be quartered on Mrs. Roger."[8] It was not until late April that the sick and baggage of the Pennsylvania Navy were ordered removed from Trenton to Lancaster and the idle seamen at Trenton were authorized for use "as guards in the interior parts of this state, or in assisting in the transporting over the greater rivers, stores & soldiers."[9] One galley sailor was a young Irishman, Mark Adams, who later served a short time in the Trenton militia company after he was discharged at Trenton from the galley service.[10]

By early February, Pulaski had dispersed his regiments to facilitate quartering and supplying them with forage and other necessities. Bland's regiment was quartered at Pennington, Sheldon's at Chatham, Baylor's at Somerset, and Moylan's at German Town. Pulaski remained in Trenton with just 40 men but still found it difficult to obtain stabling and other necessities. By March, forage had been exhausted at Trenton.[11]

Pulaski broadly interpreted Washington's instructions on procuring and maintaining equipment. Refitting his troopers required manufacturing a number of items, and several Trenton area men were exempted from active militia duty while working for the light horse. These included: a Trenton saddler to make up leather helmets and other items; saddler Benjamin Smith and his apprentice David Van Norden, to make harness; Lott Dunbar of Captain Tucker's militia company and his journeyman William Yard, to make a variety of items; saddler Stephen Burrows and his journeyman William Hepburn, to repair saddles and accoutrements; and Samuel Tucker, Jr., Thomas Hunt, and John Bellerjeau, employed by shoemaker Captain William Tucker to make and mend boots for the cavalry.[12]

Craftsmen had to be careful that they received valid orders for work to ensure they got paid. As late as October, Moore Furman, serving as Deputy Quartermaster General (DQMG) at Pittstown, received word from his assistant Peter Gordon at Trenton that cavalry quartermasters were contracting with local craftsmen to make many saddles and accoutrements without proper authorization. Gordon facetiously asked if the regimental quartermasters were "invested with such unlimited power as to order what they please made," and begged for instructions about how to handle the situation. In the same letter, he digressed to let Furman know that the sick children of Abraham Hunt were doing better that morning. Gordon was Hunt's brother-in-law.[13]

Supplying healthy horses to Pulaski's regiments was another constant concern. Trenton was designated in April as a depot to receive horses purchased for them and dispose of useless ones. On June 8 some horses being disposed of were sold at public auction at the Trenton market house.[14]

Trenton residents read on April 23 that Congress had agreed to General Pulaski's request to raise an elite legion of mixed infantry and cavalry based on the principals of the Roman Legions, whose "dress is calculated to give a martial appearance, and to secure the soldier against the inclemency of the weather and season." "Major" Betken's quarters became the recruiting station in Trenton.[15]

A number of local people produced supplies for the army. The army always needed flour, and on January 9 the Council of Safety exempted from militia duty for 30 days, four men working as millers and coopers at the Nottingham Township mill, provided they continued in the same employment. Several days later their exemption was extended to March 9.[16] A number of local people obtained, stored, issued, and transported supplies as part of the struggling supply system. Alexander Chambers, as Receiver General for Clothing, sent what clothing he had in February to headquarters for delivery to General Maxwell.[17] Clothing the troops for winter was always difficult, and on December 5 the Assembly ordered that linens at the quartermaster store in Trenton be sent to Princeton to be made up into clothes for the New Jersey regiments.[18]

Trenton resident James Paxton was appointed Assistant Commissary of Issues on September 8, 1777 and hired clerks and scale men, as well as coopers and bakers.[19] At one point, Trenton had three bake ovens, but baking was sporadic due to the periodic lack of flour.[20] Paxton convinced the Council of Safety in February to exempt from active militia duty a cooper, a commissary and his clerk, a clerk of the scales, and the superintendent of the bake houses.[21]

While making a February tour of supply depots, Washington's aide, Lieutenant Colonel Tench Tilghman, came to Trenton. Tilghman was thorough and checked quantities personally because he did not trust the accuracy of commissary returns. He sent off about 50 barrels of pork that he found and calculated the magazines then had 671 barrels of fish, 120 of pork, and 60 of bread. He arranged to send off the additional pork "as soon as the horses are shod." Needing still more pork, Tilghman scouted the farms around Trenton and encountered many farmers who had salted much of their butchered meat to feed their families through the winter and were not anxious to sell any to him. The area was exhausted of cattle and hay, although flour was plentiful and the only thing keeping it from the army was procuring enough wagons, horses, and drivers to transport it. Soon after, General Anthony Wayne at Mount Holly sent to Trenton 40 barrels of powder he had found and 150 head of cattle.[22]

While in Trenton, Tench Tilghman witnessed instances of ugly dissension similar to those arising among Whigs throughout the States, the result of mismanagement, corruption, and selfishness in both the military and civilian supply administrations.[23] Livingston felt it was "impossible for this State to cure the blunders of those whose business it is to provide the Army; and considering what New Jersey has suffered by the war, I am justly certain it cannot hold out another year if the rest [of the states] will not furnish their proportionable share of provisions." Livingston was "so discouraged by our public mismanagement, & the additional load of business thrown upon me by the villainy of those who pursue nothing but accumulating fortunes to the ruin of their Country, that I almost sink under it."[24]

Tilghman talked with members of the Assembly from every part of New Jersey and found that they all agreed "the failure in the

Commissary department has been entirely owing to neglect." Many of the purchased provisions had been consumed by employees of the commissary and quartermaster departments who "like locusts oppress the people" by consuming "what they gather up." There were too many employees and "there is not a cross road or a village of three houses but a deputy Commissary and Quarter Master is fixed there, to do nothing."[25]

Washington decided to make changes and appointed Nathanael Greene to replace Thomas Mifflin as Quartermaster General. Although Greene deeply wanted to keep his combat command, he finally agreed on condition that he keep his military rank and have two assistants of his choice, John Cox and Charles Pettit. Cox was a well-known businessman whose interests included the iron works at Batsto in New Jersey. Cox relocated his family to Trenton and purchased the home of Dr. Bryant, the Kingsbury manor house originally built by William Trent, and renamed it Bloomsbury. Trenton merchant Moore Furman became a DQMG when the new structure took over on March 2.[26]

The new supply department officials had to clean up the mess left by their predecessors, as well as build and oversee a more efficient system. The Legislative Council met at Trenton on March 5 and advised Governor Livingston of the many complaints that supply officials had been "guilty of oppressions, in seizing by violence what they might have peaceably procured either by voluntary consent of the proprietors, or in the mode prescribed by law." The laws had not been well communicated to either the people or the government officers, and it was hoped that things would change under the new leadership.[27]

Trenton was in the delicate position of being outside the immediate vicinity of Philadelphia, but not so far away that it was completely safe. However, the Council of Safety still ordered on March 22 that some cannon be sent to Trenton as part of removing artillery, ammunition, rigging, and sails belonging to the Navy Board of Pennsylvania from the enemy's reach.[28]

The Legislative Council also passed an act on March 24 to better regulate soldier quartering and the people of Trenton must have read about this act with great interest given the demands constantly being made on them. This law spelled out the prohibition against unlawfully impressing property or billeting soldiers in private homes. When a military unit needed quarters, the commanding officer was to apply to a justice of the peace, specifying the number of soldiers involved. If the local barracks could not accommodate them, the officers and men were to be quartered "in taverns, victualing-houses, the houses of persons retailing strong liquors, and also in barns and other out-houses fitting for the purpose." If the available spaces were not sufficient, then commanders could contract with the owners of houses and public buildings not in use and mutually agree on the number of soldiers to quarter in each structure. Building owners would be reimbursed for any damage done to property by quartered troops.[29]

Colonel Samuel H. Sullivan served as DQMG at Trenton until March 2. Even though he settled his accounts to January 1, 1778 with outgoing Quartermaster General Mifflin, there were still many unpaid debts owed to people who had supplied many necessities for the Continental army. In July, Sullivan was confronted daily by people presenting demands he could not satisfy. He had not been provided with money to pay these bills and the men now serving in the department refused to pay them. Sullivan requested that Congress either order the current department officials to pay the debts incurred by previous department officials or name someone to pay them. He was desperate to be "relieved from the imputation of dishonesty which ignorant persons" accuse him of and "from the danger of imprisonment with which he is threatened."[30]

Sullivan was succeeded as DQMG at Trenton by Major Peter Gordon, who had been serving from the beginning of the war in the militia, mostly as brigade major. He was 29 years old and the husband of Susannah Hunt, younger sister of Abraham Hunt, and father of a seven-year-old son.[31]

Transportation issues were never ending. Shortly before leaving office, DQMG Sullivan encouraged men to enlist for three years as wagoners in the Continental army. As inducement, they were offered a $20 bounty, £6 per month, "a suit of new clothes every year, and a great coat (if possible) and shoes or boots." Volunteers were scarce, so on February 16, Governor Livingston urged the Assembly to authorize impressing wagons and teams for 14 days or three weeks. The Assembly and Council approved short-term impressment, limiting impressed wagons, teams, and drivers to 15 days service at a time, and wages to be paid with "all possible dispatch, after the services are performed." The Council of Safety ordered Major Hoagland of the Nottingham Township militia to immediately impress wagons, horses, teams, carriages, and drivers to transport pork from several locations to Trenton and deliver them to Assistant Commissary James Paxton. The next day, the Council of Safety authorized Major Peter Gordon to impress wagons and teams with drivers to transport provisions from Trenton to the army; he could call on any militia officer for assistance if necessary.[32]

Impressment was rife with possibilities for oppression. Governor Livingston proclaimed on March 9 at Trenton that any impressment should be done legally and respectfully, and published his proclamation on page one of the March 18 *New Jersey Gazette* to help people understand the law and how it should be implemented.[33] Wagons could only be impressed for military necessity, such as transporting baggage, provisions, military stores, removing sick or wounded, and none of the carriages, teams, or drivers could be detained in service for more than six days at any one time unless the owner consented. Horses needed for express riders could be similarly impressed. Provisions for troops and horses, as well as firewood, could be impressed under equally protected circumstances. Any items taken and not returned had to be paid for, and the services of teams and drivers had to be compensated. Farmers tried to avoid officials who might impress them, disrupting Trenton's economy, so the Council of Safety reassured them that they could bring their provisions into town "without the fear of having their wagons, horses & cattle taken from them for the service of the army."[34]

Forage, "fuel" for the horses, was a major source of distress for Moore Furman and Peter Gordon. Both hay, also called long forage, and grain, also known as short forage, were needed in very large quantities for the many horses they were responsible for feeding. Grains preferred for forage were oats, corn, and rye, saving wheat for flour. Trenton had one of the 14 forage magazines in New Jersey. Forage Master Phillips, with an assistant and a measurer, oversaw a complex, convoluted, and constantly shifting operation, periodically employing men to store and forward forage, as well as cut straw, load and unload, and perform other tasks. The forage master kept a detailed written log of all forage received and issued, purchased forage of the type designated by the Board of War or commander in chief, and made a monthly report to the Board of War, the quartermaster general, and the commissary general of forage.[35] In late March, Nathanael Greene noted 40,000 bushels of grain and large quantities of hay within eight or 10 miles of Trenton, but also noted the drain on forage caused by

Pulaski's cavalry and the supply wagon horses, requiring that forage be drawn from Burlington or Monmouth County.[36]

Wagoners were still needed in the spring, and Trenton inhabitants read in the *New Jersey Gazette* on May 6 that the Continental army immediately needed men "well skilled at driving teams and taking care of the cattle." Interested men now only had to enlist for at least one year's service and should apply to the Wagon Master General at Valley Forge.[37] Because of the shortage of volunteers, militiamen had been impressed or encouraged to sign on for short periods of time. However, impressed men were sometimes then fined for not turning out for militia duty, even though they were performing a public service. Militia duty had also interfered with the ability to get supplies made for the army, because the craftsmen making various items were called away for militia duty so often. In late May, Governor Livingston requested changes in the militia law to exempt men from active militia duty while serving as wagoners or making military supplies.[38]

The nature of the war greatly diversified the tasks given militiamen, several of which brought them to Trenton. The Council of Safety directed Colonel Bowes Reed on February 28 to send to Trenton, under proper guard, all the prisoners at Burlington charged with trading with the enemy or going into enemy lines without proper passports and the militia guards needed accommodations at local taverns such as Williams's.[39] Two classes[40] of Colonel Phillips' First Hunterdon Regiment were diverted from heading east towards Elizabethtown for their monthly tour, to be part of a 100-man guard for the Legislature while it sat at Trenton. Throughout March, local militiamen were stationed at Trenton as express riders for the Council of Safety and at the end of March, the Assembly resolved that the governor could call out six light horse and six foot militia as a personal guard when and where he thought it was necessary.[41]

The fears of British incursions from Philadelphia kept local militiamen ordered out as individuals to guard various Delaware River crossings and militia companies passed through town on their way to areas south of Trenton. Trenton residents became used to hearing about British forays in Bucks County, Pennsylvania just across the Delaware River from them.[42] On March 21, Captain Clunn's artillery company was ordered south to Haddonfield to assist Colonel Joseph Ellis' militia. However, because the area was so "miserably infested with Tories," Ellis wrote that it was not safe for Clunn to come until the slowly arriving militia had sufficient numbers to support him.[43]

In May, everyone expected the British to leave Philadelphia soon, with Trenton as a possible target. First Hunterdon militiamen, including Captain Tucker's company, were stationed at and just south of Lamberton to watch for enemy movements on the river.[44] Captain Robert Quigley's Nottingham company guarded the public stores and prisoners at Trenton for 54 days in April, May, and June. On April 1, the Council of Safety ordered Captain Tucker to supply 150 cartridges for use by Quigley's guard. Quigley optimistically promised to return them "within a month." Shortly after, Quigley was ordered to remove some prisoners to Princeton.[45] Captain John Mott led a company on a scouting patrol to the Bordentown area and in the words of Maidenhead militiaman John V. K. Taylor, they "scouted up and down the River watching the motion of the enemy and took up the bridges between Burden Town [Bordentown] & Trenton in order to prevent the enemy from crossing & flung up redoubts between said towns." Other men helped remove military prisoners from Trenton to Easton.[46]

The strain on militiamen was great, and Trenton men continued to appeal fines for not turning out for active militia duty. At the May term of the Hunterdon Court of Common Pleas, several men, including John Bellerjeau, John Howell, William Robinson, Samuel Bellerjeau, and William Rose, appealed their fines for not turning out the previous November. After hearing their appeals, the court ordered their fines to be repaid.[47] For Quakers taking their religious exemption of militia service, paying the legislated fee in lieu of militia duty was a problem. On May 4, the Burlington Monthly Meeting heard a report that Trenton printer Isaac Collins had "transgressed the rules" of the Quakers by effectively paying a fine "in lieu of personal service in the militia" for which he had been asked to account several times and had "not cleared himself thereof to satisfaction." He was disowned by the Meeting in September and refused his right to appeal, remaining an outsider for almost 10 years.[48]

Lacking sufficient recruits to fill the New Jersey Continental regiments, the Legislature authorized drafting men from the militia. In April and May, Benjamin Yard and Rensselaer Williams served on a commission to draft 29 recruits from the First Hunterdon Regiment. The regiment was divided into 29 classes of 18 men each. Each class had to provide one man; a volunteer from the class, someone hired by the class, or a man chosen by lot from the 18 men in the class. At least one man from Trenton, twenty-year-old John Alcott, was one of the men recruited.[49]

The Assembly and Legislative Council began sessions at Trenton on February 16, after a weather delay, and as usual requested Rev. Spencer to attend each morning to open meetings with prayer.[50] A committee that had been formed to investigate the papers lost by Samuel Tucker in 1776 reported that the papers probably included lists of suspected Loyalists who gave their parole and submitted bonds for good behavior. The committee found no clear order for who was responsible for receiving these papers but believed it would have been Tucker as the President of the Provincial Congress. They could not find that he had accounted for any of the papers.[51] Tucker appeared before the Council of Safety on March 10 and took the oaths of abjuration and allegiance, as prescribed by law.[52]

The Council of Safety met in Trenton during the winter and brought a number of people to town charged with damaging the patriot cause by selling items at higher than set prices, trading with the enemy, or enlisting in the service of the enemy. On February 26, four British army deserters were brought before the Council and it was agreed to turn them over to General Pulaski and give them 60 dollars for the arms they brought over from the enemy. Three additional British deserters came before the Council on March 1 and were sent on to army headquarters.[53]

Concern for the vulnerability of Trenton caused the Council of Safety and the Assembly to move their meetings to Princeton and then Morristown.[54] The Assembly formed a committee on April 13 to settle the accounts of Alexander Chambers, William Tucker, Abraham Hunt, and Joseph Ellis, commissioners appointed by the Provincial Congress for purchasing arms and military stores. Tucker and Chambers produced their accounts of purchases and disbursements, but few vouchers, because many had been taken by the enemy. Some of the vouchers could be replaced by applying to the people involved, but it would take time. The committee recommended to postpone settlement in order to achieve a more complete accounting.[55]

Fears of an attack on Trenton were not unfounded. A large British force carried by 20 to 30 flat-bottomed boats sailed up the Delaware from Philadelphia in early May, intent on destroying ships and rebel property near the river as far up as Trenton. After destroying vessels and several houses at Bordentown, the flotilla continued up river to Biles Island where it spent the night. General Dickinson ordered his small force of militiamen at Lamberton to keep more fires than needed going all night, to give the impression he had a larger force. When the British advanced on the morning of May 8, Dickinson ordered Captain Clunn's two field pieces to the edge of the river, where they exchanged shots with the British galleys while Dickinson kept the militia "paraded to the most advantage on the hill."[56] Hopewell militiaman Benjamin Titus of Clunn's artillery company recalled, "We got down on the bank with our two four pounders [and] fired at them as they came up, with good success. They shot at us but couldn't bring their guns to bear & fired over our heads. We drove them to the Pennsylvania side, and they soon went back" down the river. James Bowen from Trenton reported that the artillery "did good execution and hulled some of the enemies boats as they were attempting to get up to Lamberton." Alexander Douglass of Nottingham could "hear the shot strike very distinctly against a galley," while militiaman John Borrows saw a galley that ran aground but floated free so that the British "pushed her down the river."[57] A week later, news of the declaration of war by France against England was celebrated in Trenton with an illumination on Friday evening May 15.[58]

By mid-May, Washington at Valley Forge knew the British were preparing to leave Philadelphia and return to New York. He instructed Nathanael Greene to "immediately have the boats on the Delaware inspected and got ready in all respects to transport the army across" at Coryell's Ferry. Militiamen from the Third Hunterdon Regiment, in whose territory Coryell's Ferry was located, came down to Trenton to take boats up to Coryell's.[59]

General Dickinson commanded several militia regiments at Trenton by June 1 and ordered guard posts set up with the main guard at the courthouse, a second post at Trenton Ferry, and a third post at the Lower Ferry at Lamberton. Dickinson ordered regimental commanders to establish parade grounds and "exercise their men, morning and afternoon and practice them in wheeling, marching, advancing in columns, & quick fireings – they will be particularly attentive to their mens arms." He instructed regimental adjutants to ensure that their drummers and fifers "attend their duty" and make sure their men assigned for guard duty turned out each morning at 9:00 am on the general parade ground "just above Head Quarters" and submit their returns. Dickinson had to remind the officers of the day to "pay particular attention, to the guards, & see they challenge properly."[60]

Dickinson ordered regimental commanders to furnish their men with provisions for three days and make an immediate report on the ammunition needed to bring their men's cartridge boxes up to full capacity. To stop unnecessary musket firing, Dickinson made soldiers accountable for the ammunition cartridges they received from the commissary of military stores. When discharged from his tour of duty, each man would return unused cartridges to the Commissary and any missing cartridge not "expended in actual service" would result in a deduction from their pay.[61]

Colonel Joseph Phillips of Maidenhead had served with British engineers during the French and Indian War, and Dickinson put him in charge of building redoubts at Lamberton. Each day, a work party, consisting of one junior officer and 20 privates, worked for him on the redoubts. A second fatigue party of four privates split wood at the baker's and two men baked biscuits. Beginning June 9, the regimental adjutants were ordered to assign any man without a musket to the work party at the redoubts. Enough men lacked muskets that a few days later only unarmed men were to be assigned to it.[62]

The militia turnout was weak in numbers and slow, causing Dickinson to combine incomplete battalions "until further orders." Troops always brought wagons that often led to crowding, so Dickinson ordered militia wagons and horses to be kept in the enclosed quartermaster's lot, which was part of the supply depot, to prevent civilian complaints. Officers neglecting their duty caused Dickinson to command adjutants on June 8 to submit regular returns "or they will most certainly be put under arrest, which would be so great a reflection upon them, that it would give the General pain, to inflict a just punishment - but order must take place." He had to continually remind his battalion commanders to "have their mens arms put into the best order & see them supplied with ammunition."[63]

Nancy Shippen received a letter at school dated June 7 from her father at Valley Forge explaining that, "An expectation of being in Philadelphia very soon has prevented your Mamma's & my visiting you at Trenton which we are very desirous of doing, ever since we have heard you behaved so well. The enemy are preparing to leave

Philadelphia and 'tis thought here they will go tomorrow. If so, you may expect to see us in a few days. Many people from the city say all the ships are gone down below the Cheveaux de Frize[64], & that many of the inhabitants are gone with them. Your Mamma has bought you many clever things for ye summer & longs to see you much."[65]

Trenton inhabitants and militiamen read on June 10 in the *New Jersey Gazette* that the British in Philadelphia were clearly making preparations to leave the city. They were destroying defensive works, rendering heavy cannon useless, impressing wagons and teams from farmers to carry military baggage across New Jersey to New York, and making plans to exchange prisoners. The British army had been ordered to be ready to march "at a minute's warning." To keep his militiamen ready for them should they come up to Trenton, Dickinson ordered "that no officer, nor private now on duty at this post, shall presume to cross the river with arms, without orders for that purpose, under the severest penalty, a court martial can inflict." The next day, he again reminded battalion commanders to pay particular attention to their men's muskets and the adjutants to turn out their unarmed men for fatigue duty at the redoubts each day.[66]

Dickinson did not hesitate to admonish officers by name in his general orders and on June 14 was obviously frustrated with Captain Tucker, whom he singled out and "desired to be more attentive, to the parading of his men, as they come on very irregular." The officers in charge of guard details had also been slack, and Dickinson instructed them as a group to "instruct their respective centinals, that they may not plead ignorance of their duty, when posted." He found this order necessary "as many centries were seen yesterday, seting on the ground – a shameful, unsoldier like position, for a man on duty, & reflects the highest disgrace, both on officers & privates."[67]

By June 15, neither officers nor privates were to absent themselves from their posts for any reason. Dickinson ordered Adjutant Bishop to furnish the fatigue party on June 16 to work under Colonel Phillips and complete the redoubts. The same day, the Assembly ordered Dickinson to send out one or more discreet officers with detachments of militia to impress and pay for lead in Hunterdon, Burlington, and Gloucester counties.[68]

The British departure from Philadelphia on June 18 coincided with the monthly militia exchange at Trenton. The men currently on duty at Trenton were ordered mustered before their replacements came into camp.[69] Those men expecting to be discharged had to remain and join with the new arrivals when the alarm was sounded that the British had marched from Philadelphia.

When Isaac Quigley of Nottingham heard the alarm guns signaling the British departure from Philadelphia, he "repaired to the alarm post near [his uncle] Captain Robert Quigley's" where he received orders to "warn out"[70] John Clutch, Uriah Clutch, Patrick Lamb, James Rakale, David Kelley, Samuel Read, and several other men to appear for duty. Isaac was only 15 years old but "enlisted as a volunteer" in the company.[71]

Joseph Clunn's artillery company turned out, marched to Crosswicks Creek, engaged some Hessians at the bridge, and returned to Trenton. They drew rations and marched to Stony Brook near Princeton where they spent the night before setting off to Allentown and then Freehold. However, Lieutenant Henry Chambers brought the two cannon and some of the men back to town. The returning men told their families and friends that Clunn had been ordered to bring the cannon back, but he had asked the men to voluntarily join the army as infantrymen. Many men did, including Jabez Ashmore, William Robinson, and David Van Norden. However, Lieutenant Isaiah Yard attached himself to another artillery unit. When these men later returned home, they told of their experiences at the Battle of Monmouth on June 28. Ashmore was engaged throughout the battle as an infantryman under Colonel Shreve on the left flank of the British and suffered excessively due to the extreme heat and lack of water. Two of the volunteers from Clunn's company were wounded, but no one was killed in the battle. After the Monmouth campaign, Clunn resigned as captain and Isaiah Yard replaced him.[72]

The day after the battle, 27 British prisoners, mostly grenadiers, were brought to Trenton.[73] Shortly after, John Borrows rode into town on a horse borrowed from George Washington and carrying a Continental army discharge personally signed by the general. Borrows had been serving Washington as an express rider since joining the army at Morristown about May 1777. The Battle of Monmouth marked his last day working for the General because his horse dropped dead during the action from heat and fatigue. Borrows was always proud of his service to Washington but later said, "I never got any pay for the one [horse] that I lost on the day of Monmouth battle." Taking up residence in Trenton, Borrows became an apprentice blacksmith and fulfilled his militia obligation by volunteering for service with the artillery company. Young Isaac Quigley was brought home on the 29th to begin three-months recovering from a "flesh wound just below the hip joint" suffered in the battle. He would always be a little lame from the wound.[74]

After the Battle of Monmouth, Dr. Wilson Waters was ordered to Trenton, where he assisted Dr. James Tilton at the barracks military hospital until August 1779. One of the men he treated in Trenton was no doubt Gideon Viah of the Tenth Virginia Regiment, sent back to Trenton after the Battle of Monmouth with camp fever and confined there for five or six weeks while recuperating. Men who became ill after the Battle of Monmouth were cared for in Trenton, after being carried along in wagons for a short time, and some were probably among the 60 or so Continentals discharged from the hospital on July 28 and marched off to camp to join their regiments.[75]

The perceived threat to Trenton had caused Isaac Collins to stop printing the June 24 issue of the Gazette and seek temporary safety along with other Trenton residents. The paper was distributed on July 1 carrying the date of June 24 because page one had been printed before the alarm. Collins' paper allowed Trenton inhabitants to read about how the Battle of Monmouth had come about and been conducted, and how their local militia had participated. Prior to the battle, General Washington had detached a large body of troops under Major General Lee to support General Maxwell's brigade and the militia under Generals Dickinson and Heard. The militia under Dickinson were those that had been at Trenton, and they had joined with troops harassing the British on their march before the battle on June 28.[76]

Apparently not all the boats borrowed to cross the army at Coryell's Ferry were properly returned. Patrick Colvin of Trenton Ferry petitioned Congress on July 24 complaining that without sufficient boats he could not handle the heavy traffic and had become "the object of insult and threats." He heard there were "a number of boats and flats at some of the other ferry's on the River Delaware at this present time not in use" and asked Congress to move some of those boats to his ferry, and his request was granted.[77]

So much military traffic crossed at the Trenton ferries during the war years that one or the other became designated the "Continental

Ferry" where authorized military traffic could cross at a reduced rate charged to Congress. In September 1778, it was the lower ferry near the supply depot, formerly run by Elijah Bond and now owned by William Trent, who was trying to sell the 600-to-700-acre ferry property with its orchards, fishery, and large fish pond capable of holding 1,000 sturgeon. Trent also touted it as a fine location for a town.[78]

Trenton was a beehive of activity in the months after the Battle of Monmouth. A number of American prisoners from New York arrived in town in July after being exchanged and told the people of Trenton that New York was experiencing a great shortage of bread. On Sunday and Monday, July 19 and 20, about 100 men recently enlisted in the Continentals for the duration of the war passed through town on their way to the American camp, and about the same time 12 British prisoners captured near Sandy Hook arrived in town to be kept in the jail. Towards the end of July, about 40 recruits for Colonel Bland's light dragoon regiment arrived from Virginia on their way to camp. On Sunday, August 9, about 100 neatly uniformed and well mounted light dragoons, mostly new recruits, commanded by Major William Lee arrived from Virginia. Lee probably thought back to when he was wounded in Trenton on December 26, 1776. About 600 "fine healthy troops" of the Third North Carolina Regiment commanded by James Hogun passed through on August 25 on their way to headquarters at White Plains, followed by the Provost Troop of Light Dragoons on September 9, and recruits for the light dragoons from Virginia and North Carolina a short time later.[79] Colonel Hogun's Third North Carolina Regiment came back through Trenton when ordered to march from camp at Middle Brook to Philadelphia in December. Washington ordered Hogun to leave a captain, two lower ranking officers, and 50 men at Trenton to guard the military stores there. Hogun also left a number of sick and convalescent men too ill to proceed further at the hospital.[80] Other troops passing through Trenton in December included the light dragoons of Major "Light Horse" Harry Lee on their way to Burlington for winter quarters.[81]

In addition to American soldiers on their way to the army, deserters from the enemy came through town occasionally. Several British deserters from Staten Island passed through on August 30, and four Hessian deserters from Kingsbridge on September 11.[82]

Privateers captured a number of small vessels and several State courts of admiralty were held in Trenton, usually at taverns, to determine their fate.[83] On March 27, the Council of Safety at Trenton dealt with various cases of men accused of trading with the enemy, providing provisions to the enemy, spying, or otherwise aiding the enemy. Some offenders were offered enlistment in the Continentals rather than face jail and some cases were dismissed after the men took the oaths of abjuration and allegiance. One man who took the oaths and was dismissed was a slave of John Cox.[84]

Trenton residents read in the August 19 *New Jersey Gazette* about court inquisitions held on August 1 concerning individuals from their town who had joined the army of the King or had "otherwise offended against the form of their allegiance to this State." Daniel Coxe was accused of joining with the British army at Philadelphia on April 9, 1778 and serving it "by acting as a magistrate of the police" of that city. Isaac Allen, John Barnes, Charles Harrison, Joseph Taylor, and Jesse Waln were charged with "joining the army of the King of Great Britain" on or about December 8, 1776. Alexander Carr, "late of Trenton," was charged with coming back to Trenton from Philadelphia on or about December 1, 1777 and speaking "disrespectfully of the American army by calling them Rebels" and afterwards returning to Philadelphia in March while it was in possession of the British Army. Brereton and Mary Poynton, late of Trenton, were accused of joining with the army of the King of Great Britain about October 1, 1777. Rensselaer Williams was the presiding justice and other justices and judges included William Clayton, Moore Furman, and Benjamin Yard. The jury, including Joseph Higbee, Alexander Chambers, William Tucker, Joseph Clunn, Hezekiah Howell, Isaiah Yard, Charles Axford, Jr., and men from the nearby area, found the charges true. Confiscated Loyalist property sold at public auction at Rensselaer Williams's tavern on December 9 included the library of Daniel Coxe, over 100 titles, many of multiple volumes, and some valuable household furniture of John Barnes.[85]

Articles of impeachment against one of the judges, William Clayton, were presented to the Assembly on October 1, accusing him of misbehavior as a magistrate. The case originated in April, and the first article accused him of "commonly and uniformly" showing "a disposition to favour persons disaffected to the present Government." The second article accused him of directing the clerk of the Hunterdon Court of Quarter Sessions to make "a false and erroneous entry of a judgment in the case of a certain William Frazer, fined for refusing to take the oaths to government." The third article accused him of "voluntarily" seeking a protection paper from the British in December 1776 and encouraging other people to do likewise. He appeared before the Legislative Council on October 6 when evidence from both the prosecution and defense was heard. He was found guilty of the first article. The vote was equally split and the governor, a man with a strong dislike for "disaffected" persons, broke the tie. He was found innocent of the second charge but unanimously found guilty of the third. A vote to remove him from office as a judge and justice of the peace failed to pass, but he resigned on October 31.[86]

In early November, several Joint Meetings at Britton's tavern discussed New Jersey's position on approving the Articles of Confederation. The committee recommended to approve them even though there were concerns about "unequal terms of the Articles of Confederation between the several States." This recommendation passed by a very close vote on November 20 and was announced in the *New Jersey Gazette* on November 25.[87]

Problems caused by the British and Hessian occupation of December 1776 lingered into 1778. During the Hessian occupation, a daybook, ledger, and several dockets, books and other papers from the estate of Abraham Cottnam were taken from the office of Ebenezer Cowell, and they were believed to be in the possession of a person in or near Trenton.[88] David Pinkerton petitioned the Council of Safety on September 19 for permission to go to New York to seek payment for several items taken from him by the enemy in December 1776. Pinkerton was directed to attend the Council of Safety before permission could be granted, and several days later he received it.[89]

Pulaski's Legion was in Trenton on September 29 when Washington ordered Pulaski to assist Lord Stirling with an operation in eastern New Jersey. Pulaski was having several conflicts with Congress and did not leave until some of those issues were resolved and he was ordered to Little Egg Harbor by Congress on October 5. The events in the east did not go well for Pulaski, but he did all he could to put them in a good light.[90] Trenton's newspaper publisher, Isaac Collins, encouragingly told his readers that Pulaski and his troops had driven the enemy back on board their vessels and they had retreated to New York. He left out any unflattering details.[91]

Concerned about his men's fatigue from their actions at Little Egg Harbor, Pulaksi wanted to bring them back to Trenton. By Saturday, October 24, he was back in town and planning to set off the coming Monday to join the main army, but very concerned about his lack of a quartermaster and about 100 blankets needed to replace those lost in a surprise attack.[92] During their short time in Trenton, the Legion experienced desertions and missing horses. For example, on October 28, two dragoon horses either strayed or were stolen from a fence near Stacy Potts' bark house. Some exchanged prisoners of war from Baylor's cavalry, taken prisoner at the Baylor Massacre at Old Tappan and transported to New York, arrived in Trenton the last week of October. Pulaski's Legion left Trenton on October 31 and marched to Sussex Courthouse. On November 16, Colonel Bland's cavalry regiment came back through Trenton and left the next day for Virginia to spend the winter.[93]

After the Pulaski Legion went south, his surgeon, Nicholas de Belleville, who had personally served Pulaski, as well as being a surgeon for the military, came back to Trenton to make it his home. Belleville was 28-years-old and had come to America with Pulaski in 1777. While serving in Trenton with Pulaski, he lived with Dr. Bryant at Kingsbury and worked at the military hospital. Mary Yard later recalled seeing him walk by her house daily from Dr. Bryant's to the barracks military hospital. Dr. Bryant encouraged him to leave the army and practice in Trenton. He did not do so immediately but he came back to Trenton and married Ann Britton, daughter of Charity, in January 1780 and lived the rest of his life in Trenton, earning an outstanding reputation as both a doctor and person. He became known for considering as a sacred trust the confidence patients placed in him. "He was cautious and minute in investigating - keen in observing - careful and deliberate in deciding – accurate in judgment – prompt and efficient in the administration of remedies – candid and conscientious in advising – kind and soothing in deportment."[94]

Local resident Hugh Runyon had taken on the duties of assistant quartermaster at Trenton and in July was dealing with the usual frustrations of purchasing forage. He was uncertain just what price to pay and conferred with Abraham Hunt, who recommended he check with Moore Furman to find out what price was being paid in Philadelphia and use that. He was also confused about his title. Was it DQMG or Assistant DQMG (ADQMG)? Apparently Furman and John Cox were not consistent when addressing letters to him. He noted in a letter that he did not really care about the title but to carry out his job with dignity he desperately needed to be provided with the required money. It was important to him that when the war was over, he would merit the title of "good person." He was doing what he could in issuing hay but needed instructions on how to deal with the problems faced by his department, especially the lack of money, at a time when business was heavier than it had ever been.[95]

About this time, Furman dismissed Runyon, which greatly disturbed John Cox and Peter Gordon. Gordon wrote to Furman, noting Cox's displeasure because he held Runyon in high regard and thought he had been treated "in the crudest manner." While Cox understood that Furman could hire or fire whomever he chose, Cox felt the way things had been handled "reflects much disgrace on Mr. Runyon" and Cox "cannot reconcile the inhuman part you [Furman] have acted in turning such an industrious active gentleman out of employ." Fortunately, Gordon understood that Runyan had been offered a deputy quartermaster position in Bucks County just across the river.[96]

Contributing to the money problems was the waste and questionable practices that Gordon saw all around him. He was dismayed that General Dickinson was keeping unneeded artillery horses at his estate for which Gordon had to pay for pasture and grain. In addition, he had to give Dickinson's "Negro one ration a day for feeding them & two quarts rum a week." Not only were these horses a great expense to the public but the general was also drawing forage for all his other horses.[97]

Runyon had commented that quartermaster activity was extremely busy and Gordon reinforced this in a July 28 letter to Moore Furman. He wrote, "I assure you we have had a busy time since you left us. Saturday I suppose there was 150 teams to be loaded which was accomplished before sunset and indeed every day since our hands & heads has been fully employ'd." He was displeased that "Mr. Paxton went to Philada Saturday last which I think was not altogether right considering our business." Gordon felt the trip was more for pleasure than business and had left Gordon to act as "almost QM[,] Commissary & everything."[98]

He continued the theme in a July 31 letter, commenting, "There is no less than six boats now laying at the wharf to unload with commissary stores & forage – a busy time." Adequate forage was not to be had for anyone needing it, and Gordon sarcastically commented that those who expected him to magically find forage "might as well order bricks made without the necessary materials."[99]

In early September, large quantities of corn and oats passed through Trenton on route from Virginia and Maryland to camp. This short forage from southern states was essential, because supplies in the middle States had been greatly drained. High prices demanded by farmers were part of the problem, but officials understood that something also needed to be done "to get the farmers to work and grain threshed, etc.", while also acknowledging that "militia duty gets in the way of threshing."[100] By the fall, Furman had been doing everything in his power to collect a good quantity of long forage at Trenton, "the starting post from whence all the flour and many other necessaries goes on to our army."[101]

Although stationed at Pittstown, Furman went to Trenton in mid-October where he encountered Captain John Stith of Colonel Baylor's light dragoons with about 100 men and horses on their way to winter quarters. To save local forage for the wagon horses Washington ordered the light horse to avoid traveling on the wagon route. Furman worried that if all these cavalry horses were quartered at Trenton or at any of the posts along the wagon route, all the available forage would be consumed within a month or two at the most, and it could not be replaced "unless taken out of the mouths of man & beast and they perish."[102] Stith promised Furman he would not remain at Trenton. However, after Furman left town, Stith ordered his men to stay and only he left.

Gordon told Furman that Captain Stith had gone to headquarters and feared he was lobbying to keep his troopers at Trenton for the winter again. Gordon was also concerned that 30 men from Pulaski's Legion were stationed at Trenton and feared more would come. Gordon had done all he could to get Baylor to "cull out all the horses not fitting for their service" and push Baylor to Bristol, Pennsylvania, both without success. Gordon summed up his situation saying, "We have had for several days near two hundred teams in town waiting for forage to proceed—this number of horses with the cavalry horses has made great havock in the forage yard. But providence has once more favored us with some forage boats and hope to have this busy town a little thinner very shortly." The cavalry horses couldn't leave soon enough. Gordon wrote Furman on October 24 that, "Yesterday afternoon Baylors Regt Dragoons march'd for Mr. Runyans Post – a pleasing sight – and gave us all much pleasure – but of short duration – for about two hours afterwards Polaskeys Legion arrived, which sunk our spirits ten degrees lower than they was in having Baylors Regt with us – However as man is born to trouble we must bear our proportions."[103]

Furman believed New Jersey farmers would willingly supply forage if they had it, but "they have been under the hands of the foragers for three years past and are now very bare indeed." Furman had enough wagons to transport flour and other supplies to the army, but if additional horses, such as the cavalry mounts, were put into the equation, he would not have enough forage to keep the wagons going. He was already dependent on other states for short forage. Furman notified everyone involved and hoped disaster could be avoided. All forage within 15 to 20 miles of Trenton had already been collected and he suggested it would be better to quarter horses, other than the wagon horses, in places nearer to where forage could still be collected. One of his contacts at Trenton informed Furman that General Pulaski's quartermaster had declared he had orders to "secure what oats and other forage" he needed, even if he had to use force, which he was prepared to do. Furman hoped "no such conduct will be put in execution or the country will soon be in a flame." The situation was indeed bad and quartermasters Gordon and Furman received desperate letters from military posts stating that they could not keep supply wagons moving without more forage.[104]

By November 7, Gordon was again desperate for forage. He wrote Furman, "I know not what will be done for forage – we have been entirely out for four days – I have advised Mr. Owen Biddle [of the forage department] almost every day of our distress – but no releaf as yet – Bad situation indeed – the Commissarys calling out for provisions to be forwarded with all dispatch. Fifteen or twenty brigades now here laying idle for want of forage – but so it is and can only hope for better times." He had to send teams off without even forage for their own horses, much less the army. He wrote, "I have persuaded several brigades to sett off and try to buy their forage on the road but expect it will come very high – yet it may be better to pay three dollars for corn than to be laying idle here & destroying our hay."[105]

Three days later, he followed up with another letter to Furman lamenting that "I hardly know how to begin to give you still more uneasiness and have been contriving[,] waiting[,] studying for several days to help ourselves out of our difficulty – but am fairly beat out – our trouble is for want of forage." Nothing had been received for 10 days and "our brigades had almost all collected here in a drove so that our hay has melted away like butter in summers day." Gordon held a council and it concluded "to send the brigades all out of town Empty." He had given the orders that morning. Brigades raised between 15 and 20 miles away were sent home until Trenton got forage. Brigades from further away were sent away to seek pasture, "for to keep them here eating up our hay would answer no good purpose." He assured Furman, "This is justly and truly our situation – Bad – Bad & even worse than Bad." However, he had received word that at least some forage might arrive by boat soon. Money was another concern, and he lamented, "My cash is almost run out for I have been oblig'd to advance large sums for the brigades which is gone forward to buy their forage." Desperate to raise some money, he told Furman, "Next Saturday I intend to sell some old horses and expect you will send some."[106]

By November, Quartermaster General (QMG) Greene was concerned that "the complaints are so loud and so numerous from New Jersey that I am almost afraid to go there. Trenton must save us, as it has done once before or else there will be an end of the poor quarter master." Greene did stop in New Jersey on December 21 on his way to Philadelphia and stayed in Trenton at least a week, where he and his wife Caty were the guests of John Cox at Bloomsbury. He was delayed due to the river being impassable with ice. When conditions allowed him to cross on the ice, Nathanael went on to Philadelphia, arriving December 31, while Caty remained in Trenton until mid-January.[107]

Rev. James Caldwell of Springfield was appointed to settle debts of the previous supply department in several counties, including Hunterdon. He announced in December that he had money to discharge debts contracted between October 5, 1776 and March 3, 1778 and would be at Trenton on January 8 and 9, 1779 to settle properly certified accounts.[108]

In December, Gordon's letters continued to stress frustrations with forage and he used phrases like "we shall as usual be in distress before many days" and "I hope they will be able to contrive some kind of beasts that will answer to go without forage." Gordon really felt the burden of the Continental light horse and commented on December 11 that, "We have been surrounded for two days past with the whole of Moylans Regt Horse – which has hurt us. They are now parading and [I] hope in a few minutes to be clear of them – if the wind and frost will admit of their crossing the River." But he had to write as he finished the letter, "To my great grief the cavalry cannot cross the River and are swarming around us again." Gordon felt the need to justify what might be interpreted as his failures and added, "We are striving to help our army as much and as soon as possible – but cannot do more than we can. I shall write to Gen Green today and inform him of our situation."[109]

By mid-December, Gordon was feeling "pressed[,] drawn and hurried on every hand, almost out of our sinces." He was receiving constant expresses "crying out in the greatest distress for forage," boards for winter huts, and provisions. It was a "distressd situation indeed & sorry I am not to be able to afford them immediate releaf – but so it was – I can only comfort myself that I have done my might." The weather was not cooperating either, and "there has been such severe rains that the teams has met with much difficulty in crossing the rivers & creeks which has lately kept us some back." One piece of good news was the expectation that "by tomorrow morning there will be fifteen or twenty boats up with Commissary stores – but cant find there is any forage on the way." He was also running out of money, because "nothing can be bought without immediate payment." He expected to be out of money in three days because "I have been paying up the [wagon] brigades from 17th Sept to Novemb 1st which takes a monstrous sum of Continental to accomplish and find I shant have near enough to go through. The brigades which has been discharg'd I concluded ought in justice to be paid off to enable the owners to procure forage for their horses, which I have done, especially those of a distance."[110]

With the British back in New York, the end of 1778 found Trenton much less threatened than at the end of the previous year, but the town still provided a busy supply depot and hospital, and a continuing flow of dignitaries and troops made demands on the citizens, as well as benefiting them by spending money and reporting news.

Chapter 11

1779

On June 29, 1779, several days after resigning as New Jersey's Deputy Quartermaster General, Moore Furman sat down at his desk in Trenton to write to John Cox and Charles Pettit, Quartermaster General Nathanael Greene's top assistants. Furman had resigned in total frustration on June 24 but at Greene's request, and from his sense of duty, was continuing to serve as a volunteer. Lack of money provided to the quartermaster department and depreciation of the currency were two primary factors leading to his resignation. The small sums of money given to him fell far short of the amount needed to procure necessary supplies and pay "what has been long due to the good people of this State" for previous purchases. The army, headquartered at Middlebrook, had been dispersed to West Point, the Hudson Highlands, and Danbury, Connecticut, necessitating more teams to haul its supplies and increasing the already heavy demands for forage. Because New Jersey law now required that farmers be paid before officials took forage from them, Furman could not just give receipts and "this circumstance alone you must suppose sufficient to prevent my being able to collect it."

He explained that the problem was not just the lack of necessary funds, but that the "farmers begin to loose all confidence in the money; the rapid and continued depreciation of it; impresses stronger and stronger on their minds." In spite of these difficulties, he had been able to provide the army with a regular supply of provisions, "but its only from day to day, and should a want of confidence in the money, or any other cause make but a few days stoppage at an unlucky moment the consequences may be fatal."

These difficulties were compounded by the fact that prices fluctuated in some locations but were fixed in others. Farmers naturally looked for the best deal, so a unified pricing system throughout the state and among the states would be very helpful. Furman found that farmers often held back urgently needed forage until they could learn about prices nearby, or they demanded "such high prices as they think will not be exceeded by others." New Jersey farmers would willingly sell at reasonable prices if they knew the price was comparable to other areas.

Because of the unsolved problems he faced, Furman found it "impossible to do the business of the Army with the least appearance of prudence or economy." Something must be done soon, because it was now time for mowing hay and the grain harvest was approaching. Furman told Cox and Pettit that they should feel free to forward his thoughts and analysis of the problems to Congress if they thought it would help things. Meanwhile, he would dutifully continue to operate as a volunteer for the department "until the cause of my resignation be removed or another is appointed."[1]

Trentonians stayed current with the changing nature of the war from talking with the many individuals and military units passing through town during the year. In 1779 the war was shifting to the southern States, and while people often came through town from the south on their way to Washington's army, a number of regiments from that army came through heading south.[2] The town still served as an important military supply depot and the Continental hospital at the barracks continued to function. Although few documents survive, the hospital was functioning in December with four officers, 20 sick soldiers, three horses, and one wagon.[3] Those local people working for the supply departments continued to struggle with a lack of resources and everyone had to deal with the inflation.

Throughout the year, various military officers and dignitaries came through town. General and Mrs. Washington passed through on their way to headquarters at Middlebrook on Wednesday, February 3. Washington had been in Philadelphia since January 6, meeting with Congress about the 1779 campaign. General De Kalb and General Woodford of Virginia arrived in town from Philadelphia on March 30, stayed overnight, and then set out for Middlebrook.[4] Just a few days earlier, Maryland Captain William Beatty came through Trenton on his way back to the huts near Middlebrook after a two-month furlough home.[5]

French ambassador Conrad-Alexandre Gerard and his suite arrived in Trenton on their way to Middlebrook on Tuesday evening, April 27, accompanied by Spanish representative Don Juan de Miralles and escorted by some Philadelphia Light Dragoons.[6] Lord Stirling and Governor Livingston greeted the dignitaries and they lodged that night at John Cox's Bloomsbury manor house. General Greene arrived at 7:00 pm and noted that "Col Cox sends off immediately a light wagon with a sturgeon and some shad for headquarters. It will travel all night and arrive seasonably to have the fish for dinner."[7]

Ambassador Gerard came again from Philadelphia on Sunday evening, September 19, and on September 21 the Count De La Luzerne, who was replacing him as ambassador, arrived with his secretary and large retinue escorted by a troop of Baylor's light dragoons. The Governor and Legislature were meeting in town and paid their compliments to the count. After a short stay, the two emissaries set out to return to Philadelphia.[8] Ambassador Gerard passed through town again during the first week of October on his way to headquarters to pay his respects to Washington before leaving for France.[9] In addition to these dignitaries, a wide variety of people spent time in town during the year including paroled American officers and British and Hessian deserters and prisoners.[10]

On January 1, a one-year lease for the house Peter Gordon rented from Philadelphia merchant George Davis went into effect. In the agreement, Gordon agreed to put in good repair, at his own expense, any part of the property that required it, including doors, windows, fences, porches, gates, racks, and mangers. He also agreed not to put hay or straw into "any part of the buildings except the stables."[11]

Supplying the army with food and forage during the winter produced another litany of impending disaster. Although the winter proved mild overall, ice on Chesapeake Bay and the Delaware River in early January greatly hampered getting food supplies to the army. The commissary department was ordered in January to procure as much wheat and flour as possible and have it ready to forward to Trenton when navigation reopened on the Delaware because "we shall want every barrel." Gordon was concerned that high prices for corn were being demanded by, and paid to, "disaffected" persons while those people "always ready to spare anything that may be wanted for support of our army" were paid a lower price. He wished for a set price to be published in the newspaper and supported by local magistrates.[12]

Some relief was promised to citizens who had been given receipts rather than cash for items purchased or services provided for the army. Hugh Runyon, serving as DQMG at Bristol, stationed himself at Jonathan Richmond's tavern on January 11, 12, and 13 to pay holders of certificates received for transporting baggage, forage, or wood for the militia since March 2, 1778. Former DQMG Sullivan was at Captain Joseph Clunn's tavern between January 19 and 21 and February 8 and 11 to settle accounts for expenses incurred between October 5, 1776 and March 2, 1778 and for forage department debts for deliveries to Trenton before March 2, 1778. Benjamin Smith, the post master at Trenton, was authorized in March to receive properly attested accounts to forward to Rev. James Caldwell who had been designated to settle accounts incurred under previous QMG Mifflin from October 5, 1776 to March 2, 1778.[13]

The stresses placed on supply officials made interpersonal relationships fragile. Peter Gordon got into a dispute with John Cox over manure in February. Manure was a saleable commodity produced in large quantities by the horses employed by the quartermasters. Manure that accumulated on horse lots rented by the local quartermaster could be collected and sold by him as one of his benefits. When John Cox sent five or six wagon teams to a lot owned by Benjamin Yard to remove the manure, Yard confronted them and forced them to leave empty because Gordon should be the one to profit from it. Cox was furious and wrote to Peter Gordon "a tolerable severe letter" stating his "determination to have the manure" and explaining his rationale for why he was entitled to it. Gordon told Furman, "I have not seen him [Cox] and don't care if I never do – but expect when I do a severe scold which I am determined not to bear if he says too much – but at the same time will make matters as easy as I can." Gordon believed that Cox was actually trying to get him removed from office, which he said would be "agreeable to me for I see a large field [of] trouble opened." However, that evening he wrote Furman again and commented that, "Since I wrote you this morning Col. Cox has been with me and was exceeding pleasant, and told me he did not expect nor mean to take the manure off any lott belonging to the inhabitants - So that I am in hopes there will be no more said on that score."[14]

However, the incident became a topic of conversation in the community, and a week later Gordon wrote Furman that "I believe our friend Col Cox is a little asham'd of his spunk about the dung and hopes to hear no more of it. He is now at camp and before he left me told me he did not pretend to claim a single handful as his right for he knows it had always been the custom that the acting quartr mastr of every post was to have the profit of it and he ment to make me full satisfaction for its value." Cox asked Gordon to make this known widely "for the damn'd dung (using his expression) was in every bodys mouth." After making this request, Gordon said Cox "very complisantly took his leave."[15]

Gordon was also under pressure from Cox in February over the need to forward some corn at Coryell's Ferry to camp but he lacked resources to do it. He asked Furman for help because otherwise "I shall have the Col. on my back." He also notified Furman that the Bristol, Pennsylvania post that Hugh Runyan had taken when removed by Furman was now closed and that Runyan had moved to the lower Trenton Ferry at Lamberton operated by Widow Janney. Gordon found all of this to be "strange manoevers indeed." Three days later, Gordon reminded Furman, "Pray have you thought and given orders to have the flour at Coryells Ferry taken on to camp. I wish it could be removed for the Commis[sary] &c keeps every day bawling about it and if there should be any blame laid any where by its not being forwarded, I may be assured it will fall on my back as Col. Cox has given me orders" to move it. He expected criticism even though "There has been a large quantity of all kind provision sent to camp within two weeks so that they cannot be in much want at present."[16]

Gordon's life was further complicated at this time because his landlord, George Davis, wanted him to be out of the house he rented by the first of May, because Davis wanted it for himself. Gordon did not know where he would find housing for his family and was fearful he would not find a place close enough to Trenton for him to continue in his position. He promised to give Furman timely notice if he needed to find a replacement, "which perhaps may please Col Cox better than I do."[17] Things came together rapidly for him, and by February 20 he had purchased a 270-acre farm in Hopewell Township near the Baptist Meeting House. While somewhat removed from Trenton, he was looking forward to "settle for life – and not be runing & renting every year or two."[18]

Samuel Tucker was searching in February for papers belonging to an estate for which he was executor. He opened a small trunk for the first time since December 1776 and was surprised to find it contained many important papers he thought had been packed in the trunk that was taken by the British from the Abbott farm. Among the papers were "all the bonds of paroles taken as President of the Convention" from known and suspected Loyalists. He informed Assembly Speaker John Hart of his find and that the bonds and paroles were ready to deliver to the Assembly. This discovery cleared up the Assembly's question raised in 1778 about the location of these documents.[19]

At the annual town meeting in March, Stacy Potts and Charles Axford, Jr. were again chosen clerk and assessor. Conrad Kotts was elected a county freeholder, while Isaac DeCou was chosen one of the constables and Benjamin Smith overseer of the Trenton town roads. Other business included dealing with the poor and replacing several men who declined to hold offices to which they had been elected.[20]

Confiscated Loyalist property continued to be sold to raise money to pay for the war, and at 10:00 am on Thursday, March 25 a public vendue was held at Britton's tavern to sell parcels of land taken from Isaac Allen, Daniel Coxe, John Barnes, and Brereton and Mary Poynton.[21] Another former Trenton resident who lost his land was Captain Samuel Rutherford, who served 23 years in the British Sixtieth, or Royal American, Regiment of Foot. He lost several lots, including a "brewhouse lot, totaling more than 16 acres, located "in the middle & centre of the town."[22]

Nathanael Greene told Washington in April that he was considering resigning his position because "My reputation I value more than any advantages of gain; and I consider it in great danger." He was totally exasperated with the inability of Congress to remove the difficulties that prevented him from fully supplying the army honorably and he found "The politicks of Congress are really alarming and the state of the financeing astonishing, where they will end time only can unfold."[23]

By May, some of Moore Furman's staff had resigned and he was afraid he would lose others unless their pay was increased, as John Cox also feared. Furman had no pork or flour at Trenton and felt there was so little forage in New Jersey that even legislating higher prices for it could not secure enough. He feared that if inflation was not controlled soon, "it will take more Continental money to purchase than can possibly be made." Lack of money continued to limit Furman's ability to transport the supplies needed by the army, and by May he had about 200 private teams of horses in service at Trenton but not enough forage. He had about 60 wagons ready to go, but no drivers, because civilians were paying them higher wages than the army.[24] Furman was also furious because many of the provisions, including large amounts from Trenton, were being so mismanaged that "much more carting is done then necessary – [and] I know not at whose door to lay this."[25] On May 25, Peter Gordon commenting on the money problems complained, "Our Assembly is very busy and am afraid do but little."[26]

Notice was given on May 26 that inquisitions against former Trenton residents John Tabor Kemp and his wife, Grace, had been returned at the last Inferior Court of Common Pleas for Hunterdon County and that anyone with information that might reverse the judgment that the Kemps were Loyalists and should suffer the consequences must appear at the next Court of Common Pleas to be held at Trenton when final judgement would be made.[27]

Governor Livingston found it increasingly difficult to turn out sufficient numbers of militiamen for monthly tours of active duty. He knew a pay increase would encourage them since the Continentals had received one recently. However, Washington objected to increasing militia pay on the grounds that it would "occasion disgust and desertion, if not mutiny, among those already in the [Continental] Army; and would be a new discouragement to others from entering into it."[28] In order to get Continental volunteers, political and military leaders always wanted to ensure that militia duty was more disagreeable than service in the Continentals. Livingston agreed with Washington that men should obey the militia law as a civic duty simply because it was the law and not because of the pay received for active service. However, enticements might help because the legislature had "uniformly manifested a disinclination to use compulsion" to enforce the militia law. He also felt the small increase suggested would not result in the consequences Washington feared. Besides, the situation was getting desperate and without some modest pay increase or bounty, he believed so few men would turn out that "our frontiers would be entirely left to the mercy of the enemy."[29] He was convinced that the number of classes scheduled for duty in May was not enough because so many men would simply refuse to serve. His appeals to call out additional classes were unsuccessful so he had to tell militia Colonel John Neilson, in command at Elizabethtown, that he would just have to do the best he could with whatever men showed up.[30] Livingston ordered out the classes on May 26, including one class of the First Hunterdon, to defend northeast New Jersey against enemy incursions from New York.[31] However, on May 30 Livingston received word from Neilson that he had only received about 14 men from the Hunterdon County regiments, none from the First Hunterdon, and the total of about 140 militiamen who turned out from the designated county classes was but a fraction of what he required.[32]

Perhaps because of the difficulty in getting militia to turn out to guard the military supplies, five First Virginia soldiers, including a sergeant, were absent from their regiment and on guard duty in Trenton in May. One of these men had been on command there in April with two other men, perhaps for the same duty.[33]

Men serving the patriot cause in public offices continued to petition the Assembly for exemption from militia duty, such as saddler Benjamin Smith who had been appointed postmaster at Trenton and requested exemption on May 14. The same day, the inhabitants of Trenton petitioned for the incorporation of the town. Neither petition was acted on at this time. The incorporation petition was officially turned down on September 27 at a Joint Meeting at Britton's tavern. The Joint Meetings this year were mostly held at Britton's, although several in May and June were held at the Methodist Meeting House. The June 10 Joint Meeting passed an act for relief and support of maimed or disabled soldiers and widows and children of soldiers killed, such as Rezine Anderson, widow of Ephraim Anderson.[34]

Several units of the Continental army came north through town on their way to join Washington's army. Major Henry Lee and his light dragoons came the first week of June.[35] Jabez Ashmore of Nottingham was stationed at the Lamberton Continental Ferry for six months after enlisting under Quartermaster Hugh Runyon.[36] In June, it was announced that the Continental Ferry had moved to the upper Trenton Ferry. However, an ad promoting the lower ferry noted the upper ferry had no tavern, "which makes it very inconvenient for travelers." The tavern there, where John Adams had stopped in 1774, had been burned down during the Hessian occupation in December 1776. The lower ferry had a tavern on the Pennsylvania side and touted that "it is well known that the lower ferry is a good easy ferry with good shores to land at on each side the river, and good attendance is given, where there is no danger of getting upon the rocks as at the upper ferry."[37]

By June 12, the Assembly was very concerned about receiving almost daily complaints respecting the behavior and use of public money by officials in the commissary, quartermaster, hospital, and other departments. The assemblymen were also concerned that there were no methods in place to prevent and punish those who abuse their offices or to "rescue the faithful servants of the publick from that undiscriminating censure, which the bad and unworthy bring upon all." It was resolved that the members of the Assembly and Legislative Council, aided by justices of the peace, should make inquiries in their home counties and collect any evidence to present to proper authority.[38]

The first week of June, Furman was hearing the cry of "No money - No money - what shall we do."[39] He came to Trenton to consult with Cox and Gordon, and applied to the governor, Legislative Council, and Assembly for aid with the supply problems. When he returned to Pittstown, he was relieved that two brigades of wagons appeared from Trenton going to Chester with flour. He also heard that Major Gordon hoped to load 100 wagons that week for Pittstown, besides those going to Morristown, so perhaps the army would be supplied in time. To stretch the supplies of forage for the horses pulling wagons, he planned to reduce the quantity of grain given to the teams for a while and have them subsist solely on grass.[40] However, horses need the protein and nutrients from grain to stay in working condition. When Peter Gordon heard of this plan, he told Furman, "This much I am sure that no teams will continue in the service if they are not to be allowed ... short forage and I think if that should be ordered we shall soon bring ourselves in trouble. I know it is Col Biddles plan - to starve our horses here that their horses may be full fed when at the same time they depend upon our teams pushing (and that hard) for every thing they stand in [need] off - Can it be possible that any person can expect teams to travel 100 miles with loads without forage when there is any here in store - No - and if they positively so order it - they may come and have the total management themselves for it will be out of my power."[41]

John Cox received a letter from Greene in mid-June that quantified the need for horse teams. Greene calculated that it would require 340 teams to deliver daily about forty wagons loaded with stores and provisions sent from Trenton and Easton to the camp at Smiths Clove,

New York. In addition it would require about 70 additional teams just to transport forage for the supply and forage wagon teams. More would have been needed, except no grain forage was available, just hay.[42] This estimate was just for meeting the needs for one post and illustrates the magnitude of the transportation problem, on top of any problems in obtaining supplies to send.

Governor Livingston needed to call up militia in April to replace Continental troops that Washington had removed from Elizabethtown and Monmouth to send with General Sullivan on a campaign against the Iroquois in New York State.[43] On June 2, the Legislature authorized raising a force of 1,000 militiamen to serve full-time until December 15 and reduce the need for monthly call outs. While hoping to fill this six-month levy with volunteers, each militia regiment was divided into classes and each class was to furnish one man or contribute money to pay a substitute. Only men over the age of 21 were eligible and men who volunteered, such as Captain Joseph Clunn, received a $50 bounty.[44]

The Continental Congress and New Jersey Legislature had failed to take effective measures to reduce the problems facing the supply departments and men were leaving the service out of frustration. Nathanael Greene wrote to John Cox at Trenton on July 29 that he understood Furman's and Colonel Robert Lettis Hooper's staffs were resigning and inquired about the resignations of his top assistants, Cox and Charles Pettit, asking if there was 'no accommodation to be had." Greene asked for information on the staff situation.[45]

Trenton merchant David Pinkerton had helped procure supplies beginning early in the war. He wrote to William Churchill Houston and James Mott of the Assembly on July 29, informing them that he had received their letter of the 27th "respecting the settlement of my publick accounts." Pinkerton told them that he could not "produce a single paper or voucher" toward this settlement, because all such papers, along with his other papers, cash, and personal effects "to a considerable amount" were taken from him by British troops in December 1776. Pinkerton had received "several sums from Mr. [Samuel] Tucker" amounting to some £70 that he needed for the public service, but he seldom received more than he had advanced from his own money. He believed he could pay Doctor Cowell between £40 and

£50 and use what remained to pay for express horses, wagons, and boatmen. Pinkerton promised to collect any paperwork and vouchers he could get and transmit them to the committee.[46]

Greene was also dealing with Washington's concern that the enemy might make a foray into New Jersey to destroy some flat-bottomed boats then at Trenton, so the boats should be moved towards Pittstown. On June 16, Gordon wrote to Furman that he could not send them up because he was only provided with "bare wagons ... without horses or any thing else." He didn't really "know what to do or how to get them forward – It seems that every day brings its trouble."[47] Somehow he procured enough heavy duty wagons and teams to carry the boats, and a return made by Benjamin Eyre on July 31 of boat department assets at Trenton showed that 20 "waggon boats" (the flat bottom boats) had been moved from Trenton to camp, leaving Trenton with six scows, one skiff, and one wherry belonging to the army.[48]

Everyone was suffering from the rampant inflation and many were looking for local ways to restrain it because the Legislature seemed unable to do so. Peter Gordon reported to Moore Furman that "This Township is notified to meet this day [July 14] and expect they will get a Committee. Mr. [Samuel] Tucker seems very warm and determined to have it done. We expect a long harangue from him." Gordon was not enthusiastic because he was not convinced the actions being contemplated were entirely legal. After the meeting, Gordon wrote, "At our Town meeting on Wednesday last, we had the pleasure of hearing Mr. Tucker hold forth for half an hour, and [I] assure you it was a studied flowery speech." During his "harangue he mentioned that no friend of liberty and freedom could have the least timidness or fear in his breast, but must always speak his mind freely without any regard to whom it gave offense, and as for myself (says he), I can and will speak my sentiments freely. I feel no bashfulness, and am ready & willing to spend life and fortune for support of the great grand cause we are engaged in (Look back thinked I to the day of sneaking in to the British aside)." Gordon had clearly not forgotten, or forgiven, that Tucker had taken British protection in December 1776. Gordon was not impressed by the meeting, noting that "Indeed there was but very few met and the business went on with much confusion," and that "after much disputing" several men had been "appointed for no other purpose than to correspond by letter with the gentleman Committee in Philada. and assist the majistrates in examining persons passing through without proper passports agreeable to our laws – they are also to form a petition to be signed by the inhabitants & presented to our Assembly at their next setting."[49]

The results of the meeting appeared in the *New Jersey Gazette* on July 28. In a letter to the people of Trenton, the committee strongly recommended "that we all unanimously agree to ask, demand, or receive no greater price for any article of produce, manufacture, labour, or merchandize" than would have been expected on or before July 14. This could help "prevent the further depreciation of the currency, until the Legislature of the United States may adopt some mode of appreciating it throughout the whole Continent." Alexander Chambers signed the letter for the committee on July 24.[50]

Two companies that had been raised in Gloucester and Salem counties to serve until December 15 for the six-month militia, marched from Trenton for Elizabethtown on August 8. About 150 light dragoons on their way to camp under Lieutenant Colonel Washington of Baylor's regiment arrived from Philadelphia on August 24.[51]

Moore Furman wrote to Stephen Lowrey at Trenton in late August that he had heard of problems with flour coming from Trenton. He checked and found that some barrels had been tampered with and were not full. He told Lowrey that all provisions at Trenton should be inspected because partially filled containers cost just as much to transport as full ones and that they should get their money's worth and it was important to deliver a full supply to the army. If the barrels were known to be properly filled when they left Trenton, then it should be easy to find out who was plundering them. Furman reported to Lowrey that when he asked a wagoner how it happened that his load was faulty, the man replied that he had "objected to it when it was delivered to him but was told he would be paid for carting a barrel and had nothing to do with what was in it." Furman was clearly not happy and wanted things tightened up at Trenton.[52]

Captain Edward Gale's company of the Maryland Continentals came up by water in September and then marched on to join Washington's forces monitoring the British in New York.[53]

Commissary Stephen Lowrey enticingly advertised in September that he offered the highest prices for items needed at the supply depot, including white oak pipe staves and heading, barrels of marketable pork, hogs lard, and bees wax. Materials leaving Trenton in September included 1,000 feet of boards carted to Princeton by David Olden, one of the commissioners for providing clothing for the New Jersey Brigade, to be made into boxes for packing clothing for the brigade.[54]

Like Moore Furman, department officials were resigning but continuing to act as volunteers. John Cox and Charles Pettit had resigned in protest over a tax laid on them by the New Jersey Legislature as assistant quartermaster generals for the Continental army. At the discretion of the local assessor and county freeholders, they were subject to a tax of between £1,000 and £10,000 in addition to their regular assessment. They had appealed to Congress in June to intercede, but nothing had been done even though both men had resigned (although continuing to serve while Congress tried to straighten things out). Pettit told Congress that he had been assessed £1,000, in addition to the regular taxes on his estate, and the assessor was demanding it from him. He was in hopes that Congress would provide relief.[55]

The problems in the quartermaster department became so frustrating that Peter Gordon was ready to resign in August. On August 14 he wrote to Furman that "I am willing to quit tomorrow or continue (purely for the sake of our army) until January first next."[56] On top of everything else, he was feeling disrespect for the department from Congress that had recently passed a law enabling States to levy taxes on upper level department officials in addition to taxing them like other citizens and the law made statements showing they did not understand the actual structure of the department. In addition, on July 9 Congress had empowered "the Legislature to displace us when they please (without trial)."

Gordon was concerned about fighting within the department caused by the July 9 resolves. In another letter of August 26 he wrote Furman that, he had fears that a recent "very extraordinary complaint" from a "very extraordinary insignificant" clerk in the forage department was made on behalf of "some larger enemy who keeps behind the curtain." Altogether, "It goes sharper & sharper for staff gentlemen and fear we shall not all be able to stand the tempest, for my own part [I] rest quite easy."[57]

Gordon knew that Moore Furman had resigned but was working as a volunteer for the good of the cause. Gordon told him "for my part I am determined to quit the first of January at farthest and as much sooner as you should determine to make a close." He also needed to vacate his rented house, which also served as his office, by January 1. If Furman could find someone to replace him before the end of the year he should hire him because "ten thousand pounds wont tempt me to stay another year."[58] The actions of Congress hoping to build more public confidence in the department were unfortunately perceived as demeaning threats by men such as Furman and Gordon who believed they had worked extremely hard and deserved to be treated with more respect.

The money problem was so serious in October that Moore Furman determined to come to Trenton and meet with the Assembly to seek changes. He arrived in Trenton the evening of October 26 but was unable to get the Assembly's attention because it was busy reelecting Livingston as governor and with other ceremonies. He planned to return the following week but worried that if he could not get some money he would be unable to secure grain.[59]

Wages for men serving in the forage department had been increased, but not enough for them to support themselves and still lower than could be earned in private employment. Men hired, even temporarily, demanded pay equal to that of Continental army officers with equal responsibility. This was an admittedly complex equation to solve fairly because of the differing levels of responsibility at different posts for men with similar titles. For example, men serving at supply magazines had more responsibility than men with an equal title at a common army post. The clerks, stackers, hay pressers, and laborers serving at Trenton were caught in the middle of this issue.[60] Moore Furman received a petition from six wagon masters in Continental service at Trenton, dated November 3. They had worked for some time at a low rate of pay, much less than they could get outside the service, in the hope that an adequate adjustment would be made, and because no raise had been authorized they were prepared to quit on November 15.[61]

Obtaining supplies went better in the fall and on October 10 it was estimated that there were 300 tons of hay in Trenton, and although all the grain had not been harvested, it was beginning to come in. More than 3000 bushels of grain had been forwarded from Philadelphia and more was coming. By October 18, Major Peter Gordon reported he had sent forward to the army more than 300 barrels of flour, but there were no Commissary supplies left in Trenton.[62]

At a Joint Meeting of the Assembly and Legislative Council at Britton's tavern on October 30, William Livingston was reelected governor. Philemon Dickinson received nine votes, while 29 voted for Livingston. At three o'clock on the afternoon of November 2, a joint Council and Assembly committee met at Britton's tavern to discuss making further provisions for wounded officers and soldiers and widows and children of those killed. Two days later another joint committee met at Britton's to discuss price regulation. Charity Britton's son, Isaac, had taken over the operation of her tavern. Charity had retired in 1777 and the tavern had been operated by Francis Costigin and then Samuel Bellerjeau before twenty-eight-year-old Isaac applied for a tavern license in July 1779, stating that he "has settled himself in his own house, lately and long occupied by Mrs. Charity Britton as a tavern."[63]

In October the Legislative Council dealt with the issue of a satirical article that had appeared in the *New Jersey Gazette* attacking the governor in the form of "hints" about how to conduct the election process so as to elect a proper person. The Legislature ordered Isaac Collins to identify the author, who had signed the article as "Cincinnatus." However, in this early case involving the principle of freedom of the press in New Jersey, Collins refused and was supported by a 17-to-11 vote in the Assembly. A note sent by Collins to the Legislative Council was described in its minutes as "an impertinent refusal to the requisition made to him" on October 29, but a move to insert this note in the minutes was voted down.[64]

The last week of November, the light dragoons under Colonel William Washington passed through town again on their way to Bristol.[65]

Peter Gordon reflected on the critical situation in New Jersey in a letter to Moore Furman on November 3. "Poor New Jersey [it] seems must bear a large proportion of the burden of the war. We have not one bushel of forage on hand & have no less than six [wagon] brigades in town. But must push them out." He also told Furman, "I beg you will remember the first of January I quit the department and think you had better provide one to take my place in time[,] and if he was to be here the middle of next month to see a little in the business of the post would be an advantage." Gordon had little use for the Legislature and told Furman on November 12, "I know not what our Assembly is at. But hope they are not asleep as usual." Commenting on some discouraging news from the South he wrote, "No doubt it will raise the drooping spirits of the disaffected – and sink the timmid Whigs. But the firm and determinate will stand unshaken, with this class I will at present rank myself."[66]

Furman reported on November 22 from Trenton that he had had the pleasure of "seeing several hundred barrels flour go out of town for camp" and hoped they would "arrive in time to prevent the Army from too long [a] fast." However, he warned that supplies were short and he did not have even 20 barrels of provisions at Trenton to send on. Furman had met with the Assembly and "informed them of the impossibility of supplying the Army with forage without their aid." He was infuriated when told the Assembly wanted to work in coordination with other states, because he knew such an approach would take a long time while the problem demanded immediate solution.[67]

Before leaving Trenton to return to Pittstown, Furman sent out two men to purchase forage from local farmers. He specifically wanted rye, corn, oats, and buckwheat in sufficient quantities to supply the needs of his post at Trenton and also the army. He authorized his men to purchase forage at the prices set for that area, but his foragers found that farmers would not sell to them because prices in other counties were higher and the farmers were willing to travel some distance for them. Furman lamented that this resulted in the farmers carrying forage "from the army to carry it to the army."[68]

What military stores there were at Trenton were vulnerable to theft in spite of the militiamen routinely guarding them. Beginning about the middle of October, men from Captain Quigley's company from Nottingham provided guards at Lamberton for about five months. In spite of these guards, on the night of November 5 the Continental store house at Trenton Landing was broken into and nine barrels of flour were stolen. The wagon taking it away left tracks for some distance up the road towards town. Commissary Lowrey very optimistically offered a reward for return of the flour, in whole or in part.[69]

In mid-November, the Continental army was preparing to go into winter quarters near Morristown and needed a supply of building materials for huts. Nathanael Greene went on ahead of the troops to mark out the ground and told Moore Furman to expect instructions on "where to direct the boards and other materials for hutting the army. I wish you to hasten on the boards from Trenton and other quarters as fast as possible."[70] However, there was still some uncertainty about exactly where the winter quarters would be located, so some things were sent to Morristown and some to Middlebrook.[71]

Meeting at Mount Holly on November 15, the Assembly agreed to a motion made by Benjamin Van Cleve of Maidenhead that benefited Trenton residents. His proposal was to appoint committees in each county to appraise the damages suffered "from the ravages of the British troops, and from the waste committed by the army of the United States, or the militia of this or any of the neighbouring States." Trenton residents had suffered much property destruction from all the troops passing through and spending time there, and now there was hope for some compensation.[72]

Moore Furman was in Trenton on November 22, expeditiously procuring boards and other supplies to Morristown. He had forwarded 100,000 feet of boards to different locations, pending the final decision on the encampment site. He wanted to send another 100,000 feet but noted that dry weather had "prevented the saw mills from going nor has the late rain raised the springs the ground being so dry it has drank up all that fell."[73]

At Morristown, Nathanael Greene found that carting boards for huts from Trenton and points south was so difficult that he wanted Furman to stop contracting for them but send on immediately all that he currently had. Ultimately, the troops at Middlebrook used the boards, while the huts at the Jockey Hollow encampment at Morristown were constructed of logs. The hutting was progressing well for the troops, although the officers were still camped in the open. Maryland Captain William Beatty worked on the huts until December 26 and then set out for Maryland to do some recruiting, passing through Trenton on his way south.[74]

In December, Peter Gordon continued to be dismayed by the failure to alleviate problems. He wrote Furman, "I am astonished at the enormous price given for forage in Pennsylvania ... . Poor Continental and I may say poor America what will become of you, for it really appears as clear as the sun at noon day that we are working our own ruin fast and very fast – and which almost turns my brain." He could not understand how people in the department could live with themselves when they used the poorly regulated system for their own benefit. All he could do was "sett it down fast that all the servants of the public are no better than they ought to be. He believed the government purchasers "who are the public servants should buy as low as we possibly can - or be unfaithfull."[75]

Late in the year, Continental units came through town under orders to join the southern army. Washington ordered the North Carolina regiments in late September to march by the shortest route to South Carolina and, due to some uncertainty about the developing situation, they were ordered to "proceed slowly towards Trenton" and halt there until further orders.[76] The North Carolina Brigade under Colonel Clark finally came through town on its way south in the first week of December. Peter Gordon commented, "The North Carolina troops left us this morning [December 4] they came here day before yesterday and cluttered us much. However they behaved well and look hearty – about 600. Their light infantry past through some days ago."[77]

Troops of the Virginia Continental line arrived in town on December 12 and were noted by Isaac Collins as being in high spirits and making "a martial appearance." Peter Gordon noted, "The Virginia Line is marching through. Two regts is here now, expect two more this evening." A number of enlistments were approaching their end and men were being discharged, such as William Dollar who was discharged while they were in Trenton.[78]

While Nathanael Greene felt there was a good possibility for obtaining adequate supplies of long and short forage, he was concerned that supplies of all kinds at Trenton were "likely to be reduced very low in every necessary for man & beast by General [William] Woodfords [First Virginia] Brigade which is halted here and wait for further orders." Woodford arrived in Trenton the evening of December 13, not feeling well and needing a rest, as well as orders for his troops. Furman commandeered his wagon conductors, wagons, and drivers because they were needed immediately at camp to bring in forage, or the army would shortly be in distress.[79]

Furman's major concern was for adequate forage, but there was also the need for a great quantity of firewood in the cold season, and wood was "exceedingly difficult to get within any moderate distance of the town." However, lack of flour was a greater problem than wood. Rice had been substituted for flour, but was running low. Luckily, the troops sent to the south would allow the provisions "collected hereabouts [to] be forwarded to camp where it is much wanted." Because of the shortages, "everything that can be called bread that falls in my power shall go on as fast as possible for I shall be under the greatest uneasiness till I hear of a supply being arrived there." Furman found there were almost 200 teams employed at Trenton, more than were absolutely necessary and more than could be supported with the available forage unless there was "considerable aid from Pennsylvania." However, he had no reason to expect help from that quarter and sought orders for how many teams he should retain in service. If there were not sufficient numbers of oxen at camp for hauling and more could not be gotten, he could make up the shortage with horse teams.

By the end of the month, Washington was hopeful that the Virginia troops had marched from Trenton, not only because it was reported that British troops were sailing for the south but to reduce the demands on the supply system struggling to provide provisions and forage to the army. The Virginia troops were scheduled to start leaving on December 22; however, Furman found he had to juggle the teams needed to carry provisions to camp with those needed to haul baggage for the Virginians, so the Virginians were delayed. The lack of money forwarded to Furman had put him at considerable personal expense to keep things going and he was again considering leaving his post. He was very disappointed to learn that Nathanael Greene had resigned as quartermaster general and wondered who would succeed him.[80] The Virginians did not leave until the last week of December. Woodford divided them into three divisions to make marching on the road easier and sent the divisions off on December 27, 29, and 31.[81] Part of the Virginia troops were still in Trenton on December 28 when Martha Washington came through town on her way from Virginia to Morristown, and they formed up and greeted her.[82]

By the end of the year, Furman was getting requests from his subordinates to help them settle accounts, but he had to use whatever small amounts of money he received to get at least some supplies to camp. Those money sources were now drying up and he had no idea how to replace them. If things did not change quickly, he planned to "go to Philadelphia & lay my distressed circumstances before the Board of War, Treasury Board or wherever is most likely to give relief." Debts incurred for "necessaries called for by the Army" increased "much faster than the supplies of money came in and for some weeks past notwithstanding my most earnest solicitation for money [I] have not been able to obtain any." Even in this distressed situation, he was determined "to persevere to the end for no man has more feelings on these occasions," and he continued to hope that ultimately "we may be enabled to pay off our contracts with honour."[83]

The weather was extremely cold and by December 22 navigation on the Delaware between Trenton and Philadelphia was completely stopped, delaying the arrival at Trenton of shipments of southern flour badly needed by the soldiers suffering at Morristown. By the end of the month, Furman was grateful to hear that there were reasonable supplies of forage at camp and that some grain would be sent from Hunterdon and Somerset counties to increase the supply.[84] The early severe weather presaged what became the coldest, snowiest, and most miserable winter encampment of the war.

As the year drew to a close, Greene was glad that Furman planned to spend the winter at his home in Trenton rather than Pittstown, believing this would improve communication. This was good news to Peter Gordon, who wrote him that "I rejoice at your determination of moving down and you may be assured every thing shall be provided that this quarter will afford – hay and wood you shall have in abundance." He reported that "Mrs Furman safe arrived last evening [December 12] but complains of being much fatigued."[85] Furman had stationed himself at Trenton by December 20.

Innkeeper Joseph Clunn had resigned his command of the Hunterdon militia artillery company to accept a captain's commission in the six-month State militia under his friend Colonel Sylvanus Seely. One of Seely's duties was to prevent illegal trade with the enemy at New York. In late November, Seely was accused of being involved in the illegal trade himself.[86] Joseph Clunn found himself involved in this case, accused of seizing two trunks that belonged to two known Philadelphia Loyalists. These trunks were supposedly delivered to Captain John Clunn, Joseph's merchant and ship-captain relative, at Trenton and then taken to Philadelphia.[87]

Governor Livingston asked Rensselaer Williams to assist Pennsylvania with the inquiry, telling him that the investigator from Philadelphia would meet with him when he came to Trenton "to seize two trunks with merchandize from New York imported contrary to law, & now in the possession of Capt. Clun. There is the strongest reason to believe that the goods were brought out for some Tories in Philadelphia, & that Capt. Clun means to protect them for their benefit under pretence of their having been condemned to him, which from many circumstances is supposed to be altogether fraudulent." Livingston considered this a very important matter and told Williams to call on Justice Benjamin Yard if he needed help. He said this case fell under a law recently passed by the Legislature putting the burden of proof on the defendant to prove the goods did not come through enemy lines.[88]

Livingston met with Joseph Clunn and reported to Pennsylvania President Joseph Reed that Clunn "declares positively that the goods were condemned to him without any collusion; & that they never were in Philadelphia, nor have ever been removed from Trenton." Clunn complained that he had been confined "and at last held to such high bail by a state [Pennsylvania] which [he] supposes had no jurisdiction in the matter." Livingston expressed hope that "we may be able to develop the mystery, as there really seems to have been a design of passing the goods as the property of Mrs. Bergen, for which he does not account to my satisfaction."[89] However, in March 1780, the court martial results of the case against Colonel Seely were announced and he was not only acquitted but praised.[90] This also exonerated Clunn.

The Legislature passed an act in December moving the location of State Supreme Court meetings to the Trenton courthouse on the first Tuesday of April and September and the second Tuesday in May and November. Each session was to last not less than three days nor more than 11 days, excluding Sundays.[91]

As 1779 came to a close, Trentonians were beginning to experience the worst winter weather of the century as well as dealing with rampant inflation and a war with no end in sight, even though France had become an ally of the young United States.

Chapter 12

1780

The Marquis de Chastellux, a member of the French Academy and Major General of the French Army under the Count de Rochambeau, visited Trenton on November 29, 1780. He enjoyed visiting the battlefields at Princeton and Trenton, and commented in his travelogue that "all my steps were on martial ground, and I was in the same morning to see two fields of battle." He noted that when approaching Trenton, "the road descends a little, and permits one to see at the east end of the town the orchard where the Hessians hastily collected, and surrendered prisoners." After a day exploring battlefields, Chastellux wrote, "it was but right to think of dinner. I found my headquarters well established in a fine inn kept by Mr. [Rensselaer] Williams." This was the Royal Oak Tavern, on the corner of Queen and Third Streets, and Chastellux found "the sign of this inn is a philosophical, or, if you will, a political emblem. It represents a beaver at work, with his little teeth bringing down a large tree, and underneath is written, perseverando."

Shortly after his arrival in town, Chastellux was visited by fifty-seven-year-old Governor William Livingston, whom he described as "a much respected old man, and considered a very sensible one. He was pleased to accompany me on a little walk I took before dinner, to reconnoiter the environs of the town and see the camp on Mill Hill occupied by the Americans before the affair of Princeton." Afterward, Chastellux "returned to dinner with Colonel Moylan, M. De Gimat, and two aides-de-camp of M. De La Fayette, who had arrived some time before me. We were all acquainted, very happy to be together, to dine at our ease, when a justice of the peace, who was at Trenton on business, and an American artillery captain came and sat down at the table with us, without any ceremony; it being the custom of the country for travelers when they meet at the hour of dinner, to dine together." Chastellux found the dinner excellent and "there was wine on the table, a very rare and dear article in America," but he was somewhat miffed after dinner because he had ordered the dinner charged to him, and his companions "learned this on going out, but set off without saying a word" to him about it. Chastellux noted, "I have often had occasion to observe that there are more ceremonies than compliments in America. All their politeness is mere form, such as drinking healths to the company, observing ranks, giving up the right of way, etc. But all this comes only from what they have been taught, none if it arises from feeling; in a word, politeness here is like religion in Italy, all in practice and nothing from principle." He set out from Trenton at 4:00 pm and crossed the river at one of the Trenton ferries, then on to Bristol.[1]

The year 1780 produced great uncertainty and growing frustration. No end to the war was in sight and although a French army finally arrived at Rhode Island, it was unclear whether these allies would help Washington attack the British at New York City. Chastellux was not the only French dignitary to come through town. In mid-April, His Excellency the Chevalier De La Luzerne, Minister Plenipotentiary from the Court of Versailles, Mr. Marbois, and Mr. Merailles, a "Spanish Gentleman of distinction," came through on their way to headquarters at Morristown, escorted by a troop of light horse. Luzerne passed through again on September 19 on his way to headquarters. LaFayette, passed through on his way to Philadelphia the first week of December. Continental and militia troops continued to march through or occupy the town, while the hospital and supply depot remained active.[2] Public morale was eroding due to the continuing financial crisis, lack of success in the southern campaign, and perceived caution on the part of Washington.

Dr. David Cowell placed what appeared to be a routine notice in the January 12 *New Jersey Gazette* advertising the sale of "a sober, healthy, able bodied Negro man of about 32 years of age, who has had the small pox, and understand all kinds of farming business, and the care and management of horses, equal to any in the country." Cowell would also consider exchanging the man for a "suitable Negro boy of about 16 years of age." However, there was nothing routine about the announcement, and a letter instigated by it and simply signed "Adam" appeared in the February 2 edition of the paper. This letter purported to be from the man advertised for sale by Cowell and warned the public that he had purchased his freedom but that Cowell was trying to deny it. Adam expected that, should anyone try to purchase him from Cowell, he would be protected by the "freedom, justice, and protection which I am entitled to by the laws of the state, altho; I am a Negro."[3]

Cowell defended himself in a follow-up letter on February 23 that denied there had ever been any agreement concerning Adam's freedom. He named Quakers Nathan Beakes and Stacy Potts, although "without any desire to expose" their conduct, as encouraging Adam since the previous October 30 to leave Cowell's service. Adam had been unfaithful by attempting to escape to New York the previous summer, which cost Cowell "great expence in gaol fees, money paid the guards, and riding more than two hundred miles after him." Cowell said he had brought action in the Supreme Court against Beakes and Potts, one of whom now employed Adam. He was only able to begin court action after locating an attorney who had not already been given a retaining fee by Beakes or Potts.[4]

This letter certainly did not end the issue. Another long, legal-sounding letter reasserting the validity of his claim and signed by "Adam" appeared the next week. He said that exposing the conduct of Beakes and Potts would actually result in "rendering their characters more amiable." While those two men would not stoop to attack the character of Cowell, Adam felt he "might be justified in exposing his conduct by open design, when perhaps attempting to violate his solemn engagement with me would appear the least exceptionable part of his character." He then referred to old accusations that Cowell had "become notorious for having defrauded his father, robbed his brothers and sisters of their patrimony, and by venality and debauchery, render[ed] his person as nauseous as his character is contemptible." Of even more importance was that investigation would reveal the "negligence and misconduct" that caused "numbers of brave soldiers" to be "sent to eternity, at a time when their services here were most necessary." This statement indicated that Cowell had treated soldiers at the military hospital established at the Trenton barracks. In closing, Adam wished "that every foot may wear the shoe that fits it, while I continue to pray for the prosperity of that government which protects the rights of a poor Negro."[5]

The letters signed "Adam" were in fact, according to Cowell, written by Beakes, Potts, and someone else not identified. Cowell's next letter appeared the following week and, referring to their religion, he attacked "the three quaking authors of the two illiberal pieces of calumny signed Adam." He demanded they write the truth and "no longer act the hypocrite to me and their too indulgent country." They should know that they "are so well known by their friends, and their characters and cause blacker than the slave they want to keep in their debt, and consequently in their service his life time." They are "miscreants, who having lost all sense of truth and decency, have rendered their persons fit companions only to runaway negroes, and their congenial spirits amiable only to demons." Defending his work as a military doctor, Cowell claimed to have in his possession "from the head of the department, authentic credentials of having 'acted in the military hospitals near two years as an industrious, humane and skillful Senior Physician and Surgeon, and always manifested great zeal to the American cause.'" He called for someone to use force, if necessary, to effect the just return of his "unfaithful disobedient negro" to his master.[6]

Although Cowell was very critical of Stacy Potts, Potts was again elected town clerk at the annual town meeting in March, while Cowell was not elected to any office. Other leading Trentonians elected included Charles Axford, Jr. as assessor, Joseph Britton as an overseer of the poor and collector, Benjamin Smith as a freeholder, and Abraham Hunt as a commissioner of appeal and overseer of the Trenton roads.[7]

Cowell apparently won his case in court, but in June 1783, almost three years later, he wrote another letter for the paper stating that Adam continued to be absent from his service. The constables had been unable to take him, even though he was still suspected of being "employed, protected, secreted and encouraged, by the same evil-minded advisers as formerly." He had been seen recently by several witnesses "mowing in the meadow of Nathan Beakes, in company with a young man who lives at his house." He noted that Adam did not stay in one place for long and was constantly being moved by his protectors. He forbade all people from harboring, employing, or dealing in any way with Adam and hoped that someone might apprehend him and deliver him to Cowell, the constable, or the jail keeper. To encourage a non-judicial resolution, he offered a generous reward to anyone who successfully encouraged Adam to return "to his duty, which will prove much to the advantage of the negro."[8] Nothing further is known about Adam but his story reveals the mixed feelings about slavery in Trenton at this time, as well as some of the tensions between members of the community.

In addition to their opposition to slavery, the militia law put the pacifist Quakers in a difficult position. Several Quakers found themselves in conflict with their meeting because they payed fines in lieu of militia service or actively participated in militia duties. Several men were disowned from the Chesterfield Monthly Meeting, including John Appleton, Josiah Appleton, Nathan Beakes, Jr., and William Yard. The Appletons had also been accused of neglecting to attend religious meetings of the Friends and John of holding a Negro in bondage and not manumitting him. Fulling mill owner Abraham Skirm was one of the men assigned to inform the Appletons of these charges and let them know their rights of appeal.[9]

Conditions at the winter encampment at Morristown were already desperate in early January due to lack of food. Washington wrote to the New Jersey magistrates on January 8 that for the past two weeks, both officers and privates "have been almost perishing for want. They have been alternately without bread or meat, the whole time, with a very scanty allowance of either and frequently destitute of both." All had suffered patiently, but "they are now reduced to an extremity no longer to be supported." Out of desperation, some men had plundered property from nearby civilians and, instead of punishing them, Washington could only lament their actions as "an unfortunate necessity." The "early commencement and uncommon vigor of the winter" made it almost impossible to transport supplies to camp and the magazines near camp had been exhausted. Additional supplies from beyond New Jersey would take more than five weeks to arrive, and he was worried that "unless an extraordinary exertion be made within the State to supply the wants of the Army during that space, fatal consequences must unavoidably ensue." The unprecedented harsh winter weather made it almost impossible for supplies to get there all winter. However, in spite of Washington's deep concerns, the people of Trenton read in the *New Jersey Gazette* a week later the overly optimistic assessment and conflicting message that due to "the spirited exertions now making," the army was "likely to be well supplied."[10]

Because of this extremely perilous situation, Washington announced quotas of bushels of grain and heads of cattle for each county to collect and deliver to the army in several locations near Morristown. Hunterdon County's quota was 1,500 bushels of grain and 150 cattle, to be collected within six days. The weights of cattle brought in would be estimated by the local magistrates, in conjunction with the commissary, to ensure fair prices were given. Washington warned that if his request was not complied with in short order, the only alternative would be chaos and suffering because the starving soldiers would have to seek food wherever they could in a random rather than organized way. Washington did not want to confiscate food supplies and proclaimed the commissary department would work with the magistrates to set up places where supplies could be delivered and the owners given receipts for future payment, either at the price at time of delivery or at the time of actual payment, at the owner's choice. However, farmers, craftsmen, and merchants would soon have to pay a heavy state tax enacted to support the war and they needed cash, not receipts.[11]

Moore Furman continued to believe in late January that "as things are now circumstanced no man can do business for the public with credit to himself or advantage to the public." He had done all he could to get food to the army, but because of those efforts there were now millions of dollars owed to citizens of New Jersey for many months and he was "exceedingly alarm'd now and under great anxiety least it will not remain long in my power, to perform the task set me under my present circumstance." Beside himself, Furman told his boss, General Greene, that he would follow the order to cease purchasing items on credit at the end of the month and focus on paying department debts. But, he sarcastically asked, should he also discharge wagon teams in service, which would stop delivery of food to the army? Furman had recently sent on 150 wagons to help transport supplies from Philadelphia and believed he had done everything humanly possible to get food for the army.[12]

On any given day in mid-January, Furman might send off anywhere from 20 to 60 wagons but found it difficult to hire farmer's teams, except for short trips. The horses were available because there was less farm work for them in the winter, but the farmers would only agree to work if they could be home at night. To conserve forage, Furman looked for any opportunity to reduce the number of horses he had to feed and wrote to Nathanael Greene in February that he had assisted Pennsylvania with wagons, but now they were able to perform the needed service themselves so he was going to reduce the number of teams in his service. Because forage supplies always fluctuated and were seldom plentiful, the quartermaster at Trenton was constantly faced with the puzzle of how many horses to keep in service. Horses ate every day, whether or not they worked. They could not just be parked and left alone until needed.[13]

On top of his other problems, Furman was dealing with legislated changes to his department, and in January he wrote to Greene that he had "for some time feared that such continual change of men and measures in the conducting our public affairs would bring on great confusion and now think it near. For my own part, while I continue [temporarily] in the service, I wish to be directed and to pursue that which will really serve my country, and the present great cause at issue, and may God unite us all in these measures."[14] Furman didn't even know how much money, if any, had been advanced by Greene to Furman's assistants and asked him for an accounting, so he could hold them accountable for it. In February and March, the Assembly considered additional laws to regulate the quartermaster department, adding to the uncertainties.[15]

Furman worried in February that his forage supply would not hold out until the river unfroze and he could get more from the south, and without forage "the teams must stop." Furman experienced two difficulties, one bureaucratic and the other supply. He wrote Greene on February 19 that "If I cannot be supplied [with money] so as to do the business with some credit I had better decline before trouble comes for I fear few will look beyond the Q Master if there be any deficiency." He discharged a large number of wagons for want of forage but by mid-February was still virtually destitute of it. Besides horses at Trenton, he had to feed a number of cattle that were fit for slaughter but being kept alive for future butchering and meanwhile consuming forage needed for horses. The Assembly finally ordered Furman to have someone drive the cattle to a part of the state containing more forage.[16]

While food for soldiers and forage for horses may have been a problem, Furman reported to Greene on February 9 that the previous week he had received "two pipes of wine for his Excellency." He had inspected it immediately and "found it in a very cloudy or rather muddy state & in my opinion of an indifferent quality," but felt that some time in a warm cellar would improve its taste and appearance. He sent on the pipes in closed wagons because he didn't trust their successful arrival at camp in an open wagon.[17]

Opportunities to settle the accounts of the supply departments were announced in the newspaper in February. James Ewing, an auditor of accounts, set up office at the tavern of Mrs. Ann Janney at Trenton Landing, and all persons who had "demands upon this state" were required to see him to adjust and settle accounts.[18] The next week, Moore Furman announced that anyone with "any demands against me as Deputy Quartermaster General of this state, either for monies due, or that will become due by the first of March next, are requested to send in the accounts to the Quartermaster in whose district the debt was contracted" to settle those accounts. Former quartermaster Peter Gordon, now living in Hopewell, made himself available in Trenton to settle accounts on Mondays during March. Without money to pay debts, these men could only provide certificates promising future payment. Large numbers were needed and the blank certificates arrived slowly from Philadelphia, so Furman hired Trenton printer Isaac Collins to print some locally.[19] Azariah Dunham, Superintendent of Purchases, was directed to attend the Assembly at Trenton on March 11 "and to lay before them an account of his proceedings in the execution of his office, since his appointment." In his testimony, he stressed that some contractors purchased supplies at higher prices than others.[20]

At the end of March, Furman sent Assistant Quartermaster General Charles Pettit a summary of the winter situation. He warned, "My difficulties increase and will soon I fear be insurmountable." For some time, the army had been on half rations some days "and but few days the whole ration." He had forwarded 300 or 400 barrels of flour that week and now had about 100, but knew that his work did no more than simply keep the soldiers alive. Feeling helpless, Furman wrote "I hope and expect provisions sufficient will be produced but how it will be transported to them I know not, for more than the half the teams in the service has given me notice that they are under a necessity of quitting it. The wages being so very low it will not support them." Unless he got more money and permission to pay a reasonable price for carting, Furman insisted, "I now desire you to take notice that I will not hold myself accountable for the consequence after this present month of March runs out and this I beg you will not fail to communicate *immediately* to those who can grant relief in the premises."[21]

A February advertisement for a teacher vacancy at the Trenton school solicited candidates "qualified to teach reading, writing, arithmetic, and some of the branches of the mathematicks." Good references were essential and candidates should apply to Isaac Collins. Because it was felt that the teacher should be able to devote his full energy to his teaching, it was noted that "a single man, or one with a

George Bradshaw's c1929 etching of the original Trenton schoolhouse next to the Presbyterian Church on Second Street. (THS, Trenton)

small family, will answer best." A few months later Collins printed a want ad for "a good schoolmistress, who can teach reading, and most kinds of needle-work, knitting &c." Collins' shop also was the local source for school books, such as the *New England Primer*.[22]

The General Assembly and Legislative Council began sessions at Trenton in mid-February, although it took several days to get a quorum, due to the weather and bad roads. An early action approved $20 per month for widow Rezine Anderson. The Assembly heard complaints from a group of Trenton residents asking that the town no longer be used for an army hospital, but took no action. Departing from the usual practice of meeting at a tavern, the Joint Meeting of the Legislative Council and Assembly met at the school house on March 17.[23]

For many years, the location of Trenton at the extreme southern end of Hunterdon County had raised complaints that it was an inconvenient county seat. The legislature voted on March 4 to move the county seat to Henry Mershon's tavern, formerly John Ringoe's tavern in Amwell Township. This moved the county court and meetings of the freeholders, but not the Legislature, and only reduced crowding in town a little. The Legislative Council and Assembly adjourned on March 21 until their next meeting on May 10 at Trenton.[24]

The expansion of the war in the south, Washington's continued hope to attack the British in New York, and British forays from Staten Island into northeastern New Jersey brought a variety of military units through Trenton during the year. The Maryland Continental Line led by Brigadier General Gist came through town on their way south in April and "made a very martial appearance." They were part of some 2,000 reinforcements being sent at General Lincoln's urgent request to reinforce the Southern army in the expectation of General Clinton bringing an army from New York to South Carolina.[25] These Maryland Continentals may well have been the "throng of the soldiery" that prevented at least one meeting of the Trenton Friends. The soldiers took over the meeting house and only a few Friends attended meeting at an alternate location, the house of Stacy Potts. The Trenton Quakers had been having difficulty holding regular, well-attended meetings because of all the activity in town, and a committee of the Chesterfield Monthly Meeting was formed to visit Trenton and "endeavor to strengthen and encourage them to a discharge of their religious duty of keeping up their meetings on first and other days of the week with reputation."[26]

Most of the men working at the supply depot were local residents who obtained government jobs but then had to deal with all the financial restraints and low salaries of the supply departments. The following is a snapshot from April 1780 that shows the complexity of the work at the supply depot and the deep involvement of Trenton men. Commissary General of Issues Stephen Lowrey employed Aaron Howell as clerk, James Brown as superintendent of unloading vessels and loading wagons, cooper Josiah Appleton on an occasional basis, four laborers, and one four horse team used for carting from the wharf to the store. James Paxton of the commissary department employed as a scale man Arthur Howell, the man who said he was almost hung by the Hessians in December 1776. Howell was assisted beginning in early July by Jacob Hall who had served in the New Jersey Continental Line and been wounded in the shoulder at the battle of Springfield. He carried his arm in a sling and only had use of one arm and hand but ably assisted Howell until June 1781.[27] Jesse Roscow may also have been serving as assistant commissary of hides at this time. These men all worked alongside the men employed by the quarter master and forage master departments: Quartermaster Ellett Howell and Daniel Yard his assistant; Assistant Deputy Quartermaster General Furman Yard; Forage Master Thomas Yard and Charles Axford his assistant; Barrack Master Jonathan Richmond assisted by Philip Bowne; Superintendent of the Continental Stable Daniel Gano; Hostler Joseph Oatman; Measurer of Forage William Campbell; and, hay stackers Jeremiah Frankford and Jasper Hawse. James Burnside, Furman Yard, William Christy, and William Tindall were employed "making out the accounts for the State to receive reasonable pay according to the depreciation of the money."[28]

The supply depot at Trenton Landing contained a number of buildings belonging to the United States but located on lots rented from Abraham Hunt or Moore Furman, including a 25-by-60 foot stable, an 80-foot-long horse shed, a commissary store, an office, and a guardhouse. Rented facilities on private property included a store and usage of Abraham Hunt's wharf at Trenton Landing, a store for forage from Richard Waln, an office for a quartermaster and forage master from Widow Janney, an office for two quarter masters from Moore Furman, a house and lot for issuing forage from Thomas Yard, and a lot for a hay magazine from Samuel Tucker.[29]

Supplies coming into the depot in April included corn from Worcester County, Pennsylvania, while supplies going to the army in May included 45 dozen canteens. In May and June, Moore Furman was paid for two cattle and Furman and Hunt for 106 gallons of rum, both requisitioned by General Washington.[30]

In early April, Moore Furman, as usual, had only a few days' supply of forage and the owners of horse teams in the Continental service were on the verge of leaving because wages were so low, when they were paid at all. He had notified Congress of the problems without response, and although very frustrated, he vowed that as long as he had "a team at command they shall be employed carrying on something to Head Quarters for man or for beast."[31]

To save trouble and expense, Furman encouraged Philadelphia officials to send stores by water on government-owned vessels. On their return trips to Philadelphia, the boats could carry, at no cost, poor soldiers and released prisoners, saving them a long walk. However, stores arriving in river vessels at Trenton Landing were not always handled properly. If the commissary officials did not feel authorized to accept a shipment, it just sat there. In May, for example, a quantity of flour and Indian corn was sent from Salem County and the Continental agents refused to accept it. Nicholas Keen, the boatman, notified the Assembly of this problem, and it ordered him to offer the flour and corn to Stephen Lowrey and Moore Furman and take their receipts for it. If they declined, Keen was to inform the Legislature.[32]

Dealing with forage supply issues in May, Washington suggested to Clement Biddle that Trenton would be "a proper place for collecting a large quantity of forage."[33] However, Furman was completely frustrated in May and wrote to Nathanael Greene that he had been unable to conduct any of his personal business because of constant attendance to his quartermaster duties. In order to agree to continue, he needed a higher salary, forage for two horses, traveling expenses, and the authority to appoint his subordinates. He was adamant that if the department was not staffed to his satisfaction, "I do not hold my self bound to act any longer than is sufficient to settle up my accounts and it be convenient to you to appoint [someone] to succeed me." In June, Furman petitioned the Legislative Council to provide relief for several of his assistants who were being prosecuted for situations they could not control.[34]

Because horses were so expensive to obtain and keep, the Assembly and Legislative Council appointed a committee in June to determine just how many horses were being kept at Continental expense "in and about the post at Trenton" belonging to the agencies of the Continental Congress or employees at the post, and how many of these horses could be "spared for the immediate use of the army." Continental Stable Superintendent Daniel Gano worked with this committee when it met at Jacob Bergen's tavern the evening of June 2. Bergen had relocated about a month earlier to Trenton from his tavern at the Sign of the Confederation in Princeton. His Trenton tavern was a large house rented from Samuel Henry at the corner of the market house. The committee determined that a number of horses could be spared for other public duties.[35]

Joseph Jenkins of Trenton was appointed Sergeant at Arms when the Assembly began its May 10 session, and it voted unanimously "that the doors of this House be kept open, and that the inhabitants of the State be permitted to be present at the transacting the business of the House, except on such particular occasions as in the opinion of the House shall require secrecy." Jacob Bergen's tavern was again used for Joint Meetings on May 15 and June 17 before the Legislature adjourned on June 19.[36]

The food situation at Morristown was a constant concern and on May 9 it was estimated that the meat supply would last no more than a week and flour, if made into bread, perhaps two weeks. However, there were 1,500 barrels of flour at Trenton or on the road to camp from there. Later in the month, a supply of pork arrived from Trenton, but in June some 1,700 barrels of flour were "detained at Trenton for want of carriages."[37]

Army food supplies became so depleted that by June 20 the Assembly authorized State officials "to purchase or impress every article produced in this State and to transport the same for the use of the army." In addition, the magistrates of areas adjacent to Trenton had been "directed to issue warrants for the impressment of wagons, teams and drivers for the immediate conveyance of the stores now lying there." The Assembly communicated these actions to Congress to emphasize the desperate situation of New Jersey farmers trying to feed their families when the army encamped in their state also experienced shortages of food. New Jersey needed significant help, especially with transportation, to get stores out of Trenton. Because the army was so short of wagons, Washington requested Pennsylvania to immediately supply 250 and that number was sent to Moore Furman at Trenton. By June 28, officials at Trenton were again advertising for wagoners and promising to provide them with grain for their horses and payment for hired wagons.[38]

The quartermaster department also transported military items needing repair. During June and July, Furman forwarded to a repair facility large numbers of unusable armaments, including over 1,800 muskets that were damaged or missing various parts such as ramrods, lock plates, trigger guards, cocks, and butt plates. He also sent parts of guns (including barrels, locks, and ramrods) and hundreds of old cartridge boxes, cartridge box blocks, and bayonet belts.[39]

When the British made a foray from New York towards the army at Morristown in June, militiamen from Trenton were among those called out to counter them. The Gazette reported that the men turned out "with unanimity and resolution" and in the effort to repulse the British foray, Philemon Dickinson commanded the New Jersey militia at the battles of Connecticut Farms and Springfield. The Legislature authorized Hunterdon County to purchase a hogshead of rum for the militiamen who turned out.[40]

In mid-June, Generals Arnold and Wayne came through on their way to Morristown along with Major Henry Lee and his light dragoons.[41] On a Sunday evening in late June, a troop of 38 Philadelphia light dragoons arrived under the command of Lieutenant James Budden, a veteran who had distinguished himself during the January 2 battle at Trenton and at Princeton. The *Gazette* reported that "they were exceedingly well mounted, and made a very martial appearance." Over the next several days, a total of 10 Hessian deserters from Elizabethtown Point, including a corporal, came into town bringing their arms with them. They had been part of the enemy force that fought the Continentals and militia that month. Earlier, 34 Hessian prisoners had been brought to Trenton.[42]

The *Gazette* reported on June 28 that the ladies of Trenton and adjacent areas had "instituted a subscription to be applied as a donation to the soldiery, for the purpose of rendering their situation more easy and comfortable." They had been inspired by the recent actions of Pennsylvania women led by Esther Reed, wife of the President of Pennsylvania, Joseph Reed, who had initiated a fundraising drive to aid the soldiers of the army. A committee of women was formed in Trenton on July 4 to raise contributions by subscription in a similar statewide effort. The committee included: Moore Furman's wife Sarah as treasurer; Miss Mary Dagworthy as secretary and committee members Mrs. Isaac Smith, Mrs. John Cox, Mrs. Philemon Dickinson, and Miss Elizabeth Cadwalader. Mary Dagworthy would "receive and answer all letters that the ladies of the different counties may think proper to favour her with on the occasion, and to furnish them with proper subscription papers as soon as possible."[43]

Within days, requests to use some of the money raised began to come in. Abraham Clark of the Medical Committee of Congress wrote to Sarah Furman asking for help securing bandages and lint for dressings for sick and wounded officers and soldiers in the hospital near Basking Ridge, many of them wounded at the recent engagements at Springfield.[44] However, Mary Dagworthy wrote to General Washington on July 17 that by order of Mrs. Dickinson and the ladies of the committee, she was sending him $15,488 raised by subscription to be disposed of as Washington thought proper to benefit the Continental soldiers. Additional sums would be sent as they were received. Washington graciously thanked the ladies on August 6 but asked them to hold any additional sums until it was known how the money from the Philadelphia ladies would be used, or, if they wished, to combine their contributions.[45] Washington actually preferred that the ladies would send articles of clothing or cloth rather than money. Giving the soldiers money would inevitably cause behavior problems. With this in mind, and while they continued raising money, at the end of the year, Mary Dagworthy, on behalf of the New Jersey ladies, sent 380 pairs of stockings to DQMG Neilson, to be forwarded to Washington for the Continental soldiers.[46]

Supplies were needed at West Point in early summer in expectation of a British attack. Moore Furman forwarded about 2,800 barrels of flour about July 2. As always, forage for the horses was in short supply and he sent some people to help with it so that enough flour could get to West Point before a British attack. Furman was still frustrated by the problems of funding and staffing that convinced him he could not satisfactorily perform his job much longer. He felt he had to continue, though, and not stop after the campaign opened, when "every mans assistance, be it ever so small, will help." Wagon brigades were again on the verge of quitting and then he would only have militia teams, which could not be used more than six days at a time.[47]

The Second Delaware Regiment (militia), enroute to Dobbs Ferry on the Hudson River, arrived by water at Lamberton in July and marched through town on its way to Princeton.[48]

A camp was established at Trenton on July 28 as a staging area in anticipation of a joint American and French campaign against New York City but abandoned on September 2 when those plans faded. A variety of Pennsylvania militia units, totaling about 1,500 men, arrived over several days in mid-August. President of Pennsylvania Joseph Reed came to Trenton as commander of this large body of troops camped on the common below the town.[49] One unit, the Second Troop Philadelphia City Cavalry had been ordered into active service along with other Philadelphia units to "take part in the New Jersey campaign which centered in and around Trenton." For about five weeks these men were "called upon to perform numerous and arduous tasks which were all cheerfully and ably carried out, and that without any compensation, at the time, from the Government." John Cox had warned Greene that military supplies were very scarce at Trenton and throughout their stay the Second Troop had to rely on its own resources for provisions, "supplemented by the generous liberality of its officers," who must have approached the already stressed local merchants and area farmers. Adding to the burden, in late August, a regiment of 251 Delaware militiamen, enlisted for four months, came through the congested town on its way to camp and stayed several days.[50]

The full Pennsylvania militia brigade formed up about 9:00 am on the morning of September 1 and was reviewed by President Reed. The troops "performed a variety of military manoeuvres with great ease and exactness. They then marched thro' the town in proper military order; and after they had returned to their camp, were dismissed by His Excellency." Isaac Collins found them exemplary militiamen who were "well clothed and equipped, and made a truly martial appearance." The officers addressed President Reed, expressing their disappointment at not seeing any action against the enemy but declaring their loyalty and admiration to Reed and their State. Reed, in turn, complimented them on their conduct while in camp, especially for not causing problems with the local population, and assured them of future contact with the enemy.[51]

Edward Giles procured a great deal of clothing for the Maryland troops and expected to procure vests at Trenton, but he found they had all been forwarded to camp and issued out. By the first week of August, the magazine at Trenton was empty and wagons sent there for supplies found "not a barrel of flour." At the end of September, Charles Stewart at Tappan had only a one-day supply of flour and his deputy at Trenton informed him that there was none there.[52]

By mid-September, Moore Furman had completely run out of patience and was about to finally leave his position. He had resigned over a year earlier and periodically threatened to leave. Furman received a letter from Colonel Charles Stewart dated September 14 telling him, "You must have made up your mind by this time; I hope it is to continue the campaign. But if your usage has been such as not to permit you, for God's sake get a successor to your liking and do not let the public suffer more than you can." Furman had done well, but if he was succeeded by "an ill-inclined fellow … it may be ruinous to the public before they are aware of it."[53]

Congress had reorganized the supply departments on July 15 and turned much of the work over to the states, in addition to reducing the number of positions. There was to be only one assistant quartermaster general and Cox was let go. There could be no more than one deputy quartermaster general for each state, and other reductions in staff and their benefits were made. For Nathanael Greene, the cuts were the last straw and he was replaced by Colonel Timothy Pickering. So Greene and Cox were out and Moore Furman was described by Cox on August 7 as "determined not to continue an hour longer than is necessary to forward on to camp the provisions received at this post previous to the new arrangement."[54]

Furman was getting rid of excess horses and equipment in September and held a public auction of several horses, old wagons, and sets of harness at the Continental stables in Trenton on Saturday, September 30. He also asked all people who had horses or other United States property in their possession to bring it in immediately. In the advertisement he was listed as the former deputy quartermaster general. He also wanted to settle his accounts and announced that he would be at his Trenton office throughout the month of October to settle debts of the quartermaster and forage departments incurred between March 2, 1778 and September 20, 1780, his time in office. However, things had not been settled by mid-November causing Furman to announce that officers in counties would continue to "receive the vouchers and give certificates all the present month of November, after which the books will be closed, and any demands not made by that time must wait another opportunity for settlement."[55]

In mid-September, several deserters from the enemy passed through town about the same time as 110 Continental army recruits from Cumberland County, Pennsylvania. Deserters were not always well treated in Trenton. In September, jail keeper John James was convicted by the Supreme Court of mistreating a deserter from the British troops captured at Saratoga. James was found guilty of placing the man in irons and depriving him of "the necessaries of life" in an effort to extort his "hard money." He also promised the man his liberty and gave him a travel pass. James was removed from office, paid a £10 fine, and was imprisoned himself for four months. James had served in the five-month levies in 1776, was wounded at White Plains, and then served as a forage master, supplying the hospital staff first at Trenton and then at Valley Forge. After his discharge in October 1778, he returned to Trenton and served the remainder of the war as a sergeant in the militia artillery company to fulfill his military obligation.[56]

Several days after beginning its session on September 13, the Legislature heard a message from the governor highlighting the problems of providing the army with provisions and raising men for the army. John Bellerjeau was named Sergeant at Arms to the Assembly. One of his main duties was chasing down absent members to get them to attend. Charles Axford rode express for the Legislature for four days in September. Joint Meetings of the Legislative Council and Assembly were held at Bergen's tavern on September 22 and 23, and then on September 26 and 27 when it settled on the arrangement of officers in the New Jersey Continental regiments.[57]

New QMG Timothy Pickering commissioned Colonel John Neilson as Moore Furman's replacement as DQMG for New Jersey on September 18 at Trenton. Neilson wrote to the Board of War on October 27, detailing continuing concerns about provisions and forage. Personnel had changed but the problems persisted. Thomas Carpenter at Trenton found himself too busy procuring provisions for the army to deal effectively with settling his accounts expeditiously. The Legislative Council received a letter from Pickering describing the crucial need for forage and requesting that some method be devised for procuring it. A committee of three from the Legislative Council was appointed to meet at Jacob Bergen's tavern with members of the Assembly to consider the letter and also the problems of guarding the state frontiers during the coming winter. The Legislature dealt in early November with the issues raised by Pickering, noting that because of the summer drought and the large supplies of forage already furnished, hay was so scarce that every horse "that can possibly be spared from the army" must be sent out of New Jersey "as early this season as convenient." States neighboring New Jersey must be called on to fill the magazines so that forage could be sent to the army.[58]

The competition and controversy over designation as the Continental Ferry continued and the *New Jersey Gazette* announced in September that the deputy quartermasters for Pennsylvania and

New Jersey would hold public meetings "at Patrick Colvin's ferry on Monday the 9th of October next, from 10 o'clock to 12, and at Capt. John Clunn's tavern from 2 o'clock to 4." Those attending the meetings would discuss whether to keep the Continental Ferry at Trenton Ferry or move it back to the lower ferry. After this meeting, it was moved back to the Lower Ferry "of which all persons in public employ having occasion to pass the said ferry are to take notice – Where good boats and careful attendance is continued for the convenience of private travellers also."[59]

By late November, New Jersey's desperate supply shortages not only prevented farmers from voluntarily selling goods to the army but threatened the survival of their families. Supplies were being impressed in exchange for certificates, rather than cash, making it difficult for people to purchase needed items and pay their taxes. New Jersey desperately needed help from the Congress.[60]

At a Joint Meeting on October 30 and 31 at Bergen's tavern, William Livingston was re-elected governor and on November 23, also at Bergen's, the Legislature elected representatives to the Continental Congress.[61] In December, a joint committee of the Legislative Council and Assembly was formed to settle the accounts of Samuel Tucker during his tenure as treasurer of the former Provincial Congress. The committee reported on December 30 and accepted Tucker's account. The only question was the loss of the unsigned money taken by British Lieutenant Colonel Abercrombie in December 1776 from the John Abbott house. For everything else there were proper vouchers.[62]

Everything had seemed so favorable at the beginning of the year but now things looked bleak and army enlistments for many soldiers were about to end. The war in the south not been going well, money problems continued, militia callouts continued to be a heavy burden, and activity in Trenton remained high. In a letter to John Cadwalader in October, Washington expressed what many people in Trenton were no doubt feeling. "We are nearing drawing an inactive campaign to a close. The beginning of which appeared pregnant with events of a favourable complex'n. I hoped but hoped in vain that a prospect was displaying which wd enable me to give a period to my military pursuits, and restore me to domestic life." Just as Washington wanted to get back to his farm, militiamen wanted to get back to full-time farming or their business. Looking to the future year, Washington wrote "I see nothing before us but accumulating distress. We have been half of our time without provision and are like to continue so. We have no magazines, nor money to form them, and in a little time we shall have no men, if we had money to pay them. We have lived upon expedients till we can live no longer. In a word, the history of the war is a history of false hopes and temporary devices, instead of system and economy."[63]

Washington was also concerned that "the enemy seem to be practicing the arts of corruption so extensively that we cannot be too much upon our guard... The policy of the enemy to distract us as much as possible by sowing jealousies." The people of Trenton would certainly get caught up in the efforts to combat the enemy's perceived economic warfare and efforts to expand corruption over the next several years.[64]

Chapter 13

1781

Trenton shoemaker and militia captain William Tucker had worn a number of hats as a leader in the war for independence from its beginning. He had served constantly, often in harm's way, and sat down on April 4, 1781 take care of some militia business dating from January, a hectic month due to the January 1 mutiny of the Pennsylvania Continental regiments at their winter encampment at Morristown. The mutineers had marched off towards Philadelphia intending to confront the Continental Congress over issues of enlistment lengths, pay, and items promised to them such as food and clothing that had not been delivered. Adamant that they had not abandoned the cause of independence, they remained essentially peaceful on their march and when they encamped at Princeton on January 3. Companies of the First Hunterdon were called out to help make sure local civilians were not plundered and that the mutineers remained peaceful. Captain Tucker's men had been warned out on December 28 for a routine one-month tour beginning January 2.[1] The usual difficulties in getting the men together, the news of the mutiny, and fear the mutineers would pass through Trenton, caused a series of delays and the company did not march until January 9, when the mutineers were only a few miles from town. In the midst of this unsettling situation, the Legislature passed a new militia law on January 8 that increased the fine for not turning out. Three months later, Captain Tucker called together Lieutenant James B. Machett and Ensign David R. Chambers to help take care of the paperwork to levy fines on those militiamen who had not turned out for duty during recent months, including on January 9. Tucker placed a £20 fine on Isaac DeCou, who had resigned his major's commission in the First Hunterdon militia in 1776 and was a prosperous Trenton merchant. He also fined respected Trenton resident Micajah How £15. Both men had probably been paying fines since 1776 and symbolized to Tucker and his officers that class of citizen who, although supporting the patriot cause, found ways to avoid militia duty, placing a heavier burden on those willing to turn out.

Micajah How was not going to quietly accept this particular fine. He had been a judge under the colonial government and understood well the current laws in effect. He believed Tucker fined him an excessive amount and was going to appeal it. He created a document stating that when he was warned out on December 28 to appear on January 2, the law then in effect, dating from April 1778, called for a fine of £6. How stated that he was never informed of the change in marching date from January 2 to January 9, and that the new law was not published in the newspaper until more than 10 days after the company marched. Therefore, he should not be liable for the fine of £15. He had a point and probably won his appeal. He did not say whether having knowledge of the new, higher fine would have caused him to turn out, which was its purpose. Had the new law been passed a month earlier, he probably would have paid the higher fine with no problem. It was just a question of fairness, and Tucker, who was probably fed up with those he felt were slackers, appeared to be deliberately and unfairly hard on him. While How and DeCou probably performed little, if any, active militia service during the war, they remained respected citizens. But the long war was fraying everyone's nerves.[2]

This was a critical year. The war had dragged on inconclusively for six years since Lexington and Concord, runaway inflation brought several states close to bankruptcy and made life extremely difficult for everyone, and as the year began the Articles of Confederation were not yet in effect. New Jersey had accepted them over two years previously, but ratification had to be unanimous before they could take effect. Maryland, the last holdout, finally ratified and the Articles of Confederation became effective on March 1. The lack of a strong central government and the jealously guarded prerogatives of the states had prevented coordinated action on conducting the war. On the positive side, there was a French alliance and the promise of French military support, but how it would play out was not clear. It was generally understood that events of 1781 would determine the outcome of the long, tiresome war. In January, the ladies were still collecting pledges of money to help the soldiers and Rensselaer Williams was trying to reestablish the Trenton Library Company.[3] The people of Trenton were trying to rebuild their community while continuing to accommodate individuals and groups using their town as a thoroughfare.[4]

As the New Year began, Trenton residents became alarmed that a large group of disgruntled soldiers of the Pennsylvania Continental Line, who had mutinied at Morristown on January 1, was heading their way. The mutineers left Morristown intending to march on Philadelphia, by way of Trenton, to seek redress for their grievances. They were not a violent mob and maintained their military order and discipline under their sergeants, not their commissioned officers.

The mutineers marched "through the country with great regularity and good conduct, and perhaps less damage than is common on the passing of troops." They stopped at Princeton, and Princeton's Reverend Samuel Smith told Governor Livingston on January 3 that although the soldiers were very well behaved, he was concerned for the people of Trenton. Reminiscent of December 1776, part of an army was preparing to cross the Delaware at Trenton and descend on Philadelphia. Smith had been informed that, just as in 1776, some officers had been ordered to Trenton "to secure the boats upon the Delaware, in order to prevent these troops from passing." Smith was convinced that such an action would enrage the mutineers and put the people of Trenton and Nottingham in danger of reprisals. Smith recommended helping the mutineers get across the river to Pennsylvania and thereby distance them from any influence by British agents. The people of Trenton undoubtedly would agree with him. While at Princeton, the mutineers seized a messenger and his guide carrying proposals to them from General Clinton. "These they rejected with so much honour and indignation that they seized the messengers and delivered them to General Wayne, who put them under guard."[5]

Rather than allow the mutineers to reach Philadelphia to negotiate their grievances, a committee of the Council of Pennsylvania and a committee of Congress came to Trenton, arriving after dark on the night of January 6, to meet with the Pennsylvania soldiers. The mutineers arrived in Trenton the afternoon of January 9, and General Sullivan believed that "the unhappy dispute will be brought to a favorable Issue." By that evening, Sullivan could write to Washington that the troops appeared willing to accept the terms offered and the dispute would soon be resolved.[6] The principle problem was that some men had enlisted for three years or for the duration of the war, while others had enlisted for exactly three years period, and others for the duration of the war, so that it was not always clear which situation applied to each man. The problem was solved by not extending enlistments beyond three years. Still, each man had to be examined individually for any exceptions and to determine his enlistment date.

The two British "spies" turned over at Princeton were tried and executed at 9:00 am on January 11 "at the crossroads near the upper ferry." The committee of Congress appointed commissioners to hear and settle the claims of each soldier and returned to Philadelphia on January 15. Isaac Collins summed things up for his readers with an appropriate patriot focus by saying, "upon the whole, this affair, which at first appeared so alarming, has only served to give a new proof of the inflexible honour of the soldiery, and their inviolable attachment to American liberty; and will teach General Clinton that tho' he could bribe such a mean toad-eater as [Benedict] Arnold, it is not in his power to bribe an American soldier."[7]

On January 15, General Sullivan reported that two regiments had settled their enlistment issues and that things were proceeding in "as peaceable and quiet a manner as could possibly be expected." However, "their board of sergeants still continues to set and issue orders - and absolutely refuse to give up their authority to their officers until the whole matter is finally settled[,] indeed there seems to be an impassable breach between the men and their officers, and a total want of confidence in them."[8]

During the last two weeks of January, the people of Trenton found themselves interacting with newly discharged soldiers as individual cases were settled between January 15 and 28.[9] While the mutineers were in and about Trenton, a number of residents provided services for the government negotiators and the soldiers. For example, the Continental Congress reimbursed Rensselaer Williams $5,545 for expenses incurred by the committee of Congress at his tavern.[10] Francis Witt, Thomas Tindall, George Beatty, and others provided large quantities of firewood for the Pennsylvania soldiers, while David Brearley was reimbursed for posts and planks they took and used as firewood. William Trent supplied a ton of hay to the commissioners. Jonathan Richmond quartered some soldiers and also used his horse daily in procuring firewood for the Pennsylvania troops between January 9 and 29.[11]

DQMG John Neilson was responsible for obtaining these services from local people. Neilson moved his family to Trenton in January, renting a house from Moore Furman, and made Trenton his home as well as his headquarters. He had at least two children of school age and he made several payments to James Burnside for schooling his son John. Under the new department arrangement, Neilson was the only DQMG for New Jersey. He hired Cornelius Ten Broeck, a man in his early sixties, as one of his clerks. Neilson had known him in Somerset County and convinced Cornelius to come to Trenton to work for him. His other clerk was Philip Lott, a young man who had fled New York with his family when the British came in 1776 and became a resident of Trenton.[12]

*E*veryone was concerned about spies and individuals losing their passion for the cause. Gershom Johnson operated one of the stage lines between Philadelphia and Elizabethtown in 1781; it made round trips twice each week, passed through Trenton four times a week, and stopped for meals at Jacob Bergen's tavern.[13] In January 1781, he announced that because of concerns about Loyalists, deserters, and illegal trade with the enemy, he would only carry freemen of the United States or others who could produce proper passes. He would not carry any prohibited goods, no matter how much money he was offered, or any sealed letters, unless they were addressed to a commissioned officer belonging to the United States.[14]

The Legislative Council and Assembly met for a regular session on January 1 and voted on salaries for government officials. The next day, the Assembly heard a memorial from "sundry Inhabitants of Trenton" asking that when salaries for such officials were voted on in the future that "the Yeas and Nays may be entered on the Minutes of the House, in order that they may be informed by whom their Money is given." The memorial was ordered filed.[15]

The Assembly appointed Rensselaer Williams to take charge of the Trenton barracks "and to close up the doors and windows thereof, as well to prevent the same as far as may be in his power from being damaged, as to render them the more comfortable for quartering of troops." He was empowered to draw up to £20 from the state treasurer to defray his expenses and was "allowed such compensation for his time and trouble as the Legislature shall deem reasonable." He purchased 200 shingles from Stacy Potts in April and boards from Joseph Milnor in May, when he also paid carpenters for their work and for nails.[16]

On January 8, the Legislative Council and Assembly met jointly at Bergen's tavern and late in the day passed a very extensive militia law; the one that increased fines and caused Micajah How to appeal his. Copies of the militia act were printed by Isaac Collins and a set number were delivered to each regiment, including the First Hunterdon; but, as Micajah How would say, this was too late for him to be held accountable to it.[17]

Nottingham militiaman Samuel Wooley returned to Trenton in January after signing onto and experiencing adventures on a privateer out of Philadelphia in the summer and fall of 1780. Wooley entered into Captain Robert Quigley's company of Burlington County militia a few days after the British messengers to the Pennsylvania mutineers were executed. He found himself frequently in service because the men in Quigley's company lived near the meetings of the Legislature, the governor's residence, and the jail, all of which needed guards. As a little girl, Prudence Vandergrift often went to see Quigley's company parade, as did young John Morris, brother of militia drummer William Morris. Governor Livingston frequently sent out members of the company to break up suspected plots to capture him or to bring in prisoners being sent to Trenton, not just Loyalists but also horse thieves, counterfeiters, and other criminals. On one occasion, Wooley helped Adjutant Alexander Douglass bury, at Lamberton with full military honors, a soldier killed by Loyalists.[18]

Isaac Collins and about 20 citizens from Trenton and its environs met on February 10 to form the Trenton School Company. They met "sensible of the great importance of education to the well-being of individuals, and the good order of government, and of its peculiar use in early life, and judging the present means of it in this place inadequate." They felt the current school on the Presbyterian Church lot did not provide everything that Trenton needed. They agreed "to purchase a lot, erect a commodious building thereon, and form a permanent school under proper regulations." The original board of trustees consisted of five quite prominent men, including Stacy Potts, who served as its clerk, Moore Furman, James Ewing, William Churchill Houston, and Isaac Collins. To raise money for the school, 36 shares of stock were sold and parents not owning a share had to pay a half dollar each quarter in addition to tuition. The original stock purchasers were a Who's Who of Trenton society: Joseph Higbee, David Brearley, James Milnor, Jr., Rensselaer Williams, Joseph Paxton, Isaac Smith, William Tucker, Conrad Kotts, Stephen Lowrey, Abraham Hunt, Robert Neil, Micajah How, Jacob Benjamin, John Neilson, and Francis Witt. Each student had to pay extra charges for several things, such as firewood which cost three-quarters of a dollar per quarter. The trustees purchased land in May on Third Street and began work on a two-story building, 20-by-26 feet, with a cellar under the whole. The old schoolhouse by the Presbyterian Church continued in use, and a December 5 notice informed the inhabitants that "an English Night School will be opened on Monday evening the 10th day of December." Those interested were directed to inquire about terms to the school master there.[19]

Captain William Tucker sat on the March 21 court martial trying the Third Hunterdon's Lieutenant Colonel William Chamberlain at John Cape's tavern.[20] Cape had taken over Jacob Bergen's tavern, The Thirteen Stars, in February, after Bergen left Trenton to operate the Bunch of Grapes Tavern in Philadelphia.[21]

The annual town meeting in March was routine. Stacy Potts and Charles Axford, Jr. were, as usual, chosen clerk and assessor, respectively. Saddler Benjamin Smith was chosen a county freeholder and Abraham Hunt as overseer of the Trenton town roads, as well as one of the commissioners of appeal. Money for care of the poor was increased.[22]

James Ewing, serving as Auditor of Accounts at Trenton, was having difficulty in March getting county contractors to make returns of their purchases and settle accounts. He placed a notice in the *New Jersey Gazette* ordering them to obey the law and take care of these things immediately, and this included those who had resigned their positions and not yet made final settlement of their accounts.[23]

The war in the south had been very active in the early months of 1781 where Lord Cornwallis commanded a British army fighting against troops commanded by General Nathanael Greene. Washington had counselled Greene to conduct his campaign in a manner that would avoid the loss of his army and keep the South involved in the war while Washington and Rochambeau aimed for a decisive action against New York. The important battle of Cowpens was won in South Carolina in mid-January followed by the larger and crucial victory at Guilford Courthouse, North Carolina in mid-March. Cornwallis then marched his greatly depleted and battered army into Virginia.[24]

In mid-March at Trenton, General Philemon Dickinson was preparing for the coming campaign and expecting it would include a major effort to take back New York City, a long held desire of General Washington's. He alerted militiamen in a newspaper notice to hold themselves "in the most perfect readiness to march on the shortest notice; it being probable their services may soon be required." He ordered officers to "pay the strictest attention to their men's arms and accoutrements, that their appearance in the field may reflect honor on themselves." Field officers were directed to make returns of their regiments and brigades "agreeably to the direction of the last militia law, passed at Trenton, January 8, 1781." As a leader, he had to make morale-boosting statements, but he must have winced when he wrote that he expected the men to "turn out with that spirit which characterizes the Militia of New Jersey." The militia had a very mixed reputation for turning out with any kind of spirit. His final comment in the notice certainly did not point to the desired spirit. A citizen had sent Dickinson an "account of the 'conduct of a guard'" who was apparently stealing things from people. Dickinson supported the writer's suggestion that any militia guard engaged in such activity should be taken "to a safe place, there to remain until they shall be taught that their duty is to protect, not plunder, the good people of the state."[25]

A petition to the Assembly on May 28 from some inhabitants of Trenton sought remedies to some of the issues with inflation and trade. Except for trade with the enemy, the people wanted removal of restraints on trade, revisions to the powers given to purchasers of items for public use, a tax raised to pay the interest on bills of credit, and a date set "after which the Continental Money shall not be receivable in taxes or in debts or contracts payable to the State." They wanted the money collected from forfeited Loyalist estates used to pay off "certificates given to the inhabitants for supplies, or to the troops for the depreciation of their pay." They also wanted Congress to "regulate the alloy of the precious metals for the purposes of coinage." Clearly, money issues were primary in the minds of many citizens of Trenton.[26]

William Chambers applied for a tavern license in May, testifying that he "hath procured that large and convenient house wherein Joseph Clunn lately kept tavern for the same purpose, except a small part totally unconnected with the rest which is a separate tenement."[27]

By May, Moore Furman, with two or three clerks, had constantly attended his office in Trenton for about six months just to settle accounts. Then, for the support of his family, he needed to remove to his farm at Pittstown where he would continue "to adjust and settle such demands as may hereafter be made until they are all come in, or until some other mode of settlement be adopted." He hoped "that some expedient may be fallen on to discharge said debt as it will greatly contribute to the convenience and advantage of the inhabitants of the State and most certainly encourage them again to take up and bear the burdens of the present hour with more cheerfulness and alacrity."[28]

In May, Governor Livingston asked First Hunterdon Colonel Joseph Philips to provide a guard for some prisoners to be taken from Trenton to Morristown. Philips advised him that he had ordered his adjutant to have the captain of each company send two men "properly armed & equipped to Trenton" at 10:00 am the next morning, "to parade at the gaol in order to take charge of, and march the prisoners etc." Phillips did this even though he believed the sheriff, who could hire local men for the job whether or not they were active in the militia, should provide the guard. Phillips did not want to intrude on another official's duties and was increasingly tired of his militiamen being called out for so many diverse reasons that it increased his difficulty in getting the men to turn out when they were really needed.[29]

DQMG John Neilson announced in May "that the Continental ferry, at present kept across Delaware river at the lower landing, will be discontinued after the sixth day of June next ensuing; and that attendance will be given at the upper or old ferry below the falls, for transporting the publick across."[30] Regardless of which ferry was designated the Continental, both ferries continued to compete for business. In July 1781, the New Jersey Gazette carried the notice that "the owner of the ferry known by the name of the Trenton Old Ferry, on the post road leading to Philadelphia, and where the publick all crosses, has provided the said ferry with the best boats that ever have been constructed for the safety of transporting passengers, horses and carriages, in time of freshes, wind or ice, and a number of careful hands that have nothing else to do but work the boats, and are always ready on the spot." He also announced his fees for ferriage: a wagon and four horses, 5 shillings; a wagon and two horses, 3 shillings and 9 pence; a riding chair, 1 shilling and 6 pence; a man and horse, 6 pence; a person on foot, 3 pence, "and all other ferriages in proportion." About a month later the ferry was described as having two ferry boats and some sailboats available to make the crossing.[31]

The war was now concentrated on the southern theater and American troops under the Marquis de Lafayette traveled south in March to reinforce General Greene in North Carolina.[32] Lieutenant Ebenezer Wild of the First Massachusetts Regiment marched in this force. On February 28, the troops set out about sunrise from Princeton to Trenton with Wild in the rearguard that prevented straggling. They arrived at Trenton about 1:00 pm, and Wild found quarters with "Mr. Barnes" about a quarter of a mile north of the market house. On March 1, the troops again paraded at daylight and about sunrise marched to Trenton Landing, where they boarded vessels provided by Thomas Ashmore to take them downriver. Wild embarked aboard a large schooner that sailed at 9:00 am when the tide and wind were favorable.[33] This turned out to be the precursor to a much larger operation six months later.

Five months later, Trenton residents read in the *New Jersey Gazette* on Saturday, August 11 that during the previous week, the French troops from Rhode Island had joined with the American army on the east side of the Hudson River and the New Jersey Continentals had been ordered to march to Kingsbridge. The notice commented that "from these movements it is natural to conclude that some military operations, of a serious nature, will very shortly take place." The natural expectation was an attack on New York City. However, Washington decided by August 27 not to proceed with a campaign against New York but instead to take his combined American and French army to Virginia. He wanted to keep this plan a secret, and keep the British in New York on alert, for as long as possible, but people in Trenton must have become aware of it sooner than most. In another reprise of his actions taken in late November 1776, Washington ordered boats to be collected at Trenton to transport his troops. He ordered DQMG

Samuel Miles at Philadelphia "to have the greatest possible number of sloops, shallops and river craft of all kinds, fit for the transportation of men, artillery and baggage collected from every quarter where they can be found, and brought to Trenton by the 31st. Inst. at which time the head of the column is expected to arrive: Let others be procured and ordered to follow to the same place, as fast as may be, untill orders are received to the contrary." Miles was to carry this out in such a way that "neither labour or expence may be wanting in the performance of the *important business* now committed to you." He also dispatched a messenger to Trenton to make provisions for transporting the troops by water to Christiana Bridge, now Christiana, Delaware.[34]

Washington planned to be in Trenton on August 29. On August 28, he gave General Benjamin Lincoln the order of march for three columns that would converge on Trenton and arrive on August 31. Washington already knew that there would not be enough watercraft at Trenton to transport all the troops to Christiana Bridge and while he wanted the American troops to be in the advance, the available vessels should be provided equally to the French and American armies. He warned Lincoln that "some delicacy must be used in effecting the latter, without the appearance of selfishness, and giving umbrage to our Allies by taking more care of ourselves than them." Washington was not only concerned about boats but also having enough wagons, especially covered wagons, and teams to carry army baggage from Trenton to Head of Elk and then Virginia.[35]

Baron von Closen, a young aide-de-camp to Rochambeau, arrived in Trenton on August 29 after traveling 45 miles, dining at Princeton with General Washington, and then accompanying him to Trenton where they slept that night. Von Closen commented that "the trip with the General was the more interesting, because it gave me the opportunity to learn from General Washington himself, while we were traversing the very terrain, the dispositions, movements, and other circumstances of the famous battles of Trenton and Princeton in 1776 and 1777, the details of which I very faithfully recorded in my collection."[36] When von Closen left the next morning to continue south, he commented that Trenton was "on a charming site a half mile from the left bank of the Delaware. In spite of the ravages of the Hessians (who made themselves hated by their lack of discipline or consideration for the peaceful inhabitants during their winter quarters in the Jerseys), there are still, nevertheless, several fine houses in Trenton." He found the General Assembly meeting place, the residence of Governor Livingston, and two churches to be very fine buildings.[37]

Lamb's artillery was camped at Princeton on August 30 and his troops were told that drums would awaken them at 4:00 am the next morning, assembly would be beaten at 4:30 am, and the march to Trenton begin a half hour later.[38] Washington knew that not all the troops, supplies, and baggage would fit on the available boats and some would have to travel by land. He ordered General Lincoln to consult with Colonel Lamb about "the heavy cannon, carriages, stores and baggage, and find what will be most cumbersome and heavy to transport by land and let that have the first chance in the transports by water." The type of craft he procured would determine just how much of the heaviest items he could load. Perhaps all the covered and other wagons would have to go by land along with the light cannon and perhaps some cannon carriages. The heavy cannon, mortars and howitzers, clothing, and entrenching tools should go by water, with the heavy cannon barrels removed from their carriages. Quartermaster Neilson had told Washington that there was reportedly a ford in the Delaware River at Trenton "by which the wagons and carriages might be easily passed at that place." Washington advised Lincoln to consult with Neilson about this ford, but it was apparently not used much for this crossing. He told Lincoln that the troops designated to proceed by land should be "the lightest and best able to march, and such as are least suspected of desertion from disaffection, want of pay, or any other cause." Washington ordered Lincoln to send 100 picked men to assist with the loading and "appoint an active officer to superintend the embarkation at Trenton, whose arrangements must be calculated for dispatch and to save confusion." The craft sent up to Trenton numbered some 31 vessels, consisting of four wood flats, four schooners, and 23 sloops with an estimated capacity of 4,150 men.[39] There were about 3000 American and 5000 French soldiers, so these boats could accommodate no more than half of them.

General Lincoln, leading the van of the army, arrived about noon on August 31 and informed Washington that "our van has passed" and "the rear will be at the ferry in about one hour. ... No moment will be lost in loading the artillery stores &c. ... As soon as I can ascertain the time I can have the ferry I will inform your Excellency of it. I shall encamp tonight on the banks of the river [and] by this I hope to prevent all deserting." However, several men did desert, including fifer Anthony Bremer of Colonel John Lamb's artillery regiment and two others, followed by two men the next day. Altogether, about 10 men deserted from the regiment.[40]

Amid the high level of activity at Trenton on August 31, officers attempted to figure out how best to use the available boats to satisfy changing requirements. In his second letter to Lincoln on August 31, Washington told him that "upon consultation with Count Rochambeau, I find that he is inclined to have the French troops march by land from Trenton to Head of Elk, which will give a larger proportion of craft for the American baggage and troops." Therefore, disregarding his previous letter, Lincoln was to allot space on the vessels for the French baggage, load heavy stores and baggage, clothing, tools, and garrison carriages in consultation with Colonel Lamb, and then embark troops and send them down river to Christiana Bridge as soon as possible while keeping only enough men to accompany the wagons and baggage. He noted that General Knox now thought that the artillery pieces and stores would best go by land to prevent delay. While Washington was not opposed to using the ford in the Delaware for wagons and carriages, he may have ended interest in using it when he ordered Lincoln to "be particularly careful that no accident happens by miscrossing, as that will create much trouble and delay." The quartermaster general would give Lincoln instructions on the number of spare wagons needed to transport the army from Christiana Bridge to Head of Elk. The Assistant Quarter Master at Trenton should "give every assistance in his power to the French troops, in crossing the ferry, or in any other circumstance in which they may need his aid."[41]

The Artificers Company marched to Trenton on August 31, crossed the Delaware and encamped, but then crossed back to New Jersey and encamped there until September 3, perhaps because their services were needed to assist with crossing.[42] Sergeant-Major John Hawkins of Hazen's Canadian Regiment wrote in his journal that at day break on August 31 the drums sounded, and soon Hazen's and Lamb's regiments paraded and marched. They passed through Trenton and halted, encamping at the lower ferry. He reported that "about an hour after we encamped Col. Scammel's Corps of Light Troops, the Rhode Island and New Jersey Lines, and part of the New York Line and Sappers and Miners passed us and encamped in our front between us & the river." The French troops were still encamped between Princeton and Trenton. Hawkins noted that about 6:00 pm part of the army was embarked aboard shallops with the artillery and baggage, while the wagons and horses went by land. His regiment was "among those that first embarked."[43]

Sergeant Joseph Plumb Martin of the Sappers and Miners arrived about sunset on August 31 after a series of "rapid marches" from Chatham. They expected to camp for the night but were "ordered immediately on board vessels, then lying at the landing place, and a little after sunrise found ourselves at Philadelphia."[44] The Fifth Connecticut Regiment came to Trenton on August 31 and crossed the river on September 1.[45]

According to Dr. James Thacher, a surgeon in the Massachusetts Continental Line, those troops traveled to Trenton rapidly because their destination was no longer a secret, and they crossed at Trenton Ferry on September 1. He recalled that Washington had made Trenton "famous to the latest times, by a victory in which he so happily displayed the resources of his genius, in the severe winter of 1776. Great indeed must be the resources of that man who can render himself the most formidable to an enemy, when apparently he is the most destitute of power."[46]

Lincoln reported to Washington at 5:30 pm that they were in the process of putting the artillery and its stores on board the vessels. He would send the corps of artillery, the sappers and miners, and Colonel Hazen's regiment in the same vessels and expected them to leave about 7:00 pm in order to be at their destination by early morning. The light infantry, the Jersey Brigade, and the First New York Regiment would leave Trenton in the morning. The First New York Regiment found there were not enough boats to transport them, so they continued to march after crossing the river. There were so many empty wagons at Trenton that the troops which had to march would do so easily. The American troops had all crossed by 6:00 am the next morning when Lincoln reported to Washington that the last four wagons were then passing.[47] The First Brigade of the French Army arrived about 10:00 am and camped along Broad Street in Bloomsbury.

Frenchman Abbe Robin wrote on September 2 that "we were yesterday encamped in the vicinity of a very agreeable little town [Princeton]: and although we are today but twelve miles from it, we are come in view of another not at all inferior to it, in pleasantness and the salubrity of the air, and situated to much better advantage."

He observed that its "advantageous situation, makes it a place of considerable trade, and intercourse with the capital of Pennsylvania, especially in the article of provisions. The Delaware is navigable thus far up, for vessels of some tolerable burden, but afterwards becomes all at once so shallow, that a little above the town carriages may pass safely over at the fording places, when the tide is out." The French found the ford's greatest depth to be two-and-half feet and that "care must be taken to face upstream against the current as far as a point above the little island, after which you can head straight for the opposite bank." They got across to Pennsylvania with their baggage by 7:00 am the next morning and the Second Brigade arrived shortly after they completed crossing and crossed with its baggage by 6:00 am on September 3.[48]

When Claude Blanchard came to Princeton on September 3, he intended to stay the night, "but the weather was fine and I proceeded to Trenton, going forty miles in the day." He found Trenton to be "a pretty considerable village," more a "little city" that "seems to announce the vicinity of a capital." He left quickly the next day, having learned that the army had arrived in Philadelphia. He crossed at the ferry and described the Delaware as "neither broad nor deep at this place, but at the distance of four leagues it becomes as broad as the Loire below La Fosse. I had heard Americans say that these rivers resembled each other; this resemblance also struck me owing to the colors of the white and limpid water and the low and agreeable banks."[49]

Colonel Philip van Cortlandt of the Second New York Regiment had been ordered to construct 34 boats in preparation for carrying the army from Elizabethtown to Staten Island as part of the planned attack on New York. He was told personally by Washington of the change in plans and to proceed to Chatham with his regiment, the boats, and entrenching tools to be the rearguard of the army. On his way to Chatham, van Cortlandt received orders on September 2 to march quickly to Trenton and the next morning he marched his men 21 miles instead of the usual eight or nine. They stopped and encamped at Maidenhead, broke camp early the next morning and marched to Trenton Landing, arriving about 8:00 am. Then they put their boats in the river, loaded them, and departed about 1:00 pm, while the vessels carrying stores sailed about 4:00 pm.[50]

While at Trenton, at least some American soldiers were paid part of the money due to them with French specie. The French brought

14 wagons loaded with gold and silver coins through town. Achmet Hamet, a native of Africa who had enlisted in the Connecticut line as a drummer, was one of the soldiers paid and remembered the men assembled around wagons. The French army contributed to the local economy through its purchases, made with specie instead of paper money of questionable value or a receipt, and this was very pleasing to everyone. A few men also found employment with the French army, such as Isaac Quigley who had been driving his father's wagon and team, pressed into service by Hugh Runyon in early July, along with other wagons bringing wood and hay to Trenton. When the French army came to town, he signed on as a wagoner and went with them to Virginia.[51]

Several Trenton men later received payment for services they provided to the American and French armies. Isaac Yard supplied 170 cords of wood burned by the army and Benjamin Yard another 100 cords. Several men supplied yokes of oxen or teams of horses to help move artillery from Raritan Landing or Princeton to Trenton. Hugh Runyon ferried the army across the Delaware. Other men pastured animals or rode express delivering messages. Thomas Ashmore freighted in his vessel 38 chests of arms and three tons of lead from Trenton to Philadelphia and for 10 days transported the artificers of the Army, their tools and baggage to Christiana Bridge as well as passengers and their baggage to Philadelphia.[52] Hugh Runyon also ferried nearly 4,800 men, over 600 horses, and 399 wagons drawn by over 2,000 oxen of the French army on September 2 and 3. About half the wagons and animals were privately owned by French officers.[53] While the armies may have damaged roads and property due to so many men, animals, and wagons passing through, the economic benefits at least partially compensated for it.

A legislative Joint Meeting held at Princeton on September 28 elected John Cox second judge for Burlington County and Moore Furman a Justice of the Peace for Hunterdon County. The Assembly and Council met on October 23 at Trenton and a Joint Meeting at John Cape's tavern in Trenton on October 30 unanimously reelected William Livingston as governor. John Cox was one of two men appointed to notify Livingston of his election. Other Joint Meetings at Cape's were held in November and December. On December 20, the legislature passed an act for assessing damages sustained by citizens of the State from "the waste and spoil committed by the troops in the service of the enemy and their adherents, by the Continental army, or by the militia of this or of the neighbouring states." The men chosen to appraise damages in Hunterdon County were Peter Gordon, Sidney Berry, and Colonel Joseph Phillips.[54] A number of Trenton residents benefited from this act.

On Monday afternoon, October 22, an express from Philadelphia rode through Trenton on his way east and dropped off a letter to Colonel Neilson from DQM Samuel Miles in Philadelphia with "truly great and interesting" news, preliminary information about the victory over Cornwallis at Yorktown.[55] This news spread like wildfire and the surrender was joyously celebrated on Saturday, October 27, beginning with the beating of drums and the display of the American colours in various parts of town. At 11:00 am, the governor, the Legislative Council and Assembly, together with people from the town and vicinity "attended divine service at the Presbyterian Church, where a discourse adapted to the occasion was delivered by the Reverent Mr. Spencer." After this dignified service was over, the celebration got louder, and at noon "a proper discharge of cannon was fired" by Captain Yard's artillery company on the town common, where the governor, General Dickinson, members of the Legislature, and people from the town and neighborhood assembled. At 3:00 pm, there was "an elegant entertainment" complete with 13 toasts, each accompanied by cannon fire, to the various people, dates, and ideas associated with Yorktown and the revolution. The full day of festivities ended at 7:00 pm with a "brilliant illumination," candles in every window, and torches and lighted braziers on the streets.

Isaac Collins reported that "every thing was conducted with the greatest good order and propriety; and we mention it with pleasure, that not the least disturbance or irregularity happened during the whole festivity." He recognized the contributions of the French troops and judged the alliance with France was "now more firmly cemented by the united effusion of French and American blood, in a conquest the more agreeable to both nations, for being obtained by their combined efforts as fellow-soldiers and fellow-victors in the same triumphant cause."[56]

The ferry competition was so cutthroat that negative advertising appeared in the *New Jersey Gazette* in November 1781. A letter to the public from two unnamed men of New Jersey and one of

Philadelphia told of their experience on November 3 attempting to cross at Trenton Ferry from the Pennsylvania side managed by Patrick Colvin. According to the letter, "There happened at that time to be a fresh in the river, but the weather temperate, and after unnecessarily detaining us for some time, [Colvin] absolutely refused to put us over, unless we would pay him twenty shillings hard money for the ferriage of a one horse chair and sulky." Unwilling to pay that inflated price, "we proceeded to the New Ferry kept by Mr. John Burrows, about three quarters of a mile higher up the river, where we found no kind of difficulty, but was immediately put over for the accustomed ferriage of one shilling and six pence for a one horse chair or sulky. We therefore, in justice to Mr. Burrows, recommend him to the publick for their custom, as a person ready and willing to serve them, in preference to the said Patrick Colvin, so notoriously known for his repeated impositions and disobliging behavior."[57]

Working with Burrows on the New Jersey side was George Beatty. Their ferry, just above the falls, established a third Trenton ferry. Its creation was announced in August 1781 with the statement, "The subscribers having furnished themselves with good boats at the new ferry a little above the Falls, and almost opposite to Trenton, and the distance being nearly the same from Bristol to Trenton to go by this or Colvin's." They promised "an easy and safe passage" at rates "as low as they were twenty years ago." The rates published were the same as for the other Trenton Ferry but slightly cheaper for wagons and horses. This ferry was on the outskirts of Trenton where George Beatty had a good sized piece of land enabling him to offer "good hay and pasture" for the horses of travelers. To get to the ferry from Trenton, travelers were told to "turn to the right at the market house in Trenton, which is about one quarter of a mile from the ferry."[58]

DQMG Neilson at Trenton sent off a shipment in early February to the Quartermaster General Department that included 34 muskets, 32 bayonets, and 31 cartridge boxes for the Pennsylvania Line.[59] In March, Trenton had about 500 barrels of flour on hand.[60] During the fall, several Trenton merchants sold supplies to the army. Furman and Hunt supplied 25 bushels of salt, flour, barrels of beef and pork, and other items as well as labor and storage. Joseph Milnor supplied over 22 barrels of flour, beef, pork, and labor and storage. William Trent supplied two tons of hay.[61]

John Cox no longer held office in the quartermaster department, but General William Alexander, Lord Stirling, wrote him on October 7 about paying for iron he purchased from Alexander two years previously. Cox had pledged to pay on delivery and Stirling did not want to hear again that it was a public, not a personal, debt. Since this was not his first request, Stirling begged Cox to provide the bearer of his message "with some means of being immediately paid, and not put me to the disagreeable necessity of seeking redress some other way."[62] This was an example of how the men who worked in the quartermaster department felt they were being held responsible for the debts of Congress.

At a public auction held in August 1781 at the Trenton jail, 22 men were sold. They had been part of the cargo of a British brig captured by an American privateer and were sold along with the ship, its guns, tackle, furniture, apparel, and other cargo. Group sales of slaves in Trenton were not common but did take place on occasion, such as when Isaac Collins had facilitated the sale of "sundry negroes of different ages, sexes and qualities, all good in their kind" in December 1780.[63]

The American troops returning north from Yorktown came back in several groups. Ebenezer Wild of the Light Infantry departed Yorktown with a detachment of invalids on November 2 and traveled by water in a succession of small vessels. For the last leg, they boarded a sloop and sailed at about sunrise on November 18, but only got as far as Bordentown by 4:00 pm because their vessel was difficult to handle. They landed and marched to Trenton, arriving "a little after dusk." Lieutenant Wild recorded, "after getting our men into quarters, I walked with Capt. Bradford to Mr. Copes [Capes] tavern, where we spent the evening and supped; but the lodgings being all taken up before we arrived, walked to a private house and lodged with several other officers of the army." The next day they drew rations and about 10:00 am began their march to Princeton.[64]

On October 22, an Alexandre Blaias who described himself as a "prisonnier" crossed with "un cheval" at the lower ferry. On October 24, Lieutenant Thomas Adams of the Fourth Battalion Philadelphia Militia ferried 86 prisoners and their guard, and five days later he crossed with 19 men, perhaps the returning guards. Commissary of Prisoners Abraham Skinner also crossed that day.[65]

In November, young Isaac Quigley of Nottingham Township returned home from Virginia after being away about five months. He had gone south with the French army as a wagoner when it passed through Trenton and been sent to work on the entrenchments at Yorktown.[66]

On November 28, Lieutenant John Mix of the Second Connecticut Regiment, accompanying quartermaster general stores and baggage, crossed the lower ferry with three wagons, 10 horses, 8 oxen and 4 men. Various groups of men with a non-commissioned or lower rank commissioned officer crossed at the ferry almost daily from late October to early December. Groups ranged in size from two or three up to 53, but most were small groups. Jonathan Trumbull, Jr. also crossed November 30 with a chair and three horses.[67]

Regiments from New York, New Jersey, and Rhode Island, as well as Moses Hazen's regiment, were assigned to accompany British prisoners northward and departed from Yorktown beginning November 4. Colonel Van Cortlandt was put in charge of the New York and New Jersey brigades taking 700 prisoners to Fredericksburg. After delivering them, the Continentals continued marching toward Trenton. The first week of December, they crossed the Delaware at Trenton where the New Jersey troops departed and the New Yorkers encamped one mile beyond the town.[68]

Some 681 troops of the light infantry and the artificers, with 15 four-horse wagons; four two-horse wagons; 75 saddle horses; and 21 eight-ox teams crossed at the ferry on December 1. Thomas Graton of the Company of Artificers recalled that they crossed by ferry and went one mile past town and encamped. The Second New York Regiment camped two miles from the Trenton Ferry, and the next day its men crossed at the ferry and marched through town to camp one mile beyond and then proceed to Princeton on December 6. Hugh Runyon's ferry ledger has New York troops crossing on the 3rd – 345 foot, 16 four-horse wagons, one chair, 32 saddle horses, and four cattle. There were also 600 foot, 17 four-horse wagons, and 12 riding horses – perhaps the New Jersey brigade.[69]

The hospital at Trenton appears only sporadically in hospital reports between mid-1778 and the end of 1781. It had just 10 patients at the end of March and then nine in April. After Yorktown, General Lincoln learned that the sick and wounded had been ordered to hospitals in Philadelphia. He told Washington that this was the wrong place to send them, because "the expences will be great indeed, it will be difficult to procure vegetables for the men, the orderly men we leave to attend them, cannot with ease be kept to their duty, besides as the sick recover they must be confin'd to the hospital, for if they are suffered to go at large in the City they will be ruined by the vices of it or lost by desertion." He much preferred they be sent to Burlington or Trenton because both had good barracks "which will make excellent hospitals." They could be supplied with wood, vegetables, straw & every convenience and recovered men can "be more securely kept and with less trouble sent to their respective corps."[70]

Commissary James Paxton received a letter from Colonel Matthias Ogden of the First New Jersey Regiment "informing him that all the sick and invalids of the army from York in Virginia, amounting to 1600 men" had been ordered to Trenton for hospital care and directing him to procure food for them. The Assembly ordered the superintendent of purchases for the state "to purchase beef, pork, mutton and flour, together with such other articles of supplies as are necessary for the use of the sick and invalids of the Army." However, the Assembly wisely noted that Trenton could not provide suitable quarters for so many men, so about 1,000 should be sent to Burlington instead, leaving Trenton to deal with approximately 600 to recuperate at the barracks and other buildings used by the hospital. Dr. Bodo Otto crossed the Trenton Ferry on November 11 with his horse.[71]

Anticipating the arrival of the sick and wounded from Yorktown, DQMG Neilson hired workmen and distributed materials "for repairing the public buildings and repairing & fixing the barricks at this place for a hospital." Included were 250 bundles of straw for the sick in the barracks. Trenton carpenter John Creamer received 861 feet of pine scantling, 17 large pieces of scantling, and 27½ pounds of nails for work on the barracks.[72] The Trenton hospital had 72 American patients and 23 British prisoners at the end of November and 38 Americans at the end of December.[73] Private Prince Rodman, a "man of color" in the Rhode Island regiment, was brought to Trenton after Yorktown and died there on November 24. Lieutenant Reuben Sanderson of the Fifth Connecticut Continental Regiment marched north with the Rhode Island regiment after Yorktown and recorded in his diary that by December 14 the sick men had been distributed to several hospitals, including 36 in Trenton.[74]

Yorktown was the last major land engagement of the war between the British and Continental armies, but the civil war continued with smaller, but still bitter, engagements between Loyalists and various Continental and militia units. The reduction in troop movements allowed Trenton's people to focus on rebuilding the Trenton community. Life was getting back to normal, and Isaac Smith announced in October that the New Jersey Medical Society was being reestablished.[75] Still, the people of Trenton became involved in measures being taken to prevent losing the war economically or politically, even though the British had been unable to win militarily.

Chapter 14

1782

On Thursday, July 4, the fifth anniversary of declaring independence was celebrated in Trenton "with every mark of joy and festivity." The value of the French alliance and the victory at Yorktown since the previous year's celebration gave added meaning and happiness to the festivities. However, fear of fire on a very warm day made it too dangerous to illuminate the town that evening, so "the doors and windows of the houses were handsomely decorated about noon with flowers and green boughs, in the disposition of which the ladies did great honour to their taste." Governor Livingston and the principal men of Trenton and vicinity met for "an elegant dinner" at Rensselaer Williams's tavern, where an American flag was displayed. Thirteen toasts were made, including, to the "glorious 4th of July 1776," the United States of America, the Congress, the French King, Queen and family, General Washington and the American army, Rochambeau and the French army, the Netherlands, the King of Spain and other friendly European powers, and the memory of all the heroes who had fallen in support of independence. The last three toasts were to: "peace consistent with our independence and our alliance with France, or war for ever"; "May eternal infamy stigmatize the wretch who dares to suspect the sacred honour and inviolable faith of America"; and "the State of New Jersey, may her star shine bright in the new constellation." The festivities concluded about 8:00 pm, everyone "having spent the day with that sociability and joy which we hope will ever mark the anniversary of a day which declared our eternal separation from Great Britain, and gave us the prospect of an alliance, the advantages of which every day's experience confirms to us the propriety of."[1]

The victory at Yorktown did not end the war, but ultimate victory and independence seemed very probable to the people of Trenton, even though the February 20 edition of the New Jersey Gazette printed King George's November 27, 1781 speech to Parliament about the war in America in which he expressed his hope for ultimate victory. He expressed his frustration saying, "The war is still unhappily prolonged by that restless ambition which first excited our enemies to commence it, and which still continues to disappoint my earnest desire and diligent exertions to restore the publick tranquility."[2] However, with no direct threat from a British military force, life in Trenton was a bit less stressful. The military hospital and supply depot began winding down their activities, but the people continued to be entwined in the economic and political aspects of the war along with the efforts to keep citizens engaged in the seemingly endless conflict.

At the annual town meeting in March, Stacy Potts and Charles Axford were again chosen clerk and assessor. Tavernkeeper Francis Witt was chosen overseer of the poor, merchant Joseph Milnor a freeholder, saddler Benjamin Smith and merchant Samuel Tucker as two commissioners of appeal, Isaac Yard and Isaac Collins two of the constables, Rensselaer Williams as an assistant to the assessor, Isaac DeCou as one of the two surveyors of roads, and James Paxton as overseer of the Trenton roads.[3]

In January and February, options for consolidating the Continental military hospitals, including removing the sick soldiers from the Trenton barracks hospital to Philadelphia, were being considered. But Robert Morris questioned closing the Trenton hospital because it was closer to the army still facing the British at New York, so that it might be less expensive to keep patients there. He wanted exact estimates of the costs and what had been expended in the past, along with a return of medicines on hand and an estimate of needs for the coming year.[4] On February 15, carpenter John Creamer received "114 feet scantling, 1782 feet pine boards, 800 feet cedar, 6 shingles, 36 lights glass, 43 lbs nails, 1 barrell tarr," for an unidentified government project, perhaps more repairs to the barracks.[5]

Several Rhode Island soldiers remained in the Trenton hospital in January and February. Privates Isaac Michaels and Samuel Niles, both men of color, had been at Yorktown and died in Trenton on February 7, presumably from their wounds. Three other Rhode Island privates were sick at the hospital and died during February. Two had been at Yorktown.[6]

The quartermaster department was downsizing, but the Trenton post was one of the few to remain open. The army still needed its usual supplies and the supply departments continued to seek provisions, forage, and other items, while also trying to manage expenses. Robert Morris reported to Secretary at War Benjamin Lincoln in January that there were six or eight horses at Trenton left by traveling officers, whose expenses were paid for by the public, yet the horses did no work. In addition, the surgeon and steward of the hospitals kept their horses at the public stable. Valuable forage could not be wasted on privately owned or surplus horses. About the same time, James Thompson advertised surplus French army horses for sale. In January and February, Thompson was also willing to pay a generous price in cash for beef, pork, mutton, and whisky for the troops stationed at Burlington and Trenton.[7]

Sometime that winter, Sergeant Joseph Plumb Martin and the Sappers and Miners came back through New Jersey heading for quarters at Burlington. Martin noted the commissary and public stores at Trenton and recalled, "I concluded, although we were in a thanksgiving country, yet, as we should soon be where we should not find so much to be thankful for, that I would endeavor to supply the deficiency in some degree." Martin made out an order for three days of rations for three men. The commissary told them "he had no kind of meat on hand nor any other provisions but flour, that if we chose to take that, he would allow us a pound and a quarter of flour [as substitute] for a pound of beef." Martin said, "We took it and exchanged it at the baker's, pound for pound, and went on" to Burlington.[8]

When the campaign season approached, advertisements began appearing in the *New Jersey Gazette* for wagoners to serve with the main army. Because the low wages and irregularity of pay had discouraged men in the past, recruits were promised a month's pay in advance and a month's pay before the army took the field, with the remainder paid when discharged at the end of the campaign. Interested men could apply to DQMG John Neilson before the middle of May. Men not already known to the quartermaster were required to provide a certificate from a magistrate or well-known person, giving their place of residence and qualifications.[9]

With military activity in the north winding down, the Trenton supply depot declined in importance. In November, DQMG Neilson placed a notice in the New Jersey Gazette announcing that his office was to be discontinued after January 1, 1783, and he requested "all persons who have any demands against him as a publick officer, to present them before that time for settlement" because it would be very difficult to settle things once he no longer held office.[10]

Closing the supply depot meant selling off a huge number of items being used at the depot or held there in need of repair or no longer fit for use. Neilson had an extensive inventory made, dated October 1. There were a number of wagons, horses, and harness components. Boats included two scows, one batteau, one yawl and miscellaneous ropes, blocks, and sails. Camp equipment for the troops included knapsacks, camp kettles, canteens, axes, tent poles, entrenching tools, and 10,315 sandbags. There were many artificer tools, including broad axes, adzes, various types of saws, planes, and various carpenter's and cooper's tools, in addition to wood and iron building materials. Items for the barracks department included iron stoves and stove pipes, andirons, tongs, tables, benches, desks, stools, and sweeping brushes. Forage had always been an issue, and there were 154 ½ bushels of rye, 122 1/3 bushels of corn, and eight and-one-quarter bushels of oats and spelt along with tools used to prepare and measure forage.[11]

DQMG Neilson sold off these items at a public auction held at his office on the morning of November 21. Buyers mostly had well-known Trenton surnames such as Bellerjeau, Yard, Beatty, Douglass, Ashmore, Trent, Henry, and Huleck. Missing from the list were several important surnames such as Tucker, Williams, Cox, Hunt, Clunn, Britton, Potts, and Axford. More than 20 wagons and carts were sold and Conrad Kotts bought the batteau. Aside from the wagons, horse equipment in various quantities was purchased by a variety of people. Phillip Lott purchased the scow and some lumber, and clerk Cornelius Tenbroeck apparently purchased his desk to take back to New Brunswick.[12]

Even with the war winding down, Trenton continued to serve as a thoroughfare for a wide variety of individuals and groups. Jeremiah Greenman, taken prisoner during the campaign for Quebec, was released and on his way to Philadelphia to rejoin the Second Rhode Island Regiment when he came through Trenton on January 16 with others from the regiment, including some recruits. He recorded in his diary, "This morning after getting 2 teams proceeded to the Ferry – where could not cross without giving an extravegent price for the ferrage / went back & took the Jersy shore for Coopers ferry" further south. They left several of the recruits at the Trenton barracks hospital to be inoculated against smallpox. After some time in Philadelphia, the

Rhode Island regiment arrived in Trenton on May 30. They crossed at the ferry and six companies encamped, while three others took shelter in barns because they had no tents. After eating breakfast the next morning at daybreak, they struck their tents and marched off to Maidenhead and then Princeton. General Washington and his suite came through town in March on the way to camp on the Hudson.[13]

The people of Trenton saw firsthand the low morale of the British deserters from New York and Staten Island who came through town periodically. In October, the *Gazette* reported that more than a dozen had passed through within a few days.[14]

In November, Nathaniel Moore owned and operated the Lower Trenton Ferry at Lamberton. He placed an ad in the *New Jersey Gazette* describing the ferry for those not acquainted with it. He noted, "In this part of the river there are no obstructions, the water is deep and smooth, and the shores gravelly, so that the boats may at all times be brought so near the shores as to land their passengers without ever wetting the soals of the shoes." He touted the Lamberton location as "where most of the vessels that pass up and down the river load and unload their cargoes." There were two good taverns at the ferry, "one kept by Capt. John Clunn, the other by Mr. Abraham Waglum." Moore lived about a quarter mile from the ferry and promised ferry men would always be in attendance and rates would be as low as the other ferries. To make sure potential passengers traveling through Trenton got to his ferry and not the upper Trenton Ferry, he gave clear directions for after crossing the Assunpink Creek bridge.[15]

George Beatty, operating the third and northernmost ferry, expanded his business concerns. In October, he announced that he had completed a large set of stills at his ferry and "also a large set of fermenting tubs, containing five hundred gallons each, to receive the cyder of any person who favours the subscribers with their custom; the convenience of emptying the cyder into those large tubs, will enable all persons immediately to take back their hogsheads." He promised to produce high quality spirits and said no parts of the distillery were copper, "which ever throws up verdigris that is prejudicial to the spirit." He also noted that "the publick may be supplied by the 10th October with excellent cask beer, Irish stingo, and porter; also bottled beer at twelve shillings per dozen; Irish stingo at fifteen shillings, and porter at fifteen shillings; empty bottles to be brought in exchange, by applying to Neil and Pool, at their store in Trenton."[16]

After so many years of sacrifice and the huge success at Yorktown, maintaining a high level of commitment to the war effort among the citizenry was difficult. Governor Livingston found it increasingly difficult to get militiamen to turn out for active duty, whether from lack of pay or other causes. He found those who did turn out were not properly disciplined, due to "the insignificance & unfitness of their officers." Additionally, older, experienced militiamen were suffering from being called out so frequently and the men turning out were more likely to be those closer to the minimum militia age with little or no experience but looking for some adventure. Livingston also found the men who turned out served little purpose, because often they became "corrupted after being stationed on the lines by the alluring profits of the illicit trade" with the enemy. The patriotic zeal that supported community-wide boycotts during the protests of the 1760s and early 1770s was fading as victory seemed certain and people were looking out more for their own profit and to recoup losses they suffered earlier in the war. The Legislature was forced to pass a series of acts designed to prevent illicit trade and other "intercourse" with the enemy that threatened the ultimate successful outcome.[17]

On July 11 a group of 153 Trenton residents met to form an association to prevent trade with the enemy, essentially a reprise of the earlier Continental Association established to boycott British goods in protest to the acts of Parliament. They called for a general meeting of residents of the town and adjoining country to be held at the courthouse on Friday afternoon July 19 at 4:00 pm. Unable to win militarily, leaders believed Britain and the Loyalists were using "cunning" to cut off funding by the Americans for their war. They believed that Britain was introducing large quantities of goods to draw money from the Revolution supporter's pockets to disable them from paying taxes and disrupt the economy. The legislative acts to prevent this trade had been well intended but too many people acted in self-interest or were unconcerned about destroying the Revolution, so that "the evil is become so dangerous and inveterate, that it will not be in the power of the magistrates to correct and remove it, unless the citizens in general exert themselves to bring offenders to justice." The group joined together to detect and bring to justice any offenders, assist civil and military officers to stop the trade, help local authorities to restrain and punish suspicious persons without proper passes or carrying illegal goods, and avoid any dealings with people known to have engaged in illegal trade. Knowing certain people would resist them, they pledged to oppose anybody who believed such actions were "inconsistent with honour and good citizenship," but would not resort to "acts of oppression and violence," except where they may become "indispensably necessary."[18]

At the general meeting on July 19, the vocal Samuel Tucker was elected chairman of the association. The people accepted the draft association document of July 11 with only minor wording changes. Nine men were chosen for a committee to meet on July 22 to oversee the execution of the association's resolves for two months. This committee consisted of Samuel Tucker, William C. Houston, Robert L. Hooper, Jr., Colonel John Neilson, Robert Neil, Benjamin Smith, Captain John Mott, Captain Israel Carle, and John Reeder. At the July 22 committee meeting, Robert L. Hooper, Jr. was chosen chairman, and he placed a notice in the paper about the need for every citizen to be vigilant in helping to stop illegal trade and information going to the enemy. After two months, a meeting was held at the Trenton courthouse on September 28 to elect a new committee and transact any other necessary association business.[19]

The inhabitants of Nottingham met on August 2, with John Cox as chairman, and agreed to a very similar document of association. The main difference was calling for publishing in the *New Jersey Gazette* the names of anyone "detected in violating the laws passed in this state relating to the trade with our enemies, that they may be publickly known, and branded with the odium justly due to their crimes." The coordinating committee that met on August 5 consisted of John Cox as chairman, William Trent, Hugh Runyon, John Hutchinson, David Chambers, Richard Mount, Alexander Douglass, James Ewing, Thomas Janney, and John Clunn. They published a similar call for all people to assist in the effort to identify and catch violators. The inhabitants of Nottingham met "on public business" at the request of their committee on September 2 at Chambers' tavern.[20]

The Trenton associators met on Saturday, October 5 at 2:00 pm at the courthouse with Stacy Potts as chairman. The committee unanimously reinforced its commitment to "discourage the use of all British manufactures whatsoever, except prize goods legally condemned, and encourage the use of those of such nations as are in alliance with the United States, and friendly to their cause." The goal was to stop "all traffick and intercourse with the enemy" not only as sound policy, but also as a political duty and a way to show gratitude to those countries who had given the United States assistance by buying their goods. In addition, the committee resolved to do its utmost to promote payment of taxes. This would help "to put a speedy end to the present war, and disable the enemy from making further attempts upon our liberties." The coordinating committee was enlarged by six members, including John Bell, Charles Axford, Jun., Conrad Kotts, Ebenezer Rose, John Howell, and Joseph Tindal, "in order more fully and certainly to carry the design of this association into effect." However, the problem of trading with the enemy continued, and on November 30, Robert L. Hooper, Jr., now chairman of the association, placed a notice in the *New Jersey Gazette* encouraging everyone to help suppress this activity.[21]

Avoiding British goods was difficult for people who were used to having a wide variety of products available in the colonial consumer economy. The British had suppressed the production of many goods in the colonies, and with independence local production would need to increase to supplement imports from France and other friendly countries.[22]

Like people throughout the 13 states, the people of Trenton were pleased with the French alliance and thankful for its essential contribution to the victory at Yorktown. When the French Minister Plenipotentiary, Chevalier de la Luzerne, announced on May 13 that an heir to the crown of France had been born, Rev. Elihu Spencer, John Witherspoon, and Joseph Montgomery prepared "an address to the Minister of France, congratulating him on the birth of a Dauphin, son and heir to the crown of his royal Master; expressing the pleasure the [Presbyterian] Synod feel on this happy event." Trenton celebrated the birth on May 24 "with every mark of respect, joy and congratulation" in a manner very similar to what would take place a few weeks later to mark the anniversary of independence on July 4. The American flag was displayed at noon, and the artillery company paraded at the market place. "An elegant entertainment" began at 3:00 pm, appropriately at the French Arms Tavern, attended by Governor Livingston, the Legislative Council and Assembly, "several gentlemen of the army and others occasionally present and the gentlemen of the town and vicinity." Toasts were drunk after dinner, each accompanied by a discharge of artillery. The toasts emphasized the French royal family and military, and especially the alliance – "May the alliance between

France and America subsist as long as the Delaware shall continue to flow." There were toasts in the hope of peace – "Unanimity in council and vigour in the field" and "Peace on the terms of the alliance, or war forever." The tone of Isaac Collins' article in the *Gazette* was that the alliance had been instrumental in securing independence.[23]

The Legislature began a session at Trenton on May 15, and the Assembly resolved that "the doors of this House be kept open, and that the inhabitants of the State be permitted to be present at the transacting the business of the House, except on such particular occasions as in the opinion of the House shall require secrecy." Trenton's residents would benefit the most from this opportunity. The two houses held Joint Meetings at John Cape's tavern several times in May and June.[24]

Almost exactly one year since passing through Trenton on its way south, the French army returned north and Rochambeau's aide-de-camp Baron von Closen wrote in his journal that on September 4 they left the Red Lion Tavern north of Philadelphia and when they got to Trenton the troops and artillery caissons crossed by ferry. He wrote, "There were 7 boats, of which 5 were fit for some vehicles." At least some of the wagons bravely crossed at the winding ford a mile north on the river at the falls. Rochambeau made his headquarters at the Bloomsbury home of John Cox, and the army camped on the commons below the town at Bloomsbury, organized in two brigades. The Lauzun Legion proceeded beyond Trenton and made camp at Kingston. The French officers called on Governor Livingston. Claude Blanchard, commissary of the French army, had developed a fever in Baltimore and was not fully recovered when he arrived in Trenton on September 6. Therefore, he wrote, "after having run about and attended to my official duty, as soon as I arrived at the lodging which was intended for me, I rested and kept quiet." It was extremely hot and a number of the soldiers were also sick. Rochambeau gave the order to march from Trenton in battle formation, and the First Brigade proceeded to Princeton on September 7 with the Second Brigade following the next day.[25]

The French encampment had lasted three days and it is probable that the officers spent some time shopping. The officers have been described as acting like "tourists" in America who "delighted to find the shops full of merchandise of every description."[26] Trenton was home to a number of merchants whose general stores were well stocked with a wide variety of textiles, household items, and many other things attractive to both visitors and the local population. An ad for Robert Singer's store was typical, offering sugar, tea, coffee, pepper and ginger, calicoes, chintzes, broad cloths, moreens, red flannel, linens, Russia sheeting and duck, buckles and knives, mohair, silk and buttons, nutmegs, mode, Persian, lawn and cambric, gauze handkerchiefs, silk and linen handkerchiefs, and earthen ware. The ad also exemplified the attitude that slaves were a commodity, stating "also to be sold, a likely negro wench, eighteen years of age, has had the small pox, a horse and riding chair, a new cart and gears complete, a riding saddle, and a large open stove."[27]

Merchant William Richards had perhaps that greatest variety of items at his stores at Lamberton and Philadelphia. He was very well known for the large variety of medicines he carried, along with West Indies goods, hardware, groceries, rum, tea, coffee, chocolate, spices, grains, sturgeon, Castile and English hard soap, earthen and stoneware, building materials, fishing gear, scythes, grindstones, oils, lampblack, and "some very fine hair powder."[28]

Many craftsmen also had shops, such as Jacob Maus who made and repaired clocks and watches. He appeared first in 1780 with his shop in the house of John Reynolds and then later at William Roscow's. His shop was broken into on June 18, 1781, and a number of items were stolen, including: one silver watch without chain or crystal, one movement put together and repaired, one movement in pieces in a small box, two boxes of small tools, one silver scissors chain, one dozen plain silver coat buttons, and one pincushion hook made of silver. In 1782 he moved again, to the house of potter Bernard Hanlon opposite Joseph Milnor's store. In addition to making and repairing clocks and watches, he also had for sale "ladies and gentlemens steel chains, seals, keys, etc." State and Continental officials living temporarily in Trenton frequented the craftsmen, as did DQMG John Neilson in April when he had tailor Conrad Kotts make him a double breasted jacket.[29] The variety of craftsmen included tailors, shoemakers, hatters, stay makers, silversmiths, blacksmiths, leather workers, wood turners, potters, snuff makers, distillers, and weavers, and often more than one of each type.

Printer Isaac Collins did much more than just print the *New Jersey Gazette*. He also published government journals and laws along with other items of interest to the public. In November, he advertised that he had a few copies of Allinson's edition of the *Laws of New Jersey*.[30] Each year, he published and sold The *New Jersey Almanack* in both full size and pocket size editions. He described his almanacs as containing "besides the usual astronomical observations, a variety of useful, instructive, and entertaining matter, in prose and verse."[31] Like other merchants, he accepted produce, including wheat, wool, flax, beeswax, and other items, in-lieu of cash.[32] In November, he offered for sale a work by Thomas Paine correcting mistakes in an account of the American Revolution by Abbé Raynal.[33] By 1782, Collins' print shop had grown into a general store and instead of brief notices, he placed large ads in his paper for such items as drinks, spices, sewing supplies, textiles, dishes, drinking mugs, and glasses.[34]

Drugs and medicines were sold by Mary and Sarah Barnes at the house of Thomas Barnes nearly opposite the printing office. Some of the items they sold included compound purging powder, eye waters, spirits hartshorn, Anderson's Pills, Hooper's Pills, Bateman's drops, Daffy's elixir, Godfrey's cordial, Turlington's balsam, mouth water for the canker, and "an extraordinary ointment for corns, warts, tooth ache, and pain in the face, scald head and breaking out in children, for burns or scalds, and where the fever has settled in any part of the human body." They also sold some non-medicinal items such as china, sewing silks, thread, needles, and brass furniture for carriages.[35]

Public vendues or auctions were held periodically at various locations, often a tavern or the market house. In May, a vendue was held at John Cape's French Arms Tavern to sell items captured by privateer Captain Adam Hyler and ordered sold. They included "a number of muskets, one swivel gun, one blunderbuss, several barrels of gunpowder, a valuable chest of medicine, two cases surgeons instruments, one cask raisins, some bohea tea, a quantity of wearing apparel, a great number of mens shoes." In May, Hugh Smith was preparing to leave the area to go to sea after the death of his wife, so he sold off his belongings. A number of items put up by the Nottingham sheriff were auctioned at Jonathan Richmond's tavern in December.[36] On June 1, an auction at John Cape's sold nine male slaves captured from the British cutter *Alert* sailing from New York to Bermuda.[37]

All the economic activity at Lamberton, such as Richards's store, encouraged its growth. It was known as a healthy and beautiful location at the head of navigation, with good wharves accommodating vessels operating between Trenton and Philadelphia. There was also good wood-land in the area, providing cut wood to ship to Philadelphia on shallops and flats from John Watson's landing. A number of people had sought building lots and the owner of a level piece of ground there laid out a "number of lots from 50 to 60 feet wide, running from the present road to Lamberton to the river Delaware, and along the bank of said river to the several landings, with a back street from the centre of this to the present main street." A plan of the lots could be viewed and terms of sale or rental learned at John Watson's or Randle Mitchell's in Nottingham, Captain John Clunn's in Lamberton, and Rensselaer Williams's tavern in Trenton. The demand was so great that a public auction of the lots was scheduled for noon on Saturday, May 4 at Captain John Clunn's tavern.[38]

Quakers continued to work on ending slavery, at least among themselves. In 1782, Mary Dury, who had freed two male slaves in 1774, inherited rights from her father, late of Barbados, to a Negro woman Cornelia, two children, and two grandchildren. She gave her rights to them to Israel Morris and Nicholas Waln, who then freed the women. This manumission was witnessed by Daniel Bellerjeau and Samuel Downing of Trenton.[39]

By February 11, the new schoolhouse was not yet complete, but teacher James Burnside could begin classes. At this time, Isaac Collins had six children either already in school or coming of school age. Collins and Rensselaer Williams were appointed to be "visitors" to oversee things. A formal announcement about the new school, which appeared in the *New Jersey Gazette* on September 13, noted that "in order to render the means of education more easy and certain," several residents of Trenton and the adjoining country had established a Trenton Academy and that a "commodious handsome stone building has been erected" and is now ready for scholars. Trenton had long been home to a school with a good teacher instructing students in reading, writing, common arithmetic, and bookkeeping. To elevate the level of learning, the new school taught English, Latin and Greek languages grammatically, geography, practical mathematics, the principles of natural philosophy and astronomy, public speaking, and the rudiments of any other subject required to prepare a student for college or business. The trustees were "determined to spare no pains to render it as beneficial as possible; to which they have put it under the care of George Merchant, B.A. a gentleman graduated at the college of New Jersey several years ago. He went on to further study and has been teaching with great approval." Students could board with respected families on reasonable terms, if necessary, and "strict attention will be paid to the morals and behavior of the youth." A school to teach French was promised when there was sufficient interest to support a teacher.[40]

The school was the cooperative effort of its shareowners, who met on Wednesday, November 20, at 4:00 pm to elect trustees for the coming year. Shortly after, an employment want ad appeared in the paper for a writing master and accountant at the Trenton Academy, who were needed immediately. Only candidates who were "well qualified to teach writing, arithmetic and book keeping" and could be well recommended for their "sobriety, industry and capacity" would be considered.[41]

At 9:00 am on December 24, even though school had only been in session a short time, the academy grammar school was examined and "the scholars on this occasion acquitted themselves greatly to the satisfaction of the Trustees, and other gentlemen present." In the afternoon, children of both sexes "exhibited a specimen of their improvement in the art of speaking, in the presence of a crowded assembly of ladies and gentlemen of the town and neighbourhood, several members of the Hon. The Court of Commissioners now sitting here, and other strangers of distinction, all of whom expressed the highest approbation of the performances." Expectations were exceeded and "the conduct and success of the institution reflect honour upon the abilities and care of the teachers." The court of commissioners was meeting at Trenton between November 12 and December 30 at the order of the Continental Congress to resolve a land dispute between Pennsylvania and Connecticut dating back to 1757.[42] The commissioners included two local men, David Brearley and William Churchill Houston, and issued *The Trenton Decree,* which found no basis for Connecticut's claim and declared the land belonged to Pennsylvania. The dispute continued after the Revolution, but Pennsylvania maintained ownership. These meetings at Trenton were just one part of a decades-long series of events known as the Pennamite Wars.[43]

The Trenton jail had seen heavy usage throughout the war years, including the first week of October when seven British prisoners from Cornwallis's army were lodged there.[44] Stay maker Peter Huleck was keeper of the jail when he alerted the Assembly in November that the jail was not in "proper condition to hold a large number of prisoners." He presently had 21 prisoners of war, "being deserters from the troops which surrendered under Lord Cornwallis, and have escaped from the guards and been apprehended in endeavouring to get to New York. 13 prisoners who have been taken on the water by American cruisers; besides a number of civil prisoners from this county and elsewhere." The prisoners were so crowded as to cause suffering and he feared daily that some might escape. Eight of the prisoners were sick and six of them did not even have a blanket. He noted that the prisoners taken at sea were "totally destitute of clothing, and without means of relief, and many of them have been long confined." Some of them had even expressed their willingness to sign on for service in the frigate South Carolina now "manning at Philadelphia if it could be allowed." Huleck asked for the means to hire a guard to take the prisoners to Philadelphia where they could be confined and provided for at the expense of the United States.[45] Huleck had the prisoners until November 17 and was later reimbursed by the Assembly for money he spent to care for several sick prisoners, pay the funeral expenses of one, board 51 prisoners, and transport 28 of them to Philadelphia.[46] Just after getting rid of these prisoners, Huleck received two New York Loyalists on November 19 who had been taken in a boat near Bergen Point with about 60 quarters of beef; this represented an instance of trading with the enemy because the beef had been purchased from local inhabitants.[47]

A Joint Meeting of the Legislature met at Francis Witt's tavern on October 2 and both houses closed their session on October 5. Francis Witt had advertised in June that he was now "at the sign of the Blazing Star" where he "has laid in hay and liquors of the first quality." Both houses then opened session on October 22 with John Cox serving as a member of the Legislative Council from Burlington and Samuel Tucker as a member of the Assembly from Hunterdon.

William Livingston was re-elected as governor and John Stevens as treasurer. At a Joint Meeting at Witt's tavern on October 30, Cox was elected vice president of the Legislative Council and chairman of the Joint Meeting. Tucker was chosen for a joint committee to settle the accounts of the treasurer.[48]

The Assembly unanimously voted down in November a bill to annex Nottingham Township to Hunterdon County. It continued to work on bills to better limit illicit trade and intercourse with the enemy. When voting on salaries for state officers, including the governor, Samuel Tucker consistently voted against the initial proposed salaries, except for 25 shillings per day for delegates to the Continental Congress. He was fiscally conservative and served on a committee to determine how much to pay Isaac Collins for printing government documents. At a Joint Meeting at Francis Witt's tavern on December 18, Rensselaer Williams was elected a justice of the peace for Hunterdon.[49]

The Legislature conducted business on December 25 and received several reports from committees on which Samuel Tucker was a member, which concerned money and accounting issues. It then adjourned to meet next at Burlington on May 15, 1783.[50] It was now safe to meet at one of the actual State capitals.

As the year ended, the people of Trenton were eager for an official peace agreement.

Chapter 15

1783

About February 11, Isaac Collins composed his February 12 column of Trenton news for his New Jersey Gazette. It had been a long, drawn-out peace process since the important victory at Yorktown in 1781, but now he could write, "By letters from New York we are informed of the arrival of the King of Britain's speech, which announces an approaching peace. – That Capt. Barry, in the Alliance, who was arrived in Martinico from France, brought news that the preliminaries of peace were signed – And that several letters from the West Indies declare peace to be actually concluded." Just before putting the paper to press, he received a copy of the King's speech and printed it in a supplement. The story of peace was unfolding but not yet complete. Then, six weeks later Collins headlined the Trenton column, "Peace, Liberty, and Independence" and reported that "Sunday last arrived at Philadelphia, after a passage of 32 days from Cadiz, a French sloop of war, commanded by M. Du Quesne, with the agreeable intelligence of peace, on the return of which we most cheerfully and heartily congratulate the citizens of New Jersey." The key words from the document received were that "Great Britain acknowledges the Sovereignty and Independence of the thirteen United States of America."[1] Governor Livingston issued a proclamation on April 14, stating, "we strictly charge and command all our officers, both by sea and land, and other, subjects to these United States, to forbear all acts of hostility, either by sea or by land, against his Britannick Majesty or his subjects."[2]

Peace was gratefully and joyfully celebrated in Trenton the next day. At about 11:00 am the governor, the vice-president of the state, several members of the Legislature, judges of the Supreme Court, and other magistrates, along with a huge number of people from the town and vicinity met at Rensselaer Williams's tavern and paraded in company with the trustees, director, and students of the Trenton Academy to the courthouse where they heard the governor's peace proclamation confirming their independence that Samuel Tucker had read the declaration of on the same spot in July 1776. Thirteen cannon shots *were fired by the militia, followed by boisterous "huzzas of the people." At 12:00 pm a dignified church service was held and Rev. Spencer spoke to "a very numerous audience." At 3:00 pm the Governor and many of the gentlemen of the town gathered at Francis Witt's tavern, as well as Williams's and John Cape's, for dinner, followed by patriotic toasts accompanied by artillery discharges. At 7:00 pm the houses of the town were illuminated with candles in each window "which added great brilliancy to the festivity." The celebration continued the following evening with a ball at the French Arms tavern.*[3]

Three days later on April 19, eight years to the day from the opening shots at Lexington and Concord, Governor Livingston was ready to depart Trenton for his home at Elizabethtown. Before leaving, he was addressed by a committee of local men consisting of Rev. Spencer, Isaac Smith, John Cox, Samuel W. Stockton, and William C. Houston. After praising his work during the war, these men offered their thanks for "the affability and attentions we have experienced from your Excellency during your residence in this place, which have called forth our unfeigned esteem for your private and social virtues." While sincerely regretting his departure, they knew he longed to return home.[4] *Livingston had spent a great deal of time in Trenton during the war, because his home at Elizabethtown was constantly in danger from the British on Staten Island.*

Although independence had not yet been officially confirmed in January, everyone was confident that it was a reality. A meeting of the congregation of St. Michael's Church on January 4 adopted the following resolution: ..."the American States have become Free, Sovereign and Independent; And the Congregation being deeply impressed with the duty, the necessity and the propriety of revising and continuing the public worship according to the Evangelical doctrine of Episcopacy, have therefore proceeded to the election, and appointment of the officers of the Church." The Church congregation had been badly split by the war with the rector and a number of parishioners remaining loyal to the Crown and church services had been suspended for six-and-a-half-years beginning July 7, 1776. The congregation now elected Rensselaer Williams and Isaac DeCou as wardens and Elijah Bond, Robert Pearson, Charles Axford, Robert Singer, Francis Witt, Charles Axford, Jr., John Singer, James Emerson, William Cannon, Micajah How, William Trent, and Robert L. Hooper, Jr. as vestrymen.[5] These new officers faced the challenge of leading the church during its struggle to abandon those elements of polity and worship that had characterized the State Church of England, as well as repair the heavy damage done to the building during the war.

The Committee of the Trenton Association continued its work of discouraging trade with the enemy. On Sunday, January 26, at Howell's Ferry just north of town several members seized a wagon with a false bottom that was carrying contraband goods. The driver was charged with trading with the enemy and put in the Trenton jail.[6] When the Trenton committee met on March 8, it voted to give thanks to those members of the association who had captured the wagon and driver and had the information published in the Gazette, no doubt to encourage others to stay alert to this activity.[7] The next meeting of the committee was held on Saturday, June 28 at Jacob Bergen's tavern.[8] John Cape had announced in January that he was leaving the state,[9] and Bergen had returned to Trenton and announced in April that he had taken over Cape's "French Arms Tavern, at the corner of the markethouse, where he is building good sheds for carriages, &c. and is provided with every thing necessary for the entertainment of a large number of travelers, and is determined to shew the utmost attention and assiduity to those who are pleased to favour him with their custom."[10]

At the annual town meeting in March, Stacy Potts was once again elected clerk and merchant Joseph Milnor was chosen assessor. Potts had been elected every year of the war, in spite of his refusal as a Quaker to take the oaths of loyalty and abjuration. Isaac Collins was chosen as overseer of the poor, Conrad Kotts as a freeholder, Alexander Calhoun as an overseer of the Trenton roads, Benjamin Yard as one of the commissioners of appeals, William Yard as one of the constables, and Rensselaer Williams as an assistant to the assessor.[11]

The end of the war did not end animosity towards many Loyalists. On April 9, just a few days before peace was celebrated in Trenton, Isaac Collins expressed in his Trenton column what were undoubtedly the feelings of many people, stating, "We deem it an act of humanity, and therefore an indispensable duty, in order to prevent the effusion of blood, to caution all persons within the British lines, who have taken an active part or in any manner distinguished themselves in favour of the cause of Britain, not to return or remain among the citizens of America. They may rely upon it that nothing can save them from retaliation for the many cruelties wantonly exercised in the course of the war upon our citizens, such as murders, burnings, plunderings, and starvings on board of loathsome ships, and in horrid dungeons."[12] All Loyalists had become tainted with the excesses of the British army and the Loyalist military forces. The diversity that characterized Trenton would not include those who actively supported the losing side in the war.

The Assembly and Legislative Council met at Burlington on May 15. The Council heard a report on June 12 from the committee appointed the previous December 13 to finally settle the accounts of Samuel Tucker as treasurer of the Provincial Congress in 1775 and 1776. This included the accounts Tucker had submitted to the Assembly in February 1777. The Council did not accept his accounting for the £5818.16.3 taken from the Abbott house by the British in December 1776, and voted that Tucker should pay that amount to the State Treasurer. John Cox voted with the majority on both votes. Several months later, on December 12, the Council resolved that the attorney general of the state should recover the money from Tucker. The vote was six-to-five with Philemon Dickinson voting against the resolve. The Assembly did not confirm the Council's resolution so it was void.[13] Tucker was clearly a controversial figure, but still had supporters and was serving again as an elected official. Tucker continued to defend himself from public attacks in the newspaper after the war was long over and sought relief from the Legislature. He particularly noted its precedent of releasing other individuals from responsibility for public money that was taken by the British, or lost or stolen, and argued his situation was no different.[14] But many people could not stop questioning why he had not sent the money across the Delaware to Pennsylvania when the army crossed during the first week of December 1776.

The Legislature learned that the five barracks in the State were "much impaired and continually receiving damage" for want of proper oversight. It appointed men on June 19 to make repairs to the five barracks and lease them out, along with any houses and lands belonging to them. Charles Axford, Jr. was appointed commissioner for the Trenton barracks and ordered to "dispose of all the publick furniture belonging to" it and keep a regular account of the money raised and expended, settling accounts with the Legislature annually.[15] As part of dismantling the supply depot, a 25-by-60 foot stable was sold at a public vendue at Trenton on April 22. A store house and two small houses were sold at Trenton Landing the same day.[16]

On June 18 and 19, the Legislative Council and Assembly both agreed to invite the Continental Congress to choose New Jersey as the site for its permanent residence. This action coincided with the threat to Congress by armed Pennsylvania veterans demanding their back pay. John Cox learned about the incident from Elias Boudinot, President of Congress, and summoned citizens from Trenton and vicinity to a meeting the next day at the French Arms tavern. After hearing about the "most gross and daring insult" to Congress "by a number of lawless people in arms," the attendees expressed their "resentment and indignation at so flagitious a proceeding." They proclaimed it to be an act of anarchy and they were resolved to resist such acts whenever they emerged, just as they would acts of tyranny. They "consider the support of civil government and the majesty of the law as one of the first of social duties, and riotous citizens who disturb the public order and violate the dignity of the Union as the worst of enemies." They may have missed the irony that similar words had been used by people to justify remaining loyal to the British government during the recent revolution. The citizens pledged their "lives and fortunes to the government under which we live, in whatever way our services may be required, whether in resisting foreign invasion or quelling intestine tumults." Lastly, they would deem themselves "highly honored by the presence of Congress, and by an opportunity of testifying our zeal in support of their dignity and privileges, should they in their wisdom, think proper to adjourn to or fix their residence in this State." The resolves were signed on behalf of the inhabitants by John Cox, David Brearley, Philemon Dickinson, Samuel Tucker, William Houston, and Samuel W. Stockton. Moore Furman, Stacy Potts, and Benjamin Smith were appointed a committee to collect, as quickly as possible, information on how many people from Congress the town could accommodate. Their report the next day estimated that at least 60 people, and perhaps more, could be housed. William Livingston also wrote to Budinot expressing the same sentiments and promising to defend the Congress if it removed to New Jersey.[17] However, Congress chose to merely pass through Trenton and establish itself at Princeton.

Although Congress decided to meet at Princeton, in October the people of Trenton still created a list of over 27 inhabitants willing to help accommodate Congress should it decide to adjourn to Trenton. Some people offered complete houses, such as Stacy Potts who offered his dwelling house of 42-by-33 feet, two stories, 10 rooms (six with fire places), a kitchen, and stabling for six horses. Others offered one or more rooms in their houses, such as Samuel Tucker who offered two rooms with fireplaces. Some could only offer furniture or rooms for offices but could not lodge or board anyone. Others could stable horses. Mr. Bergen's tavern could provide a room 43-by-20 feet with two fire places for meetings. Five men, including Moore Furman and Stacy Potts, pledged to supply good hay in any quantity. These people had gone through so much, but now at the end of the long war they were still willing to have strangers invade their homes and use up local resources.[18] The people of Trenton were now patriotic promotors, envisioning their town as the focal point and center of an independent confederation of 13 States.

As a necessary post and major thoroughfare during the war, Trenton had experienced economic stress but also some economic benefit. Soldiers passing through town might cause damage to property, but legislators living in town spent money at local businesses. Some of the many travelers did likewise. Now that the war was over, the Legislature would no doubt return to the pattern of meeting alternately at Perth Amboy and Burlington, removing an economic benefit from Trenton. What better way to compensate for that loss than by inviting the Continental Congress to make its home in Trenton. The congressmen and many visitors coming to town on legislative business would continue to spend cash. In addition, Trentonians had experienced so many interactions with the people who had managed and fought the war that they no doubt developed a deep sense of identity with and loyalty to the Confederation.

Possibly because the peace had been celebrated just three months earlier, July 4 was observed more quietly than in previous years. In reality, it was the second celebration of independence that year. A curt notice appeared in the *New Jersey Gazette* on July 9 that "Friday last being the 4th of July, the citizens of this town met at the house of Isaiah Yard, innholder, to celebrate the anniversary of American independence. About noon thirteen cannon were discharged; after which the company partook of a genteel cold collation, and retired about one o'clock."[19]

Settling the accounts of the commissary department continued, and former commissary officer Aaron Dunham announced he would be at Captain Clunn's tavern at Trenton Landing between March 11 and 14 to settle accounts with men he had hired to cart flour and other stores from Trenton to Morristown and the Hudson River posts during the previous August, September, and October.[20]

At the end of the year, Benjamin Thompson, Commissioner of Accounts, gave notice that he would hold office at the house of Stacy Potts beginning December 22 to settle claims for purchases and services provided to the government. The office would be open from 9:00 am to 1:00 pm and from 3:00 pm to 6:00 pm. The problems that continued to prevent final liquidation of these government debts were part of the issues that led to replacing the Articles of Confederation with a stronger central government under the Constitution in 1787. Accounting continued long after the war and in May 1786, William Tucker was still awaiting reimbursement for money he had spent on arms, accoutrements, and tents for the militia in 1776. His papers, like those of Alexander Chambers and others, had been taken or destroyed by the British who occupied his house in December 1776. He hoped the Legislature would accept his daybook as sufficient evidence of purchases in-lieu of official receipts.[21]

Problems associated with independence were already emerging. On December 24, the Assembly dealt with a British proclamation declaring that produce of the United States could only be carried to the West Indies in British-built ships that were owned and operated by British subjects and navigated according to the laws of Britain. This especially hurt New Jersey and many in Trenton who had built long-standing trade relationships with the West Indies. In words very reminiscent of the protests against the acts of Parliament in the 1760s and early 1770s, the Assembly unanimously resolved that the Confederation Congress alone should have the power to regulate "trade and commerce throughout the United States of America and it should prohibit "British vessels from being the carriers of the growth or produce of the British West India Islands to these United States."

Likewise, it should prohibit British ships from carrying United States produce to any British West Indies island. These policies should be in effect until the British proclamation was rescinded in full.[22]

The Legislature began a session at Trenton on October 28. Samuel Tucker was a member of the Assembly and Philemon Dickinson was elected Vice President of the Council.[23] Francis Witt had announced in June that he kept an inn at the sign of the Blazing Star for the entertainment of man and horse.[24] A Joint Meeting was held at Witt's tavern and Philemon Dickinson was unanimously elected chairman of the Joint Meeting for the coming year. William Livingston was re-elected governor with only one dissenting vote, Samuel Tucker's. There was still ill feeling between the two men because Livingston could not forgive Tuckers actions in December 1776. Another Joint Meeting was held at Witt's on November 25.[25]

The Assembly apparently met regularly in a room at Francis Witt's and on the night of December 2, between 9:00 and 10:00 pm the room caught fire from an open stove, "the hearth of which had been laid too close to the floor." Before the fire made much progress, it was discovered and extinguished by men gathered at the tavern for the evening. There was no material damage, but it was necessary to remove "chests, books and papers" of the Assembly, so it postponed meeting until 3:00pm on the 3rd.[26]

Just three days after the fire, on Saturday, December 6, General Washington came through town on his way home to retirement in Virginia. He was met by Governor Livingston and a committee of Legislative Council and Assembly members who told him they could not miss the opportunity to congratulate him on his arrival in the town he had "rendered famous to the latest posterity, by the most unexampled effort of military genius; and your signal victory over an enemy till then, through the great superiority of their numbers, the triumphant possessors of this part of the country." While thanking "that all wise and most gracious Providence" which guided the events of the Revolution to a glorious conclusion, they said the pages of history "will immortalize the innumerable hardships you have endured; the almost insuperable obstacles you have surmounted; the numerous disappointments to which you have risen superior, and the infinite resources of your genius in the most unexpected and trying emergencies." They believed that the citizens of America were unanimous in respecting him more than they could any other man, and "While heroes and warriors are dazzled with the lustre of your martial achievements, the citizen and the patriot will remember your particular attention to the rights of the subjects, too often wantonly violated by military men."

Washington appreciated their sentiments and "their flattering allusion to an event which hath signalized the name of Trenton." He had no doubt that history would record the services and sufferings of his army, but it should never forget "the efficacious exertions of the State of New Jersey, or the almost unrivalled bravery of its militia." Through the rose-colored lenses of victory, he proclaimed, "Let it be remembered for ever as an example to succeeding ages, that after a large extent of country had been overrun by a formidable enemy, and thousands of citizens driven from their possessions; the virtuous freemen of New Jersey, recovering from the temporary shock, stung by the remembrance of what their wives, their children and friends had already suffered, by the thought of losing all they yet held dear and sacred, animated by an enthusiastic hope of success, and buoyed by a reliance on the aid of Heaven, above the fear of danger and death, then began to stem the tide of adversity; and, in concert with our other force, recoiling like an impetuous torrent on our lately victorious foes, confined them within narrow limits, till compelled to take their final departure from the state." He closed with great wishes for the future of New Jersey and the country as it embarked into an unknown future as an independent confederation of 13 States.[27] He did not mention the specific, numerous contributions and sufferings of the people of Trenton. Washington then continued his journey, riding across the Assunpink Creek bridge and then crossing to Pennsylvania at the ferry just as John Adams had done in August 1774 on his way to the First Continental Congress.

Epilogue

During a heavy rain at about 10:00 am on April 21, 1789, George Washington departed Philadelphia in a closed carriage. The Articles of Confederation had proven deficient and the Constitution had been written in 1787 to strengthen the central government. George Washington's had been elected as the first President under the Constitution and was now on his way to New York City to be inaugurated. He hoped the journey would be low key in nature but found that people along his route wanted to celebrate and acknowledge him.

He arrived at Colvin's Ferry about 2:00 pm, and Patrick Colvin personally ferried his party over the river, where they were met by the leading citizens of Trenton, Bloomsbury, and Lamberton, including General Philemon Dickinson and Dr. Isaac Smith. Companies of militia escorted them, including Captain Bernard Hanlon's artillery company (formerly Joseph Clunn's) and the light horse troop of Captain Israel Carle of Trenton Township. Washington and his companions exited the carriage, mounted horses, and with their escorts headed up towards town. As they crossed over Mill Hill, Washington came within sight of the Assunpink bridge; the one crossed by delegates to the First Continental Congress in 1774, crossed by American militiamen and Continentals throughout the war, crossed by an endless stream of supply wagons during the war, crossed by Hessians escaping town on the morning of December 26, 1776, defended so heroically on January 2, 1777, and crossed by the French and American armies on their way to and from Yorktown. He saw the 18-foot tall, 15-foot wide, and 10-foot long triumphal arch constructed on the center of the bridge supported by 13 pillars, seven on one side and six on the other, and gaily festooned with a variety of flowers and evergreens. On the front was a sign with golden letters on a blue background proclaiming "The defender of the mothers will also protect their daughters" and also the dates December 26, 1776 and January 2, 1777. The arch had been constructed the previous day by a group of men supervised by Benjamin Yard and decorated with flowers that morning by women of the town. The whole thing was topped by a large sunflower to symbolize the American people's belief that Washington was the "sun" that would give life and warmth to the people of the United

States. On one side stood six little girls and on the other side stood 13 young women, both groups in white dresses and holding baskets of flowers. Behind them on both sides were a large number of women from Trenton and nearby areas. As Washington entered the arch, the women and girls sang a song written for the occasion by Major Richard Howell of Trenton. After the last line, the young women and little girls spread flowers in his path. Washington could not conceal his deep emotion.

Among the women and girls taking part in this event were a number who experienced and contributed to the cause for which Washington had led the fight during the war. These included: Esther Cox, wife of Colonel John Cox of Bloomsbury; her daughters Esther and Mary; Mary Dickinson, wife of General Philemon Dickinson; her daughter Mary; Sarah Furman, wife of Moore Furman; her daughter Maria; Susanna Gordon, wife of Peter Gordon; Elizabeth Chambers, wife of Alexander Chambers who had done so much to obtain supplies for the army and militia; Sarah How, wife of Micajah How; her daughter Sarah; Keziah Howell, wife of Richard Howell who had served in the New Jersey Continental Line; Ann Richmond, wife of Jonathan Richmond, whose house Washington had used as his headquarters on January 2, 1777; Sarah Collins, daughter of Isaac Collins; Mary Keen, daughter of Hannah Keen who had stood up to the Hessian invaders of Trenton in 1776; and Mary Smith, wife of Dr. Isaac Smith. Of particular interest was Mary Dagworthy Hunt, wife of merchant Abraham Hunt. Hunt's first wife, Theodosia, died in 1784 and he had married Miss Dagworthy. Given Mary Dagworthy's record as a patriot leader supporting the American soldiers, it seems unlikely she would have had anything to do with Hunt if he had been in any way disloyal to the cause in December 1776, when he remained in town, took a British protection, and entertained Hessian officers.

Washington, with his party and escort, proceeded on to Samuel Henry's City Tavern on the southwest corner of Second and King Streets and shared a meal with Trenton's most prominent people, as well as a reception in the inn's parlors before setting off for Princeton. Washington left a letter at Princeton expressing his appreciation for the reception in Trenton and especially the "innocent appearance of the white-robed chorus who met him" with their song. It left "such impression on his remembrance as, he assures them will never be effaced." The following afternoon, the letter was read to a gathering of ladies at the home of Dr. Isaac Smith.

After further ceremonies along his route, Washington arrived in New York and was inaugurated President on April 30. Somewhat ironically, one of the tunes played during the ceremony was "The President's March," written for the occasion by Philip Phile, a German man brought to America as a musician in Colonel Rall's Hessian regiment, was captured at the Battle of Trenton, and had stayed in America when released. This tune was later arranged with lyrics, and we know it as "Hail Columbia."

George Bradshaw's c1929 etching of George Washington on his way to be inaugurated in New York City in April 1789 and his reception by the people of Trenton at the Assunpink Creek bridge. The townspeople had decorated an arch at the bridge commemorating the two battles at Trenton. (THS, Trenton)

Conclusion

Our story has revealed how Trenton and its people experienced the political and military events of the Revolution and supported General Washington's strategy for winning the war for independence. Washington's efforts to keep his army manned and in the field can be clearly seen in the troop movements through Trenton and the work of the supply depot and hospital established there. These military support facilities were cogs in the wheels of systems established by the Continental Congress, and the many difficulties confronting the men working at the Trenton facilities were indicative of problems experienced by the confederation of new states. After the 13 diverse colonies protested the acts of Parliament and then declared independence, they had to figure out how to work together to create a political and economic entity they could all support. Many problems resulted from the unclear and evolving working relationship between the individual 13 states and the Continental Congress. The people who lived in or spent time in Trenton during these years, in the words of the ironic prophecy, lived in interesting times.

Trenton had been built by people utilizing the great potential of its location at the head of navigation on the Delaware River and on the main road between New York and Philadelphia. During its first century, Trenton became the home of such industries as milling, tanning, iron working, fishing, and pottery, as well as many crafts. After the Revolution, Trenton became the state capital in 1790, grew into a city during the 19th century, and became a prime manufacturing center noted for its potteries and steel works that proudly proclaimed on one of its bridges across the Delaware that "Trenton Makes, the World Takes." In the mid-nineteenth century the town separated from the rest of Trenton Township that became Ewing Township. When Mercer County was formed in 1838, Trenton left Hunterdon County and the areas of "functional Trenton" south of the Assunpink left Burlington County and joined with the city in the new Mercer County. Since then, Trenton has been the county seat of Mercer as well as the New Jersey State capital. Trenton thrived into the 20th century but, after World War II, like many industrial cities it experienced a gradual economic decline. Except for Amtrak, Trenton is no longer on a primary communication route. Today the city struggles as commerce has shifted to economic centers outside the city. Instead of county and state government activity supplementing Trenton's economy as they did at the time of the Revolution, government facilities and workers are in many ways the life-blood of Trenton. Diversifying and developing more local businesses and attracting people to live in or visit the town to contribute to the culture and economy are real challenges that many local people struggle mightily to achieve.

In spite of all the changes made over the past 200 years, one can still walk the same streets known to the people of Trenton and visitors between 1774 and 1783; streets known to political leaders and messengers such as John Adams and Paul Revere; streets that carried troops of all the armies engaged in the war; streets that were used by wagons carrying supplies to the Continental army; and, streets that brought sick and wounded soldiers to Trenton for treatment. Street names may have changed but the pattern of the streets of the market town of Trenton remain basically unchanged. One can stand at the battle monument at the site where five streets came together in 1776 and look down the two main streets of 18th century Trenton and then turn around to see the Maidenhead Road that led to Princeton, Pennington Road that led to Hopewell, and Beakes Lane that led to the large Beakes farm. After reading this book, one can imagine themselves back in Trenton during the Revolution and create a mental image that strips away the modern structures built on the colonial foundation of the town. While very few buildings from the Revolution era survive, one can visit the Old Barracks Museum and the adjacent Petty's Run archaeological site. The William Trent House, formerly Kingsbury and then Bloomsbury, is now a museum. The important Assunpink Creek bridge site is now hidden under South Broad Street and crossed by hundreds of vehicles each day just as countless individuals, groups, stage coaches, supply wagons, and army units did in the 1770s. Visitor guides provide information on these and other remnants of Revolutionary era Trenton that can be visited.

The importance of the story of Trenton in the years of the Revolution is captured in a story told by Washington's step-grandson, George Washington Parke Custis. In his recollections, Custis describes a dinner shortly after the victory at Yorktown and quotes a toast made by Lord Cornwallis to Washington in which he says, "When the illustrious part that your Excellency has borne in this long and arduous contest becomes matter of history, fame will gather your brightest laurels rather from the banks of the Delaware than from those of the Chesapeake." This story may be apocryphal, Custis was born in 1781 so he was not an eyewitness, but at least it represents sentiments passed down in Washington's family and perhaps reflects what Washington himself felt. While the statement refers specifically to the events of December and early January 1776-1777, it could just as easily refer to the decade of actions in and about Trenton that reflected the skills and actions of Washington and the constant activity of people living in and spending time in Trenton working for the Revolution.[1]

Trenton is just one of the many locales whose history has much to tell us about the American Revolution. Each story is unique and was often accurately perceived by people at the time, just as Trenton people described their disrupted town in 1778 as "so necessary a post and so much a thoroughfare" as a crossroads of the Revolution.

Citation Abbreviations

Microform identifications - r – roll, i – image, p - page, f – frame

AO12 - Great Britain, Exchequer and Audit Department. *American Loyalist Claims.* Series 1, 1776-1831, AO 12 [microform] Exchequer and Audit Department

AO13 - Great Britain, Audit Office. *American Loyalist Claims.* Series 2, 1780-1835, AO 13 [microform] Exchequer and Audit Department

Assembly Votes – *Votes and Proceedings of the General Assembly of the State of New Jersey,* various dates beginning 1776, organized and paginated by sessions

GWPLOC – *George Washington Papers at the Library of Congress, 1741-1799,* available on line at memory.loc.gov

JCC – *Journals of the Continental Congress*

Joint Meeting - *Minutes and Proceedings of the Council and General Assembly of the State of New-Jersey, in joint-meeting, from August 30, 1776 to October 29, 1799,* Trenton: 1780.

Legislative Council Journal – *A Journal of the Proceedings of the Legislative Council of the State of New Jersey,* various dates beginning 1776, organized and paginated by sessions

NJG – *New Jersey Gazette*

NJSA – New Jersey State Archives

PC&CS – *Minutes of the Provincial Congress and Committee of Safety*

PCC – *Papers of the Continental Congress*

PF - Pension File

Provincial Assembly Votes – *Votes and Proceedings of the General Assembly of the Province of New Jersey,* various dates through the colonial period

THS – Trenton Historical Society

Notes

Introduction

1 For more on the diversity of the Middle Colonies and its effect on people during the Revolution, see: Ned C. Landsman, *Crossroads of Empire: The Middle Colonies in British North America* (Baltimore: Johns Hopkins University Press, 2010); Liam Riordan, *Many Identities, One Nation: The Revolution and Its Legacy in the Mid-Atlantic* (Philadelphia: University of Pennsylvania Press, 2007); and, Michael Zuckerman, "Introduction: Puritans, Cavaliers, and the Motley Middle" in Michael Zuckerman, ed., *Friends and Neighbors: Group Life in America's First Plural Society* (Philadelphia: Temple University Press, 1982).
2 Named for the Pettit family that settled early in Trenton.
3 Fulling mills were used to finish homespun textiles. The presence of a fulling mill indicated that significant quantities of cloth were being produced locally, even as local people participated in a developing commercial revolution that brought them a large variety of textiles from England.
4 Oxen were male cattle of any breed that had been castrated, making them steers, and trained to work. They became official oxen at age four when they achieved full growth. The term oxen should be considered a job description, not an animal species, and in some times and places can refer to trained female cows or species other than dairy cows.
5 THS, *A History of Trenton, 1679-1929; Two Hundred and Fifty Years of a Notable Town with Links to Four Centuries* (Princeton: Princeton University Press, 1929), 4-5.
6 Eleanor Nolan Shuman, *The Trenton Story* (Trenton: MacCrellish & Quigley, 1958), 23-25; Rebecca White, Nadine Sergejeff, William Liebeknecht and Richard Hunter, *A Historical Account and Archaeological Analysis of the Eagle Tavern, City of Trenton, Mercer County, New Jersey* (Trenton: 2005), 2-1; Nadine Sergejeff, *The Assunpink Creek in Mill Hill: A History and Consideration of Interpretive Opportunities: City of Trenton, Mercer County, New Jersey* (Trenton: Hunter Research, 2002); THS, Trenton, 40-41.
7 Shuman, *Trenton Story*, 28, 32-33.
8 Stephanie Smith Toothman, *Trenton, New Jersey, 1719-1779: A Study of Community Growth and Organization*. A Dissertation in American Civilization Presented to the Graduate Faculty of the University of Pennsylvania (1977), 5. Toothman uses the term "functional Trenton" to describe the relationship between the market town of Trenton and the area south of the Assunpink to Lamberton. Determining the exact population is very difficult. Any number must be an estimate based on number of households, average size of families, unknown numbers of tenants, slaves, servants, etc. who don't always show up in the records. Trenton no doubt also had some level of transient laborers and others. Another factor complicating a population figure is the political division and determining who considered themselves residents of "functional" Trenton in Nottingham Township and in Trenton Township

Chapter 1

1 This description follows one made by French observers on the march to Yorktown in 1781 and recorded in Howard C. Rice, Jr., and Anne S.K. Brown, trans. and ed. *The American Campaigns of Rochambeau's Army, 1780, 1781, 1782, 1783* (Princeton: Princeton University Press, 1972), II: 71
2 Williams announced he had relocated his Royal Oak Inn to the Ferry in an advertisement in the *Pennsylvania Gazette*, May 12, 1773, supplement 4. In the ad he noted the convenience of eating or lodging at the ferry as a time saving measure when needing to cross the river.
3 Paul H. Smith, ed., *Letters of Delegates to Congress, 1774-1789* (Washington: Library of Congress, 1976-1985), I: 3; John Adams, *Diary and Autobiography of John Adams*. L.H.

Butterfield, ed. (Cambridge: Belknap Press of Harvard University Press, 1962), II: 114; Robert Treat Paine's diary with similar information is in Smith, *Letters of Delegates*, I: 12. Newspaper articles giving some information on their journey include the *Boston Gazette, and Country Journal*, August 15, 1774.

4 Silas Deane to Elizabeth Deane, August 31, 1774, Silas Dean, *Correspondence of Silas Deane, Delegate to the First and Second Congress at Philadelphia, 1774-1776* (Hartford: Connecticut Historical Society, 1870), 163-165. A condensed version of the letter is in Smith, *Letters of Delegates*, I: 14.

5 *Provincial Assembly Votes*, Session beginning May 25, 1763, 5, 22; THS, *Trenton*, 243-244.; Frederick W. Ricord, ed. *Documents Relating to the Colonial History of the State of New Jersey* (Trenton: John L. Murphy, 1892), XVII: 397-98; *Provincial Assembly Votes*, Session beginning May 21, 1765, 42-43; *The New-York Mercury*, August 19, 1765, 3; *The New-York Gazette or The Weekly Post-Boy*, January 1, 1767, 4.

6 *Provincial Assembly Votes*, Session beginning October 10, 1769, 30; Session beginning November 10, 1773, 208; THS, *Trenton*, 249.

7 This mill was on the site of Mahlon Stacy's original grist mill. Over the years it had grown, been rebuilt, and changed hands several times. It was commonly referred to as Trenton Mills.

8 Sergejeff. *The Assunpink Creek in Mill Hill.*

9 *Provincial Assembly Votes*, Session beginning November 15, 1763, 22; Session beginning February 14, 1764, 6; Session beginning May 21, 1765, 14, 16; Ricord, *Colonial Documents*, XVII: 425, 428, 435; Bernard Bush, *Laws of the Royal Colony of New Jersey. New Jersey Archives*, Third Series (Trenton: New Jersey State Library, Archives and History Bureau, 1986), IV: 350.

10 Samuel Allinson, *Acts of the General Assembly of the Province of New Jersey* (Burlington: 1776), 402. 11 Delaware River ferries were typically guided by an overhead cable that allowed the flat, scow like boat to use the river current for power in combination with men using long poles pushing against the river bed, and sometimes a sail. A complete description of the technology of the Trenton ferries has not been found.

12 *New York Gazette and Weekly Mercury*, October 1, 1770, 3; B. F. Fackenthal, Jr., "Improving Navigation on the Delaware River with Some Account of the Ferries, Bridges, Canals and Floods." *A Collection of Papers Read Before the Bucks County Historical Society* (Easton, PA: Fackenthal Publication Fund, 1932), VI: 133, 134. In newspaper ads, Colvin gives his location as Trenton Ferry. See for example: *Dunlap's Pennsylvania Packet or, the General Advertiser*, April 18, 1774, Supplement 1. On the Delaware it was typical to have separately owned ferries on opposite sides of the river.

13 Petition of Cortland Skinner to Governor William Franklin, September 15, 1773, NJSA, Department of Education, New Jersey State Library, Bureau of Archives and History, Manuscript Collection, 1680s-1970s, Box BAH 1-01, #54; Ricord, *Colonial Documents*, XVIII: 356-357, 360-361.

14 *Dunlap's Pennsylvania Packet*, April 18, 1774, 1; THS, *Trenton*, 268-269.

15 For example, burning tea at Greenwich in protest against the Tea Act did not take place until December 22, 1774, a year after the "Boston Tea Party."

16 John O. Raum, *History of the City of Trenton, New Jersey* (Trenton: 1871), 393-394. On the evening of February 7, 1747, five men proposed to form a fire company and appointed Obadiah Howell to procure the necessary buckets, baskets, fire-hooks, and ladders. Two men were appointed to write up a constitution that was adopted the next day, along with the name Union Fire Company.

17 *New York Gazette*, May, 20, 1765, 2.

18 *New York Gazette*, February 10, 1772, 3 – letter is dated February 2; *The Pennsylvania Packet*, February 3, 1772, 2 – the letter is dated January 30; *Pennsylvania Chronicle*, February 3 to February 10, 1772, 11. By 1774, the Union Fire Company had been joined by the Hand-in-Hand Company formed at Rensselaer Williams's tavern in 1772, several months after a major fire that began in the store and home of snuff maker Dunlap Adams. One witness said, "never had a fire a more terrible appearance in so small a

town: I believe for a considerable time, we expected nearly the whole town to have been destroyed." No doubt as a result of this fire, the Union company purchased a small fire engine from James Gibbs of Philadelphia. Reflecting lessons learned, the Hand-in-Hand Company constitution required each member, under threat of fine, to provide himself, within three months and at his own cost, "two leather buckets, one bag, and one convenient basket," each marked with the owner's and the fire company name and "hung up near the front door, as conveniently as may be." Raum, *City of Trenton*, 395, 399-400. Charter members were Joseph Toy, David Cowell, Rensselaer Williams, Isaac Pearson Rodman, Archibald William Yard, Joseph Clunn, Richard Borden, and Samuel Bellerjeau.

19 *Philadelphia Gazette*, February 20, 1766, 3; *New York Mercury*, February 24, 1766, 3.

20 Richard P. McCormick, *New Jersey from Colony to State, 1609-1789* (New Brunswick: Rutgers University Press, 1964), 113.

21 For more on the New Jersey colonial government see: McCormick, *Colony to State*, 58-63.

22 Journal of the Provincial Council, VI, 1769-1776, 432; *Provincial Assembly Votes*, Session beginning November 10, 1773, 118.

23 Only Pennsylvania and North Carolina remained.

24 *Provincial Assembly Votes*, Session beginning, November 10, 1773, 122; *PC&CS*, 1-2.

25 John Ferling, *A Leap in the Dark: The Struggle to Create the American Republic* (Oxford: Oxford University Press, 2003), 92-93.

26 *Provincial Assembly Votes*, Session beginning November 10, 1773, 126 – agreed to by governor March 8 – 209; For example, March 2, 1774, 186; March 8, 1774, 199, 155, 178, 180, 190, 210.

27 Darold D. Wax, "Negro Imports into Pennsylvania, 1720-1766," *Pennsylvania History: A Journal of Mid-Atlantic Studies* 32 (1965), 258. Cites Thomas Riche to Samuel Tucker, August 1, 18, 1761, October 18, 1762, *Thomas Riche Letter Book*, I (1750-1764), Historical Society of Pennsylvania.

28 *Reynell (John) Papers, 1753-1775*, AC902, Rutgers University Libraries, Special Collections and University Archives. This collection contains a number of letters dated 1755-1775 between the Reynell and Tucker families. These are letters clearly to a "friend" as well as a business associate.

29 Toothman, *Trenton, 1719-1779*, 234, 239; Certificate of Mr. Warrell, Attorney General and Notary Public in New Jersey, as to the character of Samuel Tucker. November 4, 1751 in William A. Whitehead, *Documents Relating to the Colonial History of the State of New Jersey.* Archives of the State of New Jersey, First Series (Newark: 1883), VII: 639-640; See also the accompanying document "Deposition of Samuel Tucker" as to the Character of William Morris Esquire Judge of the Court of the Common Pleas for the County of Hunterdon in the Province of New Jersey, November 2, 1751 in which Tucker gives clues to the extent of his business interests. *NJG*, November 24, 1779, 3. Example of his land interests, 625 acres of woodland in Cumberland County, NJ.

30 For more on the Coxe family and the land disputes see: Brendan McConville, *These Daring Disturbers of the Public Peace: the Struggle for Property and Power in Early New Jersey* (Philadelphia: University of Pennsylvania Press, 1999).

31 Holding annual town meetings during March was a long-standing tradition begun under the Julian calendar, when March 25 was the first day of the year, and electing officials on the second Tuesday of March set things up for the next government year. Beginning in 1752, when the Gregorian calendar was adopted, January 1 began the year, but the traditional time for the town meeting was maintained.

32 *Minutes of the Township of Trenton, 1755-1818*, copied by the Federal Writers' Project, Works Progress Administration, 1937, from original record found in City Hall. Typescript in Trentoniana Room at the Trenton Free Public Library, Trenton, New Jersey, 34-35; John Fitch's Account Book, Historical Society of Pennsylvania, John Fitch Papers 1763-1828, Collection No. 0208. Records that silversmith Fitch paid to Ralph Jones a sum described as a tax on January 1, 1774. Jones had been the tax collector for several years.

33 *Minutes of Trenton*, 34-35; THS, *Trenton*, 243-247. The March 11, 1774, road act, passed just a few days after the town meeting, established the number of days each man was responsible to contribute to road maintenance.

34 *NJG*, February 28, 1781, 3. Marguretta was of the Yardley family. The family continued to develop during the war years. Their second son was born in November 1775, but died in September 1776. Their son Stacy was born March 4, 1777 and daughter Anna on February 20, 1779. Stacy was not a young father and was in his mid to late fifties during the main years of the war. He was almost sixty when his 23 year old daughter, Polly, died in 1781 after a lingering illness and was buried at the Friends Meeting House.

35 See Stacy Potts Tannery Day Book, NJSA, Old Barracks Museum Association Manuscript Collection, 1771-1809, POLDB001, passim.

36 The *Pennsylvania Chronicle*, July 13 to July 20, 1772, 107; July 12 to July 19, 1773, 316; *Pennsylvania Gazette*, Thursday, September 26, 1765, 6 for advertisement for sale of the tan yard where he was the tenant and that he later purchased. Stacy Potts Tannery Day Book.

37 Stacy Potts Tannery Day Book.

38 Jayne E. Triber, *A True Republican: The Life of Paul Revere* (Amherst: University of Massachusetts Press, 1998), 98; See: "Boyle's Journal of Occurrences, May 13, 1774," *New England Historical and Genealogical Register* 84 (October 1930), 374 – for the arrival of the Boston Port Act in Boston; Boston Gazette, May 16 and May 30, 1774; *New York Gazette and Weekly Mercury*, May 23, 1774; *The Newport Mercury*, May 23, 1774, 2; Esther Forbes, *Paul Revere and the World He Lived In* (Boston: Houghton Mifflin, 1943), 208.

39 For more on this see: Ray Raphael and Marie Raphael. *The Spirit of '74: How the American Revolution Began*. (New York: The New Press, 2015), 25.

40 See: Derek W. Beck, *Igniting the American Revolution: 1773-1775* (Naperville, IL: Sourcebooks, 2015), 366 n39 discussing the term Coercive Acts and the 19th century introduction of the term Intolerable Acts.

41 John Ferling, *Whirlwind: The American Revolution and the War That Won It* (New York: Bloomsbury Press, 2015), chapter 5.

42 John Fitch, *The Autobiography of John Fitch*, Frank D. Prager, ed. (Philadelphia: American Philosophical Society, 1976), 54-55. Fitch later gained notoriety as a steamboat entrepreneur.

43 Thomas Westcott, *The Life of John Fitch the Inventor of the Steamboat* (Philadelphia: J.B. Lippincott, 1857), chapter 3; Thomas Boyd, *Poor John Fitch: Inventor of the Steamboat* (New York: Putnam, 1935), 46; Fitch, *Autobiography*, 50-52; Julia Sabine, "Silversmiths of New Jersey, 1623-1800" Vol 61 no 3, July 1943, *Proceedings of the New Jersey Historical Society* 61 (1943), 164.

44 John Fitch Account Book, John Fitch Papers 1763–1828, Historical Society of Pennsylvania, Collection Number 0208.

45 *PC&CS*, 4, 6-8.

46 NJSA, Legislature, Papers relating to the Barracks at Trenton, 1758-1793, Receipts for Money Paid to the Inhabitants of Trenton for Billeting Soldiers, 1757-1758. John Baker is the only soldier mentioned by name.

47 The original petition is located in NJSA: Legislature, Papers relating to the Barracks at Trenton, 1758-1793.

48 John Hall, *History of the First Presbyterian Church in Trenton from the First Settlement of the Town*, Second Edition (Trenton: MacCrellish & Quigley, 1912), 95-96.

49 Hunter Research. *The "Trenton in 1775" Mapping project, City of Trenton, Mercer County, New Jersey*. (Trenton: The Trenton Historical Society, 2008).

50 Furman's wharves were at the foot of modern Lalor Street.

51 Richard W. Hunter, *Fish and Ships: Lamberton, the Port of Trenton*, (Trenton: Hunter Research, 2005), 11-12.

52 *The New-York Journal*, February 27, 1772, 562. In 1771-72, he provided this service for a lottery raising £3000 for Presbyterian churches in New York City, and New Castle and Christiana Bridge in Delaware. See also: The *Pennsylvania Chronicle*, Monday, January

2, to Monday, January 9, 1769, 435; *The New-York Journal*, December 19, 1771, 519; *The Pennsylvania Packet*, March 8, 1773, 3; *The New-York Journal*, May 21, 1772, 628.

53 Bush, *Laws of Royal Colony*, IV: 330-332; Ricord, *Colonial Documents*, XVII: 433-34.

54 For more specific information see *Provincial Assembly Votes*, Session beginning June 25, 1766, 17-19, 39; Ricord, *Colonial Documents*, XVII: 459-462, 467, 470, 491-92, 494-95; Bush, *Laws of Royal Colony*, VI: 397-98, 431-34, 475-477, 577-580. See also: NJSA, Papers relating to the Barracks at Trenton, 1758-1793. This collection contains a number of statements concerning work done to maintain the barracks and especially the fence around the barracks yard between 1766 and 1771. There are several references to white oak posts and work for fence repair. From these statements it is clear that the barracks were almost constantly in need of attention. Again, a number of men who would be active during the years 1774-1783 were involved in building and maintaining the barracks.

55 *PC&CS*, 13-15; McCormick, *Colony to State*, 114; Ferling, *Whirlwind*, 81.

56 Kevin Phillips, *1775: A Good Year for Revolution*. (New York, Viking, 2012), 253.

57 Beck, *Igniting the American Revolution*, 42-43; *PC&CS*, 25-27; for letters between New Jersey and Boston regarding this aid see *PC&CS*, 28-30; for the letter of commission to the delegates to the First Continental Congress from New Jersey see *PC&CS*, 30-31; Jack Rakove. *Revolutionaries: A New History of the Invention of America*. (Boston: Houghton Mifflin Harcourt, 2010), 25, 31.

58 David Hackett Fischer, *Paul Revere's Ride*, (New York: Oxford University Press, 1994), 27; appendix C, 299-300; *New York Journal*, September 22, 1774, 3; *Boston Evening Post*, October 17, 1774, 2; He also made a trip between Boston and Philadelphia between November 12 and 24; John Adams to William Tudor, October 7, 1774 in Smith, *Letters of Delegates*, I: 157; L. H. Butterfield, ed. *Adams Family Correspondence* (Cambridge: Belknap Press of Harvard University Press, 1963+), I: 164-65.

59 Broadside printed by W. and T. Bradford, Philadelphia dated In Congress, Thursday, September 22, 1774 in collection of the Old Barracks Museum, Trenton, New Jersey. Text identified as an extract the minutes of Congress signed by Charles Thomson, Sec.

60 Rakove, *Revolutionaries*, 65; Ferling, *Whirlwind*, 98.

61 THS, *Trenton*, 51-52.

62 Elizabeth Satterthwaite, *History of the Religious Society of Friends in Trenton and Vicinity* (Typescript, 1925), I: 199. Trenton Free Public Library, Trentoniana Room. Collection of document transcriptions from various sources; Hubert Schmidt, "Slavery and Attitudes on Slavery Hunterdon County, New Jersey," *Proceedings of the New Jersey Historical Society* 58 (1940), 151-169. Schmidt looks at slavery before, during, and after the Revolution.

63 Schmidt, "Slavery and Attitudes," 151. For examples of male slave sales mentioning skills see: *Pennsylvania Packet*, January 1, 1776; August 20, 1776, 1, 3; October 20, 1779, 3; *NJG*, January 3, 1781, 4; February 7, 1781, 3; March 7, 1781, 3; July 31, 1782, 3; August 21, 1782, 3; January 29, 1783, 3; April 9, 1783, 3; June 4, 1783, 3.

64 For examples of female slave sale advertisements listing skills see: *NJG*, April 19, 1779, 3; July 12, 1780, 3; March 7, 1781, 3; March 14, 1781, 3; February 20, 1782, 3; October 23, 1782, 3; June 4, 1783, 3; February 19, 1783, 4; December 20, 1783, 3; March 19, 1783, 3.

65 For example: *NJG*, November 25, 1778, 3; *NJG*, March 14, 1781, 3; May 19, 1779, 3; July 12, 1780, 3; *NJG*, March 7, 1781, 3; April 4, 1781, 3; June 4, 1783, 3; January 3, 1781, 4.

66 *NJG*, January 3, 1781, 4.

67 For example: *NJG*, April 4, 1781, 3.

68 *NJG*, November 28, 1774, supplement 2; *NJG*, October 30, 1782, 3.

69 *NJG*, August 28, 1782, 3; *NJG*, July 19, 1780, 3; *NJG*, April 27, 1780, 3; August 9, 1780, 3.

70 *NJG*, November 15, 1780, 3; *NJG*, June 3, 1778, 3; *NJG*, December 5, 1781, 4.

71 McCormick, *Colony to State*, 113.

72 See Phillips, *1775*, chapters 1-7 for a fuller discussion.

Chapter 2

1 Ricord, *Colonial Documents*, XVII: 479-480. See: 487-488 for Council's response. *Provincial Assembly Votes*, Session beginning January 11, 1775, 5-7; *PC&CS*, 63-67.

2 See: Phillips, *1775*, for an interesting and detailed discussion of the changes taking place that year.

3 Dagobert D. Runes, ed. *The Selected Writings of Benjamin Rush* (New York: Philosophical Library, 1947), 325-326, 329.

4 *Pennsylvania Packet*, December 26, 1774, 3; January 9, 1775, 4; January 2, 1775, 1; *Pennsylvania Gazette*, January 25, 1775, 4.

5 Hunter, Richard W. and Ian C. Burrow, *Petty's Run Archaeological Site: Iron, Steel, Cotton and Paper in Historic Trenton*, Volume 1 Narrative, (Trenton: Hunter Research, 2014), 4-9. Beginning in 1762, the steel furnace went through a succession of Philadelphia owners, while Yard continued to own and operate the plating mill. However, even under different ownership the various parts of the complex were connected and assisted each other by exchanging raw materials, completed and partially completed products, and sharing tools, water for power, and perhaps labor. Through shared experience, the men involved in the work undoubtedly participated in a heady exchange of technological know-how. Benjamin Yard was a son of early settler and innkeeper, William Yard.

6 *New York Gazette*, June 15, 1772, 4; *The Pennsylvania Packet*, March 15, 1773, 3.

7 John Fitch Account Book.

8 *Pennsylvania Packet*, March 6, 1775, 1.

9 *The Pennsylvania Evening Post*, March 25, 1775, 108; additional praise in *Pennsylvania Journal*, March 22, 1775, 3.

10 *Pennsylvania Packet*, March 20, 1775, 3.

11 *The Pennsylvania Evening Post*, March 23, 1775, 104; *Pennsylvania Journal*, April 19, 1775, 4. The letters tell the story of Abelard and Eloisa, a famous tragic love affair between 12th century theologian Peter Abelard and his student Eloisa.

12 *PC&CS*, 49-50, 67-69; *Provincial Assembly Votes*, Session beginning January 11, 1775, 8-9, 15; Ricord, *Colonial Documents*, XVII: 484; Peter Force, *American Archives*, Series 4 (Washington: 1834), I: 1164.

13 *Provincial Assembly Votes*, Session beginning January 11, 1775, 15-16.

14 Ibid., 331-332.

15 Ibid., 51. NJSA, Department of Education, New Jersey State Library, Bureau of Archives and History, Manuscript Collection, Box 5-1, #70.

16 *Provincial Assembly Votes*, Session beginning January 11, 1775, 58-62.

17 *Pennsylvania Gazette*, April 12, 1775, 1. Interested parties could apply to either Potts or William Jackson in Trenton.

18 Ricord, *Colonial Documents*, XVII: 531-533.

19 Hall, *Trenton Presbyterian Church*, 322.

20 *Pennsylvania Packet*, April 24, 1775, supplement page 2

21 Ferling, *Whirlwind*, 118. See also: Fischer, *Paul Revere's Ride*, for detailed information on how the news travelled.

22 James Lockwood, Wallingford, Ct. to ?, April 24, 1775, Force, ed., *American Archives*, Series 4, II: 366.

23 For more on the rage militaire see: Charles Royster, *A Revolutionary People at War: The Continental Army and American Character, 1775-1783* (Chapel Hill: The University of North Carolina Press, 1979), chapter 1.

24 See - Phillips, *1775*, Introduction for overview of the importance of the year 1775 in the Revolution. 25 See McConville, *Those Daring Disturbers*, and Larry Kidder, *A People Harassed and Exhausted: The Story of a New Jersey Militia Regiment in the American Revolution* (CreateSpace: 2013), chapter 2.

26 *PC&CS*, 108-109; also announced in The *New York Journal*, May 11, 1775, 2; and *Pennsylvania Gazette*, May 10, 1775, 3; also Force, *American Archives*, Series 4, II: 467-468.

27 Phillips, *1775*, 228-229.

28 Deane, Correspondence, 227; also Smith, *Letters of Delegates*, I: 345-347; Rivington's *New York Gazette*er, May 11, 1775; 3.

29 *Pennsylvania Journal*, June 7, 1775, 3.

30 Hunter, *Fish and Ships*, 2-4.
31 *Pennsylvania Journal*, May 25, 1774, 4.
32 Force, *American Archives*, Series 4, II: 586-587; also see, *New-York Journal*, May 4,1775, 2; July 27, 1775, 1; *The Connecticut Courant*, and *Hartford Weekly Intelligencer*, May 8,1775, 3.
33 Ferling, *Whirlwind*, 118.
34 Ricord, *Colonial Documents*, XVII: 540–552; *Provincial Assembly Votes*, Session beginning May 15, 1775, 3, 5-12.
35 *Provincial Assembly Votes*, Session beginning May 15, 1775, 13, 23-28.
36 *PC&CS*, 170; Satterthwaite, *History of Society of Friends*, I: 197.
37 Hall, *Presbyterian Church*, 125-137 passim.
38 Great Britain, Audit Office, *American Loyalist Claims*, Series 2, 1780-1835, AO13, [microform] Exchequer and Audit Department, bundle 19.
39 *PC&CS*, 170-177.
40 Robert A. Becker, *Revolution, Reform, and the Politics of American Taxation, 1763-1783* (Baton Rouge: Louisiana State University Press, 1980), 166-169.
41 *PC&CS*, 179-183; Phillips, *1775*, 15, 160-163.
42 Force, *American Archives*, Series 4, II: 1114.
43 Hunter, *Fish and Ships*, 16; "Muster Rolls and Papers Relating to the Associators and Militia of the City and County of Philadelphia," *Pennsylvania Archives*, Series 2, XIII: 556.
44 Samuel Tucker, Trenton, to John Reynell, Philadelphia, June 28, 1775, *Reynell (John) Papers, 1753-1775*, AC902, Rutgers University Alexander Library, Special Collections and University Archives.
45 John Fitch Account Book.
46 Josephus Leander Sooy, *History of State Street Methodist Episcopal Church Trenton, N.J.* (Trenton: MacCrellish & Quigley, 1886), 14.
47 "An Ancient Sanctuary," *Trenton Times*, August 30, 1887, 1. A more complete list is given in "Trenton Methodists Celebrate Progress," *Trenton Times*, June 27, 1903, 8.
48 Sooy, *Methodist Church*, 11-13.
49 *Pennsylvania Journal*, June 28, 1775, 4.
50 John Fitch Account Book.
51 William Nelson, "New Jersey Biographical and Genealogical Notes from the Volumes of the *New Jersey Archives*," *Collections of the New Jersey Historical Society* IX (Newark: New Jersey Historical Society, 1916), 84; Hamilton Schuyler. *A History of St. Michael's Church Trenton: In the Diocese of New Jersey from its Foundation in the Year of Our Lord 1703 to 1926* (Princeton: Princeton University Press, 1926), 77; Great Britain, Exchequer and Audit Department. *American Loyalist Claims*. Series 1, 1776-1831, AO 12 [microform] Exchequer and Audit Department v13, 181; AO13 bundle 2.
52 Franklin's statement is in AO 13 bundle 2.
53 *JCC*, II: 204; Force, *American Archives*, Series 4, II: 1890.
54 *PC&CS*, 184-185.
55 *Minutes of Men's Meeting, Chesterfield Monthly Meeting*, Ancestry.com. U.S., Quaker Meeting Records, 1681-1935 [database online]. (Provo, UT: Ancestry.com Operations, Inc., 2014), 503, 505, 507, 512.
56 John Fitch Account Book.
57 *PC&CS*, 187-192; NJSA, Adjutant General's Office, Revolutionary War Manuscripts, New Jersey: Numbers 110811 [microform], #719.
58 *The New-York Gazette*, October 10, 1768, 1. He was still serving as secretary the next year - *The New-York Gazette*, October 16, 1769, 1.
59 *List of the Members of the American Philosophical Society, January 17, 1890*, 10; Stephen Wickes, *History of Medicine in New Jersey, and of its Medical Men, From the Settlement of the Province to A.D. 1800* (Newark: Martin R. Dennis, 1879), 399.
60 *PC&CS*, 194.
61 Benjamin Franklin to Peter Livingston, August 29, 1775, Benjamin Franklin, *The Complete Works of Benjamin Franklin*, John Bigelow, ed. (New York: G.P. Putnam's Sons, 1887), V: 538-39; Force, *American Archives*, Series 4, III: 450.

62 Roster of Captain Ross's Company, pages 41-42 – "Col. William Thompson's Battalion of Riflemen," *Pennsylvania Archives*, Fifth Series, Volume II, Harrisburg: 1906; James Thacher, *Military Journal During the American Revolutionary War, from 1775 to 1783* (Boston: Richardson and Lord, 1823), 4, 6 description of company made when it reached Cambridge. In September, thirty-two men of the company participated in the first mutiny of the Continental army, but were not seriously punished. See: Derek W. Beck, *The War Before Independence: 1775-1776*, (Naperville, IL: Sourcebooks, 2016), 198.

63 *JCC*, III: 277; Force, *American Archives*, Series 4, III: 1890.

64 Christopher Marshall, *Extracts from the diary of Christopher Marshall, kept in Philadelphia and Lancaster, during the American Revolution, 1774-1781*. William Duane, ed. (Albany: Joel Munsell, 1877), 34.

65 Stryker, William S. Stryker, *Trenton One Hundred Years Ago* (Trenton: 1878), 5-6; THS, *Trenton*, 321, 327; Toothman, *Trenton 1719-1779*, 270-271. On the August, September 1779 Tax List, Charles Axford, jr. is a householder with one acre, one horse, and two cows. Stryker says near his door two Hessian cannon were captured at the Battle of Trenton. See: NJSA, Hunterdon County Tavern Licenses for both Axford and Richard Cox. This tavern was kept by Richard Cox in the 1760s and Axford announced on May 3, 1768 that – he "hath taken the house where Richard Cox lately dwelt in Trenton." On May 4, 1774 he applied to continue his license to keep a tavern and "public house of entertainment." *NJG*, January 22, 1783, 3. Charity Britton's license applications continue to at least 1779 and express her desire to continue "keeping a public house in that ancient licensed house in which she now lives."

66 Stryker, *One Hundred Years Ago*, 7; Toothman, *Trenton 1719-1779*, 270; THS, *Trenton*, 321. On the August, September 1779 Tax List she is a house holder with 7 acres, one cow, and a tavern. Isaac is a householder with ¼ acre and tavern. Both Charity and her son, Isaac, operated the tavern at that time.

67 NJSA, Hunterdon County Tavern Licenses, May 2, 1774, image 1208. Additional license application are found for 1775 to 1779. The 1777 application indicates the property had formerly been owned by William Morris.

68 Stryker, *One Hundred Years Ago*, 12; Toothman, *Trenton 1719-1779*, 268-269; "Trenton A Century Ago," Supplement to the *Daily True American*, April 30, 1889, building #61.

69 THS, *Trenton*, 315-317; Thoothman, *Trenton 1719-1779*, 182. Rachel was the sister of John Barnes who became a Loyalist in 1776. Her husband, Pontius, died in 1770 and the Pontius Stille who appears in later records was her son. She died June 16, 1783 at the end of the war. Stryker, *One Hundred Years Ago*, 9; Toothman, *Trenton 1719-1779*, 185, 200, 202, 204, 269.

70 *Pennsylvania Gazette*, November 29, 1764, 1 – sheriff's sale advertisement. Was then property of Robert Rutherford. The building was owned by John Johnston who lived near Spotswood, New Jersey and put the property up for sale in March 1778. *NJG*, March 18, 1778, 3. It was apparently purchased by William Plaskett who put it up for sale in 1779. *NJG*, March 24, 1779, 3. William Plaskett was selling a house and lot in Trenton, fronting the main street and church alley – four rooms on a floor, two stories high, good cellar under the whole, kitchen on the backside of the house and joined to it by a shed. Six or seven sorts of pears, plumbs, cherries, and peaches. Plaskett lived on the premises. Toothman, *Trenton 1719-1779*, 185, 200, 202, 204, 269. Owned by William Plaskett, 0.125 acre deed WJ AT 456 1779. Hunter Research, *1775 Map Project*.

71 *The Pennsylvania Ledger*, September 16, 1775, 1.

72 White, *Eagle Tavern*, 2-1; THS, *Trenton*, 294-95 – citing *Pennsylvania Journal*, March 12, 1767.

73 Nelson, "New Jersey Biographical and Genealogical Notes," 56.

74 *PC&CS* 198, 200, 220-221. See: Toothman, *Trenton 1719-1779*, 164-171 for the story of the development of Kingsbury. See: *Pennsylvania Gazette*, March 9, 1774, 4 for Dr. Bryant's advertisement for Kingsbury lots. *PC&CS*, 205; – petition of Amwell residents to be part of First Hunterdon that was not allowed.

75 *PC&CS*, 224, 232; NJSA, Revolutionary War Mss #713.

76 *JCC*, III: 285.
77 *PC&CS*, 209.
78 NJSA, Revolutionary War Mss #709. October 5, 1775 muster.
79 NJSA, Department of Education, New Jersey State Library, Bureau of Archives and History, Manuscript collection, 1680s – 1970s, State Library Mss Coll box 5-1, #75; Old Barracks Museum Association, Manuscript Collection, 1771-1809, New Jersey State Archives Accession #1968.011, #7, #16.
80 *PC&CS*, 215-216, 222-223; *PCC*, New Jersey State Papers, r82, I68, p19, p21; Old Barracks Museum Association, Manuscript Collection, 1771-1809, at the New Jersey State Archives, accession number 1968.011- Petition of Thomas Ryerson.
81 John Fitch Account Book; John Fitch. *The Autobiography of John Fitch*. Frank D. Prager, ed. (Philadelphia: American Philosophical Society, 1976), 55.
82 *PC&CS*, 233.
83 Thomas Yard petition, n.d., in private collection.
84 NJSA, Revolutionary War Mss 2522, 7269, 6; NARA M246, Revolutionary War Rolls, 1775 – 1783, Muster Roll of Captain Joseph Braleys [sic] company in Barracks at Trenton January 15, 1776, roll 57. Also in manuscript collection of the Old Barracks Museum, Trenton, New Jersey.
85 NARA M246, Muster Roll of January 15, 1775 – Scott is given as enlisting October 4, but that is clearly an error. James Monjoy says he enlisted in Brearley's Company and is probably the James Joy on the muster roll.
86 NJSA, Revolutionary War Military Records [microform], Series #8, r5, i2, 80, 82, 84, 88.
87 *PC&CS*, 221, 238- 255; *JCC*, III: 310; Force, *American Archives*, Series 4, III: 1920.
88 Force, *American Archives*, Series 4, III: 1757.
89 Ricord, *Colonial Documents*, XVII: 564-570; *Provincial Assembly Votes*, Session beginning November 15, 1775, 3-6, 19-20.
90 Beck, *War Before Independence*, 217-219. For more on Prescott's treatment of Allen and the American response, see: Christian M. McBurney, *Kidnapping the enemy: The Special Operations to Capture Generals Charles Lee & Richard Prescott* (Yardley: Westholme, 2914), 84+.
91 November 1, 1775 – Philip Schuyler at Ticonderoga to John Hulbert, *PCC*, New Jersey State Papers, r82, i68, p55; see also Force, *American Archives*, Series 4, III: 1426-27, 1520-1521. *The Providence Gazette*, November 25, 1775, 3; *Pennsylvania Evening Post*, November 23, 1775, 539; *New York Journal*, November 30, 1775, 2. Captain Hulbert who took the prisoners to Trenton reported on his mission to Congress on November 20.
92 *JCC*, III: 359; Force, *American Archives*, Series 4, III: 1588, 1608. For notice that the paroles were received by Congress on December 12 see page 1950. Paroles were sworn promises that a person left at liberty would behave in a prescribed manner to avoid imprisonment. It was quite common for military officers to be put on parole when prisoners, less common for soldiers. In the case of Loyalists, it prevented the cost of imprisonment and also kept the person contributing to the economy. British Lieutenant James Smyth Symes, held in Philadelphia, was allowed to join the prisoners in Trenton on the same parole. *JCC*, III: 359-360, 367; Force, *American Archives*, Series 4, III: 1844-45. His release from confinement in Philadelphia was reported in the *New York Gazette* and Weekly Mercury, December 4, 1775, 2.
93 Lord Stirling to the President of Congress, Head Quarters, Elizabethtown, December 3, 1775. Force, *American Archives*, Series 4, IV: 164-165. Samuel Tucker at Trenton to Lord Stirling, December 10, 1775; Thomas Lowrey at Trenton to Lord Stirling on December 10, 1775; Force, *American Archives*, Series 4, IV: 228-230.
94 John G. Waite, et. al., *The Old Barracks Historic Structure Report* (Albany: John G. Waite Associates, 1998), 12.
95 November 23, 1775 - Petition of diverse freeholders of Burlington County to the General Assembly. NJSA, Department of Education, New Jersey State Library, BAH, State Library Mss Coll box 5-1, #82.
96 Rakove, *Revolutionaries*, 32-33, 75-77.
97 *Provincial Assembly Votes*, Session beginning November 15, 1775, 27-29; *Story & Humphreys's Pennsylvania Mercury, and Universal Advertiser*, December 9, 1775, 3.

98 *JCC*, III: 402.
99 *PCC*, New Jersey State Papers, r82, i68, p29; the letter was received by Congress on December 12. *JCC*, III: 424.
100 Butterfield, *John Adams Diary*, II: 224. *Pennsylvania Evening Post*, November 25, 1775, 544; *Pennsylvania Journal*, December 20, 1775, 1.
101 Force, *American Archives*, Series 4, IV: 166. erie
102 Doyen Salsig, ed. *Parole: Quebec; Countersign: Ticonderoga: Second New Jersey Regimental Orderly Book 1776* (Rutherford, NJ: Fairleigh Dickinson University Press, 1980), 39-40.
103 Force, *American Archives*, Series 4, IV: 294-296.
104 Ibid.; Muster Rolls of Captain Joseph Braleys [sic], Captain John Scott's, Captain Joseph Stout's, and Captain James Lawrie's companies in Barracks at Trenton January 15, 1776, NARA M246, Revolutionary War Rolls, 1775-1783.
105 Colonel William Maxwell, Woodbridge, to Lord Stirling, December 17, 1775, Force, *American Archives*, Series 4, IV: 294-296. One of the Canadian prisoners, Mons. Reconville, received permission from the Continental Congress on December 21 to go to Philadelphia and await the orders of Congress. However, he was probably housed at an inn rather than the barracks. Force, *American Archives*, Series 4, III: 1957.
106 Colonel William Maxwell, Trenton, to Lord Stirling, December 26, 1775, Force, *American Archives*, Series 4, IV: 463. Lord Stirling sent a captain to Maxwell on January 12, with "one of the frocks of his company which you may use as a pattern." William Alexander to William Maxwell, 12 January 1776, *PCC*, r179, p405.
107 Hall, *Trenton Presbyterian Church*, 159-60; *JCC*, III: 438.
108 See: Phillips, *1775*, 20-24.
109 Ferling, *Whirlwind*, 119.

Chapter 3

1 William Maxwell, Trenton, to John Hancock, January 23, 1775, *PCC*, [Miscellaneous] Letters Addressed to Congress, 1775-89, r99, i78, p3.
2 Trenton Committee to John Hancock, January 30, 1776, *PCC*, New Jersey State Papers, r82, i68, p59.
3 William Maxwell, Trenton, to John Hancock, January 31, 1776, *PCC*, [Miscellaneous] Letters Addressed to Congress, 1775-89, r99, i78, p7.
4 Muster Rolls of Captain Joseph Braleys [sic] Company, Captain Joseph Stout's Company, Captain John B. Scott's Company, and Captain James Lawrie's Company in Barracks at Trenton January 15, 1776, NARA M246, Revolutionary War Rolls, 1775-1783. An original manuscript of Captain Joseph Stout's Company muster is in the Old Barracks Museum Association archives collection.
5 Philip Bevan PF S5271. On February 5, the Provincial Congress resolved that no apprentice could be enlisted without the written consent of his master. *PC&CS*, 352.
6 *JCC*, IV: 17-18.
7 Return of men enlisted for one year in Captain John Polhemus' Company, First New Jersey Regiment, Ticonderoga, June 13, 1776, NJSA, Revolutionary War Mss #2243.
8 Samuel Tucker for Committee of Safety to President of Congress, Trenton, January 19, 1776, Force, *American Archives*, Series 4, IV: 772, 849-850. Tucker did provide several small amounts of money in January and February to the four captains of the Second New Jersey Regiment for arms. NJSA, Revolutionary War Military Records [microform], Series 8, reel 5, item 2, 80, 82, 84, 88.
9 Salsig, *Parole*, 50.
10 Ibid., 43, 45-51.
11 Old Barracks Museum Association, Manuscript Collection, 1771-1809, New Jersey State Archives Accession 1968.011, #23. Read in Congress February 6, 1776 noted on back.
12 Ibid., #15. The officers signing were Captain John B. Scott, Captain Joseph Brearley, Captain James Lawrie, Captain Joseph Stout, and Lieutenant Ephraim Anderson.

13 *PC&CS*, 339, 344. John Denis was the Eastern Treasurer. Order of Continental Congress, February 21, 1776, Force, *American Archives*, Series 4, IV: 1580-1581.

14 These would be muskets purchased by counties for use by their militiamen. Although each man was required by law to have a musket, it was not always possible for a man to afford one or to replace one temporarily or permanently out of commission from use.

15 Maxwell to Hancock, February 3, 1776, *PCC*, Miscellaneous letters addressed to Congress, 1775-89, r99, i78, p11. See also *PC&CS*, 342.

16 Salsig, *Parole*, 50-51. Lowrie's company did not leave until February 7 for some reason.

17 *Pennsylvania Packet*, February 19, 1776, 1. He had inherited this land from his father. NJSA, John Anderson of Maidenhead Probate File J84 - 1773.

18 NJSA, Ephraim Anderson Probate File 1740J.

19 George Ewing, *The Military Journal of George Ewing (1754-1824) a Soldier of Valley Forge* (Yonkers: Thomas Ewing, 1928), 1.

20 *JCC*, IV: 17-18, 30, 31n, 51-52; *PC&CS*, 338. The costs of keeping the prisoners in Trenton kept growing and on April 24 the Continental Congress noted that Furman and Hunt were due $183.8 for provisions and other items for the prisoners. Force, *American Archives*, Series 4, IV: 1687; *JCC*, IV: 305. . Congress also authorized payment to Abraham Hunt for provisions, fire wood, etc. for the prisoners, as well as hiring horses for the public service. *JCC*, IV: 220-221.

21 *PCC*, New Jersey State Papers, r82, i68, p57; New Jersey Committee of Safety, Trenton, to President of Congress, January 23, 1776, (read in Congress on January 24), Force, *American Archives*, Series 4, IV: 815; Petition of the Officers of Chambly held prisoner in Trenton, Force, *American Archives*, Series 4, IV: 816-817; *JCC*, IV: 62; *PCC*, New Jersey State Papers, r82, i68, p47; *PCC*, Misc Letters to Congress 1775-89, r96, i78, p11.

22 Order of the Committee of Safety, January 12, 1776, Force, *American Archives*, Series 4, IV: 663.

23 Samuel Tucker of Committee of Safety, Trenton, to President of Congress, January 19, 1776. Force, *American Archives*, Series 4, IV: 772.

24 Trenton Committee to John Hancock, January 30, 1776, *PCC*, New Jersey State Papers, r82, i68, p59; *JCC*, IV: 81.

25 Return of lost clothing belonging to men of the 7th Regiment, Force, *American Archives*, Series 4, IV: 818.

26 *PCC*, Misc Letters to Congress 1775-89, r96, i78, p11.

27 *PCC*, Reports of Committees on Applications of Individuals, 1776-89, r27, i3, p215. Printed in *JCC*, IV: 87-88.

28 *JCC*, IV: 78. See also IV: 77 and *PCC*, r68, i35 for communications from Trenton. Trenton, New Jersey Committee of Safety to President of Congress, January 23, 1776, Force, *American Archives*, Series 4, IV: 815.

29 *PCC*, New Jersey State Papers, r82, i68, p47.

30 *PCC*, Reports of Committees on Applications of Individuals, 1776-89, r27, i3, p215. Printed in *JCC*, IV: 87-88.

31 *JCC*, IV: 101. For more on the Prescott and Chase situation see: McBurney, Kidnapping the Enemy, 86-87. Prescott was exchanged for General Sullivan, but was later apprehended on a raid in Rhode Island in July 1777 to be a suitable candidate for exchange with General Charles Lee who had been captured in December 1776. Other items in the *PCC* relating to the prisoner issues at Trenton can be found on microfilm r82, i68, p41, 45, 47, 51; i78, p9, 13 and see also *JCC*, IV: 87.

32 *PCC*, Letters of John Hancock, and Miscellaneous Papers, 1774-85, r71, i58, p424-6.

33 Ibid., 429.

34 Trenton Committee, Trenton, to Richard Smith, February 24, 1776, *PCC*, Letters of John Hancock, and Miscellaneous Papers, 177485, r71, i58, p431. Prescott and Barrington had been captured when the schooner Gaspée was captured by troops of General Montgomery in the St. Lawrence River on its way to Quebec. McBurney, Kidnapping the Enemy, 122.

35 *JCC*, IV: 19.

36 Ibid., 19-21.

37 *PC&CS*, 337.
38 *PCC*, New Jersey State Papers, r82, i68, p43; New Jersey Committee of Safety, Trenton, to President of Congress, January 23, 1776, (read in Congress on January 24), Force, *American Archives*, Series 4, IV: 815. Edmund C. Burnett, ed. *Letters of Members of the Continental Congress* (Gloucester, MA: P. Smith, 1963), I: 339 – from diary of Richard Smith.
39 *PC&CS*, 389.
40 Absalom Hart PF W425 – supporting statements of Joshua Furman and several of Absalom's siblings. When Absalom and Susan were married in Monmouth County in February, Henry Drake brought word of the wedding back to Trenton.
41 *New York Journal*, April 4, 1776, 3.
42 *Minutes of Trenton*, 37-38.
43 On February 6, April 13, and August 17 Ben Franklin recorded receiving cash from Hunt related to his postmaster duties. "Ben Franklin's Post Office Ledger," *Proceedings of the New Jersey Historical Society*, IX, (1864), 85.
44 *PC&CS*, 376, 396-397, 410; NJSA, Revolutionary War Mss #4359; Old Barracks Museum Association, Manuscript Collection, 17711809, New Jersey State Archives, Accession 1968.011, #39.
45 Account of William Tucker as Barracks Master in Trenton by appointment of Provincial Congress February 28th 1776, Old Barracks Museum Association, Manuscript Collection, 1771-1809, New Jersey State Archives, #39. On April 1 Samuel Tucker paid barrack master William Tucker £25 1s for boards and repairs to the Trenton barracks. This is a separate manuscript receipt in the Old Barracks Museum Archives collection. Tucker and Alexander Chambers had been named barrack masters in the Ordinance for appointing Barrack masters in this Province, and making provision for defraying the expense of repairing said Barracks. Force, *American Archives*, Series 4, IV: 1610.
46 Double bridled locks were firing mechanisms containing a flash suppressor to protect the adjacent soldier in the formation when firing. This type had become standard in the British army.
47 Robert Treat Paine, *Robert Treat Paine Papers*, [microform], Massachusetts Historical Society, roll 3, 115-117. A "worm" was a device for cleaning the powder residue that collected in the barrel of a musket.
48 *PCC*, Transcript Journals, 1775-1779, September 5, 1775-May 14, 1776, III: 340; *JCC*, IV: 192.
49 *Robert Treat Paine Papers*, roll 18, 32; roll 3, 175-179.
50 *Pennsylvania Journal*, Wednesday, April 3, 1776, 4.
51 John Fitch Account Book; Fitch, *Autobiography*, 55-56.
52 *Minutes of the Women's Meeting of Chesterfield Friends, Chesterfield Monthly Meeting*, Ancestry.com. U.S., Quaker Meeting Records, 1681-1935 [database on-line]. (Provo, UT: Ancestry.com Operations, Inc., 2014), 349.
53 NJSA, Department of Education, New Jersey State Library, Bureau of Archives and History, Manuscript Collection, 16801-1970s, State Treasurer's Records, 1760-1844, BAH Box 1-11, #14.
54 NJSA, Revolutionary War Mss #4259.
55 *JCC*, IV: 384.
56 *PC&CS*, 459.
57 NJSA, Revolutionary War Mss #4259.
58 Hunter, *Fish and Ships*, 15; John W. Jackson, *The Pennsylvania Navy 1775-1781: The Defense of the Delaware* (New Brunswick: Rutgers University Press, 1974), 336.
59 Jackson, *Pennsylvania Navy*, 391-2. George Edward Reed, ed., *Pennsylvania Archives*, Series 4 (Harrisburg: State of Pennsylvania, 1900), III: 602-603.
60 Richard Veit and David Orr, eds. *Historical Archaeology of the Delaware Valley, 1600-1850* (Knoxville: University of Tennessee Press, 2014), 345.
61 Hunter, *Fish and Ships*, 4-7.
62 *New York Gazette* and Weekly Mercury, June 4, 1770, 2.

63 White, *Eagle Tavern*, 2-7, 2-8, 4-1.
64 Hunter, *Fish and Ships*, 7-8.
65 *NJG*, July 12, 1780, 4. Repeated in clearer table form on July 19, page 4. See also: *NJG*, September 16, 1778, 4 for an earlier ad referring to his packet with which he transported both goods and passengers.
66 New York Committee of Safety Minutes, April 12, 1776, Force, *American Archives*, Series 4, V: 1436+. The testimony in this investigation of Peter Dubois is much longer and quite interesting. He was ultimately let off with a reprimand. Just who this Peter Dubois was is unclear, but there are several possibilities, mostly men who became acknowledged Loyalists.
67 *JCC*, V: 351, 379, 422.
68 *PCC*, Miscellaneous letters to Congress, 1775-89, r103, i78, p63.
69 "Trenton A Century Ago," Supplement to the *Trenton True American*, of April 30, 1889, 4.
70 William Henry Rawle, "Col. Lambert Cadwalader, a Sketch." *Pennsylvania Magazine of History and Biography* (1886), X: 5, 13-14.
71 James Fergus PF W25573.
72 *PC&CS*, 445-449, 548-551.
73 William Morris PF S1061; John Jemes/James PF S5603; John McCollum PF S2769.
74 Asa Adams PF W133.
75 John Inskeep PF W4703; Thomas Flowers PF S22773.
76 Samuel Wooley PF R11850 – including deposition of Matthew Mount. Wooley and Mount say they enlisted in the summer of 1775, but the wagon department was not organized until 1776.
77 *PC&CS*, 454-458. The resolves of the Continental Congress on May 15 declared it irreconcilable to swear an oath of loyalty to the British government and the necessity of suppressing all powers of the British government in the colonies.
78 Ibid., 461-462, 470. Franklin was kept in Connecticut until his release in 1778, whereupon he took up residence in British controlled New York until the end of the war.
79 *PC&CS*, 446, 473.
80 Mark V. Kwasny, Washington's P*artisan War*, 1775-1783 (Kent, OH: The Kent State University Press, 1996), 6; Committee of Safety of New Jersey, Trenton, to the Continental Congress, January 23, 1776, *PCC*, r82, i68, p41.
81 *PC&CS*, 478.
82 William Livingston, *The Papers of William Livingston* [microform] (Ann Arbor, MI: University Microfilms, [1986]) r1, f310, 314.
83 David Van Norden PF W6341; John R. Hart PF S2282.
84 Toothman, *Trenton 1719-1779*, 237-238 – citing letter of June 14, 1776 from Coxe, Furman, and Coxe in Philadelphia to James Parsons in New York.

Chapter 4

1 "Extracts from the Diary of Dr. James Clitherall, 1776," The *Pennsylvania Magazine of History and Biography* XXII (Philadelphia: The Historical Society of Pennsylvania, 1898), 468-474. Clitherall had been in Philadelphia as escort to the wives of two congressmen from South Carolina, Edward Rutledge and Arthur Middleton.
2 Shuman, *Trenton Story*, 46; *PC&CS*, 488, 492. The Provincial Congress had been meeting in Burlington.
3 *Dunlap's Pennsylvania Packet*, July 15, 1776, 3; Larry R. Gerlach, *New Jersey in the American Revolution, 1763-1783: A Documentary History* (Trenton: New Jersey Historical Commission, 1975), 219-220. On July 22 Rachel Stille was reimbursed by Samuel Tucker, one of the Treasurers of the Provincial Congress, for "expenses on declaring independence." No doubt for providing food at her inn for the celebration. See NJSA, Auditor Book B, 15.
4 *PC&CS*, 492; NJSA, Revolutionary War Mss #671.
5 *PC&CS*, 496. For more on Harrison's career with Loyalist forces and his settlement in New

Brunswick, Canada after the war, see: William S. Stryker, *"The New Jersey Volunteers" (Loyalists) in the Revolutionary War* (Trenton: Naar, Day & Naar, 1887), 49; and E. Alfred Jones, *The Loyalists of New Jersey; Their Memorials, Petitions, Claims, etc., from English Records* (Boston: Gregg Press, 1972), 88.

6 Schuyler, *St. Michael's Church*, 70, 71, 75; Dr. Carlos B. Godfrey, *St. Michael's Church*, Trenton, New Jersey, 1704-1920: A Research. Typescript, 1920, (Trenton Free Public Library, Trentoniana Room), 5.

7 *Pennsylvania Evening Post*, July 4, 1776, 332.

8 *PC&CS*, 559-561. Voting in Trenton would take place at the courthouse.

9 *PC&CS*, 511; Innkeepers Rachel Steele and Rensselaer Williams were reimbursed for expenses. Report of a committee of Friends inquiring into the use of the Meeting House in Trenton as a barracks, August 1, 1776, NJSA, Department of Defense, Adjutant General's Office, Copies of Miscellaneous Records, 1774-1837, Box 1, #9; Minutes of the Men's Meeting, September 5, 1776, 541.

10 Kwasny, P*artisan War*, 49, 60.

11 *William Livingston Papers* [microform], r2, f031.

12 Samuel Tucker to John Hancock, Trenton, July 6, 1776, Force, *American Archives*, Series 5, I: 37.

13 *JCC*, V: 518-523, 529. See *Pennsylvania Gazette*, July 10, 1776 for publication of resolutions.

14 T. Stone to Council, Philadelphia, July 12, 1776, William Hand Browne, ed., *Archives of Maryland: Journal and Correspondence of the Maryland Council of Safety, July 7 – December 31, 1776* (Baltimore: Maryland Historical Society, 1893), 35.

15 Marshall, *Diary Extracts*, 84, 85, 89 passim.

16 John Cox, Philadelphia, to Jasper Yeates, July 13, 1776, Force, *American Archives*, Series 5, I: 254.

17 Francis E. Divine, "The Pennsylvania Flying Camp, July – November 1776," P*ennsylvania History: A Journal of Mid-Atlantic Studies*, vol 46, no 1, January 1979, 61.

18 John Cochran PF R2083) See: Marshall, *Diary Extracts*, 84-85; Force, *American Archives*, Series 5, I: 557 and corrected on 1:574.

19 Peter Yokum PF S22616.

20 NJSA, Department of Defense, Adjutant General's Office, Copies of Miscellaneous Records, 1774-1837, Box 1, #9, Report of a committee of Friends inquiring into the use of the Meeting House in Trenton as a barracks, August 1, 1776; *Minutes of the Men's Meeting*, September 5, 1776, 541.

21 *PCC*, New Jersey State Papers, r82, i68, p183-84; Force, *American Archives*, Series 5, I: 138-139.

22 For more on this total community disruption, see: Kidder, *A People Harassed and Exhausted*, passim.

23 *PCC*, New Jersey State Papers, r82, i68, p187; Force, *American Archives*, Series 5, I:172; James H. Levitt, *New Jersey's Revolutionary Economy* (Trenton: New Jersey Historical Commission, c1975), 12.

24 George Washington to President of Congress, New York, July 14, 1776, Force, *American Archives*, Series 5, I: 330. Washington's order to commanding officer of the Pennsylvania Troops from Head Quarters, New York, July 14, 1776, Ibid., I: 333.

25 *PC&CS*, 563-566.

26 *PC&CS*, 568-572; Fitch, *Autobiography*, 56; Westcott, *John Fitch the Inventor*, 58-59.

27 Jesse Moore PF W1307; Edmund Roberts PF S4778 – supporting statement of Jesse Moore; Henry Simmons PF S4838; Robert James PF W4461 – supporting statement of Joshua Furman; Oliver Hunt PF S2638; Absalom Hart PF W425 – supporting statement of Joshua Furman; John Bellis PF R733; NJSA, Revolutionary War Mss #9977, Reading Howell Account Book,1.

28 William Livingston, *The Papers of William Livingston*, Carl E. Prince, ed. (Trenton: New Jersey Historical Commission, c1979-1988), I: 97; Salsig, *Parole*, 157.

29 *JCC*, V: 558.

30 Coin valued according to a proclamation of Queen Anne in 1704 attempting to unify the various silver currencies used in the colonies.

31 *PC&CS*, 507-508; Force, *American Archives*, Series 5, I: 369.

32 NJSA, Revolutionary War Mss #4259; *PC&CS*, 496; Daniel Yard PF W2399. Yard served tours

in Captain William Tucker's Company and then in 1778 became Assistant Quarter Master at Trenton.

33 William S. Stryker, The Battles of *Trenton and Princeton* (Boston: Houghton, Mifflin and Company, 1898), 123. Original document in the collection of the Swan Historical Foundation.

34 *PC&CS*, 477-478; 487-488; Kwasny, *Partisan War*, 50.

35 *The New-York Gazette*, February 15, 1768, 4. Esopus mill stones came from Ulster County, New York and were considered the best in the colonies. Other stones were imported from Europe.

36 *PC&CS*, 508; Toothman, *Trenton 1719-1779*, 245. Henry retained ownership of his mill until his death in 1784.

37 *PC&CS*, 515. This arrangement is also recorded in NJSA, Legislature, Petitions, Resolutions, Transactions, Accounts and Misc papers 1700-1845, #89 – Report of private committee respecting papers in the hands of [Samuel] Tucker, 1778. There was a question whether Tucker ever accounted for this bond and others.

38 For example, see: *PC&CS*, 498 and NJSA, Department of Education, New Jersey State Library, Bureau of Archives and History, Manuscript Collection, 1680s-1970s, Box 5-02, #103.

39 *PC&CS*, 498, 501,502, 508, 510, 511, 515, 574; Hall, *Trenton Presbyterian Church*, 332; NJSA Auditor's Book B, 15. Howell was authorized 18 shillings, which he got on August 21 - *PC&CS*, 574.

40 *PC&CS*, 513, 515; NJA Auditor's Book B, 15; Stryker, *"The New Jersey Volunteers,"* 31-32; Jones, *New Jersey Loyalists*, 20-22.

41 New Jersey Provincial Congress, Trenton, to John Hancock, July 6, 1776 – signed by Samuel Tucker, *PCC*, New Jersey State Papers, r82, i68, p175; *PC&CS*, 494-495.

42 Ibbetson Hamar, Kingsberry near Trenton, to John Hancock, July 9, 1776, *PCC*, Miscellaneous letters to Congress 1775-89, r96, i78, p63. On November 30, Hamar married Sarah Howard, widow of William Howard of the British 17th Regiment of Foot who owned a 200 acre estate known as Castle Howard near Princeton. Hamar had been exchanged and was no longer a prisoner of war and his first wife must have died. See: AO12, vol 14; AO13, bundle 61.

43 *JCC*, V: 610. Rachel Stille was also reimbursed by the New Jersey Provincial Congress in 1776 for "expense of prisoners." See NJSA, Auditor's Account A, 105.

44 This was the same John Dickinson who had refused to vote for independence, but had joined the American army. He was Philemon Dickinson's brother.

45 Carpenter Wharton, Trenton, to John Hancock, July 15, 1776, *PCC*, Miscellaneous letters addressed to Congress, 1775-89, r104, i78, p297-298.

46 Lancaster County Committee of Inspection and Observation, July 25, 1776. Received a letter from Colonel Philip Greenwalt of the Ninth Battalion of Lancaster about the needs of his men who were scheduled to march for Trenton the next Monday. The men were in need of muskets, cartridge boxes, field kettles, canteens, and other items. Force, *American Archives*, Series 5, I: 572.

47 "Extracts from the Diary of Nathan Sellers, 1776-1778," *Pennsylvania Magazine of History and Biography* 16 (1892), 191.

48 Hall, *Trenton Presbyterian Church*, 145, 328. Hall notes that Roberts did not copy the inscription completely accurately, mostly spelling and punctuation errors. Algernon Roberts, "A Journal of a Campaign from Philadelphia to Paulus Hook" The *Pennsylvania Magazine of History and Biography* VII (Philadelphia: The Historical Society of Pennsylvania 1883), 456-458. See also: Philip Conrad R2235, Jacob Latch PF W2131, John Young PF W3488. Both Conrad and Latch were in Captain John Young's Company of Col Jonathan Paschale's Regiment. Algernon Roberts was First Lieutenant, Joseph Price Second Lt, and Amos Johnson, Ensign. They were called out in August, met in Philadelphia and remained there for one to two weeks before they "left in sail Boats, which carried them to Trenton New Jersey where they landed and marched to Princeton, ..." They were out about two months. Latch says they lodged at Trenton before marching on the Princeton the next morning.

49 General Mercer, Perth Amboy, to General Washington, August 10, 1776, Force, *American Archives*, Series 5, I: 885.

50 *Legislative Council Journal*, Session beginning August 27, 1776, 5; *Assembly Votes*, session beginning August 27, 1776, 1-2. The receipt for payment by Congress Treasurer Samuel Tucker dated September 14, 1776, NJSA, Department of Education, New Jersey State Library, BAH Manuscript Collection, 1680s-1970s, Rev War Docs box 4-1a, #17. He was also paid for riding express to Samuel How at Burlington and for hiring a horse and the necessary expenses. Charles W. Parker, "New Jersey Supreme Court of September Term, 1776," *Proceedings of the New Jersey Historical Society* 50 (1932), 257, 264.

51 Address of the Grand Jury of Burlington County to Samuel Tucker, November 13, 1776, and Tucker's response, Force, *American Archives*, Series 5, III: 662.

52 *Joint Meeting*, 4, 6-7. On September 12, Samuel Tucker was mentioned as one of the "late Treasurers" - on 18 September he signed as a treasurer. *Assembly Votes*, Session beginning August 27, 1776, 9, 25. Cowell was sworn in on October 11. NJSA, Hunterdon County Court of Common Pleas Minutes, [microform] vols 11-13 (1767-1788).

53 NJSA, Revolutionary War Mss #676 – Tucker's note for Dougherty dated October 4, 1776.

54 Peter Force, *American Archives*, Series 5, II: 550.

55 Philemon Dickinson, Perth Amboy, to William Livingston, September 23, 1776, *William Livingston Papers* [microform], r3, f236. General Dickinson had informed the Assembly on September 2 that a number of militiamen had deserted, taking their arms, &c with them and a number of the militia were without arms. *Assembly Votes*, Session beginning August 27, 1776, 3.

56 Fitch, *Autobiography*, 57. John Fitch Account Book – these men included James Houston, Henry Fulford, William Torance, Richard Wilson, Frances Mills, Daniel Martin, Richard Alboy, Peter Yeatsman, William Jackson, Menoah Yeatsman, Thomas Carr, David Chambers, Nathan Wright, and James Hadden.

57 Receipt Clement Biddle DQMG in Philadelphia to John Shaw ADQMG at Trenton, August 3, 1776, Swan Historical Foundation mss #1989.1.775.

58 Swan Historical Foundation mss #1989.1.774.

59 Clement Biddle, Perth Amboy, to John Shaw, Assistant Deputy Quarter-Master at Trenton, September 11, 1776, The Sol Feinstone Collection of the American Revolution [microform] (Philadelphia: Historic Publications; Wilmington: Scholarly Resources, 1969-1975), Mss #2328.

60 *PC&CS*, 542. Whether or not John Fitch's demands for this caused it to happen is not stated.

61 Stryker, *Trenton and Princeton*, 123. Original mss in the collection of the Swan Historical Foundation.

62 William Richards to Committee, August 19, 1776, directed to Council of Safety, Samuel, Hazard, ed., *Pennsylvania Archives*, Series 1 (Philadelphia: Joseph Severns, 1853), V: 13. Two months later, Richards wrote again that the "commodore was with me this morning and says the fleet has not any colors to hoist if they should be called on duty. It is not in my power to get them until there is a design fixed on to make the colors by." When he could finally contract for flags to be made, one supplier was Betsy Ross. Marla Miller, Betsy Ross and the Making of America (New York: Henry Holt and Company, 2010), 167, 175. On February 23, 1777 William Richards's store was selling red, white and blue bunting and on May 29 the Pennsylvania Navy board paid Betsey Ross £14 12s. 2d. for "making ship's colours." For the complete story of how this fits into the possibilities of the Betsy Ross story see chapter 11, Signals of Independence. The ledgers of Philadelphia merchant John Nixon for 1776 and 1777 also show large sums of money paid to William Richards for flags.

63 *PC&CS*, 540.

64 Butterfield, *John Adams Diary*, II: 251.

65 Fitch, *Autobiography*, 57-58. While Fitch says he was appointed to be captain, he would not have been commissioned with that rank. Because this was a temporary, composite company he would have rather been designated as the company commander with the rank of lieutenant.

66 *JCC*, 5: 843; Nathanael Greene, Fort Lee, to John Hancock, October 20, 1776, Richard K. Showman, ed. *The Papers of General Nathanael Greene* (Chapel Hill: The University of North Carolina Press, 1976), I: 319.

67 William Richards to Pennsylvania Council of Safety, Philadelphia, October 15, 1776, Samuel Hazard, ed., *Pennsylvania Archives*, Series 1, (Philadelphia: Joseph Severns, 1853), V: 46; William Richards to Council, November 12, 1776, Ibid., 63; David Pinkerton to Pennsylvania Council of Safety, November 16, 1776, Ibid., 69. The Pennsylvania Council of Safety had resolved on October 17 to send the salt. Force, *American Archives*, Series 5, II: 89.

68 Lowry's petition is in Force, *American Archives*, Series 5, III: 661-662.

69 Nathanael Greene, Fort Lee, to General Thomas Mifflin, October 27, 1776; Nathanael Greene, Fort Lee, to George Washington, October 29, 1776, Showman, *Greene Papers*, I: 322, 326-327.

70 John D. Cushing, *The First Laws of the State of New Jersey*, (Wilmington, DE: Michael Glazier, 1981). Facsimile of Wilson, Peter. *Acts of the General Assembly of the State of New Jersey from the establishment of the present government, and Declaration of Independence, to the end of the first sitting of the eighth session, on the 24th day of December 1783* (Trenton: Isaac Collins, 1784), 4-5. This was supplemented June 7, 1777 with a law specifying details of enforcement not covered in the original. Cushing, *First Laws*, 27.

71 Charles Lee, Amboy, to President of Congress, October 12, 1776, *PCC*, Letters from General officers, 1775-89, r177, i158, p85-87.

72 *JCC*, VI: 874 – order repeated October 24, page 901.

73 *Pennsylvania Evening Post*, November 5, 1776, 555.

74 Sol Feinstone Collection Mss #791.

75 *JCC*, VI: 901.

76 Nathanael Greene, Fort Lee, to George Washington, November 7, 1776, Showman, *Greene Papers*, I: 336-338.

77 *PCC*, Letters from General Officers, 1775-89, r179, i162, p221. Mercer had ordered the Virginia troops at Trenton to "move on with all possible expedition" to Amboy and Washington had told him to join Greene at Fort Lee, but Stephen replaced Mercer at Amboy instead of joining Greene. Showman, *Greene Papers*, I: 344, note – attached to November 8 letter from Washington at White Plains; See Mercer to Board of War in Force, *American Archives*, Series 5, III: 600-601.

78 See: Force, *American Archives*, Series 5, I: 1199-1200 for a soldier in August. Mary C. Gillette, *The Army Medical Department, 1775 – 1818* (Washington, D.C.: Center of Military History, United States Army, 1981), 69-70; Dr. William Shippen to Board of War, November 1, 1776, Force, *American Archives*, Series 5, III: 463. Throughout the army there were many more men sick than wounded in the hospitals. Captain John Chilton to his brother, Charles Chilton, Brunswick, NJ, November 30, 1776, on Third Virginia men in the hospital, quoted in: Michael Cecere, *They Behaved Like Soldiers: Captain John Chilton and the Third Virginia Regiment 1775-1778* (Bowie, MD: Heritage Books, 2004), 87-89.

79 John Beatty was commissioned captain October 12, 1776 in Fifth Pennsylvania Regiment – exchanged May 1778 – appointed commissary general of purchases, with rank of colonel, May 23, 1778 – resigned March 31, 1781 – died at Trenton May 30, 1826 age 78 – buried in First Presbyterian churchyard in Trenton. Thomas Jenny/Janney of Trenton was commissioned second lieutenant January 5, 1776 in Fifth Pennsylvania Regiment – promoted to First lieutenant October 12, 1776 – exchanged October 25, 1700. See: Return of American officers and others prisoners on parole on Long Island – commissioned January 5, 1776, PA, taken November 16, 1776 at Fort Washington – NARA M246 Revolutionary War Rolls, 1775-83, r136, f6, p24. Hamilton Martin of Trenton and Timothy Ryan of Trenton paroled December 26, 1776. "Fifth Pennsylvania Battalion, Colonel Robert Magaw, January 3, 1776 - January 3, 1777," John Blair Linn and William H. Egle, eds., *Pennsylvania Archives*, Series 2 (Harrisburg: State of Pennsylvania, 1880), X: 154.

80 Rawle, "Col. Lambert Cadwalader," 13.

81 Isaac Smith, Trenton, to William Livingston, November 20, 1776 and reply, Prince, *William Livingston Papers*, I: 182-183.

82 Samuel Tucker, Trenton, to William Livingston, November 18, 1776, *Livingston Papers* [microform], r3, i557.

83 John Anderson PF S798; Joshua Furman PF W543. Due to the heavy activity caused by the British occupation, Anderson was out for three months under Captain Tucker and also Captain Phil Phillips at different times.

84 *Joint Meeting*, 12.

85 AO12, vol 15, 110-116; AO13, bundle 20, 210-219. His secreted property was later found and was taken away by the Commissioners for dealing with Loyalist property. Taylor believed that part of it was plundered and part was sold by the Commissioners.

86 *PC&CS*, 513, 515; NJSA Auditor's Book B, 15; Stryker, "The New Jersey Volunteers," 31-32; Jones, New Jersey Loyalists, 20-22. On August 22, 1777, Barnes was mortally wounded in the attack by General Sullivan on Staten Island and died a few days later. His wife, Mary, remained in Trenton until after his death, leaving in 1778. See her testimony in the AO13, bundle 2 file of Daniel Coxe. In her statement she says she resided in Trenton until 1778.

87 George Washington to William Livingston, November 30, 1776, *Livingston Papers* [microform], r3 f667.

88 Stryker, *Trenton and Princeton*, 22-24, 314-316.

Chapter 5

1 AO 13 bundle 2; AO 12, v13, 181; Franklin's statement is in AO 13 bundle 2.

2 A phaeton was the general name for a type of one or two horse sporty carriage with a light body and four very large wheels. It was fast and could be dangerous. Its name comes from the Phaeton of mythology who almost set the earth on fire attempting to drive the chariot of the sun.

3 Tucker sworn statement of February 15, 1777; Samuel Abbot sworn statement, Assembly Minutes, February 17, 1777, *Assembly Votes*, Session beginning August 27, 1776, 68-70; also NJSA, BAH, Box 50-02, #115; Tucker letter to John Hart, Speaker of the Assembly, January 20, 1777, NJSA, BAH, Box 5-02, #113.

4 Ewing, *Military Journal*, 2, 3, 4, 9, 12.

5 William Morris PF S1061.

6 General Return of the Army. Trenton, December 1, 1776. Force, *American Archives*, Series 5, III: 1035-1036.

7 George Washington. *The Papers of George Washington. Revolutionary War Series*. Philander D. Chase, ed. (Charlottesville: University Press of Virginia, 1985-1997), VII: 248,250. These actions were also mentioned in a letter George Washington to John Hancock, December 1, 1776, Ibid., VII, 244; George Washington to William Livingston, December 1, 1776, New Brunswick, *GWPLOC*.

8 George Washington to Colonel Humpton, December 1, 1776, Stryker, *Trenton and Princeton*, 310. Original in the collection of the Swan Historical Foundation and on display at Washington Crossing State Park, New Jersey. Washington also wrote to Congress that he had done this. George Washington, New Brunswick, to Continental Congress, December 1, 1776, *PCC*, Letters from George Washington, r167, i152, p287.

9 George Washington to William Maxwell, December 8, 1776, *GWPLOC*; Stryker, *Trenton and Princeton*, 15. Stryker says, without citing a source, that he ordered General Putnam to build rafts from timber found at the Trenton ferry landings, but there is no documentary evidence found to support this. General W.W.H. Davis, "Washington on the West Bank of the Delaware, 1776." The *Pennsylvania Magazine of History and Biography*, vol 4, issue 2, 1880, 136, also says this without attribution.

10 Joshua Mersereau PF S7224 – father also Joshua; brother John L. Mersereau PF S7217; Barbara Mercereau PF W17137. The Mersereau's had reputedly been part of a spy network working for Washington since July 1 and continued throughout the retreat across New Jersey. He says in his pension statement that this happened after the troops had crossed, but it is more likely earlier.

11 After the Battle of White Plains, Washington had divided his army into four parts. Lee had a large command that did not accompany Washington on the retreat across New Jersey. Washington had sent orders to Lee to join him to help defend against a British advance on Philadelphia.

12 Council of Safety, December 1, 1776, *Pennsylvania Archives*, Series 1 (Harrisburg: State of Pennsylvania, 1852), XI: 24-25.

13 George Washington, at Brunswick, to Continental Congress, 7:30pm, December 1, 1776, *PCC*, Letters from George Washington, r167, i152, p291.

14 Allen served throughout the war in positions of command and fought in New York, New Jersey, North and South Carolina and at the siege of Savannah, Georgia in 1779. He never returned to Trenton and his property was confiscated, so after the war he resumed his legal career in St. John, New Brunswick where he served on courts and in the House of the Assembly as a highly respected citizen. Stryker, *New Jersey Volunteers*, 28; Jones, *New Jersey Loyalists*, 9-10. Coxe later went to New York where he helped establish the Board of Refugees in 1779. The Board consisted of delegates from each of the colonies who met once a week. Christopher Sower, an important Pennsylvania Loyalist wrote on December 5, 1779 that Coxe had been appointed chair of the group "to deprive him of the opportunity of speaking, as he has the gift of saying little with many words." Lorenzo Sabine, *The American Loyalists, or Biographical Sketches of adherents to the British Crown in the War of the Revolution* (Boston: Charles C. Little and James Brown, 1847), 232.

15 David Hackett Fischer, *Washington's Crossing* (New York: Oxford University Press, 2004), Appendix K, 399.

16 George Washington to John Hancock, December 3, 1776, Chase, ed. *Papers of George Washington*. Revolutionary War Series, VII: 255; *PCC*, Letters from George Washington, r167, i152, p303; also *GWPLOC*.

17 William R. Green PF W7560 - supporting statement of John Burroughs.

18 Force, *American Archives*, Series 5, III: 1034.

19 Israel Hunt PF S1024; Benjamin Morrell PF S2871; Jacob Williamson PF W2393. See also: *Assembly Votes*, Session beginning August 27, 1776, 116-117, 119. Petition from Timothy Hunt and six other Inhabitants of the Township of Hopewell. They had not received any Pay for their Services. They were directed to apply to the Quarter Master General to receive Pay for the services they mentioned.

20 William M. Dwyer, *The Day is Ours! November 1776-January 1777: An Inside View of the Battles of Trenton and Princeton* (New York: Viking Press, 1983), 101; Jackson, *Pennsylvania Navy*, 15-17, 76; Resolution of the Council of Safety, December 2, 1776, Samuel Hazard, *Pennsylvania Archives*, (Philadelphia: Joseph Severns, 1853), V: 84; William James Morgan, ed. *Naval Documents of the American Revolution*, (Washington: Naval History Division Department of the Navy, 1972) VII: 352; *JCC*, vol 6, 1000 – also in Morgan, *Naval Documents*, VII: 351. Regarding flags flown by the gallies, see Jackson, *Pennsylvania Navy*, 408 n39. Jackson believes that the "Pennsylvania fleet used the so-called "Floating Batteries Flag," or one similar. In the case of the Pennsylvania Navy, this flag was made by Mrs. Bridges from a copy submitted to her. A somewhat conflicting picture as to what colors were used is revealed in a letter of William Richards ..... August 19, 1776 and then October 15 ... Richards further requests that the Council establish a design acceptable to the State navy. It would appear that the State navy wanted their own flag as distinguished from one copied form another state. This probably prompted the decision to ask Betsy Ross to design a flag for the fleet – a request which was granted five months later. Others than Mrs. Ross and Mrs. Bridges were employed to make colors for the fleet."

21 Jackson, *Pennsylvania Navy*, 75.

22 Stryker, *Trenton and Princeton*, 18.

23 John Coleman PF R2163 – Coleman gives Brearley's name as Brady but Brearley makes much more sense and the transformation to Brady would be natural given the pronunciation of Brearley as Bralley. When Brearley returned from Canada he very likely formed a scouting party between Trenton and Princeton based on his home township of Maidenhead. He was in the scouting party two months and soon after the Battle of Princeton he volunteered under Quigley and went to Princeton until discharged about the last of March 1777.

24 Fischer, *Washington's Crossing*, Appendix K, 399.

25 George Washington, Trenton, to President of Continental Congress, December 4, 1776, *PCC*, Letters from George Washington, r167, i152, p303; Nathanael Greene, Trenton, to Governor Nicholas Cooke, December 4, 1776, Showman, *Greene Papers*, I: 360.

26 James E. Gibson, Dr. Bodo Otto and the Medical Background of the American Revolution (Springfield, ILL: Charles C. Thomas, 1937), 123; Gillette, *Army Medical Department*, 69-70; George Washington to Board of War, December 4, 1776, *GWPLOC*.

27 Nathanael Greene, Trenton, to Catharine Greene, December 4, 1776, Showman, *Greene Papers*, I: 363.

28 George Washington, Trenton, to President of Congress, December 5, 1776, *PCC*, Letters from George Washington, r167, i152, p317; Washington to Hancock, December 6, John C. Fitzpatrick, ed., *The Writings of George Washington: From the original Manuscript Sources, 1745-1799*. (Washington: Government Printing Office, 1931-1944), VI: 333-334; Fischer, *Washington's Crossing*, Appendix K, 399.

29 Fitch, *Autobiography*, 58-59; Westcott, *John Fitch the Inventor*, 60-61; Boyd, *Poor John Fitch*, 50-51. He would later return to Trenton and make a name for himself with his steamboat pursuits.

30 William Young, "Journal of Sergeant William Young," The *Pennsylvania Magazine of History and Biography*, vol 8, no 3 (Oct. 1884), 257. Meredith was major of his Third Battalion of Associators and his wife was a Cadwalader, so he may have been staying at the Cadwalader residence.

31 George Washington, Trenton, to President of Congress, December 6, 1776, *PCC*, Letters from George Washington, r167, i152, p323.

32 Fischer, *Washington's Crossing*, Appendix K, 400.

33 George Washington, Trenton, to John Cadwalader, December 7, 1776, NJSA, Department of Defense, Adjutant General's Office (Revolutionary War), Copies of Correspondence, 1777-1782, #54.

34 George Washington, Sommerseat, to President of Congress, December 8, 1776, *PCC*, Letters from George Washington, r167, i152, p327; Nathanael Greene, Princeton, to George Washington, December 7, 1776, Showman, *Greene Papers*, I: 366-367; James McMichael, "Diary of Lieutenant James McMichael, of the Pennsylvania Line, 1776-1778," The *Pennsylvania Magazine of History and Biography* 16 (1892), 139; For weather see - Fischer, *Washington's Crossing*, Appendix K, 400.

35 Enoch Anderson, *Personal Recollections of Captain Enoch Anderson, An Officer of the Delaware Regiments in the Revolutionary War* (Wilmington: The Historical Society of Delaware, 1896), 27-28. Reprint: Arno Press, Eyewitness Accounts of the American Revolution.

36 Young, Journal, 257.

37 Stryker, *Trenton and Princeton*, 53. See: McBurney, Kidnapping the Enemy, for the complete story of Lee's capture and eventual exchange.

38 Hall, *Trenton Presbyterian Church*, 161.

39 *Dunlap's Pennsylvania Packet*, March 20, 1775, 3.

40 Miller, *The Life of Samuel Miller, 147-148*; Dwyer, *Day is Ours*, 89-90. It is good that Margaret was able to get away because when the British were in Princeton her recently completed house was burned, either by accident or deliberately. Dwyer, *Day is Ours*, 185. Dr. Absalom Bainbridge was actually a Loyalist who joined with the British army when it got to Princeton, left town, had his land confiscated, but lived out his life in the new United States. He was the father of Commodore William Bainbridge of naval fame in the War of 1812.

41 Horace Wells Sellers, "Charles Willson Peale, Artist – Soldier." *Pennsylvania Magazine of History and Biography* 38 (1914), 257-286 – also has his journal excerpts on pages 271-286 – December 1776- January 1777.

42 Various writers include portions of this statement citing Charles Willson Peale, manuscript Autobiography, American Philosophical Society. For example: Fischer, *Washington's Crossing*, 133; Dwyer, *Day is Ours*, 102; Richard M. Ketchum, *The Winter Soldiers* (Garden City, NY: Doubleday, 1973), 204; Arthur S. Lefkowitz, *The Long Retreat: The Calamitous American Defense of New Jersey, 1776* (New Brunswick: Rutgers University Press, 1999), 121.

43 Nathanael Greene to George Washington, December 7, 1776, Chase, ed., *Papers of George Washington. Revolutionary War Series*, VII: 269-270; Showman, *Greene Papers*, I: 366-67 – also talks of possibility of using pontoon boats.

44 Council meeting December 8, 1776, *Colonial Records of Pennsylvania, Minutes of the Supreme Executive Council* (Pennsylvania. Harrisburg: Theo. Fenn, 1852), XI: 39.

45 McMichael, *Diary*, 139.

46 George Washington to President of Congress, December 9, 1776, *PCC*, Transcripts of letters from George Washington 1776, r186, i169, p391.

47 AO 13 bundle 2 – Daniel Coxe.

48 Henry Knox to Lucy Knox, Trenton Ferry, December 8, 1776, Henry Knox, *The Papers of Henry Knox, 1719-1825* [microform]: Owned by the New England Historic Genealogical Society and Deposited in the Massachusetts Historical Society (Boston: 1960), r3, i92.

49 Tucker sworn statement of February 15, 1777, *Assembly Votes*, Session beginning August 27, 1776, 69; Samuel Tucker to John Hart, Speaker of the Assembly, January 20, 1777, NJSA, BAH Box 5-02, #113.

50 NJSA, Legislature, Petitions, Resolutions, Transactions, Accounts and Misc papers 1700-1845, #89 – Report of private committee respecting papers in the hands of [Samuel] Tucker, 1778

51 NJSA, Revolutionary War Mss #4259 – accounts of Alexander Chambers – December 7, 1776.

52 Fischer, *Washington's Crossing*, Appendix K, 400.

53 The jägers were special Hessian troops, a form of light infantry, recruited from hunters.

54 *Hessian Documents of the American Revolution*, Morristown National Historical Park, Von Donop Report Trenton, December 10, 1776, AA 23–25. As is common, statements of time of the British arrival vary. See also: Rodney Atwood, *The Hessians: Mercenaries from Hessen-Kassel in the American Revolution* (Cambridge, Eng.; New York: Cambridge University Press, 1980), 86.

55 Friedrich von Meunchausen, *At General Howe's Side 1776-1778: The diary of General William Howe's aide de camp, Captain Friedrich von Meunchausen*, Ernst Kipping, trans. (Monmouth Beach, NJ: Philip Freneau Press, 1974), 6 – diary entry for December 8, 1776. Von Donop says only one Light Infantryman killed and two wounded. *Hessian Documents of the American Revolution*, Morristown National Historical Park, Von Donop Report Trenton, December 10, 1776, AA 23–25.

56 McMichael, *Diary*, 139

57 Meunchausen, *Diary*, 6 – diary entry for December 8, 1776. Referenced by Fischer, *Washington's Crossing*, 135; Stryker, *Trenton and Princeton*, 28; Dwyer, *Day is Ours*, 110; Harry M. Lydenberg, ed. *Archibald Robertson, Lieutenant-General Royal Engineers, His Diaries and Sketches in America: 1762-1780* (New York: New York Public Library, 1930), 115. Accounts of the time the British troops arrived at Trenton vary from about 11:00 am to 2:00 pm. Von Donop says they arrived about 2:00 pm and were greeted by cannon fire and fortunately no one in his brigade was killed or wounded, even among the jägers "who received the full force of the grape shot down by the river." The Light Infantry lost one man killed and two wounded, the only losses known to him. *Hessian Documents of the American Revolution*, Morristown National Historical Park, von Donop Report Trenton, December 10, 1776, AA 23–25.

58 Dwyer, *Day is Ours*, 111.

59 AO12, vol 15, 110-116.

60 Atwood, *Hessians*, 86.

61 Jay Luvaas, ed. and trans., *Frederick the Great on the Art of War*, (New York: The Free Press, 1966), 131.

62 *Order Book*: 17th Regiment of Foot, Oct. 11 – December 28, 1776, *Early American Orderly Books, 1748-1817* [microform] (New Haven: Research Publications, 1977), reel 4 item 41.

63 Samuel Adams to Elizabeth Adams, Smith, *Letters of Delegates*, V: 590-591; Michael A. Davis, *The Trial of Abraham Hunt: An American Christmas Story* (Denver: Ghost Road Press, 2006), 40-42.

Chapter 6

1 *Pennsylvania Evening Post*, July 26, 1777, 394 - Translation of part of a Hessian journal found at Trenton in December 1776. The writer sounds like an officer and his friend may well have been Lieutenant Colonel Francis Scheffer of the von Lossberg Regiment.
2 Fischer, *Washington's Crossing*, Appendix K, 400.
3 AO13, bundle 25, 532-534.
4 Dwyer, *Day is Ours*, 113.
5 17th Regiment of Foot Order Book.
6 Samuel Tucker February 15 sworn statement and Samuel Abbott affirmed statement, February 14, 1777, *Assembly Votes*, Session beginning August 27, 1776, 69, 70; Samuel Tucker sworn statement, February 15, 1777, NJSA, BAH Box 5-02, #115, #117; John Abbott protection paper, NJSA, Department of Defense, Adjutant General's Office (Revolutionary War), Copies of Miscellaneous Records, 1774-1837, Box 1, #19. Signed by M. Fox, Aid de Camp to the Commander in Chief, Headquarters, Trenton, December 9, 1776 – von Munschausen, Adjutant. AO12 Daniel Coxe statement in Brereton Poynton file, vol 13, 302-14.
7 Tucker sworn statement February 15, 1777; Randle Mitchel sworn statement, February 14, 1777; Samuel Abbot sworn statement, *Assembly Votes*, Session beginning August 28, 1776, 69-70. See also: NJSA, BAH Box 5-02, #116. Some of the money that Tucker did not sign got into circulation. The law required three signatures and these bills only had two – John Hart and Samuel How. In early 1777 newspapers carried warnings that these bills were not legal tender and should not be accepted. They had been plundered by the British from the person appointed to sign them, i.e. Samuel Tucker, before he could do so. Warnings appeared as far as Baltimore. See: *Dunlap's Maryland Gazette*, Tuesday, March 4, 1777, 3; and, The *Pennsylvania Journal*, February 26, 1777, in William S. Stryker, *New Jersey Archives*, Second Series, Trenton: John L. Murphy, 1901), I: 295-296.
8 AO13, Bundle 19.
9 Fischer, *Washington's Crossing*, Appendix K, 400.
10 Balch, Thomas. *The Examination of Joseph Galloway, Esq. By a Committee of the House of Commons* (Boston: Gregg Press, 1972), 38. Photographic reprint of 1855 work published by the Seventy-Six Society in Philadelphia, reproduced from an original copy in the Boston Public Library; Stryker, *Trenton and Princeton*, 37; Dwyer, *Day is Ours*, 114.
11 Meunchausen, *Diary*, 7 – diary entry for December 10.
12 Dwyer, *Day is Ours*, 113.
13 Charles Wilson Peale, "Journal by Charles Wilson Peale." *The Crayon*, 3, (New York: Stillman and Durand, 1856), 37.
14 17th Regiment of Foot *Order Book*.
15 Fischer, *Washington's Crossing*, Appendix K, 400.
16 Stryker, *Trenton and Princeton*, 42; Dwyer, *Day is Ours*, 121; *Hessian Documents of the American Revolution*, Morristown National Historical Park, Journal of Colonel von Donop, 1776, Letter C Fiche 27 page C.1; Meunchausen, *Diary*, 7 – entry for December 11.
17 Colonel Joseph Reed to General Washington, December 12, 1776, Force, *American Archives*, Series 5, III: 1182.
18 17th Regiment of Foot *Order Book*.
19 Sir William Howe, September 26, 1776 – June 2, 1777; *Early American Orderly Books, 1748-1817* [microform] (New Haven: Research Publications, 1977), reel 4 item 41. Repeated in 17th Regiment of Foot *Order Book*.
20 Dwyer, *Day is Ours*, 119.
21 William Howe, *The Narrative of Lieut. Gen. Sir William Howe, in a Committee of the House of Commons, on the 29th of April, 1779, relative to his Conduct, during His Late Command of the King's Troops in North America: To which are added, some observations upon a pamphlet, entitle, Letters to a Nobleman.* Third Edition (London: H. Baldwin, 1781), 7-8; Stryker, *Trenton and Princeton*, 38-39.

22 *Hessian Documents of the American Revolution*, Morristown National Historical Park, Journal of Colonel von Donop, 1776, Letter C Fiche 27; Meunchausen, *Diary*, 7 – entry for December 12.

23 Charles W. Ingrao, *The Hessian Mercenary State: Ideas, Institutions, and Reform under Frederick II, 1760-1785* (New York: Cambridge University Press, 1987), 130- 140 – and the book in general; G. Paul Moser, ed., Johannes Schwalm, *The Hessian* (Millville, PA: The Johannes Schwalm Historical Association, 1976), 7-11. It is a common myth that the British army was made up of draftees, prisoners, etc. However, only the Royal Navy could impress men into service and the army was all volunteer. When the army was understrength it was normal to hire foreign regiments rather than resort to a draft.

24 Atwood, *Hessians*, 40, 47-49.

25 Ibid., 43.

26 Lefferts, *Uniforms*, 267.

27 Moser, *Johannes Schwalm*, 12-14.

28 Stryker, *Trenton and Princeton*, 40-41, 96. Stryker overstates the number of companies at six and says the Lossberg and Knyphausen regiments each had a company of grenadiers. The Trenton Prisoner List gives only five companies for each regiment and no grenadiers in the regiments other than Rall's grenadier regiment. See: "Copy Letter from Capt Bock[ing] in Battle of Trenton, 26 December 1776, Reports from the Von Jungkenn Papers," Burgoyne, Bruce E. and Hans Mayer, Trans., *Journal of the Johannes Schwalm Historical Association* 5 (1996), 26.

29 AO 13, bundle 2.

30 *Hessian Documents of the American Revolution*, Morristown National Historical Park, Rall letter, Trenton, December 16, 1776, AA 28.

31 Elliot Wheelock Hoffman, *The German Soldiers in the American Revolution*, PhD diss., University of New Hampshire (1982), 375, 377, 378.

32 Atwood, *Hessians*, 40-43.

33 Johannes Reuber, "A Hessian Diary", *Journal of the Johannes Schwalm Historical Association* 1 no. 2 (1978), 7. He has the date wrong saying they arrived in Trenton on December 19.

34 Stryker, *Trenton and Princeton*, 94-95; Reuber, "Diary," 7.

35 Stryker, *Trenton and Princeton*, 95-96, 203.

36 Stryker, *Trenton and Princeton*, 95-96, 203; Robert Oakley Slagle, *The Von Lossberg Regiment: A Chronicle of Hessian Participation in the American Revolution*, PhD diss., The American University (1965), 71, 73, 74, 214. Their regimental flag was a white, four foot square of silk with embroidery and letters worked in gold silk. On one side was a crown, various letters, and the date 1775 and on the other was an eagle with an olive branch and the motto "for prince and country" in Latin.

37 Stryker, *Trenton and Princeton*, 96-98; Lefferts, *Uniforms*, 252, 266; Berhhard A. Uhlendorf, trans., *Revolution in America; Confidential Letters and Journals 1776-1784 of Adjutant General Major Baurmeister of the Hessian Forces* (New Brunswick: Rutgers University press, 1957), 75; Atwood, *Hessians*, 45.

38 Satterthwaite, *History of Society of Friends*, I: 187. Citing *Chesterfield Monthly Meeting Miscellaneous Records*.

39 Stryker, *Trenton and Princeton*, 96-97; Lefferts, *Uniforms*, 150, 175-181, pull-out page between pages 192-193; Uhlendorf, *Baurmeister Letters and Journals*, 75.

40 Richard C. Barth, William E. Dornemann, and Mark A. Schwalm. "The Trenton Prisoner List." *The Hessians: Journal of the Johannes Schwalm Historical Association* 16 (2013), 75.

41 Lawrence R. Schmidt, *The Old Barracks Museum, Trenton, New Jersey: Barracks and Officers' House Historic Furnishing Plan* (Trenton: Old Barracks Museum, October 1991), 207-210.

42 David Howell, Oath of allegiance 12 December 1776, Sol Feinstone Collection of the American Revolution Mss #565.

43 Davis, *Trial of Abraham Hunt*, 44.

44 NJSA, New Jersey Supreme Court Case 36037, October Term 1778. Apparently, the accusers did not pursue it so the case was dismissed.

45 Uhlendorf, *Baurmeister Letters and Journals*, 75.

46 Uhlendorf, *Baurmeister Letters and Journals*, 75; Meunshausen, *Diary*, 7 – entry for December 12.

47 *PCC*, British plundering and ravaging, r66, i53, p45; Uhlendorf, *Baurmeister Letters and Journals*, 75. 17th Regiment of Foot *Order Book*; Sir William Howe *Order Book*.

48 Susan Pindar Embury, A *Grandmother's (Martha Reed, wife of John Shannon) Recollections of the Old Revolutionary Days. 1875*. Typescript in Trentoniana Room at the Trenton Free Public Library, Trenton, New Jersey. The timing and manner of the creation of this document raises questions about its accuracy and legitimacy. However, most of her comments are consistent with what would be expected. If nothing else, it represents the way in which the memory of the Hessian occupation of Trenton was handed down in local families. Another copy of this memoir is: Embury, Susan Pindor; 1875; General Manuscripts Miscellaneous Collection, Box 15; Manuscripts Division, Department of Rare Books and Special Collections, Princeton University Library, and gives her father as Thomas Reed, a private in the New Jersey Continental Line.

49 NJSA, Revolutionary War Mss #709 – Brearley's company muster; John W. Barber and Henry Howe. *Historical Collections of the State of New Jersey* (Newark: B. Olds, for Justus H. Bradley; New Haven: J.W. Barber, 1852), 263. Gregory B. Keen, "The Descendants of Joran Kyn, The Founder of Upland." The *Pennsylvania Magazine of History and Biography* 4 (1880): 356.

50 Dwyer, *Day is Ours*, 184. See also: AO12: 13, AO13, bundle 2.

51 General Howe, Trenton, to Colonel von Donop, December 13, 1776, Stryker, *Trenton and Princeton*, 316-317 – referred to on pages 46-47; Also in: *Hessian Documents of the American Revolution*, Morristown National Historical Park, von Donop Journal, C.54.

52 Dwyer, *Day is Ours*, 151; Atwood, *Hessians*, 90.

53 Atwood, *Hessians*, 43.

54 17th Regiment of Foot *Order Book*; Sir William Howe Orderly Book; *Hessian Documents of the American Revolution*, Morristown National Historical Park, von Donop Journal, C. 4.

55 Atwood, *Hessians*, 87; Munchausen, *Diary*, 7 – entry for December 14.

56 *Hessian Documents of the American Revolution*, Morristown National Historical Park, von Donop Journal, C. 4.

57 *Assembly Votes*, Session beginning August 27, 1776, 68-69 for Tuckers sworn statement; Samuel Tucker to John Hart, January 20, 1777, *William Churchill Houston Papers*, Princeton University Library, Department of Rare Books and Special Collections, Manuscripts Division, CO315, Box 4, Folder 4; *NJG*, July 20, 1784, 2. This paper printed a series of affidavits concerning the Tucker affair.

58 Prince, *Livingston Papers*, I: 301, 304-305, 310-311. See also: NJSA, New Jersey Council of Safety Records, 1776-1781, loose papers, items 33, 39 (deposition of William Imlay for statement made by Woodward in Trenton that he had disarmed rebels), 52 (deposition of William Imlay for statement that he was "an old Presbyterian"), 53 (deposition of Lewis Bestedo for Robins statement of rebel accountability for British deaths), 60 (deposition of Thomas Forman for statement of rebel self interest).

59 David J. Fowler, *Egregious Villains, Wood Rangers, and London Traders: The Pine Robber Phenomenon in New Jersey During the Revolutionary War*. PhD diss., Rutgers The State University of New Jersey (1987), 73; Thomas Page affidavit, enclosure in Israel Putnam, at Princeton, to William Livingston, March 10, 1777, *Livingston Papers* [microform], r4, f276.

60 Sir Guy Carleton, *British Headquarters (Sir Guy Carleton) Papers, 1777-1783*, [microform] (Washington, Microfilming Service, Recordak Corp., 1957), item 7445; Prince, *Livingston Papers*, I: 304-305. See also: NJSA, New Jersey Council of Safety Records, 17761781, loose papers, items 35.

61 AO12 vol 15 - Richard Robins deposition.

62 AO13 bundle18; AO12: vol 15, 42-54, 434. Leonard's property was confiscated and he ended up at St. John, New Brunswick after the war. He helped guide the British army across New Jersey in June 1778. See: New Jersey Gazette, March 12, 1779, 3 for notice of court action against him for "joining the army of the King of Great-Britain, and other treasonable

practices." John Horner were also part of the group and assisted them. AO13: bundle 18 for John Horner. AO13, bundle 21. For these actions Jesse Woodward was charged in April 1777 with high treason, fined £344.16.7, and committed to jail at Newtown.
63 Stryker, *Trenton and Princeton*, 97.
64 For a complete discussion of the Woodward groups activities see: Fowler, Egregious Villains, Chapter 3: "Now the Staff is in our Hands": The Woodward Insurrection.
65 David J. Fowler, "'Loyalty is Now Bleeding in New Jersey': Motivations and Mentalities of the Disaffected", in Joseph S. Tiedemann, Eugene R. Fingerhut, and Robert W. Vanables, eds., *The Other Loyalists: Ordinary People, Royalism, and the Revolution in the Middle Colonies, 1763-1787* (Albany: State University of New York Press, 2009), 55.
66 Stryker, *Trenton and Princeton*, 42, 92; *Pennsylvania Gazette*, September 26, 1765, 6; November 22, 1750, 4 – for descriptions of house and lot.
67 Stryker, *Trenton and Princeton*, 97-98.
68 Andreas Wiederholdt, "Rall at Trenton." The *Pennsylvania Magazine of History and Biography* 22 (1898): 463.
69 Dwyer, *Day is Ours*, 166-168; Wiederholdt, "Rall at Trenton," 463.
70 Stryker, *Trenton and Princeton*, 99-100; Scheffer account May 5, 1778 in "Reports from the von Jungkenn Papers," *Journal of the Johannes Schwalm Historical Association*, 5 no 4 (1996): 21.
71 Stryker, *Trenton and Princeton*, 100-101.
72 Wiederholdt, "Rall at Trenton," 462-463; Dwyer, *Day is Ours*, 169.
73 Schmidt, *Old Barracks Historic Furnishing Plan*, Appendix C, 201-210.
74 Stryker, *Trenton and Princeton*, 101-104.
75 AO 13, bundle 2. In addition to the large tract south of the Assunpink, Coxe also owned a small 52 acre farm on the edge of Trenton that he called Busy Cottage Farm.
76 Stryker, *Trenton and Princeton*, 103.
77 Stryker, *Trenton and Princeton*, 47, 106; Atwood, *Hessians*, 46.
78 Fischer, *Washington's Crossing*, Appendix K, 400.
79 This is the site of the battle monument today. Wiederholdt, "Rall in Trenton," 463. Wiederholdt attributes the suggestion for the earth-works to Major von Dechow.
80 Fascines were bundles of sticks tied together at about two foot intervals and were a component in building earthwork fortifications, such as redoubts. The bundles could be of different lengths for different situations. For more see: Captain George Smith, *An Universal Military Dictionary or a Copious Explanation of the Technical Terms &c. Used in the Equipment, Machinery, Movements, and Military Operations of an Army (1779)*, 87. Reprinted by Museum Restoration Service, Ottawa, Ontario, Canada, 1969.
81 Wiederholdt, "Rall at Trenton," 463; Stryker, *Trenton and Princeton*, 106-107; Max Von Eelking, *The German Allied Troops in the North American War of Independence, 1776-1783*. J.G. Rosengarten, trans. (Albany: Joel Munsell's Sons, 1893), 61. Atwood, *Hessians*, 84, 88-89. Also: Luvaas, *Frederick the Great*, 131.
82 Stryker, *Trenton and Princeton*, 107-108, 110.
83 Stryker, *Trenton and Princeton*, 323-324; Fischer, *Washington's Crossing*, Appendix K, 400. *Hessian Documents of the American Revolution*, Morristown National Historical Park, Von Donop Journal, C.8; Rall letter, Trenton, December 16, 1776, AA28; von Donop to Heister from Bordenton, December 16, 1776, AA 33; von Donop Journal, C7.
84 She was related to Loyalist David White.
85 Tucker sworn statement, February 15, 1777, *Assembly Votes*, Session beginning August 28, 1776, 60, 69.
86 Runes, *Selected Writings of Benjamin Rush*, 333.
87 Fischer, *Washington's Crossing*, Appendix K, 400; Stryker, *Trenton and Princeton*, 50-51, 323-324; Rall had sent a letter to von Donop earlier on the 17th describing these two incidents. See also *Pennsylvania Evening Post*, July 26, 1777, 391 from portion of Hessian diary printed in the newspaper that mentions this incident; *Hessian Documents of the American Revolution*, Morristown National Historical Park, von Donop Journal, C.8

88 *Hessian Documents of the American Revolution*, Morristown National Historical Park, von Scheffer and von Dechow to Baron von Heister, Trenton, December 17, 1776, Letter B – Reports of the North American War. General von Heister, 1776-77, Fiche 22, B. 210211. Heister wrote to Frederick on March 21, 1777 commenting on the poor condition of uniforms due to the sea voyage and hard campaigning. Lace had been removed from the uniforms when they arrived at State Island. The tailors and shoemakers were privates given temporary assignments for these duties. This was common practice in all armies at the time.
89 Fischer, *Washington's Crossing*, Appendix K, 400.
90 *Hessian Documents of the American Revolution*, Morristown National Historical Park, von Donop Journal, C.8-9. Von Donp confusingly says the mortally wounded man was brought in and also that a wagon was sent out under escort to get the wounded.
91 *Hessian Documents of the American Revolution*, Morristown National Historical Park, von Donop Journal, C. 8.
92 Stryker, *Trenton and Princeton*, 105, 326; Fischer, *Washington's Crossing*, 196; *Pennsylvania Evening Post*, July 26, 1777, 394 - from portion of Hessian diary printed in the newspaper
93 Reuber, "Diary," 7 - This was more likely the 18th rather than the 22nd.
94 *Hessian Documents of the American Revolution*, Morristown National Historical Park, Von Donop Journal, C. 8.
95 Sir Guy Carleton, *British Headquarters (Sir Guy Carleton) Papers, 1777-1783*, [microform] Washington, Microfilming Service, Recordak Corp., 1957, item 7445.
96 Stryker, *Trenton and Princeton*, 105-106; Fischer, *Washington's Crossing*, Appendix K, 400.
97 Letter of Rall to von Donop, Stryker, *Trenton and Princeton*, 329; *Hessian Documents of the American Revolution*, Morristown National Historical Park, von Donop Journal, C.17.
98 Stryker, *Trenton and Princeton*, 80 – Stryker mistakenly says it was published in the *Pennsylvania Journal* on December 19, but that paper had suspended publication temporarily.
99 Fischer, *Washington's Crossing*, Appendix K, 400.
100 Colonel Rall to Colonel von Donop, December 20, 1776, Stryker, *Trenton and Princeton*, 329; *Hessian Documents of the American Revolution*, Morristown National Historical Park, von Donop's Journal, C.10, C. 16-17.
101 Arthur Howell PF W14944 – especially affidavits of Leah Howell, William Coleman, Rachel Slack, William Fisher. His widow was applying for the pension so there is no statement of Arthur's.
102 Reuber, "Diary," 7.
103 AO13, bundle 92.
104 Fischer, *Washington's Crossing*, Appendix K, 400.
105 Philemon Dickinson to George Washington, December 21, 1776, *GWPLOC*.
106 Reuber, "Diary," 7.
107 Stryker, *Trenton and Princeton*, 105-106; Dwyer, *Day is Ours*, 220; Fischer, *Washington's Crossing*, Appendix K, 400.
108 Reuber, "Diary," 7.
109 Colonel Rall to Colonel von Donop, Trenton, December 21, 1776, Stryker, *Trenton and Princeton*, 332.
110 *Hessian Documents of the American Revolution*, Morristown National Historical Park, Von Donop Journal, C. 12.
111 Wiederholdt, "Rall at Trenton," 464. The weather was not good on December 20-21 so this was probably the time Wiederholdt speaks of. Fischer, *Washington's Crossing*, Appendix K, 400. Von Donop in his Journal also recounts this but without the comments on over reaction. *Hessian Documents of the American Revolution*, Morristown National Historical Park, von Donop Journal, C.12.
112 *Hessian Documents of the American Revolution*, Morristown National Historical Park, von Donop Journal, C.12, C. 19.
113 Extract of a letter from Philadelphia dated December 21 contained in Baltimore news of December 25, Virginia Gazette, Williamsburg, VA, Friday, January 3, 1777, 1; John Stevens PF W1092 mentions Anderson's attacks; Stryker, *Trenton and Princeton*, 87 also mentions these.

114 General Grant to Colonel Rall, Brunswick, December 21, 1776, Stryker, *Trenton and Princeton*, 334-335. Also commented on in: *Hessian Documents of the American Revolution*, Morristown National Historical Park, von Donop Journal, C. 20.
115 Atwood, *Hessians*, 91.
116 Slagle, *von Lossberg Regiment*, 89 - citing Heusser journal manuscript
117 *Hessian Documents of the American Revolution*, Morristown National Historical Park, von Donop Journal, C. 13-14.
118 Fischer, *Washington's Crossing*, Appendix K, 400.
119 David Lanning PF W3830; Barber and Howe, Historical Collections, 296; William S. Stryker, *The Continental Army at the Crossing of the Delaware River on Christmas Night of 1776* (Trenton: J.L. Murphy, 1896), 16. This is a story that is difficult to prove as more than local tradition. However, it is not improbable and Lanning was known to be active with the militia at this time and would be a likely man to have been sent over.
120 Reuber, "Diary," 7. Grenadier Reuber said this happened the Saturday before Christmas, making it December 21, but he entered it under December 24. Also mentioned in: *Hessian Documents of the American Revolution*, Morristown National Historical Park, von Donop Journal, C. 21.
121 Fischer, *Washington's Crossing*, Appendix K, 400.
122 Stryker, *Trenton and Princeton*, 110-111; Dwyer, *Day is Ours*, 220; Slagle, *von Lossberg Regiment*, 215; Eelking, *German Allied Troops*, 64-65.
123 *Hessian Documents of the American Revolution*, Morristown National Historical Park, von Donop Journal, C24, C. 25-26 – in the translation the Colonel is given as Climber of Hunterdon.
124 Fischer, *Washington's Crossing*, Appendix K, 401.
125 Philemon Dickinson to George Washington, December 24, 1776, *GWPLOC*. This mission would have been similar to the one of David Lanning a few days earlier. Or, it could refer to Lanning.
126 Stryker, *Trenton and Princeton*, 78, 343.
127 Uhlendorf, *Baurmeister Letters and Journals*, 78 – commenting on a letter from Rall to Colonel von Donop the day before the battle of Trenton.
128 Atwood, *Hessians*, 92.
129 Fischer, *Washington's Crossing*, Appendix K, 401.
130 Stryker, *Trenton and Princeton*, 108, 117-123; Dwyer, *Day is Ours*, 221-222.
131 The group from Stephen's brigade met up with the army on its march to Trenton that night and Washington was initially quite angry with them that they might have ruined the surprise attack. However, he later learned how the action had caused Rall to lower his guard thinking the rumored attack had already occurred that night. Stryker, *Trenton and Princeton*, 117-123; Dwyer, *Day is Ours*, 221-222.
132 Wiederholdt, "Rall at Trenton," 465. 133 Stryker, *Trenton and Princeton*, 122-125.

Chapter 7

1 Henry Melchior Muhlenberg, *The Journals of Henry Melchior Muhlenberg*, translated by Theodore G. Tappert and John W. Doberstein (Camden, ME: Picton Press, 1945), II: 771; Dwyer, *Day is Ours*, 259.
2 Muhlenberg, *Journals*, II: 771 – journal entry for December 31, 1776. The Hessians may have mistaken for civilians any American riflemen or others who got into houses and fired on their enemy.
3 Fischer, *Washington's Crossing*, Appendix K, 401.
4 Stryker, *Trenton and Princeton*, 145-146. When the Jägers patrolled to the home of Captain Mott they did not know that at that exact time he was one of the guides helping Washington's army get to Trenton in the storm. This militia captain John Mott should not, as most historians have, be confused with Captain John Mott of the New Jersey Continentals. They are completely different men. See: Kidder, A People Harassed and Exhausted, 210 for details on the identity of Mott.
5 Dwyer, *Day is Ours*, 252, mistakenly gives it as the house of Dr. David Cowell and his brother Ebenezer.

6 Wiederholdt, "Rall at Trenton," 465-466; Fischer, *Washington's Crossing*, 235.
7 Embury, *A Grandmother's Recollections*.
8 Stryker, *Trenton and Princeton*, 153-154.
9 Embury, *A Grandmother's Recollections*.
10 Dwyer, *Day is Ours*, 263. Dwyer does not give a citation for this but simply attributes it to one report of several stories about close encounters among the people of Trenton.
11 Larry Kidder, "Guiding Washington to Trenton," *Journal of the American Revolution*, May 6, 2014, https://allthingsliberty.com/2014/05/guiding-washington-to-trenton.
12 Paul Dudley Sargent PF W24894.
13 Stryker, *Trenton and Princeton*, 150-151; Dwyer, *Day is Ours*, 251.
14 White, *Eagle Tavern*, 2-2.
15 Stryker, *Trenton and Princeton*, 151-152, 189; Dwyer, *Day is Ours*, 251. Quotes Wilkinson who says the early fugitives going over the bridge were joined by some of the musicians, the surgeons, and some of the women. This is very questionable because the band was captured in total and surgeons were paroled to help the wounded left in town after the battle. The Trenton Prisoner List includes the musicians, medical officers, and some wives. It does not list any jägers.
16 John Cadwalader, Bristol, December 26, 1776, to PA Council of Safety, Force, *American Archives*, Series 5, III: 1441. Commenting on the report of a Mr. M. Lane and his observations from Trenton Ferry that morning. Cadwalader had tried to cross the night of the 25th at Dunks' Ferry but it was not possible to get their cannon across so they had returned to Bristol about 4:00 am. From Trenton Ferry, Pennsylvania side, he had heard heavy firing on the River and Pennytown roads leading to Trenton that he said was heavy for about an hour and then moderate for about three quarters hour.
17 Stryker, *Trenton and Princeton*, 152-153; Dwyer, *Day is Ours*, 252 – he quotes an unidentified aide to Washington.
18 *Hessian Documents of the American Revolution*, Morristown National Historic Park – enclosed with Heister to Landgrave Frederick, New York, February 9, 1777, Fiche 11, page 26. Heister says he heard excellent reports on Bockum including from "a nearby resident, at whose house he was posted with his detachment." This may have been Barnes.
19 Atwood, *Hessians*, 93.
20 Wiederholdt, "Rall at Trenton," 465-466.
21 Dwyer, *Day is Ours*, 253 – today known as five points, and the location of the battle monument.
22 Now Princeton Avenue.
23 Dwyer, *Day is Ours*, 253 – quoting the aide.
24 Nathanael Greene, Trenton, to Catharine Green, December 30, 1776, Showman, *Greene Papers*, I: 377.
25 Quoted in Atwood, *Hessians*, 93.
26 Dwyer, *Day is Ours*, 252, 254-255 – quoting Knox
27 Cornelius Sullivan PF S1258; Thomas Forrest to Col. Proctor, December 29, 1776 from McConkey's Ferry, Samuel Hazard, *Pennsylvania Archives*, (Philadelphia: Joseph Severns, 1853), V: 142. His comments were made about Hessian prisoners.
28 John Boudy PF W5858.
29 *Pennsylvania Gazette*, Sunday, November 22, 1750, 4; Thursday, September 26, 1765, 6.
30 Stryker, *Trenton and Princeton*, 154-156.
31 Canister was a cluster of small projectiles in a container and firing it essentially made the cannon a large, powerful shotgun.
32 Stryker, *Trenton and Princeton*, 156-158, 162-164; General James Wilkinson, *Memoirs of My Own Times* (Philadelphia: Abraham Small, 1816) Reprint AMS Press, New York: 1973, 129; Joseph White, "The Good Soldier White: A Revolutionary Veteran Speaks," *American Heritage* 7 (1956), 77. Joseph White PF W11805 – contains copy of his book narrative – seems most proud of taking off the damaged cannon at Trenton; Adam Stephen to Jonathan Seaman, January 5, 1777, Harry M. Ward, *Major General Adam Stephen and the Cause of American Liberty* (Charlottesville: University Press of Virginia, 1989), 152.

Jonathan Seaman was the overseer of Stephen's plantation. James Monroe, *Autobiography of James Monroe*, Edited by Stuart Gerry Brown (Syracuse: Syracuse University Press, 1959), 25-26.

33 Reuber, "Diary," 7-8.

34 Patrick Duffey to Col Proctor of Artillery, December 28, 1776 from McConkey's Ferry, Hazard, *Pennsylvania Archives*, V: 141.

35 *Vermont Republican* (Windsor, VT), March 31, 1832, 4.

36 Stryker, *Trenton and Princeton*, 162-164; Wilkinson, *Memoirs*, 129.

37 Stryker, *Trenton and Princeton*, 167-168, 186.

38 Stryker, *Trenton and Princeton*, 168-172; Barth, Dorneman, Schwalm, "The Trenton Prisoner List," 18, 22.

39 Loyalist Joseph Galloway later said that a number of Hessian soldiers were "more attentive to the safety of their plunder than their duty, and engaged in putting horses to and loading their wagons, became deaf to all orders." While doing this, he says they were surrounded and taken and there is no evidence that any wagons left the village. Galloway was not an eyewitness and was probably seeking a reason for the defeat. No eyewitnesses give any indication of this kind of behavior. Stryker, *Trenton and Princeton*, 172.

40 Wiederholdt, "Rall at Trenton," 466 -467.

41 Reuber, "Diary," 7-8. Reuber's is the only account of this.

42 Stryker, *Trenton and Princeton*, 174.

43 Ibid., 175.

44 Stryker, *Trenton and Princeton*, 176-182.

45 Ibid.

46 Ibid., 182-184. On December 27 Washington ordered that the swords and knapsacks that had been taken from officers and sergeants were to be returned.

47 Dwyer, *Day is Ours*, citing Major Apollos Morris.

48 Stryker, *Trenton and Princeton*, 190.

49 William S. Powell, "A Connecticut Soldier Under Washington: Elisha Bostwick's Memoirs of the First Years of the Revolution." *The William and Mary Quarterly*, Third Series, 6 (1949), 107.

50 Stryker, *Trenton and Princeton*, 185, 187 – Stryker considers the various estimates from Hessian officers.

51 Ibid., 192. When the Potts house, later the City Tavern, was demolished in 1857, newspapers noted that the pane of glass with the bullet hole was then in possession of one of the citizens and that curiosity hunters had taken pieces of the old-fashioned painted Dutch tile from under the mantle pieces. See: Newark Daily Advertiser, June 11, 1857, 2. The glass pane with the bullet hole is now part of the collections of the Old Barracks Museum in Trenton.

52 Embury, *A Grandmother's Recollections*.

53 *Carleton Papers*, item 7445.

54 AO12, vol 15, 110-116; AO13, bundle 20, 210-219. He continued to serve the British as a Deputy Commissary in New York, then in Virginia and South Carolina. He had to leave the army when he became ill and returned to New York until the evacuation in 1783. After the war he settled in Nova Scotia.

55 Death notice, *Boston Herald*, January 20, 1862, 2. She was 96 at the time of her death. The article noted that Joshua Richard then lived in the house in 1862 where her parents had lived in 1776. The clock still stood in the same corner of the same room.

56 On his way home after discharge he sold it to a young officer for $8. White, "Good Soldier," 77.

57 Dwyer, *Day is Ours*, 261; John Greenwood, *The Wartime Services of John Greenwood: A Young Patriot in the American Revolution 1775-1783* (Westvaco, 1981), 42.

58 Dennis P. Ryan, ed., *A Salute to Courage: The American Revolution as Seen Through Wartime Writings of Officers of the Continental Army and Navy* (New York: Columbia University Press, 1979), 56.

59 Moses Smith PF S23925.

60 Bostwick, "Connecticut Soldier," 102. He wrote this description after the battle when the prisoners were removed over the Delaware.

61 Fischer, *Washington's Crossing*, Appendix K, 401; Stryker, *Trenton and Princeton*, 206; Extract of a letter from an officer in the American Army from Newtown, Pennsylvania December 27, 1776. In Force, *American Archives*, Series 5, III: 1442-1443.
62 NJSA, Legislature Series, Inventories of Damages by the British and Americans in New Jersey, 1776-1782, Jacob Benjamin Damage Claim No. 13 Hunterdon, NJSA
63 White, "Good Soldier," 77.
64 Stirling submitted an account of this loss on April 30, 1778 - *PCC*, Letters from General Washington, r168, i152, p17.
65 Stephen Moylan, Newtown, to Robert Morris, December 27, 1776 – carried by Colonel Baylor, *PCC*, Pennsylvania State Papers, 1775-91, r83, i69, p299.
66 Return of Prisoners taken at Trenton the 26th December 1776, *PCC*, Pennsylvania State Papers, 1775-91, r83, i69, p155; also *PCC*, Transcripts of letters from George Washington 1776, Unknown return of German mercenaries captured at Trenton – transcript, r186, i169, p433; Stryker, *Trenton and Princeton*, 201.
67 John Cadwalader, Bristol, to PA Council of Safety, December 26, 1776, *PCC*, Pennsylvania State Papers, 1775-91, r83, i69, p303.
68 Stryker, *Trenton and Princeton*, 207, Gibson, *Dr. Bodo Otto*, 127-28.
69 Hosea Husted PF S34412; Reuben Husted PF W465; Death notice of Hosea in Washington Whig (Bridgeton, NJ), June 7, 1823, 3; Cornelius Wells PF W2503.
70 Rev. David Avery, "The Battle of Trenton from the unpublished diary of Rev. David Avery, Chaplain in Colonel John Patterson's Regiment," *The American Monthly Magazine* 19, (Washington, D.C.; National Society, D.A.R., 1901), 155. Avery also says the wounded officers were left on parole and the prisoners were marched to Yardley's Ferry, although he may have meant Johnsons.
71 Tench Tilghman, Newtown, to James Tilghman, December 27, 1776, Tench Tilghman, Memoir of Lieut. Col. Tench Tilghman, Secretary and Aid to Washington (Albany: J. Munsell, 1876. Reprint Arno Press, 1971), 149; Barth, Dorneman, Schwalm, "The Trenton Prisoner List".
72 Stryker, *Trenton and Princeton*, 172, 392.
73 Stryker *Trenton and Princeton*, 196; Barth, Dorneman, Schwalm, "The Trenton Prisoner List".
74 Stryker, *Trenton and Princeton*, 192. Oliva says Rall died the evening of the battle, December 26. The exact location is unknown.
75 Barth, Dorneman, Schwalm, "The Trenton Prisoner List".
76 *Hessian Documents of the American Revolution*, Morristown National Historical Park, Journal of the Hessian Corps... under Gen. von Heister, 1776-77, Letter AA (Part 1) – Fiche No. 3, Reports of von Donop, etc., AA 62 – 63 - letter of Surgeon Oliva, Trenton, January 13, 1777.
77 Tench Tilghman, Newtown, to James Tilghman, December 27, 1776, Tilghman, *Memoir*, 149.
78 THS, *Trenton*, 755; Shuman, *Trenton Story*, 37; letter from Baltimore, December 31, 1776, Peter Force, *American Archives*, Series 5, III: 1509-1510; Notice in a number of New England papers including *Independent Chronicle* (Boston, MA), Thursday, January 23, 1777, 3.
79 Hall, *Trenton Presbyterian Church*, 159-163. Citing damage assessment report of commissioners Joseph Phillips, Peter Gordon, and Sidney Barry acting in accordance with a 1781 New Jersey law. The accuracy of the inventory of damages was attested to by Alexander Chambers as a Trustee of the Church and sworn before Joseph Phillips September 7, 1782.
80 AO13, bundle 19. Two other witnesses were Isaac DeCou and Miss Sally Barnes, niece of Major John Barnes of the Loyalist forces. Also, Schuyler, *St. Michael's Church*, 79.
81 NJSA, Legislature Series, Inventories of Damages by the British and Americans in New Jersey, 1776-1782, Damage Report Claim No. 45 Elizabeth Pearson Burlington, NJSA
82 For example: NJSA, Legislature Series, Inventories of Damages by the British and Americans in New Jersey, 1776-1782, Damage Report Claims No. 311 Alexander Douglass Burlington; No 313 Thomas Jenney Burlington; No 318 Jonathan Richmond Burlington, NJSA.
83 NJSA, Legislature Series, Inventories of Damages by the British and Americans in New Jersey, 1776-1782, Damage Report Claim No. 10 William Plaskett, NJSA.

84 Fischer, *Washington's Crossing*, Appendix K, 401.
85 Joseph Reed, "General Joseph Reed's Narrative of the Movements of the American Army in the Neighborhood of Trenton in the Winter of 1776-77," The *Pennsylvania Magazine of History and Biography*, 8 (1884), 397.
86 Tench Tilghman (for Washington) to Thomas Mifflin, December 29, 1776, *Papers of George Washington, Revolutionary War Series*, VII: 474n.
87 Stryker, *Trenton and Princeton*, 245-6.
88 Avery, "Diary," 155.
89 Stryker, *Trenton and Princeton*, 246; Wilkinson, *Memoir*, 133.
90 General Orders, December 30, 1776, *Papers of George Washington, Revolutionary War Series*, VII: 484.
91 James McMichael, "Diary of Lieutenant James McMichael, of the Pennsylvania Line, 1776-1778," The *Pennsylvania Magazine of History and Biography* 16 (1892), 140; John Stevens PF W1092 – his deposition and the supporting deposition of Israel Clark. First Hunterdon militiaman Stevens says he went with Reed as a guide. There is no other documentary confirmation of this, but there was no reason for Stevens to lie and, even though Reed had some familiarity with the area, a guide was an appropriate and normal addition.; Fischer, *Washington's Crossing*, 279-80; Joseph Reed, "General Joseph Reed's Narrative of the Movements of the American Army in the Neighborhood of Trenton in the Winter of 1776-77." The *Pennsylvania Magazine of History and Biography* vol viii, no 4, 1884, 391-402, 399-400; See also - William B. Reed, Life and Correspondence of Joseph Reed (Philadelphia: Lindsay and Blakiston, 1847), I: 283; Joseph Lapsley Wilson, ed., *Book of the First Troop, Philadelphia City Cavalry, 1774-1914* (Philadelphia: First Troop Philadelphia City Cavalry, 1915), 8; Wilkinson, *Memoir*, 134
92 Nathanael Greene, Trenton, to Catharine Greene, December 30, 1776, Showman, *Greene Papers*, 377.
93 Fischer, *Washington's Crossing*, 281; Kidder, *A People Harassed and Exhausted*, 219.
94 Stryker, *Trenton and Princeton*, 254-255.
95 Avery, "Diary," 156.
96 How, David. *Diary of David How, A private in Colonel Paul Dudley Sargents Regiment of the Massachusetts Line, in the Army of the American Revolution*. Morrisania, NY: 1865, 41-42. He later went out as a militiaman and served at the time of the Battle of Saratoga.
97 George Washington, Proclamation to "the Friends of America in the State of New Jersey," December 31, 1776, Sol Feinstone Collection Mss #2275.
98 Fischer, *Washington's Crossing*, 281.
99 Edwin M. Stone, *The Life and Recollections of John Howland, Late President of the Rhode Island Historical Society* (Providence: George H. Whitney, 1857), 71.

Chapter 8

1 Ethel Armes, ed., *Nancy Shippen Her Journal Book* (Philadelphia: JB. Lippincott, 1935), 35-39.
2 Fischer, *Washington's Crossing*, Appendix K, 401.
3 Wilkinson, *Memoirs*, I: 133.
4 Stryker, *Trenton and Princeton*, 256; George Washington, Trenton, to John Hancock, January 1, 1777, *CWPLOC*.
5 *Pennsylvania Evening Post*, January 14, 1777, 20.
6 Joseph Reed to Council of Safety, January 1, 1777, Hazard, ed., *Pennsylvania Archives*, Series 1, V: 151. 7 Stryker, *Trenton and Princeton*, 256.
8 William S. Powell, "A Connecticut Soldier Under Washington: Elisha Bostwick's Memoirs of the First Years of the Revolution." *The William and Mary Quarterly*, Third Series, vol 6, no 1 (Jan., 1949), 103. Washington wrote to Robert Morris on August 14, 1777 that, "In looking over my private acct with the Public, I find a credit to it of a blank number of silver dollars sent me by you whilst I lay at Trenton about the first of Jany – for want of the sum, I cannot babl the acct. and shall th ask you for information on this head." Sol Feinstone Collection of the American Revolution, Mss #2216.

9 Moses Smith PF S23925.
10 Oliver Corey PF S12558. He gives his captain as head of the life guard as Captain Moody Dustin. Dustin was in a New Hampshire regiment and Sullivan was from New Hampshire. Sargent's regiment was in Sullivan's Brigade at Trenton. The story is plausible. Corey was discharged at Morristown and returned home.
11 Benjamin Rush to Richard Henry Lee, Philadelphia, January 14, 1777, L. H. Butterfield, ed., *Letters of Benjamin Rush* (Princeton: American Philosophical Society and Princeton University Press, 1951), I: 129.
12 Whitfield J. Bell, Jr. and L.H. Butterfield – introduction to Benjamin Rush, *My Dearest Julia: The Love Letters of Dr. Benjamin Rush to Julia Stockton* (New York: N. Watson Academic Publications, 1979).
13 Runes, *Selected Writings of Benjamin Rush*, introduction; Benjamin Rush to Julia Stockton, January 5, 1776 in Rush, *My Dearest Julia*, 45. See also the introduction.
14 Benjamin Rush, *The Autobiography of Benjamin Rush: His Travels through life together with his Commonplace Book for 1789-1813*, George W. Corner, ed. (Westport, CN: Greenwood Press, 1970), 125 -126.
15 Rush, *Autobiography*, 126-127.
16 Wilkinson, *Memoirs*, I: 135; Stryker, *Trenton and Princeton*, 261-263.
17 AO13 bundle 25, 532-534.
18 Rush, *Autobiography*, 127.
19 Peale, "Journal," *The Crayon*, 38; Charles Coleman Sellers, *Charles Willson Peale* (New York: Charles Scribner's Son's, 1969), 131.
20 James Johnston PF S2298.
21 William Young, "Journal of Sergeant William Young" The *Pennsylvania Magazine of History and Biography* 8 (1884), 255-278, 262-263.
22 McMichael, "Diary," 139.
23 Stone, *John Howland*, 71-72.
24 Peale, "Journal," *The Crayon*, 38; Sellers, *Charles Willson Peale*, 131.
25 James Johnston PF S2298.
26 William Morris PF S1061. The William Morris Tune Book, 1776-1777 is in the collection of the New York Historical Society and can be viewed on-line from the Society's website.
27 Thomas Rodney, *Diary of Captain Thomas Rodney, 1776-1777*, Caesar A. Rodney, intro. (Wilmington: The Historical Society of Delaware, 1888), 30.
28 Avery, "Diary," 155.
29 AO13 bundle 25, 532-534. He was kept at Newtown for three weeks and then escaped with several other prisoners who got safely to New Brunswick. He continued in Loyalist service on Staten Island and then South Carolina. He settled in East Florida after the war and then in Nova Scotia.
30 Henry Knox to Lucy Knox, Trenton, January 2, 1777, January 7, 1777, Knox, *Papers of Henry Knox* [microform], r3, i109, i112.
31 Fischer, *Washington's Crossing*, Appendix K, 401.
32 James Barnett PF W391.
33 Wilkinson, *Memoir*, 137-138.
34 Ibid., 139.
35 Henry Knox to Lucy Knox, Trenton, January 7, 177, Knox, *Papers of Henry Knox* [microform], r3, i112, 7; *Hessian Documents of the American Revolution*, Morristown National Historical Park, Von Donop to Heister, January 6 from Brunswick, AA 49 – 50.
36 Benjamin Rush to editor of the *Pennsylvania Journal*, July 4, 1782, Butterfield, *Letters of Benjamin Rush*, 276. Letter signed Leonidas.
37 Henry Knox to Lucy Knox, Trenton, January 7, 1777, Knox, *Papers of Henry Knox* [microform], r3, i112.
38 *Hessian Documents of the American Revolution*, Morristown National Historical Park, Von Donop to Heister, January 6 from Brunswick, AA 49 – 50.
39 Stryker, *Trenton and Princeton*, 246.

40 Lydenberg, *Archibald Robertson*, 119-120.
41 Henry Knox to Lucy Knox, Trenton, January 7, 1777, Knox, *Papers of Henry Knox* [microform], r3, i112.
42 Stryker, *Trenton and Princeton*, 261-263.
43 Stone, *John Howland*, 72-74; Henry Knox to Lucy Knox, Trenton, January 7, 1777, Knox, *Papers of Henry Knox* [microform], r3, i112.
44 Probably a colloquial spelling of fusil, a light flintlock musket.
45 *Pennsylvania Evening Post*, April 29, 1777, 237.
46 Ryan, *Salute to Courage*, 56.
47 Isaiah Crandall PF S12636.
48 Ryan, *Salute to Courage*, 56. Also: Custis, George Washington Parke Custis, *Recollections and Private Memoirs of Washington* (New York: Derby & Jackson, 1860), 413. In this source Scott is quoted as saying, "To the last man, your excellency."
49 "Anecdotes of Old Gen. Scott," *Daily Constitutionalist* (Augusta, Georgia), July 17, 1835, 1. This unsigned article appeared in a number of newspapers across the country between 1835 and 1860. Just when it was written is unclear.
50 Powell, *Elisha Bostwick's Memoirs*, 106. Troops firing too high was a common problem in 18th century warfare.
51 Augustus C. Parker, *Parker in America, 1630-1910* (Buffalo, NY: 1910), 251.
52 Peale, "Journal," *The Crayon*, 38; Sellers, *Charles Willson Peale*, 131.
53 James Johnston PF S2298; Stryker, *Trenton and Princeton*, 261-263.
54 Stryker, *Trenton and Princeton*, 263-264; Thomas Rodney, *Diary*, 30.
55 Wilkinson, *Memoir*, 137-138.
56 "Abstracts of Pension Applications on File in the Division of Public Records, Pennsylvania State Library," The *Pennsylvania Archives*, Series 5, IV: 586-7.
57 Stone, *John Howland*, 72-74.
58 Thomas Rodney, *Diary*, 30.
59 Stone, *John Howland*, 72-74; Henry Knox to Lucy Knox, Trenton, January 7, 1777, Knox, *Papers of Henry Knox* [microform], r3, i112; Stryker, *Trenton and Princeton*, 264-267; White, "The Good Soldier White," 77-78; Hood?, "Engagements at *Trenton and Princeton*, January 2 and 3, 1777," The *Pennsylvania Magazine of History and Biography* 10 (1886); 263-265. Also: Sol Feinstone Collection Mss #907.
60 Daniel Smith PF S11416.
61 Henry Knox to Lucy Knox, Trenton, January 7, 1777, Knox, *Papers of Henry Knox*, [microform], r3, i112.
62 For example, see: Enoch Gandy PF W4963; Other men also described the battle as a "cannonade." See for example, Joseph Sayre PF S18587. He was a Salem County, New Jersey militiaman who says he was "at the cannonade of Trenton very early in the year 1777."
63 Rush, *Autobiography*, 127-128.
64 Benjamin Rush to Richard Henry Lee, January 6, 1777, Butterfield, *Letters of Benjamin Rush*, I: 124.
65 NJSA, Legislature Series, Inventories of Damages by the British and Americans in New Jersey, 1776-1782, Charles Axford, Jr.; Caledonian (St. Johnsbury, Vermont), July 4, 1843, 3. In another account, Richmond's tavern was severely damaged by British artillery during the battle. Mrs. Richmond had refused to leave town during the events that winter. The notice commented on the recent July 4 celebration and noted that the republicans of Trenton celebrated at her house, which she still lived in, and the federalists dined where the British artillery had been placed. American Citizen (New York City), July 16, 1803, 2.
66 Moses Smith PF S23925; Moses Smith death notice National Aegis (Worcester, Massachusetts), July 22, 1846, 3. Smith's accounts contain several inconsistencies, but the loss of his right hand at Trenton on January 2, 1777 seems accurate. He gives a detailed account in his pension application that fits with known facts. In his death notice that relates stories he told of his service he mistaken says he lost his hand at the battle of Trenton rather than second Trenton, as related in his pension file. He also tells a completely different, but more heroic, story of his service after recovering. He also relates

a story about the battle of Trenton, that again was meant to be second Trenton, which is colorful but implausible. He tells a story in his pension file about capturing British horses at first Trenton that is plausible and is related in this work.

67 "Abstracts of Pension Applications on File in the Division of Public Records, Pennsylvania State Library," 514.

68 Gibson, *Dr. Bodo Otto*, 179-180.

69 Rush, *Autobiography*, 127.

70 Runes, *Selected Writings of Benjamin Rush*, 327-329.

71 Leydenberg, *Archibald Robertson*, 119-120.

72 *Hessian Documents of the American Revolution*, Morristown National Historical Park, Von Donop to Heister January 6 from Brunswick, AA 49 – 50.

73 McMichael, *Diary*, 139-141.

74 Thomas Rodney, *Diary*, 30. Rodney's published diary notes that Martinas later joined Col. David Hall's Delaware Regiment and became a brave and faithful soldier.

75 Peale, "Journal," *The Crayon*, 38; Sellers, *Charles Willson Peale*, 131.

76 The Douglas house has been moved from its original location on Greene Street on the site of the German Lutheran Church. It is now at 165 East Front Street.

77 Fischer, *Washington's Crossing*, Appendix K, 401.

78 Stryker, *Trenton and Princeton*, 269-274; Wilkinson, *Memoir*, 138-140. Benjamin Rush credits Joseph Reed for suggesting the maneuver. Butterfield, *Letters of Benjamin Rush*, 1094. Three local men selected as guides were Elias Phillips, Patrick Lamb, and Ezekiel Anderson, brother of Ephraim Anderson.

79 White, "The Good Soldier White," 77-78.

80 Jesse E. Dow, "The Life Guardsman," *Graham's Lady's and Gentleman's Magazine*. Vol xviii, (Philadelphia: George R. Graham, 1841). 277. Also in *Barre Gazette*, Barre Massachusetts, June 25, 1841, 1. Hugh Maxwell does not appear on roster of Life Guard, but it is not complete. Use of the term "life guard" does indicate he served in early part of war – which he describes – as Washington forbid use of this term later. Nothing stands out as terribly wrong – minor mistake in number of artillery captured at Trenton (9 vs 6). However, may be somewhat romanticized.

81 White, "Good Soldier White," 77-78.

82 George Yard PF R11925.

83 Stryker, *Trenton and Princeton*, 274-275.

84 Cornelius Wells PF W2503; Death notice *Southern Patriot* (Charleston, SC), August 9, 1844, 2.

85 Cary McClelland PF S9006.

86 Dow, "The Life Guardsman," 277.

87 Stryker, *Trenton and Princeton*, 274-275.

88 Peale, "Journal," *The Crayon*, 38; Sellers, *Charles Willson Peale*, 131.

89 Young, "Journal," 264.

90 Morgan, ed., *Naval Documents*, VIII: 128.

91 Thomas Rodney, *Diary*, 32.

92 Peale, "Journal," *The Crayon*, 38; Sellers, *Charles Willson Peale*, 131.

93 McMichael, "Diary," 139-141.

94 James Johnston PF S2298.

95 Rush, *Autobiography*, 127.

96 Kidder, A People Harassed and Exhausted, 227. John Stevens PF W1092.

97 Caesar Rodney to George Read, January 23, 1777, Caesar Rodney, *Letters to and From Caesar Rodney, 1756-1784*, George Herbert Ryden, ed. (New York: DaCapo Press, 1970), 170. Rodney heard this story from Tucker while he commanded at Trenton in January and February 1777.

98 The story of Rosbrugh is told by Hall, *Trenton Presbyterian Church*, 163-64; Rev. John C. Clyde, *Rosbrugh, A Tale of the Revolution; or, Life, Labors, and Death of Rev. John Rosbrugh* (Easton, Pa: 1880), 55; William Buel Sprague, *Annals of the American pulpit: or, Commemorative notices of distinguished American Clergymen of Various Denominations* (New York: Robert Carter & Brothers, 1859), III: 254-255. His widow Jean Rosbrugh

received a pension from Pennsylvania. He left five minor children. "Abstracts of Pension Applications on File in the Division of Public Records, Pennsylvania State Library," The *Pennsylvania Archives*, Series 5, IV: 547-8; *Pennsylvania Evening Post*, April 29, 1777, 237. It was later moved to the Presbyterian churchyard, although the grave is not marked.

99 *Pennsylvania Evening Post*, January 14, 1777, 20; Hunter, *Fish and Ships*, 15.

100 *Pennsylvania Evening Post*, January 21, 1777, 31.

101 Stone, *John Howland*, 71-72. John Howland also deposed for Robert Tift, Rhode Island, PF W3514 confirming their participation in these events.

102 Wilkinson, *Memoirs*, 133.

Chapter 9

1 The former house of Abraham Cottnam. The advertisement for its sale in 1779 said it had been a tavern for over two years. *NJG*, March 17, 1779, 3. See: NJSA, Hunterdon County Tavern Licenses, 1331-1336.

2 Adams, *Diary and Autobiography*, II: 265. It is likely the Mr. Thompson and lady were Continental Congress Secretary Charles Thompson and his wife. Mrs. Jackson may be Mrs. James Jackson. Adams told the story to Abigail in a letter from York, Pennsylvania on September 30. See: *Letters of Delegates* to Congress, VIII: 27.

3 Joseph Killgore PF S35509; George Bedinger PF W2992

4 *Joint Meeting*, 14.

5 Miller, *The Life of Samuel Miller*, 147-148.

6 William Richards to Council January 7, 1777, Hazard, ed., *Pennsylvania Archives*, Series 1, V: 169-170. See for example: Conrad Davis PF R2705. He entered service as a wagon teamster at Hackettstown in a twelve team brigade. He specifically mentions Hunt at Trenton as a place he went to and from delivering food and army stores.

7 John Bell PF S22642; Samuel Wooley PF R11850.

8 *Assembly Votes*, Session beginning August 27, 1776, 59, 60. On June 6 the Assembly resolved that clothing should be delivered to the Clothier General of the Army. Ibid., 143.

9 *Assembly Votes*, Session beginning October 28, 1777, 42.

10 William Robinson PF W4572 and supporting statements of Joseph Reed and widow.

11 George Washington to Continental Congress, January 5, 1777, *GWPLOC*; Israel Putnam at Bristol to Robert Morris, January 5, 1777; Israel Putnam at Bordentown to unknown, January 6, 1777, *PCC*, Letters from General Officers, 1775-89, r178, i159, p29. Also, General Putnam to Council of Safety, January 6, 1777, Hazard, ed., *Pennsylvania Archives*, Series 1, V: 168.

12 Stryker, *Trenton and Princeton*, 274 – says this was on January 9.

13 Adam Stephen to Lord Stirling, January 8, 1777, Trenton, *PCC*, Letters from General Officers, r179, i162, p233.

14 William Trout PF S2567; John Coleman PF R2163. He says General Morgan also commanded at the same place. He says he served under General Heard while in Quigley's company until Heard left the army during the harvest of 1777. James Fergus PF W25573; Israel Putnam, Princeton, to Lord Stirling, January 19, 1777, *PCC*, Letters from General Officers, 1775-89, r178, i159, p35.

15 Lord Stirling to Captain Isaiah Robinson, Continental Brig Andrew Doria, Philadelphia, January 22, 1777, Morgan, ed. *Naval Documents*, VII: 1017-18.

16 Caesar Rodney, Trenton, to General Putnam, January 21, 1777, Caesar Rodney, *Letters*, 171-172. In a post script he asked to be informed about just how many troops he should keep at Trenton as a garrison.

17 Caesar Rodney, Trenton, to George Read, January 23, 1777, Caesar Rodney, *Letters*, 156-157, 169-171. He also noted the bodies of Colonel Haslet and Major Morris, killed at Princeton on the 3rd were in Trenton on January 23 on their way to Philadelphia for interment.

18 Thomas Rodney, *Diary*, 47-49.

19 Caesar Rodney, *Letters*, 159-165,172-173, 176.

20 Sewell Elias Slick, *William Trent and the West* (Harrisburg: Archives Publishing Company of Pennsylvania, 1947), 164.

21 Caesar Rodney, *Letters*, 166, 174-175. Dickinson had earned praise for the "Forage War."

22 Ibid., 168, 177-178; George Washington to Caesar Rodney, February 18, 1777, Morristown, *GWPLOC*.

23 Gibson, *Dr. Bodo Otto*, 127-28; *Hessian Documents of the American Revolution*, Morristown National Historical Park, Journal of the Hessian Corps... under Gen. von Heister, 1776-77, Letter AA (Part 1) – Fiche No. 3, Reports of von Donop etc, AA 62 – 63 - letter of Surgeon Oliva, Trenton , January 13, 1777

24 Muller to __ New York, March 15, 1777, *Hessian Documents of the American Revolution*, Letter AA, fiche 11, p47. Muller had been ordered as early as January 1 to get organized for this relief effort and had started out on January 7. He received permission on February 11, spent night of February 14 beyond Cranberry, and arrived in New York on February 17. See: Morristown Hessian Documents, letter AA, fiche 11, p37.

25 George Washington to William Shippen, Jr., January 6, 1777, *GWPLOC*; *JCC*, VII, 110.

26 William Shippen, Jr. to General Caesar Rodney at Trenton, General Hospital, Phila., February 17th, 1777, Gibson, *Dr. Bodo Otto*, 133; Gillette, *Army Medical Department*, 75. See: Tom Shachtman, *Gentlemen Scientists and revolutionaries: The Founding Fathers in the Age of Enlightenment*, (New York: Palgrave McMillan, 2014), 105-113 for more on Washington's inoculation efforts. Also see: Elizabeth A. Fenn, *Pox Americana: The Great Smallpox Epidemic of 1775-82* (New York: Hill and Wang, 2001). Joseph Ellis, *His Excellency, George Washington*, (New York: Alfred A. Knopf, 2004), 87.

27 *Pennsylvania Evening Post*, February 18, 1777, 89.

28 NARA M246. May 16, 1777 Muster Roll, Muster rolls, payrolls, strength returns, and other miscellaneous personnel, pay, and supply records of American Army units, 1775-83. r0109, f275 11th Virginia Regiment.

29 Dr. William Shippen, Jr., from General Hospital to Gen. Sullivan at Princeton, May 29, 1777, Otis G. Hammond, ed. *Letters and Papers of Major-General John Sullivan, Continental Army* (Concord: New Hampshire Historical Society, 1930-1939), I: 346.

30 Robert Kirkwood, *The Journal and Order Book of Captain Robert Kirkwood of the Delaware Regiment of the Continental Line*. Edited by Joseph Brown Turner. (Port Washington, NY: Kennikat Press, 1970), 84-85.

31 Samuel Tucker to John Hart, Speaker of the Assembly, January 20, 1777, NJSA, BAH Box 5-02, #113. Stockton's home, Morven, later became the house for New Jersey's governors and today is a museum in Princeton.

32 *Assembly Votes*, Session beginning August 27, 1776, 52-54; *Council Journal*, Session beginning August 27, 1776, 45. The legislature had met January 22 at Pittstown, but then moved to Haddonfield.

33 Samuel Tucker to John Hart, Speaker of the Assembly, February 4, 1777, NJSA, BAH Box 5-02, #114; Samuel Abbot affirmed statement, February 14, 1777, *Assembly Votes*, Session beginning August 27, 1776, 70. After the war it was learned that a number of Tucker's possessions came with the British to Philadelphia in 1777. Elizabeth Fegan Affidavit, April 19, 1784, *NJG*, July 20, 1784, 2.

34 *Assembly Votes*, Session beginning August 27, 1776, 60, 66-67. His attendance had been required earlier and on February 7 the Assembly noted that he sent a letter saying he could not attend at that time so he was ordered to attend the following Thursday, February 13. Questions proposed for Mr. Tucker, NJSA, BAH Box 5-02, #118.

35 *Assembly Votes*, Session beginning August 27, 1776, 52-54, 68-70; *Council Journal*, 45; *Joint Meeting*, 15. In 1784 John Cadwalader and Elizabeth Fegan testified about the money not being signed by Tucker, causing him to be cursed by British officers. The money was useless to the British. *NJG*, July 20, 1784, 2.

36 *Minutes of Trenton*, 38-39.

37 A reward was offered for the return of one or both. *Pennsylvania Evening Post*, May 8, 1777, 255.

38 *Joint Meeting*, 19. Because of his election to the court, Dr. Smith was required to take the oaths of abjuration and allegiance, which he did on July 18, 177. See: *Council of Safety*

Minutes, 18 March 1777 – 8 October 1778, 38.

39 *Assembly Votes*, Session beginning August 27, 1776, 109. Also noted Isaac Smith as being appointed second Justice of Supreme Court and thereby disqualified from being Colonel and refusal of Abraham Hunt to be Lieutenant Colonel. Notes Captain Van Cleave refusing to go into service as being engaged in the Loan Office Business. Actually had been elected to office.

40 Caesar Rodney, *Letters*, 164-166.

41 Thomas Jones at Trenton to Livingston, March 26, 1777, *Livingston Papers* [microform], r4, i377.

42 Joseph Trumbull, Commissary General to Jared Tracy, Camp Middlebrook, June 5, 1777, Morgan, ed., *Naval Documents*, IX:36; NJSA, Old Barracks Museum Association, Manuscript Collection, 1771-1809, Accession #1968.011, #27.

43 August 8, 1777 – Joseph Trumbull at Germantown to William Buchanan, *PCC*, Letters and papers relative to the Quartermaster's Department, 1777-84, r199, i192, p395.

44 September 3, 1777 – Unknown return of stores – Return of stores received by Col Charles Stewart Commissary General of Issues and his deputies in the Middle Department, *PCC*, Letters and papers relative to the Quartermaster General's Department, 1777-84, r199, i192, p483.

45 Alexander Chambers to Livingston – Trenton, September 9, 1777, *Livingston Papers* [microform], r5, i704; NJSA, Department of Education, New Jersey State Library, Bureau of Archives and History, Manuscript Collection, 1680s-1970s, BAH Box 1-01, #73.

46 Gen. Benedict Arnold, at Philadelphia to Gen. Sullivan at Princeton, June 1, 1777, Hammond, *Sullivan Papers*, I: 355.

47 Benedict Arnold at Philadelphia to John Hancock, June 13, 1777, *PCC*, Letters from General Officers, 1775-89, r179, i162, p92.

48 Foreign Affairs Committee to Commissioners in France, June 14–15, 1777, *PCC*, Letters of the Committee for Foreign Affairs and of Robert R. Livingston, Secretary of Foreign Affairs, 1776-83, r105, i79, p69.

49 Benedict Arnold at Coryell's Ferry to John Hancock, June 18, 1777, *PCC*, Letters from General Officers, 1775-89, r179, i162, p96.

50 John Clutch PF S2126. Anderson is an intriguing and colorful figure. His military story is told more fully in Kidder, A People Harassed and Exhausted, passim.

51 Gibson, *Dr. Bodo Otto*, 139; John A. Otto PF S5133. He says the hospital was removed to Easton in 1778 and he served until 1780 as physician and surgeon. John Otto was born in Hanover, Germany in 1751 and came to America when one year old. Growing up, he studied medicine with his father.

52 Muster Rolls of Captain Alexander Mitchell's Company, August 1777-May 1778, NARA 246 Department of Defense, Revolutionary War Rolls, 1775-1783, Record Group 93; Folder 53.

53 Gibson, *Dr. Bodo Otto*, 205-206; Benjamin Rush to William Shippen, November 18, 1780, in Butterfield, *Rush Letters*, I: 257.

54 Gibson, *Dr. Bodo Otto*, 284. Militia private William Robinson remembered that after the Battle of Princeton, Kotts had "caused a letter to be prepared for Gen. Mercer at the time he was wounded at the Battle of Princeton." William Robinson PF W4572.

55 George Washington to John Hancock, July 16, 1777, *PCC*, Letters from Gen George Washington, r167, i152, p351, 355 – two letters of the same day.

56 George Washington to John Hancock, July 30, 1777, *PCC*, Letters from Gen George Washington, r167, i152, p406a, 409.

57 General Greene's Orders, Coryell's Ferry, July 30, 1777, Showman, *Greene Papers*, II: 129.

58 Stephen Moylan at Trenton to John Hancock, July 31, 1777, *PCC*, Miscellaneous letters addressed to Congress, 1775-89, r99, i78, p235; C.F. William Maurer, *Dragoon Diary: The History of the Third Continental Light Dragoons* (Bloomington, IN: AuthorHouse, c2005), 28.

59 Baylor Hill, *A Gentleman of Fortune: The Diary of Baylor Hill, First Continental Light Dragoons, 1777-1781*. Annotated and edited by John T. Hayes. (Fort Lauderdale: Saddlebag Press, c1995), 55.

60 George Washington to General Nash, August 21, 1777, *GWPLOC*; George Washington to General Nash, August 22, 1777, *GWPLOC*; George Washington to General Nash, August

25, 1777, *GWPLOC*; Jacob Turner, "Jacob Turner's Book 1777-1778," The State Records of North Carolina, Walter Clark, ed., (Winston, NC: M.I. & J.C. Stewart, 1895), 485-494. Turner's book is one of the copies of the *Order Book* of the brigade.

61 Maurer, *Dragoon Diary*, 31; Kirkwood, *Journal and Order Book*, 275, 155; William Beatty, "Journal of Capt William Beatty," *Maryland Historical Magazine* III (Baltimore: Maryland Historical Society, 1908), 108.

62 NJSA, Hunterdon County Court of Common Pleas Minutes [microform], vols 11-13, 1767-1788.

63 Benjamin Flower deposition re Commissary Department, August 19, 1778, *PCC*, Papers of Paymaster Pierce, r76, i62, p639+.

64 Gibson, *Dr. Bodo Otto*, 141, 169; Kirkwood, *Journal and Order Book*, 168; General Orders, September 12, 1777, *GWPLOC*; Gillette, *Army Medical Department*, 79.

65 Richard L. Blanco, Physician of the American Revolution Jonathan Potts (New York: Garland STPM Press, 1979), 163.

66 Charles Biddle, *Autobiography of Charles Biddle, Vice-President of the Supreme Executive Council of Pennsylvania, 1745-1821* (Philadelphia: E. Claxton and company, 1883), 102.

67 Philemon Dickinson to William Livingston, September 16, 1777, *GWPLOC*; George Washington to John Hancock, September 18, 1777, *GWPLOC*.

68 Eliphalet Dyer to Joseph Trumbull, Lancaster, September 28, 1777; James Duane to Mary Duane, September 21, 1777; John Hancock to Philemon Dickinson or Alexander McDougall, September 19, 1777, *Letters of Delegates* to Congress, VIII: 24-25, 8, 3.; Hiltzheimer, *Diary*, 35.

69 T*he Moravian Diary, The Memorabilia Section, Congregational Report of Bethlehem September-October of 1777*, XXXI 1776-1777, excerpt for September 24, 1777 translation by Jeannette Louise Norfleet, May 2016, provided by Don Billig to the author in January 2017; *Moravian Community Diary*, XXXI 1776-1777, entry 4157 for September 22, 1777; Moravian Archives, Bethlehem, Pennsylvania.

70 A team consisted of a wagon, the two or four horses pulling it, and the driver.

71 Robert Lettis Hooper to Quartermasters of Hunterdon County, September 27, 1777, NJSA, Old Barracks Museum Association, Manuscript Collection, 1771-1809, Accession #1968.011, #44.

72 Charles Stewart to Livingston, Trenton, September 28, 1777, *Livingston Papers* [microform], r5, i835

73 Livingston to Stewart, Princeton, September 28, 1777, *Livingston Papers* [microform] r5, f843.

74 *Joint Meeting*, 21.

75 Philemon Dickinson to Livingston from Trenton, September 16, 1777, *Livingston Papers* [microform], r5, i761; Philemon Dickinson to John Hancock, September 15, 1777, *PCC*, Miscellaneous letters addressed to Congress, 1775-89, r94, i78, p131.

76 Philemon Dickinson to Livingston, September 14, 1777, Prince, *Livingston Papers*, II: 71. See also: *Lieut. James Moody's Narrative of his Exertions and Sufferings in the Cause of Government, Since the Year 1776*, 2nd ed. London, 1783, 8-9. A group of Loyalists from Hunterdon and Sussex counties and northeastern Pennsylvania attempted to join Brig Gen Cortland Skinner on Staten Island. About 40 were captured near Perth Amboy by New Jersey militia on September 14 after a brief skirmish. Philemon Dickinson to John Cadwalader, September 14, 1777, *GWPLOC*.

77 Moses Estey PF S3339. *Assembly Votes*, Session beginning August 27, 1776, 178. Governor Livingston's request to the Assembly to arrange for guards and provisions to get them to jail in either Hunterdon or Burlington County. For follow-up on this see: Deposition of Jonathan Palmer, Princeton, October 1, 1777, Prince, *Livingston Papers*, II: 79.

78 Philemon Dickinson to William Livingston, September 29, 1777, *Livingston Papers* [microform], r5 i846.

79 Philemon Dickinson to Livingston, October 18, 1777, *Livingston Papers* [microform], r5, i1011. Previously the Assembly had dealt with a letter from Livingston regarding Dickinson having four field pieces and no artillerymen. *Assembly Votes*, Session beginning August 27, 1776, 194. On October 10 an act had been passed for raising several

companies of militia artillery and two companies of militia horse. One company of each would be raised in Hunterdon. Cushing, First Laws, 30.

80 Jabez Ashmore PF W5647.

81 Philemon Dickinson to Livingston, December 7, 1777, *Livingston Papers* [microform], r6, i442.

82 Matthew Clunn, Joseph's brother, apparently rented the Ship & Castle and applied for a tavern license on May 8, 1777. He died not long after and his widow, Mary Clunn, applied for a license to operate the Ship & Castle. She renewed in May 1779. On both her applications, Joseph Clunn was one of the subscribers recommending her. Applications of both Matthew and Mary Clunn are found in Hunterdon County Tavern Licenses. Some sources give John Clunn operating the Alexander the Great Tavern. THS, Trenton, 322; Toothman, *Trenton 1719-1779*, 270.

83 Armes, *Nancy Shippen Journal*, 36-40.

84 Ibid., 40-42.

85 George Washington to Philemon Dickinson, Head Quarters, October 1, 1777; George Washington to Deputy Quartermaster General Jonathan Mifflin, Head Quarters, October 1, 1777, *GWPLOC*.

86 George Washington to William Livingston, October 1, 1777, *GWPLOC*.

87 William Livingston to George Washington from Princeton 5 October 1777, Prince, *Livingston Papers*, II: 86; See also: William Livingston to George Washington, Princeton, October 5, 1777; October 6, 1777, George Washington to William Livingston; October 7, 1777, George Washington to Board of War, *GWPLOC* for follow-up.

88 Col Jonathan Mifflin to Col Clement Biddle, October 6, 1777, *PCC*, Letters from George Washington, r168, i152, p93-95 – copy of letter.

89 George Washington to Samuel Smith, Head Quarters, October 1, 1777, *GWPLOC*.

90 *Assembly Votes*, Session beginning October 28, 1777, 32, 33, 35.

91 Tench Tilghman to Benjamin Ayres, October 14, 177, *GWPLOC*; Pennsylvania Supreme Executive Council to William Bradford, December 9, 1777, and Pennsylvania Supreme Executive Council to Commodore John Hazelwood, December 20, 1777, Morgan, ed., *Naval Documents*, X: 689, 763.

92 Gibson, *Dr. Bodo Otto*, 285; Hall, *Trenton Presbyterian Church*, 169; *JCC*, IX: 822.

93 *Assembly Votes*, Session beginning October 28, 1777, 6, 48; *Council Journal*, Session beginning October 28, 1777, 6. On November 3, the Assembly and Council met at Princeton and continued there until adjourning on December 12 to meet February 11, 1778 back at Trenton; *Joint Meeting*, 23.

94 *Assembly Votes*, Session beginning October 28, 1777, 27, 30; *Council of Safety Minutes*, 201.

95 Cushing, *First Laws*, 32.

96 M. Lee Minnis, *The First Virginia Regiment of Foot 1775-1783* (Lovettsville, VA: Willow Bend Books, 1998), 143, 147, 168, 192, 214, 219, 245, 271, 282, 286, 298, 338, 347,406.

97 Muster Roll of Captain Jenkins's Company of the Second Pennsylvania Regiment, NARA 246, Department of Defense, Revolutionary War Rolls, 1775-1783, Record Group 93.

98 November 1, 1777 Return of the Fourth Pennsylvania Regiment in "Continental Line, Fourth Pennsylvania, January 1, 1777-November 3, 1783," *Pennsylvania Archives*, Series 5, II: 1025; NARA M246. Muster rolls, payrolls, strength returns v, and other miscellaneous personnel, pay, and supply records of American Army units, 1775-83. Roll. 0109. Folder: 275 11th Virginia Regiment. Gibson, Dr. Bodo Otto, 146; Gillette, *Army Medical Department*, 80.

99 Muster Rolls of Captain Alexander Mitchell's Company of the Fourth New Jersey Regiment for November 1777, NARA, Department of Defense, Revolutionary War Rolls, 1775-1783, Record Group 93; William Finley PF S34350; Thaddeus Rice PF S35630. These were Thaddeus Rice, a man from Connecticut; William Finley; and, John Woodcock. Finley later claimed to have been in the hospital three months.

100 Wardwell Green (Greene) PF W23161. He returned to Fort Mifflin and was furloughed back to Rhode Island until he was discharged in July 1778; John Dickinson PF 991.

101 Col Lewis Nicola to unknown person, October 2, 1777, *PCC*, Letters from General and other officers, 1776-89, r180, i163, p17.

102 Benjamin Van Cleve to Livingston, October 6, 1777, *Livingston Papers* [microform], r5 i934. Original in NJSA, Department of Education, New Jersey State Library, BAH Collection, Box 4-1a, #55; Return of Sick and Wounded, *PCC*, r102, i78, v20, p113.

103 William Livingston to Hugh James, October 8, 1777, Prince, *Livingston Papers*, II: 87.

104 NJSA, Legislature Series, Inventories of Damages by the British and Americans in New Jersey, 1776-1782, Charles Axford.

105 Hamilton Schuyler, *A History of St. Michael's Church Trenton: In the Diocese of New Jersey from its Foundation in the Year of Our Lord 1703 to 1926* (Princeton: Princeton University Press, 1926), 82; NJSA, Legislature Series, Inventories of Damages by the British and Americans in New Jersey, 1776-1782, Elijah Bond for *St. Michael's Church.*

106 Samuel H. Sullivan to Lewis Nicola, November 7, 1777; James Paxton to Lewis Nicola, *The Papers of George Washington. Revolutionary War Series*, XII: 157-158.

107 *Assembly Votes*, Session beginning October 28, 1777, 27, 30.

108 Gibson, *Dr. Bodo Otto*, 146, 285; George Washington to Jonathan Mifflin, October 1, 1777, *GWPLOC*; William Shippen Jr. to George Washington, December 12, 1777, *GWPLOC*.

Chapter 10

1 Petition of Trenton residents opposing Continental light horse in Trenton, January 2, 1778, Prince, *Livingston Papers*, II: 173; also *GWPLOC*; Washington to William Livingston, December 31, 1777, Prince, *Livingston Papers*, II: 157; also Washington to Pulaski the same day, *GWPLOC*. See also: Leonard Lundin, *Cockpit of the Revolution: The War for Independence in New Jersey* (New York: Octagon Books, 1972 [c1940]), 386-387, for a general description of the difficult situation in New Jersey at the time.

2 Minnis, *First Virginia Regiment*, 147, 214, 370, 404.

3 Richard F. Hixon, *Isaac Collins: A Quaker Printer in 18th Century America* (New Brunswick: Rutgers University Press, 1968), 55, 67+; *Assembly Votes*, Session beginning October 28, 1777, 8-9.

4 Hixon, *Isaac Collins*, 11-16, 23, 32-33, 39-40, 75, 115. John Collins, Isaac Collins, Thomas G. Morton, and Morris Earle. *Reminiscences of Isaac and Rachel (Budd) Collins, with an Account of Some of their Descendants, together with a Genealogy of the Collins Family* (Philadelphia: J.B. Lippincott, 1893), 41. See also the many ads in the *NJG* for items he had for sale at various times. Virtually every issue of the paper has one or more.

5 *Council Journal*, Session beginning October 28, 1777, 38, 78, 84; Hixon, *Isaac Collins*, 76-77; *NJG*, April 23, 1778, 3. Rags provided the fibers for making paper at this time. Wood pulp was introduced later.

6 There is a family tradition in the William Green family, who lived in what is now Ewing Township on the campus of the College of New Jersey, that Continental cavalry were lodged at William's house, and it may well have been at this time. Benjamin Tallmadge to George Washington, January 12, 1778, notes navy men. Prince, *Livingston Papers*, II: 173 – also *GWPLOC*; Mark Adams PF W2896; William Green PF R4271 for comment on house use by light horse. *NJG*, January 21, 1778, 3; *NJG*, January 14, 1778, 4.

7 George Washington, Head Quarters, to Casimir Pulaski, December 31, 1777, *GWPLOC*.

8 Casimir Pulaski, Trenton, to George Washington, January 20, 1778, *GWPLOC*; Armes, *Nancy Shippen Journal*, 62. "Mr. Barclay" was probably Thomas Barclay a well-known political figure in Philadelphia on the Pennsylvania Navy Board. Just how he could help with the Pulaski situation is unclear.

9 Minutes of the Pennsylvania Supreme Executive Council, Lancaster, April 23, 1778, Morgan, *Naval Documents*, XII: 174-76.

10 Adams had served in the Maryland Continental Line before being drafted into the row galleys and after his First Hunterdon tours he served on privateers until his ship was captured and he was a prisoner in England until the war ended. Mark Adams PF W2896.

11 William Livingston, Trenton, to George Washington, March 18, 1778, Prince, *Livingston Papers*, II: 263. Benjamin Thompson, Trenton, to Henry E. Lutterloh, February 6, 1778, *PCC*, Letters and papers relative to the Quartermaster's Department, 1777-84, r199, i192, p209.

12 George Washington to General Pulaski, December 31, 1777, *GWPLOC*; *NJG*, March 4, 1778, 3; NJSA, Council of Safety, *Council of Safety Minutes, 18 March 1777 – 8 October 1778*, 215, 303, 306, 308; NJSA, Revolutionary War Mss #4193.

13 NJSA, Revolutionary War Mss #5093 - Peter Gordon to Moore Furman, October 24, 1778. Gordon was also Hunt's brother in law.

14 *NJG*, April 23, 1778, 3; *NJG*, June 3, 1778, 3.

15 *NJG*, April 23, 1778, 4; Casimir Pulaski to George Washington, November 23, 1777, *GWPLOC*. Why he was listed as major in the ad is unclear since he served as a dragoon captain in the Legion.

16 NJSA, Council of Safety, *Council of Safety Minutes, 18 March 1777 – 8 October 1778*, 258, 263. It doesn't say which mill but probably Trenton Mills

17 *Assembly Votes*, Session beginning October 28, 1777, 63; Council concurred – *Council Journal*, Session beginning October 28, 1777, 32.

18 *Assembly Votes*, Session beginning October 27, 1778, 45. Council concurred December 7 - *Council Journal*, Session beginning October 27, 1778, 26.

19 January 30, 1778 – Thomas Jones, camp near Valley Forge, - Return of the names of the Assistant Commissaries of Issues at the several Posts & Magazines in the Middle Department, *PCC*, Letters and papers relative to the quartermaster's department, 1777-84, r199, i192, p457.

20 Unknown date – possibly 1778 - return of ovens in baker master's department, *PCC*, Letters and papers relative to the Quartermaster's Department, 1777-84, r199, i192, p449.

21 *Council of Safety Minutes*, 128.

22 Tench Tilghman, Trenton, to George Washington, February 19, 1778; Anthony Wayne, Mount Holly, to George Washington, February 26, 1778; George Washington to Anthony Wayne, February 28, 1778, *GWPLOC*.

23 Tench Tilghman, Trenton, to George Washington, February 19, 1778, *GWPLOC*; Lundin, *Cockpit*, 382.

24 Livingston, Trenton, to the Assembly, February 16, 1778, Prince, *Livingston Papers*, II: 230-231; William Livingston to George Washington, February 16, 1778, *GWPLOC*.

25 Tench Tilghman, Trenton, to George Washington, February 19, 1778, *GWPLOC*.

26 Charles Petit, Trenton, to Francis Dana, Pres of Congress, March 12, 1778, *PCC*, Quartermaster's Department letters, r199, i192, p187; Hunter, *Fish and Ships*, 16.

27 NJSA, Governor's Privy Council, Minutes, 1777-1845, 24.

28 *Council of Safety Minutes*, March 22, 1778.

29 Cushing, *First Laws*, 35-40. This act was similar to the various British quartering acts which tried to avoid quartering troops in private homes. Lack of public buildings in the colonies led to using private homes, as had happened at Trenton, and led to the petitions to build barracks, including the one at Trenton.

30 Samuel H. Sullivan Memorial to Congress, July 31, 1778, *PCC*, Memorials addressed to Congress, 1775-88, r52, i41, p52.

31 Peter Gordon PF S28743. It is interesting that his pension file indicates there is no documentary record giving his exact dates of office as quarter master and he does not have much to say about his service, attributing this to his aging memory. As indicated in this book, he was obviously quite active as quartermaster.

32 *NJG*, February 25, 1778, 4; March 18, 1778, 4; William Livingston, Trenton, to the Assembly, February 16, 1778, Prince, *Livingston Papers*, II: 230-231; William Livingston to George Washington, February 16, 1778, *GWPLOC*; *Assembly Votes*, Session beginning October 28, 1777, 54; *Council Journals*, Session beginning October 28, 1777, 28-29; *Council of Safety Minutes*, February 17-18, 1778, 205.

33 Proclamation from Trenton, March 9, 1778, Prince, *Livingston Papers*, II, 247-248, also published in *NJG*, March 18, 1778, 1, 4. On page four was another notice seeking three year recruits to drive wagons for the Continental army.

34 *Council of Safety Minutes*, March 10, 1778, 213.

35 Clement Biddle, Moore Hall, January 30, 1778, Return of persons employ'd in the Forage Department at the Magazines under my direction & with the army, *PCC*, Letters and

papers relative to the quartermaster's department, 1777-84, r199, i192, p379; Clement Biddle, Moore Hall, February 9, 1778, Plan for Magazines of Forage in the Middle Department, *PCC*, Letters and papers relative to the Quartermaster's Department, 1777-84, r199, i192, p373-377. See: NJSA, Revolutionary War Mss #4428 for an example of the monthly reports.

36 Nathanael Greene, Valley Forge, to Col Clement Biddle, March 30, 1778, Showman, *Greene Papers*, II: 327.

37 *NJG*, May 6, 1778, 3.

38 William Livingston to the Assembly, May 29, 1778, Prince, *Livingston Papers*, II: 345; *Assembly Votes*, Session October 28, 1777, 127, 149, 150, 156; *Council Journal*, Session October 28, 1777, 76, 79, 80, 85; *Assembly Votes*, Session October 28, 1777, 87-88.

39 *Council of Safety Minutes*, February 28, 1778, 208-209; *Assembly Votes*, Session beginning October 28, 1777, 71.

40 Militia companies were divided into several classes and classes could be called out rather than the full company.

41 David A. Bernstein, ed., *New Jersey Archives*, Third Series (Trenton: New Jersey State Library, 1974), I: 63. Also Minutes of the Governor's Privy Council, 1777- 1845, NJSA, p19; Benjamin Blackwell PF W839 - John Stevens statement; William Houghton PF W19816; Thomas Leonard PF W3098; Asher Hart PF S2283; *Council of Safety Minutes*, April 1, 1778, 221-222; *Assembly Votes*, Session beginning October 28, 1777, 94.

42 For example see *NJG*, March 4, 1778, 3 for an account in the Trenton news of a British foray into Bucks County that showed the need for militia ferry guards. Stephen Hart PF S2257; Jonathan Smith PF S31380 – supporting statement of Philip Smith.

43 Bernstein, *New Jersey Archives*, Third Series, I: 71-72; William Livingston to George Washington, March 22, 1778; Joseph Ellis to William Livingston, March 23, 1778, Prince, *Livingston Papers*, II: 268, 270. Ellis had requested help on February 28 and the Privy Council had advised the Governor to order out four classes of militia from a number of regiments, including the First Hunterdon. See: NJSA, Governor's Privy Council Minutes, 1777-1845, 20.

44 Israel Hunt PF S1024; Gershom Herin PF S22299; NJSA, Auditor's Book B, 183-187; Auditor's Book C, 51, 54; Edward Hart PF W7628; Israel Hunt PF S1024.

45 *Council of Safety Minutes*, April 1, 221; NJSA, Revolutionary War Mss #3959; Asa Adams PF W133 – deposition of Robert Carson.

46 John V.K. Taylor PF W9512; *Assembly Votes*, Session beginning October 28, 1777, 104.

47 NJSA, Court of Common Pleas for Hunterdon May Term Minutes 1778.

48 Hixon, *Isaac Collins*, 83-84, 136. His wife and children were admitted to the Chesterfield Meeting near Trenton, unaffected by his actions. In 1787 he was readmitted to the Burlington Meeting after acknowledging "his error in having acted inconsistently with our peaceable Testimony" by his actions during the war.

49 *Assembly Votes*, Session beginning October 28, 1777, 80-81; NJSA, Revolutionary War Mss #3613, 3614. Alcott is listed as in the service on the 1779 tax list for Trenton.

50 *Assembly Votes*, Session beginning October 28, 1777, 48, 59; *Council Journal*, Session beginning October 28, 1777, 27-28.

51 NJSA, Legislature, Petitions, Resolutions, Transactions, Accounts and Misc papers 1700-1845, #89 – Report of private committee respecting papers in the hands of [Samuel] Tucker, 1778

52 *Council of Safety Minutes*, March 10, 1778, 213.

53 *Council of Safety Minutes*, February 26, 1778, 207; March 1, 1778, 209.

54 *Council of Safety Minutes*, April 6, 28, 223; *Assembly Votes*, Session beginning October 28, 1777, 102.

55 *Assembly Votes*, Session beginning October 28, 1777, 107, 109, 112; *Council Journal*, Session beginning October 28, 1777, 60, 62-63.

56 Philemon Dickinson, Trenton, to George Washington, May 9, 1778, *GWPLOC*. Dickson believed the British force was about 1000 men, mostly light infantry, and two field pieces.

See also the report of Major John Maitland who led the British forces. Report dated May 11, 1778, Morgan, *Naval Documents*, XII: 331-332.

57 Benjamin Titus PF W6287. Douglas owned the house where Washington had held his council of war the night before the battle of Princeton. He was adjutant for the First Burlington County Regiment of militia. Jabez Ashmore PF W5647 – supporting statement of Alexander Douglas; Alexander Douglas PF S994; John Borrows PF S22134; Isaiah Yard PF S1156 – supporting statement of James Bowen; William Cannon PF W842 – second supporting statement of Jabez Ashmore. Isaiah Yard was lieutenant in the artillery company and later became its captain. John Bell PF S22642; John Clutch PF S2126.

58 *NJG*, May 20, 1778, 3.

59 George Washington, Valley Forge, to Nathanael Greene, May 17, 1778, Showman, *Greene Papers*, II: 393. See *NJG*, May 20, 1778, 3 in the column of news from Trenton for one of the letters giving intelligence that the British were preparing to leave. Amos Peters PF S1076; Richard Holcomb PF S1020.

60 Philemon Dickinson, *Order Book Major General Philemon Dickinson Commanding the New Jersey Militia, 1777-1778*, NJSA, Department of Defense, Adjutant General's Officer (Revolutionary War), Copies of Miscellaneous Records, 1774-1837, Box 1, item 27, 36-38. Hessian Major Baurmeister recorded in his diary the intelligence that Philemon Dickinson's militia was gathering near Trenton, "though in small numbers and unwillingly." Uhlendorf, *Baurmeister Letters and Journal*, 74 – May 18-June11, 1778.

61 Dickinson, *Order Book*, 37. Cartridges consisted of a paper tube containing gunpowder and a musket ball.

62 Dickinson, *Order Book*, 37-40. The lack of muskets was frequently noted throughout the war. Not everyone could afford to purchase one and wear and tear of constant call outs, sharing of muskets, etc. meant losses and damage without replacements available.

63 Dickinson, *Order Book*, 39.

64 The Cheveaux de Frize was a series of sharpened poles placed underwater in the Delaware River as a barrier against the British fleet.

65 Armes, *Nancy Shippen Journal*, 64. Sometime after the British left Philadelphia Nancy was reunited with her mother there. How much longer she attended Mrs. Rogers' school is unclear.

66 *NJG*, June 10, 1778, 3; Dickinson, *Order Book*, 40-41.

67 Dickinson, *Order Book*, 41.

68 Dickinson, *Order Book*, 41-42; *Assembly Votes*, Session beginning October 28, 1777, 149-150; *Council Journal*, Session beginning October 28, 1777, 81.

69 Dickinson, *Order Book*, 42.

70 Warning out was the word of mouth alert chain for calling men out for militia service. It let men know they were needed and when and where to join their company.

71 Isaac Quigley PF R8550.

72 Jabez Ashmore PF W5647 and supporting deposition of Alexander Douglas who was in the First Burlington Regiment and from Nottingham; John Lattimer PF S4507; David Van Norden PF W6341; Isaiah Yard PF S1156; William Robinson PF W4572; Peter Sorter PF S23933.

73 *NJG*, June 24 actually July 1, 1778, 2-3. Isaac Collins noted on his paper that "The other side of this paper having been printed off last week, previous to the alarm, and thereby prevented from being completed, sufficiently accounts for the date in the title page."

74 John Burrows PF S22134; Isaac Quigley PF R8550.

75 Dr. Wilson Waters PF S7805. He had served previously under Dr. Bodo Otto at the Yellow Springs, Pennsylvania hospital. Gideon Viah PF S6311. Gillette, *Army Medical Department*, 99.

76 Richard F. Hixon, *The Press in Revolutionary New Jersey* (Trenton: New Jersey Historical Commission, 1975), 15, 100, *NJG*, June 24 [July 1], 1778, 3

77 Petition of Patrick Colvin, Trenton, to Congress, July 24, 1778, *PCC*, Petitions addressed to Congress, 1775-89, r53, i42, p48 - notation on reverse says "prayer granted."

78 *NJG*, September 16, 1778, 3.

79 *NJG*, July 22, 1778, 3; July 17, 1778, 3; July 29, 1778, 3; August 12, 1778, 3; August 26, 1778, 3; September 9, 1778, 3; September 16, 1778, 3.

80 George Washington, Middle Brook, to William Lee Davidson of the Third North Carolina Regiment, December 19, 1778, *GWPLOC*.

81 *NJG*, December 23, 1778, 3.

82 *NJG*, September 2, 1778, 3; September 16, 1778, 3.

83 *NJG*, January 14, 1778, 3; February 25, 1778, 4; February 11, 1778, 3; March 4, 1778, 3.

84 *Council of Safety Minutes*, 308-309.

85 *NJG*, August 19, 1778, 3; November 25, 1778, 3. NJSA, Court of Common Pleas for Hunterdon, August Term Minutes 1778; NJSA, Department of Education, New Jersey State Library, BAH-Inquisition, Box 1-28, #90, 92, 93, 94, 95, 96, 97, 98, 100; *NJG*, August 19, 1778, 3 and August 26, 1778, 4. An additional inquisition against two former Trenton residents took place on May 3, 1779 at John Larrison's tavern in Hopewell, when John Tabor Kemp and wife Grace were tried for going to the enemy and taking refuge sometime in April 1776, and remaining with them.

86 *Council Journal*, Session beginning October 28, 1777, 103, 106-107. For background on this case see: *Assembly Votes*, Session beginning October 28, 1777, 111, 149-152. Also accused were Daniel Hunt and Edward Hunt two other justices of the peace.

87 *Council Journal*, Session beginning October 27, 1778, 9, 10, 12-13; *Joint Meeting*, 29; Cushing, *First Laws*, 61; *NJG*, November 25, 1778, 3.

88 *NJG*, April 8, 1778, 3. They also offered the thirteen acre estate known as Dowsdale for sale. It was a small farm with two dwelling houses located near Trenton on the road to Hopewell.

89 *Council of Safety Minutes*, September 19 and 22, 1778, 282-283.

90 George Washington to Casimir Pulaski, September 29, 1778, *GWPLOC*. See: Todd W. Braisted, *Grand Forage 1778: The Battleground Around New York City* (Yardley: Westholme, 2016), 147-155 for more on his actions. Peter Gordon mentioned Pulaski left shortly after October 7 in a letter to Moore Furman dated October 7, NJSA, Revolutionary War Mss #5087.

91 *NJG*, October 28, 1778, 3.

92 Count Pulaski, Trenton, to Henry Laurens, Pres of Congress, October 24, 1778, *PCC*, Letters from General Officers and the Count d'Estaing, 177-86, r181, i164, p25; Count Pulaski, Little Egg Harbor, to Continental Congress, October 21,1778, Ibid.. His letter was referred to the Board of War which ordered sixty blankets.

93 *NJG*, November 4, 1778, 3; November 18, 1778, 3. The troopers from Baylor's regiment had been involved in the notorious bayonet attack at Tappan. For an excellent account of that encounter see: Braisted, Grand Forage 1778, 99-112.

94 Nicholas Belleville PF R728 – especially affidavit of Mary Yard; Hall, *Trenton Presbyterian Church*, 428-431; Stephen Wickes, History of Medicine in New Jersey, and of its Medical Men, From the Obituary by Dr. F.A. Ewing, *Emporium and True American*, December 24, 1831, 3. Mary Yard referred to the barracks as White Hall. After the war parts of the barracks were a coat of stucco and it began to be referred to as White Hall.

95 Hugh Runyon, Trenton, to ?, July 5, 1778, *DeCoppet (Andre) Collection of Historical Manuscripts*; Office of Communications Records, Box 25, Folder 8; Princeton University Archives, Department of Rare Books and Special Collections, Princeton University Library, Box 4, Folder 21.

96 Peter Gordon to Moore Furman, July 12, 1778, NJSA Revolutionary War Mss #5075. Unfortunately, the details of this story have not survived.

97 Peter Gordon to Moore Furman, July 12, 1778, NJSA Revolutionary War Mss #5075

98 Peter Gordon to Moore Furman, July 28, 1778, NJSA, Revolutionary War Mss #5078

99 Peter Gordon to Moore Furman, July 31, 1778, September 1, 1778, NJSA, Revolutionary War Mss #5079, #5083.

100 Clement Biddle to Charles Pettit, September 6, 1778; Moore Furman, Pittstown, to Joseph Reed, October 23, 1778 (delivered by Mr. Coxe), *PCC*, Miscellaneous letters to Congress, 1775-89, r91, i78, p177-179, 185-187; *NJG*, September 23, 1778, 3. Letter to Pettit also: NJSA, Miscellaneous Correspondence, 1739-1941, Box 1.

101 *PCC*, Miscellaneous letters addressed to Congress, 1775-89, r95, i78, p185-87.

102 Moore Furman, Pittstown, to Joseph Reed, October 23, 1778 (delivered by Mr. Coxe), *PCC*, Miscellaneous letters addressed to Congress, 1775-89, r95, i78, p185-87.

103 Peter Gordon to Moore Furman, October 21, 1778, October 24, 1778, NJSA, Revolutionary War Mss #5090, #5093;
104 Moore Furman, Pittstown, to Joseph Reed, October 23, 1778 (delivered by Mr. Coxe), *PCC*, Miscellaneous letters addressed to Congress, 1775-89, r95, i78, p185-87; James Burnside to Moore Furman, October 28, 1778, Sol Feinstone Collection, Mss #1834.
105 Peter Gordon to Moore Furman, November 7, 1778, NJSA, Revolutionary War Mss #5094.
106 Peter Gordon to Moore Furman, November 10, 1778, NJSA, Revolutionary War Mss #5095.
107 Nathanael Greene to Charles Pettit, November 23, 1778; Nathanael Greene, Camp Middlebrook, to Griffin Greene, December 21, 1778; Nathanael Greene, Trenton, to Lord Stirling, December 27, 1778, Showman, *Greene Papers*, III: 81-82, 122-123, 125-126.
108 *NJG*, December 9, 1778, 3. This was the Reverend Caldwell who wife was infamously killed at the Battle of Springfield in 1780.
109 Peter Gordon to Moore Furman, December 4, 1778, (Gordon wrote several letters to Furman that day);Peter Gordon to Moore Furman, December 11, 1778, NJSA, Revolutionary War Mss #5102, #5103, #5105.
110 Peter Gordon to Moore Furman, December 17, 16778, nine at night, NJSA, Revolutionary War Mss #5106.

Chapter 11

1 Moore Furman to John Cox and Charles Pettit, June 29, 1779, *PCC*, Miscellaneous Letters to Congress, 1775-89, r93, i78, p367-69.
2 See: John Ferling, *Almost a Miracle: The American Victory in the War of Independence* (New York: Oxford University Press, 2007), 323.
3 December 31, 1779 – An imperfect return of established hospitals, officers, horses, and wagons necessary for the Medical Department exclusive of the Southern department. Gibson, *Dr. Bodo Otto*, 180. Gillette, *Army Medical Department*, 110.
4 *NJG*, February 10, 1779, 3; March 31, 1779, 3; Ferling, *Miracle*, 346-347.
5 Beatty, *Journal*, 17.
6 *NJG*, April 7, 1779, 3; April 28, 1779, 2. Miralles was a representative from Spain. He died of illness while visiting Washington at Morristown almost exactly one year later.
7 Nathanael Greene to Washington, Trenton, April 27, 1779 – 7 o'clock in the evening, Showman, *Greene Papers*, III: 433.
8 *NJG*, September 22, 1799, 3.
9 *NJG*, October 6, 1779, 3; Charles Pettit to Nathanael Greene, Philadelphia, September 24, 1779, Showman, *Greene Papers*, IV: 407411.
10 *NJG*, January 13, 1779, 3; August 4, 1779, 3; Arthur Dudley Pierce, *Smugglers' Woods: Jaunts and Journeys in Colonial and Revolutionary New Jersey* (New Brunswick: Rutgers University Press, 1960), 52; Uhlendorf, *Baurmeister Letters and Journal*, 308 – entry for November 8, 1779.
11 Agreement between George Davis of Philadelphia and Peter Gordon QM at Trenton January 1, 1779, NJSA, Revolutionary War Mss, #5092
12 Ferling, *Miracle*, 326; Ephraim Blaine Deputy Commissary General, to John Ladd Howell, from Philadelphia January 4, 1779, Sol Feinstone Collection Mss #094; Peter Gordon to Moore Furman, January 25, 1779, NJSA, Revolutionary War Mss #5108.
13 *NJG*, January 6, 1779, 3; January 13, 1779, 3; January 27, 1779, 3; March 3, 1779, 3. March 2, 1778 was the date the Quartermaster Department reorganized and Nathanael Greene took command from Thomas Mifflin.
14 Peter Gordon to Moore Furman, February 16, 1779, NJSA, Revolutionary War Mss #5111.
15 Peter Gordon to Moore Furman, February 25, 1779, NJSA, Revolutionary War Mss #5113.
16 Peter Gordon to Moore Furman, February 16, 1779, February 20, 1779, NJSA, Revolutionary War Mss #5109, #512.
17 Ibid.
18 Peter Gordon to Moore Furman, February 20, 1779, NJSA, Revolutionary War Mss #5112.
19 Samuel Tucker to John Hart, February 15, 1779, William Churchill Houston Papers, Box

4 Folder 4, Princeton University Library Special Collections. Hart at this time was ill at home in Hopewell and would die in just a few months. The tone of Tucker's letter is very friendly and he signs it "I am your assured friend."

20 *Trenton Minutes*, 41-45.

21 *NJG*, February 24, 1779, 3. Daniel Coxe lost a number of other parcels of land outside Trenton. For example, see: NJSA, Legislature, Petitions, Resolutions, Transactions, Accounts and Misc papers 1700-1845 concerning his 500 acre Bellmont Farm in Hopewell Township. #10 – Petition of Hunterdon County Commissioners of Forfeited Estates to the Legislature at Trenton April 21, 1779.

22 AO13, bundle 92.

23 Nathanael Greene to George Washington, April 26, 1779, Showman, *Greene Papers*, III: 429-430.

24 Moore Furman, Trenton, to Nathanael Greene, May 7, 1779, Moore Furman, *The Letters of Moore Furman: Deputy Quarter-Master General of New Jersey in the Revolution* (New York: New Jersey Society of the Colonial Dames, 1912), 3-4. For more on the money problems see: Ferling, *Miracle*, 348-356.

25 Moore Furman, Pittstown, to Nathanael Greene(?), May 10, 1779, Furman, *Letters*, 5. Furman Yard of Trenton was serving as Q.M. at Pittstown - *NJG*, May 26, 1779, 3.

26 Peter Gordon to Moore Furman, May 25, 17789, NJSA, Revolutionary War Mss #5036.

27 *NJG*, April 21, 1779, 3; May 26, 1779, 3.

28 George Washington to William Livingston, May 4, 1779, *GWPLOC*.

29 William Livingston, Trenton, to George Washington, May 8, 1779, Prince, *Livingston Papers*, III: 84-85.

30 William Livingston, Trenton, to John Neilson, May 13, 1779, *Livingston Papers* [microform], r9, i566; William Livingston, Trenton, to John Neilson, May 18, 1779, Prince, *Livingston Papers*, III: 92.

31 William Livingston, Trenton, to John Neilson, May 26, 1779, *Livingston Papers* [microform], r9, i660.

32 John Neilson to William Livingston, May 30, 1779, Prince, *Livingston Papers*, III: 100-101.

33 Minnis, *First Virginia Regiment*, 68, 71, 163, 180-181, 253, 366.

34 *Council Journal*, Session beginning October 27, 1778, 35, 82, 83, 100; *Assembly Votes*, Session beginning October 27, 1778, 69-70, 95, 98, 100, 115, 134, 156, 161, 163, 167-169, 170-171, 176, 178, 207; *Joint Meeting*, 30, 31.

35 *NJG*, June 9, 1779, 3.

36 Jabez Ashmore PF W5647. Including deposition of Alexander Douglass. During the remainder of the war he served as a wagoner under Major Peter Gordon at Trenton. When Asmore enlisted, Runyon was quartermaster at Bristol.

37 *NJG*, June 9, 1779, 3.

38 *Assembly Votes*, Session beginning October 27, 1778, 154.

39 Peter Gordon to Moore Furman, June 6, 1779, NJSA, Revolutionary War Mss #5038.

40 Moore Furman, Pittstown, to Nathanael Greene, June 9, 1779, Furman, *Letters*, 10.

41 Peter Gordon to Moore Furman, June 9, 1779, NJSA, Revolutionary War Mss #5040.

42 Nathanael Greene to Colonel John Cox, June 13, 1779, Showman, *Greene Papers*, IV: 150-151.

43 William Livingston to the Assembly, 24 April 1779 and to George Washington, April 24, 1779, Prince, *Livingston Papers*, III: 69.

44 *Assembly Votes*, Session beginning October 27, 1778, 119, 123, 134; Cushing, *First Laws*, 77.

45 Nathanael Greene to John Cox, July 29, 1779, *PCC*, Letters from Nathanael Greene, r192, i173, p9.

46 David Pinkerton to W.C. Houston & J. Mott, July 29, 1779, NJSA, Department of Education, New Jersey State Library, BAH, box 41a, Rev War Docs, #64.

47 Peter Gordon to Moore Furman, June 16, 1779, NJSA, Revolutionary War Mss #5043.

48 Return of the Schooners, Boats, &c in the Boat Department – Benjamin Eyre, B.D., to Nathanael Greene, July 31, 1779, *PCC*, Letters from Nathaniel Greene, r192, i173, p179. Hessian Baurmeister commented on these boats also. Uhlendorf, *Baurmeister Letters and Journal*, 297. August 27, 1779 - "The flatboats built in Philadelphia were taken up the river as far as Trenton, and thence transported to the army on wagons, while the boats built on the Raritan last spring lie at Elizabethtown."

49 Peter Gordon to Moore Furman, July 14, 1779, July 16, 1779, NJSA, Revolutionary War Mss #5047, #5048.
50 *NJG*, July 28, 1779, 3.
51 *NJG*, August 11, 1779, 3, August 25, 1779, 3.
52 Moore Furman to Stephen Lowrey, August 29, 1779, Furman, *Letters*, 15.
53 Gov. Johnson to Captain Edward Gale, Annapolis, September 16, 1779, William Hand Browne, ed., *Archives of Maryland: Journal and Correspondence of the Council of Maryland, April 1, 1778 – October 26, 1779* (Baltimore: Maryland Historical Society, 1901), XXI: 527.
54 *NJG*, September 1, 1779, 3; Department of Defense, Adjutant General's Officer (RevWar), Quartermaster and Commissary General Records 1776-1789, Box 1, #1 – Receipt of William Hight to David Olden of payment for carting wood, September 8, 1779.
55 Charles Pettit to Pres of Congress, October 20, 1779, *PCC*, Letters and Papers relative to the Quartermaster's Department, 1777-84, r199, i192, p253. The assessor was from Nottingham Township since Cox owned the Bloomsbury estate there.
56 Peter Gordon to Moore Furman, August 14, 1779, NJSA, Revolutionary War Mss #5051.
57 Peter Gordon to Moore Furman, August 26, 1779, NJSA, Revolutionary War Mss #5055.
58 Peter Gordon to Moore Furman, August 14, 1779, August 17, 1779, August 26, 1779, NJSA, Revolutionary War Mss #5073, #5052, #5054.
59 Moore Furman to ?, October 19, 1779, October 27, 1779, Furman, Letters, 28, 30.
60 Owen Biddle to Charles Pettit, October 25, 1779, *PCC*, Miscellaneous letters addressed to Congress, 1775-89, r91, i78, p379.
61 Petition of wagon masters in Continental service to Moore Furman DQMG for NJ. November 3, 1779 from Trenton, NJSA, Revolutionary War Mss #5943.
62 Estimate of Hay in New Jersey, October 10, 1779, *PCC*, Letters from Nathaniel Greene, r192, i173, p89; Moore Furman to ?, October 18, 1779, Furman, *Letters*, 24.
63 NJSA, Hunterdon County Tavern Licenses.
64 Hixon, *Isaac Collins*, 95; *NJG*, October 27, 1779, 2; *Council Journal*, Session beginning October 26, 1779, 6-7, 11; *Assembly Votes*, Session beginning October 26, 1779, 8. See also: NJSA mss, Legislature, Petitions, Resolutions, Transactions, Accounts and Misc papers 1700-1845, #66 – Resolution of Assembly concerning article printed in *NJG*, October 29, 1779.
65 *NJG*, December 1, 1779, 3. Washington had been wounded at Trenton on December 26, 1776.
66 Peter Gordon to Moore Furman, November 3, 1779, November 12, 1779, NJSA, Revolutionary War Mss #5062, #5064.
67 Moore Furman to ?, November 22, 1779, Furman, *Letters*, 38-40. See also: *Assembly Votes*, Session beginning October 26, 1779, 31, for notice that he attended and gave his message.
68 Moore Furman to ?, November 27, 1779, Furman, *Letters*, 41.
69 Isaac Quigley PF R8550; *NJG*, November 10, 1779, 3.
70 Nathanael Greene to Moore Furman, November 15, 1779, *PCC*, Letters from Nathanael Greene, r192, i173, p81.
71 Nathanael Greene to James Abeel, November 15, 1779, *PCC*, Letters from Nathanael Greene, r193, i173, p13.
72 *Assembly Votes*, Session beginning October 26, 1779, 10, 18-19, 26; *Council Journal*, Session beginning October 26, 1779, 9, 10; *Joint Meeting*, 32. It appears the legislature continued at Mount Holly for the rest of session until December 25.
73 NJSA, BAH, Box 41a, Revolutionary War Documents, #80; Moore Furman to Nathanael Greene, Trenton, November 22, 1779, Showman, *Greene Papers*, V: 107.
74 Nathanael Greene to Moore Furman, December 20, 1779, NJSA, Moore Furman Letter Book, Moore Furman Correspondence, 1778-1800; Beatty, Journal, 18.
75 Peter Gordon to Moore Furman, no date (page one missing), NJSA, Revolutionary War Mss #5066.
76 George Washington to John Jay, September 30, 1779, *PCC*, Letters from General George Washington, r170, i152, p57-59; John Hancock to George Washington, October 5, 1779; Hancock to Colonel Clarke of North Carolina Troops, October 5, 1779; John Hancock to George Washington, October 6, 1779, *PCC*, Letter Books of the President of Congress, 1775-87, r24, i14, p203-204; *NJG*, December 8, 1779, 3.
77 Peter Gordon to Moore Furman, December 4, 1779, NJSA, Revolutionary War Mss #5067.

78 Peter Gordon to Moore Furman, December 12, 1779, NJSA, Revolutionary War Mss #5068; William Dollar PF W22965.
79 William Woodford to Samuel Huntington, Pres of Congress, December 13, 1779, *PCC*, Miscellaneous letters addressed to Congress, 1775-89, r104, i78, p145; Nathanael Greene to Moore Furman, December 9, 1779, *PCC*, Letters of Nathanael Greene, r193, i173, p195.
80 Moore Furman to Nathanael Greene, December 20, 1779; Moore Furman to Clement Biddle, December 20, 1779; Moore Furman to Colonel John Mitchell, December 21, 1779, Furman, *Letters*, 46-48.
81 William Woodford to George Washington, December 28, 1779, *GWPLOC*.
82 December 29, 1779, 3; George Washington to Samuel Huntington, December 30, 1779, *PCC*, Letters from George Washington, r170, i152, p279-80; George Washington to William Woodford, December 24, 1779, *GWPLOC*.
83 Moore Furman to Rev. James Caldwell, December 31, 1779, Furman, *Letters*, 50-51.
84 *NJG*, December 22, 1779, 3; Moore Furman to John I. Schanck, December 28, 1779; Moore Furman to Daniel Marsh, December 31, 1779, Furman, *Letters*, 48-49.
85 Nathanael Greene to Moore Furman, December 10, 1779, *PCC*, Letters of Nathanael Greene, r193, i173, p203; Peter Gordon to Moore Furman, December 4, 1779, December 12, 1779, NJSA, Revolutionary War Mss #5067, #5068.
86 William Livingston to Silvanus Seely, November 26, 1779; December 7, 1779, Prince, *Livingston Papers*, III: 233, 255. See also: Sylvanus Seely, *The Diary of Sylvanus Seely*. Morristown National Historical Park [microform] #399, 1768-1790, cabinet 1, drawer 6. The diary entries show that Seely traveled to Trenton a number of times and usually stayed at Joseph Clunn's tavern. They also did some business together.
87 Joseph Reed to William Livingston, December 24, 1779, Prince, *Livingston Papers*, III: 281-282.
88 William Livingston to Rensselaer Williams, December 25, 1779, Prince, *Livingston Papers*, III: 282. Privy Council Minutes for December 1779 do not record a discussion of this matter.
89 William Livingston to Joseph Reed, December 28, 1779, *Livingston Papers* [microform], r10, i909 - also printed in vol 3 of the *Livingston Papers*. Clunn had separately been accused of discouraging desertions from the British from Staten Island. See: Kidder, *A People Harassed and Exhausted*, 311.
90 *NJG*, May 31, 1780, 3.
91 *NJG*, December 15, 1779, 3; *Assembly Votes*, Session beginning October 26, 1779, 56; *Council Journal*, 59; Cushing, First Laws, 102, 221.

Chapter 12

1 Marquis de Chastellux, *Travels in North America in the Years, 1780, 1781 and 1782*, Howard C. Rice, Jr. Trans. (Chapel Hill: The University of North Carolina Press, 1963), I: 127. The tavern sign image appears to have been borrowed from the Continental sixdollar bill that had a beaver gnawing down a tree with the same motto (291-292). The Royal Oak Tavern was located on premises formerly owned by Abraham Cottnam. Williams had first rented and then purchased it from Cottnam's executors in April 1779.
2 *NJG*, April 19, 1780, 3. Miralles died while at Morristown on April 28. *NJG*, September 20, 1780, 3; *NJG*, December 6, 1780, 3; Blanco, Physician of the American Revolution, 202. A reorganization of the hospital department was made September 8, but no changes were made to the general hospitals at several locations, including Trenton.
3 *NJG*, January 12, 1780, 3; February 2, 1780, 3. The original notice by Cowell was also repeated in this issue.
4 *NJG*, February 23, 1780, 3.
5 *NJG*, March 1, 1780, 3.
6 *NJG*, March 8, 1780, 4.
7 *Minutes of Trenton*, 45-46.
8 *NJG*, June 25, 1783, 3.
9 *Chesterfield Monthly Minutes*, October 7, 1779, 616; January 6, 1780, 618, 619; February 3, 1780, 620-623.

10 *NJG*, January 19, 1780, 3.
11 George Washington to the New Jersey Magistrates, January 8, 1780, *GWPLOC*.; See also: Furman, *Letters*, 51-53.
12 Moore Furman to Charles Petit, January 26, 1780, Furman, *Letters*, 55-56; Moore Furman to Nathanael Greene, January 28, 1780, *PCC*, r193, i173, p51.
13 John Mitchell to Nathanael Greene, January 2, 1780, *PCC*, r193, i173, p217; Charles Pettit to Nathanael Greene, January 12, 1780, *PCC*, r193, i173, p249; Moore Furman to Charles Pettit, January 26, 1780, Furman, *Letters*, 55-56; Moore Furman to Nathanael Greene, February 9, 1780, *PCC*, r193, i173, p57.
14 Moore Furman to Nathanael Greene, January 28, 1780, *PCC*, r193, i173, 51.
15 Moore Furman to Nathanael Greene, January 6, 1780, Furman, *Letters*, 54; *PCC*, r193, i173, p47; Moore Furman to Nathanael Greene, February 19, 1780, *PCC*, r193, i173, p61. See also: *Council Journal*, Session beginning October 26, 1779, 54+, and *Assembly Votes*, Session beginning October 26, 1780, 133+.
16 Moore Furman to Nathanael Greene, February 9, 1780; Moore Furman to John Cox, February 16, 1780; Moore Furman to Nathanael Greene, February 19, 1780, *PCC*, r193, i173, p57, 35, 61; Clement Biddle to Nathanael Greene, February 24, 1780, *PCC*, r170, i152, p431-434; *Assembly Votes*, Session beginning October 26, 1779, 137, 143.
17 Moore Furman to Nathanael Greene, February 9, 1780, *PCC*, Letters from Nathanael Greene, r193, i173, p57. A pipe, also called a butt, of wine held about 126 gallons, so two pipes would be 252 gallons.
18 *NJG*, February 9, 1780, 3. While the advertisement said Trenton, her tavern was at Trenton Landing in Nottingham.
19 *NJG*, February 16, 1780, 3; *NJG*, March 15, 1780, 3. Andrew Lytle, Lieutenant of 5th PA Regt at Philadelphia to Major Peter Gordon, A.D. QMG at Trenton, March 23, 1780, Sol Feinstone Collection Mss #837. Lytle had been appointed to take over as distributor of state stores to the Pennsylvania troops. He requested that wagons be ordered to be ready for him when he arrived at Trenton. Lytle knew very little about how much a wagon could carry so he left it up to Gordon to decide how many to procure. From this, it seems that Gordon was still functioning as ADQM. at Trenton. For follow-up on the need for people to settle accounts see: *NJG*, April 19, 1780, 4; Moore Furman to Nathanael Greene, February 19, 1780, *PCC*, Letters from Nathanael Greene, r193, i173, p61.
20 *Assembly Votes*, Session beginning October 26, 1779, 152, 163.
21 Moore Furman to Charles Pettit, March 29, 1780, Furman, *Letters*, 59.
22 *NJG*, February 23, 1780, 3; May 24, 1780, 1; Hixon, *Isaac Collins*, 116.
23 *NJG*, February 16, 1780, 3; *Council Journal*, Session beginning October 26, 1779, 49, 50, 64-65; *Assembly Votes*, Session beginning October 26, 1779, 115-116, 128, 135; *Joint Meeting*, 34; THS, *Trenton 1929*, 709.
24 Cushing, *First Laws*, 119; *Assembly Votes*, Session beginning October 26, 1779, 140, 182; *Council Journal*, Session beginning October 26, 1779, 73; *NJG*, March 22, 1780, 3.
25 *NJG*, April 27, 1780, 3; Timothy Pickering, [jr.] to Henry Hollingsworth, April 19, 1780, Sol Feinstone Collection, Mss #1151. Also: Bernard Christian Steiner, Editor, *Archives of Maryland*, XLIII, (Baltimore: Maryland Historical Society, 1924), 474.
26 *Monthly Men's Meeting at Chesterfield* May 4, 1780, 615, 625-626.
27 Stephen Lowry to Phillip Schuyler and Nathaniel Peabody, April 25, 1780, *PCC*, Miscellaneous Letters Addressed to Congress, 1775-89, r98, i78, p317; Return of the persons employed under me [Stephen Lowry] at the Magazine at this post [Trenton], April 25, 1780, *PCC*, Letters of the Committee to Headquarters, r46, v3 , p372; A Return of the numbers of persons employ'd by James/John Paxton, April 25, 1780, *PCC*, Letters of Committee to Headquarters, r46, v3, p404; Arthur Howell PF W14944 and deposition of Jacob Hall.
28 Return of Persons employed at this post of Trenton in the Quarter Master Generals & Forage Departments - April 1780, *PCC*, Letters of Committee to Headquarters, r46, i39, p405. For receipts signed by Ellet Howell as Quarter Master see: Nicholas Okerson/Okeson

PF S7279; NJSA, Department of Education, New Jersey State Library, BAH, box 4-1a, Revolutionary War Documents, #92. A similar list of persons employed on May 5, 1780 is in Daniel Yard PF W2399 and also receipts and other documents relating to Yard's service in the quartermaster department. Jesse Roscow affidavit in this file gives his service as assistant commissary of hides under Paxton.

29 NJSA, Account of buildings belonging to and rented for the use of the United States in the State of New Jersey, May 6, 1780, Department of Education, New Jersey State Library, BAH, Manuscript Collection 1680s-1970s, Box 41a, Revolutionary War Documents, #89.

30 Council to the Commissioners for Worcester County – April 24, 1780, Steiner, *Archives of Maryland*, XLII: 151; NJSA, Department of Defense, Adjutant General's Office (RevWar), Quartermaster and Commissary General Records 1776-1789, Box 1, #26; NJSA, Department of Defense, Adjutant General's Officer (RevWar), Quartermaster and Commissary General Records 1776-1789, Box 1, #34; Robert Nesbitt to Furman Yard, July 1, 1780, NJSA, Department of Defense, Adjutant General's Office, Copies of Correspondence, 1777-1782, #39.

31 Moore Furman to Thomas Durie, April 4, 1780, Furman, *Letters*, 60-61.

32 Moore Furman to John Mitchell, May 13, 1780, Furman, *Letters*, 63-64; *Assembly Votes*, session beginning October 26, 1779, 200.

33 George Washington to Clement Biddle, May 29, 1780 *GWPLOC*.

34 Moore Furman to Nathanael Greene, May 9, 1780, Furman, *Letters*, 63; *Council Journal*, Session beginning May 10, 1780, 100.

35 NJSA, Hunterdon County Tavern Licenses; *NJG*, May 17, 1780, 3; *Assembly Votes*, Session beginning October 26, 1779, 215, 216, 222.

36 *Assembly Votes*, Session beginning October 26, 1779, 185, 189, 251-252; *Council Journal*, Session beginning May 10, 77-78, 80, 101102, 106; *NJG*, May 10, 1780, 3; May 17, 1780, 3; *Joint Meeting*, 41.

37 Charles Stewart and Ephraim Blaine to George Washington, May 9, 1780, *PCC*, Letters of Committee to Head Quarters, r46, i39, p14; George Washington to President of Congress, May 27, 1780, *PCC*, Letters from General Washington, r170, i152, p579 – 585; Account of James Gamble of the weight of Pork received of Stephen Lowry A.C.I. at Trenton, May 31, 1780, Account of provisions received at Morris Town magazine from Trenton, with a state of deficiencies, *PCC*, Letters to the Committee to Headquarters, r46, i39, p235; Phillip Schuyler to Samuel Huntington, June 17, 1780, *PCC*, Letters from General Schuyler, r173, i153, p527-529.

38 New Jersey General Assembly at Trenton to S. Huntington, June 20, 1780, *PCC*, NJ State Papers, r82, i68, p557-559; *Assembly Votes*, Session beginning October 26, 1779, 251-252; *Council Journal*, Session beginning May 10, 1780, 106; Pennsylvania Council Resolve, June 21, 1780, *PCC*, Pennsylvania State Papers, 1775-91, r83, i69, p227; *NJG*, June 28, 1780, 3.

39 NARA M853, Numbered Record Books, Journal of Military Stores, March 1780 – March 1781, r37, v133, p74, 78, 94, 105.

40 *Assembly Votes*, Session beginning October 26, 1779, 231; *Council Journal*, Session beginning May 10, 1780, 97; *NJG*, June 14, 1780, 3.

41 *NJG*, June 14, 1780, 3.

42 Lieutenant James Budden to General Washington, June 26, 1780, *GWPLOC*; *NJG*, June 28, 1780, 3; *Assembly Votes*, Session beginning October 26, 1779, 222; *Council Journal*, Session beginning May 10, 1780, 92.

43 *NJG*, June 28, 1780, 3, July 5, 1780, 3.

44 Abraham Clark to Mrs. Furman, July 11, 1780, NJSA, Department of Education, New Jersey State Library, BAH, box 4-1a, Revolutionary War Documents, #95.

45 Mary Dagworthy to Gen. Washington, July 17, 1780, *GWPLOC*; George Washington to Mary Dagworthy, August 6, 1780, *GWPLOC*. For a detailed article on this effort, see: Catherine Hudak, "The Ladies of Trenton: Women's Political and Public Activism in Revolutionary NJ," *New Jersey Studies: An Interdisciplinary Journal* 1 (2015), 39.

46 Ferling, *Miracle*, 406; Mary Dagworthy to General Washington, December 29, 1780, *GWPLOC*.

47 Moore Furman, at Trenton, to General Greene, July 2, 1780, *PCC*, r22, i11, p327.
48 Dann, *Revolution Remembered*, 154. William Hutchinson statement.
49 *NJG*, August 16, 1780, 3; August 23, 1780, 3; Ephraim Blaine to Gen. Washington, August 15, 1780, *PCC*, Letters from General George Washington, r170, i152, p73.
50 Major W.A. Dorland, "The Second Troop Philadelphia City Cavalry" *Pennsylvania Magazine of History and Biography* 45 (1921), 266-287. See also, Jacob Coxe Parsons, ed., "Extracts from the Diary of Jacob Hiltzheimer of Philadelphia, 1765-1798" (Philadelphia, 1893), 43; *NJG*, August 23, 1780, 3; John Cox to Nathanael Greene, August 7, 1780, Showman, *Greene Papers*, VI: 186-188.
51 *NJG*, September 6, 1780, 2.
52 Edward Giles to Governor Lee, September 19, 1780, Steiner, *Archives of Maryland*, XLV: 110; John Mathews to Samuel Huntington, August 7, 1780, *PCC*, Letter of Committee to Headquarters, r46, i39, p217; Ephraim Blaine to Committee at Headquarters, August 7, 1780, *PCC*, Letters from Colonels, 1776-83, r182, i165, p323; Charles Stewart to George Washington, September 30, 1780, *PCC*, Letters from General George Washington, r170, i152, p207.
53 Charles Stewart to Moore Furman, September 14, 1780, "Two Revolutionary Letters of Col. Charles Stewart," *Proceedings of the New Jersey Historical Society* 39 (1921) New Series VI: 86-89.
54 John Cox to Nathanael Greene, August 7, 1780, Showman, *Greene Papers*, VI: 186-189. Also see: VI: 150-155 for a detailed analysis of why Greene and others quit the quartermaster department.
55 *NJG*, September 27, 1780, 3; November 15, 1780, 4.
56 *NJG*, September 20, 1780, 3; September 13, 1780, 3; John Jemes/James PF S5603. James may have worked as a cooper. In his pension file he claims to have learned the trade, but not as an apprentice.
57 *NJG*, September 13, 1780, 3; *Council Journal*, Session beginning May 10, 1780, 108, 111, 113, 123; *Assembly Votes*, Session beginning October 26, 1779, 255-258, 267, 293; *Joint Meeting*, 41-43.
58 Thomas Carpenter to James Ewing, October 11, 1780, NJSA, Department of Education, New Jersey State Library, BAH, box 4-1a, Revolutionary War Documents, #100; John Neilson to Board of War, October 27, 1780, *PCC*, Letters from Board of War, r161, i148, p217; *Council Journal*, Session beginning October 24, 1780, 7, 8-9; *Assembly Votes*, Session beginning October 24, 1780, 12-13. Neilson's commission and further information about him can be found in his pension application file S4607.
59 *NJG*, September 27, 1780, 3; November 1, 1780, 3. Notice dated October 25.
60 *Council Journal*, Session beginning October 24, 1780, 20-22.
61 *NJG*, October 18, 1780, 3; *Council Journal*, Session beginning October 24, 1780, 5, 8; *Assembly Votes*, Session beginning October 24, 1780, 5, 7, 12; *Pennsylvania Gazette*, October 25, 1780, 2; *Joint Meeting*, 45; Philemon Dickinson and David Brearley were also candidates, but Livingston won handily. Representatives elected were John Witherspoon, Abraham Clark, William Churchill Houston, William Paterson and William Burnett
62 NJSA, Legislature, Petitions, Resolutions, Transactions, Accounts and Misc papers 1700-1845, #97 – Appointment of committee to settle account of Mr. (Samuel) Tucker, late Treasurer of the Provincial Congress of this State. Committee formed December 12, 1780; *Assembly Votes*, Session beginning October 24, 1780, 92.
63 George Washington to John Cadwalader, October 5, 1780, *GWPLOC*. He writes an almost word for word repetition in a letter to George Mason, October 22, 1780, *GWPLOC*.
64 George Washington to Continental Congress War Board, October 25, 1780 *GWPLOC*.

Chapter 13

1 "Warning out" was the process of notifying militiamen of their upcoming active duty, date to report, place to report, etc. It was getting hard to get the men who had been serving

for several years to turn out for the frequent calls. Younger men, especially those just reaching militia age, were more likely to turn out.

2 NJSA, Revolutionary War Mss #671, 672, 697. This story is a modified version of the one appearing in Kidder, A People Harassed and Exhausted, 347-48.

3 *NJG*, January 17, 1781, 3; January 3, 1781, 3.

4 For example, Monsieur De Letombe, Consul General of France for the four New England States passed through Trenton on July 13 on his way to Philadelphia. While in town he delivered some dispatches to Governor Livingston. Continental Congress delegate from New Hampshire, John Sullivan, came to Trenton on Saturday, August 11 from Philadelphia on his way to his home and spent the weekend in Trenton, leaving on Monday. The day Sullivan left for New Hampshire, "the celebrated" Captain John Paul Jones passed through town on his way to the east. *NJG*, July 18, 1781, 3, August 15, 1781, 3.

5 Rev. Samuel Smith to William Livingston January 3, 1781, *Livingston Papers* [microform] r14, i033. Isaac Collins gave a short summary of the entire event in *NJG*, January 17, 1781, 3.

6 John Sullivan to President of Congress, January 9, 1781, Hammond, Sullivan Papers, III: 257. Also in *PCC*, No. 152, vol 9, p461; John Sullivan to George Washington, January 9, 1781, Hammond, Sullivan Papers, III: 258; *NJG*, January 17, 3.

7 *NJG*, January 17, 3.

8 John Sullivan to Gen Washington, January 15, 1781, Hammond, *Sullivan Papers*, III: 265. For more on the mutiny see: John A. Nagy, *Rebellion in the Ranks: Mutinies of the American Revolution* (Yardley: Westholme, 2008), chapters 5-11; Hammond, *Sullivan Papers*, III: 251, 253, 254, 256, 259, 262-265; *PCC*, Letters from General George Washington, r170, i152, p439-441, 447, 455.

9 See pension application abstracts for John Dailey, Fifth Pennsylvania Regiment, Andrew Bird, Tenth Pennsylvania Regiment, Samuel McFarland Third Pennsylvania Regiment, James Ryan First Pennsylvania Regiment, Frederick Stull Second Pennsylvania Regiment, Mathias Littell Twelfth Pennsylvania Regiment, Samuel Auchmutly Third Pennsylvania Regiment, David Solt Fifth Pennsylvania Regiment, and William Howell Eleventh Pennsylvania Regiment. "Abstracts of Pension Applications on File in the Division of Public Records, Pennsylvania State Library," The *Pennsylvania Archives*, Series 5, IV: 517, 518, 522, 545-6, 551, 583. Daniel Welker PF S40669. For an example of a discharge certificate from this episode see: Discharge of David Logan signed by Anthony Wayne at Trenton, January 16, 1781. "This is to certify that the Bearer _____ having served in the ____ Regiment of Pennsylvania during the term of his Enlistment, is now discharged the Service of the United States of America. Given at ___ this ____ Day of ____ 1781. Sol Feinstone Collection, Mss #1647.

10 *PCC*, Miscellaneous papers 1770-89, r72, i59, p197.

11 Dorothy Agans Stratford and Thomas B. Wilson, *Certificates and receipts of Revolutionary New Jersey. Records of New Jersey*, volume II, (Lambertville, NJ: Hunterdon House, 1996), 24, 56-57, 109, 111, 138, 139, 143, 147-148, 158, 160, and others.

12 *Neilson Family Papers*, Rutgers University Libraries, Special Collections and University Archives, Box 2, Folder Neilson Family - Transcripts, copies & miscellany, v.d. He also made payments to a Mrs. Dunham for schooling and in December to Benjamin Coles. Box 2, Folder – Official Papers 1780-1782, Return of persons employed in QMG Department 1 October 1782 at Trenton and Morristown; Box 2, Folder – Neilson Papers Correspondence, etc. 1783-1824, Letter of John Neilson at Trenton to Samuel Hodgdon, January 11, 1783. Letter concerns payment owed to employees of QM Department.

13 *NJG*, October 25, 1780, 3; *NJG*, May 23, 1781, 3; William C. Houston to Gen Sullivan in Congress, February 1, 1781 from Trenton (conveyed by Genl Dickinson), Hammond, Sullivan Papers, III: 278.

14 *NJG*, January 31, 1781, 3.

15 *Assembly Votes*, Session beginning October 24, 1780, 93-96; *Council Journal*, Session beginning October 24, 1780, 59.

16 *Assembly Votes*, Session beginning October 24, 1780, 103, 106. Council concurred on

January 8. *Council Journal*, Session beginning October 24, 1780, 67. His accounts were settled in November 1781. *Assembly Votes*, Session beginning October 23, 1781, 43. NJSA, Misc Departments, Treasury, Revolutionary War era, Auditor's Accounts, Auditor's Book B, 117-118.

17 *Joint Meeting*, 46; Cushing, *First Laws*, 166-181; *Assembly Votes*, Session beginning October 24, 1780, 105-106; *NJG*, January 31, 1781, 3.

18 Samuel Wooley PF R11850, including depositions of Alexander Douglass, Prudence Vanderfrift, and John Morris. Stryker also lists Douglas as adjutant. Stryker, *Trenton and Princeton*, 373.

19 William L. Dayton, *Historical Sketch of the Trenton Academy* (Trenton: 1881), 3-4; *NJG*, December 5, 1781, 3.

20 See: Kidder, *A People Harassed and Exhausted*, 357-361 for a complete discussion of this case.

21 NJSA, Hunterdon County Tavern Licenses; *NJG*, January 16, 1782, 3; February 14, 1781, 3; July 17, 1782, 3.

22 *Minutes of Trenton*, 45-46.

23 *NJG*, March 7, 1781, 3.

24 Ferling, *Miracle*, 494. Ferling compares Greene's campaign decisions to Washington's in November and December 1776 and January 1777.

25 *NJG*, March 14, 1781, 3.

26 *Assembly Votes*, Session beginning May 15, 1781, 21.

27 NJSA, Hunterdon County Tavern Licenses #1207, page 27.

28 Moore Furman to Josiah Hornblower, May 15, 1781, Furman, *Letters*, 64-65.

29 Joseph Phillips to William Livingston, May 13, 1781, Prince, *Livingston Papers*, IV: 193-194.

30 *NJG*, May 30, 1781, 3. In this usage, "Publick" meant those in public service, not the general public.

31 *NJG*, July 25, 1781, 3; Rice, Jr., and Brown, American Campaigns of Rochambeau's Army, II, 71-72 – citing itineraries prepared by the quarter master corps of the French army when it came through Trenton in early September.

32 Samuel Miles to the Board of War, June 14, 1781, *PCC*, Memorials addressed to Congress, r51, i41, p239. Washington had ordered LaFayette south to reinforce Greene. See George Washington to LaFayette, April 6, 1781, *GWPLOC*.

33 "Journal of Ebenezer Wild", *Massachusetts Historical Society Proceedings* Second Series, No. 6, (Boston, 1891), 131-132. "Mr. Barnes" was probably Thomas Barnes. Stratford and Wilson, *Certificates and Receipts*, 166. Receipt for Thomas Ashmore, February 18, 1782.

34 *NJG*, July 11, 1781, 3; George Washington to Samuel Miles, August 27, 1781, *GWPLOC*.

35 George Washington to David Forman, August 28, 1781, George Washington to Benjamin Lincoln, August 28, 1781, *GWPLOC*.

36 This was based on the Wiederhold map.

37 Baron von Closen, *Journal*, 115. He wrote "two Presbyterian churches" but there was only one Presbyterian Church and he probably mistook St. Michael's for another.

38 August 30 – "Lamb's Artillery Orderly Book," *Early American Orderly Books, 1748-1817* [microform] (New Haven: Research Publications, 1977), reel 14.

39 George Washington to Benjamin Lincoln, August 31, 1781, *GWPLOC*. There are two letters from Washington to Lincoln on that date.

40 Benjamin Lincoln to George Washington, August 31, 1781, *GWPLOC*; *NJG*, September 12, 1781, 3; NARA M246, Revolutionary War Rolls, 1775-1783, Second Regiment of Artillery, 1777-1783, r110, f41. Bremer apparently returned and he appears as a fifer on a 1782 muster for the regiment.

41 George Washington to Benjamin Lincoln, August 31, 1781, *GWPLOC* from Philadelphia second letter of the day.

42 Thomas Graton PF W14824. A photocopy of his journal of war experiences is included in the file.

43 Robert A. Selig, T*he Washington-Rochambeau Revolutionary Route in the State of New Jersey, 1781-1783: An Historical and Architectural Survey* (Trenton: State of New Jersey, 2006), I: 203, citing Journal of Sergeant-Major John H. Hawkins, 1779-1781. Manuscript Guide 273, Historical Society of Pennsylvania, Philadelphia. Hawkins' journal is not paginated.

44 Martin, *Narrative*, 191.

45 "Diary of the March from the Hudson to Yorktown, and Return, by Lieutenant Reuben Sanderson, Fifth Connecticut Continental Line, on Duty with Scammell's Light Infantry Corps." In: Henry P. Johnston, *The Yorktown Campaign and the Surrender of Cornwallis, 1781* (Eastern National Park and Monument Association, 1958. Originally published 1881), 170.

46 Thacher, *Military Journal*, 325. Some of the French officers also commented on the historical event at Trenton. For example, see: Abbe Robin, *New Travels through North America* (New York: New York Times and Arno Press, 1969). Reprint of 1783 edition. Eyewitness Accounts of the American Revolution, Letter VI: Trenton, September 2, 1781, 42-43.

47 Benjamin Lincoln to George Washington, August 31, 1781, Benjamin Lincoln to George Washington, September 1, 1781, *GWPLOC*; Benjamin Lincoln to Col Courtland, September 1, 1781, Frederick S. Allis, Jr., ed., *The Benjamin Lincoln Papers* [microform] (Boston: Massachusetts Historical Society, 1977), r6, f254.

48 Robin, *New Travels through North America*, Letter VI: Trenton, September 2, 1781, 42-43. Comments on the ford are found in Rice, Jr. and Brown, *American Campaigns of Rochambeau's Army*, II, 71-72, 150.

49 Blanchard, *Journal*, 134-135. Abbe Robin also commented on the resemblance to the Loire.

50 Philip Van Cortlandt, *The Revolutionary War Memoir and Selected Correspondence of Philip Van Cortlandt*, Jacob Judd, comp and ed., (Tarrytown, NY: Sleepy Hollow Restorations, 1976), 58-60; George Washington to Philip van Cortlandt, August 28, 1781, *GWPLOC*; Tallmadge, Journal, 759; T. W. Egly, Jr., *History of the First New York Regiment, 1775-1783* (Hampton, NH: P.E. Randall, 1981), 200; John Neilson to Timothy Pickering, 4 September 1781, NARA M859, Misc. Numbered Records, r80, f38.

51 Achmet Hamet PF S38107; Isaac Quigley PF R8550.

52 John Neilson Papers, certificate no. 2270, DQM for NJ, 1780-1782, Box 2, Account Book beginning Trenton, 25 Sept. 1780 to 4 October 1782. Special Collections, Rutgers University, New Brunswick, Ac589. These and other certificates are published in: Stratford and Wilson, *Certificates and Receipts*, 46, 56, 57, 89, 111, 131, 141, 147, 148.

53 Robert A. Selig, "Rochambeau in New Jersey: The Good French Ally," in James J. Gigantino II, ed. *The American Revolution in New Jersey: Where the Battlefront Meets the Home Front* (New Brunswick: Rutgers University Press, 2015), 94-95.

54 *Joint Meeting*, 49-52; *Council Journal*, Session beginning May 15, 1781, 50, Session beginning October 23, 1781, 5-7, 25-26; *Assembly Votes*, Session beginning October 23, 1781, 5-6; *NJG*, October 31, 1781, 3; Cushing, *First Laws*, 237-240;.

55 *NJG*, October 24, 1781 3. Also quip from a Philadelphia paper of the 22nd with the announcement of the surrender on the 17th.

56 Hall, *Trenton Presbyterian Church*, 174; *NJG*, October 31, 1781, 3.

57 *NJG*, November 28, 1781, 3.

58 *NJG*, August 22, 1781, 4. Ads for this third ferry continued through the war years. For example, see: *NJG*, June 11, 1783, 4. In ads before establishing the ferry, Beatty placed ads for vendue sales at his house "near Trenton" to well work horses, breeding horses, milch cows, oxen, sheep, etc. See *NJG*, September 1, 1779, 3. In common with other prominent men of Trenton he participated in land sales, for example in Morris County in January 1781 involving a farm that had once belonged to Trenton's Isaac DeCou. See: *NJG*, January 3, 1781, 3.

59 NARA M853. Numbered record. Records of Military Stores Received and Delivered at Philadelphia, 03/1780 - 09/1784, R37, p216.

60 Ephraim Blaine to George Washington, March 23, 1781, *PCC*, Transcripts of letters from George Washington, 1781-82, r188, i169, p79.

61 NJSA, Department of Defense, Adjutant General's Officer (RevWar), Quartermaster and Commissary General Records 1776-1789, Box 1, #26 – Account book of cash received and paid by Joseph Inslee, Contractor of Hunterdon.

62 William Alexander to Col. John Cox, October 7, 1781, NJSA, William Alexander – Correspondence 1764-1782, #29.

63 *Pennsylvania Packet*, June 30, 1781, 1; *NJG*, July 18, 1781, 2; August 1, 1781, 3; December 20, 1780, 3.
64 Wild, *Journal*, 159.
65 Hugh Runyan Ferry Account 1781, *Neilson Family Papers*, Box 2, Special Collections and University Archives, Rutgers University Libraries.
66 Isaac Quigley PF R8550.
67 Hugh Runyan Ferry Account 1781.
68 Tallmadge, *Journal*, 768. Hugh Runyon's ferry log gives slightly different dates than Tallmadge, but within a day or two.
69 Thomas Graton PF W14824; Tallmadge, *Journal*, 768; Hugh Runyan Ferry Account 1781. The "chair" listed was a riding chair. A very light, four wheeled carriage bed carrying a large chair. This was a horse-drawn sports car of its age.
70 Gillette, *Army Medical Department*, 110; Benjamin Lincoln to George Washington, November 22, 1781, *GWPLOC*.
71 Shuman, *Trenton Story*, 41; *Assembly Votes*, Session beginning October 23, 1781, 17, 18; *Council Journal*, Session beginning October 23 1781, 11; Hugh Runyan Ferry Account 1781.
72 *Neilson Family Papers*, Special Collections and University Archives, Rutgers University, New Brunswick, Ac 589. Box 2, John Neilson, Papers ... kept as DQM for NJ, 1780-1782, Account Book beginning Trenton, 25 Sept. 1780 to 4 October 1782.
73 Gillette, *Army Medical Department*, 127.
74 Daniel M. Popek, *They "...fought bravely, but were unfortunate:" The True Story of Rhode Island's "Black Regiment" and the Failure of Segregation in Rhode Island's Continental Line, 1777-1783* (AuthorHouse, 2015), 534, 540 citing: December 14, 1781, Return, Returns Book, Second Rhode Island Regiment Rhode Island Regiment, RIHS mss.; Henry P. Johnston, *The Yorktown Campaign and the Surrender of Cornwallis, 1781* (New York: Harper & Bros., 1881), "Diary of the March from the Hudson to Yorktown, and Return, by Lieutenant Reuben Sanderson, Fifth Connecticut Continental Line, on Duty with Scammell's Light Infantry Corps.", 172
75 Richard Lee McClenahan, "New Jersey Medical History in the Colonial Period," *Proceedings of the New Jersey Historical Society* 43 –(1925) new series vol 10, 362+, 371-372.

Chapter 14

1 *NJG*, July 10, 1782, 3.
2 *NJG*, February 20, 1782, 2.
3 *Minutes of Trenton*, 47.
4 Robert Morris to Thomas Bond, Jr., February 9, 1782, Morris, Robert. *The Papers of Robert Morris, 1781-1784*, James Ferguson, ed. (Pittsburgh: University of Pittsburgh Press, 1973), IV: 263. Bond was in the Continental Hospital Department.
5 John Neilson, Papers ... kept as DQM for NJ, 1780-1782, Box 2, Account Book beginning Trenton, 25 Sept. 1780 to 4 October 1782. Special Collections, Rutgers University, New Brunswick, Ac 589.
6 Popek, *They "...fought bravely, but were unfortunate"*, 546-547. These three men were not listed as "man of color" so were presumably white.
7 Robert Morris to the Secretary at War, Benjamin Lincoln, January 12, 1782, *Morris Papers*, IV: 14-15; *NJG*, January 16, 1782, 3; January 23, 1782, 3; February 6, 1782, 4; Timothy Pickering to Robert Morris, February 19, 1782, *Morris Papers*, IV: 269.
8 Martin, *Narrative*, 219.
9 *NJG*, April 24, 1782, 3. Men could also apply to the quartermaster at Morristown.
10 *NJG*, November 13, 1782, 3
11 Neilson Papers, Box 2 Folder – Return of public property Quarter Master General's Dept. October 1, 1782. Spelt is a grain, often fed to horses like oats.
12 Neilson Papers, Box 2, Folder – Official Papers 1780-1782, Account of Sales sold at vendue – November 21, 1782; *NJG*, November 13, 1782, 3.

13 Jeremiah Greenman, *Diary of a Common Soldier in the American Revolution, 1775-1783: An Annotated edition of the Military Journal of Jeremiah Greenman*, Robert C. Bray and Paul E. Bushnell, eds. (Dekalb: Northern Illinois University Press, 1978), 242, 250; *NJG*, March 27, 1782, 3.
14 *NJG*, October 16, 1782, 3.
15 *NJG*, November 6, 1782, 3.
16 *NJG*, October 9, 1782, 3.
17 William Livingston, Trenton, to George Washington, January 1, 1782, Prince, *Livingston Papers*, IV: 357; Cushing, *First Laws*, 287298, 318-320. A major law was passed in June, followed by a supplement in December.
18 *NJG*, July 17, 1782, 3.
19 *NJG*, July 24, 1782, 3; September 18, 1782, 3.
20 *NJG*, August 7, 1782, 3; August 14, 1782, 3; August 28, 1782, 3.
21 *NJG*, October 2, 1782, 3; October 23, 1782, 3; December 11, 1782, 3.
22 See: T. H. Breen, *The Marketplace of Revolution: How Consumer Politics Shaped American Independence* (Oxford: Oxford University Press, 2004) for an overview.
23 *NJG*, May 29, 1782, 2; Hall, *Trenton Presbyterian Church*, 171-172, 336. The Dauphin died in childhood. For Luzerne's response see *Council Journal*, Session beginning May 15, 1782, 17; *Assembly Votes*, Session beginning May 15, 1782, 33.
24 *Council Journal*, Session beginning May 15, 1782, 4, 7, 27; *Assembly Votes*, Session beginning May 15, 1782, 50, 52-54.
25 Claude Blanchard, *The Journal of Claude Blanchard*, trans. William Duane, ed. Thomas Balch (New York: New York Times, 1969), 173-174; Baron Ludwig Von Closen, *The Revolutionary Journal of Baron Ludwig Von Closen, 1780-1783*, trans. and ed. Evelyn M. Acomb (Chapel Hill: University of North Carolina Press, 1958), 233-234; *NJG*, September 4, 182, 2; Uhledorf, *Baurmeister Letters and Journals*, 523. At least one contemporary source says the artillery crossed at the ford. Rice and Brown, American Campaigns, I: 78. Perhaps some went by ferry and some by the ford.
26 Arnold Whitridge, *Rochambeau* (New York: Macmillan, 1965), 193.
27 *NJG*, March 13, 1782, 3. Specifics on the many stores and items they sold can be gleaned from virtually every issue of the *NJG* during the years 1777 to 1783.
28 *NJG*, June 20, 1781, 3. For other lists of items for sale see: *NJG*, February 18, 1778, 3; March 17, 1779, 3; May 10, 1780, 3; April 25, 1781, 3.
29 *NJG*, September 13, 1780, 3; June 27, 1781, 3; October 30, 1782, 3; Neilson Papers, Box 2, folder Correspondence, etc. 1780-82, Receipt from April 12, 1782 – Neilson to Conrad Kotts for materials and labor for making a double breasted jacket "W. S."
30 *NJG*, November 20, 1782, 3.
31 For example: *NJG*, May 20, 1778, 3; *NJG*, November 25, 1778, 1; March 3, 1779, 4; January 10, 1781, 3; November 20, 1782, 1; December 16, 1783, 4.
32 *NJG*, August 21, 1782, 3.
33 *NJG*, November 20, 1782, 1
34 *NJG*, January 2, 1782, 3; January 30, 1782, 3; July 10, 1782, 3; December 25, 1782, 1
35 *NJG*, July 25, 1781, 3; November 14, 1781.
36 *NJG*, May 8, 1782, 3; May 1, 1782, 3; May 22, 1782, 3; June 5, 1782, 3; December 4, 1782, 3.
37 *NJG*, May 8, 1782, 4; May 29, 1782, 3.
38 *NJG*, November 13, 1782, 3; April 3, 1782, 3; April 24, 1782, 3.
39 Satterthwaite, *History of Society of Friends*, I: 210.
40 Hixon, *Isaac Collins*, 118; Dayton, *Trenton Academy*, 8; *NJG*, September 18, 1782, 3.
41 *NJG*, November 13, 1782, 3; November 20, 1782, 3; December 11, 1782, 3.
42 *NJG*, January 15, 1783, 3.
43 Frederick W. Gnichtel, "The 'Pennamite Wars' and the Trenton Decree of 1782." *Proceedings of the New Jersey Historical Society*, New Series, VI (1921), 24-34. *NJG*, November 20, 1782, 3; January 1, 1783, 3.
44 *NJG*, October 9, 1782, 3.

45 Peter Huleck petition, Trenton November 2, 1782, NJSA mss, Department of Education, New Jersey State Library, Bureau of Archives and History, Manuscript Collection, 1680s-1970s, Legislative Records, 1782-1787, BAH Box 1-15, #20.
46 *Council Journal*, Session beginning October 22, 1782, 33; *Assembly Votes*, Session beginning October 22, 1782, 71.
47 *NJG*, November 20, 1782, 3.
48 *Council Journal*, Session beginning October 22, 1782, 5; *Assembly Votes*, Session beginning October 22, 1782, 3-6, 13; *NJG*, June 19, 1782, 3; October 23, 1782, 3; October 30, 1782, 3; November 6, 1782, 3; *Joint Meeting*, 54.
49 *Assembly Votes*, Session beginning October 22, 1782, 20, 24, 37-39, 55-58; *Joint Meeting*, 55.
50 *Council Journal*, Session beginning October 22, 1782, 35-36, 38; *Assembly Votes*, Session beginning October 22, 1782, 89.

Chapter 15

1 *NJG*, February 12, 1783, 3; March 26, 1783, 3.
2 Proclamation, Trenton, April 14, 1783, Prince, *Livingston Papers*, IV: 517.
3 *NJG*, April 16, 1783, 3; Hall, *Trenton Presbyterian Church*, 174-75.
4 *NJG*, April 23, 1783, 2.
5 Schuyler, *St. Michael's Church*, 123; Godfrey, *St. Michael's Church*, 5.
6 *NJG*, January 29, 1783, 3.
7 *NJG*, March 12, 1783, 3. The members being thanked were not named in the paper, but were thanked personally by Hooper.
8 *NJG*, June 25, 1783, 3.
9 *NJG*, January 22, 1783, 3.
10 NJSA, Hunterdon County Tavern Licenses; *NJG*, April 30, 1783, 3.
11 *Minutes of Trenton*, 49-50.
12 *NJG*, April 9, 1783, 2.
13 *Assembly Votes*, Session beginning October 22, 1782, 74, 93, 95; *Council Journal*, Session beginning May 15, 1783, 42, 56.
14 *NJG*, July 20, 1784, 2. See: *NJG*, April 6, 1784, 3 and August 23, 1784, 1 for examples of the public attacks on him and his loss of the public money in 1776.
15 *Assembly Votes*, Session beginning May 15, 1783, 148-149, 150; *NJG*, July 2, 1783, 2.
16 *NJG*, April 9, 1783, 3.
17 *Assembly Votes*, Session beginning May 15, 1783, 147; *Council Journal*, Session beginning May 15, 1783, 68; John Cox to Elias Boudinot, June 25, 1783, *PCC*, Locating the seat of government, r60, i46, p79. Also printed in: *NJG*, July 16, 1783, 2; *PCC*, r60, i46, p83; William Livingston to Elias Budinot, President of Congress, June 24, 1783, *PCC*, NJ State Papers, r82, i68, p613. Petition of the inhabitants of the western part of Nottingham Township proposing their town as the site for the national government. *PCC*, r60, i46, p43.
18 Inhabitants of Trenton to Congress, October 13, 1783, *PCC*, Miscellaneous letters to the Congress, 1775-89, r103, i78, p283.
19 *NJG*, July 9, 1783, 3.
20 *NJG*, February 26, 1783, 3.
21 *NJG*, December 23, 1783, 4; May 15, 1786, 2; *Assembly Votes*, Session beginning October 25, 1785, 62.
22 *NJG*, December 30, 1783, 3.
23 *Assembly Votes*, Session beginning October 28, 1783, 5; *Council Journal*, Session beginning October 28, 1783, 5-6, 10.
24 *NJG*, June 19, 1782, 3. Witt was not a new resident of Trenton, but had been in the auction business for several years.
25 *Joint Meeting*, 57-59.
26 *Assembly Votes*, Session beginning October 28, 1783, 39; *NJG*, December 9, 1783, 3.
27 *NJG*, December 9, 1783, 3.

Epilogue

1 This story is told in: "Account of the Reception of General Washington at Trenton, April 21," *The Columbian Magazine* (May 1789), 288-290 and William S. Stryker, Washington's Reception by the People of Trenton in 1789 (Trenton: Naar, Day, and Naar, 1882).

Conclusion

1 George Washington Parke Custis. *Recollections and Private Memoirs of Washington*. New York: Derby & Jackson, 1860, 251. The story is repeated by many historians, including William S. Stryker (*Trenton and Princeton*,464) and David Hackett Fischer (*Washington's Crossing*, 362) but is argued to be apocryphal by Douglas Southall Freeman in *George Washington: A Biography*, (New York, C. Scribner's Sons, 1948-), V: 399 note 30.

Bibliography

Manuscript Collections (specific items given in the source notes)

Historical Society of Pennsylvania

Morristown National Historical Park

New Jersey State Archives

Old Barracks Museum Association Manuscript Collection

Princeton University Archives, Department of Rare Books and Special Collections, Princeton University Library

Rutgers University Libraries, Special Collections and University Archives

Swan Historical Foundation Collection at Washington Crossing State Park, Titusville, NJ.

Published documents - print and microform

"Abstracts of Pension Applications on File in the Division of Public Records, Pennsylvania State Library," *The Pennsylvania Archives*, Series 5, IV: 514.

Adams, John. *Diary and Autobiography of John Adams*. L. H. Butterfield, ed. Cambridge: Belknap Press of Harvard University Press, 1962.

Allinson, Samuel. *Acts of the General Assembly of the Province of New Jersey*. Burlington: 1776.

Allis, Frederick S., Jr., ed., *The Benjamin Lincoln Papers* [microform], Boston: Massachusetts Historical Society, 1977.

American Philosophical Society, *List of the Members of the American Philosophical Society, January 17, 1890*.

Ancestry.com. U.S., *Quaker Meeting Records, 1681-1935* [database on-line]. Provo, UT: Ancestry.com Operations, Inc., 2014.

Anderson, Enoch. *Personal Recollections of Captain Enoch Anderson, An Officer of the Delaware Regiments in the Revolutionary War*. Wilmington: The Historical Society of Delaware, 1896.

Armes, Ethel, ed., *Nancy Shippen Her Journal Book*. Philadelphia: J. B. Lippincott, 1935.

Avery, Rev. David. "The Battle of Trenton from the unpublished diary of Rev. David Avery, Chaplain in Colonel John Patterson's Regiment." *The American Monthly Magazine*, 19 (1901): 151-156.

Balch, Thomas. *The Examination of Joseph Galloway, Esq. By a Committee of the House of Commons*. Boston: Gregg Press, 1972. Photographic reprint of 1855 work published by the Seventy-Six Society in Philadelphia, reproduced from an original copy in the Boston Public Library.

Barth, Richard C., William E. Dornemann, and Mark A. Schwalm. "The Trenton Prisoner List." *The Hessians: Journal of the Johannes Schwalm Historical Association* 16 (2013: 75-90.

Baurmeister, Carl Leopold. *Revolution in America; Confidential Letters and Journals 1776-1784 of Adjutant General Major Baurmeister of the Hessian Forces.* Berhhard A. Uhlendorf, trans., New Brunswick: Rutgers University Press, 1957.

Beatty, William, "Journal of Capt William Beatty," *Maryland Historical Magazine* 3 (1908): 104-119.

Biddle, Charles. *Autobiography of Charles Biddle, Vice-President of the Supreme Executive Council of Pennsylvania, 1745-1821.* Philadelphia: E. Claxton and Company, 1883.

Blanchard, Claude. *The Journal of Claude Blanchard.* William Duane, trans., Thomas Balch, ed. New York: New York Times, 1969.

Browne, William Hand, ed., *Archives of Maryland: Journal and Correspondence of the Maryland Council of Safety, July 7 – December 31, 1776.* Baltimore: Maryland Historical Society, 1893.

Burgoyne, Bruce E., trans. D*efeat, Disaster and Dedication: The Diaries of the Hessian Officers Jakob Piel and Andreas Wiederhold.* Bowie, MD: Heritage Books, 1997.

Burnett, Edmund C., ed. *Letters of Members of the Continental Congress.* Gloucester, MA: P. Smith, 1963.

Bush, Bernard. *Laws of the Royal Colony of New Jersey.* New Jersey Archives, Third Series. Trenton: New Jersey State Library, Archives and History Bureau, 1986.

Butterfield, L. H., ed. *Adams Family Correspondence.* Cambridge: Belknap Press of Harvard University Press, 1963+.

Butterfieldd, L. H. ed. *Letters of Benjamin Rush.* Princeton: American Philosophical Society and Princeton University Press, 1951.

Carleton, Sir Guy, *British Headquarters (Sir Guy Carleton) Papers, 1777-1783,* [microform] Washington: Microfilming Service, Recordak Corp., 1957.

Chastellux, Marquis de. *Travels in North America in the Years, 1780, 1781 and 1782.* Howard C. Rice, Jr. trans. Chapel Hill: The University of North Carolina Press, 1963.

Clitherall, James. "Extracts from the Diary of Dr. James Clitherall, 1776", *The Pennsylvania Magazine of History and Biography* 22 (1898): 468-474.

Closen, Baron Ludwig von. *The Revolutionary Journal of Baron Ludwig Von Closen, 1780-1783.* Evelyn M. Acomb, trans. and ed. Chapel Hill: University of North Carolina Press, 1958.

Colonial Records of Pennsylvania, Minutes of the Supreme Executive Council – Pennsylvania. Harrisburg: Theo. Fenn, 1852.

Culter, Rev. Manasseh. "New Jersey, Pennsylvania and Ohio, in 1787-8: Passages from the Journals of Rev. Manasseh Cutler." *Proceedings of the New Jersey Historical Society,* Second Series, 3 (1874).

Cushing, John D. *The First Laws of the State of New Jersey*. Wilmington, DE: Michael Glazier, 1981.

Dann, John C., ed. *The Revolution Remembered: Eyewitness Accounts of the War for Independence*. Chicago: University of Chicago Press, 1980.

Dean, Silas. *Correspondence of Silas Deane, Delegate to the First and Second Congress at Philadelphia, 1774-1776*. Hartford: Connecticut Historical Society, 1870.

Early American Orderly Books, 1748-1817 [microform]. New Haven: Research Publications, 1977.

Embury, Susan Pindar. *A Grandmother's (Martha Reed, wife of John Shannon) Recollections of the Old Revolutionary Days. 1875*. Typescript in Trentoniana Room at the Trenton Free Public Library, Trenton, New Jersey. Another copy of this memoir is: Embury, Susan Pindor; 1875; General Manuscripts Miscellaneous Collection, Box 15; Manuscripts Division, Department of Rare Books and Special Collections, Princeton University Library.

Ewing, George. *The Military Journal of George Ewing (1754-1824) a soldier of Valley Forge*. Yonkers: Thomas Ewing, 1928.

Feinstone, Sol. *The Sol Feinstone Collection of the American Revolution* [microform]. Philadelphia: Historic Publications; Wilmington: Scholarly Resources, 1969-1975.

Fitch, John. *The Autobiography of John Fitch*. Frank D. Prager, ed. Philadelphia: American Philosophical Society, 1976.

Force, Peter, ed. *American Archives: consisting of a collection of authentick records, state papers, debates, and letters and other notices of publick affairs, the whole forming a documentary history of the origin and progress of the North American colonies; of the causes and accomplishment of the American Revolution; and of the Constitution of government for the United States, to the final ratification thereof. In 6 series*. 1972.

Franklin, Benjamin. "Selection from the Correspondence and Papers." *Proceedings of the New Jersey Historical Society* 9 (1864): 83-85.

Franklin, Benjamin. *The Complete Works of Benjamin Franklin*, John Bigelow, ed. New York: G.P. Putnam's Sons, 1887.

Furman, Moore. *The Letters of Moore Furman: Deputy Quarter-Master General of New Jersey in the Revolution*. New York: New Jersey Society of the Colonial Dames, 1912.

Gerlach, Larry R. *New Jersey in the American Revolution, 1763-1783: A Documentary History*. Trenton: New Jersey Historical Commission, 1975.

Great Britain, Audit Office. *American Loyalist Claims. Series 2, 1780-1835*, AO 13 [microform] Exchequer and Audit Department.

Great Britain, Exchequer and Audit Department. *American Loyalist Claims. Series 1, 1776-1831*, AO 12 [microform] Exchequer and Audit Department.

Greene, Nathanael. *The Papers of General Nathanael Greene*. Showman, Richard K., ed. Chapel Hill: The University of North Carolina Press, 1976.

Greenman, Jeremiah. *Diary of a Common Soldier in the American Revolution, 1775-1783: An Annotated edition of the Military Journal of Jeremiah Greenman*, Robert C. Bray and Paul E. Bushnell, eds., Dekalb: Northern Illinois University Press, 1978.

Greenwood, John. *The Wartime Services of John Greenwood: A Young Patriot in the American Revolution 1775-1783.* Westvaco, 1981.

Hessian Documents of the American Revolution, Morristown National Historic Park [microform], Boston: G. K. Hall, 1989.

Hill, Baylor, *A Gentleman of Fortune: The Diary of Baylor Hill, First Continental Light Dragoons, 1777-1781.* John T. Hayes, ed. Fort Lauderdale: Saddlebag Press, c1995.

Hiltzheimer, Jacob. *Extracts from the Diary of Jacob Hiltzheimer of Philadelphia, 1765-1798.* Jacob Coxe Parsons, ed. Philadelphia: 1893.

How, David. *Diary of David How, A Private in Colonel Paul Dudley Sargent's Regiment of the Massachusetts Line, in the Army of the American Revolution.* Morrisania, NY: 1865.

Howe, William, *The Narrative of Lieut. Gen. Sir William Howe, in a Committee of the House of Commons, on the 29th of April, 1779, relative to his Conduct, during His Late Command of the King's Troops in North America: To which are added, some observations upon a pamphlet, entitle, Letters to a Nobleman.* London: H. Baldwin, 1781.

Journals of the Continental Congress, 1774-1789. Washington: Government Printing Office, 1904.

J*ournal of the Proceedings of the Legislative Council of the State of New Jersey*, various dates beginning 1776, organized and paginated by sessions.

Kirkwood, Robert, *The Journal and Order Book of Captain Robert Kirkwood of the Delaware Regiment of the Continental Line.* Joseph Brown Turner, ed. Port Washington, NY: Kennikat Press, 1970.

Knox, Henry. *The Papers of Henry Knox, 1719-1825* [microform]: Owned by the New England Historic Genealogical Society and Deposited in the Massachusetts Historical Society. Boston: 1960.

Lauber, Almon W., *Orderly Books of the Fourth New York Regiment, 1778-1780, The Second New York Regiment, 1780-1783 by Samuel Tallmadge and others with Diaries of Samuel Tallmadge, 1780-1782 and John Barr, 1779-1782.* Albany, University of the State of New York, 1932.

Livingston, William. *The Papers of William Livingston.* Carl E. Prince, ed. Trenton: New Jersey Historical Commission, c1979-1988.

Livingston, William. *The Papers of William Livingston* [microform]. Ann Arbor, MI: University Microfilms, [1986].

Luvaas, Jay, ed. and trans., *Frederick the Great on the Art of War.* New York: The Free Press, 1966.

Marshall, Christopher. *Extracts from the diary of Christopher Marshall, kept in Philadelphia and Lancaster, during the American Revolution, 1774-1781.* William Duane, ed. Albany: Joel Munsell, 1877.

Martin, Joseph Plumb. *A Narrative of a Revolutionary Soldier.* New York: New American Library, 2001.

McMichael, James. "Diary of Lieutenant James McMichael, of the Pennsylvania Line, 1776-1778." *The Pennsylvania Magazine of History and Biography* 16 (1892): 129-159.

Meunchausen, Friedrich von. *At General Howe's Side 1776-1778: The diary of General William Howe's aide de camp, Captain Friedrich von Meunchausen.* Ernst Kipping, trans. Monmouth Beach, NJ: Philip Freneau Press, 1974.

Minutes and Proceedings of the Council and General Assembly of the State of New-Jersey, in joint-meeting, from August 30, 1776 to October 29, 1799, Trenton: 1780.

Minutes of the Provincial Congress and the Committee of Safety of the State of New Jersey. Trenton: Naar, Day & Naar, 1789.

Minutes of the Township of Trenton, 1755-1818, copied by the Federal Writers' Project, Works Progress Administration, 1937, from original record found in City Hall. Typescript in Trentoniana Room at the Trenton Free Public Library, Trenton, New Jersey.

Monroe, James. *Autobiography of James Monroe*, Stuart Gerry Brown, ed. Syracuse: Syracuse University Press, 1959.

Montgomery, Thomas Lynch, ed., *Pennsylvania Archives, Series 5.* Harrisburg: The State of Pennsylvania, 1906.

Morgan, William James, ed. *Naval Documents of the American Revolution.* Washington: Department of the Navy, Naval History Division, 1972.

Morris, Robert. *The Papers of Robert Morris, 1781-1784*, James Ferguson, ed. Pittsburgh: University of Pittsburgh Press, 1973.

Muhlenberg, Henry Melchior. *The Journals of Henry Melchior Muhlenberg.* Theodore G. Tappert and John W. Doberstein, trans. Camden, ME: Picton Press, 1945.

NARA M246. *Muster rolls, payrolls, strength returns, and other miscellaneous personnel, pay, and supply records of American Army units, 1775-83.*

NARA M247. *Papers of the Continental Congress, 1774-1789.*

NARA M804. *Revolutionary War Pension and Bounty-Land Warrant Application Files.*

NARA M881. *Compiled service records of soldiers who served in the American Army during the Revolutionary War, 1775-1783.*

New Jersey Archives, Second Series. William S. Stryker, ed. Trenton: John L. Murphy, 1901.

Paine, Robert Treat, *Robert Treat Paine Papers*, [microform], Massachusetts Historical Society.

Parker, Charles W. "New Jersey Supreme Court of September Term, 1776," *Proceedings of the New Jersey Historical Society* 50 (1932): 256+.

Pennsylvania Archives, Series 1, Samuel Hazard,, ed. Philadelphia: Joseph Severns, 1853.

Pennsylvania Archives, Series 2. John Blair Linn and William H. Egle, eds. Harrisburg: State of Pennsylvania, 1880.

Pennsylvania Archives, Series 4. George Edward Reed, ed., Harrisburg: State of Pennsylvania, 1900.

Powell, William S. "A Connecticut Soldier Under Washington: Elisha Bostwick's Memoirs of the First Years of the Revolution." *The William and Mary Quarterly, Third Series*, 6 (1949): 94-107.

Reed, Joseph. "General Joseph Reed's Narrative of the Movements of the American Army in the Neighborhood of Trenton in the Winter of 1776-77." *The Pennsylvania Magazine of History and Biography* 8 (1884): 391-402.

Reuber, Johannes, "A Hessian Diary", *Journal of the Johannes Schwalm Historical Association* 1 no. 2 (1978): 1-8.

Rice, Howard C., Jr., and Anne S.K. Brown, trans. and ed. *The American Campaigns of Rochambeau's Army, 1780, 1781, 1782, 1783.* Princeton: Princeton University Press, 1972.

Ricord, Frederick W., ed. *Documents Relating to the Colonial History of the State of New Jersey.*
Vol xvii, Journal of the Governor and Council, Vol V, 1756-1768. Trenton: John L. Murphy, 1892.
Vol xviii, Journal of the Governor and Council, Vol VI, 1769-1775. Trenton: John L. Murphy, 1893.

Roberts, Algernon. "A Journal of a Campaign from Philadelphia to Paulus Hook." *The Pennsylvania Magazine of History and Biography* 7 (1883): 456+.

Robertson, Archibald. *Archibald Robertson: His Diaries and Sketches in America: 1762-1780.* Lydenberg, Harry Miller, ed. New York: The New York Public Library, 1930.

Rodney, Caesar. *Letters to and From Caesar Rodney, 1756-1784*, George Herbert Ryden, ed. New York: DaCapo Press, 1970.

Rodney, Thomas. Caesar A. Rodney, intro. *Diary of Captain Thomas Rodney, 1776-1777.* Wilmington: The Historical Society of Delaware, 1888.

Rush, Benjamin. *The Autobiography of Benjamin Rush: His Travels through life together with his Commonplace Book for 1789-1813.* George W. Corner, ed. Westport, CN: Greenwood Press, 1970.

Rush, Benjamin. *Letters of Benjamin Rush.* L.H. Butterfield, ed. Philadelphia: American Philosophical Society, 1951.

Rush, Benjamin. *My Dearest Julia: The Love Letters of Dr. Benjamin Rush to Julia Stockton.* New York: N. Watson Academic Publications, 1979.

Rush, Benjamin. *The Selected Writings of Benjamin Rush*. Dagobert D. Runes, ed. New York: Philosophical Library, 1947.

Salsig, Doyen, ed. *Parole: Quebec; Countersign: Ticonderoga: Second New Jersey Regimental Orderly Book 1776*. Rutherford, NJ: Fairleigh Dickinson University Press, 1980.

Satterthwaite, Elizabeth. *History of the Religious Society of Friends in Trenton and Vicinity*, typescript, 1925. Trenton Free Public Library, Trentoniana Room.

Schoepf, Johann David. *Travels in the Confederation, 1783-1784*. Alfred J. Morrison, trans. and ed. Philadelphia: William J. Campbell, 1911.

Sellers, Nathan, "Extracts from the Diary of Nathan Sellers, 1776-1778," *Pennsylvania Magazine of History and Biography* 16 (1892): 191-196.

Smith, Billy G. *Life in Early Philadelphia: Documents from the Revolutionary and Early National Periods*, University Park, PA: The Pennsylvania State University Press, 1995.

Smith, Paul H., ed. *Letters of Delegates to Congress, 1774-1789*. Washington: Library of Congress, 1976-1985.

Spear, John. "The Orderly Book of Lieutenant John Spear (July 17 to December 4, 1781)", *Proceedings of the New Jersey Historical Society: A Magazine of History, Biography and Genealogy*. New Series, 1 (1916): 129-146.

Stewart, Charles. "Two Revolutionary Letters of Col. Charles Stewart," *Proceedings of the New Jersey Historical Society* 39 (1921): 86-89.

Stratford, Dorothy Agans and Thomas B. Wilson. *Certificates and Receipts of Revolutionary New Jersey*. Lambertville, NJ: Hunterdon House, 1996.

Sullivan, John. *Letters and Papers of Major-General John Sullivan, Continental Army*. Otis G. Hammond, ed. Concord: New Hampshire Historical Society, 1930-1939.

Thacher, James. *Military Journal During the American Revolutionary War, from 1775 to 1783*. Boston: Richardson and Lord, 1823.

Tilghman, Tench. *Memoir of Lieut. Col. Tench Tilghman, Secretary and Aid to Washington*. Albany: J. Munsell, 1876.

Turner, Jacob. "Jacob Turner's Book 1777-1778," *The State Records of North Carolina*, Walter Clark, ed. Winston, NC: M. I. & J. C. Stewart, 1895.

Van Cortlandt, Philip. Jacob Judd, ed., *The Revolutionary War Memoir and Selected Correspondence of Philip Van Cortlandt*. Tarrytown, NY: Sleepy Hollow Restorations, 1976.

Votes and Proceedings of the General Assembly of the Province of New Jersey. Various dates organized and paginated by sessions.

Votes and Proceedings of the General Assembly of the State of New Jersey. Various dates beginning 1776, organized and paginated by sessions.

Washington, George. *George Washington Papers at the Library of Congress, 1741-1799*, on line at http://www.memory.loc.gov/ammem/gwhtml/gwhome.html.

Washington, George. *The Papers of George Washington. Revolutionary War Series.* Philander D. Chase, ed. Charlottesville: University Press of Virginia, 1985-1997.

Washington, George. *The Writings of George Washington: From the original Manuscript Sources, 1745-1799.* John C. Fitzpatrick, ed. Washington: Government Printing Office, 1931-1944.

White, Joseph. "The Good Soldier White: A Revolutionary Veteran Speaks," *American Heritage* 7 (1956): 74-79.

Whitehead, William A. *Documents Relating to the Colonial History of the State of New Jersey. Archives of the State of New Jersey, First Series*, Newark: 1883.

Wild, Ebenezer. "Journal of Ebenezer Wild", *Massachusetts Historical Society Proceedings, Second Series*, 6 (1891): 78-160.

Wilkinson, General James. *Memoirs of My Own Times*. Philadelphia: Abraham Small, 1816.

Young, William. "Journal of Sergeant William Young." *The Pennsylvania Magazine of History and Biography* 8 (1884): 255-278.

Newspapers

Specific newspaper articles are given in the source notes.

Secondary Sources

Atwood, Rodney. T*he Hessians: Mercenaries from Hessen-Kassel in the American Revolution*. Cambridge, Eng.; New York: Cambridge University Press, 1980.

Barber, John W. and Henry Howe. *Historical Collections of the State of New Jersey*. Newark: B. Olds, for Justus H. Bradley; New Haven: J.W. Barber, 1852.

Beck, Derek W. *Igniting the American Revolution: 1773-1775*. Naperville, IL: Sourcebooks, 2015.

Beck, Derek W. *The War Before Independence: 1775-1776*. Naperville, IL: Sourcebooks, 2016.

Becker, Robert A. *Revolution, Reform, and the Politics of American Taxation, 1763-1783*. Baton Rouge: Louisiana State University Press, 1980.

Bidwell, John. *American Paper Mills 1690-1832*. Hanover: Dartmouth College Press, c2013.

Bining, Arthur C. *British Regulation of the Colonial Iron Industry.* Clifton: Augustus M. Kelley, 1973.

Blanco, Richard L. *Physician of the American Revolution: Jonathan Potts.* New York: Garland STPM Press, 1979.

Boyd, Thomas. *Poor John Fitch: Inventor of the Steamboat.* New York: Putnam, 1935.

Braisted, Todd W. *Grand Forage 1778: The Battleground Around New York City*. Yardley: Westholme, 2016.

Breen, T. H. *American Insurgents American Patriots: The Revolution of the People*. New York: Hill and Wang, 2010.

Cecere, Michael. *Captain Thomas Posey and the 7th Virginia Regiment*. Bowie, MD: Heritage Books, 2005.

Cecere, Michael, *They Behaved Like Soldiers: Captain John Chilton and the Third Virginia Regiment 1775-1778*. Bowie, MD: Heritage Books, 2004.

Chartrand, Rene. *The French Army in the American War of Independence*. London: Osprey, 1991.

Clyde, Rev. John C. *Rosbrugh, A Tale of the Revolution; or, Life, Labors, and Death of Rev. John Rosbrugh*. Easton, Pa: 1880.

Coldham, Peter Willson. *American Loyalist Claims*. Washington, D.C.: National Genealogical Society, 1980.

Collins, John, Isaac Collins, Thomas G. Morton, and Morris Earle. *Reminiscences of Isaac and Rachel (Budd) Collins, with an Account of Some of their Descendants, together with a Genealogy of the Collins Family*. Philadelphia: J.B. Lippincott, 1893.

Custis, George Washington Parke. *Recollections and Private Memoirs of Washington*. New York: Derby & Jackson, 1860.

Davis, Michael A. *The Trial of Abraham Hunt: An American Christmas Story*. Denver: Ghost Road Press, 2006.

Davis, W. W. H. "Washington on the West Bank of the Delaware, 1776." *The Pennsylvania Magazine of History and Biography* 4 (1880): 133-163.

Dayton, William L. *Historical Sketch of the Trenton Academy*. Trenton: 1881.

Divine, Francis E., "The Pennsylvania Flying Camp, July – November 1776," *Pennsylvania History: A Journal of Mid-Atlantic Studies* 46 (1979): 59-78.

Dorland, Major W.A., "The Second Troop Philadelphia City Cavalry," *Pennsylvania Magazine of History and Biography* 45 (1921): 266-287.

Dow, Jesse E., "The Life Guardsman." *Graham's Lady's and Gentleman's Magazine* 18 (1841): 275-278. Also in *Barre Gazette*, Barre Massachusetts, June 25, 1841, 1.

Dwyer, William M. *The Day is Ours! November 1776-January 1777: An Inside View of the Battles of Trenton and Princeton*. New York: Viking Press, 1983.

Egly, T.W., Jr., *History of the First New York Regiment, 1775-1783*. Hampton, NH: P. E. Randall, 1981.

Ellis, Joseph. *His Excellency, George Washington*. New York: Alfred A. Knopf, 2004.

Fackenthal, B. F., Jr. "Improving Navigation on the Delaware River with Some Account of the Ferries, Bridges, Canals and Floods." *A Collection of Papers Read Before the Bucks County Historical Society*. Easton, PA: Fackenthal Publication Fund, 1932, VI: 103-219.

Fenn, Elizabeth A. *Pox Americana: The Great Smallpox Epidemic of 1775-82*. New York: Hill and Wang, 2001.

Ferling, John. *A Leap in the Dark: The Struggle to Create the American Republic*. New York: Oxford University Press, 2003.

Ferling, John. *Almost a Miracle: The American Victory in the War of Independence*. New York: Oxford University Press, 2007.

Ferling, John. *Whirlwind: The American Revolution and the War That Won It*. New York: Bloomsbury Press, 2015.

Fischer, David Hackett. *Paul Revere's Ride*. New York: Oxford University Press, 1994.

Fischer, David Hackett. *Washington's Crossing*. New York: Oxford University Press, 2004.

Forbes, Esther. *Paul Revere and the World He Lived In*. Boston: Houghton Mifflin, 1943.

Fowler, David J. "Egregious Villains, Wood Rangers, and London Traders: The Pine Robber Phenomenon in New Jersey During the Revolutionary War." PhD diss., Rutgers The State University of New Jersey (1987).

Fowler, David J. "Loyalty is Now Bleeding in New Jersey: Motivations and Mentalities of the Disaffected." *The Other Loyalists: Ordinary People, Royalism, and the Revolution in the Middle Colonies, 1763-1787*. Edited by Joseph S. Tiedemann, Eugene R. Fingerhut, and Robert W. Vanables. Albany: State University of New York Press, 2009.

Gibson, James E. Dr. *Bodo Otto and the Medical Background of the American Revolution*. Springfield, ILL: Charles C. Thomas, 1937.

Gillette, Mary C. *The Army Medical Department, 1775 –1818*. Washington, DC: Center of Military History, United States Army, 1981.

Gnichtel, Frederick W. "The 'Pennamite Wars' and the Trenton Decree of 1782." *Proceedings of the New Jersey Historical Society, New Series*, VI (1921): 24-34.

Godfrey, Dr. Carlos B. St. *Michael's Church, Trenton, New Jersey, 1704-1920: A Research*. Typescript, 1920 (Trenton Free Public Library, Trentoniana Room)

Hall, John. *History of the First Presbyterian Church in Trenton from the First Settlement of the Town*. Trenton: MacCrellish & Quigley, 1912.

Hewitt, Louise. *Historic Trenton*. Trenton: The Smith Press, 1916.

Hixon, Richard F. *Isaac Collins: A Quaker Printer in 18th Century America*. New Brunswick: Rutgers University Press, 1968.

Hixon, Richard F. *The Press in Revolutionary New Jersey*. Trenton: New Jersey Historical Commission, 1975.

Hoffman, Elliot Wheelock. "The German Soldiers in the American Revolution." PhD diss., University of New Hampshire (1982).

Hood, ?. "Engagements at Trenton and Princeton, January 2 and 3, 1777," *The Pennsylvania Magazine of History and Biography* 10 (1886); 263-265.

Hudak, Catherine, "The Ladies of Trenton: Women's Political and Public Activism in Revolutionary NJ." *New Jersey Studies: An Interdisciplinary Journal* 1 (2015): 39-78.

Hunter, Richard W. and Ian C. Burrow. *Petty's Run Archaeological Site: Iron, Steel, Cotton and Paper in Historic Trenton*, Volume 1 Narrative. Trenton: Hunter Research, 2014.

Hunter, Richard W. *Fish and Ships: Lamberton, the Port of Trenton*. Trenton: Hunter Research, 2005.

Hunter Research. *The "Trenton in 1775" Mapping project, City of Trenton, Mercer County, New Jersey*. Trenton: The Trenton Historical Society, 2008.

Ingrao, Charles W. *The Hessian Mercenary State: Ideas, Institutions, and Reform under Frederick II, 1760-1785*. New York: Cambridge University Press, 1987.

Jackson, John W. *The Pennsylvania Navy 1775-1781: The Defense of the Delaware*. New Brunswick: Rutgers University Press, 1974.

Johnston, Henry P. *The Yorktown Campaign and the Surrender of Cornwallis, 1781*. Eastern National Park and Monument Association, 1958. Originally published 1881.

Jones, E. Alfred. *The Loyalists of New Jersey; Their Memorials, Petitions, Claims, etc., from English Records*. Boston: Gregg Press, 1972.

Keen, Gregory B., "The Descendants of Joran Kyn, The Founder of Upland." *The Pennsylvania Magazine of History and Biography* 4 (1880): 343-360.

Ketchum, Richard M. *The Winter Soldiers*. Garden City, NY: Doubleday, 1973.

Kidder, Larry. *A People Harassed and Exhausted: The Story of a New Jersey Militia Regiment in the American Revolution*. CreateSpace, 2013.

Kwasny, Mark V. *Washington's Partisan War, 1775-1783*. Kent, OH: The Kent State University Press, 1996.

Landsman, Ned C. *Crossroads of Empire: The Middle Colonies in British North America*. Baltimore: Johns Hopkins University Press, 2010.

Lefferts, Charles M. *Uniforms of the American, British, French, and German Armies in the War of the American Revolution 1775-1783*. Edited by Alexander J. Wall. Old Greenwich, CT: We, 1976.

Lefkowitz, Arthur S. *The Long Retreat: The Calamitous American Defense of New Jersey, 1776*. New Brunswick: Rutgers University Press, 1999.

Levitt, James H., *New Jersey's Revolutionary Economy*, Trenton: New Jersey Historical Commission, c1975.

Lowell, Edward J. *The Hessians and the other German Auxiliaries of Great Britain in the Revolutionary War*. New York: Harper, 1884.

Lundin, Leonard. *Cockpit of the Revolution: The War for Independence in New Jersey*. New York: Octagon Books, 1972 [c1940].

Maurer, C.F. William. *Dragoon Diary: The History of the Third Continental Light Dragoons*. Bloomington, IN: AuthorHouse, c2005.

McBurney, Christian M. *Kidnapping the Enemy: The Special Operations to Capture Generals Charles Lee & Richard Prescott*. Yardley: Westholme, 2014.

McConville, Brendan. *These Daring Disturbers of the Public Peace: the Struggle for Property and Power in Early New Jersey*. Philadelphia: University of Pennsylvania Press, 1999.

McCormick, Richard P. *New Jersey from Colony to State, 1609-1789*. New Brunswick: Rutgers University Press, 1964.

Miller, Marla R. *Betsy Ross and the Making of America*. New York: Henry Holt, 2010.

Miller, Samuel. T*he Life of Samuel Miller, D.D., LL.D*. Philadelphia: Claxton, Remsen, and Hafflefinger, 1869.

Minnis, M. Lee. *The First Virginia Regiment of Foot 1775-1783*. Lovettsville, VA: Willow Bend Books, 1998.

Moser, G. Paul, editor. *Johannes Schwalm, The Hessian*. Millville, PA: The Johannes Schwalm Historical Association, 1976.

Nagy, John A. *Rebellion in the Ranks: Mutinies of the American Revolution*, Yardley: Westholme, 2008.

Nelson, William. *New Jersey Biographical and Genealogical Notes from the Volumes of the New Jersey Archives. Collections of the New Jersey Historical Society*, IX, Newark: New Jersey Historical Society, 1916.

Parker, Augustus C. *Parker in America, 1630-1910*, Buffalo, NY: 1910.

Peale, Charles Wilson. "Journal by Charles Willson Peale." *The Crayon* 3 (1856): 37-40.

Peale, Rembrandt. "Reminiscences. Charles Willson Peale. A Sketch by his Son." *The Crayon* 1 (1855): 81-83.

Phillips, Kevin. *1775: A Good Year for Revolution*. New York, Viking, 2012.

Pierce, Arthur Dudley, *Smugglers' Woods: Jaunts and Journeys in Colonial and Revolutionary New Jersey*. New Brunswick: Rutgers University Press, 1960.

Podmore, Harry J. T*renton Old and New*. Revised and edited by Mary J. Messler. Trenton: Trenton Tercentenary Commission, 1964.

Popek, Daniel M. *They "...fought bravely, but were unfortunate:" The True Story of Rhode Island's "Black Regiment" and the Failure of Segregation in Rhode Island's Continental Line, 1777-1783*. AuthorHouse, 2015.

Rakove, Jack. *Revolutionaries: A New History of the Invention of America*. Boston: Houghton Mifflin Harcourt, 2010.

Raphael, Ray and Marie Raphael. T*he Spirit of '74: How the American Revolution Began*. New York: The New Press, 2015.

Raum, John O. *History of the City of Trenton*, New Jersey. Trenton: 1871.

Rawle, William Henry. "Col. Lambert Cadwalader, a Sketch." *Pennsylvania Magazine of History and Biography* 10 (1886): 1-14.

Reed. William B. *Life and Correspondence of Joseph Reed*. Philadelphia: Lindsay and Blakiston, 1847.

Retzer, Henry J. *The German Regiment of Maryland and Pennsylvania in the Continental Army 1776-1781*. Westminster, MD: Family Line Publications, 1996.

Riordan, Liam. *Many Identities, One Nation: The Revolution and Its Legacy in the Mid-Atlantic*. Philadelphia: University of Pennsylvania Press, 2007.

Royster, Charles. *A Revolutionary People at War: The Continental Army and American Character, 1775-1783*. Chapel Hill: The University of North Carolina Press, 1979.

Ryan, Dennis P., ed., *A Salute to Courage: The American Revolution as Seen Through Wartime Writings of Officers of the Continental Army and Navy*. New York: Columbia University Press, 1979.

Sabine, Julia, "Silversmiths of New Jersey, 1623-1800." *Proceedings of the New Jersey Historical Society* 61 (1943): 145+

Sabine, Lorenzo. *The American Loyalists, or Biographical Sketches of adherents to the British Crown in the War of the Revolution*. Boston: Charles C. Little and James Brown, 1847.

Saffron, Morris H. *Surgeon to Washington: Dr. John Cochran, 1730-1807*. New York: Columbia University Press, 1977.

Schmidt, Hubert, "Slavery and Attitudes on Slavery Hunterdon County, New Jersey," *Proceedings of the New Jersey Historical Society* 58 (1940): 151-169.

Schmidt, Lawrence R. *The Old Barracks Museum, Trenton, New Jersey: Barracks and Officers' House Historic Furnishing Plan*. Trenton: Old Barracks Museum, 1991.

Schuyler, Hamilton. *A History of St. Michael's Church Trenton: In the Diocese of New Jersey from its Foundation in the Year of Our Lord 1703 to 1926*. Princeton: Princeton University Press, 1926.

Selig, Robert A. *The Washington-Rochambeau Revolutionary Route in the State of New Jersey, 1781-1783: an Historical and Architectural Survey*. Trenton: State of New Jersey, 2006.

Sellers, Charles Coleman. *Charles Willson Peale*. New York: Charles Scribner's Son's, 1969.

Sellers, Horace Wells. "Charles Willson Peale, Artist – Soldier." *Pennsylvania Magazine of History and Biography* 38 (1914): 257-286.

Sergejeff, Nadine. *The Assunpink Creek in Mill Hill: A History and Consideration of Interpretive Opportunities: City of Trenton, Mercer County, New Jersey*. Trenton: Hunter Research, 2002.

Shachtman, Tom. *Gentlemen Scientists and revolutionaries: The Founding Fathers in the Age of Enlightenment*. New York: Palgrave McMillan, 2014.

Shuman, Eleanore Nolan. *The Trenton Story*. Trenton: MacCrellish & Quigley, 1958.

Slagle, Robert Oakley, "The Von Lossberg Regiment: A Chronicle of Hessian Participation in the American Revolution." PhD diss., The American University (1965).

Slick, Sewell Elias. *William Trent and the West.* Harrisburg: Archives Publishing Company of Pennsylvania, 1947.

Snyder, John F. *The Story of New Jersey's Civil Boundaries 1606-1968.* Trenton: Bureau of Geology and Topography, 1969.

Sooy, Josephus Leander. *History of State Street Methodist Episcopal Church Trenton, N.J.* Trenton: MacCrellish & Quigley, 1886.

Sprague, William Buel. *Annals of the American pulpit: or, Commemorative notices of distinguished American Clergymen of Various Denominations.* New York: Robert Carter & Brothers, 1859.

Stone, Edwin M. *The Life and Recollections of John Howland, Late President of the Rhode Island Historical Society.* Providence: George H. Whitney, 1857.

Stryker, William S. *The Battles of Trenton and Princeton.* Boston: Houghton, Mifflin and Company, 1898.

Stryker, William S. *The Continental Army at the Crossing of the Delaware River on Christmas Night of 1776.* Trenton: J. L. Murphy, 1896.

Stryker, William S. *"The New Jersey Volunteers" (Loyalists) in the Revolutionary War.* Trenton: Naar, Day & Naar, 1887.

Stryker, William S. *Trenton One Hundred Years Ago*, Trenton: 1878.

Thomas, Isaiah. *The History of Printing in America.* Albany: Joel Munsell, 1874.

Toothman, Stephanie Smith. "Trenton, New Jersey, 1719-1779: A Study of Community Growth and Organization." PhD diss., University of Pennsylvania (1977).

Trenton Historical Society. *A History of Trenton, 1679-1929; Two Hundred and Fifty Years of a Notable Town with Links to Four Centuries.* Princeton: Princeton University Press, 1929.

Trevelyan, Sir George Otto. *The American Revolution.* London: Longmans, Green, and Co., 1917.

Triber, Jayne E. *A True Republican: The Life of Paul Revere.* Amherst: University of Massachusetts Press, 1998.

Veit, Richard and David Orr, eds. *Historical Archaeology of the Delaware Valley, 1600-1850.* Knoxville: University of Tennessee Press, 2014.

Von Eelking, Max. *The German Allied Troops in the North American War of Independence, 1776-1783.* J. G. Rosengarten, trans. Albany: Joel Munsell's Sons, 1893.

Waite, John G., et. al. *The Old Barracks Historic Structure Report.* Albany: John G. Waite Associates, 1998.

Ward, Harry M. *Charles Scott and the "Spirit of '76".* Charlottesville: University Press of Virginia, 1988.

Ward, Harry M. *Major General Adam Stephen and the Cause of American Liberty*. Charlottesville: University Press of Virginia, 1989.

Wax, Darold D. "Negro Imports into Pennsylvania, 1720-1766," *Pennsylvania History: A Journal of Mid-Atlantic Studies* 32 (1965): 254-287.

Westcott, Thomas. *The Life of John Fitch the Inventor of the Steamboat*. Philadelphia: J. B. Lippincott, 1857.

White, Rebecca, Nadine Sergejeff, William Liebeknecht and Richard Hunter. *A Historical Account and Archaeological Analysis of the Eagle Tavern, City of Trenton, Mercer County, New Jersey*. Trenton: Hunter Research, 2005.

Whitridge, Arnold. *Rochambeau*. New York: Macmillan, 1965.

Wickes, Stephen. *History of Medicine in New Jersey, and of its Medical Men, From the Settlement of the Province to A.D. 1800*. Newark: Martin R. Dennis, 1879.

Wilson, Joseph Lapsley, ed., *Book of the First Troop, Philadelphia City Cavalry, 1774-1914*. Philadelphia: First Troop Philadelphia City Cavalry, 1915.

Zuckerman, Michael. introduction to *Friends and Neighbors: Group Life in America's First Plural Society*. Michael Zuckerman, ed. Philadelphia: Temple University Press, 1982.

Index

Hes = Hessian
Br = British
Fr = French

A

B

D

E

F

M

N

O

P

Q

R

U

V

W

Note on the Author

William L. Kidder, universally known as Larry, was born in California and raised in California, Indiana, New York, and New Jersey. He received his bachelor's and master's degrees from Allegheny College in Meadville, Pennsylvania.

Larry is a retired high school history teacher who taught for forty years in both public and private schools. He considers teaching to be both his vocation and avocation. During his 32 years of teaching at The Hun School of Princeton he enjoyed designing courses that gave his students the opportunity to develop the thinking, research, and writing skills that result from "doing history" and not just learning facts for a test.

Larry served four years of active duty in the US Navy and was assigned to the US Navy Research and Development Unit, Vietnam and then the destroyer USS Brownson (DD868) homeported in Newport, Rhode Island. In the 1980s he was the lead researcher and writer for the creation of the Admiral Arleigh Burke National Destroyermen's Museum aboard the destroyer museum ship USS Joseph P. Kennedy, Jr. (DD850) at Battleship Cove in Fall River, Massachusetts.

For over twenty-five years, Larry has been a volunteer at the Howell Living History Farm, part of the Mercer County Park System, in Hopewell, New Jersey. For varying lengths of time he has volunteered as an historian, interpreter, webmaster, and draft horse teamster This interest led to the writing of his first book that tells the story of the local schoolhouse that is now part of the Howell Living History Farm and is also a case study of a rural school in central New Jersey from the early 19th to the mid-20th century.

Active in historical societies in Ewing, Hopewell, and Lawrence townships, Larry has given a number of talks on local history to a variety of civic groups. He is also a volunteer for the Crossroads of the American Revolution National Heritage Area, coordinating its Meet Your Revolutionary Neighbors project. He is an avid member of the Association for Living History, Farm, and Agricultural Museums (ALHFAM), the Washington's Crossing Roundtable of the American Revolution, and the New Jersey Living History Advisory Council.

He can be contacted by email at larrykidder@gmail.com.

Relive the "Ten Crucial Days" of the American Revolution

Visit these historic sites:

Washington Crossing Historic Park
This Pennsylvania state park and National Historic Landmark is where General George Washington's army began its epic crossing of the Delaware River the night of December 25-26, 1776, which may have saved our nation's quest for independence when the American Revolution appeared all but lost. This was the beginning of the Ten Crucial Days. The park offers a visitor center and more than 500 acres of American history, natural beauty, and family fun.

Located less than a mile from the park is **The David Library of the American Revolution**. It is a specialized research library, open free of charge to the public, dedicated to the study of American History between 1750 and 1800. This non-profit educational institution is a valuable and welcoming resource for anyone seeking information about virtually anything related to America's war for independence. It also offers lectures and events of interest to the historical community.

Washington Crossing State Park
This New Jersey state park lies opposite its Pennsylvania sister and is part of the same National Historic Landmark. It is the site where Washington's army landed after crossing the Delaware River to attack the Hessian brigade occupying Trenton. In addition to its historical significance, the 3,500-acre park is well known for its trails and wildlife habitat.

Old Barracks Museum
This museum in Trenton has a unique history dating back to 1758, when it was built to house British soldiers during the French and Indian War. It is a remnant of Trenton that helps visitors understand both the Battle of Trenton on December 26, 1776 and the Second Battle of Trenton on January 2, 1777. From military quarters to widow's home, from brothel to museum, the building offers visitors a fascinating look at the history of the area.

Princeton Battlefield

This New Jersey state park is where the Battle of Princeton was fought on January 3, 1777 - the capstone event of the "Ten Crucial Days" campaign that altered the course of the war. It is the site of what is considered to be the fiercest fight of its size during the long conflict. The 1772 Clarke House witnessed the battle and served as sanctuary for the wounded General Hugh Mercer, who died there nine days later; it contains period furniture and Revolutionary War exhibits.

Learn more about these historic sites at:

www.tencrucialdays.org

TenCrucialDays.org

December 25, 1776 - January 3, 1777